To Major James Brown Scott
With kind regards Feb 4th 1919
Andrew Carnegie

THE SPANISH ORIGIN OF INTERNATIONAL LAW

FRANCISCO DE VITORIA
AND
HIS LAW OF NATIONS

BY

JAMES BROWN SCOTT

Secretary of the Carnegie Endowment for International Peace; Professor of International Law and of Foreign Relations of the United States in Georgetown University; Member of the Association Internationale de Vitoria et de Suarez; President of the American Society of International Law; President of the American Institute of International Law; Member and past President of the Institut de Droit International

'I love the University of Salamancha; for when the Spaniards were in doubt as to the lawfulness of their conquering America, the University of Salamancha gave it as their opinion that it was not lawful.' He spoke this with great emotion. . . .

BOSWELL'S LIFE OF DR. JOHNSON

THE LAWBOOK EXCHANGE, LTD.
Clark, New Jersey

ISBN 978-1-58477-110-4

Lawbook Exchange edition 2000, 2014

The quality of this reprint is equivalent to the quality of the original work.

THE LAWBOOK EXCHANGE, LTD.
33 Terminal Avenue
Clark, New Jersey 07066-1321

Please see our website for a selection of our other publications and fine facsimile reprints of classic works of legal history:
www.lawbookexchange.com

Library of Congress Cataloging-in-Publication Data

Scott, James Brown, 1866-1943.
The Spanish origin of international law. Francisco de Vitoria and his law of nations / by James Brown Scott.
p. cm.
Originally published: Oxford : Clarendon Press ; London : H. Milford, 1934. (Publications of the Carnegie Endowment for International Peace, Division of International Law)
Includes bibliographical references and index.
ISBN 1-58477-110-0 (cloth : alk. paper)
1. International law—History. I. Vitoria, Francisco de, 1486?-1546. II. Title. III. Publications of the Carnegie Endowment for International Peace, Division of International Law.

KZ2159 .S385 2000
341—dc21 00-036835

Printed in the United States of America on acid-free paper

THE SPANISH ORIGIN OF INTERNATIONAL LAW

FRANCISCO DE VITORIA
AND
HIS LAW OF NATIONS

BY

JAMES BROWN SCOTT

Secretary of the Carnegie Endowment for International Peace;
Professor of International Law and of Foreign Relations
of the United States in Georgetown University;
Member of the Association Internationale
de Vitoria et de Suarez;
President of the American Society of International
Law; President of the American Institute of
International Law; Member and past
President of the Institut de
Droit International

'I love the University of Salamancha; for when the Spaniards were in doubt as to the lawfulness of their conquering America, the University of Salamancha gave it as their opinion that it was not lawful.' He spoke this with great emotion. . . .

BOSWELL'S LIFE OF DR. JOHNSON

OXFORD : AT THE CLARENDON PRESS

LONDON : HUMPHREY MILFORD

1934

Printed in England
At the OXFORD UNIVERSITY PRESS
By John Johnson
Printer to the University

IN GRATEFUL REMEMBRANCE

OF

ANDREW CARNEGIE

WHOSE BENEFACTIONS HAVE MADE IT POSSIBLE TO PUBLISH

THE CLASSICS OF INTERNATIONAL LAW

Memorial Day, 1932

Washington, D.C.

IL CONVIVIO

TRATTATO IV. 4

Lo fondamento radicale della Imperiale Maestà, secondo il vero, è la necessità della umana civilità, che a uno fine è ordinata, cioè a vita felice; alla quale nullo per sè è sufficiente a venire senza l'aiuto d'alcuno; conciossiacosachè l'uomo abbisogna di molte cose, alle quali uno solo satisfare non può. E però dice il Filosofo, che 'l'uomo naturalmente è compagnevole animale'. E siccome un uomo a sua sufficienza richiede compagnia domestica di famiglia; così una casa a sua sufficienza richiede una vicinanza, altrimenti molti difetti sosterrebbe, che sarebbono impedimento di felicità. E perocchè una vicinanza non può a sè in tutto satisfare, conviene a satisfacimento di quella essere la città. Ancora la città richiede alle sue arti e alla sua difensione avere vicenda e fratellanza colle circonvicine cittadi, e però fu fatto il regno. Onde conciossiacosachè l'animo umano in terminata possessione di terra non si quieti, ma sempre desideri terra acquistare, siccome per esperienza vedemo, discordie e guerre conviene surgere tra regno e regno. Le quali sono tribulazioni delle cittadi; e per le cittadi, delle vicinanze; e per le vicinanze, delle case; e per le case, dell'uomo; e così s'impedisce la felicità. Il perchè, a queste guerre e alle loro cagioni torre via, conviene di necessità tutta la Terra, e quanto all'umana generazione a possedere è dato, esser Monarchia, cioè uno solo Principato e uno Principe avere, il quale, tutto possedendo e più desiderare non possendo, li re tenga contenti nelli termini delli regni, sicchè pace intra loro sia, nella quale si posino le cittadi, e in questa posa le vicinanze s'amino, in questo amore le case prendano ogni loro bisogno, il quale preso, l'uomo viva felicemente; ch' è quello per che l'uomo è nato.

Dante Alighieri.

THE BANQUET

TRACTATE IV. 4

The root and ground of the imperial majesty is, in truth, the necessity of man's social state, which is ordained for a single end, namely, a life of happiness; to which no one is able to attain by himself without the aid of some one else, inasmuch as man has need of many things for which a single individual cannot suffice. And therefore the Philosopher says that man is by nature a 'companionable animal'. And just as an individual in order to suffice for himself requires the domestic companionship of the family, so a household to suffice for itself requires a neighbourhood, else it will suffer from many defects which will be hindrances to happiness. And because a single neighbourhood cannot in all respects be self-sufficient, in order to satisfy all its wants there must needs be a city. Moreover a city, for the sake of its crafts and for self-defence, must needs have intercourse and brotherly relations with the neighbouring townships, and for this reason kingdoms were constituted. Wherefore, inasmuch as the mind of man does not rest content with a limited possession of land, but always desires to acquire more land, as we perceive by experience, disagreement and wars must needs arise between kingdom and kingdom. Such things are the scourges of townships, and through townships of neighbourhoods, and through neighbourhoods of families, and through families of individuals, and thus happiness is hindered. Wherefore, in order to do away with these wars and their causes, it is necessary that the whole earth, and all that is given to the race of man to possess, should be a monarchy, that is to say, a single princedom; and should have a single prince, who, possessing everything, and having nothing left to desire, should keep kings confined within the borders of their kingdoms, so that peace should reign between them, and townships should rest in peace, and while they so rest neighbourhoods should love each other, and in this mutual love families should satisfy all their wants; and when these are satisfied, a man should live happily, which is the end for which he is born.

Dante's Convivio, translated into English, by William Walrond Jackson.

PREFACE

A BOOK must be its own justification. The table of contents prefixed to the present volume may therefore be looked upon by the reader as an incentive to the text, whose purpose it is to state the services of Francisco de Vitoria and his relation to the law of nations. The volume, it is hoped, will not be considered special pleading, but it is nevertheless a volume with a thesis: that there was a Spanish school of international law in the sixteenth century, within forty years after the discovery of America; that the founder of this school was Francisco de Vitoria, *prima* professor of theology in the University of Salamanca; and that his two *Relectiones*, *De Indis Noviter Inventis* and *De Jure Belli*, set forth his law of nations, which was to become the international law not merely of Christendom but of the world at large.

The present is not an unworthy thesis. It attributes to the discovery of America the expansion of international law until it has become a universal rule of conduct. It proclaims an international community composed of all the nations, the vast majority being the small powers whose defence is righteousness, justice, and the moral standard. It gives to the great expounders of the modern law of nations, who have been silent for centuries, a voice and a control in the development of the science which they founded.

The readings of Victoria disclose that he could meet and discuss a question of international importance, even though his conclusions were opposed to the theories and practice of the Pope, the King, and the Holy Roman Emperor. In his Reading *On the Indians* he dealt with a question which, as he himself acknowledged, he had never heard discussed, as he had not attended Councils of State or similar gatherings of political advisers; nor had he read anything dealing directly with this subject. Without precedents he created precedents.

Victoria could analyse the conditions of his day, feeling the necessity for a community larger than Christendom, and foreseeing the international community of the future, even though its actual conditions must have been unknown to him—more unknown by far than they are to us.

His assertion that the righting of the wrong of a particular State should not be done if it involved a greater injury to the community at large was the view of a statesman as well as of a theologian; and his conception of the community of nations, coextensive with humanity and existing as a result of the mere coexistence of States, without a treaty or convention, is the hope of the future.

It is an integral portion of the thesis that Hugo Grotius, who has so many titles to remembrance, is, although a Netherlander, to be considered as a member of the Victorian or, as it is usually termed, the Spanish school, in that he derived his doctrine on the law of nature and of nations from members of the Spanish school, which doctrine formed the basis of his treatise *On the Law of War and Peace* of 1625.

The present tractate is but the first volume of a larger work in manuscript, shortly to be published under the general caption of *The Spanish Origin of International Law.* The second volume will consist of an examination and appreciation of the services to international law of Francisco de Vitoria's fellow countrymen, Baltasar Ayala—none the less a countryman because born in the Spanish Netherlands—whose work is largely a manual of the commander in the field; of Francisco Suarez, who has in his various writings furnished us with a philosophy not merely of international law but of law in general; and of certain other Spanish writers who, in the period between Victoria and Suarez, contributed to the further development of the doctrines of the Spanish school.

The third volume will consist of a like examination and appreciation of the writings of Pierino Belli, a predecessor of Alberico Gentili, which will serve, as it were, as an introduction to more extended comments on the works of Gentili, upon whose commentary on the law of war the great Grotius laid a heavy hand; and these sections will be followed by a detailed analysis of the two masterpieces of Grotius in the domain of international law—*De Jure Praedae* of 1604, and *De Jure Belli ac Pacis Libri Tres* of 1625. It will be observed that the third volume deals with internationalists other than Spaniards—two of them Italians (Belli and Gentili) and the other a Netherlander, if indeed Grotius is not to be considered a citizen of the world.

The three volumes are regarded as forming a single whole and, as such, they will be paged continuously and will have a cumulative index.

The present tractate, then, is the first part of *The Spanish Origin of International Law*, and it may be considered as announcing the appearance of the larger work. There is, however, another—and the best—reason for issuing it separately, in that it is a contribution to the publications of the Association Internationale de Francisco de Vitoria et de Suarez, organized at the session of the Institut de Droit International at Cambridge in 1931. The founding of this Association is in itself an act of homage to the memory of Francisco de Vitoria, who in 1532, within forty years of the discovery of America, prepared his Reading *On the Indians Recently Discovered*, and, in so doing, discussed the most important, concrete problem of international law of that day—and, as we of America are inclined to think, of any other day. In this Reading, followed as it was by the dissertation *On the Law of War*, Victoria proclaimed the existence of an international law no longer limited to Christendom but applying to all States, without reference to geography, creed, or race. In their implications and their results the readings constitute, it may justly be said, the first lay treatment of the subject by a practical yet highly spiritual theologian.

The primary purpose, then, of the separate publication of the first part of the *Spanish Origin of International Law* devoted to Victoria is to lay it before the meeting of the Association Internationale de Francisco de Vitoria et de Suarez, to be held in conjunction with the meeting of the Institut de Droit International at Oslo in the month of August on the four-hundredth anniversary of the epoch-making year 1532.

It will be observed that an extended chapter on 'The Era of Discoveries' forms the first part of the present volume. Its purpose is to show that discoveries in any one domain lead to discoveries in other domains, and how the discovery of America influenced leaders of thought in the century separating Victoria and Grotius.

After wandering, as it were, in the wilderness—when it was not a desert—the publicists of to-day are disregarding the international law based upon force, unrelated to morality and rendered futile and inoperative in the international community by a conception of sovereignty descended from the divine right of kings and its successor, the divine State. They are leaving the paths marked out by false prophets of international law and turning to Victoria's law of nations and the Victorian principles which for four hundred years have pointed the path to an international law still of the future, in which law and morality shall be one and inseparable, in which States are created by and for human beings, and every principle of international law and of international conduct is to be tested by the good of the international community and not by the selfish standards of its more powerful and erring members. In Victoria's doctrine the duty of the more powerful is to observe the law as do the weak and, through his conception of the mandate, to lend a helping hand to less favoured peoples.

The object of this Preface is, in addition to stating the reason for the present publication of the volume on Victoria, to voice in no uncertain terms appreciation of the devoted services of the members of the Division of International Law of the Carnegie Endowment for International Peace in the preparation of the Victorian part of the forthcoming volumes on *The Spanish Origin of International Law.*

The co-operation of Alan T. Hurd is to be found in every section, not to say in every line, of the volume, by suggestion, by revision, and in the analytical table of contents.

Miss Gwladys L. Williams has in many instances furnished translations of both Latin and Spanish documents quoted in the text and appearing in the appendixes.

Francis Crane Macken has rendered indispensable services in connexion with the verification of authorities in various languages, ancient and modern, of which the footnotes bear ample witness.

The publication of the Classics of International Law, to which the three volumes of *The Spanish Origin of International Law* are to be as an introduction, was proposed and begun a quarter of a century ago, in order to show that international law is not a thing of treaties or conventions but the result of centuries and centuries of experience, and that it comes to us from the Golden Age of Spain as the result of the discovery of America.

The proposal as then formulated was to 'undertake the republication of the various classics of international law' because of the 'great difficulty in obtaining any of the works of the predecessors' of Grotius, a difficulty which made it 'impossible for students of international law in our various colleges and universities to trace the history of international law to its sources. . . . To understand the law of nations as it exists and is applied to-day it is necessary to understand its past; and it is the veriest truism to maintain that the future can only be forecast by an adequate knowledge of the past as well as of the immediate present. If international law be considered as undergoing a constant growth and development, it necessarily follows that the law of nations must be studied in the light of its origin and history in order to obtain an adequate knowledge of the system at present and to predict with certainty the future development of the science.'

Not the least pleasure in publishing this volume is that it enables the undersigned to dedicate it to the memory of Andrew Carnegie, without whose benefactions the Classics of International Law would never have been undertaken.

JAMES BROWN SCOTT.

Washington, D.C.
June 3rd, 1932.

POSTSCRIPTUM

WITHIN the last few years Spanish scholars have busied themselves with those whom moderns have looked upon as forgotten glories of Spain. To speak only of the international domain, the manuscripts of Victoria have been sought far and wide. A number have come to light and are being published by Father Vicente Beltrán de Heredia, who is rendering a service not merely to his countrymen and to his country but to international law. The distinguished investigator is publishing, under the title of *Comentarios a la Secunda Secundae de Santo Tomás*, the lectures which Victoria delivered as *prima* professor at Salamanca. Of these, two volumes have already appeared, a third is in process, and others are expected shortly to follow.[1]

In Appendix F to the present volume, the interested reader will find a long extract on war, which is contained in the second of Beltrán de Heredia's volumes of the *Comentarios* (published since the above preface was written), and which supplements Victoria's formal *Relectio* on the *Law of War* without altering the fundamental doctrines there expounded.

In the meantime, the learned editor of the *Comentarios* has graciously and generously copied passages of a general nature further stating Victoria's views. These excerpts will be used here and there in the second volume of *The Spanish Origin of International Law*, which will deal with Victoria's countrymen who followed in the footsteps of the *maestro*.

J. B. S.

June 3, 1933.

[1] As these pages go to press a further tribute to Victoria has come to hand in the form of advance proofs of a new edition of his *Relectiones*, containing not only reproductions of the first (1557) and second (1565) editions, but also reproductions of manuscripts of the *Relectiones*. This admirable work is being edited by Father Luis G. Alonso Getino, whose scholarly treatise, *El Maestro Fr. Francisco de Vitoria*, is now, and bids fair to remain for many a day, the most complete and authoritative source of our knowledge of Victoria.

CONTENTS

PORTRAITS

Courtesy of the Metropolitan Museum of Art *Emery Walker Ltd ph sc*

Christopher Columbus

CHAPTER I

THE ERA OF DISCOVERIES

WE live in an age of anniversaries. We recognize that the present is but an outgrowth if it be not a mere prolongation of the past. The birth of States and nations, if we can compare their artificial creation to the natural process of creation, makes an especial appeal. Within the past few years, we of North America have rejoiced at the independence of the Latin American Republics, and representatives of our government have taken part in their various centenaries. On the 4th of July, 1926, we celebrated the one hundred and fiftieth anniversary of the independence of the United States.

The great men of other days belong to us in no uncertain sense, and their birth, the publication of their works, or the announcement of their discoveries are mileposts in the development of our civilization. To two of these more modest anniversaries I would invite your attention.

On the 17th or 18th of March, 1625, a treatise on the law of war and peace was exposed for sale at the Frankfort Fair. It was by one Huig de Groot, with the Latin form of whose name, Grotius, we are more familiar. In 1925, the third centenary of the publication of the volume was celebrated at The Hague and in many parts of the world. It was an international event of no mean importance.

On the 7th of September, 1526, a Dominican friar, one Francisco de Vitoria, was appointed Professor of Sacred Theology at the University of Salamanca. In the spring of 1926, four hundred years later, his appointment was celebrated at that most ancient and venerable of Spanish universities, in the presence, it is proper to say, of a delegation from Holland, the country of Grotius.

Now Grotius has had the good fortune to be looked upon by many as the father of the law of nations, although his title perhaps would be more secure as its first systematic expounder. In the year 1532 Victoria prepared a series of readings on the relation of Spain to America, then recently discovered; many well-informed persons there are who look upon these readings as having founded the modern school of international law, of which Grotius was the most illustrious member, and his treatise the culmination of the Spanish school. The publication of the treatise and the appointment of Victoria to Salamanca were but a century apart.

The Hollander undoubtedly felt that his name would be remembered, but hardly for the treatise on the law of war and peace, by which it appears he set no great store. As to the Spaniard, the thought that his name would survive surely never occurred to him, and he would have been dumbfounded had any one suggested that he should be remembered. Yet, as I have said, the four-hundredth anniversary of his appointment as Professor was to be celebrated with pomp by the University of Salamanca, and in the presence of a committee of Grotius's countrymen. And there was a relation between the two which the Netherlanders recognized and finely observed: each laboured in the field of international relations, although one sowed in darkness, and the other reaped in light. After the lapse of centuries, he who scattered the seed is seen to be the 'Maestro' of him who garnered the harvest. Each was of his day; each was moved from without to do what he did; and what the Spaniard began, the Netherlander continued.

The flagship of Columbus bringing, we might say, the old and the new world together, drew the line between the Middle Ages in which Europe was a commonwealth based upon a system of rigid principles and modern times in which separate and equal States compete one with another. On that side of the line is unity and universality—on this side, diversity and nationality. An adequate law of nations was needed for the competing nations; with the advent of the New World new problems presented themselves, and the new conditions needed new rules of law. The modern school of international law therefore came into being, just as a more modern law of nations will arise in the future to meet and satisfy newer conditions. Life and law keep company and progress together.

The discovery of the New World was but one of the many discoveries which have made us intellectually and, in a certain respect, materially what we are. The earth was thought to be flat, and only a part of it was known and habitable. The discovery of Columbus showed that the unknown might be habitable, and that in any event the world was round. The discovery was soon to be followed by the announcement that the earth with the New World added was not even the centre of things, but that it revolved around the sun, and was small in comparison with the other planets. The spirit of adventure begotten by material discoveries heartened men of science to push into newer realms, to wrest as it were the very secrets from the heavens, and to explain the nature of things terrestrial and celestial. The world was to act upon my Lord Bacon's advice 'against the "Naught beyond" of the ancients raise your cry of "More beyond".... Let the discovery of the new terrestrial world encourage you to expect the discovery of a new intellectual world, remembering the words of the prophet that "many shall run to and fro, and knowledge shall be multiplied."'[1]

Nothing is more trite than the remark that one discovery leads to another. There were therefore several discoveries, without which the

[1] G. C. Moore Smith, *New Atlantis by Francis Bacon* (1919), p. xvi.

great adventure of 1492 might not have taken place: gunpowder and artillery, which enabled the king to enlarge his domain and lay the foundations of the powerful modern State; the discovery of antiquity, which justified, indeed led to a desire for change; printing, which disseminated the new learning, creating everywhere a desire for the newer life; and the mariner's compass, which enabled the bolder seamen to put beyond charted routes with the expectation of finding their way home. Of these four or five discoveries antedating that of the New World, some were material and some intellectual; together they made a new world of the old. Some were of use on land, and some on unknown waters, such as the invention of gunpowder and artillery, and the mariner's compass. Of the first we shall do little but mention it in passing. Its importance cannot be overlooked, and much as we may deplore the fact, it still is a fact that wars have made and unmade nations. The employment of gunpowder not only 'altered the whole art of war', but, as a learned and accurate writer informs us, 'its influence gradually and indirectly permeated and affected the whole fabric of society'.[1]

Gunpowder, however, was only an explosive. It was to become effective through cannon and small arms. Curiously enough, two monks, one a German, Berthold Schwartz by name, the other an Englishman, Friar Roger Bacon, are competitors for its discovery, or composition. The Germans naturally lean towards their countryman, and the English have a weakness for Bacon. Unprejudiced investigations seem to incline the scales towards the Englishman. About the middle of the thirteenth century, and therefore a hundred years in advance of his German competitor, Bacon thus gives the receipt for making gunpowder: 'Let the total weight of the ingredients be 30, however, of saltpetre . . . of sulphur; and with such a mixture you will produce a bright flash and a thundering noise, if you know the trick.' The pious Friar, great scientist and forerunner of experiment as the foundation of progress, added: 'You may find (by actual experiment) whether I am writing riddles to you or the plain truth.'[2]

The elder Bacon, however, does not seem to have known the use of gunpowder as a propellant. A hundred years after his time it began to be used as such in large and small weapons of warfare. In 1346, at Crécy, the English are said to have brought guns into the open field for the first time, and with disastrous results to their enemies. The new or unusual is apt to be looked upon with disfavour, especially if it be injurious to us. Thus, during the Wars of the Roses in England, the Yorkists were denounced as having 'traiterously ranged in bataill . . . their cartes with gonnes set before their batailles'.[3] But thereafter,

[1] W. R. E. Hodgkinson, 'Gunpowder' in *Encyclopaedia Britannica*, vol. xii (11th ed., 1910), p. 723.
[2] *Ibid.*
[3] Charles Francis Atkinson, 'Artillery' in *Encyclopaedia Britannica*, vol. ii (11th ed., 1910), p. 685.

princes and feudal barons, if they could but buy, beg, borrow, or purloin 'a few pieces of ordnance', could batter down the castles of their rebellious underlings. Thus in Europe the face of things was to be changed. And firearms were likewise to change the face of things beyond the confines of Europe. This we have on the authority of Montaigne, if authority is needed, who quaintly and feelingly describes in one of his essays the astonishment and fear of the American Indians inspired by 'the flashing-fire and thundring roare of shotte and Hargue-buses; able to quell and daunt even *Caesar* himselfe, had he been so sodainely surprised and as little experienced as they were.'[1]

But the greatest instance of the use of artillery took place in the fifteenth century—a century to be gladdened by the discovery of a New World by Columbus, after being inexpressibly saddened by the fall of Constantinople and the Eastern Empire of ancient Rome under the guns of Turkish invaders. The historian Gibbon informs us that Mahomet II, who conquered Constantinople, had 'studied with peculiar care the recent and tremendous discovery of the Latins', and that 'his artillery surpassed whatever had yet appeared in the world'.[2]

It would seem that a Dane or Hungarian, who had served in the armies of the tottering Empire, 'deserted to the Moslems, and was liberally entertained by the Turkish sultan'. Mahomet asked the renegade if he could 'cast a cannon capable of throwing a ball or stone of sufficient size to batter the walls of Constantinople?' to which he replied, according to Gibbon, 'I am not ignorant of their strength, but, were they more solid than those of Babylon, I could oppose an engine of superior power'. The result was the fall of the city, and of the last outpost of Imperial Rome, through cannon manufactured for the purpose. Many of the refugees from the fallen city made their way to Italy and to other parts of the West, swelling the ranks of their countrymen who had preceded them; and through whose activity the Greek literature of other days had been imparted to an expectant and enthralled world. If the fugitives did not create the Renascence, they added to the movement which lay between the Crusades and the final fall of Constantinople.

* * *

With the fall of the Empire of the West in the last quarter of the fifth century, Italy did not cease to exist, nor did the ideas which had been prevalent in that part of the world, but they lost their prominence and, with a single exception, their attraction. That exception was the

[1] *The Essayes of Michael Lord of Montaigne*, translated by John Florio, vol. iii (Everyman ed., No. 442), p. 143.

[2] Edward Gibbon, *The History of the Decline and Fall of the Roman Empire*, vol. vii (3rd ed., 1909), p. 169.

Christian Church, which had installed itself in the Eternal City—'eternal' largely because of the Church. The interest of the Church, however, was not in Italy or Rome as such, but in a doctrine—the doctrine of the Holy Land. The language, indeed, was of Rome, and so much of the older literature as was, in the opinion of the Church, suited to its purpose. In losing touch with classical literature, the language ceased to be classic, and the new literature was couched in a tongue which was losing, if it had not already lost, touch with the ancient world and its ideals. The sun of the Empire had indeed set, and its afterglow was the only light of the newer world. In one respect, however, the Old World persisted, for there never was a time, it would appear, when Roman law was wholly neglected on the peninsula; and its so-called revival in the twelfth and thirteenth centuries seems rather to have been an increased attention to the law, its sources and its possible application, than a sudden enthusiasm for a system of law recovered after a lapse of centuries.

The laymen had taken up the law which the Church had preserved, studied for its own purposes, and made the basis of its canon law; and later, from the law of Imperial Rome, and from the canon law of the Christian Church, the law of nations was to come into being. In view of these things, some say that sooner or later it was inevitable that the old Rome should attract the newer Italy, and that later, through Italy, the old Greece should be unveiled at the hands of the modern Greeks of Constantinople. The great discovery of the ancient world and its twofold civilization was to be made in the fourteenth and fifteenth centuries.

It is generally dangerous to attribute a movement to a single event; and it is indeed rare that a movement can be summed up in the life of a single man. However, it is a pardonable exaggeration to say that the cause and the movement united in the person of Petrarch. The glory of the older Rome made an irresistible appeal to him, and his express mission was to bring into repute and ordinary use the Latin of classical Rome. Through his genius and devotion, and that of his friends and followers, he succeeded.

No scholar of the English-speaking world has a better right to be heard than the late Sir Richard C. Jebb, and the views which I have ventured to express being his, should at least be stated in part in his own words. The Latin of the early day was not to be taken bodily: 'the resemblance of a modern's work to his ancient model should not be that of a portrait to the original, but rather the family likeness of child to parent.' The study of the Classics was to be, as it were, 'the key to a larger mental life, . . . one which should educate and exercise men's highest faculties'. It was not, however, through the schoolmen of the Church that the revival of letters was to be hoped for; nor in the universities, which at the time, and after, were hostile. It was only through the acknowledgement of the powerful and the wealthy that 'humanism' could make its way. Petrarch appealed to these classes, who thus became its open patrons.

This meant much; but Petrarch's services to the new learning were even greater. 'He stimulated an inner circle of disciples', said Professor Jebb. 'He was, in his own person, the first brilliant humanist; he was also the first effective propagator of humanism in the world at large; and he inspired chosen pupils who continued the tradition.'

What was the result of it all? We live in a century in which scholars have, through excavation, discovered and made known to us the material sites and cities of the ancient world. Petrarch, his friends and successors, had discovered and made known the intellectual world. However, the discovery was the civilization of Rome and of Italy; it was not of Greece and its civilization. This was not to be the task of Petrarch, although it was but another phase of the humanistic movement which he had inaugurated. 'I have not been so fortunate as to learn Greek', he said, and Greek was not to be learned through Latin or the Italian tongue. As Professor Jebb puts it, 'The rudiments of grammar and vocabulary could be acquired only from a Greek-speaking teacher.' Greek-speaking persons were only to be found in Constantinople, and among them only a few were familiar with ancient Greek and its literature. These would need to be induced to repair to Italy. Therefore, Professor Jebb says that 'the Italian revival of Greek in the fourteenth and fifteenth centuries was effected mainly by a small number of highly-accomplished Greeks, who were induced to settle as professors at Florence or other centres'.[1]

Within the first fifty years of the fifteenth century Greek had become a living tongue, and the ancient Greece a living influence. What was the value of the accomplishment? It brought within the reach of gradually widening circles the culture and civilization of the Old World which Europe had just discovered.

New learning permeated all frontiers of thought, all branches of science; and the Church was not beyond its influence. Interesting, indeed fascinating in itself, and broadening the intellectual outlook, the new learning showed the people of the Middle Ages a different world, and the possibility of change in institutions as well as in thought. This possibility dawned upon them and, setting about to exchange the conditions with which they were confronted, the Middle Ages were transformed into the modern world. The world had indeed experienced a new birth.

Just as the origin of humanism centres around the name of Petrarch,

[1] *The Cambridge Modern History*, vol. i (1909), chap. xvi, 'The Classical Renaissance', pp. 539, 540, 541.

so its triumph is associated with the name of another man—Erasmus of Rotterdam. And in behalf of Erasmus, as previously in the case of Petrarch, I invoke the authority and I quote the very words of Professor Jebb: 'The attitude of Erasmus towards humanism had a general affinity with that of Petrarch and the other leaders of the Italian revival. . . . To Petrarch, as to the typical Italian humanist generally, the New Learning was above all things an instrument for the self-culture of the individual. To Erasmus, on the other hand, self-culture was, in itself—greatly though he valued it—a secondary object, subservient to a greater end.' What was this end? 'He regarded humanism as the most effectual weapon for combating that widespread ignorance which he considered to be the root of many evils that were around him.' The abuses of the Church, the untold misery due to the selfish aims of kings, the pedantries of the schoolmen, the low moral standards in public and private life, were to yield to 'the civilising influence of knowledge'. His aim was 'educational and ethical', and his purpose was that 'of a practical moralist, who hoped to leave human society better than he had found it'. Throughout his life there was unity of purpose, and his life-work culminated 'in his contributions to Biblical criticism and exegesis. The Scholastic Theology had been wont to use isolated texts, detached from their context, and artificially interpreted. The object of Erasmus was to let all men know what the Bible really said and meant'. His edition of the Greek Testament was the earliest in the field, and his desire was to see the Scriptures translated into every language and given to all. 'I long,' he said, 'that the husbandman should sing them to himself as he follows the plough, that the weaver should hum them to the tune of his shuttle, that the traveller should beguile with them the weariness of his journey.'[1]

We cannot estimate the influence of the new learning upon the people of the Middle Ages by any statement of the influence of the Classics upon the people of our day. We are the products of the new learning. It has entered into and made in large part our culture and our civilization. We are born into its atmosphere, and we find it difficult to conceive the joy everywhere created by the discovery of those things which to us seem commonplaces. Perhaps a figurative way of stating it is more illuminating than a comparison. The sun of the ancient world had set, and the people of the Middle Ages were living in its afterglow, as I have already said. Looking backward, it was as if they saw for the first time the moon and the stars, and the light of another world. Their mental horizon was enlarged by the freedom of thought, the freedom of expression; and the results of both became their heritage. It is often said that poets are our prophets. They are sometimes our historians. And nowhere can we find a statement

[1] *Ibid.*, pp. 569, 570.

better calculated to express the soul of Europe than the few lines of Keats:

> . . . like some watcher of the skies
> When a new planet swims into his ken;
> Or like stout Cortez when with eagle eyes
> He stared at the Pacific, and all his men
> Look'd at each other with a wild surmise,
> Silent, upon a peak in Darien.

But the Renascence would not have been what it was had it not been that it found at its disposal an agency to transmit the new learning and the new conception of things to all who had eyes to see the treasures and ears to hear the message of the older world. The printing-press, strange as it may seem, gave wings to thought and permanence to its expression.

This miracle, for such it is, was the result of a long process—inscriptions on the mountains, on temples, on monuments, and even stones, informing the passer-by of things to be remembered. They were stationary, and whatever information they conveyed had to be received on the spot. Writing, instead of inscriptions, came into vogue, and manuscripts brought knowledge to those who had the means to acquire them. They were costly because each was an original and written by hand. The material was heavy, such as papyrus, and the manuscript bulked large. Such was the state of affairs in the ancient world. A form of sheepskin specially treated, called vellum, came into use. It was permanent but expensive, and heavy. The problem was to find some way of making many copies of one and the same text by a single effort, on material so light that the separate sheets could be bound together and thus, in a handy volume, put in the hands of its possessor the wisdom of the ancients, contributions of different and sometimes widely separated countries, and often the novelties of the passing day. The first great step was taken when letters and words in reverse order were engraved upon blocks of wood, covered with an appropriate medium and impressions taken. But when the next and final stage in this process was reached—the letters engraved on small and movable blocks and combined in the order of the words sought to be reproduced—a method was at hand whereby everything could be reproduced which could be expressed in the twenty-six letters of the alphabet.

The next matter of moment was to find a suitable medium upon which the impression should be made and preserved. Many materials were tried—silk in China, cotton in Damascus, but in Spain of the thirteenth century native-grown hemp and flax replaced the cotton of Damascus and the silk of China, and produced the linen paper suitable to printer, publisher, and public. The movable type alone was needed, and it made its appearance in full flood of the Renascence, on the eve of the fall of Constantinople, and, within a year after that event, the first perfected fruits of the great discovery—a Papal brief and the Holy Bible. The paper was already at hand for the movable type, and within ten years from 1440 it came into use. If, as seems likely, it was the 'discovery' of one Lourens Coster, of Haarlem, it was improved by Johann Gutenberg, of Mainz; and, in any event, through him and his associates it became universally used. Within the fifteenth century it is estimated that from twenty-five to thirty thousand different books and editions had already been printed—one-third in Italy, an equal number in Germany, and the remainder in other countries. Three things were necessary: small type, so that much could be got within a small compass; a handy format, so that a companion might be made of the book; and a price which would enable those to purchase it who could not have acquired manuscripts. Aldus Manutius of Venice hit upon a small and acceptable type; the Elzevirs of Holland, the duodecimo volumes with which their name is identified, in the sixteenth century, and through the efforts of both, and their associates and competitors, a price was set which to us of to-day seems extraordinarily moderate. The cost of an Aldine volume ranged from about a shilling to half a crown; and many of the Elzevirs were published at eighteen pence to two shillings. Within the course of a century the masterpieces and even the lesser known writings of antiquity were to be at the disposal of those who had a mind to read them. The newer literature also was scattered abroad. In one year no less than twenty-four thousand copies of Erasmus's *Colloquia* were struck off by one printing-press, and in 1527 a Spanish version of another of his writings could be found, it is said, in many country inns throughout Spain. The middle class could thus purchase books and, like the nobles and princes of a generation ago, possess private libraries. And not the least result of it all was the accuracy of the printed page. The humble printer had indeed complied with the command of the Lord: 'Write the vision, and make it plaine vpon tables, that he may runne that readeth it.' The printing-press had made the fortune of the Renascence, which found expression in different ways in all of the countries of western Europe. 'The vigorous Iberian mind, with its strongly-marked individuality, showed the impetus given by the Renaissance in other forms than those of classical scholarship', says Sir Richard Jebb. 'It found expression in the romance of Cervantes, in the epic of Camoens, and in the dramas of Lope de Vega; or, not less characteristically, in the wistful ardour of exploration which animated Vasco da Gama and Colombo.'[1]

But 'wistfulness' or 'ardour', if it put them to sea, would not bring them back. It was one thing to hug the coasts, but quite another to put boldly out to sea. Fortunately, the discovery of the mariner's compass enabled them to do both. 'Seven cities', we are told, 'warred

[1] *The Cambridge Modern History*, vol. i (1909), pp. 578–9.

for Homer being dead.' For the discovery of the mariner's compass there are no less than six contestants—the Chinese, the Arabs, the Greeks, the Etruscans, the Finns, and the Italians; and whatever may be the case with the birthplace of Homer, that of the mariner's compass is still undecided. By each of the claimants it was used, but the relation of each to the other, and the matter of priority, are mooted points. From an interesting article on the 'Compass' published in the *Encyclopaedia Britannica*, I lift here and there a passage. An Arab writer travelling from Tripoli to Alexandria in 1242 stated in his *Merchant's Treasure*, published some forty years later, that a magnetized needle was then used which 'floated on water by means of a splinter of wood or a reed'. And he expressly adds: 'They say that the captains who navigate the Indian seas use, instead of the needle and splinter, a sort of fish made out of hollow iron, which, when thrown into the water, swims upon the surface, and points out the north and south with its head and tail.' [1]

Coming now to Europe, it appears that the first definite statement of the use of the mariner's compass is to be found in a work of the twelfth century. The needle was placed on a pivot and allowed to make its own position of repose, so that the course was shown to the mariners when the polar star was hidden. In another work of the same author, Alexander Neckam, there is a further illuminating passage: 'Mariners at sea, when, through cloudy weather in the day which hides the sun, or through the darkness of the night, they lose the knowledge of the quarter of the world to which they are sailing, touch a needle with the magnet, which will turn round till, on its motion ceasing, its point will be directed towards the north.' All that is certain, the learned article informs us, is a knowledge of the nautical use of the magnet at the end of the thirteenth century.[2]

The first authentic description of a pivoted compass is of the same period, but it is still a matter of conjecture when the compass card was added. The wind-rose is older than the compass, and 'the north point', according to the article, 'indicated in some of the oldest compass cards with a broad arrow-head or a spear, as well as with a T for Tramontano, gradually developed by a combination of these, about 1492, into a *fleur de lis*, still universal'.[3] This was the year of Columbus's famous discovery.

For many years, the invention of the mariner's compass was also attributed to the visionary doctor of Mallorca, Raimundo Lulio, who mentions in his *Félix de las maravillas del orbe* and in his *Astronomía* the characteristic of the magnet or loadstone to 'turn the needle towards the north', and also that of 'the northern star which with the magnet attracts iron'. In his *Arte de Navegar*, which is said to be the

1 vol. vi (11th ed., 1910), p. 807.
2 *Ibid.*, p. 808.
3 *Ibid.*, p. 809.

first work ever written on the subject, that very visionary spirit remarked that to the west of the Hispanic Peninsula there lay a continent of land, and in his *Cuestiones solubles por el Arte demostrativo*, that '*Terra et Mare sunt sphoericum corpus*'.[1]

But something more than the compass was needed. It was found in the astrolabe, now superseded by the sextant, for taking the altitudes of the sun, moon, and stars, for calculating latitude, for determining the points of the compass, time, and the altitude of mountains. The mariner's astrolabe dates from 1480, and with tables of the sun's declination then available it was possible to calculate latitude by meridian altitudes. This was the instrument used by Columbus. Therefore, the mariner could safely put to sea and, with compass and astrolabe, have a fair chance of returning to the home port, escaping storms and the other dangers more greatly feared from the monsters with which the unknown seas were believed to be infested. Knowledge and skill, vision, and, above all, courage, were needed. Columbus had all of these and, in addition, faith.

In his excellent volume on *L'Exotisme américain dans la littérature française au XVIe siècle*, Gilbert Chinard, Professor of French Literature at Johns Hopkins University, has an illuminating passage:

> The men who were to discover America would carry with them a heavy load of myths and prejudices. Isidore of Seville, Lactantius and St. Augustine had declared belief in the antipodes to be absurd and heretical: the world was always separated into strictly defined zones of which ours alone was habitable; to wish to pass beyond its bounds was madness, and even worse, it was impious. Nevertheless, humanity, which until that time had always lived bound up in itself, felt arising within itself a spirit of adventure that impelled it to enlarge a horizon growing daily more confined. All of Europe was sorely oppressed by a need for change, a thirst for novelty. . . . The diffusion of ancient writings, thanks to the printing press, was to reveal the knowledge and political systems of antiquity. A vague aspiration toward happiness which craved immediate realization, was to bring about an outburst of pastoral poetry in Italy, in France and even in England. For a time there was a belief in the Renaissance, that is to say, in a real regeneration of the world, a spirit of liberty and emancipation which was to sweep over all Europe. And it was at this moment that there occurred in a rather unexpected way the discovery of Islands in the Ocean of a new world.[2]

To us of the present day it seems a simple matter to have sailed from the Canary Islands on a line due west until land was discovered; and it seemed so simple and natural to Columbus that he wondered why the great of the world would not start him upon his voyage. The world might be flat to the flat-minded, but to those who used their intelligence, the world was as round as the head above their shoulders. Therefore, a course due west from Spain was bound to reach Asia with its silks, its spices, and its treasures, which the people of that day wanted to obtain. There had been land-routes to Asia, but they were becoming

[1] *Biblioteca de Autores Españoles*, M. Rivadeneyra, Editor, tomo lxv (Madrid, 1873). Discurso preliminar de Don Adolfo de Castro, p. xviii.

[2] (Paris, 1911), p. xv.

difficult because of the inroads of the Turks and the fall of Constantinople under their massive artillery. Then, too, the cities which had possessed themselves of the routes to the far east, such as Venice and Genoa, and from which they drew fabulous profits, were naturally satisfied with things as they were, and not inclined to seek a new highway which, if found, they would not be able to control. This Columbus learned, for Genoa, his native city, and Venice, were cold to his overtures. The two kingdoms of the Peninsula, Portugal and Spain, lying to the west, were shut out from traffic with Cathay. For many years Columbus had been a wanderer, much of the time in Portugal, and Spain was Portugal's neighbour. To the north of both was France, likewise looking to the west, and excluded from eastern routes; and to the north was also a small country which had not yet played a role in the world's affairs, but which was about to start on that career of discovery and conquest which has made of England more than the rival of the Roman Empire. It lay off Europe, watching, as it were, its opportunity; and like the countries to the south, its outlet was to the west. Therefore, Columbus made an appeal to each of these countries. Portugal was not likely to indulge in the western adventure; it found a route to Asia around Africa, by way of the Cape of Good Hope—a route which its steady navigators had discovered, making of Lisbon, within a few years, the acknowledged centre for the distribution of Eastern wares. France did not allow itself to be persuaded, and England was too late in taking up the Italian adventurer. He was already succeeding with Spain.

*
* *

On October 12th, 1929, I had the honour to deliver before the Institute of International Law, during its session at Briarcliff, New York, an address on 'The Discovery of America and Its Influence on International Law'. As certain passages in this address bear directly upon the present subject, it may not be inapposite to repeat them here.

'The Moors had spread as a flood from the Mediterranean to and beyond the Pyrenees. Slowly the waters of invasion subsided. On January 2, 1492, Boabdil, the last of the Moorish Kings, surrendered at Granada, to Ferdinand and Isabella. "We are Thine," he said to them, "powerful and exalted King. These are the keys of this paradise; receive this city, for such is the will of God."

'Spain had achieved territorial and spiritual unity, and its Golden Age was already in sight. Concentration within was to be accompanied by expansion without. The spirit of adventure which had expelled the Moor was to invade a distant and unknown world. The one and the other were of 1492.

'The domain beyond the seas was to be the gift of a foreigner in the service of Spain. The doer of a great deed must be, we think, a great man. We are not content to take him for what he is. He must be of ancient lineage, although he need not be the head of the house. Indeed, it is more interesting if his immediate parents have seen better days, so that the youth has had to shift for himself and make his own way.

'Therefore it is that Christopher Columbus was born in Genoa of gentle birth, although his father was a weaver. The son would thus be well connected and accorded the benefit of university training. He seems to have followed his father's trade. In any event, he was not a sailor by calling [if the views of recent authorities are to be accepted],[1] and his first venture upon the high seas appears to have taken place some three years before he made his way westward to Lisbon. Here he seems to have taken an interest in tales of the sea, and to have gone to sea himself. There is nothing strange in this, for Portugal was then rounding the western coast of Africa, and was soon to pass the Cape and make for the Indies in the East. Fortune was to have it that the Genoese, although not in the service of Portugal, was to put to sea and find a way to the West Indies.

'He took an interest in navigation, in accounts of travellers, and he dabbled in matters scientific. Mingling with sea-faring men, he learned of vessels driven westward by storms and of lands which their crews had seen. He convinced himself that there were islands to the west, and that they could be reached if only he had a "patron".[2] We are told that he unbosomed himself to the Portuguese who, furtively sailing westward but finding nothing, had no further use for the impecunious stranger in their midst.

'Thereafter he turned to Spain, where he spent a number of years in searching for the "patron" who was to speed him westward. He was presented to their Catholic Majesties and spoke of the western venture. They naturally referred him to a committee of persons having their confidence. Columbus appeared before its members, but they reported against him. This was as was to be expected, if it be true as alleged that, mindful of his Portuguese experience, he spoke guardedly of the islands, giving little or no information about them; but insisting that he, and he alone, could find them.

'This was no doubt discouraging to Columbus, but it assuredly implies neither ignorance nor bad faith on the part of the committee. Over-zealous biographers have accused their Majesties of putting off Columbus on one pretext or other, but they owed him nothing. Then,

[1] Henry Vignaud, *Études critiques sur la vie de Colomb avant ses découvertes* (Paris, 1905), pp. 306, 365. *Vide* also Ramiro Guerra y Sanchez, *Historia de Cuba*, tomo i (2nd ed., Habana, 1922), p. 133.

[2] *Vide* the account of Columbus' arrival and life in Portugal in the Introduction to *Cristoforo Colombo, Documenti e prove della sua appartenenza a Genova* (published by the city of Genoa, 1931), pp. xxi–xxii.

too, they were engaged in expelling the Moors and freeing Spain from foreign domination. When this was done, they would have time to think of other things. They thought of Columbus, who had somehow found patrons who possessed influence with the Court. It thus happened that within four months after the fall of Granada, Columbus had made his terms with their Majesties, or rather with Isabella, whose mind was more open to generous ideas than that of her royal consort, Ferdinand, King of Aragon. Within a further period of four months, Columbus was on his way westward, with three tiny ships and a motley crew, but with a stout heart and an unshakeable faith in his adventure.

'First to the south, and then to the west, farther to the west, always to the west. On October 12th, the intrepid Commander reached one of the Bahama Islands. Immediately, he took possession of it in behalf of Spain, but it is now British soil. Learning from the natives of a larger island to the south, he repaired thither. On October 28th, 1492, he landed upon Cuba, the first of the future American Republics to be touched by Columbus on the first of his western voyages.

'What were the immediate results? The ultimate consequences we shall never know. An historian has told us a part of the tale: "The world has increased in size; commerce and shipping will extend through the immensity of an ocean without shores. The ores of the New World will cause a revolution in finance, in property, in manufactures, in the mercantile spirit of nations, and the crusades against the Mohammedans will be replaced by crusades for the conversion of idolaters." [1]

'I have quoted these few lines from Lafuente because they sum up admirably the influence of the discovery of America on the material world, implying, but not stating, that the new conditions would need different policies and other laws to regulate the conduct of nations. This would mean a modern law of nations. But this is not all. The quotation ends with a suggestion that Christianity, no longer in conflict with Islam, should extend its influence beyond the confines not only of Spain, but to the pagan peoples beyond the seas.

'The Spanish Church rose to the opportunity of well-doing; its servants crossed the waste of waters, carrying to the Indians but recently discovered the doctrines and practices of the Christian religion. And through the preaching of the Gospel the newer law of nations was to come into being and assume definite form and shape.'

No incident is more familiar than Columbus's discovery of America, and he knows little of history who does not know how Isabella of Spain is said to have pledged her jewels, that the Italian adventurer might sail into the west and bring back tidings of Cathay. To the west he sailed, and, returning, laid at her feet a gift more precious than any of which she had ever dreamed—a new world.

[1] In Knapp, *Modern Spanish Readings* (Boston, 1883), p. 112.

Why did Columbus discover America? There are several reasons. One is, he set out to discover it—that is, he sailed due west without allowing himself to be diverted to the north or to the south of his chosen line, as others before him had done. Why did he take this line? He felt that it was the shortest and best line from his point of departure, and his judgement in this respect has been confirmed by the succeeding centuries. Had he taken a line to the north, the winds and the currents might have been unfavourable; and in like manner, the course to the south of the Canaries had disadvantages. He wanted the eastern wind to fill his sails and to carry him westward. It did. And on his return voyage from the West Indies (he died in the belief that he had discovered at least the island outposts of Asia), he did not follow the course which had led him westward; he turned to the north, taking the course to the Azores. Why did he go and return by different routes? Because he was the ablest sailor of his time. He had made a study of the winds and currents of the ocean, so that with all the opportunities of mistake before him, he chose the best course to the west, and the appropriate course by which to return. How was he able to do this? There need be no doubt upon this point *if we are to accept his own words as evidence*,[1] for he himself had given the reason, and it has been confirmed by Las Casas, admitted then and now to be an authority on things American: 'I went to sea very young,' he says in a letter of 1501, 'and have continued it to this day; and this art inclines those that follow it to be desirous to discover the secrets of this world; it is now forty years that I have been sailing to all those parts at present frequented; and I have dealt and conversed with wise people, as well clergy as laity, Latins, Greeks, Indians, and Moors, and many others of other sects; and our Lord has been favorable to this my inclination, and I have received of him the spirit of understanding. He has made me very skilful in navigation, . . .'[2] 'In the art of navigation,' in the opinion of Las Casas, 'Columbus exceeded, without any doubt, all others who lived in his day.'[3] What did the 'spirit of understanding' which, he said, the Lord had given him, and his own seamanship enable him to accomplish? He navigated three little vessels across the Atlantic, putting to sea on Friday, the 3rd of August, 1492, and landing on one of the Bahama Islands on the morning of Friday, the 12th of October, 1492.

The expedition numbered eighty-eight persons in all. The largest of the vessels was the *Santa Maria*, commanded by Columbus, a decked ship of a hundred tons burthen, and a crew of fifty-two men. Next in size was the *Pinta*, under the command of Martin Pinzon. It was a vessel of fifty tons, with a crew of eighteen men. The *Niña*, of forty

[1] Vignaud, *op. cit.*, p. 305 *et seq.*
[2] George E. Nunn, *The Geographical Conceptions of Columbus* (1924), p. 43.
[3] *Ibid.*, p. 44 (note).

tons, had a crew of eighteen men, and was under Pinzon's brother, Vincente Yañez.[1]

If, as has been claimed, rumours of 'Antihla', an island to the west (reported by some storm-tossed vessels in the fifteenth century, and therefore put upon the map), entered into the calculations of Columbus, he had himself on October 28th, and on his very first voyage, the consolation of putting his foot upon the soil of Cuba, then and now the Pearl of the Antilles. The great navigator also discovered the island of Haiti, and on the 16th of January turned northward and east towards the Old World. He arrived in the harbour of Palos, from which he had sailed, exactly seven months and eleven days after his departure from that port. In the middle of April he presented himself in person before their Catholic Majesties and an astonished world.

The discovery of America eventually put an end to the Renascence, for instead of contenting themselves with adventures to be found in books (of which a word later), succeeding generations sought adventure in the New World. Thus it was that, according to a witty French writer, D'Anville by name, 'the greatest of errors—the supposition that Asia extended eastward beyond the 180th degree of longitude—of Ptolemy's geography, led men to the greatest discovery of new lands'.[2]

Another Frenchman has stated the material and spiritual results of the great 'error'.

> An apparent accident, based perhaps on deep underlying causes, made the Renaissance coincide with two discoveries of the very greatest consequence: America revealed and the system of the universe envisaged. The discovery of America enlarged the habitable earth and offered to Europeans unlimited fortune in the future and world domination. At the same time the earth, dispossessed of the central place it was believed to hold in the universe, was no more than a point lost somewhere in unlimited space. These two new conceptions,—the world at once enlarged and diminished, opened to the spirit of conquest and enterprise, and in the eyes of philosophers, reduced to but a grain of dust in the infinite—overthrew in a remarkable manner the traditional proportion of things. They disposed the minds of men to a spirit of adventure, some pursuing fortune in the Islands, others, science and truth in the open and bold conceptions of a philosophy freed from the chains of authority.[3]

The process of discovering America is still going on. We have cut down the forests and cleaned away the brushwood. We have settled it from ocean to ocean, and made it a part of the world; but there is something more to do—a much greater and more difficult task lies before us: to discover ourselves, what we are, what we stand for, and, through introspection, to justify the physical discovery of America. The late Stuart Sherman called it 'The Emotional Discovery of America'.[4]

[1] *Encyclopaedia Britannica* (11th ed.), p. 742.

[2] Humboldt, *Examen critique de l'histoire de la géographie du nouveau continent*, vol. i (1836), p. 11.

[3] L. Petit de Julleville, *Histoire de la langue et de la littérature française*, vol. iii, pp. 13–14.

[4] The title of his address delivered in commemoration of the twentieth anniversary of the founding of the American Academy of Arts and Letters. Printed in *Academy Publication No. 54* (1926), p. 144.

What it would mean for all of us to embark upon the great adventure he points out in his address under this heading delivered in 1926 (the last year of his all too short life) before the American Academy of Arts and Letters, to which I would invite your attention and suggest that you read it at your earliest leisure.

* * *

The most inconspicuous of the events of the *annus mirabilis* of 1492 was the appearance—of all things!—of a grammar. But it was a grammar of the Castilian language.

Printing had come into Spain with the accession of Isabella to the throne of Castile. It was probably introduced into Salamanca by one Antonio de Lebrija, also known as Nebrija,[1] the author of the grammar in question—the first grammar of the Spanish language; the first grammar of a vulgar tongue to be published by any humanist,[2] and the first scientific grammar in any modern language. Under ordinary circumstances the appearance of a grammar could not be considered a national, much less an international event, but the circumstances under which this first of modern grammars appeared made it both.

In 1481, but seven years after the accession of Isabella, Lebrija published at Salamanca his *Introductiones latinae*—a little book which, it is said, 'marks an epoch in the history of Spanish Humanism'.[3] When it came to the attention of the Catholic Sovereign, she appears to have suggested in about 1485 that the Latin text of the *Introductiones* should be accompanied by a literal translation in Spanish, so that the nuns and 'devout ladies generally' might learn Latin 'without the intervention' of a masculine instructor.[4] The desire of the Queen was to Lebrija as a command, but he was much perplexed, as it appeared to him a difficult, if not an impossible task, 'because of the lack of an adequate vocabulary in Spanish'.[5] However, he discovered that it could be done and, as often happens, one discovery led to another and a greater. A grammar of the Spanish language was issued, with the result that one Christopher Columbus, sailing westward on his voyage of discovery, bore Castilian to America with him, where it was destined not only to survive him, but, indeed, to outlast the Imperial Domain of Spain in the New World, preserving a spiritual hegemony after the loss of its territorial possessions.

It is curious how great events are sometimes crowded within an inconceivably short space of time, and also curious how they meet and

[1] *Vide* Ig. González-Llubera, in his 'Introduction' to Nebrija's *Gramática de la lengua castellana* (Oxford University Press, 1926), p. xxiii, note (50).

[2] *Vide* Professor Foster Watson's *Luis Vives, El Gran Valenciano* (Hispanic Notes and Monographs, Oxford, 1922), Spanish Series, iv, p. 104, note 1.

[3] González-Llubera, *op. cit.*, p. xxiv.

[4] *Ibid.*, pp. xxv, xl–xli.

[5] *Ibid.*, p. xli.

mingle. In the very year of 1486, in which Columbus had his first interview with Her Catholic Majesty in Salamanca, and the question of a voyage westward was discussed, the *Introduciones latinas . . . contrapuesto el romance al latin* seems to have been issued in Salamanca; and in Salamanca, where Columbus had received his first support, the grammar of the Castilian language appeared in the year of his first expedition.

First a word of Lebrija; next of the grammar and the reasons for its composition; then of its influence.

Antonio Martínez de Cala—ordinarily called 'Antonio de Lebrija', from the little town of that name lying within almost a stone's throw from Seville—was born within the first half of the fifteenth century, some authorities preferring 1444,[1] or 1445,[2] another 1442,[3] and still another 1441.[4] After studying at Salamanca, he left Spain at the age of nineteen, it is said, to spend ten years (which some would reduce to seven)[5] in Italy, then in the full flood of the Renascence. He tells us why he went: not to obtain a stipend from the Church, nor to study civil or canon law, nor to engage in trade; but, upon his return, to reintroduce into Spain the knowledge of Latin authors who 'had been, as it were, banished from Spain for many centuries'.[6] His ambition was, as so often happens, twofold: personal, in the sense that he wished to win renown in the intellectual world and to establish a place for himself in the republic of letters, and, at the same time, ardent patriot that he was, to advance the interests of his country as he saw them, first, by eliminating barbarism through the introduction of the Renascence, choosing Salamanca, as the Apostle Peter had chosen Rome, and St. Paul, Athens, as the stronghold from which he should proclaim the new doctrine.

So much for the years spent in Italy and the purposes which he had in mind. After returning and establishing himself in Salamanca, 'as it were a fortress taken by storm',[7] from which to force the powers of darkness to surrender themselves, Lebrija presented to Her Catholic Majesty, in Salamanca, during her sojourn and that of her royal spouse in 1486–7, the specimens of Spanish grammar, which his success with the *Introduciones latinas*, arranged in parallel columns of Spanish and Latin, had encouraged him to undertake. With the encouragement of Isabella, he continued the work, completing it, apparently, in 1491, on the eve of the territorial unity of Spain, writing the preface after the surrender of Granada, because of which, and for the first time in

[1] González-Llubera, *op. cit.*, pp. xviii–xix.

[2] *Vide* Menéndez y Pelayo, *Bibliografía Hispano-Latina Clásica*, tomo i (Madrid, 1902), p. 843.

[3] This is the date suggested, but also queried, by James Fitzmaurice-Kelly, *A New History of the Spanish Literature* (1926), p. 164.

[4] *Vide* González-Llubera, *op. cit.*, pp. xviii–xix, note (22).

[5] *Ibid.*, and pp. xxi–xxii. [6] *Ibid.*, p. xix, note (28). [7] *Ibid.*, p. xxiii, note (46).

centuries, Spain felt itself to be a territorial as well as a spiritual unity; and having it issue from the press on the 18th day of August, at the very time when Columbus was speeding westward, westward, for his territorial discovery. We have a photographic reproduction, made by a German scholar, of the *editio princeps* from the copy belonging to no less a person than Columbus's son [1]—which we would like to think was the copy of the great navigator himself.

What were the purposes of Lebrija, Spanish patriot to the marrow of his bones, which caused the publication of the grammar of his native language? While Lebrija may not be said to have been an over-garrulous person, he graciously and generously took the reader, real or prospective, into his confidence, by giving items about himself [2] which enable us to construct the personality of one whom no less a judge than Menéndez y Pelayo has finely called 'the most brilliant literary personification of the Spain of the Catholic Sovereigns',[3] and of whom a contemporary, Arias Barbosa, Hellenist and Portuguese, sang in Latin verse, that he had 'mixed the sacred waters of the Permessus with those of the Tormes'.[4]

How was this done? In the introduction to his epoch-making grammar, Lebrija would have us believe that it was the most natural thing in the world for him to have published his grammar in 1492. History, of which he seems to have been very fond, and of which he assuredly made great use, had informed him, and he informed Her Majesty, to whom he dedicated the grammar, that language was always the companion of Empire, and it always happened, that as they had jointly begun, so, conjointly, they grew, flourished, and finally perished from the earth. He illustrates this by the history of the children of Israel in Egypt and in the Holy Land; by the history of Greek and Latin; and, coming to his own country, speaking as of 1492, he said explicitly: 'What we have said of the Hebrew, Greek, and Latin languages, we may illustrate much more clearly by the Castilian, which

[1] Antonio de Lebrija, *Gramatica Castellana. Reproduction phototypique de l'édition princeps (1492). Publiée avec une préface par E. Walberg*, Halle, 1909. *Vide* especially, p. v.

[2] 'Fué aquella mi doctrina tan noble (decía el mismo Nebrija con justo aunque poco disimulado orgullo), que aun por testimonio de los envidiosos y confesión de mis enemigos, todo aquesto se me otorga: que yo fuí el primero que abrí tienda de la lengua latina, y osé poser pendón para nuevos preceptos . . . y que ya casi de todo punto desarraigué de toda España los Doctrinales, . . . y otros no sé qué apostizos y contrahechos gramáticos, no merecedores de ser nombrados. Y que si cerca de los hombres de nuestra nación alguna cosa se habla de latín, todo aquello se ha de referir á mi. Es, por cierto tan grande el galardón deste mi trabajo, que en este género de letras orto mayor no se pueda pensar.' [Quoted by D. Marcelino Menéndez y Pelayo, *ibid.*, from the preface of Lebrija's *Vocabulario.*]

[3] *Op. cit.*, p. 845.

[4]
Miscuit hic sacris Tormin Permessidos undis,
  Barbaricum nostro repulit orbe genus:
Primus et in patriam Phoebum, doctasque sorores
  Non ulli tacta detulit ante diem:
Pegasidumque ausus puro de fonte sacerdos
  Nostra per Ausonios orgia ferre choros.

Reprinted by Menéndez y Pelayo, *op. cit.*, p. 843.

had its childhood in the times of the judges and kings of Castile and of León, and began to show its strength in the time of the very enlightened and worthy of perpetual remembrance, King Alphonso the Wise, by whose command were written the *Siete Partidas* and the *General Istoria*; and by whom many works from Latin and Arabic were translated into our Castilian tongue, the which later spread to Aragon and Navarre, and thence to Italy, following in the train of the Spanish Princes whom we sent to govern in those kingdoms. And thus there grew up even the peaceful monarchy which we enjoy, first by Divine bounty and Providence; secondly, by the labour, industry, and diligence of Your Royal Majesty, through whose felicitous fortune the members and fragments of Spain, scattered in many places, were reclaimed and put together into a body and a united kingdom, whose form and frame are so ordered that many centuries, injuries and tempests will be unable to break or to dissever them.'[1] To this, nothing need be added except that Alphonso X, the Wise, to whom Lebrija refers, and the Spanish sovereigns imposed Castilian as the legal language of their Spain, so that as their territory was increased, the territorial domain of Castilian was likewise enlarged.

'Therefore,' Lebrija continues, 'now that the Christian religion, by which we are friends of God and reconciled with Him, has been purified'—a reference to the recent conquest of Granada—'and since the enemies of our Faith have been conquered in war and by force of arms, wherefore we have received so many injuries and feared much greater . . . the time at length has come in which no care remains but that the arts of peace should flourish.'[2] Among the first of these arts is that which teaches us language. And on this point he says that Castilian, 'until the present age, has developed loosely and without rule, because of which it has changed very much in a few centuries, to such an extent, indeed, that if we should compare the language of to-day with that of five hundred years ago, we would find a difference and divergence which could not be greater if we were dealing with two languages'.[2] It was always his hope and desire, in his own words, 'to advance the welfare of our nation, to furnish my countrymen with books by which they could better employ their leisure than in reading novels and histories mixed up with a thousand lies and errors',[2] and consequently he resolved to formulate artificial rules for his Castilian tongue, 'in order that what should be written in that language, now and in the future, might remain in a permanent form and endure throughout the times which are to come',[3] as was the case with Greek and Latin, because they had been subjected to artificial discipline.

It was, in Lebrija's opinion, necessary that this be done, for if Castilian should not, like Latin and Greek, be given a permanent form

[1] *Vide* Antonio de Nebrija, *op. cit.*, pp. 5–6. [2] *Ibid.* p. 6. [3] *Ibid.*, pp. 6–7.

and artistic quality, it would be in vain that the chroniclers and historians of his country should endeavour to hand down to posterity the glorious accomplishments of their land; they would have to be preserved, if at all, in a foreign language, because Spanish would not offer the guarantee of permanency; and his ambition was to be the first agent through which Spanish should become adequate to patriotic endeavour and achievement. He expressed the further hope that his labours should be like those of Zenodotus in Greek, and Crates in Latin, who, 'although surpassed by those who had written later than they, nevertheless had the glory which will be ours—that we have been the first to undertake a task as imperative'.[1] The present was the opportune moment, for 'our language has reached such maturity that there is more reason to fear its decline, than to hope for its ascent'.[1]

Moreover, Lebrija was proud of his discovery, in that it would enable those who did not know Latin and found it difficult, to learn it easily and quickly, through the experience had in studying his Spanish grammar.

But there was another and, for us, a weightier reason, which he thus narrates: 'When in Salamanca, I gave the sample of this undertaking to Your Royal Majesty, who asked me what useful purpose it would subserve. The Very Reverend Bishop of Ávila took over my reply, and in my behalf said that when Your Highness had placed under her yoke many barbarous peoples and nations of foreign languages, and when, as a result of their conquests, it should become necessary for them to receive the laws which the conqueror imposes on the conquered, and with those laws, our language; then, through my book, they might acquire a knowledge of Castilian, just as we ourselves now study the Latin grammar in order to learn Latin'.[2] Thus Spanish would not merely be a means of enabling his countrymen to learn Latin, the universal language of his day, but, through his book, Castilian might, in a way, be universalized, for 'certain it is that not only the enemies of our Faith, who have the need of knowing the Castilian tongue, but the Basques, the Navarrines, the French, the Italians, and all others who have any intercourse and commerce with Spain and therefore the need of our language, unless they have learned it as children, through its use, may learn it most quickly by this, my work'.[2]

The greater use of Castilian which Lebrija sought to advance through his grammar has been vouchsafed his mother tongue in a more universal measure than he could have dared to hope, much less predict; for to-day it is not merely the language of Spain, his mother country, but that of eighteen American Republics, brought into the world by the adventure of Columbus. Castilian, as distinct from the dialects of

[1] *Ibid.*, p. 7. [2] *Ibid.*, p. 8.

Spain, was prescribed by the foresight of the Spanish sovereigns in the permission which they gave to the *conquistadores* to proceed to America and take possession of its vast tracts; and because of this foresight, it is spoken to-day by more than seventy millions of people, increasing more rapidly than the Germans of Germany, or the Russians of Russia—from the Rio Grande to the southernmost point of the American Continent. And there are at most but negligible differences in the Spanish of America, because the Castilian of Spain has been preserved. Its pronunciation is easy, because its spelling is phonetic, and to such an extent that it may one day become the international medium, if the rivalry of French and English should suggest an acceptable substitute.

It was as fortunate for Lebrija, as for us of America, that there was an Isabella. His discovery that Castilian could reproduce Latin, insignificant as it may have seemed to those of his day, may be looked upon as one of the most important discoveries of an era of discoveries, as calculated to perpetuate in a New World, 'Spain, the mother of nations, to which she has transmitted with the ferment of her blood, and the harmony of her language, an immortal inheritance'.[1]

The philologist—for is he not a discoverer in the vast domain of language?—as well as the navigator, not to speak of their Catholic Majesties, has his reward. Strange as it may seem, the humble scholar of Spain may approach at a respectful distance the great Exile of Florence, for if Dante made the Tuscan dialect the language of Italy, Lebrija gave to the Romance tongue its grammatical structure and its permanent form.

*
* *

The spirit of adventure existed, and had existed for many years. The New World, opening as it did unexpected fields of adventure, whetted, as it were, the appetite for adventure in the Old World, and for the romance of chivalry. The greatest of these was *Amadís de Gaula*, printed in the last years of the fifteenth century. It is French in incident, Portuguese in origin, and Spanish in literary form. Of it M. Brunetière felt justified in saying: 'There was never a novel more romanesque, more chivalrous, and, in consequence, more Spanish.'[2] And the late Fitzmaurice-Kelly has spoken of this famous novel in such terms as to justify a quotation of his remarks in this connexion: 'No imaginative work has corresponded more closely to the ideals of a whole epoch. It satisfied to some extent the thirst for adventures

[1] Ricardo Beltrán y Rózpide's 'Cristóbal Colón y la Fiesta de la Raza' (June 15th, 1918), *Boletín de la Real Academia de la Historia*, tomo lxxiii (Madrid, 1918), p. 200.

And if Spain be the mother of nations, Castile may properly be called, in the words of Miss Gwladys L. Williams, 'the very heart of Spain, and the mother of Spanish history'. From an unpublished doctoral thesis, 'The Peisistence of Spanish Tradition in the works of Marquina, León and Martínez Sierra'.

[2] Translated from J. Fitzmaurice-Kelly, *A New History of Spanish Literature* (1926), p. 138.

awakened by the discovery of the New World, by the commerce with strange races under strange stars, by the marvellous feats of the *conquistadores* long before Cortés saw the peak of Darien, or gazed in wonderment upon the golden cupolas of Mexico.'[1] The impressions made by the vision of the city were ineffaceable, for Díaz del Castillo, one of the followers of Cortés, recalled in his old age the adventures of his youth. 'We remained astonished and said that it resembled the things of enchantment which they relate in the book of *Amadís*, by reason of the great turrets, temples, and edifices which they had within the water.'[2] But this was not all. *Las sergas de Esplandián*—which may be freely rendered 'Scenes from the Life of Esplandián'—is the first of the many sequels to the great masterpiece of chivalry. It is said to be from the pen of Montalvo, who is generally considered responsible for the Spanish version of *Amadís*. However that may be, the sequel has, as an eminent authority on Spanish literature has recently said, 'a curious interest to the American reader'. 'When the early explorers set foot in lower California,' Professor Northup continues, in his *Introduction to Spanish Literature*, 'they were reminded of an island of that name [California], "mentioned in *Las sergas de Esplandián*, on the right hand of the Indies, and very near to the Earthly Paradise."' To us, California, the second largest State of the American Union, seems to be not merely 'very near' but to be the 'Earthly Paradise'. 'Such incidents', he concludes, 'show how fiction influenced adventure during that age of high achievement.' And since he adds, 'The reverse was also true',[3] I have felt justified in calling your attention to *Amadís* and *Las sergas de Esplandián*.

*
* *

The effect of the discovery of America upon the thought of the Old World cannot be accurately estimated, for who may hope to measure the final result of a movement which is still in progress? Only of its effect upon the legal profession may we say a word, and only of those who stand out as pre-eminent in the opinion of the world: Sir Thomas More, a Lord Chancellor of England; Erasmus, a humanist friend of More, who saw that law as well as life should be moral; Michel de Montaigne, a lawyer and Magistrate of France; and Sir Francis Bacon, a Lord Chancellor of England. In so doing I am but following *longo intervallo* in the footsteps of Mr. Edward John Payne, who, in order to show the influence of the great discovery upon the thought of the Old World, invoked the persuasive authority of More, of Montaigne, and of Bacon. I would like to have quoted his observations

[1] J. Fitzmaurice-Kelly, *op. cit.*, p. 138.
[2] George Tyler Northup, *An Introduction to Spanish Literature* (Chicago, 1925), p. 148.
[3] *Ibid.*, pp. 147, 148.

in their entirety; they are too long, however, and I may only refer you to his masterly chapters on 'The Age of Discovery' and 'The New World' in the first volume of *The Cambridge Modern History* (1909). The first of the four great men (for such, indeed, they were), Sir Thomas More, sought to redress the faults of the Old World by picturing what might be if mankind could start anew in a commonwealth free to make its own traditions; the second represents the triumph of the new learning; the third dwelt upon the social conditions of peoples unspoiled by Europe; and the fourth saw in the New World the development of science in the service of mankind. It is precisely on these lines that the New World has justified its discovery.

To More, America was the land of nowhere, or the beautiful land —Utopia. It has never been found, and it only existed in his fruitful mind and his abounding heart. There man lived, not for himself, but for his fellow, or, rather, each was a part of a whole, and the whole larger than all its parts. The individual was as nothing in himself, and he possessed nothing; lands and goods were in common for the benefit of all, and therefore of the individual, not as individual, but as part of the whole. Each produced his share of the total product, and it was but just that each should participate in the fruits of his mind or the labour of his body. But neither the one nor the other should be sacrificed in the process. All worked, men and women, and therefore they did not need to rise before the sun and toil after its setting. Six were the hours of labour: three in the morning, three in the afternoon, with two in between for food and recreation. Therefore, all were to have a chance to improve their minds, not merely those who elsewhere belonged to a preferred class; and happiness was to be the lot of all, not the privilege of the lucky few. Justice was the foundation of the society, and the common good the test of everything.

Let us look into some phases of the subject, and first of all let us see how Columbus's discovery of America led to More's discovery of Utopia. The model commonwealth of Sir Thomas More is frankly due to the discovery of the New World; it is a product of the new learning: a new picture on an old canvas, in a new frame—the background, indeed, of the past, the painting of a trained and practised hand, and the whole aglow with the inner light of a spiritual imagination.

In the summer of 1515 Sir Thomas More found himself in the Low Countries as Ambassador of England for the renewal of friendly relations between the Lowlands and the England of Henry VIII. The Lowlands were then Spanish provinces, and the King, Charles the First of Castile, as More called him, was within four years destined, as we already know, to become the most redoubtable of Holy Roman Emperors under the name of Charles V. More and his colleagues met at Bruges. After an exchange of views, the Spanish negotiators repaired to Brussels, the capital of the province, in order to confer with the Government, and More to Antwerp, where he could be in touch with English merchants whose interests he represented in the negotiations. One Sunday, after hearing mass in the Church of Our Lady of Antwerp, he was attracted by a man of weather-beaten countenance and foreign aspect whom he took for a seaman. One Peter Giles, a protégé of the great Erasmus, and therefore a friend of More, espied him, and, calling his attention to the stranger—a Portuguese by birth, and Raphael Hythlodaye by name—presented him as one who had accompanied on his voyage to the New World one Amerigo Vespucci, an Italian and later a naturalized Spaniard, as was indeed the great Columbus. From Giles's account of the stranger, it appears that Hythlodaye had taken part in 'the .iii. last voyages of thoes .iiii., that be nowe in prynte and abrode in everye mans handes'.[1] And thereby hangs a tale of interest to us of the New World. The Florentine (for Amerigo was of that city of the Renascence) had represented the Medicis in Portugal, and alleged with more or less reason that he had taken part in some four voyages to the New World, giving of them descriptions, which were printed in the little city of Saint-Dié by a group of scholars in the *Introduction to Cosmography* which they were issuing in 1507. Of the New World they made a map, and on it for the first time appears the name of America, which they were minded to give it after the shrewd adventurer who, taking the public into his confidence, received in return the name of a continent. In the fourth voyage the fortunate Amerigo left behind some twenty-four of his men in the New World, among whom was, according to More's informant, Hythlodaye, who, with five companions, set out to explore the neighbouring and far-off countries, discovering and passing five years in Utopia, and returning from the other side of the globe, antedating in fiction the circumnavigation of the world which Magellan, a Portuguese navigator in the service of Spain, actually accomplished a few years later. The stranger is invited to More's lodgings, and in the garden, seated on a bench, he tells the story of his travels to his eager listeners. Interrupted by the noon-day meal, they return to the garden in the afternoon, at which time and place Hythlodaye discourses of the manners and customs of Utopia.[2] 'A slight inspection of those four

[1] J. H. Lupton's edition of *The Utopia of Sir Thomas More, in Latin from the Edition of March, 1518, and in English from the first Edition of Ralph Robynson's Translation in 1551* (Oxford, 1894), p. 27.

[2] More's remarkable skill in the use of dialogue is evidenced in many of his writings, but it is nowhere more apparent than in his *Utopia*. 'It is this dramatic temper which gives the *Utopia* its peculiar literary attraction, whilst at the same time it enables More, without committing himself, to put the case for and, more briefly, against Communism [*vide infra*, p. 29]; to state the dangers, and, on the other hand, the duty, of serving the king, at the time when he was himself hesitating whether he should enter Henry's service or no.' *Vide* Professor R. W. Chambers's learned introduction to Nicholas Harpsfield's *The life and death of Sr Thomas Moore, knight, sometymes Lord high Chancellor of England, written in the tyme of Queene Marie*, edited by Elsie Vaughan Hitchcock (London, 1932), p. clvii.

Voyages', says the most competent of More's editors and commentators, 'will show how attentively More had studied them, and how many accessories for his picture he had borrowed from them.'[1] For our purposes we do not need to dwell upon details of this kind or to show the relations between More's narrative and the *Dialogues* of Plato or St. Augustine's *City of God*. We need only point out some of the things which were not, and which, because they had not been and might not be, are called Utopian—the very name being the greatest tribute to More's imaginary commonwealth.

Utopia, conquered by one Utopus, some seventeen hundred years before Hythlodaye's visit, was originally called *Abraxa*, a peninsula. By him it was separated from the mainland, becoming an island to which the conqueror gave his own name. Wherever Utopia may have been, the island which More had in mind was just off the coast of Europe, and the channel of fifteen miles by which it was separated was none other than the English Channel. The island was composed of fifty-four States. At that time the number of shires of England was fifty-four. More considers them as free States, which taken together formed a confederation. Amaurote was the central city and capital, and each of the States sent representatives to the general council. Here More had in mind the Parliament of his own island, of which he had been member and was destined to be Speaker. In each State there was a city with its shire, and each of the cities was but a day's journey apart. In each city there were six thousand families, and in the shires adjoining the cities many living in farmsteads. The population is therefore of two classes, urban and agricultural. They were not to be separate and distinct. There was a third class consisting of bondsmen, unfortunates who had committed offences, because of which they had lost their freedom and were bound to service. It was a punishment rather than a status, and through good conduct they might become free of the State again. Each household of the farmstead consisted of forty persons. In addition, each had two bondsmen. At the head of the household stood 'the goodman and his wife'. The unit in the city was the family, each family having numerous children, not fewer than ten nor more than sixteen, of approximately fourteen years of age. They were usually children of the father and mother or of kindred. By transfer from one family to another the required number was obtained. The lines were not closely drawn between city and country, indeed a feature of the social organization was the transfer from one to the other. But the cities might become too large; in like manner there were transfers, or new cities were formed, a day's journey from one another. But the population of the commonwealth might become too numerous for the island, in which case the land of their neighbours was laid under contribution,

[1] J. H. Lupton, *op. cit.*, p. xxxviii.

peaceably if they could, forcibly if they must, for, in More's commonwealth, 'they counte this the moste iust cause of warre, when any people holdeth a piece of grounde voyde and vacaunt, to no good nor profitable vse'.[1]

How were the families of the city, the city itself, and, indeed, the island, governed? Every thirty families were united under a 'hed baylyffe',[2] called a Phylarch, and every ten of these under a Chief Phylarch elected annually. There would be in all 200 Phylarchs. The inhabitants at large elected from each of the four quarters or wards into which the city was divided four persons, from whom the 200 Phylarchs chose the Ademus or mayor, who held office for life 'onles he be deposed or put downe for suspition of tirannye'.[3] The governing body consisted of the thirty Chief Phylarchs under the presidency of the Ademus or mayor, meeting every third day, or oftener if need be, with two different Phylarchs summoned to each of the meetings. So much for the municipal government. The government of the island was vested in a national council composed of three representatives from each of the cities, meeting once a year at Amaurote, the capital. More's conception of a perfect commonwealth is thus a Republic with a democracy at its base, governed through officials directly or indirectly elected by the people. From this it is no long cry to a government of the people, by the people, and for the people.

Community of property was the basis of the social organization of Utopia. More, however, took exception to community of goods, saying:

> But I am of a contrary opinion . . . for me thynketh that men shal neuer there lyue wealthelye, where all thynges be commen. For how can there be abundaunce of gooddes, or of any thing, where euery man with draweth his hande from labour? whome the regarde of his owne gaines driueth not to woorke, and the hoope that he hath in other mens trauayles maketh hym slowthfull.[4]

To which Hythlodaye replied:

> I maruell not . . . that you be of this opinion. For you conceaue in your mynde other none at all, or els a very false ymage and symylitude of thys thynge. But yf yow hadde bene wyth me in Vtopia, and hadde presently sene their fasshions and lawes, as I dyd, whiche liued ther .v. yeares and moore, and wolde neuer haue commen thence, but only to make that new lande knowen here; then dowteles you wold graunt, that you neuer sawe people well ordered, but only there.[5]

The Utopians, indeed, lived in families and in houses, each of which had its plot and its garden. The thirty families under a Phylarch took their meals in a great hall in the official residence of the Phylarch and his wife. At the head table they sat, and on either side two of the 'anctientest and eldest', and at every table 'iiii. at a meesse' [mess].[6] The food was simple, fresh, but adequate, obtained the very day by

[1] J. H. Lupton, *op. cit.*, p. 155. [2] *Ibid.*, p. 121. [3] *Ibid.*, p. 136.
[4] *Ibid.*, pp. 109–10. [5] *Ibid.*, pp. 110–11. [6] *Ibid.*, p. 164.

stewards from the common market. In More's conception, human life was sacred, and those unable to look after themselves were cared for. In this particular respect the best of the food, he says, was set aside for the hospitals, each of the four wards having one outside the city walls. All of the Utopians worked, some in one way, others in another. Some there were who seemed to be fitted for intellectual pursuits, and these formed what we would call the learned class, from which ambassadors, public officers, and priests were chosen, by secret election of the Phylarchs upon recommendation of the priests. Faith was, however, to be justified by works. A member of the class who idled was put to manual labour, and on the other hand those among manual labourers who showed aptitude for learned pursuits were transferred. All were encouraged. In this new world the two classes intermingled and interchanged, not by election but on the principle of natural selection. Those who laboured with their hands worked but six hours, as I have already mentioned, but where the life of a community is simple and all work, they are not the slaves of toil. They had time for other things and their minds were open to the pleasures of life, for at eight of the evening all were abed, to be up with the lark at four in the morning, if that bird were there to be found and bound to the customs of the place. For in Utopia 'this ende is onlye and chiefely pretended and mynded, that what time maye possibly be spared from the necessary occupations and affayres of the commen wealthe, all that the cytizeins sholde withdrawe from the bodely seruice to the free liberty of the mind and garnisshing of the same'.[1] Even the women were human beings. They worked, they studied, they were educated. And More practised in his own household what he preached through the mouth of the traveller beyond the seas. Was not his daughter the learned and lovely Margaret Roper? In the England of More's day there was, we might say, no end to the hours of labour. We of the present century are living in an eight-hour world, and the social order of things conceived by Karl Marx was the six-hour day of Sir Thomas More.

The resort to arms did not find favour with More, and while Utopians, both men and women, trained themselves for war, they were opposed to it in principle and practice, preferring to sacrifice others than themselves, and to defend themselves by craft and cunning:

> Warre or battel as a thinge very beastelye, and yet to no kynde of beastes in so muche vse as it is to man, they do detest and abhorre; and, contrarye to the custome almost of all other natyons, they cowntc nothingc so much against glorie, as glorie gotten in warre.[2]

And they never went to war except—

> in the defence of their owne cowntreye, or to dryue owte of theyr frendes lande the enemyes that be comen in, or by their powre to deliuer from the yocke and bondage of tyrannye some people that be oppressed with tyrannye.[3]

[1] J. H. Lupton, *op. cit.*, p. 152. [2] *Ibid.*, p. 243. [3] *Ibid.*, pp. 243–4.

The chief and principal purpose of the wars in which they found themselves engaged 'ys to obteyne that thynge whyche yf they had before obteyned, they wolde not haue moued battayle'.[1] They indulged in a practice which must indeed have seemed strange to the reader of More's day, promising 'greate rewardes to hym that will kyll their enemies prince; and sumwhat lesse gyftes, but them verye greate also, for euerye heade of them, whose names be in the sayde proclamacions conteined'.[2] The reason was bluntly stated: 'bycause that by the deathe of a fewe offenders the lyues of a greate numbre of ynnocentes, as well of their own men as also of their enemies, be raunsomed and saued, which in fighting shoulde haue bene sleane.'[3]

But this means failing, they used mercenaries in preference to their own countrymen, and they spent freely of their gold and silver which they held for this purpose. In addition to the mercenaries:

they vse the soldiours of them whom they fight for. And then the help of their other frindes. And last of al they ioyne to their owne citizeins.[4]

But even these were volunteers:

For they thruste no man furthe into warre agaynste hys wyll; bycause they beleue, yf annye man be fearefull and faynte harted of nature, he wyll not onelye doo no manfull and hardye act him selfe, but also by occasyon of cowardenes to hys fellowes.[5]

And the conduct of war must also have seemed strange to the kings and princes of his day. For More's informant had said:

They do not waste nor destroy there enemies lande with forraginges, nor they burne not vp theire corne. Yea, they saue it as muche as maye be from beinge ouerrune and troden downe, other with men or horses; thynkynge that it groweth for theire owne vse and proffyt. They hurt no man that is vnarmed, onles he be an espiall. All cities that be yelded vnto them, they defende. And suche as they wynne by force of assaute they nother dispoyle nor sacke; but them that withstode and dyswaded the yeldynge vp of the same they put to death; the other souldiours they punnyshe with bondage. All the weake multitude they leaue vntouched. If they knowe that anye cytezeins counselled to yelde and rendre vp the citie, to them they gyue parte of the condempned mens goodes. The resydewe they distribute and gyue frely amonge them, whose helpe they had in the same warre. For none of them selfes taketh anye portion of the praye.[6]

Within the island the Utopians were a law-abiding people, apparently for the reason that they had few laws and no lawyers, statements probably to be taken as a jest from one who was at the very moment a leader of the Bar, and destined a few years later as Lord High Chancellor to become titular head of the Bench and the Bar. They were, however, sceptical as to the observance of law and of promises between nations. They never made leagues because leagues between princes were 'wont to be kept and obserued very slenderly'.[7] It was different in his part of the world, More informs us, with that

[1] *Ibid.*, p. 248. [2] *Ibid.* [3] *Ibid.*, p. 250. [4] *Ibid.*, p. 255.
[5] *Ibid.*, p. 256. [6] *Ibid.*, p. 263. [7] *Ibid.*, p. 280.

irony which often rendered it difficult for members of his own household to know when he was speaking seriously or in jest, although Socrates would have understood him, as one of his commentators intimates.[1]

> For here in Europa, and especiallye in thies partes, where the faythe and religion of Christe reygneth, the maiestie of leagues is euerye where estemed holly and inuiolable; partlye through the iustice and goodness of princes, and partlye through the reuerence of great byshoppes. Whyche, lyke as they make no promysse themselfes, but they doo verye religiouslye perfourme the same, so they exhorte all prynces in any wyse to abyde by theyre promisses; and them that refuse or denye so to do, by theire pontificall power and aucthorytie they compell thereto. And surely they thynke well that it myght seme a verye reprochefull thynge, yf in the leagues of them, whyche by a peculiare name be called faythfull, faythe shoulde haue no place.[2]

This is not all, for 'the mo and holyer cerymonies the league is knytte vp with, the soner it is broken, by some cauillation founde in the woordes'.[3] There seemed therefore to be two kinds of justice:

> the one mete for the inferioure sorte of the people, goinge a fote and crepynge by lowe on the grounde, and bounde downe on euery side with many bandes, because it shall not run at rouers: the other a pryncely vertue, which lyke as it is of muche hygher maiestie then the other poore iustice, so also it is of muche more lybertie, as to the which nothinge is vnlawful that it lusteth after.[4]

It was the way of the princes with whom they came into contact which caused the Utopians to avoid leagues, but More causes his traveller to say that they 'woulde chaunge theire mynde if they lyued here'.[5] The Utopians, however, are represented as of the opinion that leagues should not be entered into, even if they were to be kept:

> For this causeth men (as though nations which be separate a sondre by the space of a lytle hyl or a ryuer, were coupled together by no societe or bonde of nature), to thynke them selfes borne aduersaryes and enemyes one to an other; and that it is lawfull for the one to seke the death and destruction of the other, if leagues were not.[6]

It was the opinion of the Utopians:

> that no man ought to be counted an enemy, whyche hath done no iniury; and that the felowshyppe of nature is a stronge league; and that men be better and more surely knitte togethers by loue and beneuolence, then by couenauntes of leagues; by hartie affection of minde, then by woordes.[7]

Few laws, the absence of lawyers, the selection of judges before whom the claimant appeared in person and argued his case, preserved peace and order within the island, and indeed made it a source of envy to the neighbours, who took 'magistrates of them, some for a yeare, and some for fyue yeares space'.[8]

And their practice in religious matters introduced by Utopus, put an end to civil commotion and enabled them to live in peace. There were many forms of religion in the island, and indeed in the cities, and

[1] J. Churton Collins, *Sir Thomas More's Utopia* (Oxford, 1904), p. xxix.
[2] J. H. Lupton, *op. cit.*, pp. 238–9. [3] *Ibid.*, p. 239. [4] *Ibid.*, p. 240.
[5] *Ibid.*, p. 241. [6] *Ibid.* [7] *Ibid.*, pp. 241–2. [8] *Ibid.*, p. 236.

even, it would seem, in parts of the cities, but all agreed with the wisest among them 'in beleuyinge that there is one chiefe and pryncipall God, the maker and ruler of the hole worlde'.[1] At the time of the advent of the European travellers Christianity was unknown among them, but they gladly listened and accepted its principles 'by the secrete inspiration of God, or els for that they thought it next vnto that opinion which amonge them is counted the chiefest'.[2] Every one could believe what he would and endeavour to convert others—

> so that he dyd it peaceably, gentelye, quyetly, and soberlye, without hastye and contentious rebuking and inuehyng against other. If he coulde not by fayre and gentle speche induce them vnto his opinion, yet he should vse no kinde of violence, and refrayne from displeasaunt and seditious woordes. To him that would vehemently and feruently in this cause striue and contend, was decreid bannishment or bondage.[3]

It was a very 'vnmete and folish thing', King Utopus thought, who introduced freedom of religious belief, 'and a pointe of arrogant presumption, to compell all other by violence and threatenynges to agre to the same that thou beleuest to bee trewe'.[4] For, although there be but one true religion, he nevertheless foresaw 'that the trewthe of the owne powre woulde at the laste issue owte and come to lyght'.[5] However, a belief in the immortality of the soul and in an after life was required. Those who did not so believe were deprived of honours and excluded from the right of holding office. But they were not punished, because 'it is in no mans powre to beleue what he lyst'.[6]

This was unacceptable doctrine to the men of More's day, but in very truth the New World was to become the refuge of men and women who could not bring themselves to believe as others in politics, as well as in religion. We may not hope in this world to overtake perfection, just as we can never catch up with the horizon, but unless we set our minds on an ideal and direct our steps towards the goal, which we may never reach, we shall fail to justify our existence. As in the past, so will it be in the future, 'no man, having put his hand to the plough, and looking back, is fit for the kingdom of God'.

* * *

The Utopia of Sir Thomas More shows the effect which the discovery of America had upon the public to which he belonged and in whose behalf he spoke as a lawyer deeply read in the Classics and fitted to appeal to the humanists of his day.

At about the same time, in the year 1515, Erasmus, More's friend and companion, although somewhat older in years and with a European reputation to which More himself could not then or indeed afterwards

[1] *Ibid.*, p. 267. [2] *Ibid.*, pp. 268–9. [3] *Ibid.*, pp. 271–2.
[4] *Ibid.*, p. 272. [5] *Ibid.*, pp. 273–4. [6] *Ibid.*, p. 275.

lay claim, had stated in general terms the enlightened views which both hoped to see become the practice of the princes whom they had in mind, young Henry VIII in England and the youthful Charles, then King of Spain and shortly to be Holy Roman Emperor.

The tractate of Erasmus known as *The Institutes of the Christian Prince* was in his mind at the very time when the *Utopia* was written, if it were not lying upon the desk before him in more or less completed form. It would be surplusage to say, even in passing, that the doctrine professed by Erasmus was humanistic in thought, conception, and form. If More's masterpiece is to be looked upon as the work of the legal mind set to a social and political task, the tractate of Erasmus is to be taken as the classic expression of the views pervading enlightened Christendom in a period when the Spanish were busily engaged in expeditions to the Americas and when the Spanish missionaries were coming into contact with the Indians recently discovered—not always to the advantage of the natives, as Francisco de Vitoria would have us believe a few years later in his disquisition on the subject prepared at Salamanca in 1532.

Dates are of secondary interest, the first interest being the matters to which they relate. Sometimes, however, they are interesting in themselves. This is especially so with these two periods, in the first of which More and Erasmus were indeed looking upon an old world, with the hope that it would be new, in the sense that it might differ from the very material world of which they were a part. At the very same time it appears that a Florentine, one Machiavelli by name, was looking at the Old World, not from a wagon hitched to a star, as an American philosopher has expressed it, but with his eyes lowered to the world at his feet. He too had written with a prince of his day in mind, none other than Lorenzo the Magnificent of the Medicean dynasty. The curious conjunction of dates is that his *Prince*, as in the case of the two works of More and Erasmus, apparently lay at this time in manuscript form upon his desk in Florence, although it was first to see the light of day some years later,[1] in 1532, the very year when Francisco de Vitoria was putting into form the conception of a society extending beyond the horizon of Christendom, which should be based upon a single moral standard, applicable alike to man and State, together with rules of law based upon principles of justice of universal application—a complete refutation of the thesis of the Florentine that the State and the relations of States had no relation to morality.

When he wrote the *Christian Prince*, Erasmus was about fifty years of age and in the full possession of the world's greatest intellect. He had been appointed a member of the council to the young King of Spain, soon to become the fifth Charles in the annals of the Holy Roman

[1] Frederic Seebohm, *The Oxford Reformers* (Everyman's Library, J. M. Dent, London), pp. 229–31.

Empire. On the surface, the tractate was Erasmus's way of expressing his appreciation of the honour which the young King had conferred upon him. Inwardly, it was, like the *Utopia* of More, the expression of his matured convictions upon the education and the duties of a Christian Prince. It was a case of prince speaking to prince; for was not Erasmus then as now the prince of humanists?

The duties of a Christian Prince could be expressed in a single phrase, 'to keep the peace', and the education of a Christian Prince was to fit him to 'keep the peace'.

The little volume is made up of eleven chapters, all dealing with the education and the duties of the Prince: the first two with the education of the Prince as a lad of tender years, and the balance more especially dealing with the activities of the Prince in the performance of his duties. The chapters are difficult to summarize, for they are in themselves a summary of the matured views of Erasmus on the great question before Europe: how the princelings of the day could become enlightened rulers. Then, too, the difficulty is enhanced by the fact that we are dealing with a masterpiece of the world's literature, in which every phrase has an artistic value.

But it is more than a work of art; it is the work of an internationalist, who from his closet expressed the views which the statesman should follow in his cabinet.

Within the compass of a few pages we may only hope to show the reader of to-day why he should read this tractate of more than four centuries ago, for if it were read and its counsel pondered and accepted, the world would be better than it is, and indeed better than it ever has been.

Perhaps it is not too much to say that the opening paragraphs of the *Christian Prince* state the thesis which Erasmus had set himself to prove, and that, short as these paragraphs are, they may be looked upon as a summary of the views which he was to express at length in the tractate. In any event, they are Erasmus at his best.

There were two kinds of princes whom he had in mind: the one elective, the other hereditary. Charles of Spain was one; he was soon to be the other. Born King of Spain, he was to be elected Holy Roman Emperor while still a youth, and this Christian Prince was no ordinary youth.

Erasmus first speaks of the qualities of the elective prince—probably in the hope of arousing the interest of the young King in the tractate, relegating to the second place the hereditary monarch, as the King of Spain no doubt thought himself sufficiently educated for a post which he already held by birth. It would not be amiss if candidates for the highest elective offices in the States of our day should file with their candidacy the first three paragraphs—hardly a page of modern print—in which Erasmus speaks of the qualities which elective officers should possess, as indicating that they realize the necessity of these qualifications and consider themselves as possessing them. What are these qualities?

1. 'In those countries in which the Prince is elected to his office, the qualities particularly to be sought in him are not aristocratic lineage, physical grace, bodily height [the *Encyclopaedia Britannica* closes its *eulogium* of Charles V with the statement that he "had an incomparable leg"], although we read that, in former times, there were barbarians who indulged in the absurd practice [of electing their rulers on this basis], nor even a mild and gentle disposition. Rather should one seek a spirit sedate and far from impetuous; neither so vehement that there is danger lest it break forth in tyranny, intolerant of admonition or advice, should fortune offer an opportunity for such behaviour; nor yet so dispassionate that it will suffer itself to be led by every whim of any person whatsoever. The experience [of the candidate] ought to be taken into consideration; and his age, which should be neither so advanced that it borders upon dotage, nor so tender that he may be carried away by his passions. Possibly some heed ought also to be paid to the matter of health, lest it should immediately become necessary to find a new Prince, and that not without expense to the State.'

2. 'In navigating, he is not placed at the helm who is superior to all the rest in ancestry or wealth or outward appearance; but rather he who excels in skill as a pilot, in vigilance, and in trustworthiness. Even so, a kingdom is preferably given into the charge of one who surpasses his fellows in kingly qualities, that is, in wisdom, justice, moderation of spirit, foresight, and zeal for the public welfare.'

3. 'Ancestral images, gold, and precious stones are of no more significance in the administration of a State, than they are of service to a skipper in the steering of his ship. The one consideration which the Prince should bear in mind in the process of government, is also the sole consideration to be borne in mind by the people when they choose their Prince, namely: the public good, entirely apart from all personal desires.'

4. 'For the very reason that it is a blameworthy act to change a ruler who has once been chosen, special care should be exercised in his selection, lest we suffer a weary length of time for one hour of recklessness.'

After paying his respects to candidates for election to the chief magistracy, Erasmus turns to the hereditary monarch.

1. 'But in those countries where the Prince holds office by virtue of his birth, and not by election, . . . the hope of securing a good ruler is chiefly bound up in the conduct of his education. It is fitting that special care should be devoted to this matter, compensation being

made for the loss in the right of suffrage, by increased zeal with respect to the education [of the ruler]. Therefore, at the very outset—"even from the cradle", to use a common phrase—the mind of the future Prince, hitherto empty and unformed, must be imbued with salutary concepts. The seeds of virtue should at once be sown in the virgin soil of his childish mind, so that gradually, as he acquires age and experience, these seeds may put forth shoots, may grow to maturity, and—once implanted in his nature—may cling to him through all his life. For no [other qualities] are so deeply and firmly rooted in us, as those whose seeds are sown in these early years; years in which the influences absorbed by all of us are tremendously significant, and therefore of even greater significance in the case of a Prince.'

2. 'In countries not empowered to choose their ruler, compensatory care must be exercised in selecting the tutor of the future Prince. It is for the Powers above to will that the Prince shall be born with honourable inclinations. On the other hand, it rests in part with us that he who is born virtuous shall not grow less so; and that he who at birth is lacking in virtue shall be rendered more worthy by education. It was once the custom to set up statues, arches, and inscriptions in honour of those who had served the state well. Yet there is no one more deserving of this honour than those persons who have toiled faithfully and zealously in educating the Prince; for they had at heart no private reward, but the well-being of their country. A nation ruled by a good Prince owes all to that good ruler. But it owes that Prince himself to the individual whose upright counsels have made him what he is. The period during which a Prince may best be formed and corrected is that time when he himself does not as yet realize that he is the Prince . . .' Apparently the reading and the experience of Erasmus had led him to doubt whether much—or indeed anything—could be hoped from a Prince who already knew that he was a Prince. However, he may have had the hope that his tractate on the education of a Christian Prince might be called to the mind of the future Prince, '"even from the cradle", to use a common phrase'.[1]

With these few paragraphs as a foreword, we pass to the chapters in which Erasmus treats of the duties of the Prince. The first of these, the third chapter—although the duties of the Prince are scattered with a generous hand throughout the tractate—is entitled 'The Arts of Peace'.

Apparently Erasmus was not satisfied that 'the whole system of State administration' should be divided 'into arts of peace and war'. His view was that 'the first and principal task' should be 'to instruct the Prince in matters pertaining to wise government in time of peace'; and

[1] The preceding quotations are translated from *Desiderii Erasmi, Opera Omnia,* ed. J. Clericus (Lugduni Batavorum, 1703–6), vol. iv, p. 561.

that 'during peace every possible effort should be made to render the arts of war forever unnecessary'.[1] The Prince should endeavour 'to make himself loved by his subjects', so that his authority should 'be respected' among men.[2]

Believing that it will be convenient for the reader to have a selection of the leading counsels of Erasmus concerning the duties of his Christian Prince, we have taken them here and there from the text and supplied them with numbers.

1. There were various methods by which Princes had been wont to make themselves loved, such as 'incantation and magic rings', but Erasmus would have none of these, boldly stating that 'no incantation is so efficacious as virtue itself';[3] that 'nothing can be more lovable, for not only is it in itself a real and immortal good, but it enlists for its possessor true and undying affection'.[4]

2. 'I should further wish', says Erasmus, 'that the Prince might be born and educated among the people which he is destined to rule, for friendship best germinates and flourishes when the origin of affection is nature itself.'[5]

The comment of Erasmus drives home the advice which he would wish to see accepted. Unfortunately we have but space for a phrase: 'The multitude hates even good qualities when they are unfamiliar, . . .' 'There is a double advantage' in the advice which he has just given, because a prince 'will be more affectionately inclined towards them [his subjects], more disposed to regard them as his own people, and they in turn will look upon him with more favour'.[6]

3. 'For this reason', Erasmus continues, 'I do not like the accepted custom of allying the Prince by marriage with foreign, especially with remote, nations.'[7]

It would seem that this statement proves itself without comment. But since, where monarchs still exist, it appears to be beneath the royal dignity to marry a countryman or countrywoman, the comment of Erasmus by which he seeks to enforce his views is still apposite: 'Race and nationality, and the common spirit they engender, are great aids in winning affection.' On this is a further comment in the nature of an unanswerable reason, 'that part of this benefit will be lost if mixed marriages disturb the native and inherent tendency'.[8]

4. 'It is no servitude to live in submission to upright laws.'[9] The reason for this submission is that the State is only tranquil when the people obey laws because they are good and not because they are imposed by a tyrant whose 'every nod' is law. But how shall we have good

[1] Erasmus's *Institutio Principis Christiani*, translated, with an introduction by Percy Ellwood Corbett (The Grotius Society Publications, London, 1921), chap. iii, p. 19.

[2] *Ibid.*, p. 20. [3] *Ibid.*

[4] *Ibid.* [5] *Ibid.*, p. 21. [6] *Ibid.*

[7] *Ibid.* [8] *Ibid.* [9] *Ibid.*, p. 25.

laws? Through education, of which Erasmus was a great advocate (as became a man who was its greatest example). In his opinion, all the people should be educated, not merely the Prince but also the boys and girls, for 'youth yields to any system of training',[1] if there are good schools and good teachers.

Having thus disposed of ignorance, illiteracy, and prejudice—still problems in our own day—Erasmus says: 'If this is done, there will be no need for many laws or penalties, for citizens will of their own accord do what is right.'[2]

The best teacher, however, is the conscience of the Prince, whose own conduct (according to his conscience) should always be 'irreproachable'.

The fourth chapter is 'On Tributes and Taxes', a subject of perennial interest. The people of his day groaned under both, and, invoking history, Erasmus found that 'many seditions have risen from immoderate taxation'.[3] Therefore the first word of advice under this section is that

5. 'The good Prince will vex the people as little as possible with such measures', and that he should 'rule, if he can, with no expense to the State'. Therefore, the Prince of Erasmus should 'reduce to a minimum his demands on the people'[4] and he should devote his attention to the accomplishment of this.

The poor should be freed as much as possible from the burden of taxation. The Prince should not take advantage of temporary circumstances in order to impose taxation; for the experience of Erasmus was to the effect that if such measures were a profit to the king or the nobles, they would 'never be abolished'.[5]

The Prince should also endeavour 'to avoid excessive inequality of riches'.[6] Although Erasmus is not opposed to private property, steps should, in his opinion, be taken 'to prevent the riches of all the people being concentrated in a few persons'[7]—for which important principles he invokes the authority of Plato, that people should be neither too rich nor too poor, 'for a pauper is no asset, and the rich man refuses to turn his ability to the public account'.[8]

6. The good Prince, therefore, should 'tax least the commodities used by the humblest of the people, such as corn, bread, beer, wine, clothing', which were in his opinion 'indispensable for the support of life';[9] and the Prince's chest is therefore 'best enriched by restricting expenditure',[10] according to the old proverb that 'Parsimony is great tribute'.[11]

But supposing that taxes be needed, what should the Prince tax most heavily? 'Barbaric and foreign goods which are not wanted as

[1] *Ibid.* [2] *Ibid.* [3] *Ibid.*, chap. iv, p. 27. [4] *Ibid.* [5] *Ibid.*, p. 28.
[6] *Ibid.* [7] *Ibid.* [8] *Ibid.* [9] *Ibid.* [10] *Ibid.*, p. 29. [11] *Ibid.*

necessities of life but as luxuries and dainties; and such as are used only by the wealthy, like fine linen, silks, purple, pepper, spices, ointment, gems, and everything else of this nature.'[1]

7. The fifth chapter is appropriately short, as it is 'On Princely Beneficence'. 'The proper glory of good Princes lies in good deeds and kindness.' Therefore the Prince 'will aid some by liberal gifts, encourage others with his favour, deliver others from oppression, and hearten others with sympathy, counting that day lost on which he has not done some one a service'.[2]

The sixth chapter deals with the enactment or amendment of laws, a chapter to be read, pondered, and mastered. There is a temptation to quote much of what he says on this matter.

8. 'The best laws under the best Prince are what render a city or kingdom most prosperous, for the State is then most happy when the Prince is obeyed by all, when he himself obeys the laws, and when the laws themselves are based on the standard of justice and truth, and aim only at the benefit of the commonwealth.

'A good and wise Prince is indeed a kind of living law. He will therefore endeavour to enact not many but the best possible laws, most calculated for the welfare of the State. For a well-ordered State under a good Prince and pure magistrates very few laws will suffice: under other conditions, no number will be enough. It is not the best treatment for a sick man to have an untrained physician prescribing drug on drug.'[3]

If Erasmus is not permitted to comment upon these passages, the reader will make his own comment, without that of Erasmus or the interposition of a third party.

9. 'The Prince should make such laws as not merely decree penalties for the guilty but exert a persuasive influence against crime.

'And as an honest doctor preparing his medicines has no thought but how the disease may be conquered with least danger to the invalid, so the good Prince, in enacting laws, will make the public advantage his sole aim, striving to remedy with as little damage as possible abuses to which the people is subject . . .

'Like the Prince, the law should always be more ready to forgive than to punish . . .

'. . . Let not the Prince compare himself with any one of his subjects, but with the whole body of the State. Thus he will see how much more important is the State, embracing as it does so many excellent men and women, than the single person of the Prince. Even if there were no Prince, the State would still be a State. The greatest have flourished without a Prince, for example the Roman and Athenian

[1] Erasmus's *Institutio Principis Christiani*, chap. iv, p. 29.
[2] *Ibid.*, chap. v, p. 30.
[3] *Ibid.*, chap. vi, p. 32.

democracies. But there can be no Prince without a State; in a word, the Prince presupposes the State, the State does not presuppose the Prince. What is it that alone makes the Prince, if not the consent of those who obey him? . . . Plato says that whereas the law is most supreme under the best Prince, the worst enemy is the despot who subordinates it to a single will.'[1]

10. 'Magistracies and Offices' are the theme of chapter vii: 'That same integrity which the Prince himself exhibits, or something very close to it, he should demand from his officials.'[2] But there are magistrates and magistrates, and it is only the good who can be considered. Invoking the authority of Aristotle, Erasmus declares that good laws are useless when they are not executed; indeed they may be so badly executed as to bring ruin upon the State. Our comment would be that Aristotle divined the future as he had illustrated the past.

11. There is no better way for a Prince 'to serve his State' than 'by appointing as magistrates and officers men who excel at once in purity and in zeal for the public service'.[3] It might be said that this statement is as a corollary to what Erasmus has previously said, but his insistence on 'purity' and 'zeal' in the public service is so important that it cannot be too often stressed.

If we consider the Prince as the physician of the State—as Erasmus not infrequently does—he must not only 'have skilled apprentices' but must himself be 'above reproach',[4] in that he may be able to select honest magistrates and to correct their shortcomings, if any they have.

12. Of 'Treaties' Erasmus has much of importance to say in chapter viii: 'In concluding treaties, as in other things, the good Prince will look only to the public advantage.'[5]

13. 'Between all Christian Princes there is the closest and most holy bond of union in the very fact that they are Christians. Why then conclude so many treaties daily, as if every one were the enemy of every one else, and we must effect by conventions what Christ cannot achieve?'[6]

14. 'Such should be the good faith of Princes in the fulfilment of their obligations, that their simple promise is more sacred than any oath by another. How base then not to abide by a treaty accompanied by forms of the utmost solemnity among Christians!'[7]

15. 'The good and wise Prince will make every effort to keep peace with all men, but especially with his neighbours, who, if incensed, can do most harm, but as friends are most useful; nay, without mutual intercourse with them, the State cannot even continue to exist.'[8] The rules which Erasmus would have Princes observe in the exercise of the treaty-making power have been brought under four headings. What he says in their justification is as weighty as the rules themselves. For

[1] *Ibid.*, pp. 33, 35, 40, 41–2, 43. [2] *Ibid.*, chap. vii, p. 44. [3] *Ibid.*, p. 45. [4] *Ibid.*
[5] *Ibid.*, chap. viii, p. 47. [6] *Ibid.* [7] *Ibid.*, pp. 47–8. [8] *Ibid.*, p. 48.

example, a treaty contrary to the interests of the people is not a treaty, Erasmus rightly says, but a conspiracy on the part of the Prince who makes it. Such a treaty divides the people into two classes: the Prince, who makes it; and the people, who lose; and where this course is followed, Erasmus says, you have no State—meaning that such a government is not worthy of the name.

If the exact language of Erasmus was not quoted in the matter of good faith, it might be thought that the commentary was of our day and that we have foisted it upon Erasmus, who has greatly suffered at the hands of his commentators. What he says is indeed applicable to-day, as he writes in full knowledge of human nature, and human nature changes so slowly that the far-sighted truth of yesterday is still the truth of to-day and will be that of to-morrow. This is what Erasmus, literally Englished, says: 'When there is good faith, and the parties to a transaction are honest men, there is no need of hard-and-fast bonds; on the other hand, when the matter is one between rascals, their very bonds provide the materials for litigation. So between good and wise Princes, even where there is no treaty, there is steadfast friendship: but where Sovereigns are foolish and evil-inclined, the treaties which were designed to make war impossible are the cause of war, for some one is always complaining that one or another of their innumerable articles has been violated. The usual purpose of a treaty is to end war, but nowadays the name is applied to an agreement to carry it on. Such leagues are but war measures; wherever expediency beckons, there an alliance is formed.'[1]

Treaties in Erasmus's day were made, it would appear, to be violated, to such a degree indeed that violation seemed to be a method of ending an inconvenient treaty. But there were violations of the letter and violations of the spirit, and it was, in the opinion of Erasmus, better to put up with what he calls 'trifling infringements', since even private persons, not to speak of nations, could not 'long survive' if the parties insisted upon standing by 'the letter of every term'.[2] In any event, the advice of Erasmus in such a case is as wise and as applicable as when given; it would not indeed be more acceptable if it had come to us from Aristotle himself. Anger, he counsels us, is an unsafe guide. 'The public interest', he laconically remarks, 'is to be considered'.

Alas and alack for the treaties of our day!

16. 'In my opinion', Erasmus says in chapter ix, 'On the Marriage Alliances of Princes', 'it would be most expedient for the State if Princes sought their marriage alliances within the limits of their own kingdoms, . . .'[3] In the omitted portion of the sentence, he admits

[1] Erasmus's *Institutio Principis Christiani*, chap. viii, p. 47.
[2] *Ibid.*, p. 48. [3] *Ibid.*, chap. ix, p. 50.

reluctantly—although it is contrary to his argument—that there might be marriages with neighbours, if they are 'faithful friends'.

Unfortunately the difficulty can be illustrated only too well in our day. Victoria, 'By the Grace of God Queen, Defender of the Faith' and, by Disraeli's intervention, Empress of India, took unto herself as consort a German nobleman (in the best sense of the word), Albert of Saxe-Coburg and Gotha. Of this marriage there were, among others, three grandchildren: George V (now of Windsor), who succeeded to Victoria's domain; an older grandson, William II, former German Emperor, now in exile in Holland; and Nicholas II, once Tsar of all the Russias.

In the summer of 1914 the so-called 'World War' broke out. George V and Nicholas II found themselves at war with their first cousin, William II.

'Such alliances', Erasmus says, 'are commonly regarded as the adamantine chains of general peace, though experience itself shows that they are the sources of our greatest woes.'[1] However, 'if Princes could secure peace for the world by marriage alliances, I could wish'—in the interest of peace, with which the sovereigns of his day doubtless considered him obsessed—'each of them six hundred wives'[2]—pushing Solomon rather hard, it may be said, for an author who was a priest and the recipient at one time and another of an offer of a bishopric and a cardinal's hat.

On still another point Erasmus's views were heterodox. He even believed—at least he so stated—that 'whatever her birth, the woman who will make a good wife for the Prince is good enough'.[3]

So much for the international 'marriage alliances of Princes'.

Chapter x treats of 'Occupations of the Prince in Time of Peace', which, according to Erasmus, should be his sole occupations, inasmuch as Erasmus looked upon war as a crime, although he did not condemn as criminals all who took part in the crime. However, he deals in this section with what may be called 'preoccupations'. The occupations were many, as will shortly appear, but their purpose was to establish 'perpetual peace among the people'.[4]

17. 'The Prince, then, instructed in Christ's commandments'—for was not Christ the Prince of Peace—'and fortified by wisdom, will hold nothing so dear as the happiness of his people, all of whom, as one body, he must love and cherish. He will devote every thought and effort to such an administration of the kingdom entrusted to him as will be approved by Christ when He demands an account, and leave his memory most honoured by all men.'[5]

After an enumeration of what a Prince would do for his people, did he act as a *paterfamilias* and think only of the good of his children,

[1] *Ibid.*, p. 51. [2] *Ibid.* [3] *Ibid.*, p. 50. [4] *Ibid.*, chap. x, p. 55. [5] *Ibid.*

Erasmus, with a pardonable exaggeration and anxious to supply the idle Prince with plenty of occupation to keep him out of mischief, not to say crime, adds: 'Six thousand such tasks there are, meet for a Prince, even pleasant for a good Prince; busied with these he need never look about for wars to vary the tedium of idleness, nor shorten the night in gaming.'[1]

A duty of the Prince to which Erasmus called particular attention is that he should strive to make his kingdom 'better', not larger, and that neither the Prince of his time nor of future time should make the mistake of the ancients in directing all his efforts towards aggrandizing his kingdom. In pursuing the shadow, they often lost what they had, according to a fable which everybody knows. The comment of Erasmus, however, was, as would be expected, more dignified: 'I think the Laconic commandment worthy to be written on the insignia of every Prince: "You have been given Sparta—adorn her."'

'The good Prince must know that he can do nothing finer than to give back, more prosperous and in all respects more beautiful, the kingdom that fate has assigned to him.'[2] Taking advantage of the dictum of Epaminondas that the man glorifies the office, not the office the man—Erasmus continues, summarizing what he had said in various places and at no little length: 'The State is most strengthened by the example, the wisdom and the vigilance of a good Prince, by the integrity of magistrates and officials, by the holiness of priests, by the careful choice of schoolmasters, by just laws and measures conducing to virtue. Let his whole task be to encourage and develop these qualities.'[3]

There was nothing so distasteful to Erasmus as war. He was a man of letters—the very prince of letters—who knew by experience how the wars of his day interfered not merely with his scholarly pursuits and with the arts, but also with the mechanical arts of industry and commerce. Indeed he made the discovery—or at least he gave it its classical form—that everybody—victor, victim, and neutral—lost by war. Assuredly we of to-day dare not say him nay. To the humanist peace meant civilization—and he was a humanist to his finger-tips; and war meant destruction of civilization—of all that he and his fellow Christians held most dear; and in the *Institutio Principis Christiani*—addressed to a lad who was to wield world power and make, as it were, a profession of war—he expressed himself with that moral courage which is so infinitely superior to the mere physical courage of the animal:

19. 'The Prince should never be hasty in counsel, but above all he must be deliberate and circumspect in entering upon war, for while other things have their attending evils, war is the shipwreck of all that is good in a sea of all iniquity. No calamity prolongs itself with more

[1] Erasmus's *Institutio Principis Christiani*, chap. x, p. 55.
[2] *Ibid.* [3] *Ibid.*, p. 56.

tenacity—war springs from war, the greatest from the least, two wars from one, fierce and bloody war from a tourney; and the plague, rising in one place, spreads its infection to the neighbouring peoples, nay, to the most remote.'[1]

This is a large indictment; but history is its justification. In the opening phrase of the indictment Erasmus speaks of a Prince in general. What should be the duty of the Prince whom he had in mind?

20. 'A good Prince will never make war until every method has been tried in vain to avoid it.'[2] What will be the consequence of this policy? 'War will scarcely ever occur.'[3]

Erasmus, however, mentions a third type, 'the Prince who is truly Christian', who has a threefold task. He 'will first weigh the difference between men, born for peace and good will', and animals, 'born to prey upon one another'.[4] Second, he will 'reflect how desirable, how beautiful, how wholesome is peace; how calamitous and accursed, war; remembering what a host of sufferings even the most just war (if any war can be called just) brings in its train'.[5] Third, he should count the cost—which in a war is the bankruptcy of mankind and the destruction in a greater or less degree of civilization.

In view of its appalling consequences, Erasmus was willing to doubt the justice and question the necessity of any war. To those (St. Augustine among the number) who maintained that war could be just—and what Prince does not think his cause as just as it is necessary—to the Prince and to St. Augustine Erasmus preferred the authority of Christ, the Prince of Peace, and Peter and Paul, who 'everywhere teach the contrary'.[6]

21. 'Accordingly, the good and Christian Prince should regard every war, however just, as a thing suspect.... A good Prince measures all things in terms of the public good, otherwise he would not be even a Prince.'[7]

It is often said by those who seem to begrudge Erasmus his place in the sun that he prostrated himself before the great and the mighty; that he flattered them for his selfish purposes; and that he was sincere only in his own behalf. This is a grave charge against a priest who, as we have said, was offered a bishopric by his Prince, to whom he had addressed the tractate on the *Christian Prince*, in appreciation of the appointment as his counsellor, and whose 'worldliness' may be appraised by his refusal of a cardinal's hat, with a prospect of the Vatican in sight. None but an enemy could maintain that the comment on the measures which a good Prince should take was only calculated to curry favour with the mighty, and especially with Charles. 'There is no such right over men', Erasmus finely declares, 'as there is over cattle.'[8] If it

[1] *Ibid.*, chap. xi, p. 57. [2] *Ibid.* [3] *Ibid.* [4] *Ibid.* [5] *Ibid.*
[6] *Ibid.*, pp. 58–9. [7] *Ibid.*, p. 59. [8] *Ibid.*

should be said that this was a general observation, merely calling attention to the difference between men and cattle, the answer is that Erasmus follows this truism with another even more displeasing to an hereditary Prince, that 'an important part of government is the consent of the people', which was, he informs us in this connexion, 'the origin of kings'.[1] The conclusion which Erasmus draws, in the form of a question, from both of these truisms, as we venture to call them, could not have been pleasing to a lad to whom the consent of the people meant little. 'If a dispute arises between Princes, why do they not resort to arbiters?'[2] For there were 'many bishops, many abbots and learned men', not to speak of 'many worthy magistrates, whose judgement, rather than butchery, robbery, and universal calamity, should settle the matter',[3] and 'a righteous and merciful Prince will also bear in mind that the great sufferings which every war entails fall in great part to the lot of persons who have no concern in the conflict, and who have done nothing to merit calamity'.[4]

Quidquid delirant reges, est periniquum ut plectantur Achivi,[5] as Francisco de Vitoria was later to say at the end of his Reading *On the Law of War*.

22. 'Let the good Prince strive always for that glory which is neither stained with blood nor built on another's downfall'; for 'in war, at the best, the fortune of one side is ruin for the other, and often even the victor weeps too dear a victory'.[6]

As in the introduction to the *Christain Prince* Erasmus stated the thesis which he was to prove, so in the closing paragraphs he sums up what he had proven. As the first paragraphs were in the language of Erasmus, so are the concluding ones:

'If we are not moved by patriotism nor by world-calamity, at least let us respect the honour of the name Christian, . . .

'How brief and fugitive is the life of man, how open to calamity, assailed as it is by infinite maladies, continual accidents, falling ruins, shipwreck, earthquakes, thunderbolts. No need was there of war to inflict suffering, yet the sufferings of war are more than all the others. The preachers should have expelled discord from the hearts of the multitude. But now Angle hates Gaul and Gaul hates Angle for no other reason than that he is an Angle. The Scot, only because he is a Scot, hates the Briton; the Italian hates the German, the Suevan the Helvetian, and so on for the rest; region hates region, and city city. Why are we divided by these stupid names, rather than bound together by the common name of Christ?

'Even assuming that some war may be just', nevertheless it would

[1] Erasmus, *ibid.*, chap. xi, pp. 59–60. [2] *Ibid.*, p. 60. [3] *Ibid.* [4] *Ibid.*

[5] The words are Horace's (*Epistolae*, I, 2, 14), but Victoria, to fit them into his sentence, used *plectantur*, the subjunctive of indirect discourse, instead of the indicative *plectuntur*. [6] Erasmus, *ibid.*, p. 61.

be the opinion of both the Christian Princes at war that 'Christ is in both camps, fighting, as it were, against Himself. . . .

'If the whole doctrine of Christ is not everywhere opposed to war, if one instance can be cited where it is commended, then let us Christians fight. . . . Even against the Turks, I think we should not go thoughtlessly to war. . . . First let us see to it that we are truly Christian, and then, if it seems good, attack the Turks.'[1]

'Peace and concord', he continues, 'may flourish among peoples linked by so many pledges. To this end let them display their genius, put forth their strength, combine in council, straining every nerve to reach the common goal. . . . As it is, every one seeks his own ends—Pontiffs and bishops worry about power and wealth, Princes are led headlong by passion and ambition, their subjects all follow them for gain, and it is no wonder that, under folly's leading, we run into tempests. But if with one mind we bent ourselves to the common task, even our own affairs would prosper more. Now we lose that for which alone we fight.'[2]

Such was the Christian answer to the Pagan Prince of Machiavelli, although Erasmus did not know it at the time, for the Florentine's *Prince* lay then in manuscript.

Later we shall have the answer of Francisco de Vitoria, moralist and jurist, prepared the year of the *Prince's* publication, in 1532.

It is difficult to say when anything first happened. Some there are who maintain that Columbus was not the first to cross the Atlantic to the New World, although through him the New World came into the ken of the Old. It might be too much to say that Erasmus discovered the opposition of humanism to war in all its forms. If, however, he was not the first, nevertheless, like Columbus, it is through him that the discovery became the common possession of the world. In any event, we as well as Charles should be the better for the *Institutio Principis Christiani*.

*
* *

It would be difficult to find a layman of his day more interested than Montaigne in America, or any one whose writings have shown more clearly than his *Essays* the effect of the great discovery upon the thought of his time and of succeeding generations. Others, indeed, had interested themselves in the discovery of America and its immediate consequences. Through the Latin of their writings they had appealed to the learned. Montaigne used his native tongue, then coming to the front and within a century to make a universal appeal. Curious and inquisitive by nature, he was bound sooner or later to discover America for himself. His knowledge of that vast Continent and of its native peoples was not first-hand, for he had not set his foot upon the promised

[1] *Ibid.*, pp. 61–2. [2] *Ibid.*, pp. 62–3.

land. He had, however, in his employ a countryman who had spent some ten or eleven years in Brazil, a simple-minded man who could be trusted, because in his master's opinion he did not have the ability required to create what he had not seen. Off and on in Bordeaux, of which he was the leading citizen, Montaigne met seafaring people who had been to America, and later he came into personal contact and converse with some natives of the New World who happened to be on exhibition in Rouen. Then, too, he had more than fingered the books and accounts of America which had come under his eye. With his knowledge his interest grew, and from a casual spectator, as it were, he entered the lists in behalf of America and its peoples. Through Montaigne the American entered the world's literature.

Disregarding many references and allusions which Montaigne makes to America and the Americans, it may almost be said that he devotes two of his essays to the subject, the first under the somewhat uninviting title of 'Cannibals', and the second on 'Coaches', in which he surprises his readers by a long digression upon the grievances of the Americans at the hands of the Old World. His interest in America seems to have been aroused by the attempt of one Villegagnon to establish in Brazil a French settlement known as 'La France Antarctique', and to this day an island off Rio de Janeiro recalls the attempt and the name of the French adventurer. Villegagnon was at the time of the outing a Calvinist, and the undertaking had the blessing as well as the support of Coligny, then the head and front of the Huguenots in France. Difficulties arose among the motley group, composed alike of Protestants and Catholics, and the settlement broke up for all practical purposes when the leader of the expedition confessed his belief in transubstantiation, thus forsaking the new love for the old. But however unsuccessful the expedition, it was the first of the attempts to find a refuge in the New World against the intolerance of the old. Montaigne's informant had been a member of Villegagnon's ill-starred undertaking, and from him Montaigne learned many things, to be supplemented by others and by the account of travels already in print. To Montaigne, America was a new world, not the old Atlantis, and its inhabitants simple-minded folk who, growing up in a new environment, were unspoiled by the peoples of the Old World. If he did not find himself in the presence of primitive man, the American was nevertheless closer to Nature, and in the essay on 'Cannibals' Montaigne endeavoured, it would appear, to show the differences between the natural man of America and the artificial man of Europe. There may be exaggeration and irony in his contrast of the social conditions of the two worlds, and it may well be that he did not take himself seriously at the time. It is, however, evident that he wondered as he wrote whether, after all, it would not be better for the world to get closer to Nature and the natural instead of the artificial way of doing things. We are so made that we are inclined to look upon our own views and the conditions surrounding us as the standard of comparison, and we are also inclined to look with suspicion upon the views of others in so far as they differ from our own, and to belittle conditions with which we are unfamiliar. To the Greeks the foreigners were barbarians, because in the first place they wore beards, and the bearded men whom they knew were different from themselves. They were competing types in civilization which neither comprehended. Not so to Montaigne, who probed beneath the surface of things.

1. 'Unless men call that barbarisme which is not common to them,' he observes, 'there is nothing in that nation, that is either barbarous or savage.'

2. 'We have no other ayme of truth and reason than the example and *Idea* of the opinions and customes of the countrie we live in.' In justification of this statement Montaigne adds: 'There' (meaning again America) 'is ever perfect religion, perfect policie, perfect and compleat use of all things.'

3. 'They are even savage,' he grants, in the sense that 'we call those fruits wilde, which nature of her selfe, and of her ordinarie progresse hath produced'. Montaigne, however, was of the opinion that 'we should rather terme savage' our own fruits, which 'are those which our selves have altered by our artificiall devices, and diverted from their common order.'[1]

4. 'We may then well call them barbarous, in regard of reasons rules, but not in respect of us that exceed them in all kinde of barbarisme.'

This must have seemed strange doctrine to Montaigne's contemporaries, and many of those of our day who read the *Essays* would be inclined to shake their heads. Montaigne doubtless felt the need of what we may call a bill of particulars, and from this we may select certain items.

'Their warres are noble and generous, and have as much excuse and beautie, as this humane infirmitie may admit.'

'They contend not for the gaining of new lands; for to this day they yet enjoy that naturall ubertie and fruitfulnesse, which without labouring toyle, doth in such plenteous abundance furnish them with all necessary things, that they need not enlarge their limits. They are yet in that happy estate, as they desire no more, than what their naturall necessities direct them: whatsoever is beyond it, is to them superfluous.'[2]

They hold their goods in common and these pass 'without other

[1] *Essayes*, Florio's translation, *op. cit.*, vol. i, p. 219.
[2] *Ibid.*, p. 224.

claime or title, but that which nature doth plainely impart unto all creatures, even as she brings them into the world'.[1]

'They require no other ransome of their prisoners, but an acknowledgment and confession that they are vanquished.'[2]

The two principles which the old men of America impress upon the youth are, according to Montaigne, '*First, valour against their enemies, then lovingness unto their wives*'.[3]

He admits that the victors 'roast, and then eat' their enemies in common, and that they send 'some slices . . . to such of their friends as are absent'. This is not done 'to nourish themselves'; but, as Montaigne is anxious to have us believe, 'to represent an extreme, and inexpiable revenge'.[4] If this stood alone, the Americans would have a hard time of it with Montaigne's readers, but bad as this habit is, the European custom is worse. 'I am not sorie we note the barbarous horror of such an action, but grieved, that prying so narrowly into their faults we are so blinded in ours.' And to drive his point home: 'I thinke there is more barbarisme in eating men alive, than to feed upon them being dead; to mangle by tortures and torments a body full of lively sense, to roast him in peeces, to make dogges and swine to gnaw and teare him in mammockes (as wee have not only read, but seene very lately, yea and in our owne memorie, not amongst ancient enemies, but our neighbours and fellow-citizens; and which is worse, under pretence of pietie and religion) than to roast and eat him after he is dead.'[5]

5. 'The lawes of nature doe yet command them, which are but little bastardized by ours.'

And in Montaigne's conception 'with such puritie, as I am sometimes grieved the knowledge of it came no sooner to light, at what time there were men, that better than we could have judged of it. I am sorie, *Lycurgus* and *Plato* had it not'.

6. 'What in those nations we see by experience, doth not only exceed all the pictures wherewith licentious Poesie hath proudly imbellished the golden age, and all her quaint inventions to faine a happy condition of man, but also the conception and desire of Philosophy.'[6]

With the 'poesie' of America he said he was so conversant that he quotes an 'amorous canzonet' which has no 'barbarism' in its invention, and which in his opinion was 'altogether Anacreontike'. The canzonet, the substance of which he quotes in his own good prose, was one day to interest the inquiring Herder, and the many-sided Goethe:

Adder stay, stay good adder, that my sister may by the patterne of thy partie-coloured coat drawe the fashion and worke of a rich lace, for me

[1] *Essayes*, Florio's translation, *op. cit.*, vol. i, pp. 224–5.
[2] *Ibid.*, p. 225.
[3] *Ibid.*, p. 221.
[4] *Ibid.*, p. 223.
[5] *Ibid.*, pp. 223–4.
[6] *Ibid.*, p. 220.

to give unto my love; so may thy beautie, thy nimbleness or disposition be ever preferred before all other serpents.[1]

7. 'They' (Lycurgus and Plato) 'could not imagine a genuitie so pure and simple, as we see it by experience; nor ever beleeve our societie might be maintained with so little art and humane combination.' Leaving Lycurgus aside, Montaigne stated the entire case for the American in a literary reply to Plato which the great Shakespeare did not disdain to appropriate literally in *The Tempest.* 'It is a nation', he says, 'that hath no kinde of traffike, no knowledge of Letters, no intelligence of numbers, no name of magistrate, nor of politike superioritie; no use of service, of riches or of povertie; no contracts, no successions, no partitions, no occupation but idle; no respect of kindred, but common, no apparell but naturall, no manuring of lands, no use of wine, corne, or mettle. The very words that import lying, falsehood, treason, dissimulations, covetousness, envie, detraction, and pardon, were never heard of amongst them. How dissonant would hee finde his imaginarie commonwealth from this perfection!'[2]

Thus was America, in Montaigne's conception, a light in an otherwise darkened world, 'the light that never was, on sea or land', or, to use Montaigne's own prose: 'Surely, in respect of us these are very savage men; for either they must be so in good sooth, or we must be so indeed: There is a wondrous distance betweene their forme and ours.'[3]

I have said that Montaigne had seen some of the natives at Rouen in the time of King Charles IX, 'who talked with them a great while'. What passed Montaigne thus recounts: 'They were shewed our fashions, our pomps, and the forme of a faire Citie; afterward some demanded their advise, and would needs know of them what things of note and admirable they had observed amongst us.'[4] In the first place 'They found it very strange, that so many tall men with long beards, strong and well armed, as it were about the Kings person (it is very likely they meant the Switzers of his guard) would submit themselves to obey a beardlesse childe, and that we did not rather chuse one amongst them to command the rest.' On this statement Montaigne makes no comment. They had a manner of phrase, Montaigne continues, whereby

[1] *Ibid.*, p. 228.

[2] *Ibid.*, p. 220. The passage referred to in *The Tempest* is Gonzalo's speech in Act II, Scene i:

> I'th' commonwealth I would by contraries
> Execute all things: for no kind of traffic
> Would I admit: no name of magistrate:
> Letters should not be known: riches, poverty,
> And use of service—none: contract, succession,
> Bourn, bound of land, tilth, vineyard—none:
> No use of metal, corn, or wine, or oil:
> No occupation, all men idle, all:
> And women too, but innocent and pure:
> No sovereignty—

[3] *Ibid.*, p. 227.

[4] *Ibid.*, pp. 228–9.

they called 'men but a moytie one of another'; and their second observation was: 'They had perceived, there were men amongst us full gorged with all sortes of commodities, and others which hunger-starved, and bare with need and povertie, begged at their gates: and found it strange, these moyties so needy could endure such an injustice, and that they tooke not the others by the throte, or set fire on their houses.'[1] On this Montaigne is likewise silent. There was a third observation which the Americans had made, but which Montaigne had forgotten. In view of the two which he has given, it is perhaps just as well that his memory was faulty.

Montaigne was not to be outdone by the King, for he had some conversation with them, but apparently did not profit as much by the occasion as he had hoped because of the interpreter's shortcomings. To the question 'what good' one of the Americans who appeared to be a captain and was called King by the French mariners, got from his position, Montaigne received in reply: 'it was to march formost in any charge of warre.' And asking whether the King's authority expired after war was ended, that worthy answered 'that hee had only this left him, which was, that when he went on progresse, and visited the villages depending of him, the inhabitants prepared paths and highwaies athwart the hedges of their woods, for him to pass through at ease'. Perhaps this is a fairly good substitute for the third question, and with a couple of phrases which furnish food for thought for us of to-day he dismisses the cannibals. 'All that is not verie ill; but what of that?' And this time he gives his own answer without the intervention of King, interpreter, or savage. 'They weare no kinde of breeches nor hosen.'[2]

The more Montaigne thought about America and the Americans, and the more he reflected upon them and their ways, the more his heart went out to them, as appears from the essay on 'Coaches', the sixth of the third book, published some eight years after the disquisition on 'Cannibals'. The cruelty with which the Americans were treated appalled him, although, as he himself tells us, he lived in an age of cruelty. He lived in a France which was convulsed by religious wars, and his observations of his own country, in his essay on 'Cruelty', are applicable to the Low Countries, where the attempts of the Spaniards to stamp out religious dissent and political rebellion were the scandal of the world. The passage therefore would seem to have for our purpose a double interest:

> I live in an age, wherein we abound with incredible examples of this vice, through the licentiousness of our civill and intestine warres: And read all ancient stories, be they never so tragicall, you shall find none to equall those, we daily see practised.[3]

[1] *Essayes*, Florio's translation, *op. cit.*, vol. i, p. 229.
[2] *Ibid.*, p. 229.
[3] *Ibid.*, vol. ii, p. 121.

Montaigne did not often yield to his feelings, for he practised the moderation which he preached. On the subject of cruelty, however, he was 'inexorable'. 'Amongst all other vices, there is none I hate more than crueltie, both by nature and judgement, as the extremest of all vices.' He was indeed so faint-hearted that he could not 'chuce but grieve' to see 'a chickins necke puld off, or a pigge stickt'. And he could not well endure, as he said, 'a seelie dew-bedabled hare to groane, when she is seized upon by the houndes; although hunting be a violent sport'.[1] Sir Thomas More had already expressed his opinion to the same effect in his *Utopia*. Not only was hunting a violent sport, but it was one much more common in his day than in ours, when many persons not addicted to that form of recreation or amusement are inclined to condemn it, especially in the New World. And in this very connexion Montaigne returns to his cannibals, saying that neither they nor savage people offend him so much 'with roasting and eating of dead bodies, as those which torment and persecute the living'. He could not even 'behold the execution' of any man, albeit the law demanded it, 'with an unrelenting eye', for even in matters of justice, 'whatsoever is beyond a simple death' he deemed it to be 'meere crueltie'. 'And especially amongst us, who ought to have a regardfull respect, that their soules should be sent to heaven, which cannot be, having first by intolerable tortures agitated, and as it were brought them to dispaire.'[2] A little later in the essay Montaigne is inclined to doubt 'that imaginary sovereigntie that some give and ascribe unto us above all other creatures', saying, in a much quoted passage, but which can assuredly never be too often quoted on this side of Heaven: 'yet is there a kinde of respect, and a generall duty of humanity, which tieth us not only unto brute beasts that have life and sense, but even unto trees and plants. *Unto men we owe Justice, and to all other creatures that are capable of it, grace and benignity.*'[3]

These were deep-seated views, and to be found in the first collection of his *Essays*, from which we may conjecture, if need there were, what his attitude would be against the opening up of America to adventurers from the Old World intent on conquest, plunder, and gain.

In the essay on 'Coaches' Montaigne confirms, to use a phrase dear to diplomacy, the views which he had set forth in his previous communication on 'Cannibals', a guaranty for his earnestness. Two passages may be lifted from the latter essay: 'Our world hath of late discovered another . . . no lesse-large, fully-peopled, all-things-yeelding, and mighty in strength, than ours: nevertheless so new and infantine, that he is yet to learne his A.B.C. It is not yet full fifty yeares that he knew neither letters, nor waight, nor measures, nor apparell, nor corne, nor vines. But was all naked, simply-pure, in Natures lappe, and lived but

[1] *Ibid.*, p. 117. [2] *Ibid.*, pp. 119–20. [3] *Ibid.*, p. 124.

with such meanes and food as his mother-nurce affoorded him.'[1] A little later he says: 'It was an unpolluted, harmeless infant world; yet have we not whipped and submitted the same unto our discipline, or schooled him by the advantage of our valour or naturall forces, nor have wee instructed him by our justice and integrity; nor subdued by our magnanimity.'

Montaigne was of the opinion that the conduct of the Americans in their negotiations with the Europeans was marked at least by an equal degree of natural wit and intelligence; that their 'hardiness and undaunted courage' could be opposed 'to the most famous ancient examples, we may with all our industrie discover in all the Annales and memories of our knowen old World'.[2] He is amazed at the 'undismaied resolution against paine, smarting, famine and death it selfe' which they were called upon to endure and suffer through the death and destruction which we call the conquest of Mexico by Cortez, and the even greater brutality and cruelty suffered by the Incas of Peru at the hands of Pizarro, who himself suffered death at the hands of his followers. So lawless were the *conquistadores*, more tolerable in retrospect than in life, that divers of their chieftains 'have beene executed to death, even in the places they had conquered, by the appointment of the Kings of *Castile*, justly offended at the seld-seene horror of their barbarous demeanours, and well nigh all disesteemed, contemned and hated'.[3] And Montaigne's earnestness is seen in his further comment that 'God hath meritoriously permitted, that many of their great pillages, and ill gotten goods, have either beene swallowed up by the revenging Seas in transporting them, or consumed by the intestine warres and civil broiles, wherewith themselves have devoured one another'.[4]

It was resentment against the claim of the Europeans of his day to superiority over the inhabitants of the New World which caused Montaigne to plead for justice to those who were different but not necessarily inferior, and it was the lawlessness of the Spanish adventurers, intent on gain, which had caused some fifty years earlier, the period from which Montaigne dated our knowledge of the New World, the law-abiding in Spain to protest against acquisition without right and warfare without law, and in so doing, to bring into being a newer law of nations which condemned and indeed outlawed such actions. Others there were who had written of America and, like the good Las Casas of Spain, had protested against the unjustified and inhuman treatment of the Americans at the hands of European adventurers coming from countries which claimed to be civilized, and indeed were universally regarded as leaders in what they were pleased to call their civilization. But they either wrote in Latin, making a large yet limited

[1] *Essayes*, Florio's translations, *op. cit.*, vol. iii, p. 141.
[2] *Ibid.*, p. 142.
[3] *Ibid.*, p. 148.
[4] *Ibid.*

appeal, or in the mother tongue which did not cross their frontiers. Montaigne alone made a universal appeal, using a language which, without displacing others, was widely read in foreign countries, and using that language in such a way as to make of his *Essays* the priceless possession of readers without regard to nationality. Our English Shakespeare felt his influence, and Florio's translation of Montaigne's *Essays*, with Shakespeare's own autograph, is the only book which we certainly know to have belonged to the supreme poet of the English-speaking world. Montaigne's influence has been hardly less in other countries, and, indeed, the preference of succeeding centuries for natural society with its natural man, to artificial society with its artificial man, dates from Montaigne. Conditions in America, real or alleged, have attracted and still attract the attention of the Old World.

*
* *

The interest of my Lord Bacon in America, although later, was none the less keen than that of Montaigne. There is a relationship between their writings in that both insisted on the facts, and from the facts derived conclusions. The experimental method was common to both, although Montaigne approached the New World from the standpoint of the moralist, and his interest lay in the social condition of the Americans; Bacon's interest was not that of the moralist, in whom character counts for much, but of the scientist, or rather of those addicted to what may be called the physical, the mathematical, or the exact sciences, and the services which they might render to mankind. From his early youth, he had been obsessed with the idea that he was reserved for great things. Money he required to carry them into effect, or great position, which would bring him money and facilitate the accomplishment of his self-imposed mission. The result has measurably justified the opinion which he had of himself; but it would have been better for him and for the world if he had devoted himself to his scientific ideal without wasting his life and ruining his character in the search for wealth and the prestige of position.

In 1592, when he was engaged in the practice of law, and but thirty-one years of age, he stated his aim and purpose, saying, 'I have taken all knowledge to be my province'; and the 'best state of that province', he himself said, consisted 'in industrious observations, grounded conclusions, and profitable inventions and discoveries'.[1] And in an interlude for the Court composed the same year, entitled 'The Conference of Pleasure', he anticipated the power 'to endow the life of man with infinite commodities'.[2] There was a 'sovereignty of

[1] *New Atlantis*, by Francis Bacon, Lord Verulam, Viscount St. Albans, edited with introduction and notes, by Alfred B. Gough (1915), p. ix.

[2] *Ibid.*, p. x.

man' which lay 'hid in knowledge', which kings could not 'buy, nor with their force command', of which their spies could give no news, and whither seamen could not sail. Nature we govern indeed 'in opinions', but are dependent upon her in necessities. We would, however, command her in action, if we were 'led by her [in ?] invention'.[1] Somewhat later Bacon, confessing that he was born 'for the service of mankind', and asking in what way he could best serve mankind according to the services which he felt himself 'best fitted by nature to perform', found, he said, 'none so great as the discovery of new arts, endowments, and commodities for the bettering of man's life'. The self-imposed mission was indeed great, and the time short at any man's disposal; but he would have been content to construct the machine, even though he should 'not succeed in setting it on work'.[2] He did construct the machine, although he did not put it to work.

In 1594, in a composition for the Christmas revels of Gray's Inn (one of the law-courts of London, of which he was then a member, and to-day one of its permanent glories), Bacon anticipated the *New Atlantis*. Addressing the sovereign, 'the Prince of Purpoole' (Bacon was always appealing to princes), he said: 'I will commend to your Highness four principal works and monuments of yourself.' The first of these was 'the collecting of a most perfect and general library'; the second was, 'a spacious, wonderful garden' to which the beasts of the field, the birds of the air, and the fish of the sea might be added—we would call it a botanical and zoological garden; the third was, 'a goodly huge cabinet'—as we would say, a museum—containing the inanimate things which 'nature hath wrought' and whatever the hand of man had made; and lastly, a laboratory, or, as Bacon has chosen to put it, 'a still-house, so furnished with mills, instruments, furnaces, and vessels as may be a palace fit for a philosopher's stone', the consequences of which, he goes on to say, shall be that 'Miracles and wonders shall cease, by reason that you shall have discovered their natural causes'.[3]

Of the many writings in which Bacon spoke of 'the new instrument' through which Nature's secrets were to be obtained for the benefit of mankind, the *New Atlantis*, written but a couple of years before his death in 1626, stands out as the best statement of his views, as admittedly the best written, and due at least in its outward form to the discovery of America, as was the *Utopia* of his great predecessor, which is in some respects the model of his own *New Atlantis*.

It is proper to premise a few observations of a more general nature before taking up the thesis of the *New Atlantis*. The wayfarers (fifty-one in number, of whom seventeen were ill at the time), seeking a port of distress, were asked if they were Christians—from which it would appear that the vast island which they had approached was a Christian

[1] *New Atlantis*, p. xi. [2] *Ibid.*, p. xii. [3] *Ibid.*, p. xi.

community, and the Christian religion had been introduced centuries ago. Judaism, as the accredited ancestor of Christianity, was tolerated. The great king who made the island what it was, was Solamona by name, who approached the original in his wisdom, but was without his prototype's foibles; for in the New Atlantis the doctrine obtained of one man, one wife, and there was not 'under the Heauens, so chast a Nation, as this of Bensalem'—for such was its official name—'Nor so free from all Pollution, or fouleness'. Indeed, Bacon would have us believe that it was 'the Virgin of the World'.

The *New Atlantis* is indeed a fiction, but as Dr. Abbott has said, 'Bacon has put into it perhaps more of his own self, his tastes, his preferences, his ideals, than into any other of his writings'.[1] Hythlodaye and his companions started from Brazil, in the east of the Continent, and made their way to the west, and to the south, until they set foot upon Utopia—the only travellers, it may be observed, who have ever found that spot. In Bacon's romance, which is related, apparently, by the leader of the expedition, the point of departure is Peru, '(wher wee had continued by the space of one whole yeare,) for *China* and *Iapan*, by the South Sea'.[2] Driven by 'Strong and Great Windes from the South, with a Point East' they were giving themselves up for lost 'in the Midst of the greatest Wildernesse of Waters in the World, without Victuall', when they saw in the distance 'thick Cloudes, which did put vs in some hope of Land'. They bent their course thither, and on the dawning of the next day, discerned the land of their hopes. It was an inhabited country, and some eight persons put out in a boat to meet them, handing them a scroll of parchment, on which these words were written 'in Ancient *Hebrew*, and in Ancient *Greeke*, and in good *Latine* of the Schoole, and in *Spanish*, these wordes; *Land yee not, none of you; And prouide to be gone, from this Coast, within sixteene daies, except you haue further time giuen you*'.[3]

'Our Answer', according to our informant, 'was in the *Spanish* tongue.' There was nothing strange in that, because they had spent a year in Peru, then the capital, so to speak, of Spanish America; and Spain itself was at that time the dominating country of Europe. And the answer was, '*That for our Shipp, it was well; For we had rather mett with Calmes, and contrary windes, then any Tempests. For our Sick, they were many, and in very ill Case; So that if they were not permitted to Land, they ran danger of their Liues.*' Some hours later 'a Person (as it seemed) of place' came to them, and 'with a loud voice, in *Spanish* asked, *Are yee Christians?* We answered; *We were*', whereupon the person, well pleased with the answer, said, '*If yee will sweare, (all of you,) by the Meritts of the* SAVIOVR, *that yee are no Pirates; . . . you may haue License to come on Land.*' They took oath, whereupon they were allowed to

[1] *Ibid.*, p. xxxi. [2] *Ibid.*, p. 3. [3] *Ibid.*, p. 4.

land, and were installed in 'the *Strangers House*'. The country was the New Atlantis, which the Australians might be inclined to claim as Australia.[1]

And what of the old, that this should be called the 'new'? In the opinion of the natives, the old was none other than '*the great* Atlantis (*that you* [addressing himself to the travellers] *call* America)'.[2] They admitted the disappearance of the island because of a flood; but they were of the opinion that with the subsidence of the waters, the 'great Atlantis' which we all call America presented itself, to be discovered anew by the Old World.

This was the belief of many, which Bacon shared. 'The discovery of America', says Mr. Gough, in his excellent edition of the *New Atlantis*, 'and especially of the strange isolated civilizations of Mexico and Peru had aroused much speculation, and Bacon's belief that America was the wreck of the submerged Atlantis was shared by many in his age. The wonderful tales brought from newly-discovered lands both in East and West, aroused in various minds the fancy that somewhere there might yet be found an ideally happy and virtuous community.'[3] Bacon's purpose was to show how the New Atlantis was not an idle hope, but a virtuous community; and he founded it, not upon political or social institutions, as had his predecessors, but upon the exalted place which he gave to science, through which, and through which alone, he professed to believe that mankind might be made prosperous and happy.

How had this happened? What one people had done, others could do. The experience of one might well be the experience of others. What was this experience? Bacon's description was interesting then, and it is now. The people of the Old Atlantis who lived in the valleys perished either by drowning or 'for want of Food, and other things necessary'.[4] Those of the mountains survived, and '*being simple and sauage People*, (*Not like* Noah *and his* Sonnes, *which was the chiefe Family of the Earth*) *they were not able to leaue Letters, Arts, and Ciuillity, to their Posterity*'. '*So as maruaile you not at the thin Population of* America, *nor at the Rudeness and Ignorance of the People; For you must account your Inhabitants of* America *as a young People; Younger a thousand yeares, at the least, then the rest of the World*.'[5] In the upper regions, they had been accustomed to clothe themselves with the skins of animals, which they discarded because of the intolerable heat of the valley. And because they '*knew no meanes of lighter Apparell, they were forced to beginn the Custome of Going Naked, which continueth at this day*'.[6]

The government of the New Atlantis was monarchical. The

[1] *New Atlantis*, pp. 5–7. [2] *Ibid.*, p. 18. [3] *Ibid.*, pp. xxiv-xxv.
[4] *Ibid.*, p. 20. [5] *Ibid.*, p. 21. [6] *Ibid.*, p. 20.

King, Solamona, 'the Law-giuer' of the island, '*had* a large heart, *inscrutable for good*' and, at least in fiction, '*was wholly bent to make his Kingdome and People Happy*.'[1] The island was to be self-sufficient, and to maintain itself without foreign aid. The laws which the King issued were so fundamental that they were still in force and vigour at Bacon's advent. He was a conservative, and for this reason the New Atlantis has nothing to do with the community of property which had been an integral part of the ideal commonwealths of Plato and Sir Thomas More.

One of the peculiarities of the New Atlantis was the prohibition of strangers unless in the case of distress, when they were treated, one might say, as wards of the island, and allowed to stay for a time which might be prolonged or become permanent. In the latter case, they became in effect naturalized subjects or 'Bensalemites' (if the term be permitted). However, while the New Atlantis was closed to strangers, the islanders possessed a knowledge of foreign parts; for it appeared that every twelve years, two ships were dispatched to obtain '*Knowledge of the Affaires*' of the countries to which they had been sent, '*especially*', Bacon is careful to inform us, '*of the Sciences, Arts, Manufactures, and Inuentions of all the World*', and of course, '*Bookes, Instruments, and Patternes, in euery kinde*'[2] were not overlooked. The ships turned homewards after landing the envoys, who were to remain in foreign parts until a new mission should be sent. The remarkable thing about it was that their commerce with the outer world was strictly intellectual and scientific. The islanders had indeed a trade, but it was not '*for Gold, Siluer, or Iewels; Nor for Silkes*'—of which Bacon himself was, it must be said, overfond—'*Nor any other Commodity of Matter*'. For what, then, did they trade, it may be asked. It was '*onely for* Gods *first Creature, which was* Light'. '*To haue* Light', Bacon reports his interlocutor as saying, '*of the Growth of all Parts of the World*'.[3]

So much for this phase of the subject, for neither the value nor the interest of the New Atlantis lies in its government, or laws; but in the one institution which was the very eye of this kingdom, or rather, we may say, the very apple of Bacon's eye from early manhood to the day of his death. This was the creation of an order, or society, which the leaders called 'Salomons House', dedicated to the '*Study of the* Works, *and* Creatures *of* God', and in their opinion—which Bacon most assuredly shared, for the institution was nothing but the realization of an imaginary commonwealth of his dream of a lifetime—'*The Noblest Foundation, (as wee thinke,) that euer was vpon the Earth; And the Lanthorne of this Kingdome*'.[4] Bacon's interlocutor remarked that the name perhaps should be 'Solamona's House', after the King who had founded it; but he was of the opinion that their great King and

[1] *Ibid.*, p. 21. [2] *Ibid.*, p. 24. [3] *Ibid.*, p. 25. [4] *Ibid.*, p. 23.

lawgiver founded it in honour of the historic Solomon, from the hand of whom the islanders possessed works which did not exist elsewhere. And he was strengthened in this view by the fact that the house was sometimes called '*the* Colledge *of* the sixe Daies Workes', '*whereby I am satisfied*', the informant continued '*That our Excellent* King *had learned from the* Hebrewes; *That* God *had created the World, and all that therein is, within sixe Dayes*'.[1]

As happens so easily in fiction, the wayfarers were to catch a glimpse of one of the Fathers—that is, a member of 'Salomons House', who was about to visit the city in which they were installed. None of the 'Colledge of the sixe Daies Workes' had visited the city within the past twelve years, and had it not been for the arrival of the strangers, there was apparently no telling when he would have honoured it with his presence. Indeed, the 'Father' of 'Salomons House' had not only taken note of their arrival, but had decided to admit them all to his presence, and to '*haue priuate Conference with one of you, that ye shall choose*',[2] and to whom he should give his blessing. Naturally, Bacon, as the leader of the imaginary expedition, was chosen.

The interview was had. The others withdrawing, the 'Father' asked the chosen of the strangers to sit down beside him, and, if Bacon is to be believed, recounted to him 'in the *Spanish Tongue*' the marvellous things of 'Salomons House' and the 'Colledge of the sixe Daies Workes'.

First of all, the Father gave Bacon his blessing, and proceeded to state the end of the foundation; the preparations and instruments which were used in their investigations; the several employments and functions to which the fellows of the college were assigned, and the ordinances and rites which were observed. Of the first, he said, 'The End *of our* Foundation *is the Knowledge of* Causes, *and Secrett Motions of Things; And the Enlarging of the bounds of* Humane Empire, *to the Effecting of all Things possible.*'[3] After which he set forth the preparations and instruments which, without going into detail, may be said to be a universal laboratory of sciences, with an imaginary equipment—for none existed in Bacon's time, although to-day it may be found everywhere.

The employments and offices of the fellows of the college are stated at length; some were to visit foreign countries, and were called 'Merchants *of* Light'; others were to 'Collect *the* Experiments *which are in all* Bookes'. These were the 'Depredatours'. Still others were to collect the experiments of mechanical arts and liberal sciences. These were the 'Mystery-Men'. Some, the 'Pioners *or* Miners', were to try new experiments; and the 'Compilers' were to 'Drawe *the* Experiments *of the* Former Foure *into* Titles, *and* Tables, *to giue the better light, for the*

[1] *New Atlantis*, p. 24. [2] *Ibid.*, p. 34. [3] *Ibid.*, p. 35.

drawing of Obseruations *and* Axiomes *out of them*'. Another group was to draw from them 'Things *of* Vse, *and* Practise *for* Mans life, *and* Knowledge, *as well for* Workes, *as for* Plaine Demonstration *of* Causes, Meanes *of* Naturall diuinations, *and the easie and cleare* Discouery, *of the* Vertues *and* Parts *of* Bodies'. These were the 'Dowry-Men *or* Benefactours'.[1]

All these things were past experiments. What of the future? The members of the House were to meet, to consult, and to consider all the former labours and collections, and out of them still another group was '*to* Direct New Experiments, *of a Higher* Light, *more* Penetrating *into* Nature *then the* Former. *These wee* call Lamps'. Some of their number, called 'Inoculatours', were to 'Execute *the* Experiments *so* Directed, *and* Report *them*'. And finally the 'Interpreters *of* Nature' were to '*raise the former* Discoueries *by* Experiments, *into* Greater Obseruations, Axiomes, *and* Aphorismes'.[2]

Novices and apprentices there were, so that the House should remain the centre of science and of experiment. Consultations were to be had, to determine which of their inventions and experiments should be published and made known, or kept secret for the time being. The first group, whose duty it was to sail into foreign parts, was twelve; all of the others were three in number.

There are two passages from the *New Atlantis* which should be quoted in Bacon's own words, inasmuch as they show what had been done, the respect in which the pioneers of science should be held, and the services which he predicted would result from his method—experiment followed by induction—services which actually have been rendered, or will be rendered in the future. The first passage, under the caption of 'Ordinances *and* Rites' is, therefore, in the informant's words:

> *Wee haue two very* Long, *and* Faire Galleries: *In one of these wee place* Patternes *and* Samples *of all manner of the more* Rare *and* Excellent Inuentions: *In the other wee place the* Statua's *of all* Principall Inuentours. *There wee haue the* Statua *of your* Columbus, *that discouered the* West-Indies: *Also the* Inuentor *of* Shipps: *Your* Monke *that was the* Inuentour *of* Ordnance, *and of* Gunpowder: *The* Inuentour *of* Musicke: *The* Inuentour *of* Letters: *The* Inuentour *of* Printing: *The* Inuentour *of* Obseruations *of* Astronomy: *The* Inuentour *of* Works *in* Mettall: *The* Inuentour *of* Glasse: *The* Inuentour *of* Silke *of the* Worme: *The* Inuentour *of* Wine: *The* Inuentour *of* Corne *and* Bread: *The* Inuentour *of* Sugars: *And all these, by more certaine Tradition, then you haue. Then haue we diuerse* Inuentours *of our* Owne, *of* Excellent Workes; *Which since you haue not seene, it were too long to make* Descriptions *of them*; *And besides, in the right Vnderstanding of those* Descriptions, *you might easily erre. For vpon euery* Inuention *of Valew, wee erect a* Statua *to the* Inuentour, *and giue him a Liberall and Honourable* Reward.[3]

In the second passage the informant likewise said:

> *Lastly, wee haue* Circuites *or* Visits, *of diuers* Principall Citties *of the* Kingdome; *wher, as it commeth to passe, we doe publish such New* Profitable Inuentions, *as wee thinke good. And*

[1] *Ibid.*, p. 45. [2] *Ibid.*, pp. 45–6. [3] *Ibid.*, pp. 46–7.

wee doe also declare Naturall Diuinations *of* Diseases, Plagues, Swarmes *of* Hurtfull Creatures, Scarcety, Tempests, Earthquakes, Great Inundations, Cometts, Temperature *of the* Yeare, *and diuerse other Things*; *And wee giue* Counsell *thereupon, what the* People *shall doe, for the* Preuention *and* Remedy *of them.*[1]

In the last passage to be quoted, Bacon himself speaks in his proper person; and if the blessing which he received at the hands of the Father is fictitious, that which posterity received from him, overlooking his shortcomings, is real:

> And when Hee had sayd this, Hee stood vp: And I, as I had beene taught, kneeled downe, and He layd his Right Hand vpon my Head, and said; God *blesse thee, my Sonne; And* God *blesse this Relation which I haue made. I giue thee leaue to Publish it, for the Good of other Nations; For wee here are in* Gods *Bosome, a Land vnknowne.* And so hee left mee; . . .[2]

The Royal Society, founded in 1662, was the first step in the realization of Bacon's dream; the Royal Institution, founded in 1779, was the second; and the Imperial College of Science and Technology at South Kensington, founded in 1907, was the third in England.

In his *Great Englishmen of the Sixteenth Century* Sir Sidney Lee makes a statement which would be immodest from an American, but which I may perhaps without impropriety venture to quote. Asking whether Bacon's idea may be realized, he says that conditions are 'not favourable for its emergency in this country' (meaning England). 'It seems'—it is still Sir Sidney Lee who is speaking—'more likely to come to birth in Germany or in America first. For both in Germany and in America things of the mind such as Bacon worshipped receive a public consideration.'[3] However, every college or university with laboratories amply equipped, whether in the Old World or in the New, and every school of science, wherever found, is but the realization of Bacon's vision. In very truth, these United States are, as a whole, the 'Salomons House' of my Lord Bacon. America is still the favourite field for experiment in government and political organization; for experiments in social relations in which human beings as such are to possess the rights which in the past were called natural; and for experiments in science dedicated to the service of mankind. 'Posterity will say', the great Napoleon predicted, 'that the old world had lost its rights and that the new world has reconquered them.'

If the discovery of America has influenced to such an extent the minds of humanists and of lawyers, and has in various ways caused them to suggest laws affecting the inhabitants of each of their fancied commonwealths, it may be asked, what has been the effect of the era of discoveries upon the law of nations, or the rules of conduct between those separate and distinct communities which, taken together, form the Community of Nations. Another Englishman, Churton Collins,

[1] *New Atlantis*, p. 47.
[2] *Ibid.*, p. 47.
[3] (London, 1904), p. 254.

has said it all in a single phrase: 'The *Intercursus Magnus* had laid the foundations of International Law.' [1]

And as interesting to internationalists, if not so spectacular as the great adventurer's discovery of America, is the consequent discovery by Francisco de Vitoria that the same principles of justice expressed in the same rules of law were applicable alike to the civilized nations of Europe, the primitive peoples of America, and indeed to all other peoples of the world.

[1] J. Churton Collins, *op. cit.*, p. xxxi.

CHAPTER II

HISTORICAL BACKGROUND OF THE SPANISH SCHOOL

THE Low Countries were bound to be the high countries—as it were the 'high spots'—of Europe during the eventful century and a half which saw the emergence of the modern law of nations. Burgundy had been a dividing line between the east and the west of Europe. The Low Countries, which had become the appanage of Burgundy, were to be the dividing line between the old and the new state of things.

It is a custom for parents to look after their children, and kings have been very generous with the property of their subjects in this regard. The Duchy of Burgundy is a case in point. John the Good, King of France, who was defeated at Poitiers—as all youngsters know who read Froissart's *Chronicles*—invested his fourth son, to be known as Philip the Bold, with the Duchy; and the House of Burgundy, as it was called, became so powerful in the course of a century as not only to overshadow France but to menace Europe. Its rise and fall is one of the interesting 'ifs' of history.

Inheritance by marriage, purchase, and conquest extended the territories of the Dukes of Burgundy, which then included Franche-Comté as well as the territory to the north and west, comprising roughly the provinces now included in Belgium and the seven provinces of the Kingdom of the Netherlands—in all seventeen—forming what was technically known as 'Les Pays Bas'.

But the House of Burgundy came to grief by a man and a woman—a condition of things not confined to the Low Countries. Charles the Bold, a competent soldier but no general, lost his life and his possessions at Nancy in 1477. If he had had a son and heir—but he had none. Alas for his House! He had but a daughter and an heiress. If Mary of Burgundy (the natural limits of which country play such an important role in French history) had married the Dauphin of France—but she did not. She married the Archduke Maximilian of Austria, and to their son the Low Countries passed, with the exception of the Duchy of Burgundy, which Louis XI, King of France, seized and held. The conflicting claims of Francis I to Burgundy (through its seizure by Louis XI) and of Charles I of Spain, the grandson of Mary of Burgundy, are used more than once by Francisco de Vitoria to illustrate how possession is more than 'nine points' of fact if not of law, and also to illustrate what should not be done under the law governing the relations of nations.

Now Mary's son was Philip, known as 'the Handsome', to whom the Low Countries passed, and Philip the Handsome married the daughter of Ferdinand and Isabella, 'Crazy Joanna', or, to give her the

Spanish name to which she is entitled, 'Juana la Loca'. She in turn as heiress of father and mother, passed the Crown of Spain, with its immense possessions in America and in Europe, including the Low Countries, to a Spanish prince, the first of the Spanish Charles's and the fifth of the Roman Emperors, who, curiously enough, happened to be born in the city of Ghent, in the territory of his grandmother, Mary of Burgundy. There can therefore be no doubt as to his title.

The seventeen provinces which formed the Low Countries were far from homogeneous. Without disrespect, they might be called 'odds and ends'. Their peoples were of Germanic origin, although the language of those to the south was French, for whatever territory the Romans conquered and held their language has left an indelible mark thereon. Religion apparently goes with the language, for the southern provinces were, and still are, of the Church of Rome. The seven northern provinces were also originally Catholic, but the tyranny of Philip, the Count of Holland, better known to history as Philip the Second of Spain, in matters governmental and religious, caused the northern provinces to declare their independence of Spain on July 26th, 1581. This they did under the leadership of William of Orange, called 'the Silent'—not that he was taciturn but because he knew when to hold his peace—who was at the time stadtholder, that is to say, the political representative of Spain, in the three provinces of Holland, Zeeland, and Utrecht, and was later to become Count of the first two of these provinces, to which the other provinces of the north attached themselves, forming the United Netherlands. And, curiously enough, in our day a woman—Queen Wilhelmina, also of the Orange line—rules over the provinces which were once those of Mary of Burgundy.

The independence of the northern provinces was not a thing of a day. Off and on there was a war of some 'eighty years', and their complete independence from Spain was only formally recognized in the Treaty of Münster of January 30, 1648, ending that phase of the calamity which we call the 'Thirty Years' War'.

More was at stake, however, than the independence of seven provinces to the north and the south of the mouth of the Rhine. The Christians of the Western Church were at swords' points. The Spanish sovereigns of the Low Countries were of the Catholic branch. William of Orange and his people were Protestants. For reasons of his own, Henry VIII had withdrawn England from the See of Rome, without himself subscribing to the new faith. His daughter, Elizabeth, Queen of England by act of Parliament and a Protestant, supported the Protestant provinces of the Netherlands in their revolt. The Spanish Armada, the supreme attempt of Philip II against Protestant England, was scattered to the winds off the coasts of the British Isles in 1588.

Henry of Navarre was King of France and a thorn in the side of

Philip. Therefore he sympathized with the northern provinces and aided them, refusing, however, their offer of sovereignty. In the interest of powerful neighbours as well as because of their prowess, the northern provinces were to become a nation. During the process one Hugo de Groot, of whom we shall hear much later, was born at Delft in 1583, at a critical moment in history as well as of international law.

*
* *

In Victoria's century there were two international events which changed and shaped history as few other events—if any—have done. Their consequences in the Old and the New Worlds, their effect on matters spiritual and temporal, are still incalculable after a lapse of four centuries.

The first involved the discovery of America, with its consequences; the second, the divorce question—which was a Spanish question. If they had not been responsible for the discovery of the New World—which they were—the Catholic Sovereigns would not have overshadowed their day and generation. They might not have acquired the Kingdom of Naples, and the hand of their daughter would likely not have been asked by no less a person than a member of the royal family of England, for, through the discovery of America, the Spanish sovereigns acquired an immense distinction and notoriety, as well as untold wealth. In simplest terms, Spain had become a world power: a double world power, in that it had discovered the New World, and claimed the exclusive right to settle it.

As to the divorce: from one standpoint, it was of no importance to the world at large whether Henry VIII married or not; but he sought the hand of a Spanish princess, Catherine of Aragon, his brother's widow, and married her. Growing tired of her and wanting to marry an English woman, one Anne Boleyn by name, at a moment when Spain was, without peradventure, the greatest and most powerful country in the modern world, he sought a dissolution of his marriage with this princess of Aragon. Even the question of the divorce might have had but a passing interest—just as is the case with many divorces of our day—had there not been more than one nation concerned. But Henry's was an international marriage, involving great issues. The dissolution of his marriage, which Rome had refused to countenance but which an English Archbishop of Canterbury had pronounced, changed the whole face of Europe, largely because the nephew of the unfortunate Catherine, the divorced queen, was the Holy Roman Emperor—at the same time King of Spain—holding in his hand the power of the world.

Even that is not the chief interest in the incident—because the displeasure of the Holy Roman Emperor was not necessarily to change the history of the world. But the refusal of the Pope to dissolve Henry's marriage with Catherine of Aragon resulted in the separation of England from the Roman See; and the passage of power into the hands of Henry's daughter, Queen Elizabeth (the daughter of Anne Boleyn and therefore illegitimate in the eyes of the Catholic world), created an international situation of vast potentialities, because of Elizabeth's immense dexterity in statecraft. The legitimate heir to the throne, after the death of Mary Tudor (Henry's only surviving child by Catherine of Aragon), was, according to the Catholic world, Mary, Queen of Scots. There was a mortal enemy to the south of England—Philip of Spain, who had been the husband of Mary Tudor and, as such, for a few years King of England as well as King of Spain, which was at the time the most powerful of single kingdoms. On the north was Scotland; and across the Channel, the Low Countries, now Belgium and Holland, and the vast domain of France, of which Mary Stuart had been the queen as the young wife of the youthful Francis II. The destruction of the Spanish Armada, which was to have conquered England and put an end to its great maritime career; and the Spanish downfall, already started by the revolt of the Netherlands—supported as they were by the Queen of England—were to mark the beginning of the end of the predominance of Spain.

Hence it is that the divorce of Henry VIII was in its consequences one of the great incidents in modern history. The question was Spanish; it was argued by a Spaniard, none other than Francisco de Vitoria; and the doctrine which he stated is still the doctrine of the Catholic world.

CHAPTER III

FRANCISCO DE VITORIA

PRIMA PROFESSOR OF THEOLOGY AT SALAMANCA

FRANCISCO DE VITORIA has long been known as a theologian, moralist and humanist; to-day his reputation is that of a jurist and a philosopher as well; to-morrow it will be that of an internationalist and a humanitarian; and many believe that he is destined to be regarded as the founder of the modern law of nations. A specialist in many fields, his specialities must be examined by specialists, and we can only touch in passing the phases of his varied activities which relate to or throw light on Victoria as an internationalist and international lawyer. It is, however, impossible to separate his work into compartments, inasmuch as he was not content to examine the subject in hand from a single standpoint but viewed it in its various aspects, in order that the solution which he proposed should be complete according to his larger—and what we may call universal—conception of things. Hence it is difficult to determine the field in which he chiefly excelled. To the churchman he was a theologian, the founder of the new school of theology, reviving it and making it adequate to the conditions of his day to such an extent that no less a person than Menéndez y Pelayo could say that Victoria had made a theologian of every Spaniard.[1] This may be what is called a pardonable exaggeration, but at least Victoria made of the Spaniards who studied theology the most competent theologians of Europe.

He was a philosopher, not merely in the technical meaning but in that larger sense which brings to the solution of a problem what we may call the philosophical nature of things, being in all things a seeker after fundamental truth, with the result that the solutions of his legal problems are not merely true but establish what may be called the philosophy of law.

Because he was a theologian, it may well be said he was a moralist, inasmuch as any system of theology should bear some definable relation to morality; but with Victoria the moral element entered to such an extent and was so stripped of technicalities that it can properly be said that with him morality in its non-technical and universal sense, which may be called ethics, was as a thing apart and formed the ultimate test, with the result that to the layman the moralist is often more evident than the theologian.

[1] *Ensayos de Crítica Filosófica* (Madrid, 1918), p. 237; *vide* also the Prólogo to Luis G. Alonso Getino, O.P., *El Maestro Fr. Francisco de Vitoria, Su Vida, Su Doctrina e Influencia* (Publicaciones de la Asociación Francisco de Vitoria, second edition, Madrid, 1930), pp. iii–x; and the Epilogo to Vicente Beltrán de Heredia, O.P., *Los Manuscritos del Maestro Fray Francisco de Vitoria,* O.P. (Biblioteca de Tomistas españoles, vol. iv), pp. 155–8.

When it is said that a philosophy of law resulted from Victoria's discussion of legal problems, it follows not only that he was a jurist familiar with texts and precedents but that he brought to their examination and application a philosophy drawn from what was then considered the law of nature; and the fact seems to be that the churchmen of Victoria's time were held to be competent to consider every legal question which presented itself from the standpoint of right reason.

To say that Victoria was a humanist means that he was a man of his day and generation, when Greek as well as Latin and the learning of antiquity had been rediscovered and the civilization of the ancient world had entered into what we may call the civilization of the medieval world, which was developing, because of humanism, into the modern world. The perfect flower of humanism was Erasmus, whom Victoria is said to have met in his early and formative days as a student in Paris, then (as now) the great centre for the scholarly world and for youth thirsting for learning and devoting itself to a scholarly, that is to say, clerical, career.

There is a French expression to the effect that who says 'society' says 'law'; and it would be equally true to say that who said Paris in Victoria's day said internationalism, for it was even then the meeting-place of the nations. And after the eighteen years which Victoria spent in Paris as student and as teacher, without ceasing to be a Spaniard, on leaving France—for which he always retained an admiration, and indeed an affection [1]—he returned to Spain as a citizen of the world, or, as we to-day would say in a single word, an internationalist, which in its simplest and best sense is one who knows that other countries exist beyond his own frontiers and, because of this knowledge, endeavours to understand them and their people as he would have them understand his own country and people.[2]

Of the capacity of Victoria as an international lawyer this volume is at once a testimony and an act of homage.

In former days it frequently happened that the place of birth supplied a surname, and so it was that one Francis, born in the little

[1] 'Sin duda en su larga estancia en la nación vecina había cobrado cariño muy intenso a Francia.' Getino, *op. cit.*, p. 219.

[2] Erasmus, speaking of another great Spaniard (Luis Vives), employed a happy phrase to the effect that he was 'Spanish with a fine strain of French in him, through having lived some years in Paris'—a phrase which might well have been coined expressly to describe Victoria. *Vide* Watson, *op. cit.*, p. 35. Concerning Victoria as an internationalist, *vide* also the comment of Professor Camilo Barcia Trelles, of the University of Valladolid: 'Pour nous, François de Vitoria est la figure qui se détache le plus vigoureusement parmi les internationalistes du XVIe et du XVIIe siècle.' Quoted from lectures delivered, under the title 'Francisco de Vitoria et l'École moderne du Droit international', at the Hague Academy of International Law in 1927, as printed in the *Recueil des Cours* of the Academy, vol. 17, p. 117. These lectures have since been published in book form in Spanish under the title *Francisco de Vitoria, Fundador del Derecho Internacional Moderno* (Universidad de Valladolid, Publicaciones de la Sección de Estudios Americanistas, Serie Quinta, Numero III, 1928).

town of Vitoria, in a Basque province, Alava, is known as Francisco de Vitoria. Now spelling is an art, and it has its own standard. 'Francis' is secure in English and 'Francisco' has a single spelling in Spanish, but 'Victoria' is spelled in various ways. Nevertheless it seems to be the practice that in speaking of Francis as a man, his surname is spelled with a 'c' (as in the case of the late Queen Victoria), whereas in speaking of him as a theologian and jurist, the 'c' is eliminated from the name. In using his full name we have given it as Francisco de Vitoria. But when the surname is used alone, it comes more easily to the Anglo-Saxon tongue to say 'Victoria'. Therefore in the following pages we are dealing with 'Francisco de Vitoria' and 'Victoria', as one or the other seems appropriate.

In 'Victoria's' day, birth seemed to be the chief element, and the time, as well as the place, an incident; that is to say, the date of his birth is uncertain. Some authorities are of the opinion that he came into this world of sin and sorrow in 1480; others, 1483; still others, 1486; and one has it, 1473.[1] For him, as well as for us, the important matter is that he was born. There seems to be what might be called a consensus of opinion that his birth could not have been earlier than the first date mentioned nor later than the third, and the year 1483 apparently has the preference. The date of 1483 is particularly pleasing to the international lawyer for sentimental as well as historical reasons, because, if it be adopted, we have the two great figures of international law, Victoria and Grotius, separated by the span of exactly one century.[2]

Victoria's brother Diego, his elder by some years, was a member of the Dominican Order, and 'Francisco de Vitoria' likewise entered the Order of Preachers while a youth of tender years. Later he repaired to the Convent of San Pablo of Burgos, where he made his formal profession and from which as a young man of promise, learned in the Classics, he was sent, as happened with the *élite*, to the college of the Dominicans in Paris. He was there to profit not only by the courses of the college but, above and beyond all, by the courses of the Sorbonne, then the admitted centre of learning, profane and sacred, of the world. He was already treading in the footsteps of St. Thomas Aquinas himself, it may be said, who had added to the lustre of the Sorbonne by professing theology there.

The Convent of the Dominicans in Paris was its principal college, as we would expect it to be. It was situated in the 'Latin Quarter', in the street of St. Jacques—a name one day destined to be heard throughout

[1] Getino, *op. cit.*, p. 13.

[2] The relationship between Victoria and Grotius was not overlooked by the good people of Holland who bethought themselves of Francisco de Vitoria, sending a mission to Spain, to lay, as it were, a wreath on the unmarked tomb of the noble Spaniard, *maestro* as well as predecessor of their great countryman. On this occasion, Father Luis G. Alonso Getino, on behalf of the Dominican Order, delivered an admirable address in Latin, which is appended in English to the present chapter, *infra*, pp. 88–93.

the world, as it was to lend its name to the party of the 'Jacobins' which met there in the stormy days of the French Revolution.[1]

The year of Francisco's arrival in Paris is put at 1506, and it is supposed that he remained there as a student in the convent and at the Sorbonne and as a teacher in the Dominican college for approximately eighteen continuous years. It is known that he taught theology in his college, and the chair of theology required its holder to have taught the arts; it thus appears that from his early years he was not only familiar with the Classics[2] but that he had professed them in the university city of Paris.

In a Dominican college the text in theology would naturally be the *Summa Theologica* of St. Thomas Aquinas—a name in the Order which overshadows even that of its founder. The method of instruction then in vogue, and which brought scholasticism into disrepute, was that of pedantic disputation and subtle distinctions: a method which nevertheless gave the student immense training in the field of disputatious controversy and logical exposition. Fortunately for scholasticism, Francisco de Vitoria was to replace the weaknesses of the method, upon his return to Spain, by systematic instruction in the fundamentals of theology, which he applied not merely to the individual student but to the world at large. He continued, however, to employ to the best effect the syllogism, which had become, as it were, indispensable to the scholastic mind. In short, he took from scholasticism its best and devised a method of instruction and of exposition which is as useful to-day as then, and is as applicable to law as it is to theology.[3]

[1] For details of Victoria's life at Paris and a discussion of theological and humanistic influences and developments in the French capital at the beginning of the sixteenth century, *vide* Getino, *op. cit.*, chap. iii; also Cardinal Ehrle's essay 'Die vaticanischen Handschriften der Salmanticenser Theologen des sechszehnten Jahrhunderts', printed in *Der Katolik* (1884, Zweite Hälfte), pp. 505–10.

Further details on this phase of the subject will be found in the Introduction to Professor Ernest Nys's edition of Victoria's *De Indis et De Jure Belli Relectiones*, published by the Carnegie Institution of Washington (Washington, 1917). This scholarly Introduction, written by Professor Nys, contains an admirable survey of the life and work of Victoria, with deftly interwoven details of historical and doctrinal background. *Vide* also Professor Nys's *Le Droit des Gens et les Anciens Jurisconsultes Espagnols* (La Haye, 1914), especially Chapter VIII 'Les Grands Publicistes du XVIe siècle et du Commencement du XVIIe siècle'.

[2] 'No solo en la Teología fué eminente, mas en todas las ciencias y artes, tanto que parecía que cada una era su propria facultad y que en solo aquella había empleado la vida.' Quoted from the *Coronica* of Juan de la Cruz by Getino, *op. cit.*, p. 284.

[3] *Vide* Cardinal Ehrle, *op. cit.*, pp. 497, 505–6, 512–13, who says of Victoria: 'Er war es vorzüglich, welcher Salamanca für das 16. Jahrhundert eine Stellung anwies, wie sich deren in der zweiten Hälfte des 13. Jahrhunderts Paris erfreut hatte; durch ihn wurde es zur Wiege der neuen Scholastik. Die so nothwendige fruchtbringende Reform, welche diese neue Aera kennzeichnet, wurde zuerst durch ihn in ausgezeichnetem Masse in's Werk gesetzt. . . . Francisco de Vitoria gilt mit Recht als der Vater wie der Salmanticenser Schule, so der neuen Scholastik überhaupt. Bei ihm findet sich nämlich zuerst deutlich und vollständig jener Fortschritt ausgeprägt, welcher jene Schule und diese Periode der speculativen Theologie kennzeichnet. . . . Offenbar bildete seine mit humanistischer Bildung gepaarte theologische Erudition seine Hauptkraft. Wir finden bei ihm nicht mehr jene einseitige Bevorzugung der philosophischen Speculation. Ohne durch Missachtung derselben in das andere Extrem zu fallen, verstand er es, die positiven Beweisquellen: die h. Schrift, die Concilien und h. Väter, in ihre Rechte wieder einzusetzen. Sie bildeten bei ihm die nothwendige und sichere Grundlage. Auf sie erst baute er dann seine dogmatische Speculation auf, mit Mass, ohne sich in vorwitzige Fragen zu verlieren. Die Schärfe und Consequenz, mit welcher er diese allein richtige Methode begründete und handhabte, gab seinem talentvollen Schüler Canus die erste Idee zu seinem classischen Werke *de Locis theologicis*. Dasselbe enthält wohl nur

The attainments of the young Basque were well known to his fellow members of the college who, on their return to Spain, were loud in his praise. The result was that he repaired to Spain to profess in the Convent of San Gregorio in the city of Valladolid, serving there a few years' apprenticeship, as it were, before his appointment to the chair of theology in Salamanca, the Sorbonne of Spain. But before he returned from France he must needs take his degree of

die wissentschaftliche und theoretische Begründung jener Topik, welche Vitoria zeitlebens in seinem Unterricht praktisch angewandt hatte.'

Vide also Getino, *op. cit.*, pp. viii–ix: 'Vitoria no abandonó por esto su labor cuotidiana de clase, que era, al fin y a la postre, por una parte su deber, y por otra la fuente de su crédito; Vitoria siguió siendo expositor de sutilezas dogmáticas y zurcidor de la urdimbre casuística en sus lecciones ordinarias, normales, de rejunteo pedagógico-doctrinal. Pero utilizó un expediente comodísimo para dar lecciones fuera de clase, para hablar al gran público de todos los dominios españoles y de cuantos tuviesen relación con sus cosas (sin que los visitadores y jueces de la escuela pudieran alegar que se salía del reglamento), dando a la Teología aires de vida, volcando la doctrina evangélica en el lecho de los nuevos sucesos sociales, lo que en un pueblo de tan ardiente religiosidad y tan creciente vida era de una importancia suma.

'Vitoria, despreciando el marchamo de las rutinas escolares en uso, agrandando el radio de la Teología y poniendo clase al mundo con sus lecciones extraordinarias o *Relecciones teológicas* acerca de la *autoridad civil y eclesiástica*, del *derecho de guerra* y de *conquista*, de la *magia*, de la *templanza*, del *homicidio* y *suicidio*, es uno de los espectáculos más grandiosos que pueden contemplarse en una época que era de decadencia teológica. Al enfocar dichas cuestiones lo hizo con esa mirada perforadora de los genios, que escruta los problemas en sus más forzosas y transcendentales derivaciones. Los hombres más sabios e imparciales del mundo reconocían su acierto y su constancia, y le llaman *creador de la Escolástica española, don singular de Dios a España, implantador de la ciencia moral, padre del Derecho de gentes*.'

In his edition of Victoria's *Comentarios a la Secunda secundae de Santo Tomas* (Salamanca, 1932, p. xvii), Beltrán de Heredia furnishes the following interesting information concerning the methods employed by Victoria in the classroom: 'Para amenizar la exposición, que resultaría monótona siguiendo la forma descarnada de la argumentación escolástica, introduce él frecuentemente una especie de diálogo improvisado con el adversario, que a veces adquiere cierto aire dramático. Puede formarse idea de la vida que sabía infundir a temas de sí áridos, por estos ejemplos que reproducimos a continuación, donde el alumno ha procurado conservar las modalidades del discurso hasta en sus ínfimos detalles.

'En la q. 1, a. 1, nn. 24–5 se entabla una discusión entre el professor y un supuesto adversario sobre el tema: an ultima resolutio fidei sit ad revelationem divinam. Según Santo Tomás, parece que sí. Pero arguye Vitoria: Sed contra, sumo istam: hoc est revelatum a Deo. Quomodo scitis quod Deus revelavit?

'*Adversario*: O quia revelavit quod ipse revelavit.

'*Vitoria*: Arguo sic: illa non est per se nota. Quomodo scis eam? Erit processus in infinito.

'*Adversario*: Credo hoc evangelium esse quia Ecclesia dicit.

'*Vitoria*: Contra, quomodo ergo scis Ecclesiam non posse errare?

'*Adversario*: O quia dicit scriptura.

'*Vitoria*: Jam videtis quomodo est circulus. Ergo ultimata resolutio videtur ad auctoritatem humanam.

'Y sigue exponiendo las soluciones dadas a esta cuestión, para terminar con una síntesis de la doctrina verdadera expresada en varias proposiciones.'

Beltrán de Heredia also furnishes other interesting examples in this connexion, in which, he says, Victoria 'discute como lo haría un comunista de hoy'.

In the words of Domingo Bañez (quoted by Getino, *op. cit.*, p. 121 note) Victoria, in method and results, was *velut alter Socrates*.

Elsewhere Bañez says: 'Tengo entendido por referencias de nuestros padres que en Salamanca ó por mejor decir, en toda España, hace sesenta años eran mucho menos peritos los teólogos escolásticos hasta que Fr. Francisco de Vitoria de gloriosa memoria, que fué insigne maestro de nuestra orden, enseño de viva voz como otro Sócrates la doctrina escolástica ilustrándola y reduciéndola en su cátedra de Prima de Salamanca, con un método perspícuo y repleto de erudición para la inteligencia de Santo Tomás.' Getino, *op. cit.*, p. 283.

Professor Ernest Nys, in his Introduction to the Carnegie Institution edition of Victoria's *De Indis et de Iure Belli Relectiones*, *op. cit.*, p. 20, says of the theology of Victoria: 'Il est incontestable que François de Vitoria ne donna pas seulement une impulsion vigoureuse à sa science de prédilection, mais qu'il lui imprima un caractère nouveau: il l'embellit et il l'élargit; grâce à lui, la plupart des théologiens espagnols renoncèrent à la forme incorrecte, rude, barbare qu'avaient employée leurs devanciers; grâce à lui, dans l'argumentation, des idées vinrent prendre la place occupée précédemment par des phrases; grâce à lui également, dans l'étude de la théologie d'autres sciences furent mises à profit. C'est ainsi

licentiate in theology at the Sorbonne, which he did on March 24th, 1522.[1]

It is supposed that he spent three years in Valladolid, then the favourite residence of the royal court and the seat of the councils for the Indies.[2] Francisco was the senior lecturer on theology at Valladolid, or, as we might say, dean of studies. He was not rector of the college, as has been supposed, nor was he at any time rector of the University of Salamanca; for, although taking an active part in university matters, he was, body and soul, a professor of theology and an instructor of youth.

In 1526 the *prima* chair of theology at Salamanca became vacant. It was the custom then, as it still is in some quarters, for candidates to step forward and to propose themselves; and strange as it may seem to us of other days and other ways, it was the students who chose the professor from among the candidates whose reputation, whose personality, and whose exposition of an assigned topic were most acceptable and pleasing to them.[3] An odd method it seems to us; but, if a tree is to be known by its fruit, there is something to be said for a democratic method of selection which could confer on Francisco de Vitoria the *prima* professorship of theology in Salamanca, the most sought for chair in the greatest of Spanish universities. It is no slight tribute to democracy that a small democratic, intellectual group should have chosen from among the intellectuals the one person best able to defend democracy for the entire world.

The expression '*prima* professor' throws a light on the customs of the day. The holder of the first or prime chair was so named because he first professed theology in the course of the day. In Salamanca there were two chairs, the *prima* and the *vespera*, indicating the hours of the day when the course should be given. That of the *prima* professor began at the prime hour, according to canonical custom, which was none other than six o'clock in the morning, following the meeting for prayers; and that of vespers at what would be considered even by pagans as the more Christian hour of four or five in the afternoon. The earlier the hour, the greater the honour. It is evident from the hour of the *prima* lecture that education must have been taken seriously in that age, both by the student body and the professorate. Francisco de Vitoria's colleague in the *vespera* chair, it should be stated, was none

que, dans ses leçons consacrées aux droits des Indiens et au droit de la guerre, les problèmes sont traités, non comme s'ils étaient sans intérêt pratique et actuel, destinés uniquement à exercer la raison et à fournir l'occasion d'objections et de réfutations, mais comme des questions soulevées par de graves événements et dont la solution intéresse tous les hommes de cœur, puisque dans la pratique immédiate elle produit des effets souvent redoutables. De plus, l'illustre publiciste ne se contente pas d'un vain étalage de connaissances: il est plein de générosité et plein de bonté et son enseignement respire les plus nobles sentiments.'

[1] Getino, *op. cit.*, p. 43; Cardinal Ehrle, *op. cit.*, p. 510.

[2] As to the members of these councils, Getino (*op. cit.*, p. 154) tells us that 'El Consejo de Indies [estaba] compuesto principalmente de juristas y hombres de negocios.'

[3] *Vide* Barcia Trelles, *Recueil des Cours, op. cit.*, p. 125.

other than Domingo de Soto, whose reputation was very great and who was later to succeed to Victoria's chair.

The duty of the professor of theology, first or second, was to comment on the *Sententiae* of one Peter Lombard[1] and the *Summa Theologica* of St. Thomas Aquinas.

It is evident that Victoria had devoted himself—we might say consecrated himself—to St. Thomas Aquinas, teaching the *Summa* in Paris and in Valladolid; and, notwithstanding the fact that the *Sententiae* of Peter Lombard was prescribed, he was permitted to base his instruction upon the teaching of the great Dominican Summist.

The professors of Salamanca were elected by the students, and their influence did not cease with the election, for later their will—if not law—apparently decided the sources of the law which should be expounded. They were pleased—as well they might be—with Victoria's exposition of the *Summa*, and he continued to base his instruction upon the *Summa*, with the result that the *Sentences* eventually gave way to the *Summa*.

Some of the professors contented themselves with reading the *Sentences* of Peter and the articles of St. Thomas—in which practice they do not seem to have differed greatly from some of their successors of more modern days. Francisco de Vitoria was not one of those who read—that is to say, in class.[2] He prepared himself elaborately in advance. He prepared himself as carefully for subsequent courses on the same subject, saying that he did so and that he wrote with his own hand the lecture of the day;[3] and it appears that the labour of prepara-

[1] Peter Lombard (*circa* 1100–*circa* 1160), as his name indicates, was probably born in that part of Italy known as Lombardy. He made his studies at Bologna, Rheims, and Paris, where he came into contact with the great minds of his day. He knew St. Bernard, and probably studied under Abelard. Peter Lombard's greatest work is the *Book of the Sentences*, which was probably written between 1145 and 1151—while he was a professor at the school of Notre Dame. In 1158 his name appears as Archbishop of Paris; it is improbable, however, that he held that office for very long. Shortly thereafter we begin to read of him as having lived in the past, and so it may be concluded that he died *circa* 1160. His original copy of the *Sentences* was bequeathed by Stephen Langton, Archbishop of Canterbury, to the Library of Notre Dame.

The *Catholic Encyclopaedia* says: '. . . the success of the book was incontestable; down to the sixteenth century it was the textbook of the University courses, upon which each future doctor had to lecture during two years.'

[2] Getino (*op. cit.*, p. 127) says of Victoria in this connexion: 'Su gran relieve es el de filósofo y pensador cristiano, en independencia y generosidad por nadie superado, y sobre todo profesor *que no leía*, que no se atenía a leer las *Sentencias* y la *Suma* y a explicarlas siguiendo servilmente sus lineas, sino que las trazaba nuevas; encarnaba en los principios de la vieja escolástica las nuevas direcciones; enfocaba por diferentes puntos los problemas que podríamos llamar gastados, porque se discutían de una manera estática y predeterminada; removía la enorme congeries filosófico-teológica, oreándola con el soplo vivificante de las múltiples y vitales cuestiones planteadas ante el derecho nuevo.'

[3] *Vide* Beltrán de Heredia, *op. cit.*, pp. ix–x: 'Vitoria acostumbraba preparar sus lecciones con el mayor esmero. La enseñanza era para el, más que una profesión, un culto, un apostolado. Leía mucho—hombre de lectura *pene infinita* le llama Vaseo—meditaba, organizaba las conclusiones y luego lo ponía por escrito. Cada vez que comenzaba a explicar una materia, aunque la tuviera ya muy trillada en ciclos anteriores, volvía a estudiarla, fijando posiciones y escribiéndola de nuevo, como si entonces inaugurase su profesorado. No rezaba con él proceder de tantos catedráticos, que una vez confeccionado su manual de texto, se contentan con repetir en años sucesivos la misma cantinela, como si la ciencia hubiera logrado encerrarse en fórmula definitiva. "Ne putetis me.—decía él a sus alumnos al comenzar el curso de 1539–

tion was so severe and burdensome that it prevented him from doing other things. From his chair he spoke freely from the fullness of knowledge, and it may be with notes in hand.

The classroom which we of to-day would say he honoured with his presence is still a classroom in the University of Salamanca and it still rings with the voices of students and professors. The comforts of Francisco's day were fewer than those of ours: a large, oblong room, a passage in the centre and one on each side and, in between, wooden benches with wooden planks as desks, showing the marks of the absent-minded through many a generation. The *cathedra*, or as the Anglo-Saxons would say, the desk, from which the *prima* professor spoke is a sort of pulpit. The chair upon which he sat was a plain wooden bench.

The room and the benches and the platform, with its pulpit and bench, were used on the 7th day of November, 1927, some four centuries after the *prima* professor had himself inaugurated his courses, when the Francisco de Vitoria chair was inaugurated: the room being filled with students—not so many as he would have had, because he admitted that they numbered 'one thousand, less one'[1]—and also honoured by the Government, represented by its Minister of Education. On the day of the chair's inauguration, the street through which the *prima* professor of theology had repaired daily (in his last years upon the shoulders of his devoted students) from the Convent of San Esteban to the university was formally christened with the name of Francisco de Vitoria.

To the internationalist the classroom is not merely that of Francisco de Vitoria; it is the cradle of international law.

The *prima* professor gave regular courses which were called *Lectiones*—we would say readings, although they were lectures based upon notes rather than readings. It was, however, the duty of the professor of theology to give a public reading during the course of the year and, as it was based upon the course which he had professed, it was called a *Relectio*, or, as one might say, a re-reading. Fortunately for us it happened that Victoria was accustomed to profess courses which had a direct connexion with the conditions of his day, and very often with

40—eamdem qua hucusque cantilenam recantaturum. Non enim hoc est ingenii mei, nec instituti; sed novo sermone, nova diligentia omnia pro viribus explicabo, ac si hodierna die primo legere inciperem." En conformidad con esto, nos hace saber de paso en otro lugar, que escribía previamente sus lecciones. "Hoc dixi pro nunc, quia latius dicam infra q. 180, a. 4. Et licet omnia ista *habeam ego iterum scripta, ideo nunc scripsi*, quia clara erunt mihi et omni legenti." (q. 79, a. 3.)'

In his volume *Los manuscritos del Maestro Fray Francisco de Vitoria, O.P., op. cit.*, p. 16, Beltrán de Heredia quotes Victoria as saying in the course of his lectures: 'Quod ideo dixi ne putetis me eamdem qua hucusque cantilenam recantaturum, et ea quae millies forte dixi iterum repetiturum. Non enim hoc est ingenii mei nec instituti. Sed novo sermone, nova diligentia omnia pro viribus explicabo ac si hodierna die primo legere inciperem. Ita tamen ut et vos pro vestra me virili animetis et vestro diligenti studio adjuvetis, quod quidem hucusque optimum et mihi beneplacitum sensi.'

[1] Victoria's words, as quoted by Beltrán de Heredia, in his edition of Victoria's *Comentarios* (*op. cit*, p. xii, note 1), are: 'Sicut si jurat quod hic [in aula] sunt mille, et non sum tot, sed deest unum.' *Vide* also Getino, *op. cit.*, p. 270.

matters either of an international nature or with an international implication.[1] It appears also to have been his habit to devote a course to a question which had been submitted to him or to the university for a professional opinion and to make it later the subject of a public reading. This was in accordance with his conception of the place which theology should occupy.[2] It was the greatest and most inclusive of all the sciences, as it was called in earlier days. In his opinion, nothing could be settled without reference to theology; indeed, he held that the jurists by themselves were incompetent to pass judgement upon questions of law because every legal question involved philosophy as well as theology, and the jurists as such were in his opinion not sufficiently familiar with either. His practice was in accordance with a conviction that theology was not merely for the churchman or for the individual member of the Church; its moral tenets applied to all individuals, irrespective of the offices which they held. An act was wrong in itself, not wrong in the lowly and right in the prince. Therefore the act of the State—as the act of the individual—would as a matter of fact be right or wrong according to its nature rather than according to the rank and position of him who performed it. The standard was thus impersonal, in that it was no respecter of persons or of frontiers; being impersonal, it was universal and therefore it was law. It was, however, law in its highest sense. An accepted rule is of course law, whether it regulates the material or spiritual concerns of life. If it is law it is law, and it cannot be said to be the more or the less law because it regulates the imponderables. The fact that law regulates both the spiritual and the material renders it applicable to the human being, as such. But for this application, there should be in the general principle and in the special rule an ethical content as well as a spiritual element. In Victoria's conception, all these essentials were united.

By brushing aside the accidental—because a political post, even that of the Catholic sovereign, was an accident of birth—and by clinging to the nature and the consequences of the act, irrespective of the person who committed it, Victoria had a firm and a sure foundation for his system and a standard by which to test the conduct of the State as well as of the international community. As these various elements are present in his discussions of the larger questions of the day, involving kings and governments, States and their international

[1] 'Une des marques charactéristiques de son enseignement, c'est qu'il s'occupe des grandes questions politiques qui étaient à l'ordre du jour et qu'il est ainsi animé et vivant.'—Professor Ernest Nys, 'Les Publicistes Espagnols du XVIe Siècle et les Droits des Indiens' published in the *Revue de Droit International et de Législation Comparée,* tome xxi (1889), p. 556.

[2] *Vide* note 2, p. 95, *infra*. *Vide* also the statement of Professor Nys in his introduction to the Carnegie Institution's edition of Victoria's *De Indis et de Iure Belli Relectiones, op. cit.*, p. 35: 'Il [Victoria] soutient que l'office et la charge du théologien s'étendent à ce point que nul argument, nulle controverse ne paraissent étrangers à la profession et à l'institution de la théologie.' Victoria's statement on this point is discussed *infra*, p. 253.

activities, it follows that he must have regarded the elements to which we have already referred as the essence of his system, so that, when he applied the *Sentences* of Peter the Lombard or the *Summa Theologica* of St. Thomas Aquinas to a concrete situation, although of an international import, the jurist was not to have the last word. There was the law, and there was the spirit of the law. The large examples appealed to him because of his large conception of things. How could he show the universality of the system which he was professing better than by taking the concrete facts of international life, and above and beyond all the concrete facts to which Spain was a party? For the rule of conduct for his country, if correct, should be applied as well to all countries; and the principles upon which the rule was based were the same principles that applied to the acts of all individuals.

If we take 1483 as the date of Victoria's birth, he was at the impressionable age of nine when the astounding news of the discovery of a New World reached the little town of Vitoria, in which he was born and passed his early years. It happened during the year of his birth that no less a person than Isabella the Catholic honoured the community with her royal presence,[1] a fact that would be a tradition in the little town.

Years later, while he was a youth of fourteen dwelling in Burgos, and shortly before he entered the monastery of San Pablo, Isabella the Catholic with her husband, one Ferdinand by name, received Columbus at Burgos upon his return from his second voyage in 1497.[2] This incident would be more than a tradition; it was something which entered into what we may call Victoria's personal experience, becoming a part of his life and no doubt awakening for the first time that abiding interest in the Americas which was to play such a dominant part in the development of international law. To this youth of the Old World the New World had become very real.

There was still another reason for his interest in America. The Dominicans, whose official name is 'Order of Preachers'—inasmuch as they prepare themselves for spreading the Gospel through preaching—had chosen America as a field for their labours. The reports of the missionaries, describing not only the spiritual but the material conquests beyond the seas, doubtless passed from house to house, especially in Spain, so that the conduct of the *conquistadores* became a matter of common knowledge; in a word, the Dominicans specialized in things American, and the reports which came from America became a subject of great concern to the Order. The apostle of the Indians was none other than a Dominican, Bartolomé de las Casas. No less than seven times he crossed the ocean in order to plead with the King of Spain,

[1] Getino, *op. cit.*, pp. 12, 379.

[2] *Ibid.*, p. 379.

a distinguished Dutch publicist of our day tells us,[1] 'to put an end to these atrocities; six times he returned to his second country to reconquer and to make of it a veritable City of God;' and of his career not only Spain, not only the Dominicans and the Catholic Church, but humanity should be proud.

The Dominicans appear to have taken their mission seriously. The reports and protests which came from their missionaries on the conditions resulting from the conquest became not merely common knowledge but common property, so that the Catholic sovereign, Ferdinand of Aragon (for Isabella, who belongs to America as well as Spain, had died in 1503), submitted the charges to a commission of theologians and jurists for investigation and report. The conclusions which they presented and the reasons therefor, as expounded, on behalf of the theologians, by Fray Matías de Paz, then a Dominican professor of theology at Valladolid and later a professor at Salamanca (who subsequently prepared a treatise on the subject),[2] were the forerunners of those to which Victoria was to give a classical and more human expression. The question was therefore one in which Victoria had a personal and above all a professional interest. Hence it is not astonishing that after many years of reflection—because his was a reflective nature—he should have made the conduct of the Spaniards in America the subject of professional readings.[3]

In a letter to Father Arcos,[4] to which the date of November 8th, 1534, has been assigned, Victoria dwelt at some length upon the activities of his fellow countrymen in the New World, although the letter, it appears, was occasioned in particular by their actions in Peru: 'With regard to Peru, I assure Your Reverence that, owing to my

[1] 'Sept fois Las Casas traverse l'océan—voyage dangereux et de longue durée—pour aller conjurer le roi d'Espagne de mettre fin à ces atrocités; six fois il retourne à sa seconde patrie pour faire ce qu'il pourra pour la reconquérir pour une véritable cité de Dieu. La campagne persévérante de cet homme isolé, homme sans autorité ni puissance, contre les crimes envers Dieu et envers la conscience qui se commettent la-bas au nom respecté de Sa Majesté Catholique, compte parmi les exploits dont doivent être fiers, non seulement l'Espagne, non seulement l'ordre des dominicains ou l'Eglise catholique, mais l'humanité.' C. Van Vollenhoven, *Du Droit de Paix—De Iure Pacis* (La Haye, 1932), p. 60.

[2] *De dominio Regum Hispaniae super Indos. Vide* Beltrán de Heredia's article on Matías de Paz, published in *La Ciencia Tomista* (1929), and also in pamphlet form, under the title *Un Precursor del Maestro Vitoria. Vide* also Getino, *op. cit.*, who in chapters x and xi gives an authoritative survey of the questions which arose in connexion with the work of the Dominican missionaries among the Indians.

[3] Of Victoria's interest in the Indians of the New World, Dr. C. Van Vollenhoven (*op. cit.*, pp. 61–2) says:

'Il recherche de toute son originalité vigoureuse, s'il peut être vrai qu'il n'y ait pas de droit international envers ces peuples de la-bas; s'il peut etre vrai que le régime de la guerre permette de faire la guerre a qui l'on veut et de guerroyer avec une liberté et un arbitraire absolus. Et dans ses deux séries de cours publiées après sa mort, le "De iure belli" et le "De bello Indicorum", il fait avec droiture, simplicité et hardiesse l'analyse des problèmes qui se réfèrent à l'action d'outremer des descubridores et des conquistadores. L'œuvre de Vitoria, honnête, habile, courageuse, originale, ne nous montre guère cette houle d'émotion et de compassion qui pénètre l'œuvre de Las Casas; son travail a lui, c'est le travail d'un érudit; sa campagne à lui, c'est une campagne pour réaliser la paix européenne.'

[4] Printed in Beltrán de Heredia's lecture, *Ideas del P. Vitoria sobre la Colonización de América, según documentos inéditos*, as reproduced in the *Anuario de la Asociación Francisco de Vitoria*, vol. ii (1929–30), pp. 32–4.

lengthy studies and extensive experience, I am no longer startled or shocked by any of the questions which come to my attention, with the exception of benefices held through trickery, and events in the Indies,' at the mention of which 'my blood runs cold'.

He avoided discussing the question of benefices and he endeavoured 'to preserve the same attitude with regard to the conquerors of Peru, some of whom—although not many—visit these parts' (the letter was written from Salamanca). He was unwilling to 'cry out, or stir up tragic conflicts, against either of the two groups under discussion', but he was incapable, as he informs us, of concealing his 'true feelings', and, as ordinarily happens with people of conscience and of profound conviction, he added that he could 'say merely that the matter passes my understanding'.

The first group betook themselves to the Pope, on the ground that Victoria was questioning the acts of the Holy Father. The second group sought the Emperor, 'to inform him that both His Majesty and the conduct of affairs in the Indies are being subjected to criticism . . . Consequently,' Victoria said, 'I acknowledge my fault; for in so far as I am able, I avoid quarrelling with these people.' Victoria was, as we shall see, a man of patience as well as of peace, but in his opinion there were times when a private quarrel, as well as a public war, was permissible and patience ceased to be a virtue. 'But if, in the end,' he adds, 'I am absolutely compelled to give an unequivocal answer, I shall state my true opinion.' The end came, and with it the Readings *On the Indians Recently Discovered* and *On the Law of War*.[1] These two readings are the 'onlie begetter' of the present volume.

However, Victoria could not refrain from giving his opinion in a friendly way in reply to a letter from a friend, a brother churchman, and indeed Dominican. He was later to express his doubts as to the method employed by the *conquistadores*, but in the present instance he contented himself with saying that they had 'set their heart upon riches', and appropriately he referred to the maxim concerning the difficulty which many rich men are said to have experienced in entering 'the kingdom of heaven'—a maxim which we have on higher authority even than that of Francisco de Vitoria.

One of the charges against the conquerors was the unlawful taking of property—although this was not the greatest charge and cannot after all be compared with the spiritual damage done to the natives.

[1] *Vide* Getino, *op. cit.*, p. 167: 'En la historia del pensamiento humano será difícil encontrar nada que pueda compararse a la valentía de Vitoria, echando un jarro de agua fría sobre los entusiasmos ardientes que en Españo habían levantado las hazañas de Hernán Cortés y levantaban las de Pizarro, y diciendo al Emperador que poco miraban por su salvación los que le aconsejaban la conquista de Indias. No menos enérgico estuvo, como luego veremos, contra otras luchas que encendían más aún la sangre del Emperador, contra las luchas con los franceses. En especial, miraba con enojo al héroe de Pavía, Antonio Leiva.' [*Vide* Victoria's statement regarding Leiva in his letter to the Constable of Castile, *infra*, pp. 82–83.]

Victoria stated bluntly that the property in question could only be claimed under 'the right of war'. But a war to be permissible should have a just cause, and in his own words, 'the justice of this war [in the New World] passes my understanding'.

As it would be an injustice to the memory of Victoria to paraphrase or to quote in part his indignant language in condemnation of the conduct of the Catholic sovereign and his fellow countrymen, his very words are reproduced in a literal translation: 'I do not, indeed, dispute the fact that the Emperor can conquer the Indies, for I presume that, strictly speaking, he can do so. But I infer from the accounts of those very persons who took part in the recent battle with Tabalipa, that neither Tabalipa nor his people had at any time or in any way injured the Christians, or committed any other act for which war might justly be waged against them. To this point, those who champion the cause of the conquerors reply that the soldiers were under no obligation to investigate that phase of the matter, but were, on the contrary, obliged to obey the commands of their captains, and to act in accordance with those commands.

'I grant the force of this reply,' he continues, 'with respect to those persons who did not know that the sole motive for the war was robbery; and all, or the majority [of the soldiers] were indeed ignorant of this fact. Furthermore, I believe that the other conquests, taking place between that time and the present, have been still more despicable.'

Victoria had, as he said, made up his mind and it was inevitable that the thesis which he was to maintain in the public Reading *On the Indians* would be that of justice, without regard to king or country. He had an open mind, and the ability to see all sides of a question was one of his characteristics; and his conception of right and wrong involved a knowledge of the wrong or the means of such knowledge within the reach of him who was to commit the wrongful act. The soldiers could not know, as Victoria has stated, 'that the sole motive for the war was robbery'.

Bad as were the early misdeeds of his countrymen, however, the later conquests were, in his opinion, 'still more despicable'. Yet, grave though these charges were, there was one still graver, involving the legal and political relations between the Spaniards and the aborigines. The Indians 'newly discovered' could not be treated as aliens, for simple-minded folk that they were, they had accepted the dominion of the Spaniards, so that, if not countrymen, they were at least vassals, and neither slaves nor outcasts but nationals as the Filipinos are nationals of the United States of to-day. Therefore violence which might be legitimate against an alien people should not be used against the Indians. The employment of such measures against them was nothing less than a wrongful injury, and those who sought to inflict it could, in Victoria's opinion, justly be taxed with knowledge; but the Indians, in their capacity as vassals, were not wrong in resisting force unjustly applied, for to the best of their knowledge and belief, the Spaniards were 'oppressing and attacking them unjustly'. Had the vassals misbehaved themselves, force could have been used as a corrective measure but not 'for the purpose of robbing and despoiling the latter of their temporal goods'.

The word of Victoria suffices for us of to-day, for has it not stood the test of four centuries? But Victoria himself invoked two classes of authorities in behalf of his views, however unanswerable they might seem to him. The first of the authorities consisted of the saints and doctors of the Church and the wise men of the profane world; and the second and not the least of the authorities, the nature and the dignity of the human being.

First of Victoria as a churchman. 'For, if there be any truth in "the sayings of the prophet"—in the words, that is, of the saints and doctors [of the Church]—wars, and especially those waged against vassals, must be undertaken and conducted for the sake of the vassals, and not for the sake of the Prince. Neither am I aware of any pretext on which one may rob the poor wretches who are conquered, stripping them of all that they possess and do not possess.'

Second of Victoria as a humanitarian. 'If the Indians are not human beings, but monkeys, they are not susceptible to injury. But if they are human beings and fellowmen, and—as they themselves declare—vassals of the Emperor, I see no ground on which these conquerors may be acquitted of extreme impiety and tyranny.' Here we have, as it were, the Spaniards brought before a court of conscience, to be convicted of a mortal sin; for to him as a churchman impiety would naturally be such, and to him as a humanitarian tyranny would also be as a mortal sin. 'Neither do I see', Victoria concludes, 'that they are rendering His Majesty such a great service in bringing ruin upon his vassals.'

So far the letter discloses Victoria as well informed of events beyond the University of Salamanca. It also discloses the method which he was to employ in his Readings; but it has an even greater interest in that it shows us the man Victoria as he was, more than do his formal writings, convincing us that the inner voice of conscience can be heard above the din and the noise and the turmoil of the world. 'If I earnestly desired', he adds, showing how untainted he was by worldly ambition, although he must have been aware of his fitness for place and position, 'the archbishopric of Toledo, which is now vacant, and if that office were to be granted me on the condition that I should affirm orally or in writing the innocence of these conquerors, I should certainly not dare to make the affirmation.' This would be a strong statement, even if it stood alone. But his soul was on fire: 'May my tongue and my hand wither away, before I say or write a thing so inhuman and so thoroughly unchristian.' The way of the world was not Victoria's. He knew it; he shunned it; and he already saw the outline of Sepúlveda[1] and his kind in the distance. 'Let those persons go their way, and leave us in peace. They will not lack for some one, even from among the Order of the Preachers [such as Sepúlveda], to exonerate them—nay, more—to praise their deeds, and their butchery, and their plundering.'

So much for happenings over seas. That Victoria was equally intent on the things nearer home is apparent from two letters addressed, not to a fellow Dominican—to whom he might unbosom himself—but to no less a person than the Constable of Castile, and containing observations and expressions of his personal opinion which, as he must have known, would sooner or later pass into other hands. The hands were those of Charles I, King of Spain, who was likewise Charles V, Holy Roman Emperor. The letters, in the handwriting of Victoria, are supposed to have been written within two years of the date of that to Arcos.

In the first of the letters Victoria speaks as a churchman, and the language is that of the court of conscience:

> We were already informed of the fact that Your Excellency had departed for the Queen's Court, since the Count of Siruela had written me to that effect. I presume that you have returned to the Court in order to await the coming of His Majesty. God grant that, on this occasion, you may not wait in vain, for the time grows long to all of us.
>
> And may He ever preserve Your Excellency for many benefactions, both public and private; for they who do good after this manner are the truly great, in the sight of heaven, and in the language of the Gospel, Our Lord has said: 'Whosoever therefore shall break one of these least commandments, and shall teach men so, he shall be called the least in the kingdom of heaven: but whosoever shall do and teach *them*, the same shall be called great in the kingdom of heaven.' It would be a mockery, indeed, if the great men of this world should prove to be the least in the kingdom of heaven, having but acted as in a farce the parts of kings or nobles! God forbid that this should come to pass.
>
> I saw a letter, written from the field of battle, and declaring that Antonio Leiva met his death, far more renowned as a gentleman and a captain, than as a Christian. In fact, I believe that, according to this letter, he did not even make a last confession of his sins. May the Lord be merciful to him, and to us, every one; for we are in sore need of His mercy; and He possesses secret wisdom, knowing those who are righteous in their deeds, and those who are not so. If the contents of the letter be true, there was good reason to mourn for Leiva

[1] For a discussion of Sepúlveda's arguments supporting the Spanish conquest and subjugation of native peoples, and also of the condemnation of his doctrine by Spanish theologians and jurists, *vide* Barcia Trelles (*Recueil des Cours, op. cit.*, pp. 142–3); and Aubrey F. G. Bell, 'Juan Ginés de Sepúlveda' in *Hispanic Notes and Monographs,* Oxford, 1925, Spanish Series IX. Perhaps the best account of the controversy, however, is given by Professor Ernest Nys in his admirable essay 'Les Publicistes Espagnols du XVIe Siècle et les Droits des Indiens', published in the *Revue de Droit International et de Législation Comparée* (1889), *op. cit.*, pp. 542–55; this essay was later published, with slight alterations, in his *Études de Droit International et de Droit Politique* (Brussels and Paris, 1896), p. 219.

in his passing to that other world, wherein he may have proved to be no captain, but a private soldier. Reflection given to such a matter at the moment of death, comes late indeed.

John the Baptist, when the soldiers inquired of him what they must do in order to enter the kingdom of heaven, did not demand that they abandon their profession or the interests they supported, but answered thus: 'Do violence to no man, neither accuse *any* falsely; and be content with your wages.' However, they that keep this commandment are few, for [the greater number] do not believe themselves to be men of valour, unless they display more ferocity towards their countrymen and friends than towards their enemies. The precept laid down by John is, in a measure, pertinent and directly applicable to nobles in their relations with their vassals, as well as [to professional soldiers]. God has lavished upon these nobles riches which they may spend without injury to any man; neither does He command that they forfeit any part of that which is their right; but in every doubtful case, as Aristotle said, 'It is better to be injured, than to commit an injury.'...

May God ever prosper and guard in His service, the life and fair fortunes of Your Excellency.

The Chaplain and servant of Your Illustrious Excellency,

Fray Francisco de Vitoria.[1]

In the second letter, Victoria appears as an internationalist familiar with the doings and undoings of princes, spiritual as well as temporal:

The news I send Your Excellency from Salamanca must needs be slight, since you yourself are at the source of all news. God grant that every good report be true, and that the rest may all prove false. Above all, I pray that the report which we have at hand with respect to the coming of His Majesty may not be fallacious. May God lead him hither, not only for the well-being of these his domains, but for the sake of all Christendom, which is in such dire straits. It is a well-known fact that princes are not wont to defer to the opinion of any man, and least of all to those opinions which are opposed to their own desires; but if there be any person whose judgement may have weight in the eyes of His Majesty, you are that person, and for many reasons. At times, I reflect upon the great folly that I and my kind commit, not only in speaking, but even in thinking of public affairs and matters of government; and such an act seems to me more incongruous than an attempt on the part of [political] leaders to discuss our philosophical questions. But when I remind myself that they whose decisions control these affairs of state are nevertheless men of flesh and blood, such as we are ourselves; and when I remember that men may perchance be found outside their circle as wise as those included therein: then, I no longer think it madness to assume that the latter are neither infallible nor all-sufficing. I realize that conditions are unfavourable [for such an outcome], but if it were possible to find some means of effecting a compromise between His Majesty [Charles V] and the King of France, that achievement would seem to me even more auspicious than the conquest of Tunis. At this time, I ask of God no greater blessing than that He should make of these two princes, true brothers in good will, as they are brothers by marriage. For if this event should come to pass, there would be no more heretics within the Church, and no Moors [within its domains] save those under the sufferance [of the two monarchs]; and the Church would be reformed, whether the Pope so willed, or no. And until I behold such a state of things, I shall carė not a farthing for Councils, or for all the remedies and devices that may be contrived. Yet the blame should not be cast upon the King of France, much less upon the Emperor; for it would seem that all have sinned. War was devised, not for the benefit of princes, but for the

[1] Translated from the Appendixes to the *Discursos leídos ante la Real Academia de la Historia in la recepción pública de D. Eduardo de Hinojosa, el día 10 de marzo de 1889* (Madrid, 1889), pp. 65–6. The delicate and difficult letters in this volume, disclosing as they do in every phrase the moral and unworldly characteristics of Victoria, have been put into literal but impeccable English by Miss Gwladys L. Williams.

welfare of whole peoples. If this be true—as, indeed, it is—let honest men say whether our wars promote the well-being of Spain, France, Italy or Germany; or whether such wars tend to destroy all these nations, and to swell the numbers of Moors and heretics. Let those who will, swear that we have no blame in this matter! And I would that God might pardon the princes, and those who prompt the actions of the princes; but He will not pardon them.

However, I am writing to Your Excellency of these matters as if they were novelties, and as if they were not better known to Your Excellency than to any other person! But the worst of the matter is that these facts are clear to all, save only to the princes....

May God ever prosper and guard in His service, the life and fair fortunes of Your Excellency.

The Chaplain and servant of Your Illustrious Excellency,
Fray Francisco de Vitoria.[1]

Victoria's letter to Arcos more than intimates that his views on the Indians and on the attitude of the Emperor and the Pope in regard to them were known to those distinguished personages.

The highly personal views contained in the letters to the Constable of Castile were too interesting not to reach a larger public.

The Readings *On the Indians* and *On the Law of War*, in which he handled without gloves, as we would say to-day, the personalities of their 'Holinesses', the Holy Roman Emperor and the Holy Father, were delivered in public and would therefore necessarily be called to their attention. As a matter of fact, the book of Readings, when published, only escaped the Index by the unexpected and not untimely death—so far as Victoria was concerned—of Pope Sixtus V.

The Emperor waited for no publication of the Readings before he took action. In the course of the year 1539 an imperial and imperious letter reached the Prior of the Convent of San Esteban, who happened to be none other than Domingo de Soto, *vespera* professor of theology at that time and destined in due course to succeed to Victoria's chair of *prima* professor of theology. De Soto was, if a colloquial expression be permitted, 'tarred with the same brush';[2] for he shared Victoria's views and had himself proclaimed them.

The letter is from the Emperor as King and is signed by his imperial and royal hand.

The King, to the reverend Prior of the Monastery of San Esteban, in the city of Salamanca:

I have been informed that certain clerics who are teachers in your monastery, have taken it upon themselves to discuss, in their sermons and dissertations, Our right to the isles of the Indies and to the lands across the ocean; and also the force and validity of the reparations which have been and are being made within Our domains, under the authority of our Most Holy Father, [the Pope]. Since the treatment of these matters, unknown to Us and without previously advising Us of such a discussion, is not only extremely pernicious and scandalous, but might also result in grievous impiety toward God, in disrespect towards the Apostolic See and the Vicar of Christ, and in injury to the Royal Crown of these domains, We have resolved to recommend, and do recommend and command, that hereupon and without delay, you shall summon to your presence the said teachers and clerics who have dealt with the above-mentioned subjects or with any phase of those subjects,

[1] Translated from Hinojosa, *op. cit.*, pp. 66–7.

[2] *Vide* Getino, *op. cit.*, p. 160, note.

whether in sermons, or in dissertations, or in any other manner whatsoever, either publicly or secretly; and that you shall receive from them a deposition, made under oath, concerning the times, places, and auditors of the discussions and affirmations aforementioned (both those drawn up in finished form, and those in the shape of rough drafts and briefs), together with a declaration as to whether or not they have given a copy of such comments to any other person, whether ecclesiastical or secular. The deposition which they make, and also such written material as they may have on this subject (of which material neither they nor any other person may retain a copy), shall be delivered by you, together with a statement bearing your signature, to Fray Nicolás de Santo Tomás. We are sending the latter to you for this purpose, and also in order that he may bring these documents to Us and may, acting under Our orders, make such investigations and provisions touching the matter in hand as shall be best fitted for the service of God and for Our own service. You shall command the [clerics and teachers] in question to refrain, now and at all future times, from engaging in discussions, sermons, or debates, without Our express permission, regarding the topics above mentioned; and likewise from causing any composition on those topics to be printed. And if my bidding in this matter be disregarded, I shall consider that a grave offence against me has been committed, and shall take such steps as the nature of the case demands.

Given in Madrid, on the tenth day of the month of November of the year 1539.

I the King.
Countersigned by his hand.[1]

In order to understand fully the courage of Victoria in proclaiming limitations on the power of Emperor as well as of Pope, it is necessary to say a word on his relations with Charles V in the period immediately preceding the delivery of the public lecture on the Indians. It is clear that the Emperor recognized Victoria's remarkable qualities—and such recognition on the part of the Holy Roman Emperor of that day would have been of tremendous import to any man of worldly ambition with an eye to the main chance. The Catholic sovereign for example, under date of April 18th, 1539, transmitted a request from the Bishop of Mexico—showing how Victoria was regarded in the outposts of empire—that Victoria should select a number of his disciples in order that they might be sent by the Government as missionaries to the New World.[2]

There is a still earlier letter of the same year, under date of January 31st, countersigned by the King, and addressed directly to Victoria, requesting his opinion and that of his colleagues regarding a matter then before the Council of the Indies on certain doubts as to the instruction and conversion of the natives in New Spain,[3] as the Spanish territory was then and for many years thereafter to be called. Courteous as was the letter, and flattering as it was to Victoria, it is nevertheless to be looked upon as a warning of an impending change of the royal attitude towards the distinguished and highly respected *prima* professor, who was to be directed later, as we have seen, to confine his opinions to the spiritual side of questions and not to meddle

[1] Translated from the Spanish text as given by Getino, *op. cit.*, pp. 150–1.

[2] Getino, *op. cit.*, p. 149.

[3] *Ibid.*, pp. 152–3.

with matters political and governmental, as to which the members of the royal council were held to be better informed.

But even royal wrath cools, and it is to the infinite credit of the Catholic sovereign that he could later see and fully recognize the merits of Victoria. Some two years afterwards, in a communication to the *prima* professor of theology at Salamanca dated March 31st, 1541, Charles V again requested an opinion on the conversion of the Indians, particularly with reference to their baptism—a matter upon which no one was better qualified to give an opinion than the author of the Reading *On the Indians Recently Discovered.* The reply was signed, under the date of July 1st, 1541, by eight theologians, and among the signatures were those of 'Franciscus Victoria' and 'Dominicus Soto'. Although the document was several pages in length, the conclusion of the theologians is contained in a single paragraph:

> Barbari illi infideles non antea sunt baptizandi, quam sint sufficienter instructi, non solum in fide, sed etiam in moribus christianis, saltem quantum necessarium est ad salutem, nec priusquam sit verisimile eos intelligere quid recipiant, aut respectent, et profiteantur in baptismo, et velint vivere et perseverare in fide et religione christiana.[1]

A few years later, on the eve of the Council of Trent, the Emperor bethought himself again of the two theologians of Salamanca, Francisco de Vitoria, *prima* professor, and Domingo de Soto, *vespera* professor of theology. Both had been the subject of his imperial wrath, but he turned to them as best fitted to uphold the temporal dignity and the spiritual doctrine of Spain. Therefore under date of February 15th, 1545, he wrote to his son Philip[2] (destined to succeed him in his Spanish dominions, and to be known as Philip II of Spain):

[1] *Colección de Documentos Inéditos Relativos al Descubrimiento, Conquista y Colonización de las Posesiones Españolas en América y Oceania, Sacados, en su Mayor Parte, del Real Archivo de Indias, bajo la dirección de los Sres. D. Joaquin F. Pacheco y D. Francisco de Cárdenas, miembros de varias reales academias cientificas; y D. Luis Torres de Mendoza, abogado de los Tribunales del Reino, con la Cooperación de Otras Personas Competentes* (Madrid, 1865), Tomo iii, p. 545.

At the end of their report the theologians stated a corollary which was to be 'inferred from the conclusion':

'Ex conclusione infertur et patet corolarium, quod temerarium et periculosum videtur ita, passim et sine majore diligentia et examinatione, baptizare barbaros, unde multa absurda neque satis pia accidere necesse est, quale est illud quod in Hispania videmus, ut multi qui ad baptismum recepti sunt, excludantur et repellantur ab omnibus ecclesiasticis sacramentis, qui tamen, ut dictum est, statim post baptismum eucharistie sacramento communicari debuissent, si antiquam ecclesie traditionem retineremus. Atque ita fit ut, dum quam plurimos festinamus habere baptizatos, paucos habeamus vere christianos, non solum quo ad mores, sed etiam quo ad fidem. Proverbium est, "sat cito si sat bene"; et incredibile dictu est quantum more rebus et negotiis festinatione adjiciatur, et ut est in adagio hispaniensi "sepe compendium, dispendium est", quod si hec diligentia in aliis infidelibus observanda est, multo magis necesaria videtur erga istos barbaros, qui suapte nature dicuntur hebetes, et parum considerantes quid illis expediat, et mirum in modum inconstantes. Hec nobis de re proposita visa sunt, salva semper saniore sententia et judicio. Salmantice, prima Julii, anni 1541. Fr. Cordubensis, decanus facultatis. Fr. Franciscus Victoria. Magister Joannes de Sant Millan. Fr. Dominicus Soto. Fr. Andreas Vega, magister. Magister Franciscus Sancho. Magister G. Gallo. Magister Joannes Ægidius de Nava.'

For a very interesting narration and discussion of the relations between Victoria and Charles V, *vide* Getino, *op. cit.*, pp. 148–53, 159 and note, 222–5. The Emperor's letter of 1541 to Victoria is printed in the 1914 edition of Getino's volume, pp. 114–15.

[2] Translated from the Spanish text as found in *Los Manuscritos . . . de Vitoria, O.P.*, by Beltrán de Heredia, *op. cit.*, pp. 163–4.

Since it is necessary that other and special theologians should attend, and in view of the favourable reports which have reached Us regarding Fray Antonio de la Cruz, a provincial Superior, and Fray Francisco de Vitoria, prime professor in Salamanca, We are writing to bid them attend the said Council. It is possible that Fray Francisco may ask to be excused because of his illness, in which event, it would be advisable that some other person should take his place, and that this person should be Fray Domingo de Soto, vesper professor and Prior in Salamanca. . . .

This invitation, both from the Emperor and Prince Philip, Victoria was obliged to decline, although his views were destined to prevail through the presence of his colleagues and disciples:

To His Serene Highness[1] [Prince Philip]:

I have received the missive from Your Highness, together with that in which His Majesty and our Sovereign, the Emperor, bids me attend the holy assembly of the Council, to be held, God willing, in Trent. In addition to the service that I should render His Majesty in performing this task—a service which would in itself be a source of great happiness and solace to me—I should indeed rejoice to form part of an assemblage which, as we hope, will labour to the glory of God, and to the great benefit and relief of all Christendom. However (blessed be the name of the Lord in all that He brings to pass!) I find myself in a condition better suited to one who departs for the next world, than to one who would set forth on a journey to any region of this world; since I have not been able to take a single step for a year, and it is only with extreme difficulty that I can be moved from one spot to another. From day to day, I have been approaching the state in which it will be impossible to move me by any device whatsoever; and for six months I have lain on my bed as one crucified. Truly, no obstacle would deter me from undertaking the journey [which you propose], if there were any possible means by which I might make the trip; but there is no such means.

I beg that His Majesty and Your Highness will accept my excuses.

May our Lord watch over the lives of His Majesty and Your Highness for the good of Christendom, and further exalt your fortunes in His service.

The humble servant of Your Royal Highness,
Fray Francisco de Vitoria.

To His Serene Highness, the Prince;
to be transmitted to His Majesty.

Within a twelvemonth, in 1546, Victoria had taken the journey of which he forewarned his imperial correspondent; and, bearing the *Maestro* upon their shoulders, the various professors of *prima*, accompanied by his colleagues of the university, the clergy, and indeed the populace of Salamanca, 'pusieron la luz debajo de la tierra'.[2]

[1] Translated from the Spanish text as found in Getino, *op. cit.*, p. 277.
[2] Hinojosa, *op. cit.*, p. 19.

APPENDIX TO CHAPTER III

ADDRESS OF LUIS G. ALONSO GETINO, O.P., ON THE FOURTH CENTENARY OF VICTORIA'S APPOINTMENT AS *PRIMA* PROFESSOR OF THEOLOGY AT SALAMANCA IN 1526[1]

I BEG that this distinguished assemblage, so earnestly devoted to the learning of Holland and of Spain, will permit me to couch my humble speech of greeting, not in the vernacular—although that might be more in keeping with our customs—but in Latin: the language in which the wisdom of our ancestors spoke, and won renown; in which both Victoria and Grotius—in whose honour this festival is celebrated—composed their glorious and unforgotten readings.

They wrote, not with artifice and suavity, not in words chosen to enchant the ear; but rather with clarity, and in language fitted to the exposition of truth. It is that purity of style, that clarity, that perspicuity, which I—their disciple—would seek to imitate, in so far as I am able; in other respects, my spirit does not aspire to imitation.

Most reverend Sirs, I am gratified by the opportunity of delivering to-day's address, in which it behoves me to unite the glory of the Flemish with that of the Spanish people; the fourth centenary of Victoria's advent to Salamanca's fount of wisdom, with the tercentenary of the publication of Grotius' work, *De jure belli ac pacis*; the unveiling of this tablet to Victoria, with the presentation of the Grotian medal; and all these things, with a matter which may be known to very few, the commemorative celebration of the erection of this exquisite cloister of San Esteban, where we are holding solemn session.

The task which falls to me on this day is one to inspire timidity; but duty constrains me, on many grounds: I am the Chronicler of Salamanca, the official historian of Victoria, a Dominican Provincial, deeply devoted to the Basque country, and—the thought that is uppermost in my mind to-day—I was sixteen years ago a guest of Holland, where I cultivated the closest friendships with wise men of that nation.

Allow me to recall these names, dear to me and familiar to almost all; the name of the Most Reverend Father Theissling, who was in Salamanca some years ago, and who passed away last year, having attained to the most exalted position in our Order; that of De Groot, Father and Master, whose work was used in connexion with the *De locis theologicis* in the very home of the latter volume, the Convent of San Esteban, where the author of that work, the illustrious Melchior Cano, a famous pupil of Victoria, took his religious vows. This Father De Groot, at the time a professor in the University of Amsterdam, to-day no longer among the living, was my travelling companion in Holland. To his name I should add that of Father ter Maat, who so frequently contributed chronicles on the affairs of Holland, to our journal *La Ciencia Tomista*, and who at one time dwelt in our midst.

[1] Translated, with one or two corrections of misprints, from the address as delivered in Latin, and published in the *Anuario de la Asociación Francisco de Vitoria*, vol. i (Madrid, 1929), pp. 31–9.

Distinguished orators of Holland, you desire to unite our glory with your own, and since you acknowledge our Father Victoria as the precursor and inspiration of your Grotius, you are eager to weave for them crowns doubly adorned with flowers from Spain and from Holland.

Striving to imitate you in gratitude and nobility, we in turn have taken pains to find your glory reflected in our Victoria.

Francisco de Vitoria, when still a youth—not to say, a mere boy—was sent to Paris, that he might study philosophy and theology in the College of our Saint James; and at that time there shone like a star, in this celebrated College, the teacher Petrus Crockart, a source of pride to the Flemish people.

Under the choice guidance of the Flemish preceptor, our youth made such great progress, and acquired such high esteem for his Master as the event later proved. For in the year 1512, the pupil, preparing an edition of his Master's work, joined thereto an enthusiastic preface. Thus first the genius of our Franciscus bore fruit for the world, and in this fruit were blended the Spaniard and the Fleming: both of the Sorbonne, and both devotees of theology.

Hearken to the pupil speaking with his Master at the very portals of the work:

'Father always to be revered: even though I numbered you not among the most illustrious of men, still you would be assigned a place as one of them, because of the writings, destined to imperishable fame, in which you have invaded all the regions of philosophy, natural and theoretical; because of the notable discussions that you conducted for so long a period and to your great renown, in this celebrated College; and finally, because of your triennial exposition of Saint Thomas, to which so many pupils flocked. However, since your modesty forbids me to say more, I shall mention in conclusion one matter, which heaps to overflowing the measure of your glory: the fact that, after a goodly number of years devoted to writing, teaching and debating, you had earned the right to a more tranquil way of living; and nevertheless, because of your faith in the holy Doctor and your devotion to him, you undertook—heedless of the labour involved, and of the state of your own health—to bring to a conclusion your work on the *Secunda Secundae* of Saint Thomas, the interpretation of which you had begun in the preceding year.'

While our Cantabrian was in Paris, he also edited the *Opera Moralia* of Saint Anthony of Florence, the ardent champion of justice (an edition which was inaccessible to me when I composed a biography of Victoria in 1912), as well as the *Conciones* of his friend Pedro de Cobarrubias, of Burgos. If time permitted I should dwell at length upon these works and their influence, which is insufficiently recognized. Indeed, I cannot refrain from calling to your attention the brief preface affixed to the works of Saint Anthony, for it is like a song of youth, and of faith in the newer learning:

'From the Brother Francisco de Vitoria, Bachelor of the Order of Preachers, to the reader: Greetings.

'Gentle reader, I do not propose to eulogize Saint Anthony to you. For it might so happen that I should not prove my point to all, and especially not to certain disdainful persons who find pleasure only in that which springs from their own Muse, although there is no one more ignorant than those very persons. But I do desire to offer you one admonition, and not even that, on my own authority: do not imitate the many who measure their esteem for authors, as for wine, by age.

For there are certain [critics] who have made a law to deter us from reading the work of any writer, "Who has not aged for at least four hundred years". But if this law is just, we should not read, and therefore should not hearken to, these legislators themselves; yet they seek not merely to be read but even to be committed to memory by all. However, it is obviously absurd to brand so shamefully all these centuries that have passed, to reproach them with being so ill-starred, declaring that in all these ages there has appeared not one mind whose creations are worthy to be glanced at, much less read, by the [critics] in question. I grant you that it is ridiculous to linger over the books of some recent writers who do but toy with trifling compositions, and whom we should scarcely find endurable in a conversation or a formal discussion. But even from such a source, one may deduce what [works] are profitable to a virtuous man, and how vast is the difference between an intelligent person and one who is stupid; while the works of the writers in question, once they have lost the charm of novelty for a scanty handful of readers, find no purchaser, and so can never again be forced upon the printers. On the other hand, the works of an author who has won approval, though they are everywhere printed again and again, can hardly satisfy the multitude of their zealous readers. It is for this reason that Joannes Parvus, an honourable and trustworthy man, has prepared a new impression of the *Summa* of Saint Anthony, at the request of numerous theologians and teachers of this Parisian academy, and in spite of the fact that the work in question has been repeatedly issued from almost every press. Moreover, this new edition is something of an improvement. For the form of the book is more convenient [than that of the older impressions], and therefore more pleasing; while many passages whose text is corrupt in the other editions, have been restored to their original language. Wherefore, kind reader, you owe a debt of gratitude to him who prepared this edition. Farewell.'

The zealous pupil of Petrus Crockart returned to his native land in 1524, himself a teacher now; and at the College of Saint Gregory, in Pincia [Valladolid], he taught theology throughout the year, before coming to Salamanca, where he sought and obtained the principal Chair of Theology, vacant owing to the death of Petrus de León.

With the happy advent of Victoria to our midst, there dawned for us a day worthy to be recorded in red letters, according to the words of the wise Cano, who witnessed the consequent transformation: 'Spain received, by the special gift of God, the greatest teacher of theology.' Azpilcueta praises the *lectiones* of Victoria because of their great novelty and utility. Báñez divides Spanish theology into two epochs: before Victoria, and after Victoria. Nicolaus Antonius describes the subsequent theologians of Spain—who were numerous, and indubitably great—as blossoms of the Victorian tree.

So it is that we should commemorate this event in 1526, as the rising of our sun.

For twenty years—until the day of his death—Victoria toiled in our Salamancan Academy, with the greatest applause from both students and strangers. A thousand and more auditors came seeking the treasure of his words in the great hall of the School. The Emperor Charles attended the *lectiones* of Victoria, although that sovereign later took offence because of certain doctrines expounded by the Master. Erasmus desired Victoria's friendship, and wrote a lengthy letter to the Salamanca teacher.

The Pope[1] and the Prince Regent of Spain[2] nominated him as a Theologian of the Council of Trent, when he was already suffering from a grave malady.

[1] On April 9th, 1537. *Vide* Getino, *op. cit.*, 1914 edition, pp. 213–14.
[2] In 1545. *Vide* Beltrán de Heredia, *Los Manuscritos de . . . Vitoria, op. cit.*, pp. 163–4.

We do not possess Victoria's reply to the Pope, but lend your attention for the moment to a Latin translation of his reply to the Prince. . . .[1]

He whose counsel was so widely sought, who was learned in so many sciences, must needs be instructed in the greatest science of all, in the school of sacrifice and infirmity. For without such instruction, all knowledge languishes; as our Lord says: 'He that knoweth not sorrow, what doth he know?'

He lay wellnigh motionless on his couch, and crucified with pain; yet he uttered no complaint because of his bodily suffering, but rather the sweetest words of thankfulness for the afflictions of illness.

The eager desire to hear a teacher so pleasing, infirm of body, but possessed of a clear—and fruitful—mind, impelled the students to carry him in his chair to his beloved lecture hall. What an amazing spectacle was that, to see him borne on the shoulders of youths thirsting for the divine wisdom that flowed from his lips! In the classroom of so great a master, vacations were not desired.

Neither did they spare him on holidays, not even on the most important, lest they be deprived of his explanations.

Hearken to the Master as he complains gently and most affectionately in his Preamble to the Reading *On Homicide*: 'Not without reason does the Preacher say: "He that increaseth knowledge increaseth sorrow." Farmers, labourers, artisans, have their periods of leisure, and after days of toil in which they provide for the necessities of life, on days of festival they rest, and delight in whatsoever way they will their minds and hearts, which are forgetful of all labour. But we may not be idle, whether on feast-days, or on workdays; we enjoy no vacation from our studies, no holiday from the practice of letters. For lo! we have gathered together, most pious Fathers and distinguished auditors, on this signal festival, because of this *Relectio*, which I was not allowed to postpone until the following year as I had planned, nor even until some other day. Therefore, in order that we may not increase our necessary labour by the added task of a preamble, let us go at once to the heart of the matter; and may Heaven be our guide.' (*De Homicidio*, Introduction.)

Moreover he gave of himself generously not only to the public, but also to individual students.

In confirmation of this assertion, I am reminded of the fact that a certain Flemish writer, Joannes Vaseus, at one time a professor in Salamanca, acknowledges at the beginning of his work the aid which Victoria lent his friends: 'And at this point, kind reader, I shed tears of just sorrow, because I may not include in the list, the venerable Brother Franciscus a Victoria, who, when he lived, was prime professor of Sacred Theology at Salamanca, and whom I shall ever cherish in my memory. Before I had imparted knowledge of my purpose to him by whose will I was ruled, upon whose counsel I relied, in whose goodwill I rejoiced, he was delivered from the sorrows of this life and transported, as I do not doubt, to the company of the saints. If he had lived, he would have aided my efforts to an

[1] As an English translation of this letter from the original Spanish is given *supra*, p. 87, the Latin translation is not included here.

amazing extent; for his erudition was incredible, his reading wellnigh boundless, his judgement extremely accurate, his memory most ready: so that he rightly seemed a prodigy of nature. The illustrious and pious Order of Saint Dominic has cause for self-congratulation in that it acquired such a member; and indeed, I doubt if [that Order] has possessed in many years an individual more skilled in Sacred Theology. He himself would have left testimony to this effect if he had been as desirous of writing as he was remarkable for learning. It seems to me, indeed, that I may make the following assertion, without any hesitation: that for many years there has been in all Spain no one more learned in every good art and in all the humanities.' (*Chronici rerum memorabilium Hispaniae*, vol. i, Salamanca, 1552, chapter i.)

While comforting those close at hand, he did not fail the absent, whom he zealously cheered in so far as he was able, with letters full of solace.

Another witness [to these facts] is a writer from Lower Germany, Nicolaus Clénard, the glory of your land, and the shining ornament of our own. 'I have known no person', he says, 'from among the number of those who have passed their lives in the study of Latin literature, whose letters have pleased me so greatly as those of Victoria; if he had applied his mind to writing, the whole world would be filled with his fame.'

But why do I recall these qualities, which could be more credible to none than they are to you, who are yourselves aware of them ?

Matamorus, a pupil of the opposing Complutensian School, calls Francis our 'divine, incomparable glory, and the ornament of Theology'.

He was the defender of the poor, the champion of justice, and entirely free of any respect for persons.

Amid such tumult in the minds of men, when the trumpet of the Emperor Charles was sounding for the combat, when the whole 'machine' of warfare was inspiring terror in Spain, Upper and Lower Germany, France, Italy, America, Africa—the Salamancan teacher, the poor Dominican, bore aloft with invincible spirit the standard of peace, and provoked the wrath of the Emperor, so that the latter threatened the Prior of this Monastry because of the doctrines expounded therein.

The fourth centenary of a structure such as this in which we stand—a building that is strong, spacious, beautiful—is not unworthy of remembrance in this day; for in the time of Victoria, this monastic monument arose like a glorious apparition; in this cloister of the dead, the joy of the very building [upon the present occasion] makes joyful the earthly remains of the Brothers and of our Francis, who awaits, beneath these stones, the universal resurrection.

In our Constitution, this Cloister is called 'the Cloister of perpetual silence', and such it is. Only the murmur of prayers may be heard therein. And in truth, praise and exultation are most unbefitting a monument so great.

In Christian piety, let us revere the dust of the dead; let us imitate their virtues; and in addition to the honours we bestow on them, let not those supplications be forgotten, to which God in His compassion gives heed, and which in some degree bring us into communion with the dead:

'Eternal rest grant unto them, O Lord: And let perpetual light shine upon them.'

Your Excellency: God grant that, as your hand draws back the veil from this tablet, the professors and students of the University and Convent may be inspired with the purpose of imitating the fruitful and life-giving Master. Unless this comes to pass, the memorial of the year 1526, so exquisitely wrought in marble, shall be a tablet on which accusation is written, rather than a record of glory. We may not truly be called the heirs of the Master, unless, as best we may, we follow in his footsteps.

DIXI

CHAPTER IV

ANALYSIS OF THE READING *ON THE INDIANS RECENTLY DISCOVERED.* SECTION I

The University of Salamanca, to mention only the seat of learning in which Victoria passed the last twenty years of his life and where he made an appeal to the world of his own as well as of our day, based its instruction in theology, which, in the conception of Francisco de Vitoria, had an international implication as well as a theological content, upon the *Sentences* of Peter Lombard and the *Summa Theologica* of St. Thomas Aquinas. If the international implication had not been evident to Victoria, editions of his works would not be appearing in the *Classics of International Law* and, if he had not made the implication express and applied it to the relations of nations as well as to individuals, he would not be in a fair way to be considered as the founder of the modern law of nations.

The 'schoolmen' had apparently passed away. A new generation had arisen 'that knew not Joseph', as happens in the New World as well as in the old; and the new generation seemed intent on a method of exposition of the truths of the past in a way which would impress the oncoming generations. Francisco de Vitoria believed in the new order of things. He was a reformer, but he was intent on proving all things and holding 'fast that which is good'. The truth which he appreciated was that the scholastic method had been sufficient in the past, when the theologians of his Church had something to say; and that the trouble with the theologians of the century in which he lived was that they had nothing to say, either according to the method of the schoolmen or of any other method.[1]

He was himself to show in the classroom, in personal intercourse with students and on public occasions through his disquisitions, which were technically called *Relectiones*, that scholasticism was not dead but sleeping, needing only to be awakened by the voice of the master, the master in this case—although he would have been the last to admit it—being himself.

[1] 'Vitoria, à Paris, se modèle moins sous l'influence du milieu que par réaction en face de son entourage. Qu'on n'oublie pas qu'à cette époque de l'histoire, l'enseignement de la théologie offert dans la capitale de la France était caractérisée par l'absence de curiosité, par l'attachement inconditionnel au passé, par les disputes sans épilogue sur des mots ou à propos de mots. Érasme disait de ces maîtres: "Y a-t-il quelque chose de plus imbécile que le cerveau de ces théologues? Je ne connais rien d'aussi barbare que leur langage, rien de plus grossier que leur esprit, rien de plus épineux que leur doctine, rien de plus violent que leurs discours." Ernest Nys (*Le droit des gens et les anciens jurisconsultes espagnols*, La Haye, 1914), se référant à Vitoria, porte sur l'enseignement donné à Paris ce jugement sévère: "On voit bien que ce ne fut point avec les maîtres de philosophie ou de théologie de Paris que Vitoria put acquérir ce fonds précieux où se trouvaient réunis l'esprit d'investigation, la tendance au progrès, l'amour du prochain, le sentiment de la solidarité. La nature l'avait doué de qualités exceptionnelles, il portait en lui-même une force que rien ne pouvait ni comprimer, ni asphyxier." ' Barcia Trelles in *Recueil des Cours, op. cit.*, p. 120.

He was reputed to have been the best instructor of his day, not merely in Salamanca but in all Spain[1]—Spain then being the newer Spain fashioned by the hand of Isabella the Catholic.

He discoursed, as did others, upon the *Sentences* and the *Summa*, but apparently, unlike others, he separated the spirit from the text and applied it to the world in which professor and student lived.[2] That world was a larger world than Spain had ever known; indeed, it included an altogether new world because of the westward voyage of Columbus, which in very truth was due to Isabella, whose eyes were open to the invisible, even though it lay beyond the horizon of the new and enlarged Spain of which she was the foundress.

Victoria's custom was to examine the new questions of the day in the light of that past which had made the present. A mere enumeration of the Readings shows that they were, as we would say, current questions[3]—one of which has not ceased to be current: that of the divorce which arose in the case of Henry VIII and Catherine of Aragon. But the outstanding and impersonal question was the relation of the Old World to the New World discovered by Columbus, the discussion of which Victoria undertook and treated in such a way that his Reading *On the Indians Recently Discovered* is the proclamation of the new international law, and indeed of the law of nations which is yet to be.[4]

Victoria respected facts, and none treated them with greater care than he; but to him they were important, not in themselves, but as a means to an end—the discovery of truth.[5] He dealt in fundamentals and his fundamentals are the fundamentals of the system of international law for which he is responsible; and they are the fundamentals in which is implicit, if not expressed, the newer international law beginning with the individual, to end with the international community.

Unfortunately we do not have the views of Victoria precisely as he himself stated them. His business was the saving of souls—the souls

[1] Of Victoria's great ability as a teacher Melchior Cano, who succeeded him in the *prima* chair of theology at Salamanca, said that 'Diez discípulos más sabios que él no enseñarían como él'. Getino, *op. cit.*, p. 243, note 2.

[2] Getino (*op. cit.*, pp. 5, 32–3), speaking of Victoria's treatment of theology, says: 'El profesor de Salamanca . . . la humanizaba applicándola a la Política, al Derecho, a la Sociología. . . . Vitoria empezaba a acercarse al pueblo, a utilizar de la Teología lo más humano, lo más inteligible, lo que luego le había de dar tanta influencia y tan alto relieve en la colonización de Indias, en los asuntos de Derecho internacional, en la reforma de la enseñanza teologica. Vitoria se ladeaba ya por el lado práctico, relegando a un segundo lugar las arideces en que se abroquelaba una Escuela ya decadente.' *Vide* also Barcia Trelles in *Recueil des Cours, op. cit.*, p. 124: 'En outre, Vitoria, par son intelligence, va humaniser la théologie en insufflant dans son enseignement de l'intérêt et de l'émotion.' *Vide* also p. 76, *supra*.

[3] Concerning his Readings Barcia Trelles (*Recueil des Cours, op. cit.*, p. 128) says: 'Vitoria les prononçait chaque fois qu'une grave question, difficile à résoudre, se posait devant sa conscience ou lorsqu'on sollicitait son opinion autorisée. Voilà comment la chaire de théologie occupée par Vitoria à Salamanque en vint à constituer un véritable tribunal, où l'on examinait les problèmes qui passionnaient l'opinion.'

[4] 'Vitoria ne se propose pas d'écrire *a priori* un traité de droit des gens. Dans sa chaire de l'Université de Salamanque, il étudie ces problèmes dont l'apparition inquiète le monde; il parle pour ses élèves; il est modeleur de consciences.' Barcia Trelles in *Recueil des Cours, op. cit.*, p. 118.

[5] 'No dejamos de advertir que Vitoria asienta más firme el pie tratándose de las teorías que tratándose de los hechos.' Getino, *op. cit.*, p. 154.

entrusted to him in the classroom—and, giving all that he had to give to his students, he did not have the time to put his views in form for publication either in his lifetime or after his death.[1] His students, however, saved him, where he would not save himself, for an unending posterity, by taking notes of his Readings, which give the substance, if not the form, of his lectures.[2]

It would be unjust to the memory of Victoria to make a summary of what is in fact but a summary of his Readings; and therefore the language of the notes as printed will be here and there reproduced, in order that Victoria may speak for himself.

* * *

The outlook of Victoria was as large as the world. The question before him, in the opening lines of his first Reading *On the Indians*, was whether the children of unbelievers could be baptized against the wishes of their parents.[3] In his hands, the discussion of this question became the first treatise on the modern law of nations.[4]

How did this happen? The question was controversial. The discussion, he informs us, was 'started on account of the aborigines of the New World, commonly called Indians, who came forty years ago into the power of the Spaniards, not having been previously known to our world'.[5]

[1] *Vide* Beltrán de Heredia, *op. cit.*, p. 18: 'Las horas tranquilas de su retiro conventual, en que otros solían redactar sus escritos destinados a la imprenta, él las ocupaba en el estudio y preparación de las lecciones o se prestaba a dictar en las aulas domésticas a propios y extraños, sin cuidarse de fijar por si mismo en un comentario en forma las ideas que iba derramando en la enseñanza. A juzgar por su conducta, parece que se propuso reprobar con el ejemplo el afán innato de publicidad del ambiente renacentista en que se había educado.'

[2] Beltrán de Heredia (*op. cit.*, p. 13) considers that this practice of taking notes was introduced in Victoria's time and indeed was adopted because his listeners wished to retain every word of his brilliant lectures. 'También se introdujo en tiempo de Vitoria entre los escolares salmantinos la costumbre, importada probablemente de París, de tomar por escrito la explicación del profesor. La fama del doctor sorbónico, la originalidad y brillantez de sus lecciones, sugirieron el recurso de esta medida excepcional para fijar mejor las ideas fecundas, los comentarios luminosos que iba trazando en torno a los argumentos de la *Suma*. A ninguno entre los que le precedieron en aquella cátedra ni a los que por entonces enseñaban en nuestras ya numerosas Universidades, sabemos que se hiciese esa demostración de aprecio.'

On this point Getino (*op. cit.*, p. 122) says: 'Francisco Vitoria es al primer profesor español, y no sé si extranjero, cuyas lecciones fueron recogidas en clase por sus alumnos y transmitidas a la posteridad...' *Vide* also Barcia Trelles in *Recueil des Cours, op. cit.*, p. 126.

[3] *Victoria, Relectio ... de Indis, infra*, Appendix A, p. i. The English translation of the two Readings *On the Indians* and *On the Law of War* used for the present analysis, and reproduced in the Appendix, is that by John Pawley Bate as published in *De Indis et de Ivre Belli Relectiones, Being Parts of Relectiones Theologicae XII*, with an introduction by Ernest Nys (the Classics of International Law, published by the Carnegie Institution of Washington, 1917). Citations and quotations from the Latin text of these Readings are from the photographic reproduction of Simon's edition (1696) of Victoria's *Relectiones* published in the Carnegie Institution edition above mentioned. The Latin text as there reproduced is preceded by an exhaustive editorial commentary and a carefully revised and extended text prepared by Herbert Francis Wright, which has been of no small assistance in tracing Victoria's references.

Victoria had discussed various phases of the status and rights of unbelievers in his lectures on the *Secunda Secundae* of St. Thomas, but without specific reference to the American Indians. *Vide* Beltrán de Heredia's edition of the *Comentarios a la Secunda Secundae de Santo Tomás*, vol. i, pp. 160–212.

[4] The question was not a new one to Victoria. He had already discussed various phases of the status and rights of unbelievers in his lectures on the *Secunda Secundae* of St. Thomas Aquinas, although without specific reference, as in the present instance, to the American Indians. *Vide* Beltrán de Heredia's edition of Victoria's *Comentarios a la Secunda Secundae de Santo Tomás*, vol. i, pp. 160–212.

[5] *De Indis, infra*, Appendix A., p. ii.

Of course he had in mind Columbus, but apparently he concealed nothing from his students and in fact the students show us in a later passage that the master had in mind none other than 'Columbus the Genoan'.[1]

Victoria might have said, had he been other than Victoria, that he was opposed to the baptism of the aborigines in the New World discovered by Columbus, and let it go at that, with a reference to the *Sentences* of Peter Lombard[2] and the *Summa Theologica* of St. Thomas.[3] This, however, would have been merely an appeal to the past. Victoria was a man of the present, with his eyes turned towards the future. That future was America. The question in his hands was not merely as large as America—large as it is—but as large as our world. But if ever Victoria should be heard in his own behalf, it is on this point, because his appreciation of the subject and the manner in which he treated it are the reasons, and the sole reasons, why we of to-day are interested in the *prima* professor of theology in the University of Salamanca.

'This present disputation about them', his students have him say, 'will fall into three parts.'[4] Such a method might well have followed the *Sentences* and the *Summa* of an earlier day. However, this was not his purpose. 'In the first part we shall inquire by what right these Indian natives came under Spanish sway'[5]—a part which deals with nothing smaller than title by discovery.

'In the second part,' he continues, 'what rights the Spanish sovereigns obtained over them in temporal and civil matters.'[6] Here is more than a suggestion of the rights and duties of a material kind resulting from colonization.

But Victoria was not merely a jurist. He was that and something that every jurist should be—a moralist as well, for whom the spiritual world existed, not only in the printed pages of the New Testament but in very fact.

'In the third part, what rights these sovereigns'—the sovereign he had in mind was Charles I, King of Spain, who likewise was the Holy Roman Emperor, Charles V—'or the Church obtained over them in matters spiritual and touching religion.'[7]

That the answer of the past, whether it be that of the *Sentences* of Peter Lombard or the *Summa* of the Angelic Doctor, was not sufficient for Francisco de Vitoria, is shown by the words immediately following—'in the course of which'—meaning the third part, which he had just stated—'an answer will be given to the question before us'.[8]

It is not until we have read and pondered these opening lines that

[1] *Ibid.*, p. xxv. [2] Bk. IV, dist. iv.

[3] *Secunda Secundae*, question 10, article 12; *Tertia Pars*, question 68, article 10. Readers desirous of reading St. Thomas in English translation should see *The 'Summa Theologica' of St. Thomas Aquinas*, Literally translated by Fathers of the English Dominican Province (London, 1915–).

[4] *De Indis, infra*, Appendix A, p. ii. [5] *Ibid.* [6] *Ibid.* [7] *Ibid.* [8] *Ibid.*

we understand the nature and the vast extent which the problem could, and actually did, acquire at the hands of one of whom we might properly observe that he saw the universe in a grain of sand.

Victoria was confronted on the threshold with a difficulty which might have prevented the discussion of any one of the three parts into which he divided the subject at hand; or at least, if the difficulty were not circumvented, the discussion would be academic and for his purposes futile—and he had a very definite purpose in mind: to reopen the question which the world of the wise considered as settled.

What was this difficulty? Before considering it in detail, it is well to examine in a broad way not only the importance but the implications of the question before him, and his method of approaching it.

We know, for various reasons, how important the question was to Victoria; but we may not suppose that he had in mind the creation of the law of nations. Yet for us the importance of the Reading lies in the fact that, together with the Reading *De Jure Belli*, it did create a law of nations, which is still in existence and which is developing along Victoria's lines, for is not his conception of the international community, possessing the power to make laws and to punish their violation, more than the conception of the Society of Nations in the Covenant of 1920?

For present purposes, the importance which Victoria attached to the Reading *On the Indians* is evident only to those who are familiar with the method of approach employed in his other Readings. An examination of these will show that his custom was to plunge *in medias res*, with at most a word or two by way of introduction. But in the present instance he was intent first of all, it would seem, upon convincing his students (and by their Summary they have enabled him to convince us) that, although the question was in form theological, it was in substance juridical, and that the solution of the problem by either the jurist or the theologian alone would be fragmentary and therefore unacceptable.

Why was it necessary to argue the point? Was it not that the view of the theologian, tied down by authorities, would necessarily be a narrow and therefore an inadequate solution, and that the examination by the jurist would also be narrow and unsatisfactory, because the jurist dealt only with the text of the law? In either case the word would kill, whereas the spirit could make alive. There is a philosophy of theology—indeed theology is philosophy; there is a philosophy of law. There was a natural theology; there was a natural law. The natural law, whether it was synonymous with the Divine or revealed law, was, it appears, the patrimony of the churchman, and the philosophy of law sprang from the conception of natural law; therefore it was that the juridical phase of the question could only be adequately examined from the spiritual point of view of the theologian as well as from the material point of view of the jurist.

Nothing better shows Victoria's determination, as well as his earnestness, and the method which he was to bring to the discussion of international questions and their decision—not merely in accordance with the canons of the Church of which he was destined to be the most conspicuous ornament of his country but in accordance with the reason of the thing which he always applied, and, in this case, in accordance with the nature and the dignity of the human being as such—than his way of meeting the difficulty and, in so doing, justifying, if not actually founding, a new school of thought. The method is sometimes as important as the matter, and here as elsewhere with Victoria, they went hand in hand. But he did not let method becloud his vision.

His introduction is, as it were, an exposition of the new method and the foundation of the philosophy for which his name stands. The method, therefore, not only opened up the three parts of the discussion which the world had considered closed; it went to the essence of the entire question. But in the case of Victoria—with whom brevity may be said to be one of the cardinal virtues—the introduction might be called a disquisition on method less elaborate than that of Descartes in justification of his philosophy, but fully as serviceable to Victoria and to those of the older school of thought for whom he spoke.

Here, as elsewhere, his views will be stated as far as possible in his own words, because his very words are winged. What then, in his own language, was the difficulty which stood in the way of treating anew the question?

'It might seem,' he said, 'at the very outset, that the whole of this discussion is useless and futile, not only for us who have no concern either to inquire whether the men in question have conducted their administration with propriety in every detail or to raise any doubts about that business or to correct any fault that may have been committed, but also for those whose concern it is to attend to and administer these matters.' [1]

Here we have an admirable example of the schoolman's method: to present first of all, and as strongly as possible, the case which barred his way. From the reign of Isabella and Ferdinand until the reign of the then occupant of the Spanish throne Spanish sovereigns had been 'in bona-fide occupation and peaceful possession'.[2] Why, then, examine their rights and titles which had already been passed upon by what the Spanish sovereigns doubtless considered as the appropriate organs of the State? Not content with the bald statement of the case against him, Victoria cites the authorities upon which it rests. The very first of these is the prince of political philosophers.[3] 'Because,' in Victoria's own language, 'as Aristotle says, "if any one were to be

[1] *De Indis, infra,* Appendix A, p. ii. [2] *Ibid.*
[3] Aristotle, *Nicomachean Ethics,* III. iii. 16: εἰ δὲ ἀεὶ βουλεύσεται, εἰς ἄπειρον ἥξει.

continually inquiring, settlement would be indefinitely postponed"; and sovereigns and their advisers could not attain security and certitude of conscience, and, if they had to trace the title of their rule back to its origin, they could not keep anything they had discovered.'[1] The history of the world is with the Dominican's opponents on this statement, which is in the nature of an axiom; but the purpose of Victoria, as we shall later see, was to get rid of title by discovery.

Here, then, is the first difficulty, strongly stated.

The second, however, is even stronger. The sovereigns who had claimed under title of discovery were none other than Ferdinand and Isabella, and they were 'most Christian'; and then too the Emperor—Charles I in Spain and Charles V in the vast domain of the Holy Roman Empire—was their grandson and, according to Victoria, 'a most just and scrupulous sovereign'.[2] Therefore, because they were Christian or just and scrupulous, it was 'not to be believed', Victoria adds, strengthening the case of his adversaries—as was the wont of the schoolmen—'that they did not make a thoroughly complete and exact investigation into everything that could affect the security of their estate and conscience.'[3] The conclusion would seem to be inevitable and is aptly stated: 'it may seem not only useless but also presumptuous to raise any question about the matter'; and, still strengthening the argument which he was about to demolish, he added that it was 'like looking for a knot in a bulrush and for wickedness in the abode of the righteous'.[4] It is perhaps open to question whether a more perfect example of the scholastic method of stating and, if need be, making the case of the adversary is to be found in the books.

Victoria, than whom no man was better qualified to stand alone, always invokes an authority, his authorities showing the nature, the capacity, and the strength of his mind. If Aristotle had been invoked in behalf of the 'most Christian, most just and scrupulous' sovereigns, the edge of his authority was to be turned against the thesis which Victoria must needs refute, for Aristotle's authority was a two-edged sword. If, on the one hand, as the Greek philosopher had declared, 'deliberation' were to be excluded 'about matters either impossible or necessary' and if, on the other hand, there could be no 'investigation' of matters 'certainly and notoriously lawful and seemly' or of those 'certainly and notoriously unlawful and unseemly',[5] the reason is that there can be no doubt, reasonable or unreasonable, about them. But what if one or the other be doubtful? In doubt the case of Victoria lies, and without doubt what would become of our philosophy?

In such a case, indeed, the mere presence of doubt opens up the entire question, and Victoria loses no time in pressing through the

[1] *De Indis, infra,* Appendix A, p. ii. [2] *Ibid.* [3] *Ibid.*
[4] *Ibid.* [5] Aristotle, *Nicomachean Ethics,* III. iii.

breach. But he is not content with a breach in the argument of his opponent, nor is he satisfied with merely pressing through. A powerful man intellectually, he must overwhelm and crush his foe with a series of arguments which are like rapid and irresistible blows. 'When, however, some project is on foot concerning which there is a genuine doubt'—obviously the doubt of a reasonable human being—'whether it be good or bad, just or unjust', what is to be done? The answer of Victoria is the answer of the ages: 'It is then advantageous to take advice and to deliberate and to abstain from premature action before finding out and determining how far it is or is not lawful.'[1] The entire question is thus transferred from the lawyer to the moralist, and Victoria has brought the question within the ethical domain.

His first illustrations are from the material world, but to the spiritually minded there is always, fortunately for us, a spiritual element even in the most material transaction. 'And in all these cases the circumstances', Victoria continues, 'are such that, even if the thing in question were in itself lawful, it would be sinful for any one to do it before deliberating and assuring himself of its lawfulness; and he would not be excused on the ground of ignorance, for the ignorance would manifestly not be invincible, since he does not do what in him lies to inquire into the lawfulness or unlawfulness of the matter.'[2] That is the counter-case of Victoria. It is a positive statement going to the root of the matter. Just as the *Ethics* of Aristotle were invoked in their behalf, his opponents are again to feel the double edge of the sword. 'For in order that an act, the goodness of which is otherwise uncertain, be good, it must be done in accordance with the investigation and determination of the wise, it being (*Ethics*, Bk. II)[3] one of the conditions of a good act that it be done in accordance therewith.'[4] As in the case, so in the counter-case, the conclusion follows: 'Accordingly, when, in a doubtful case, the doer omits to take the advice of the wise, he is without excuse. Nay, even if we grant that the act in question is lawful in itself, yet, if there be any doubt thereon, the doer is bound to take the advice, and to act in accordance with the award, of the wise, even though they be themselves in error.'[5]

The greater the doubt, the greater the need of investigation—to use the proverbial form, of which our Spanish friends are so fond.

If Victoria, practical man that he was, had not been a philosopher, he might have stopped here, having presented both sides of the case in a manner not to be misunderstood, for his own opinion, which meets the most exacting standard of clearness, is so clear that it cannot be misunderstood. Omitting illustrations of the appositeness of

[1] *De Indis, infra*, Appendix A, pp. ii–iii. [2] *Ibid.*, p. iii.
[3] Chapter vi: *ἐν μεσότητι . . . ὡρισμένῃ λόγῳ καὶ ὡς ἂν ὁ φρόνιμος ὁρίσειε.*
[4] *De Indis, infra*, Appendix A, p. iii. [5] *Ibid.*

the doctrine which he had laid down, we observe that the philosopher in Victoria gets the upper hand, disclosing his strength alike as a theologian and a jurist: 'In those matters which belong to his salvation a man is bound to yield credence to the teachers appointed by the Church, and in a doubtful matter their ruling is law.'[1]

So much for the churchman. Now for the man of law: 'For just as in the contentious forum', he adds, 'the judge is bound to judge in accordance with what is alleged and proved, so in the forum of conscience a man is bound to base his judgement, not on his own sentiments, but on demonstrable reason or on the authority of the wise.'[2] Indeed we have Victoria not in a twofold, but in a threefold and therefore irresistible role, that of theologian, of jurist, and of moralist, and from this threefold point he examines and decides every question which presents itself.

Passing by an apt quotation from the Old Testament[3]—the first reference to that authority which he has made—we have Victoria's conclusion reinforced, as not infrequently happens, by the New Testament, by Aristotle, and by a poet whose authority Aristotle invokes: 'In doubtful matters,' he asserts, 'a man is bound to seek the advice of those whom the Church has appointed for that purpose, such as prelates, preachers, and confessors, who are people skilled in divine and human law'—for which statement Victoria had invoked, from the Old Testament, Deuteronomy,[4] 'For in the Church, some are eyes, some feet, and so on (I Corinthians, ch. xii); and in Ephesians, ch. iv, "And he gave some, apostles; . . . some, evangelists; and some, pastors and teachers", and in St. Matthew, ch. xxiii, "The Scribes and the Pharisees sit in Moses' seat; all therefore whatsoever they bid you observe, that observe and do."'[5]

This certainly was authority enough for a churchman. But Victoria was more than a churchman; he was a humanist. In the present instance he invokes the first book of Aristotle's *Ethics*, stating that the philosopher 'lays this down as a precept, following Hesiod, "The man who is ignorant in himself, yet does not listen to another in order to know what is good, is a foolish and empty person".'[6] And he had doubtless read his Aristotle in the Greek, for elsewhere he corrects an erroneous view concerning the great philosopher by referring to the Greek text.[7]

It might seem that Victoria had made his counter-case, but it was so fundamental to his contention and to his system that he felt it

[1] *De Indis, Infra*, Appendix A, p. iii. [2] *Ibid.* [3] Deuteronomy, xvii. 8–11.
[4] *Ibid.* [5] *De Indis, infra*, Appendix A, p. iv.
[6] *Ibid.* Aristotle, *op. cit.*, I. iv. 7; Victoria refers only to the last two lines of the following verses which Aristotle quotes from Hesiod, *Works and Days*, lines 293, 295–97.

οὗτος μὲν πανάριστος ὃς αὐτὸς πάντα νοήσῃ,
ἐσθλὸς δ' αὖ κἀκεῖνος ὃς εὖ εἰπόντι πίθηται·
ὃς δέ κε μήτ' αὐτὸς νοέῃ μήτ' ἄλλου ἀκούων
ἐν θυμῷ βάλληται, ὁ δ' αὖτ' ἀχρήϊος ἀνήρ.

[7] Getino, *op. cit.*, p. 15.

needed an additional and conclusive restatement, and he therefore expressed his final conclusions in a paragraph of three pointed sentences. These, however, are preceded by tentative conclusions, the first of which must be stated in full: 'It is, therefore, not enough for security of life and conscience that a man should deem himself to be doing right, but in doubtful matters he must needs rely on the authority of others whose business is therewith.'[1] This doctrine he applies not merely to life and to conscience in general, but, as an illustration, to merchants who enter 'into illegal contracts without the advice of the wise'.[2]

Here he found himself face to face with an authority of the Church, a glory of the Dominican Order—of which he considered himself an humble member—who had been head of the Order and later a Prince of the Church (Tommaso de Vio, Cardinal Cajetan),[3] whose authority could hardly have been less convincing then than it is now after some four hundred years. But a man who could criticize the policy of the Holy Roman Emperor and King of Spain, of which country he was a subject, and could controvert the Pope, the very head of the Catholic Church, was not likely to bend the knee even to the Cardinal Cajetan. 'And so,' he says, 'I do not agree with Cardinal Cajetan'—mentioning expressly his name—'when he says that if a doubt arises about something which really is lawful in itself and some preachers or confessors who otherwise have authority to pronounce thereon declare it unlawful or declare it mortal sin when it is venial, yet the man who, following his own inclination in the matter, disbelieves them and determines in his own conscience that it is not a mortal sin, does not sin.'[4] After a further illustration he continues, 'if in a doubtful matter a man has taken counsel with the wise and has accepted their ruling that the thing is lawful, he is safe in conscience—at any rate until he receives a second opinion and is driven to doubt or to believe the contrary by a person of such authority, or by reasons of such cogency, as ought to affect his judgement'. Why? 'This is notorious,' is Victoria's answer, 'for he does all that in him lies and so his ignorance is invincible.'[5]

From all of which—each statement being as a link in a faultless chain—he concludes:

'First. In doubtful matters a man is bound to seek the advice', not merely of the well-informed but 'of those whose business it is to give it, otherwise he is not safe in conscience, whether the doubt be about a thing in itself lawful or unlawful.

'Second. If after a consultation in a doubtful matter it be settled by the wise that the thing is unlawful, a man is bound to follow their opinion, and if he act contrary thereto he is without excuse, even if the thing be otherwise lawful.

[1] *De Indis, infra*, Appendix A, p. iv. [2] *Ibid.* [3] 1469–1534.
[4] *De Indis, infra*, Appendix A, p. iv. [5] *Ibid.*

'Third. On the other hand, if after such consultation it be settled by the wise that the thing is lawful, he who follows their opinion is safe, even if it be otherwise unlawful.'[1]

Victoria does not ask the impossible, nor does the philosophy which he professed. Ignorance was to be condemned because it was vincible; ignorance which could not be enlightened was invincible, and therefore was neither to be condemned nor to affect the conscience of one who had acted in good faith.

*
* *

It has been said on excellent authority that Victoria's Readings *On the Indians* and *On the Law of War* are in the nature of manuals of confession.[2] Therefore it is that the conscience weighs with him, and the effect of the act upon the conscience is paramount. Without further comment upon these conclusions as such, might we not say with the poet, for the poet is a prophet: 'The world is too much with us'—not merely in business, but in all things which, material in outward form, have nevertheless a spiritual content?

These were general observations important in themselves, if they had no other purpose than to enlighten. They had, however, a further purpose, and Victoria, having reached his conclusions, immediately applies them to the concrete case before him, in order that the question which was thought to have been decided by sovereigns 'most Christian' and 'most just and scrupulous' might be put to the test of the Christian conscience.

Therefore, returning at once to 'the matter of the barbarians',[3] Victoria declares: 'We see that it is not in itself so evidently unjust that no question about its justice can arise, nor again so evidently just that no doubt is possible about its injustice, but that it has a look of both according to the standpoint.' The standpoint, in other words, is double, for it was possible to believe that under the circumstances, and given the character of the sovereigns and their representatives, everything had been done properly and justly. From that standpoint there would be no doubt. However, without invoking the scriptural phrase, 'by their fruits ye shall know them', Victoria proceeded with a skilled hand to draw, from the consequences of the acts of the best of sovereigns

[1] *De Indis, infra*, Appendix A, pp. iv–v.

[2] *Vide* the lecture of Mr. Willem Van der Vlugt (former Professor of the Philosophy of Law, in the University of Leyden): 'L'Œuvre de Grotius et son influence sur le développement du Droit international', published in the 1925 *Recueil des Cours* of the Hague Academy of International Law, vol. 7 (Paris, 1926), p. 418: 'Nous avons déjà dit à plusieurs reprises que, à commencer par le passage cité de saint Thomas, toute la littérature traitant des droits et des devoirs en matière internationale, en tant qu'elle a exercé sur les contemporains et les générations suivantes une profonde influence, a été inspirée par les manuels à l'usage du confessionnal. Manuel de confesseur la partie traitant de la morale dans la "Somme" de Thomas d'Aquin; manuels d'un caractère analogue les travaux des "sommistes" qui depuis "le docteur angélique" se sont succédé en l'imitant; manuels de même tendance les *Relectiones* de Victoria et leurs copies plus ou moins originales dont Grotius, tout jeune qu'il fût, avait déjà quelque connaissance.'

[3] *De Indis, infra*, Appendix A, p. v.

and their advisers, the conclusion that fact is to overcome presumption. 'We hear of so many massacres, so many plunderings of otherwise innocent men, so many princes evicted from their possessions and stripped of their rule, that there is certainly ground for doubting whether this is rightly or wrongly done.' [1] Therefore he concludes, with entire confidence, that 'the discussion in question does not seem at all superfluous'.[2]

This is Victoria's justification in answer to the objections to reopening the question; but lest some one should say that there was no need of a fresh inquiry, because the question had been discussed and settled by the wise and the whole matter was being administered by the advice of those, to quote Victoria's words, 'whose business' [3] it was to settle it, he replied: 'I assert'—for here Victoria is voicing his utmost convictions as a theologian, although he was also a jurist—'that it is not for jurists to settle this question or at any rate not for jurists only, for . . . jurists are not skilled enough in the divine law to be able by themselves to settle questions of this sort' [4]—meaning questions involving disputed matters of morality and, above and beyond all, the human conscience.

Paying his respects to the theologians whose opinions might have been requested, he bluntly says that he is not sure that among them those who may have been called upon were 'competent to pronounce on so grave a matter', for 'the issue concerns the forum of conscience'.[5] The conclusion of the whole matter is a highly personal one, Victoria declaring what was apparently his measured judgement that he is 'doing something which is not only not futile and useless, but well worth the trouble, if I am enabled to discuss this question in a manner befitting its importance'.[6] The answer of posterity is that what he did was not 'futile and useless' but that it was indeed 'well worth the trouble', and that in discussing it 'in a manner befitting its importance', he laid the broad and sure foundation of modern international law, leaving it to his successors to enter in and take possession. Indeed, these Readings not only signalize the foundation of international law but mark the rebirth of scholasticism. And these two facts demonstrate beyond question that Victoria was fitted to discuss the gravest of international questions according to the doctrine of the Christian Church, a secular standard of morality and the requirements of the human conscience. Victoria would doubtless have accepted as his own view the happy and truthful statement of President Lincoln that 'nothing is settled until it is settled right'.

After the conclusion of his introduction, in which he stated that view, in effect if not in so many words, and justified it by the reason of the thing, his purpose was to reopen the question, which he does at once.

Who, we may ask, were these barbarians recently discovered, and

[1] *Ibid.* [2] *Ibid.* [3] *Ibid.*, p. iv. [4] *Ibid.*, p. v. [5] *Ibid.* [6] *Ibid.*

what was their standing in private and in public law 'before the arrival of the Spaniards'? With the question opened, he asks 'whether they were true owners of private property and possessions and also whether there were among them any who were the true princes and overlords of others'.[1] That is to say, was the status of the barbarians that of the Spaniards and of the French in these matters? For it is these two peoples which Victoria has in mind for purposes of comparison and analogy when he discusses the status of the aborigines of the New World.

In dealing with such questions the great Spaniard appears to have had a single and impersonal standard. Later in his Readings he discloses in a single sentence his large and generous thought, stating simply and without argument that the Europeans discovering the Americans could not have greater rights because of their discovery than the Americans would have had if they had discovered the Spaniards and the French; and it is well to state his view here and now, in order that we may have at the very beginning Victoria's conception of the relations which he was seeking to establish between the peoples of the Old and the New Worlds, a conception based upon the fundamental principles that possession should follow discovery to confer a title, and that the barbarians held title to their 'principalities', to use his expression, upon an equality with the kingdoms of Spain and of France.

To return to the question at hand and to follow Victoria step by step until he reaches, according to his scheme, the inevitable conclusion. His method, here and elsewhere, is that of the schoolmen: to state in full the view which he opposes before he crushes and utterly destroys it. With this purpose he sets forth the argument that the unfortunate Americans could not own property, for, according to the *Institutes* and *Digest* of Justinian, 'a slave can have nothing of his own',[2] and whatever acquisitions a slave may make, belong, according to the *Institutes*,[3] to the master. This is the major premise of the case against him.[4] 'But', he continues, stating the opponents' case in full, 'the aborigines in question are slaves', from which he draws the seemingly triumphant and damning conclusion: 'Therefore the matter is proved; for as Aristotle[5] neatly and correctly says'—still according to the view of his opponents—' "Some are by nature slaves, those, to wit, who are better fitted to serve than to rule." '[6]

[1] *De Indis, infra*, Appendix A, p. vi.

[2] Justinian's *Institutes*, II. ix. 3 (*Inst.*, Per quas personas nobis adquiritur, § *item vobis*): 'Ipse enim servus qui in potestate alterius est, nihil suum habere potest.'

[3] *Digest*, XXIX. ii. 79 (l. *placet* ff., De acquirenda vel omittenda hereditate): 'Placet, quotiens adquiritur per aliquem hereditas vel quid aliud ei cuius quis in potestate est, confestim adquiri ei cuius est in potestate, neque momento aliquo subsistere in persona eius per quem adquiritur et sic adquiri ei cui adquiritur.' *Institutes*, I. viii. 1 (*Inst.*, De his qui sui vel alieni iuris sunt, § *nam apud omnes* [*in potestate itaque*?]): '.. et quodcumque per servum adquiritur, id domino adquiritur.'

[4] *De Indis, infra*, Appendix A, p. vi.

[5] Aristotle, *Politics*, I. ii. 15: *Ὅτι μὲν τοίνυν φύσει τινὲς οἱ μὲν ἐλεύθεροι οἱ δὲ δοῦλοι, οἷς καὶ συμφέρει τὸ δουλεύειν καὶ δίκαιόν ἐστιν.*

[6] *De Indis, infra*, Appendix A, p. vi.

It would be possible and easy to summarize in a few words the argument advanced in behalf of the holders of this view. However, the case is so interesting and so all-embracing, and Victoria puts the views of his opponents so fully and fairly, that it is well here and now to quote it as perhaps the most interesting example of the scholastic method to be found in the Readings, and which, when pondered, will enable us to treat somewhat cavalierly the arguments, wherever advanced, which are contrary to the nature and dignity of the human being in any quarter of the world. 'Now these are they who have not sufficient reason to govern even themselves, but only to do what they are bidden, and whose strength lies in their body rather than in their mind. But, of a surety, if there be any such, the aborigines in question are pre-eminently such, for they really seem little different from brute animals and are utterly incapable of governing, and it is unquestionably better for them to be ruled by others than to rule themselves. Aristotle says it is just and natural for such to be slaves. Therefore they and their like cannot be owners. And it is immaterial that before the arrival of the Spaniards they had no other masters; for there is no inconsistency in a slave having no master, as the glossator on *Dig.*, 40, 12, 23, notes. Nay, the statement is expressly made in that passage of the *Digest* and it is the expressed case set out in *Dig.*, 45, 3, 36, pr., where it is said that a slave who has been abandoned by his master and not taken into possession by any one else can be taken into possession by any one. If, then, these were slaves they could be taken into possession by the Spaniards.'[1]

It is fortunate for us that human liberty is not a thing of logic.

The passage is, however, not interesting merely as a perfect example of the scholastic method. It is interesting as showing the authorities upon which such premises and such conclusions rest. There is here no reference to the Old or the New Testament with a promise of a better and a happier existence. The references are to the past—a past which had ceased to exist, and which we of to-day think never should have existed—to the hard and relentless texts from Roman law and to a passage from Aristotle's *Politics*. In each, the attempt was made to justify an existing state of affairs. Victoria himself was fond of invoking the *Institutes* and the *Digest* of Justinian, and he was an Aristotelian; but he did not subordinate his judgement to a relentless and unacceptable past. With him the New Testament prevailed, whenever the classic texts of Roman law were opposed to the Victorian conception of human progress and of justice. And to the case of what we of to-day would call the 'reactionaries', Victoria's answer is one of fact, consisting of but a single paragraph of two short sentences: 'On the opposite side we have the fact that the people in question were

[1] *Ibid.*

in peaceable possession of their goods, both publicly and privately. Therefore, unless the contrary is shown, they must be treated as owners and not be disturbed in their possession unless cause be shown.'[1]

But Victoria was not satisfied with a solution of fact and, as was his wont, he discussed the question not merely as a jurist, bound by legal authority, but as a theologian, with whom the things of the spirit were of supreme moment. An attempt might be made to show cause that the Americans did not possess dominion, on the ground that, to quote his exact language, 'they were sinners or were unbelievers or were witless or irrational'.[2] If this argument were to be invoked and strictly applied against the Americans of to-day, it may be said in passing, we might find ourselves without dominion or possessions or anything else. After setting forth the arguments of those (such as the Waldenses[3] and John Wycliffe[4]) who believe that 'sinners, at any rate those in mortal sin, have no dominion over anything',[5] and of those who accept that doctrine declaring that 'the barbarians had no dominion, because they were always in mortal sin', Victoria replies, in the manner of the schoolmen, to that line of reasoning. The answer is an emphatic denial, a carefully reasoned and authoritative denial in a single sentence: 'Against this doctrine I advance the proposition that mortal sin does not hinder civil dominion and true dominion.'[6]

As a specimen has been given of the way in which Victoria set forth the views of the opponent which he was about to refute, it seems advisable at the very beginning of this analysis of the disquisition on the Indians to give an example of the ease and grace and the skill with which Victoria employed the scholastic method in its most perfect and technical form, in order to reach a conclusion which leaves to us sinners the property which we may have earned by the sweat of our brow.

'First, if a sinner has not civil dominion (which is what they seem to be speaking of), he, therefore, has not natural dominion; but the consequent is untrue; therefore, &c.'[7] It is to be observed that Victoria is meeting the argument of scholastics by a scholastic argument, and that he does not at times give himself the trouble of completing the syllogism, leaving it to the intelligence of the reader. 'I prove the con-

[1] *De Indis, infra,* Appendix A, p. vi. [2] *Ibid.*

[3] A sect which bears the name of its supposed founder, Peter Waldo *or* Waldes (*fl. circa* 1150), and which first made its appearance among the people of Lyons. The ban of excommunication was pronounced against its members at Verona, in 1184. The Waldenses were reactionaries against the splendour and outward display of the medieval Church; their doctrines condemned war, the infliction of the death penalty, and the taking of oaths. They held the view that the validity of the Sacraments depended upon the worthiness of the minister, and that sin or even unworthiness destroyed the validity of ownership of temporal things. Most of the Waldenses were swallowed up by the other sects in the Protestant Reformation; there are, however, still a few thousand who profess to hold the original doctrines of the sect.

[4] English heretic (1324–84). He was a member of John of Gaunt's anti-clerical party. His teachings, embraced in twenty-four propositions, were condemned by an ecclesiastical court sitting at Blackfriars in 1382. Aside from his heretical holdings regarding the Sacrament, his principal doctrine was that 'Dominion is founded in grace', i.e. that no respect is due to the commands or the property of the wicked. [5] *De Indis, infra,* Appendix A, p. vi. [6] *Ibid.*, p. vii. [7] *Ibid.*

sequence; for natural dominion is a gift of God, just as civil dominion is, nay, more so, for civil dominion seems an institute of human law. Therefore, if for an offence against God a man loses civil dominion, he would for the same reason lose his natural dominion also.'[1] It will be seen that in this passage Victoria refers both to human and to natural law, no doubt having in mind the epoch-making statement of St. Thomas that the unaided eye of reason could discover natural law without revelation, thereby laicizing law. 'But the falsity of the consequent', Victoria proceeds, 'is demonstrated by the fact that the man in question does not lose dominion over his own acts and over his own limbs, for a sinner has a right to defend his own life.'[2]

'Secondly, Holy Scripture often names as kings those who were wicked and sinners, as appears in the case of Solomon and Ahab and many others; but one cannot be a king without having dominion; therefore, &c.

'Thirdly, I employ against the opposing party their own argument: Dominion is founded on the image of God; but man is God's image by nature, that is, by his reasoning powers; therefore, dominion is not lost by mortal sin. The minor is proved from St. Augustine (*De Trinitate*, bk. 9) and from the doctors.'

This is the first reference which Victoria makes to St. Augustine, who in the Church universal is said to occupy a position only inferior to that of St. Paul.

'Fourthly, David called Saul his lord and king even when he was persecuting him (1 Sam., ch. 16, and elsewhere). Nay, David himself sinned at times, yet did not lose his kingdom on that account.

'Fifthly (Genesis, ch. 49), "The sceptre shall not depart from Judah, nor a leader from between his feet, until he that is to be sent shall come," &c.; yet there were many bad kings; therefore, &c.

'Sixthly, spiritual power is not lost by mortal sin; therefore not civil, for it seems much less assuredly to be founded in grace than spiritual power is. Now, the antecedent is obvious, because a bad priest consecrates the Eucharist and a bad bishop consecrates a priest, beyond all doubt. Although Wycliffe[3] denies this, Armachanus[4] admits it.

'Seventhly, it is not at all likely, seeing that we are bidden to obey princes (Romans, ch. 13; and 1 Peter, ch. 2: "Be subject to your masters,

[1] *Ibid.*, pp. vii–viii. [2] *Ibid.*, p. viii. [3] *Vide supra*, p. 108.

[4] Richard Fitzralph, Archbishop of Armagh (1295–1360), was one of the great scholastic luminaries of his day. He was Chancellor of Oxford University (1333); Chancellor of Lincoln Cathedral (1334); Canon and Prebendary of Lichfield (1335); and was consecrated Archbishop of Armagh (1346). He visited the papal court at Avignon, and while there, presented a petition on behalf of the English clergy, reciting certain complaints against the mendicant orders. He was almost immediately involved in a dispute which lasted until the end of his life. In 1357 he was cited from England to Avignon to defend one of his works (*Defensorium Curatorum*). His holdings were never directly condemned. He died in peace at Avignon.

not only to the good but also to the forward"), and not to take what belongs to another, that God meant that there should be any uncertainty as to who were true princes and owners.

'And, in sum, this is manifest heresy. And in the same way that God makes His sun to rise on the good and on the bad and sends His rain on the just and on the unjust, so also He has given temporal goods alike to good and to bad.'[1]

There is but a single observation which may be made, although it seems hardly to be needed and it applies not merely here but throughout his readings: one cannot but admire and wonder at the extraordinary learning of Victoria, the skill with which he frames his syllogism, the familiarity with the saints and the doctors of the Church and the extent to which the Bible—the Old Testament as well as the New—was constantly at his finger-tips. It would be unpardonable to dwell, because they are so obvious, upon the sureness, rapidity, and penetration of his thought.

In his opinion, unbelievers are to be allowed their dominion and the possession of things temporal. A concession which he seems to make to his opponents, in order to state their case in all its strength, is that heretics having no dominion, unbelievers should not, inasmuch as their condition should not be better than that of heretics. His answer here is short, very interesting, and invokes, as heretofore, proof from the Scriptures in behalf of the view which he accepts in contradistinction to the views of his opponents. Here we have, as it were, the official appearance of St. Thomas Aquinas who, with St. Augustine, is to be regarded as furnishing the materials which, through Victoria, have entered into the structure of the modern law of nations. Omitting the Biblical illustrations, such as Joseph's making all the land of Egypt tributary to Pharaoh, we may turn at once to the conclusions which must be reproduced in Victoria's own words: 'Unbelief does not prevent any one from being a true owner',[2] he says, and the reasoning upon which this statement is based is that of St. Thomas Aquinas.[3] In summary form later Victoria invokes the reason of St. Thomas that 'unbelief does not destroy either natural law or human law; but ownership and dominion are based either on natural or on human law; therefore they are not destroyed by want of faith';[4] and in the form of a corollary Victoria states his further conclusion in strict accord with the doctrine of the Church, and with the humanitarianism which we are pleased to consider as of our day: 'Hence it is manifest that it is not justifiable to

[1] *De Indis, infra,* Appendix A, p. viii.

[2] *Ibid.*

[3] *Secunda Secundae,* question 10, article 12; but 'The words in qu. 12, art. 2, are more to the point: "Respondeo dicendum quod, sicut supra (qu. 10, art. 10) dictum est, infidelitas secundum se ipsam non repugnat dominio eo, quod dominium introductum est de iure gentium, quod est ius humanum; distinctio autem fidelium et infidelium est secundum ius divinum, per quod non tollitur ius humanum."' [Revised Latin text (by H. F. Wright) in Victoria, *De Indis et de Ivre Belli Relectiones,* Carnegie Institution edition, p. 226, footnote no. 3.]

[4] *De Indis, infra,* Appendix A, p. ix.

take anything that they possess from either Saracens or Jews or other unbelievers as such, that is, because they are unbelievers; but the act would be theft or robbery no less than if it were done to Christians.'[1]

It is not to be supposed that Victoria, with his largeness of soul and liberality of mind, would deny to 'heretics' dominion over property, either by divine or human law, and in according the right to heretics he completely overturned the premise of the reactionaries in the matter of unbelievers. For our purpose it is sufficient to state what he calls the 'generally accepted' and 'notorious' doctrine that 'from the standpoint of the divine law a heretic does not lose the ownership of his property'.[2]

Heresy, it is to be observed, is a spiritual offence. It is not, however, by divine law that the property of heretics might be confiscated; but they may by statute be deprived of the fundamental right of ownership. Without dwelling upon this matter or following Victoria in his line of argument, it suffices to say that even in the most advanced countries of the present day, anarchists may be deprived of what, we shall see later, Victoria also considered a fundamental right—to reside in a country and to acquire its citizenship. This is the temporal consequence of a belief for which there is fortunately no spiritual penalty.

The conclusion which Victoria draws in the matter of sinners and unbelievers, considered from various points of view, is 'that the barbarians in question cannot be barred from being true owners, alike in public and in private law, by reason of the sin of unbelief or any other mortal sin, nor does such sin entitle Christians to seize their goods and lands, as Cajetan proves at some length and neatly (*Secunda Secundae*, qu. 66, art. 8)'.[3] This statement of Victoria is interesting inasmuch as it shows his open and discriminating mind in that he here accepts the authority of Cajetan, which in an earlier passage he had rejected as not being in accordance with his own scheme of things.

But the great question to the lay mind remained unanswered: 'whether the Indians lacked ownership because of want of reason or unsoundness of mind'[4]—which raised the ultimate question, according to Victoria, 'whether the use of reason is a precondition of capacity for ownership in general'.[5] It is a matter which concerns us who do not always make that impression upon others which we inwardly cherish.

But what then is ownership? 'Nothing more', replies Victoria, 'than the right to put a thing to one's own use.'[6]

As was the wont of St. Thomas Aquinas, Francis of Victoria uses the first person in the most important matters. 'I answer', he says,[7] 'by the following propositions: . . . Irrational creatures cannot have dominion'; adding that the proposition which he advanced is also

[1] *Ibid.* [2] *Ibid.* [3] *Ibid.*, p. xi. [4] *Ibid.* [5] *Ibid.* [6] *Ibid.* [7] *Ibid.*

confirmed by the authority of St. Thomas Aquinas,[1] 'to the effect that only rational creatures have dominion over their acts, the test of a man's being master of his acts being . . . that he has the power of choice'.[2] However, choice, we are justified in saying, indicates the possession of reason and judgement on the part of the one making the choice, although 'there might seem some doubt', according to Victoria, 'whether a boy, who has not yet the use of reason, can have dominion, inasmuch as he seems to differ little from irrational animals'.[3] But Victoria's reply is as convincing to-day as then, stating as it does the law and the practice of the entire civilized world: 'Boys, even before they have the use of reason, can have dominion.' Why should this be so? 'Because they can suffer wrong; therefore they have rights over things'; and 'therefore also they have dominion, which is naught else than a right'.[4]

It is no doubt true that the guardian of the child may exercise the right of the child, and his action must therefore be in the interest of the ward, not in his own; for however limited the exercise of this right over the property because of the tenderness of their years and the feebleness of their judgement, 'the wards are the owners'.[5]

This reasoning might suffice. It was not, however, sufficient for Victoria, who had the habit of going to the root of things, his purpose being to show that the child, however young it may be, may acquire property as an heir 'who succeeds to the rights of the deceased and who has dominion over the inheritance'. For this statement, as true then as now, he invokes the authority of the *Digest* and the *Institutes* of Justinian.[6]

It is to be observed that there were two alleged reasons why the Americans of that day might not possess property, the second of which was unsoundness of mind. The disability in this case is not slenderness of reason but its total absence, 'whereby they neither have nor is there any hope that they will have the use of reason'. Nevertheless, in the Victorian conception, 'they can still have dominion, because they can suffer wrong'; and 'therefore they have a right'.[7]

Having established a principle, it did not seem necessary to Victoria to press the matter further, and he left it to the jurists by profession to determine whether those of unsound mind should or should not be held to possess civil dominion.

[1] *Summa Theologica, Prima Secundae,* question 1, articles 1 and 2; *ibid.,* question 6, article 2; *Summa Contra Gentiles,* Book III, chap. cx.

[2] *Prima Secundae,* question 1, article 2: 'Illa ergo, quae rationem habent, seipsa movent ad finem, quia habent dominium suorum actuum per liberum arbitrium, quod est "facultas voluntatis et rationis". Illa vero, quae ratione carent, tendunt in finem per naturalem inclinationem, quasi ab alio mota, non autem a seipsis.'

[3] *De Indis, infra,* Appendix A, p. xii. [4] *Ibid.* [5] *Ibid.*

[6] *Ibid.,* p. xiii. Justinian's *Digest,* XLIV. iii. 11 (1. *cum heres, ff.,* De diversis temporalibus praescriptionibus et de accessionibus possessionum). *Ibid., Institutes,* II. xix. 7 (*Inst.,* De heredum qualitate et differentia, § *fin.*).

[7] *De Indis, infra,* Appendix A, p. xiii.

Victoria, concerned with universal principles, dealt in generalities, frequently leaving to others what he would doubtless have called their narrowing application.

That this particular matter was incidental and immaterial to a man of Victoria's outlook is evident from what follows: 'However this may be, . . . the Indian aborigines', in his opinion, 'are not barred on this ground from the exercise of true dominion.' Why should this be so? Here Victoria uses as a proof the doctrine which he had previously established, that they have, 'according to their kind, the use of reason'.[1] In other words, they are not of unsound mind. Why are the barbarians credited with reason and its use? 'They have polities which are orderly arranged and they have definite marriage and magistrates, overlords, laws, and workshops, and a system of exchange, all of which call for the use of reason.' Last, but not least in his conception, 'they also have a kind of religion'.[2] It was a matter of vast importance to Victoria, too, that they saw things as other human beings, and therefore had the premises upon which reason should be exercised and from which apposite conclusions could be derived, for in the Victorian philosophy 'the most conspicuous feature of man is reason, and power is useless which is not reducible to action'.[3]

Victoria, it will be observed, accredits the barbarians with a kind of religion, but states that it was only 'a kind of religion'—not the form to which he devoted his life—going on to say 'that it is through no fault of theirs that these aborigines have for many centuries been outside the pale of salvation, in that they have been born in sin and void of baptism and the use of reason whereby to seek out the things needful for salvation'. What then is the conclusion to be drawn from the premises in which this section abounds? 'Accordingly I'—it is Victoria who is speaking—'for the most part attribute their seeming so unintelligent and stupid'—to what?—'to a bad and barbarous upbringing'[4]—the complaint, unfortunately, which has also been common to so-called civilized peoples throughout recorded history. Now Victoria, while far-sighted, was not short-sighted. If from his chair in Salamanca he could look across the waste of waters and recognize in the Americans his fellow human beings, he was not too short-sighted to say that 'even among ourselves'—meaning the Spaniards—'we find many peasants who differ little from brutes'.[5]

Victoria was not merely a humanist; he was also a humanitarian. The humblest of God's creatures was to him God's creature, whether a Spaniard or an Indian, whether an opponent of the religion which he professed, or whether too simple, it might seem, to comprehend the message of the Gospel. The toleration of our day may be said to be a mark of indifference. The toleration of Victoria was that of the great

[1] *Ibid.* [2] *Ibid.* [3] *Ibid.* [4] *Ibid.* [5] *Ibid.*

heart and of the balanced mind. Therefore the conclusion to which he seemed impelled: 'The upshot of all the preceding is, then, that the aborigines undoubtedly had true dominion in both public and private matters, just like Christians, and that neither their princes nor private persons could be despoiled of their property on the ground of their not being true owners.' Why? Because it would be unchristian, for 'it would be harsh to deny to those, who have never done any wrong, what we grant to Saracens and Jews, who are the persistent enemies of Christianity'. For this statement there was unanswerable authority: the law and practice of Victoria's day. 'We do not deny that these latter peoples are true owners of their property, if they have not seized lands elsewhere belonging to Christians.'[1]

There is, however, a question still outstanding—double in fact, though but one in the conception of Victoria—stated by him in the beginning of his disquisition, and which could apparently, in his opinion, only have an adequate answer in the light of the fundamental principles which he advanced and established. Reactionaries of every age have declared their less-favoured countrymen incapable of self-government, and if this were true, there would needs be, in the opinion of those whom Victoria refutes, 'slaves by nature because of their incapability of self-government'.[2] The difficulty might impress the layman as being 'invincible'—to use a theological term—in that the argument and the conclusion were none other than Aristotle's.[3] The truth of the matter appears to be that Aristotle was in fact guilty of the charge of denying natural rights,[4] and it was only by an interpretation of what Victoria thought Aristotle meant rather than what he said, that the 'pagan saint' was not stricken from his calendar.

How did the Spaniard extricate the Greek from the embarrassing position which the latter was considered to occupy? 'Aristotle', he explains, 'certainly did not mean to say that such as are not over-strong mentally are by nature subject to another's power and incapable of dominion alike over themselves and other things; for this', he declares roundly, 'is civil and legal slavery, wherein none are slaves by nature.'[5]

The second step in Victoria's rehabilitation of Aristotle is the statement that the 'Philosopher' did not mean that 'if any by nature are of weak mind, it is permissible to seize their patrimony and enslave

[1] *De Indis, infra,* Appendix A, p. xiii. [2] *Ibid.* [3] Aristotle, *Politics,* I. ii.

[4] Aristotle's view was commonly held throughout pagan times. It conceived slavery to be a natural state—i.e. that by the natural law some were born to be slaves, just as others were born to be free. The idea was based upon the assumption that physical, mental, or moral inferiority (that is, with reference to the warlike virtues and vices, such as courage, fear, &c.), as evinced by being conquered in battle, made the conquered only worthy to be the victor's chattel. Slavery by birth was a later development. Some modern writers hold that this system was introduced in order to preserve racial purity among the slave-owning class—the slaves being originally of 'subject races', or at any rate, foreigners.

[5] *De Indis, infra,* Appendix A, pp. xiii–xiv.

them and put them up for sale'; but what Victoria insists he (the Philosopher) means is 'that by defect of their nature they need to be ruled and governed by others and that it is good for them to be subject to others, just as sons need to be subject to their parents until of full age'.[1]

The proof of Aristotle's intent is found by Victoria in the Philosopher's 'corresponding remark that some are by nature masters, those, namely, who are of strong intelligence'.[2] Admitting that this 'corresponding remark' is that of Aristotle, Victoria again comes to the defence of the Philosopher, alleging it to be clear that he does not mean thereby 'that such persons can arrogate to themselves a sway over others in virtue of their superior wisdom, but that nature has given them capacity for rule and government'.[3] In these half-dozen lines he unhorses the reactionaries and gives us all hope of dominion and of human and political freedom, for does he not say, 'even if we admit that the aborigines in question'—he is speaking of the Americans—'are as inept and stupid as is alleged, still dominion cannot be denied to them, nor are they to be classed with the slaves of civil law'.[4] Therefore 'the conclusion stands sure'—and with this he ends the first section of the first Reading—'that the aborigines in question were true owners, before the Spaniards came among them, both from the public and the private point of view'.[5]

They and their successors still are.

[1] *Ibid.*, p. xiv. [2] Aristotle, *Politics*, I. ii. [3] *De Indis, infra*, Appendix A, p. xiv.
[4] *Ibid.* [5] *Ibid.*

CHAPTER V

ANALYSIS OF THE READING *ON THE INDIANS RECENTLY DISCOVERED.* SECTION II

HAVING explained the origin of the question which he was about to resolve and his method of treating it in three parts, and having followed this by an exposition of what may be called his legal and moral philosophy, ending with a statement which accorded to the Indians, lately come to the knowledge of the Old World, dominion over and possession of their territories on a footing of equality with the kingdoms of Spain and France, Francisco de Vitoria proceeds to examine the titles which had been alleged by both temporal and spiritual sovereigns, by virtue whereof the Americans might come under European dominion. Some of these titles were, in his opinion, inadequate; others might or might not be adequate, depending upon the circumstances of the case; and he ends his consideration of these matters, which may be called his disquisition on the law of nations, by setting forth his views on the conduct of war.

It is not material to our purpose to determine the number of readings into which the entire question was divided in Victoria's presentation of his views: whether there were originally but two readings—the first in several parts, and the second, devoted to war—is a question of extreme nicety and one for classical scholars rather than international lawyers to determine. It is enough that the readings were delivered at the University of Salamanca by Victoria; that they were published (unfortunately not until a quarter of a century after their preparation, the first edition appearing posthumously at Lyons in 1557); and that, however the various editions appearing from time to time may have differed, the law of nations which they announced remained in essence, if not in form, unchanged. It is a matter of indifference, therefore, to the international lawyer what edition of Victoria's Readings fell under the eye of the learned Grotius. For the present purpose, the first Reading is to be considered as composed of three sections: the first which we may call an introduction; the second which deals with the illegitimate titles by which the Spaniards claimed the New World; and the third which treats of the lawful titles by which the Americans could have come into the power of Spain. The second and third sections set forth what may be called the law of peace. A separate Reading is on the law of war, which is intended to apply to the war made by the Spaniards on the barbarians, and the two readings taken together, irrespective of their subdivisions, form what may properly be termed Victoria's treatise *On Peace and War*, antedating Grotius's treatise *On War and Peace* by wellnigh a century.[1]

[1] The reader who desires information on the interesting question of the number of lectures which

The method of Victoria was, as the reader already knows, direct and to the point. Therefore he begins the second part which we call 'section' with a statement of but a couple of lines: 'It being premised, then, that the Indian aborigines are or were true owners, it remains to inquire by what title the Spaniards could have come into possession of them and their country.'[1]

This section is devoted to the inadequate or illegitimate titles. Of these there were, in Victoria's opinion, seven.

The question which he was about to discuss was one beset with difficulties. Charles V, the Holy Roman Emperor, was involved, and of Charles, as King of Spain, Victoria was a temporal subject. The question also involved the supreme head of the Church, and as a churchman he was a spiritual subject of the Pope. No language better than Victoria's can show the question involved and the spirit in which he approached it. 'The first title that might be alleged, then, is that the Emperor is the lord of the world, and in such a way that, even if it be granted that in time past there was a defect in his claim, it would by now be purged as regards our present, most Christian Emperor. For, even if we assume that the Indian aborigines may be true owners, yet they might have superior lords, just as inferior princes have a king and as some kings have the Emperor over them. There can in this way be many persons having dominion over the same thing; and this accounts for the well-worn distinction drawn by the jurists between dominion high and low, dominion direct and available, dominion pure and mixed. The question, therefore, is whether the aborigines had any superior lord. And, as this question can only arise with regard to either the Emperor or the Pope, let us speak of these.'[2]

Here again, as is the habit of the schoolmen, he sets forth the allegation, which it is his purpose to disprove, that the Emperor is 'lord of the world', and therefore of the barbarians; and it must be admitted that the case for the Emperor was of long standing,

went to make up these Readings and the probable dates at which they may have been delivered will find the information in Beltrán de Heredia's *Los Manuscritos del Maestro Fray Francisco de Vitoria, O.P.*, *op. cit.*, pp. 109–10, 132–3, 144–51, 153; and in Getino's *El Maestro Fr. Francisco De Vitoria, op. cit.*, pp. 142–51, 157–60, 162–3. The latter says (p. 143): 'La primera redacción de sus conferencias o Relecciones *De Indis*, de las que llegaron hasta nosotros, la hizo en 1532, como él terminantemente lo confiesa.

'"Toda la disputa y Relección que tenemos entre manos, dice al empezar estas materias, se ha tomado por estos bárbaros del Nuevo Mundo, que llaman indios, que hace cuarenta años vinieron a poder de los españoles y antes eran desconocidos en nuestro Mundo; *qui ante quadraginta annos venerunt in potestatem Hispanorum ignoti prius nostro orbi*."

'Pudiera alguien argüir que Vitoria, en vez de precisar el número de años que hacía desde que los indios fueron conocidos en nuestro Mundo, buscó el cuarenta, como número redondo aproximado; más es bien llano que colocándonos en el año de 1539 en que dió la Relección citada, más próxima y exacta tenía la decena inmediata de cincuenta, que era además más redonda, por marcar medio siglo. En tan corta distancia y tratándose de suceso de esa magnitud, en el que intervenían de una manera u otra la mitad de los españoles, y no habiendo usado el gran Maestro la partícula de aproximación *circa, propre, proxime*, el año que él señala de 1532 es la efeméride gloriosa de la primitiva redacción que no quita retocase antes de la lectura.'

[1] *De Indis*, section II, *infra*, Appendix A, p. xv.

[2] *Ibid.*, p. xvi.

with Roman and Canon law in its behalf. Was not Maximilian, the grandfather of Charles V, known as 'lord of the world'? Therefore the claim was a very living and real one, even though it was based upon a musty title wrested from the past—for it dates, in theory, at least, from the proclamation of Charlemagne, as Holy Roman Emperor, at Rome on Christmas Day of the year 800.

Omitting the texts of the Scripture with which the reader is doubtless familiar, we note that Victoria quotes the great Bartolus, prince of commentators, to the effect that 'the Emperor is the rightful lord of the whole world'.[1]

It is to be expected that St. Thomas and St. Thomas's Aristotle would make their appearance on behalf of monarchy as the best system;[2] from which Victoria's opponents drew the conclusion that there should be one Emperor divinely instituted in the world.

However, there is a further argument of a kind more common then than in our day: that Nature ought to be imitated; that 'in things natural there is'—so it is said—'always one governor; as in the body, it is the heart; in the soul, it is reason'—with the inevitable conclusion that there should be 'one governor, just as there is one God'[3]—a contention which would be agreeable to the Emperor Charles, 'ever August', and to the head of the Church.

But irrespective of the merits of claims on behalf of the spiritual and temporal potentates, Victoria roundly asserts that such a contention is 'baseless', and, dismissing the Supreme Pontiff for a moment, he discloses his conclusion, before proceeding to argue it, that 'The Emperor is not the lord of the whole earth'. The reason for this is that 'dominion', in the opinion of the great Dominican of Salamanca, 'must be founded either on natural or divine or human law'. It was not founded on natural law, inasmuch as, according to the greatest of Dominicans, St. Thomas, 'dominion and pre-eminence were introduced by human law';[4] and 'they, therefore, were not [introduced] by natural law'; and Victoria very properly adds to the words of the doctor saint (for St. Thomas was both): 'Nor would there be any greater reason why this dominion should be more proper for Germans than for Gauls.' Again he invokes the authority of St. Thomas, who shares the doctrine

[1] *De Indis, infra*, p. xvi. Bartolus of Sassoferrato (1314–57), an Italian jurist, was the most famous master of the dialectical school. His method gained such wide acceptance that for two hundred and fifty years—or until the close of the sixteenth century—he was regarded as the very prince of lawyers. He taught law at Perugia, and made that school as renowned as its sister university at Bologna. His best known works are those *On Evidence* and *On Procedure*—and of course his *Commentary on Justinian's Code*, which, the reader will recall, was regarded as second in authority only to the *Codex* itself. On the doctrine of Bartolus and his school, and Victoria's refutation of it, *vide* Alfred Vanderpol's admirable study, *Le Droit de Guerre d'après les Théologiens et les Canonistes du Moyen-âge* (Paris and Brussels, 1911), pp. 177–85.

[2] St. Thomas Aquinas, *De Regimine Principum*, Book I, chap. ii; Aristotle, *Politics*, III. xviii.

[3] *De Indis, infra*, Appendix A, p. xvii.

[4] *Summa Theologica, Secunda Secundae*, question 10, article 10.

of Aristotle that 'man being a political animal', civil power 'is founded not on nature, but on law'.[1]

So much for natural, what of divine, law?

Among the many authorities invoked, one statement from Victoria is sufficient for the present purpose, and furnishes an interesting example of his method of fitting Holy Writ to temporal needs. In this case he seems to have anticipated the advice of a French dramatist of a later day—'to pass on to the Deluge'—inasmuch as Victoria says that 'to omit everything that happened before the Flood, the world was certainly divided after Noah into different provinces and kingdoms, whether this were by ordinance of Noah himself—for he survived the Flood three hundred and fifty years (Genesis, ch. 9), and sent colonies into different regions, as appears in Berosus of Babylon—or whether, as is more likely, different family-groups by the common agreement of mankind occupied different provinces'. Omitting an entertaining colloquy between Abraham and Lot, 'We are', in the words of Victoria, 'accordingly told (Genesis, ch. 10) that through the descendants of Noah came diversities of peoples and countries, whether in some regions they first assumed lordship by usurpation, as Nimrod seems to have done, . . . or whether by accord of several to unite in one State they appointed a prince over themselves by common agreement'.[2]

Perhaps it would not be amiss to remark that Victoria was peculiarly apt in his choice of Noah as an authority upon which to base colonization and the creation of nations, because by mere length of days he had a longer experience than any other political philosopher in such matters. And indeed we are told that he was only surpassed in length of years by one Methuselah.

At any rate the reference to Noah as a colonizer is interesting, inasmuch as Victoria, although not having as free a hand as his sovereign lord and king in the matter, nevertheless was professionally occupied with it. And not only was Noah's authority on colonization persuasive but Victoria credits him and his descendants with modern ideas concerning the origin of the State, for does not the last clause of the passage suggest the social contract one day to become famous in political and constitutional theory?

But to continue the reference to Noah: 'For it is sure that either in these or in other like modes sovereignty and lordship began in the world and that afterwards, either by right of inheritance or of war or by some other such title, they were continued unto our own day, or at any rate up to the time of the Saviour's coming.'[3] Although these passages are not formally set in the form of a syllogism, with a major and minor premise and conclusion, nevertheless each is there, and the

[1] *De Indis, infra,* Appendix A, p. xvii. Victoria is here referring to the *De Regimine Principum* of St. Thomas, Book I, chap. ii.
[2] *De Indis, infra,* Appendix A, p. xviii.
[3] *Ibid.*

conclusion settles the matter up to the time of the Christian Era: 'Before the coming of Christ no one was vested with world-wide sway by divine law'; and therefore 'the Emperor'—even though it should be the 'most Christian' Emperor Charles V, 'ever August'—'cannot at the present day derive therefrom a title to arrogate to himself lordship over the whole earth, and consequently not over the barbarians'.[1]

No comfort, however, was to accrue to the advocates of the Emperor from the coming of Christ, Who informs us that His 'Kingdom is not of this world'.[2] Victoria himself says that 'even if we grant that He was temporal Lord, it is guess-work to say that He bequeathed that power to the Emperor, there being no mention of any such thing in the whole Bible'. Here he invokes the gloss of St. Thomas Aquinas on 'My Kingdom is not of this world' who 'expressly says that Christ's Kingdom is not temporal or such a kingdom as Pilate conceived, but a spiritual kingdom, inasmuch as our Lord declares in that passage: "Thou sayest that I am a King. To this end was I born and for this cause came I into the world, that I should bear witness unto the truth"'[3]—a passage upon which Victoria remarks by more than a gloss that it is therefore 'a mere fiction to say that by express grant of Christ there is one Emperor and lord of the world'.[4]

The notes in the margin of the text are not those of Victoria but of the original editor; nevertheless the one in the margin on this phase of the subject is as true as it is apt: 'The author demolishes this reasoning.'[5]

Here we might leave the subject. Not so, however, Victoria, who proceeds to demolish further the reasoning by supplementing Holy Writ with history. 'If there had been any such institution by divine law, how comes it', he asks, 'that the Empire was divided into Eastern and Western, first among the sons of Constantine the Great and then, later, by Pope Stephen, who conferred the Empire of the West on the Germans, . . . ?'[6] After a homily on the Greek emperors, Victoria answers his own question by two examples which are as interesting to us as they were to him: the first concerned 'the patrimony of the Church', which not only the jurists, but even the greatest among them, Bartolus, that arch-supporter of empire, admitted was not 'subject to the Emperor';[7] and in our proper person we may also add that small, not to say infinitesimal, as is the patrimony of the Church of our day, it is still independent of any temporal power.

The second example is drawn from the current history of the day,

[1] *De Indis, infra*, Appendix A, p. xviii. [2] St. John, xviii. 36. [3] St. John, xviii. 37.
[4] *De Indis, infra*, Appendix A, p. xix. [5] *Ibid.*, p. xviii.
[6] *Decretals*, I. vi. 34 [Innocentius III duci Caringiae '*Venerabilem fratrem*']: . . . Verum illis principibus ius et potestatem eligendi regem, in imperatorem postmodum promovendum, recognoscimus, ut debemus, ad quos de iure ac antiqua consuetudine noscitur pertinere; praesertim, quum ad eos ius et potestas huiusmodi ab apostolica sede pervenerit, quae Romanum imperium in personam magnifici Caroli a Graecis transtulit in Germanos. [7] *De Indis, infra*, Appendix A, p. xix.

as was Victoria's custom when it suited his international purpose: 'Also, the Kingdom of Spain is not subject to the Emperor, nor is France'[1]—both of them are republics to-day, and there is no emperor to claim authority over them if he would. On this point Victoria was able to rely upon the Doctors of the Church, who agreed 'that States, which have in times past been subject to the Empire, might be freed from that subjection by prescription; which would not be the case, if this subjection were in virtue of a divine law'.[2]

As for the third of the trinity falsely invoked, Victoria holds that by human law 'it is manifest that the Emperor is not lord of the world, because either this would be by the sole authority of some law'—and in his opinion 'there is none such; or, if there were, it would be void of effect, inasmuch as law presupposes jurisdiction'.[3] Here we have the founder of international law displaying to the full his mastery of the law which he was creating; for he had already examined the baseless claim from the twofold standpoint of natural and divine law, both of which entered into his system of international law. He completes the sources of his law of nations by an examination of the question at hand from the standpoint of human law, declaring that man-made law did not exist on behalf of the Emperor, and after the manner of the jurists he adds that if it did, it would be of no effect because jurisdiction was lacking. 'If, then, the Emperor'—Victoria is his own best commentator —'had no jurisdiction over the world before the law, the law could not bind one who was not previously subject to it. Nor, on the other hand, had the Emperor this position by lawful succession or by gift or by exchange or by purchase or by just war or by election or by any other legal title.' Victoria was human, as the best of international lawyers should be. It would appear that at this point patience had ceased to be a virtue with him. To get rid of the preposterous claim he sweepingly denied it any legal title whatsoever. And without further ado he delivered himself of a conclusion as unpalatable to his lord and master, as it is unanswerable, that the 'most Christian' and 'ever August' Emperor 'never was the lord of the whole world'.[4]

However, Francisco de Vitoria was not through with the Emperor, to whom he was unwilling to accord a throne in America, although he could not deny him two in Europe. 'Granted', he says, 'that the Emperor were the lord of the world, still that would not entitle him to seize the provinces of the Indian aborigines and erect new lords there and put down the former ones or take taxes.' This might seem to be taking away with one hand what he gave with the other. The reason is, however, that, admitting the case of the Emperor's advocates, it was that of jurisdiction, not of ownership. His statement on this point is especially interesting if we are to believe the original editor's note in

[1] *Ibid.* [2] *Ibid.*, pp. xix–xx. [3] *Ibid.*, p. xx. [4] *Ibid.*

the margin that it is 'as the gloss on the preface to the *Digest*'. 'Even those who attribute lordship'—the language is Victoria's—'over the world to the Emperor do not claim that he is lord in ownership, but only in jurisdiction', and the latter right does not warrant the Emperor 'in converting provinces to his own use or in giving towns or even estates away at his pleasure'. The last support of the title was thus removed. 'This, then, shows', in the opinion of Victoria as churchman, historian, and lawyer, 'that the Spaniards cannot justify on this ground their seizure of the provinces in question.'[1]

The Emperor's claim of title was single and simple in comparison with that of the partisans of the Church to which Victoria belonged. It was twofold; for the Pope was a temporal monarch, then possessing the large and important papal States, as well as a spiritual sovereign. The claim of the Supreme Pontiff was, according to Victoria the churchman, 'vehemently asserted', for, if the Pope was a temporal monarch, as claimed, whose power extended 'over all the world', he could of course 'make the Kings of Spain sovereign over the aborigines in question', and, in the opinion of those holding that view, this had been done.[2]

This theory was popular with the churchmen and with some jurists, who held that the Pope had 'full jurisdiction in temporal matters over the whole earth', and as Victoria points out, 'they even add that the power of all secular princes comes to them from the Pope'.[3]

According to his analysis the authors of this opinion maintained: 'In the first place, that the Pope has free power, on the footing of supreme temporal lord, to make the Kings of Spain rulers over the Indian aborigines. Secondly they say that, even if it be assumed that he could not do this, at any rate if these aborigines refused to recognize the temporal power of the Pope over them, this would warrant him in making war on them and in putting rulers over them.' This was not mere argument. 'Each of these things', Victoria informs us, 'has been done.' And continuing the analysis he summarizes the proofs alleged in favour of the opinion in question. The first is that 'the Supreme Pontiff granted the provinces in question to the Kings of Spain'. In the second place 'the aborigines were notified that the Pope is the vicar of God and His vicegerent on earth'; this being the case 'it was claimed that they should . . . recognize him as their superior'; and finally it was held that 'their refusal furnishes a good ground for making war on them and seizing their lands, &c.'[4]

The Dominican friar was here on delicate ground, because superiors do not ordinarily recognize the right of inferiors to question their authority or action; but he was sure of his ground because he had already, as he informed his listeners, discussed the temporal power of

[1] *De Indis, infra,* Appendix A, p. xx. [2] *Ibid.* [3] *Ibid.* [4] *Ibid.*, p. xxi.

the Pope in his Reading *On the Ecclesiastical Power*, and he could, therefore, put his 'answer to the above into a few brief propositions'. The first of his propositions was that 'the Pope is not civil or temporal lord of the whole world in the proper sense of the words "lordship" and "civil power"'. The proof of this is that 'if Christ the Lord had not temporal power, . . . much less has the Pope it, he being Christ's vicar'. And in Victoria's opinion 'the proof is sufficient, like that given above concerning the Emperor, for no lordship can come to him save either by natural law or by divine law or by human law';[1] the assertion, therefore, of such lordship is 'ungrounded and arbitrary'[2] (strong language, this, for a man in orders), in the case of the Pope, as in that of the Emperor, since 'it is certain that none comes to him by natural or by human law, and none is shown to come to him by divine law'.[3]

In the next place, 'the Pope', as even Victoria's 'opponents' grant, 'has no spiritual jurisdiction over unbelievers'. Therefore, he concludes that the Supreme Pontiff does not have it 'in temporal matters'. Here again Victoria appears to have been visibly annoyed and his language is more pointed than one would expect towards the head of the Church: 'Of a truth there is nothing in the argument', he asserts, 'that, as Christ had temporal power over the world, therefore the Pope also has it.'[4] Admitting that the founder of the Christian religion could exercise spiritual jurisdiction over the whole world, Victoria denied that the Pope had power 'over unbelievers'.

So much for the first proposition.

The second is like unto it. Even admitting that the Supreme Pontiff already possessed the temporal power in question, he could not pass it on to secular princes, because under such an assumption power 'would be annexed to the Papacy' and hence could not be separated from it.

The fact that the Pope had temporal power Victoria could not think of denying; but such temporal power was limited, although it was possessed by the Pope as far as it was 'necessary for the administration of spiritual affairs'.[5] It might seem strange that pagan authority should be vouched to bolster up the power of the Pope—but to the schoolmen Aristotle was both an uncanonized saint and a sage counsellor in the things of the spirit. The proof of Victoria's statement, therefore, lay in Book I of Aristotle's *Ethics*, that 'an art to which a higher end pertains is imperative and preceptive as regards the arts to which lower ends pertain';[6] and it follows that the 'temporal power is subject to spiritual power', because 'the end of spiritual power is ultimate felicity',

[1] *Ibid.*, pp. xxi–xxii. [2] *Ibid.*, p. xxii. [3] *Ibid.* [4] *Ibid.* [5] *Ibid.*

[6] A paraphrase of the Aristotelian *ὅσαι δ' εἰσὶ τῶν τοιούτων ὑπὸ μίαν τινὰ δύναμιν—καθάπερ ὑπὸ τὴν ἱππικὴν ἡ χαλινοποιικὴ καὶ ὅσαι ἄλλαι τῶν ἱππικῶν ὀργάνων εἰσίν, αὕτη δὲ καὶ πᾶσα πολεμικὴ πρᾶξις ὑπὸ τὴν στρατηγικήν, τὸν αὐτὸν δὲ τρόπον ἄλλαι ὑφ' ἑτέρας—ἐν ἁπάσαις δὴ τὰ τῶν ἀρχιτεκτονικῶν τέλη πάντων ἐστὶν αἱρετώτερα τῶν ὑπ' αὐτά. τούτων γάρ χάριν κἀκεῖνα διώκεται.* *Nicomachean Ethics*, I. i.

while that of civil power is 'political felicity'.[1] Moreover, appealing to the authority of the third Innocent,[2] Victoria adds that anybody entrusted with an office is by implication 'granted everything without which the duties of the office cannot rightly be discharged'[3] and, as the discharge of this office 'cannot be hindered by the civil power . . . it is beyond doubt that power over things temporal has also been left to him so far as is necessary for the government of things spiritual'.[4] This, it may be said in passing, is the justification even to-day for the existence of that smallest of States known to international law as Vatican City.

This reasoning of Victoria, sound in itself, has an implication of vast possibilities, vesting the Supreme Pontiff with arbitral functions, even in temporal disputes, to be exercised among those recognizing his jurisdiction, and indeed beyond the confines of the Church, if States in controversy should care to avail themselves of the judgement of one who is in very fact the supreme moral authority in the Christian world.[5] 'When princes are at variance with one another about some right of sovereignty and are rushing into war,' Victoria adds that the Pope 'can act as judge and inquire into the claims of the parties and deliver judgement, a judgement which the princes are bound to respect, lest those numerous spiritual evils should befall which are the inevitable results of a war between Christian princes.'[6] Is it too much to hold that the head of Christendom, with no temporal ambitions and in a very real sense the 'servant of the servants of God', could render inestimable services in these and in less weighty disputes, since he is the only temporal sovereign who does not have territorial ambitions and whose only purpose would be a spiritual gain for humanity?

Turning now to the immediate question in hand, that of the second title based on the claim of the Pope, Victoria dismisses it rather

[1] *De Indis, infra,* Appendix A, p. xxii.
[2] *Decretals,* I. xxxiii. 6; and I. xxix. I.
[3] *De Indis, infra,* Appendix A, p. xxii.
[4] *Ibid.,* p. xxiii.
[5] Many examples of papal arbitrations and mediations may be drawn from the history of the past. Among the successful ones may be mentioned those of:

(*a*) Pope Gregory XIII between Bathory of Poland and Ivan the Terrible of Russia, resulting in the cession of Polotsk and all of Livonia to the Poles (1583).

(*b*) Leo XIII between Haiti and San Domingo (1897).

(*c*) Leo XIII between Germany and Spain—at the invitation of Bismarck—over the Caroline Islands and the Pelew Group (including Yap). This is a most important case of the modern world, as it involved the interests of great nations. Spain claimed the islands by right of discovery, Germany by right of colonization. England took Germany's part, and a solemn farce—of planting the German and Spanish flags on the islands, each of the parties thus claiming them—ensued. A few weeks later the warships of all three nations sailed into the Pacific and manœuvred about the islands. Bismarck presented the case to the Vatican on the 24th of September, 1885; on the 22nd of October of the same year the award was made, giving the islands to Spain, with certain important concessions—such as a naval base—to Germany. A treaty was signed at the Vatican on the 17th of December of the same year between the two parties, carrying out the award in full.

Vide John Bassett Moore, *International Arbitrations. . . .* vol. v (Washington, 1898), p. 5042 *et seq.*; also, article on 'Papal Arbitrations' in *Catholic Encyclopaedia* (New York, 1907).

[6] *De Indis, infra,* Appendix A, p. xxiii.

cavalierly with a conclusion in the form of a syllogism: 'The Pope has no temporal power over the Indian aborigines or over other unbelievers. . . . For he has no temporal power save such as subserves spiritual matters. But he has no spiritual power over them. . . . Therefore he has no temporal power either.'[1]

If this be so, it necessarily follows, that 'even if the barbarians refuse to recognize any lordship of the Pope, that furnishes no ground for making war on them and seizing their property',[2] a demonstration on spiritual, as well as on temporal, grounds 'that at the time of the Spaniards' first voyages to America they took with them no right to occupy the lands of the indigenous population'.[3]

This, we may say, closes the first series of Victoria's 'titles', which were coextensive with Christianity, and existed even before the Americas had been discovered by the Spaniards.

The third title is one which makes an appeal to the churchman and layman, not merely of the Old World but to the descendants of the barbarians of either class in the Western World. 'The whole of this controversy and discussion was started on account of the aborigines of the New World, commonly called Indians, who came forty years ago into the power of the Spaniards.'

The third title (considered, apparently, by Victoria in 1532[4] exactly 'forty years' after the westward voyage of Columbus) was that of discovery. No other title was 'originally set up', and he informs us that 'it was in virtue of this title alone that Columbus the Genoan first set sail'.[5] At first sight the title seemed adequate, 'because those regions which are deserted, become', as Victoria well knew, 'by the *jus gentium* and the *jus naturale*'—which were obviously familiar to one who was then engaged in founding international law—'the property of the first occupant'.[6] If the premises were correct, there could be no doubt of the conclusion which the advocates of this title drew, that, 'as the Spaniards were the first to discover and occupy the provinces in question, they are in lawful possession thereof, just as if they had discovered some lonely and thitherto uninhabited region'.[7]

But Victoria did not belong to the casual class. Even if the region were lonely and uninhabited, discovery seemed to him to convey no more title than that which a globe-trotter could claim to territory seen by the naked eye from the deck of a pleasure craft. International

[1] *Ibid.* [2] *Ibid.* [3] *Ibid.*, p. xxiv.

[4] On the year 1532 as the date when this *Relectio* was originally prepared, *vide* Getino (*op. cit.*, p. 143). The *Relectio* may have been delivered at a later date (*vide* Beltrán de Heredia, *op. cit.*, pp. 132–3, 144–51, 153), but for us the important fact is that Victoria speaks as from 1532, specifically referring to a date forty years after the American Indians were first discovered by the Spaniards and came into their power. *Vide* also *supra*, note, pp. 116–17.

[5] *De Indis, infra*, Appendix A, pp. xxiv and xxv.

[6] *Ibid.*, p. xxv. Victoria's reference here is to Justinian's *Institutes*, II. i. 12 (*Inst.*, De rerum divisione, § *ferae* [*igitur*] *bestiae*): quod enim ante nullius est, id naturali ratione occupanti conceditur.

[7] *De Indis, infra*, Appendix A, p. xxv.

law should have a firm foundation, and such he gave it in his comment upon discovery. The suggestion of this title seems to have irritated him, for he brushed it aside with a curtness and withering dryness from which it has never recovered. 'Not much, however,' he observes, 'need be said about this third title of ours, because, as proved above, the barbarians were true owners, both from the public and from the private standpoint.'[1] Nothing could be more categorical, nothing more disrespectful, than such language to their Christian Majesties. But he knew whereof he was speaking—and he spoke of nothing other than the law of nations, which this very Reading was to make a living thing and an inestimable blessing to mankind. 'Now the rule of the law of nations' to which he had already referred was 'that what belongs to nobody is granted'—not to the first discoverer or indeed to any discoverer, as such, but 'to the first occupant':[2] a statement so at variance with the claim and the policy of his country as to require authority, and that authority must be such as could not be gainsaid. He therefore based his doctrine on 'the aforementioned passage of the *Institutes*'—meaning, of course, of Justinian. Having proved that the object in question, to wit, the Western World, 'was not without an owner', Victoria declared that 'it does not fall under the title which we are discussing'.[3] Under certain circumstances the title might 'produce some effect', but mere discovery 'in and by itself' gave, and rightly in Victoria's opinion, 'no support to a seizure of the aborigines any more than if it had been they who had discovered us'[4]—the 'us' being not merely Spain and France, but each and every State of the Old World.[5]

So much for what may be called the material aspect.

The fourth title raises the spiritual issue, involving the barbarians who refused 'to accept the faith of Christ, although it is set before them and although they have been adjured and advised to accept it'.[6] If Victoria had been a man of lesser breadth of mind this title might

[1] *De Indis, infra*, Appendix A, p. xxv.

[2] This is such an important point in Victoria's proof, and a point so frequently overlooked—especially by those not trained in the law—that we have thought best to quote the passage from the *Institutes* (*vide supra*, p. 125, footnote 6) in full:

'Ferae igitur bestiae et volucres et pisces, id est omnia animalia, quae in terra mari coelo nascuntur, simulatque ab aliquo capta fuerint, iure gentium statim illius esse incipiunt: quod enim ante nullius est, id naturali ratione occupanti conceditur. nec interest, feras bestias et volucres utrum in suo fundo quisque capiat, an in alieno: plane qui in alienum fundum ingreditur venandi aut aucupandi gratia, potest a domino, si is providerit, prohiberi ne ingrediatur. quidquid autem eorum ceperis, eo usque tuum esse intellegitur, donec tua custodia coercetur: cum vero evaserit custodiam tuam et in naturalem libertatem se receperit, tuum esse desinit et rursus occupantis fit. naturalem autem libertatem recipere intellegitur, cum vel oculos tuos effugerit vel ita sit in conspectu tuo, ut difficilis sit eius persecutio.'

[3] *De Indis, infra*, Appendix A, p. xxv.

[4] *Ibid.*

[5] For an illuminating discussion of titles by discovery and occupation, *vide* Professor Ernest Nys, *Le Droit International, les Principes, les Théories, les Faits*, tome ii (Brussels, 2nd ed., 1912), pp. 64 *et seq.*; also Dr. Julius Goebel's *The Struggle for the Falkland Islands* (New Haven and London, 1927); and, above all, Judge Max Huber's masterly decision rendered on April 4, 1928, in the Island of Palmas case, which was submitted to arbitration by Spain and the United States. This award was published by the International Bureau of the Permanent Court of Arbitration at The Hague; also in the *Hague Court Reports* (second series) published by the Carnegie Endowment for International Peace (New York, 1932), pp. 84–131.

[6] *De Indis, infra*, Appendix A, p. xxv.

have seemed to be 'a lawful one for occupying the lands of the barbarians'—as it did to many a churchman of his day—on the scriptural ground that 'Whoso believeth and is baptized shall be saved, but he who believeth not shall be damned'.[1] The Pope, as the Vicar of Christ, might grant authority to compel the aborigines 'to receive the faith of Christ', and to resort to war in case they rejected the faith, according to those who claimed under the fourth title; for in their opinion those did evil who did not accept the faith of Christ, and the princes might, by resorting to war, execute 'wrath upon them that do evil'.[2]

The second argument advanced in behalf of the fourth title is broader and indeed all-inclusive but of a material nature, capable of being pressed into a spiritual service. The King of Spain could, in the view of the advocates of this title, compel the French to obey their King should they refuse to do so: from which it would follow that Christian princes could compel the aborigines to obey the Christian God, since the cause of God, according to this argument, 'ought not to be in worse condition than the cause of men'.[3]

But there is no end to an argument such as this on the part of an opponent, because of its all-inclusiveness. Baptism might be forced upon the children of unbelievers on the simple ground that they should be compelled to obey a superior rather than an inferior lord—and unquestionably Christ and God were superior to infidel chiefs.

The third argument in favour of the title is that if the barbarians could be punished for publicly blaspheming Christ, they could undoubtedly be punished for unbelief, which is a graver sin because 'directly opposed to faith'. Therefore, the argument runs, 'seeing that Christians can proceed by war against unbelievers for their blasphemy of Christ, so they can for their unbelief itself'.[4]

Victoria was opposed to the fourth title, and therefore to each one of these arguments just advanced—and indeed for the best of reasons. The barbarians could not commit the sin of unbelief before Christianity had come to their knowledge, for, as St. Thomas said, 'unbelief does not wear the guise of sin' to 'those who have not heard of Christ'.[5] His exact words, as quoted by Victoria, were that 'such unbelievers as these are indeed open to condemnation for other sins, . . . but not for the sin of unbelief'.[6]

The doctors might hold to the contrary, and Victoria quoted those who did,[7] but the doctor whom he preferred and to whose authority he pinned his faith was St. Thomas, who held that those to whom the

[1] St. Mark, xvi. 16. [2] *De Indis, infra,* Appendix A, p. xxv. [3] *Ibid.* [4] *Ibid.*, p. xxvi.

[5] *Ibid.* The quotation from St. Thomas is from the *Secunda Secundae,* question 10, article 1.

[6] *De Indis, infra,* Appendix A, p. xxvi.

[7] Such as Altissiodorensis (*Summa Aurea Sententiarum,* fol. cxxxv, col. 4 at end); William of Paris; Gerson (*De Spirituali Vita Animae,* lect. 4); Hugo de Sancto Victore (*De Sacramentis Christianae Fidei,* Bk. II, pt. VI, ch. v); Cornelius (*Acts,* ch. x); and to some extent, Adrian (*Quodlibeta,* qu. 4). *De Indis, infra,* Appendix A, pp. xxvi–xxvii.

Christian religion had not been made known are 'under an invincible ignorance', and invincible ignorance 'is not sin'—a point of view and a philosophy which Victoria had been careful to point out in the introduction to the first section of the disquisition.

Now what is this invincible ignorance? For ignorance to be a sin —even though it be vincible—it must be accompanied by negligence, as, for example, that the person involved 'refused to hear or did not believe what he did hear'. In the case of invincible ignorance, on the other hand, it is 'enough that the man bestowed human diligence in trying to learn, even if in other respects he is in mortal sin'. We thus end the quotation of this phase of Victoria's argument 'in mortal sin'. But what of 'the aborigines to whom no preaching of the faith or Christian religion has come'? They will not be damned 'for the sin of unbelief', for does not St. Thomas say the essential thing is that they should do what in them lies and lead a good life according to the law of nature? 'It does not therefore follow', Victoria continues, 'that if their life be bad, ignorance or unbelief in baptism and the Christian faith may be imputed to them as a sin.'[1]

But Victoria went beyond this; he was not prepared to believe that the Indians were to be held to commit mortal sin because they rejected the Christian religion after it had been merely declared and announced to them as the true religion and after they had merely been told that 'Christ is the Saviour and Redeemer of the world', without any 'proof or incentive to belief'. What he wanted was proof by miracle or other proof or persuasions, for he held that 'where there are no such signs nor anything else of persuasive force, the aborigines are not bound to believe'.[2] Wherefore it follows that 'if the faith be presented to the Indians in the way named only'—that is, without the aid of miracle or other incentive to belief—'and they do not receive it, the Spaniards cannot make this a reason for waging war on them or for proceeding against them under the law of war', because 'they are innocent in this respect and have done no wrong'.[3]

We are here face to face with war, and, while Victoria has devoted a Reading to the subject, nevertheless the statement here made is a summary of the doctrine which he later treats of at length, and as it is so short and pertinent to the present argument, it would be unjust to Victoria to omit it. St. Thomas and St. Augustine (upon whose views the justification of war was based from the early days of Christianity until war ceased to require a reason other than a declaration) are invoked. First, St. Thomas says that for a just war, 'there must be a just cause', that is to say, 'some fault must deserve the attack'.[4] St. Augus-

[1] *De Indis, infra*, Appendix A, p. xxviii. [2] *Ibid.*, p. xxix. [3] *Ibid.*

[4] *Ibid.* The passage of the *Secunda Secundae* of St. Thomas regarding war (question 40, article 1) to which Victoria here refers is discussed at length elsewhere in this tractate, especially pp. 191 *et seq.*, *infra*.

tine, whose authority was even greater than that of St. Thomas—and the authority of both was, with Victoria, necessary in defining a just war—required that such a war should involve the avenging of some wrong, 'as where a people or state is to be punished for neglect to exact amends from its citizens for their wrongdoing or to restore what has been wrongfully taken away',[1] that is to say, there is neither cause nor justification for war unless a wrong has previously been committed. 'This', Victoria informs us, 'is the received opinion of all the doctors, not only of the theologians, but also of the jurists.'[2]

'Cajetan', he continues, turning to one whose authority with the Dominicans and indeed with the Church of to-day is second only to that of St. Thomas, 'lays it down clearly'. And speaking in the first person, Victoria adds: 'I know of no doctor whose opinion is to the contrary.' Whence it follows that the mere refusal to accept the faith in and of itself 'would not be a legitimate title to seize the lands of the aborigines or to despoil the former owners'.[3]

There are two propositions, each true in itself; but as to their application, in the then condition of affairs, Victoria had grave doubt. They are, first: 'If the Indians, after being asked and admonished to hear the peaceful preachers of religion, refused, they would not be excused of mortal sin.' And second: 'If the Christian faith be put before the aborigines with demonstrable and reasonable arguments, and this be accompanied by an upright life, well-ordered according to the law of nature (an argument which weighs much in confirmation of the truth), and this be done not once only and perfunctorily, but diligently and zealously, the aborigines are bound to receive the faith of Christ under penalty of mortal sin.'[4]

However, it was not 'sufficiently clear' to Victoria 'that the Christian faith has yet been so put before the aborigines and announced to them that they are bound to believe it or commit fresh sin'. What, it may be asked, was the way in which it should be put and announced, in order to overcome invincible ignorance? 'I say this because . . . they are not bound to believe unless the faith be put before them with persuasive demonstration.'[5] This is a general statement, about which there might be argument and doubt. However, the great Dominican rendered it specific for all time. 'I hear of no miracles or signs or religious patterns of life; nay, on the other hand, I hear of many scandals and cruel crimes and acts of impiety.' Therefore it did not appear to Victoria that the Christian faith had 'been preached to them with such sufficient propriety and piety that they are bound to acquiesce in it'. Here not merely his heart was enlisted but his conscience, and last,

[1] *De Indis, infra,* Appendix A, p. xxix. *Vide* also p. 185, *infra.*
[2] *De Indis, infra,* Appendix, A, p. xxix. [3] *Ibid.* [4] *Ibid.,* pp. xxix, xxx.
[5] *Ibid.,* p. xxx.

but not least, his pride of country suffered. He granted that 'many religious and other ecclesiastics seem both by their lives and example and their diligent preaching to have bestowed sufficient pains and industry in this business', but unfortunately they had been 'hindered therein by others who had other matters in their charge'.[1] The 'others' were doubtless the laymen, who had gone to the New World not for the 'greater glory of God', but for unworthy motives which, unfortunately, are not unknown in the history of colonization.

A man of ordinary calibre might have been satisfied with the refutation of the title which he had already made. But with Victoria a mere answer to an adversary was not sufficient. A favourite method of his was to strengthen the opponents' best statement of their case, and to grant their contentions in full, only to overwhelm them by a statement of fundamental and unanswerable principles. Of this there is no better example to be found in the disquisition than the concluding paragraphs in the fourth title, dealing with those who refuse to accept the faith of Christ. 'Although', he says, granting everything to the opposing argument, 'the Christian faith may have been announced to the Indians with adequate demonstration and they have refused to receive it, yet this is not a reason which justifies making war on them and depriving them of their property.'[2]

His first step in the process of ultimate refutation is the statement of St. Thomas Aquinas 'that unbelievers who have never received the faith, like Gentiles and Jews, are in no wise to be compelled to do so'. What is the authority for this? 'The doctors alike in the canon law and in the civil law.' Where does the proof lie? 'In the fact that belief is an operation of the will.' What influence does force have upon the will? Here Victoria invokes the 'pagan saint': 'fear detracts greatly from the voluntary (*Ethics*, bk. 3),[3] and it is a sacrilege to approach under the influence of servile fear as far as the mysteries and sacraments of Christ.'[4]

Turning from St. Thomas and Aristotle, whose authority was individual, to that of the use and custom of the Church, which was universal, he continues: 'For never have Christian Emperors, who had as advisers the most holy and wise Pontiffs, made war on unbelievers for their refusal to accept the Christian religion.' That is not all. War he considered as 'no argument for the truth of the Christian faith',[5] even in a day when religious wars were not unknown. 'Therefore the Indians cannot', in his opinion, 'be induced by war to believe, but rather to feign belief and reception of the Christian faith, which is monstrous and a sacrilege.'[6]

[1] *De Indis, infra*, Appendix A, p. xxx. [2] *Ibid.*

[3] Aristotle, *Nicomachean Ethics*, III. i. 4 *et seq.*: ὅσα δὲ διὰ φόβον μειζόνων κακῶν πράττεται ἢ διὰ καλόν τι, οἷον εἰ τύραννος προστάττοι αἰσχρόν τι πρᾶξαι κύριος ὢν γονέων καὶ τέκνων, καὶ πράξαντος μὲν σῴζοιντο, μὴ πράξαντος δ' ἀποθνήσκοιεν, ἀμφισβήτησιν ἔχει πότερον ἀκούσιά ἐστιν ἢ ἑκούσια.

[4] *De Indis, infra*, Appendix A, p. xxx. [5] *Ibid.*, p. xxxi. [6] *Ibid.*

After the authority of such persons as St. Thomas Aquinas and Aristotle and the 'most holy and wise Pontiffs', it is clear, in the judgement of the broad-minded Dominican, 'that the title which we are now discussing is not adequate and lawful for the seizure of the lands of the aborigines'.[1]

The sins of the aborigines are made by Victoria's opponents to cover a multitude of inequitable propositions; for example, although war should not be made upon them because of their unbelief, 'yet', in the language of Victoria, 'they may be attacked for other mortal sins which (so it is said) they have in numbers, and those very heinous'.[2]

There is, however, a distinction in the matter of mortal sins. The assertion is made by some, Victoria implies, that 'there are some sins which are not against the law of nature, but only against positive divine law'. For these sins the Indians could not 'be attacked in war'. But there were other sins which were indisputably contrary to nature's law, 'such as cannibalism,[3] and promiscuous intercourse with mothers or sisters and with males'. And for such sins it was generally held that the aborigines could 'be attacked in war and so compelled to desist therefrom. In the case of sins which are against positive law', Victoria

[1] *Ibid.* [2] *Ibid.*

[3] Victoria has discussed the practice of anthropophagy further in his *Relectio De Temperantia*, and also in an unpublished and fragmentary manuscript which Father Beltrán de Heredia discovered, and which he believes is a portion of the above-mentioned *Relectio*. *Vide Anuario de la Asociación Francisco de Vitoria*, vol. ii (1929–30), article 'Ideas ... de Vitoria anteriores a las relecciones "de Indis" ... por el R. P. Fray Vicente Beltrán de Heredia', pp. 23 *et seq.* *Vide* also Getino, *op. cit.*, p. 142.

In dealing with this subject the late Ernest Nys says in his Introduction to the Carnegie Institution edition of Victoria's *De Indis et de Iure Belli Relectiones*, *op. cit.*, p. 41:

'Nous pouvons observer d'ailleurs que les reproches formulés contre les Indiens étaient fondés. Un passage de Bernal Diaz del Castillo, un des compagnons de Fernand Cortez dans son expédition du Mexique offre quelque éclaircissement. Diaz reproduit le langage tenu par son chef à des caciques qui implorent sa protection. Cortès, écrit-il, leur dit qu'ils devaient abandonner les idoles et ne plus leur sacrifier. "Il ajouta qu'ils devaient se rendre purs des vices honteux dont leurs jeunes hommes donnaient continuellement le scandale; que d'ailleurs on sacrifiait chaque jour sous nos yeux quatre et cinq Indiens dont on offrait les cœurs aux idoles, lançant le sang sur les murailles, coupant les jambes, les cuisses et les bras pour les manger comme viande qui sortirait de nos boucheries (je crois même qu'on les vendait en détail dans leurs marchés)." Il finit par leur promettre que "pourvu qu'ils abandonnassent leurs mauvaises habitudes et ces usages, non-seulement nous serions leurs alliés, mais nous ferions en sorte de les rendre seigneurs d'autres provinces." '

In a footnote Professor Nys cites as his authority the *Histoire véridique de la conquête de la Nouvelle-Espagne*, écrite par le capitaine Bernal Diaz del Castillo, l'un des conquistadores; traduction par D. Jourdanet (Paris, 1877), p. 121.

Quoting another author, Edward John Payne, in his *History of the New World Called America*, vol. I (Oxford, 1892), p. vii, Professor Nys continues:

'Un historien confirme ce qui a été dit au sujet du degré de civilisation des peuples du Nouveau Monde. "The Mexicans and Peruvians," écrit-il, "were barbarians: that is, while possessing a material basis sufficient to support a low degree of civilization, their habits of thought and life remained essentially savage. The Mexican warriors, the most advanced class found in America, were cannibals; in both Mexico and Peru regular human sacrifices formed an essential part of the scheme of life. Cannibalism was unknown in Peru, though it existed among the Indians of the forest districts to the eastward of the Andes (the *montaña*) and to the northward of Los Pastos, the northern limit of the Inca dominion: this may reasonably be ascribed to the fact that the Peruvians possessed large domesticated food-animals, which were wanting in Mexico. In most other respects the Peruvians were at a lower level than the Mexicans." "In Mexico," ajoute le même auteur, "there existed a rudimentary commerce.... Slavery, an important element in the earliest advancement, had come into existence.... In Peru, so far as appears, commerce was unknown ... nor was there any division of labour, except that between the warrior and the cultivator." '

continues, explaining these views, 'it cannot be clearly shown to the Indians that they are doing wrong'. But it is a different matter as regards sins of the aborigines against the law natural, for they can be 'shown' that by such acts 'they are offending God, and they may consequently be prevented from continuing to offend Him'. This, however, was not all: according to this doctrine the Indians could 'be compelled to keep the law which they profess. Now, this law is the law of nature'. Such was the view of no less a person than Innocent III whose word was as the law, and indeed became the law on many matters.[1] But Victoria's measured opinion is directly to the contrary. 'Christian princes cannot, even by the authorization of the Pope, restrain the Indians from sins against the laws of nature or punish them because of those sins.'[2] The reason for this follows from what he had previously said: that the Pope had no jurisdiction over the aborigines, for did not St. Thomas say, 'The prelates have received power over those only who have submitted themselves to the faith'?[3] To hold otherwise would be as much as to say, which Victoria refused to do, 'that the aborigines may be warred into subjection because of their unbelief, for they are all idolaters'.[4]

This, however, did not include all the sins against Nature, but, as the Pope could not engage in war against Christians 'on the ground of their being fornicators or thieves or, indeed, because they are sodomites', he could not for such reasons confiscate their land and give it to other princes, for, if this were done, 'there would be daily changes of kingdoms, seeing that there are many sinners in every realm'; and if confirmation on this point were needed it would be that 'these sins are more heinous in Christians, who are aware that they are sins, than in barbarians who have not that knowledge'. Assuredly Victoria was on firm ground when he more than intimated that 'it would be a strange thing that the Pope, who cannot make laws for unbelievers, can yet sit in judgement and visit punishment upon them'.[5]

But Victoria was not willing to dismiss the subject with this ex-

[1] Innocent III [Lotario de' Conti 1160–1216], one of the greatest popes of the Middle Ages, was the son of Count Trasimund of Segni, and nephew of Clement III. He obtained his early education at Rome, studied theology at Paris, and jurisprudence at Bologna. He was the author of various literary works, epistles, and decretals, and the historically important *Registrum Innocentii III super negotio imperii.* Perhaps the greatest—and certainly the best known—of his decretals is the famous *Venerabilem,* called forth by the imperial elections of 1198, and promulgated in May, 1202, in the Cathedral at Cologne. It defines the legal status of Papacy and Empire, and reforms the manner of imperial election. When Innocent ascended the papal throne, Philip Augustus of France and Richard of England were engaged in a cruel war. Innocent sent legates to each, and threatened them and their kingdoms with interdict—absolute separation from the rest of the Christian world—unless they declared peace or made a truce of five years within two months. Within the appointed time the two kings met, and the five years' truce was negotiated and agreed upon. The Christ Church controversy in England over the legality of the election of an archbishop of Canterbury resulted in the happy choice of Innocent's candidate—one Stephen Langton—in spite of King John's insistence upon the election of his candidate, John de Grey.

[2] *De Indis, infra,* Appendix A, p. xxxii.

[3] St. Thomas Aquinas, *Commentarii in Epist. ad Corinth.,* I, ch. v, lect. 3. *De Indis, infra,* Appendix A, p. xxxii.

[4] *De Indis, infra,* Appendix A, p. xxxii.

[5] *Ibid.*

pression of opinion on his part. He not only knew whereof he was speaking but also that he had 'a further and convincing proof' in support of his views. As the matter seemed so important to Victoria, and as there is perhaps no more closely reasoned argument in his dissertation on the Indians—assuredly not in the present section—it is only fair to the memory of that great man that the passage upon which he set such store should be quoted in its entirety. 'The aborigines in question', he says, 'are either bound to submit to the punishment awarded to the sins in question or they are not. If they are not bound, then the Pope cannot award such punishment. If they are bound, then they are bound to recognize the Pope as lord and lawgiver. Therefore, if they refuse such recognition, this in itself furnishes a ground for making war on them, which, however, the writers in question deny, as said above. And it would indeed be strange that the barbarians could with impunity deny the authority and jurisdiction of the Pope, and yet that they should be bound to submit to his award. Further, they who are not Christians cannot be subjected to the judgement of the Pope, for the Pope has no other right to condemn or punish them as a Vicar of Christ.[1] But the writers in question admit—both Innocent and Augustinus of Ancona, and the Archbishop and Sylvester, too—that they cannot be punished because they do not receive Christ. Therefore not because they do not receive the judgements of the Pope, for the latter presupposes the former.'[2]

It will be observed that the arguments for warring against the Indians are based upon the law of nature. Therefore it is of the essence that there should be no doubt as to the definition and the application of so serious a matter which would authorize punishment, war, conquest, and subjection. The importance of the law and its meaning were not lost upon Victoria who himself asks 'What is it that the writers in question call a profession of the law of nature?' Upon this as a text he comments, and his comment relieves the Indians from responsibility. 'If it is mere knowledge, they do not know it all; if it is a mere willingness to observe the law of nature, then the retort is that they are also willing to observe the whole divine law; for, if they knew that the law of Christ was divine, they would be willing to observe it. Therefore, they make no more a profession of the law of nature than they make of the law of Christ. Further, we certainly possess clearer proofs whereby to demonstrate that the law of Christ is from God and is true than to

[1] *Vide* St. Thomas Aquinas, *Summa Theologica, secunda secundae*, question 10, article 9, where he says with regard to communication between Christians and unbelievers that it cannot be forbidden by the Church as a method of punishing the latter 'who have not in any way received the Christian faith ... because she has not the right to exercise spiritual judgement over them, but only temporal judgement, in the case when, while dwelling among Christians, they are guilty of some misdemeanour, and are condemned by the faithful to some temporal punishment'. This whole question is extremely involved, and has been the subject of dispute in the schools throughout the centuries.

[2] *De Indis, infra*, Appendix A, p. xxxiii.

demonstrate that fornication is wrong or that other things which are also forbidden by natural law are to be shunned. Therefore, if the Indians can be compelled to observe the law of nature because it admits of proof, they can, therefore, be compelled to observe the Gospel law.'[1]

Victoria must have been sure of his system when he would not justify an attack upon the aborigines even to the extent of preventing them from committing what he considered the most revolting of crimes. A system which can stand this test could come only from a man of profound convictions, for loathsome as the offences are, they must have been especially loathsome to a churchman.[2]

The sixth title is that of 'voluntary choice'. If peoples of the Old World should be willing, and should actually wish, to unite themselves with the peoples of another country, they could do so; and, in the opinion of Victoria, the barbarians should have the same rights which the Europeans possessed. However, both the peoples of the New as well as the Old World should know what they are doing.[3] We of America—I may only speak of the United States—are familiar with the argument that the Europeans who came to North America did so in a spirit of brotherly, and indeed sisterly, kindness, and that they wished to extend to the natives the manifold rights and privileges of native-born English subjects of Her Majesty Queen Elizabeth, the Charles's, and the rest of the English line; and we equally know that the natives who believed in the fair promises of the early comers, did so to their sorrow. Human nature was very much the same in England as it was in Spain, the antagonist of the English-speaking world of that day.[4]

What was the inducement offered to the barbarians ('recently discovered' by one 'Columbus the Genoan') by Francisco de Vitoria's fellow-countrymen? 'On the arrival of the Spaniards we find them declaring to the aborigines how the King of Spain has sent them for their good and admonishing them to receive and accept him as lord and king'; and the aborigines—in the centre and south of America and in the Caribbean—replied, as did their unfortunate countrymen of the north, 'that they were content to do so'.[5] There was a text to validate the result of this transaction: 'There is nothing so natural'—according to Justinian's *Institutes*, II. i. 40—'as that the intent of an owner to

[1] *De Indis, infra,* Appendix A, p. xxxiii.

[2] Concerning the opinions of Victoria and others on this subject, *vide* the quotations given in Alfred Vanderpol's *Le Droit de Guerre d'après les Théologiens et les Canonistes du Moyen-âge, op. cit.*, pp. 161–4.

[3] *De Indis, infra,* Appendix A, p. xxxiii.

[4] According to Salvador de Madariaga, in his *Spain* (New York, 1930), p. 81: 'It is fair to say with an English historian [F. A. Kirkpatrick in the *Cambridge Modern History*, vol. x, p. 271] that "it may safely be alleged that so vast a region of savagery has never elsewhere been pacified with so much patience and so little violence, and that an immense indefensible frontier has never won comparative security at so little cost of life and treasure."'

[5] *De Indis, infra,* Appendix A, p. xxxiii.

transfer his property to another should have effect given to it.'[1] This was the text for the transaction, but to Victoria it was but a pretext. He points out the total absence of anything like real freedom in the so-called 'voluntary' choice of the Indians. To him, freedom implied a full knowledge of the cause, the circumstances, and the result of any action before the action had taken place; it implied also the power—independent of influence from without—to perform the action. Because of the absence of all these elements, Victoria finds himself forced to 'assert that this title, too, is insufficient'.

We have just had an example of the closeness of Victoria's reasoning in matters theological. We have in the comment which follows an example of Victoria the jurist. The two combined fitted him to be the incomparable protagonist of justice between nations as between individuals, and hence the founder of the only adequate system of international law which has ever been proposed. Therefore Victoria, the jurist, expresses his views without interruption, as did Victoria, the theologian: 'This appears, in the first place, because fear and ignorance, which vitiate every choice, ought to be absent. But they were markedly operative in the cases of choice and acceptance under consideration, for the Indians did not know what they were doing; nay, they may not have understood what the Spaniards were seeking. Further, we find the Spaniards seeking it in armed array from an unwarlike and timid crowd. Further, inasmuch as the aborigines, as said above, had real lords and princes, the populace could not procure new lords without other reasonable cause, this being to the hurt of their former lords. Further, on the other hand, these lords themselves could not appoint a new prince without the assent of the populace. Seeing, then, that in such cases of choice and acceptance as these there are not present all the requisite elements of a valid choice, the title under review is utterly inadequate and unlawful for seizing and retaining the provinces in question.'[2]

It would seem that Victoria's refutation of the alleged titles under which the Pope or the Spaniards might claim was more than sufficient to convert the open-minded; but he was after another class of opponents, those who claimed under a seventh and a final title, 'by special grant from God'. To those—and he passed them by curtly—who asserted the grant and insisted that the barbarians of the New World were to be given over hand and foot to the Spaniards, he exclaims that 'it would be hazardous', without miracles—and none were adduced—'to give credence to one who asserts a prophecy against the common law and against the rules of Scripture'. If the grant could be

[1] The exact words of the *Institutes* (*Krueger Recognovit. Berolini, Apud Weidmannos, MCMXI,* vol. i, p. 12, col. b) are as follows: nihil enim tam conveniens est naturali aequitati, quam voluntatem domini, volentis rem suam in alium transferre, ratam haberi.

[2] *De Indis, infra,* Appendix A, pp. xxxiii–xxxiv.

proved, it did not follow—and in behalf of his assertion he invoked the Old Testament—that those 'who wrought their ruin would be blameless'; and from the bottom of his Christian soul he cried, 'would that, apart from the sin of unbelief, there might be no greater sins in morals among certain Christians than there are among those barbarians!'[1]

'And so,' he concludes, standing as it were upon the threshold of the Temple of International Justice—of which, in the following section, he was to show himself the incomparable architect—'if there be no other titles than those which I have discussed', and he knew of no others,[2] 'it would certainly be of ill omen for the safety of our princes, or rather of those who are charged with the discovery of these matters; for princes follow advice given by others, being unable to examine into these matters for themselves.'

Victoria, in concluding this phase of his self-imposed task, rose, as our Milton would say,

> to the height of this great argument,

involving the question of all the ages: '"What is a man advantaged", so saith the Lord, "if he gain the whole world and lose himself, or be cast away?"'[3]

[1] *De Indis, infra*, Appendix A, p. xxxiv.

[2] *Ibid.*, p. xxxiv: 'I have seen nothing written on this question and have never been present at any discussion or council on this matter. Hence it may be that others may found a title and base the justice of this business and overlordship on some of the passages cited and not lack reason in so doing. I, however, have up to now been unable to form any other opinion than what I have written.'

[3] *Ibid.*, p. xxxiv. The Biblical quotation is from St. Matthew, xvi. 26; St. Mark, viii. 36; and St. Luke, ix. 25.

CHAPTER VI

ANALYSIS OF THE READING *ON THE INDIANS RECENTLY DISCOVERED*. SECTION III

THE sections already dealt with have an importance which would no doubt impress the casual reader, but their implications are as large as the world and cover the world. They not only state the questions which the readings were to discuss and to resolve but also the philosophical point of approach, the fundamental importance attached to knowledge and the means of acquiring knowledge, without which liability did not accrue (Victoria's phrases in this connexion are 'vincible' and 'invincible ignorance'), the rights which peoples grouped together (whether in empire, kingdom, or principality) for a material purpose possess of necessity, irrespective of geographical situation, and the interrelation of the spiritual and material conception of things—once, but no longer, coextensive with Christendom. In a word, we are confronted with the rights of nations, if we speak in terms of the law of nations, or the rights of peoples, if we speak in terms of humanity, which rights, consciously or unconsciously, Victoria was formulating.

We need only to turn again to a single sentence in Victoria's text, to see that equality of peoples and of States is the very life and soul of his scheme of international relations. 'Although, then, this title,' Victoria says, speaking of discovery, 'when conjoined with another'—such as occupation, for example—'can produce some effect . . . yet in and by itself it gives no support to a seizure of the aborigines any more than if it had been they who had discovered us' [1]—the 'us' being not merely Spain and France but the Christendom of that day.

It will be observed that the learned and innovating professor has from time to time referred to law in support of his contentions: natural law, divine law, and man-made law. The equality to which we have called special attention was apparently, in Victoria's mind, an inherent condition.[2] It was to be preserved in the international relations of peoples and of States, and it could only be preserved by law; and the law to preserve it was international law—to use the phrase of our day, but the 'law of nations' in the older terminology.

Therefore, having demonstrated the equal rights alike of their Catholic majesties and of the American princes within their respective

[1] *De Indis, infra*, Appendix A, p. xxv.

[2] The Roman Catholic theology, and the interpretation which it places upon the natural law, will not admit of predestination; consequently, in its eyes, all men are equal before God, having an equal opportunity for salvation. The Church will, on the other hand, admit that inequality may justifiably exist in other ways; for instance, the illiterate should be governed in the field of learning by the literate, and should be subject to them; the soldier should be subject to the officer, for the maintenance of order, and because the latter represents the State to the former; citizens should be subject to the head of the State, for the maintenance of order, because the ruler is chosen by the majority to act for them, or as in the case of monarchy, rules with their consent—tacitly given, or otherwise expressed.

dominions, Victoria passes at once to a consideration of that law which was to be the law of fundamental duties as well as of rights.

The fundamental conception of that law, which it is the glory of Victoria to have proclaimed, is 'that of natural society and fellowship'.[1] It is to be observed that Victoria had in mind not merely the individual but the individual in society; and that society involved an intimate relationship appears from his use of the word 'fellowship' in its immediate connexion.

We do not need to discuss whether society is natural or not. The great unquestionable—at least unquestioned—authority on this subject was Aristotle. As a matter of fact, man could not and cannot live in isolation if mankind is to survive. Nature had provided a society for the perpetuation of the species. But in point of fact, the natural society of man and woman was not enough, according to Aristotle, for their daily needs and for the protection of the society formed by their mere coexistence. The society was therefore to be preserved, and the conduct of the members not merely towards one another but towards the society resulting from that coexistence necessitated of itself a rule of conduct which was, in form and effect, a social rule, and, because it applied equally to every member of the entire society, it was a rule of law instead of a social privilege.

This state of things seemed to Victoria to be so general, so common, and so fundamental as to be natural: hence it was that he spoke of natural society and natural fellowship. For our purposes it is therefore sufficient to say that we are not dealing with the abstract question —if such there be—but with human beings in society; and that the rule of conduct in such a case should be that which is consistent with the nature and dignity not alone of human beings, as such, but of human beings in a state of society, and which changes to meet changed conditions and the needs of a progressive civilization.

It is, however, a fact (to which Victoria does not here advert, although his discussion of it elsewhere may be considered as his greatest contribution to the modern law of nations) that no society consisting of any one group of individuals is sufficient unto itself; that is to say, however separate and distinct the societies or groups may be, and however much they may prefer to exist in isolation as regards other societies, their mere existence, whether in the Iberian Peninsula or in the New World 'recently discovered', forms the international community, whether we consider it as made up of the groups which we call States or of the individuals whom we call humanity. Slowly and painfully and by cruel experience, we of to-day are beginning to see with

[1] *De Indis, infra*, Appendix A, p. xxxvi. Of this conception proclaimed by Victoria, Professor Ernest Nys says: 'François de Vitoria est peut-être le premier des internationalistes qui ait exposé cette thèse.' *Vide* Nys's masterly essay 'Les Publicistes Espagnols du XVIe Siècle et les Droits des Indiens,' published in the *Revue de Droit International et de Législation Comparée*, tome xxi (1889), p. 559.

our own eyes what Victoria, centuries ago, because of the discovery of America, both felt and proclaimed.

Here, however, it was not necessary for him to dwell upon the matter for he had already given full expression to his thought in his Reading *De Potestate Civili.*[1]

What he had in mind in the present Reading was a series of duties and the law which was to render those duties effective, with the consequences attendant on the violation of that law. In a sentence he gave expression to the very essence of the matter: 'The Spaniards have a right to travel into the lands in question and to sojourn there, provided they do no harm to the natives, and the natives may not prevent them.'[2] Of these three phrases each is important in itself; but all three are necessary for the rule of social conduct, that is to say, the rule of the international community, or, in plain words, of international law, which he wished to lay down. Let us dwell somewhat on this sentence which is so fundamental to his system of law. It is to be observed in the first of the three phrases that the Spaniards are possessed of a right. In the second and third phrases it becomes clear that that right involves duties not merely on the part of those in relation to whom the right is to be exercised but on the part of the beneficiaries of the right. Let us state the right separately, so that there may be no doubt about its nature and extent. It is 'a right to travel into the lands' of the Americans and there to sojourn. What are the duties? It being the right of the Spaniards to travel and to sojourn there, it is the duty of the natives to permit the exercise of that right or, as stated in a negative way, not to 'prevent them'. But in Victoria's view right and duty are not merely correlative in the sense that the one pertains to the first party and the other to the second party; they are correlative in the further sense that right and duty are present in the same party. Therefore a duty arises in respect to the beneficiary, or rather beneficiaries—for the rule, as is necessary in law, is universal—that 'they do no harm to the natives'.

However, this sentence of Victoria's, which is as the law and the prophets, required to be proved, and the proof was at hand; it was none other than the law of nations. There were, as it will appear, several proofs, but the first was doubtless the most important to him, and it assuredly is to us. But his language here must not be paraphrased. 'Proof of this may in the first place be derived from the law of nations (*jus gentium*), which either is natural law or is derived from natural law. "What natural reason has established among all nations is called the *jus gentium*."'[3] This sentence, like the one already quoted, is made up of various parts and each part is essential to form the whole.

[1] For a discussion of this *Relectio, vide infra*, p. 253. For a translation of the text, *vide infra*, Appendix C, p. lxxi.

[2] *De Indis, infra*, Appendix A, p. xxxvi.

[3] *Ibid.* Victoria is here quoting *Institutes*, I. ii. I (*Inst., De Iure Naturali*, I. *Ius autem*), but he adapts the passage to his purpose by substituting *inter omnes gentes* for the *inter omnes homines* of the *Institutes*.

The phrase, *jus gentium*, may be Englished as the law of peoples, and these peoples, taken together, form humanity as made up of all peoples. It is a law for each and for all—not merely of each individual and of all individuals but of each State, which is but a group of people, and of all the States forming the international community of States, which is synonymous, and indeed identical, with humanity. '*Jus gentium*' therefore appears to be used in the double sense of law for people and for States: the law of humanity on the one hand and, on the other, the law of each and every fraction of humanity as expressed in the term 'nation' or 'nations'.

Now Victoria had made a specialty of this *jus gentium*, of which the incontrovertible proof is the Reading under consideration. Into this conception at least two elements entered: one, natural law—of which volumes have been written; the other, a derivation from natural law, which appears to mean the law of nature in action.

Perhaps the American reader would not be averse to a phrase from the Declaration of Independence, which is a classic statement of the Victorian law for human beings—'life, liberty and the pursuit of happiness'. Of course he did not have before him the authority of Jefferson, but he did have an authority which he would have considered equally good, if not better—that of Justinian, whom we have just quoted to the effect that 'What natural reason has established among all nations is called the *jus gentium*'. In other words, reason is the ultimate source of the law of nations of both the Roman and the Spaniard. While definitions are dangerous, nevertheless it may properly be said that the 'reason' that Victoria had in mind was that form or quality which was natural to man as distinct from the animal creation.

Reserving for later consideration this phase of the matter—which goes to the essence, be it said in passing, of the law governing human relations—we need but say that natural reason, governing peoples as it governed individuals within the group, is the source of the law between and among nations, that is, international law, in the sense in which we of to-day use the term. That Victoria had in mind, not the ancient *jus gentium* (identical in fact if not in name with conflict of laws), but rather the law both of the individuals composing humanity and of the individuals socially organized in States, is evident from the fact that the purpose of the observation which he has made is to state the law and its content and to apply it to the very matter in hand. 'For', he says, 'congruently herewith, it is reckoned among all nations' —the Latin text being *apud omnes nationes*—'inhumane to treat visitors and foreigners badly without some special cause'—which he

Vide Professor Ernest Nys in his Introduction to the Carnegie Institution edition of Victoria's *De Indis et de Ivre Belli Relectiones, op. cit.*, pp. 42–3. *Vide* also J. Barthélemy in *Les Fondateurs du Droit International* (Paris, 1904), p. 7; Herbert Francis Wright, *Francisci de Victoria, De Iure Belli Relectio* (Washington, 1916), pp. 15–16; and the statement by the distinguished Cuban statesman, publicist, and judge of the Permanent Court of International Justice, Antonio Sanchez de Bustamante y Sirvén, in his *Derecho Internacional Publico* (Habana, 1933), p. 21.

had expressed as harm done to the natives—'while, on the other hand, it is humane and correct to treat visitors well.'[1]

His definition of international law, its nature, its origin, and its application, should not be looked upon as pedantry on the part of the Spaniard; it goes to the genesis of our modern international law, for the first proof of this first title of the third section of the Reading under consideration was regarded by no less a person than Grotius as a primal axiom of the law of nations, and the second of Victoria's proofs was, as expressly stated by Grotius, the foundation of his tractate on the *Freedom of the Seas*,[2] which is regarded by not a few as his greatest contribution to international law. Indeed it need only be said in passing that this entire section (Titles 1–7) is the source of that international law which Grotius set forth in his commentary on the *Law of Prize*, and elaborated in his large treatise upon which his reputation as an international lawyer rests.

Victoria accepted as a further proof the tradition of natural law that, property having been originally held in common, everybody was 'from the beginning' free to travel and to settle 'wheresoever he would'. And he maintained that the right and the permission were not lost by the subsequent division of property and that it would have been inhumane to deprive Noah's descendants of travelling and settling and thus creating the modern peoples and States.[3]

A further proof is in the form of a syllogism, compressed within the narrowest possible limits: 'Everything is lawful which is not prohibited or which is not injurious or hurtful to others in some other way.' This is the major premise. 'But (so we suppose) the travel of the Spaniards does no injury or harm to the natives.' This is the minor premise. The conclusion inevitably follows: 'Therefore it is lawful.'[4] Short as is this statement, it is to be observed that setting forth the right, it also makes it dependent upon the duty of exercising the right without prejudice. The right to travel and sojourn is, however, universal, as is revealed in his next proof. If, to use his favourite example, the French and the Spaniards possessed this right as consistent with the nature and dignity of the human being, then the Americans must respect their right. In other words, a right valid in the Old World was equally valid in the New World so recently discovered; and the corresponding duty was likewise applicable to the peoples of both worlds.

[1] *De Indis, infra*, Appendix A, p. xxxvi. On Victoria's conception of the *jus gentium*, *vide* Professor Ernest Nys, *Le Droit International, op. cit.*, tome i, p. 56, and especially note 1.

[2] Grotius, *The Freedom of the Seas*; translated by Ralph Van Deman Magoffin, published by the Carnegie Endowment for International Peace (New York, 1916), ch. i, p. 7: 'I shall base my argument on the following most specific and unimpeachable axiom of the Law of Nations, called a primary rule or first principle, the spirit of which is self-evident and immutable, to wit: Every nation is free to travel to every other nation, and to trade with it' (Fundamentum struemus hanc iuris gentium, quod primarium vocant regulam certissimam, cuius perspicua atque immutabilis est ratio; licere cuivis genti quamvis alteram adire, cumque ea negotiari). *Vide* also Grotius's reference on page 9 to *De Indis* II [III], notes 1–7.

[3] *De Indis, infra*, Appendix A, p. xxxvi.

[4] *Ibid.*

Equality, with Victoria, is a matter of right, not of privilege; and, as this proof goes to the very root of the system, it is stated in Victoria's own words, showing how the syllogism and analogy of the schoolmen could be employed to frame our modern law and even the law of the future: 'It would not be lawful for the French to prevent the Spanish from travelling or even from living in France, or vice versa, provided this in no way enured to their hurt and the visitors did no injury. Therefore it is not lawful for the Indians.'[1]

In these two syllogisms right and duty are established as correlative, or rather as different phases of one and the same thing. Why does not the community possess the right, should it so desire, to withdraw permission for the stranger to remain within its jurisdiction? Because this would be banishment and banishment is a capital form of punishment for a crime, and, no crime having been committed, the expulsion would be without the sanction of law or justice. It is, however, more than that. To look upon the foreigner as a 'barbarian', and therefore an enemy, and to refuse admittance to him, as well as to order his expulsion, could be viewed as acts of war. The application of this to the matter in hand is inevitable, that, 'as the Indians are not making a just war on the Spaniards'—again upon the assumption that the Spaniards are doing no harm—'it is not lawful for them to keep the Spaniards away from their territory'. Natural law, the law of nations, the reason of the thing, the advisability of travelling and the necessity of living somewhere—all establish the right and the duty, primitive and modern, which Victoria had in mind; but, as he was a humanist, he invoked Virgil, who was the patron saint of the humanists just as Aristotle was their pagan philosopher:

> Quod genus hoc hominum? quaeve hunc tam barbara morem
> Permittit patria? hospitio prohibemur arenae.[2]

We come now to a second series of proofs, culminating (with apologies to the late President Wilson) in what might be called Victoria's fourteenth point. In this section we have Victoria at his best—the theologian and the jurist, the philosopher and the moralist. First Ecclesiasticus is invoked: 'Every animal loveth its kind',[3] the conclusion from which will be obvious to the reader.

Next St. Matthew appears upon the scene: 'I was a stranger and ye took me not in'[4]—invoked by Victoria in order to show that such an action is not in accordance with natural law.

So much for the moralist.

Next for the jurist; and what authority could be more convincing than the *Institutes* of Justinian? 'By natural law running water and

[1] *De Indis, infra,* Appendix A, p. xxxvi.

[2] 'What race of men is this? or what country is barbarous enough to allow this usage? We are driven off from the hospitality of its shore.' *Aeneid,* Book I, lines 539–40.

[3] *De Indis, infra,* Appendix A, p. xxxvii. Victoria (edition of 1696) cites *Ecclesiasticus,* chap. xvii; according to the Vulgate, the citation should be Ecclesiasticus, xiii. 19.

[4] St. Matthew, xxv. 43.

the sea are common to all, so are rivers and harbours, and by the law of nations ships from all parts may be moored there';[1] that is to say, in the words of Victoria, 'they are public things', and 'therefore it is not lawful to keep any one from them', with the inevitable conclusion that 'the aborigines would be doing a wrong to the Spaniards, if they were to keep them from their territories'.[2]

It is permissible perhaps to break the thread of Victoria's argument to remark that if we do not recognize these absolutely as natural rights, we recognize them indirectly through treaty provisions.

Recurring to Victoria and to his further statement that the aborigines in question admitted 'all other barbarians', we find his conclusion follows naturally that it would therefore be wrong to exclude the Spaniards, who should at least be treated upon a plane of equality with the 'other barbarians'.[3]

In the next two proofs Victoria continues in the role of jurist, stating that 'if it were not lawful for the Spaniards to travel among them', and to sojourn, 'this would be either by natural law or by divine law or by human law'; but it was 'certainly lawful', he maintained, 'by natural and by divine law', and, if there were human law existing which 'took away rights conferred by natural and divine law', it would be, in his opinion, 'inhumane and unreasonable and consequently would not have the force of law',[4] because it would be inconsistent with the nature and dignity of the human being, Spaniard or barbarian.

A further, and the last link but one in the series of proofs, is logical to a fault: 'Either the Spaniards are subjects of the Indians or they are not.'[5] If they are not, they would enter by natural right; if subjects, then the Indians should treat their subjects well—at least as well as would the Spaniards, it may be added.

In a syllogism which of itself would for ever justify scholasticism, Victoria's fourteenth and final proof discloses the Spaniard not merely in the fourfold role of theologian and jurist, philosopher and moralist, but as the perfected type of humanitarian in which the four qualities are merged in their fullness: 'The Spaniards are the neighbours of the barbarians, as appears from the Gospel parable of the Samaritan.[6] But they are bound to love their neighbours as themselves.[7] Therefore they may not keep them away from their country without cause: "When it is said 'Love thy neighbour', it is clear that every man is our neighbour" (St. Augustine's *De doctrina Christiana*).'

[1] *Institutes*, II. . I (On the Division o Property—*De Rerum Divisione*): 'Et quidem naturali iure communia sunt omnium haec: aer at aqua profluens et mare et per hoc litora maris. nemo igitur ad litus maris accedere prohibetur, dum tamen villis et monumentis et aedificiis abstineat ,quia non sunt iuris gentium, sicut et mare. . . . (2) Flumina autem omnia et portus publica sunt: . . . (4) Riparum quoque usus publicus est iuris gentium, sicut ipsius fluminis: itaque navem ad eas appellere, funes ex arboribus ibi natis religare, onus aliquid in his reponere cuilibet liberum est, sicuti per ipsum flumen navigare.'

[2] *De Indis, infra*, Appendix A, p. xxxvii.

[3] *Ibid.* [4] *Ibid.* [5] *Ibid.* [6] St. Luke, x. 29–37. [7] St. Matthew, xxii. 39

So much for what may be called the natural and the inherent right of the human being to travel and to choose his place of sojourn. But if that were all, he might starve. Having entered a foreign country, he must be granted the right to carry on his legitimate business and should be treated in other respects as the native, provided, of course, he commits no wrong. Thus—to consider the Spaniard as representing the foreigner in general—he 'may lawfully carry on trade', he may import 'wares which the natives lack', and indeed export what we are bound to say the Spanish travellers, in common with travellers and sojourners the world over, had a weakness for—'either gold or silver or other wares of which the natives have abundance'.[1] Here as in previous passages the right and the duty are correlative and reciprocal. The barbarian is not to forbid the Spaniard so to trade, nor 'may the princes of Spain prevent commerce with the natives'.

The proof of this? The first proposition, with its 'fourteen points', Victoria has just set forth. In the present instance, he reinforces the matter by again invoking the *jus gentium*—meaning international law—together with divine law and natural law.[2] This was the threefold law; but there was still a higher law—a category by itself: 'Thou shalt not do to another what thou wouldest not wish done to thyself'; and in the fifth and last of the proofs of his second proposition Victoria sums up the matter from the standpoint of the Christian and the jurist and clinches his argument, as it were, with the authority of the poet. 'The aborigines', he declares, 'can no more keep off the Spaniards from trade than Christians can keep off other Christians.'[3] This is true, but it is general; it is equality of right irrespective of religion. But Victoria is dealing with a particular situation; hence he brings into the picture his stock examples, Spain and France. 'It is clear', he says, 'that if the Spaniards kept off the French from trade with the Spaniards, and this not for the good of Spain, but in order to prevent the French from sharing in some advantage, that practice would offend against righteousness and charity.'[4]

So much for his countrymen and their neighbours, in the matter of righteousness and charity.

It is now the turn of the jurist. 'If, then,' he insists, 'there can be no just legal ordinance to this effect, it also cannot be accomplished in actual fact.' Pausing for a moment to remind us parenthetically of what we too often forget, that 'the injustice of a law consists solely in the execution of the law', since a law not unjust in itself may become so because of its execution, he continues with a quotation from the *Digest*, and a better one for the point in hand would have been hard to find: 'Nature has established a bond of relationship between all men.'[5]

[1] *De Indis, infra,* Appendix A, p. xxxvii. [2] *Ibid.*, pp. xxxvii–xxxviii. [3] *Ibid.*, p. xxxviii.
[4] *Ibid.* [5] *Digest,* I. i. 3: '. . . et cum inter nos cognationem quandam natura constituit, . . .'

Wherefore, in Victoria's language, 'it is contrary to natural law for one man to disassociate himself from another without good reason'.[1] Why should this be so? Is not the inevitable answer that of Ovid, if a poet may be invoked in a legal matter: 'Non enim homini homo lupus est, sed homo.'[2]

The third proposition is that of the lawyer, or rather that of the first international lawyer of our time dealing consciously with the law of nations, and with that phase of it known in our modern parlance as the 'favoured nation' clause. It is thus stated: 'If there are among the Indians any things which are treated as common both to citizens and to strangers, the Indians may not prevent the Spaniards from a communication and participation in them.'[3]

The extent to which Victoria was a master of the principles which, set forth by him, have entered into and made the law of nations, cannot be better shown than by the proof in behalf of the proposition which he has stated: 'If, for example, other foreigners are allowed to dig for gold in the land of the community or in rivers, or to fish for pearls in the sea or in a river, the natives cannot prevent the Spaniards from doing this, but they have the same right to do it as others have, so long as the citizens and indigenous population are not hurt thereby.'

Hence, in accordance with his first and second propositions—showing how closely knitted is the argument, an argument as inexorable in its implications as in its conclusions—he stated that 'if the Spaniards may travel and trade among' the aborigines, they may, of a consequence, invoke the 'laws' and enjoy all 'advantages' possessed by any and all foreigners.[4]

From his illustrations of digging for gold and fishing for pearls Victoria drew a definition and statement of the law of nations in terms as acceptable to-day as when he framed them, and it is not surprising, therefore, that they are to be found in effect if not in so many words in the memorable three books *On the Law of War and of Peace*, the masterpiece of Grotius, who was destined to be the most illustrious member of the Spanish school. Victoria considered that a general right to dig for gold and to fish for pearls had not been acquired by and vested in any particular individual. Neither the gold-bearing land nor the fishing-ground was subject to occupation for the purpose in hand to become the exclusive property of the first occupant, as might be the case with ordinary unoccupied lands. The right to the gold and the pearls in question vests in the first occupant thereof—that is, the first person who found them—according to the law of nations, as stated in a passage from the *Institutes* (II. i. 12), which had already been quoted only to be rejected in the case of the great discovery by Columbus.[5]

[1] *De Indis, infra*, Appendix A, p. xxxviii.
[2] 'For a man is not a wolf to his fellow man, but a man.'
[3] *De Indis, infra*, Appendix A, p. xxxviii.
[4] *Ibid.*
[5] *Vide supra*, p. 125, and footnote 6.

'There are many things in this connection', Victoria says, 'which issue from the law of nations.' But what is this law of nations? The description very properly precedes the definition: 'It has a sufficient derivation from natural law'; it 'is clearly capable of conferring rights'; it possesses the power of imposing (Victoria says 'creating') obligations; although there are some things which find their origin in natural law—a statement which necessarily implies that the contrary is also true, namely, that there are rights created and obligations imposed in the law of nations which are not derived from natural law. Whence do they come? Victoria's answer is a pregnant phrase or two which describes and defines our modern international law: 'A consensus of the greater part of the whole world, especially in behalf of the common good of all.'[1] Francisco de Vitoria was apparently a believer in the fundamentalness of 'the pursuit of happiness' before the phrase had been coined and minted from American gold.[2]

Clear as is the statement, unmistakable as are the nature and the import of the definition, Victoria, perhaps unaware of the epoch-making nature of his words and of the science which they were to found, was not willing to have the definition rest upon a supposition. It was the law of nations—not of a nation; and it was the law which the international community itself imposed upon mankind, although there might be those who would dissent from it. In the illustration with which he follows the statement and the definition, he embraces the entire world, both as to time and extent, applying it to the original creation and to the people of the world descended from Noah. If there is any occasion upon which the exact language of Victoria should be quoted, with the original text in a footnote, it is here: 'For if after the early days of the creation of the world or its recovery from the flood the majority of mankind decided that ambassadors should everywhere be reckoned inviolable and that the sea should be common and that prisoners of war should be made slaves'—instead of being put to death, as in primitive times—'and if this, namely, that strangers should not be driven out, were deemed a desirable principle, it would certainly have the force of law, even though the rest of mankind objected thereto.'[3]

Having stated and defined international law, Victoria proceeds, in the fourth proposition, to state who are the objects, the subjects, and the beneficiaries of international law. Throughout the present

[1] *De Indis, infra,* Appendix A, p. xxxviii.

[2] *Vide* the American 'Declaration of Independence' which states the philosophical propositions—'truths self-evident'—that 'all men are created equal'; that 'they are endowed by their Creator with certain unalienable rights, that among these are Life, Liberty, and the Pursuit of Happiness....'

[3] *De Indis, infra,* Appendix A, p. xxxviii. The Latin of this passage is: 'Si enim post prima tempora creati orbis, aut reparati post diluvium, major pars hominum constituerit, ut legati ubique essent inviolabiles, ut mare esset commune, ut bello capti essent servi, & hoc ita expediret ut hospites non exigerentur: certè hoc haberet vim, etiam aliis repugnantibus.' Quoted from the facsimile of the edition of 1696, page 391, in Victoria, *De Indis et De Ivre Belli Relectiones*... Carnegie Institution edition.

title, and indeed throughout the entire disquisition, he has been speaking of natives and of foreigners, and of their respective rights and duties, which in his opinion were the same in both Europe and the Americas. What does he mean by 'natives', and by what means, if any, may foreigners acquire the status of natives—that is, become citizens of another country, or, to use the technical expression, nationals by naturalization? The passage in which this matter is discussed is of peculiar interest to us of the United States, stating as it does, in unmistakable terms, a principle of law which was some centuries later to find its classic expression in an amendment to the Constitution of the United States, giving a definite form and content to the term 'citizens' and to their rights—matters which had greatly troubled the good people of the United States, and the settlement of which was destined to come through a civil war. The amendment in question was the fourteenth,[1] to the effect that all persons born or naturalized in the United States and subject to their jurisdiction are citizens of the United States and of the State in which they reside. Victoria's conception, the same in substance, was, as is to be expected, different in form: 'If children of any Spaniard be born there'—meaning in the land of the barbarians—'and they wish to acquire citizenship, it seems they cannot be barred either from citizenship or from the advantages enjoyed by other citizens.'[2] Upon this he places a limitation which is not to be found in the amendment to the Constitution of the United States: that the prospective citizens were to be children of foreigners having their domicile in the American principalities—not merely children who might happen to be born in transit.[3] What is the proof of this doctrine? It is none other than the law of nations which he had stated and defined in the third of his propositions; to quote his exact language, 'by the rule of the law of nations, . . . he is to be called and is a citizen who is born within the State'. This was not merely the opinion of Victoria as *prima* professor of theology at the University of Salamanca; it was the doctrine of Justinian's *Code*.[4]

[1] 'Article XIV, Section I. All persons born or naturalized in the United States, and subject to the jurisdiction thereof, are citizens of the United States and of the State wherein they reside. No State shall make or enforce any law which shall abridge the privileges or immunities of citizens of the United States; nor shall any State deprive any person of life, liberty, or property, without due process of law; nor deny to any person within its jurisdiction the equal protection of the laws.' [Proclaimed as a duly ratified Article (Amendment) to the Constitution of the United States on July 28th, 1868.]

[2] *De Indis, infra*, Appendix A, p. xxxix.

[3] *Ibid.*, pp. xxxix. For the Latin text *vide* Victoria: *De Indis et de Ivre Belli Relectiones*... Carnegie Institution edition, p. 391: 'Immo si ex aliquo Hispano nascantur ibi liberi et velint esse cives, non videtur quod possint prohiberi vel a civitate vel a commodis aliorum civium—dico ex parentibus habentibus illic domicilium.'

[4] In the Latin text this citation appears as follows: 1. *cives ff.*, De appellationibus. This should be a reference to the *Code* rather than to the *Digest*; at the former place (*Code*, VII. lxii. 11) in the Kreuger edition, a footnote tells us that 'Herrmann iungit 10, 40, 7' which is apparently the passage Victoria intended to cite. It reads as follows: 'Cives quidem origo manumissio adlectio adoptio, incolas vero, sicut et divus Hadrianus edicto suo manifestissime declaravit, domicilium facit. Et in eodem loco singulos habere domicilium non ambigitur, ubi quis larem rerumque ac fortunarum suarum summam

To Victoria the matter seemed simple, as great truths generally are. Man being 'a civil animal', it followed as a matter of course that whoever was born 'in any one State' was not to be considered as 'a citizen of another State'.[1] The child was to have a nationality; he was not to be stateless; and it was to be a single, not a double, nationality. In this simple way Victoria evaded two of the greatest problems of modern international jurisprudence. The principle here is as a corollary of the doctrine which he had laid down, apparently so simple as not to require the threefold statement of the syllogism. This being the case it appeared sufficient to him, as it does to us, to state merely the conclusion: 'Therefore, if he were not a citizen of the State referred to'—meaning the State in which the child was born—'he would not be a citizen of any State', that is to say, he would be a stateless person, a condition of affairs which would be 'to the prejudice of his rights under both natural law and the law of nations'.[2] There is no doubt about it. Citizenship by birth was a right under the twofold authority of the law natural and the law of nations. Without conscious intention, perhaps, on the part of its author, but none the less surely, the doctrine of Victoria—which was doubtless unknown to its beneficiaries by its name in the language of international law, the *jus soli*—has endowed each and every person born within any American Republic, and subject to its jurisdiction, with a separate and distinct nationality by the mere fact of birth within the republic.[3]

So much for citizenship by birth.

But what of naturalization? 'If there be any persons', Victoria says, 'who wish to acquire a domicile in some state of the Indians, as by marriage or in virtue of any other fact whereby other foreigners are wont to become citizens, they cannot be impeded any more than others, and consequently they enjoy the privileges of citizens just as others do, provided they also submit to the burdens to which others submit.'[4]

Under this doctrine, the children of foreigners would become citizens by birth; foreigners themselves would become naturalized citizens upon a footing of equality with any and all other foreigners, upon compliance with the laws which, in the American principalities

constituit, unde rursus non sit discessurus, si nihil avocet, unde cum profectus est, peregrinari videtur, quo si rediit, peregrinari iam destitit.'

[1] *De Indis, infra*, Appendix A, p. xxxix. [2] *Ibid.*

[3] 'Probatur, quia hoc videtur esse de jure gentium, ut civis dicatur et sit, qui natus est in civitate (*ff.*, De appellationibus, 1. *cives*).' [*Vide supra*, footnote 4 on page 147.] 'Et confirmatur, quia, cum homo sit animal civile, talis natus in una civitate non est civis alterius civitatis. Si ergo non esset civis illius, non esset civis alicuius civitatis, per quod impediretur a iure naturali et gentium.' (Victoria, *De Indis et de Ivre Belli Relectiones* . . . Carnegie Institution edition, p. 391.)

[4] *De Indis, infra*, Appendix A, p. xxxix. The Latin text is as follows (Victoria, *op. cit.*, p. 392): 'Immo si qui vellent accipere domicilium in aliqua civitate illorum, ut accipiendo uxorem vel alia ratione, qua alii peregrini solent fieri cives, non videtur quod possint prohiberi plus quam alii, et per consequens gaudere privilegiis civium sicut alii, modo etiam subeant onera aliorum.'

in question, would confer nationality. We are here in the presence of the most important 'favoured nation' clause, and there was not to be—and indeed there should not be—any discrimination in the laws of the States in the mind of Victoria, whose language expressly excludes it. And finally, because the principle is so fundamental, it is worth repeating that here, as elsewhere, we have right and duty correlative, for the rights of citizenship depend upon the performance of its duties.

The law of Victoria is a perfect law—as perfect, at any rate, as any human law can be which is designed for the welfare and happiness of an imperfect world. It eliminates from citizenship by birth the children of transients. It endows each and every other person born within the territory with a single nationality, that of the principality in which the birth takes place; and it expressly excludes from such nationality children of its nationals born abroad, thus avoiding, as it were, both the Scylla of statelessness and the Charybdis of dual nationality. There is no room here for the trouble-breeding term *jus sanguinis*. Victoria's first word is the last word, and it is not too much to hope that nationality may yet be determined by a single and impersonal standard.

Admitting that there is such a thing as international law and that it confers rights and imposes reciprocal duties; and that the right under discussion is that of the foreigners to travel to, and to settle in, any State, to become its subjects by naturalization—or, in the case of their children, by birth—and to engage in industry and commerce upon a footing at least of the most 'favoured nation', what is the consequence of the violation of the right? In the first place, it is evident that the right must be used with moderation, in such a way as not to prejudice the State or the community against which the right is exercised. But if it is so exercised, what is the recourse, in the Victorian conception, against the State, community, or persons violating the right? The application of international law is as important as its existence. In such a case the foreigners—that is, the Spaniards—should 'use reason and persuasion . . . , according to the saying, "It behoveth the prudent to make trial of everything by words first".'[1] But if fair words be of no avail, and the barbarians themselves 'propose to use force'? The right of self-defence comes into play, provided, however, that, in accordance with Victoria's supposition, the conduct of the Spaniards is right and proper. We are here on the threshold of war in the international sense. However, Victoria allows but a step at a time. Even under the provocations he has described, he would have the foreigners or Spaniards make war only 'on the authorization of their sovereign'.[2]

It is to be observed in passing that in international as well as in

[1] Victoria, *op. cit.*, p. 392: 'omnia sapientes prius experiri decet.' Terence (*The Eunuch*, line 789, *or* Act IV, scene vii, line 19) has: '. . . omnia prius experiri quam armis sapientem decet.'

[2] *De Indis, infra*, Appendix A, p. xxxix.

private law, no authorization is required to resort to self-defence and it is not to be considered as war; but as war is a matter of grave consequence, involving the State as such as well as its citizens or subjects, it is a sovereign matter and it can only be declared or carried on legitimately by authorization of the sovereign power. The location of this power may differ in different countries and in different systems of government, but its intervention is essential to war as distinct from the use of forcible means employed by private persons to redress an injury. Unlike Grotius, who accepted the theory of private war—which, if permitted, would either plunge the community into anarchy or would increase the anarchy if it already existed—Victoria held no brief for private war—indeed he held no brief even for his country.[1]

As we shall also see later, the cause or causes of war should be just, but for Victoria's present purpose a syllogism, with a reference to St. Thomas, suffices: 'Warding-off and avenging a wrong', he declares, following St. Thomas, 'make a good cause of war. . . .[2] But when the Indians deny the Spaniards their rights under the law of nations they do them a wrong. Therefore, if it be necessary, in order to preserve their right, that they should go to war, they may lawfully do so.'[3] Thus the remedy for the violation of the right owes its existence to the law of nations; indeed, without the law of nations, there would be no right to travel and to sojourn, no nationality by birth or naturalization, and no redress by force if reason and persuasion had failed. Victoria was a man of system; his system is the law of nations; and the law of nations is here in action.

But Victoria was not merely a man of law. The heart counted as much as the head, and he tempered justice with mercy. The barbarians were, in the view of the Spaniards, a poor folk; they were an ignorant and stupid, a timid and fearful folk. These things were, in his opinion and in that of his countrymen, facts, and in the assertion of right they were to be borne in mind. To the legally minded, a right is a right and a remedy is a remedy. The powerful plaintiff may sue and dispossess the powerless defendant in the law court, but the moralist has a different standard: the court of conscience. And what the court of conscience meant to Victoria, as well as the way in which his international law was to be enforced, is immediately set forth in a passage which does infinite honour to the man and the system which he was propounding. His contribution to humanity is as great as his contribution to law. This is what he says: 'It is, however, to be noted that the natives being timid by nature and in other respects dull and stupid, however much

[1] Getino (*op. cit.*, p. 168) observes that: 'Vitoria tratando temas que a los españoles afectaban singularmente, eleva la discusión y la reduce a principios que pueden aplicarse a todas las naciones y gentes. Sus puntos de vista sirven para dar luz en las discusiones habidas en España a cuenta de la colonización americana; pero no se identifican con ellos.'

[2] *Secunda Secundae*, question 40.

[3] *De Indis, infra* Appendix A, p. xxxix.

the Spaniards may desire to remove their fears and reassure them with regard to peaceful dealings with each other, they may very excusably continue afraid at the sight of men strange in garb and armed and much more powerful than themselves.' Therefore, if the Indians should 'unite their efforts to drive out the Spaniards or even to slay them, the Spaniards might, indeed, defend themselves, but within the limits of permissible self-protection'.[1] It would be wrong for them, however, 'to enforce against the natives any of the other rights of war (as, for instance, after winning the victory and obtaining safety, to slay them or despoil them of their goods or seize their cities)'. Why? Because according to Victoria's hypothesis 'the natives are innocent and are justified in feeling afraid'. And the conclusion sums up the whole matter in a single sentence: 'Accordingly, the Spaniards ought to defend themselves, but so far as possible with the least damage to the natives, the war being a purely defensive one.'[2]

War is for the redress of injury, for the protection of rights, not for conquest. This is the war of St. Augustine, of whom later.[3] In the meantime, however, we may say that we are in the presence of the law of nations dealing with peace and with war, each under the control of a sound and secular morality, and the passage which has just been quoted is in itself a demonstration of Victoria's theory that the jurist alone was not competent to discuss questions with a moral implication.

Implicit in this passage is the question whether the war can be just on both sides; for, if the Spaniards, although they are in the right, comport themselves as superior beings, the war which the simple-minded may wage against them may be just because of their belief in the injustice of the Spaniards; for does not Victoria say that 'the natives are innocent and are justified in feeling afraid'?[4] This question goes to the essence of the whole matter, inasmuch as war is not a right in itself but a means of enforcing a right, and if the right be absent, the remedy should be non-existent. Therefore Victoria mentions as it were in passing, the justification, on the one side and on the other, of that force which is war, reserving the complete discussion of the question for the Reading on war. However, it was of such importance to the matter in hand that he indulged in an illustration and, as we would expect, Spain and France, his favourite countries, were involved. The illustration, which concerned the province of Burgundy, was apt in itself, but it had a special interest for one in Victoria's position; for was not Charles V, Holy Roman Emperor and King of Spain, a grandson of Mary of Burgundy, whose duchy had been overrun and was held in the possession of France, although in the imperial and Spanish conception of things it belonged of right to Charles? There was, however—in the

[1] *Ibid.*, pp. xxxix–xl.
[2] *Ibid.*, p. xl.
[3] *Vide infra*, pp. 179 *et seq.*
[4] *De Indis, infra*, Appendix A, p. xl.

broadmindedness of Victoria—a right or a claim of right on both sides, so that it was conceivable that each might defend what he sincerely believed to be his right by force of his arms.[1] To apply the illustration to the matter in hand, the conduct of the Indians towards the Spaniards, as set forth by Victoria, may have been wrong; nevertheless they were right in resisting the Spaniards. And this being the case there would be no justification for employing all the rights of war against them. 'For', in Victoria's language, 'the rights of war which may be invoked against men who are really guilty and lawless differ from those which may be invoked against the innocent and ignorant.'[2]

So far the moralist.

What was the conclusion of the jurist, supposing that the Spaniards were right in law and right in their conduct, and that all efforts to settle matters peaceably with the hostile Indians had failed, so that they could no longer be considered as 'innocent folk'? Under those circumstances it was lawful to wage war in the international sense, the means and consequences of which were later to be set forth by Victoria himself in his tractate on war. However, as a moralist he required not only that the war should be just but that the object or end of the war likewise should be just, and that end, in the language of St. Augustine, was 'peace and safety'.[3] Therefore all the means necessary to secure that 'end and aim of war' were to be considered as lawful, among which Victoria enumerates 'despoiling' the enemy 'of their goods, reducing them to captivity, deposing their former lords and setting up new ones'. There is, however, a limitation. These rights of war must be exercised with a due observance of proportion 'as regards the nature of the circumstances and of the wrongs done to them'.[4] In other words, the punishment is to be made to fit the offence.

In this connexion, the barbarians were to be treated as equals of Christian peoples. Their inferiority, real or alleged, was not to give them either a preferred or a subordinate position in international war. The law of nations was to be the standard, to be legally applied to the unbeliever or the Christian, the forward or the backward people.[5]

[1] *De Indis, infra,* Appendix A, p. xl. [2] *Ibid.*

[3] *Epistola (ad Bonifaciam), n.* 189 [*vel. n.* 205], § 6. *Vide* also *infra,* p. 182, where this letter is discussed with relation to its author's views on war and peace. [4] *De Indis, infra,* Appendix A, p. xl.

[5] *Ibid.,* p. xl. 'It is a universal rule of the law of nations that whatever is captured in war becomes the property of the conqueror, as is laid down in *Dig.* 49, 15, 28 and 24, and in *Decretum,* Pt. 1, dist. 1, can. 9, and more expressly in *Inst.* 2, 1, 17, where it is said that "by the law of nations whatever we take from the enemy becomes ours at once, to such an extent that even men may be brought into slavery to us".'

The *Decretum* reference cited contains an interesting definition of the law of nations which is derived from St. Isidore of Seville's *Etymologiae.* The definition will serve to dispel the doubts which some may have had regarding the way in which the medieval scholars understood the term *jus gentium.* It should be noted, however, that there was another division of law—which, though it contains many things that we of to-day would place under international law proper—can best be approximated by the rendering 'Law of War'—the *jus militare.* The canonical definition of *jus gentium*

Omitting for the time being the application of international law to persons and property captured in war, with which Victoria deals at length in his Reading *On the Law of War*, we come to a passage which is so fundamental that we can but consider it as being at once the cornerstone and the arch of the Victorian doctrine. 'A prince', he declares, 'who has on hand a just war is *ipso jure* the judge of his enemies and can inflict a legal punishment on them, condemning them according to the scale of their wrongdoing.'[1] The statement is indeed that of Victoria; the authority is that of the doctors of the Church. In this conception, war is not only to be conducted according to law but also for a lawful purpose and a lawful end, for its only justification, in the opinion of Victoria and of the authorities which he invokes, is the absence of the court of a superior between the contending parties to which they would be obliged to refer the dispute. And, it is proper to observe, there was to be no superior and no court until the American experiment of the Supreme Court of the States, a tribunal established by agreement, should endow the nations of the world with the model for a Permanent Court of International Justice for the settlement of all disputes between them of a legal nature. But Victoria and the doctors knew no such court; for them war was the only legal process for the assertion and the rendition of justice between nations.

Victoria concludes with this statement: 'This, then, is the first title which the Spaniards might have for seizing the provinces and sovereignty of the natives.' But before he leaves the subject he wishes to emphasize once more his conception of the equality of Christian and non-Christian before the law. Therefore he adds that 'if the natives allow the Spaniards to traffic peaceably among them, the Spaniards could not allege in this connexion any just cause for seizing their goods any more than the goods of Christians'.[2]

However, Victoria was favourable to the propagation of Christianity as a possible and second lawful title. The propagation of Christianity which he had in mind, however, was the right 'to preach and declare the Gospel in barbarian lands',[3] a right which we of to-day insist is the right of the Christian missionary in every land, whether barbarian or not. As a churchman, he naturally accepted, in theory and practice, the injunction to 'preach the Gospel to every creature'.[4] There were many reasons which might be invoked in behalf of this title, for, if the Spaniards were to be permitted to travel in the New

is as follows: 'Ius gentium est sedium occupatio, edificatio, munitio, bella, captiuitates, seruitutes, postliminia, federa pacis, induciae, legatorum non uiolandorum religio, conubia inter alienigenas prohibita. Hoc inde ius gentium appellatur, quia eo iure omnes fere gentes utuntur.' Professor Ernest Nys characterizes this definition, or description, which approaches the modern conception, as 'un phénomène assez curieux' in that it was written in the seventh century, some hundreds of years before our modern international law came into being. *Vide* Nys, *Le Droit International*, *op. cit.*, tome i, p. 54; *vide* also his *Le Droit de la Guerre et les Précurseurs de Grotius* (Brussels and Leipzig, 1882), p. 12.

[1] *De Indis*, *infra*, Appendix A, p. xli. [2] *Ibid.* [3] *Ibid.* [4] St. Mark, xvi. 15.

World and to settle there and engage in trade, they should assuredly be permitted to engage in spiritual commerce and be heard by those willing to hear them, even though their words should fail of any result. In the Christian conception of things, the natives were 'not only in sin, but outside the pale of salvation',[1] and it was the duty of the Christians, according to Victoria, to bring to them the Gospel of salvation, not only because they were ignorant of it but because they were 'our neighbours' and because, to quote a further phrase of the master: 'Brotherly correction is required by the law of nature, just as brotherly love is.'[2]

Who should make known the Gospel? The Christians—the Christians, according to Victoria, being those who recognized the Pope as their spiritual head. As to the preaching of Catholic Christianity—Victoria spoke as a Catholic—this task, common and permitted to all, might nevertheless be entrusted by the head of the Church of which Victoria was a member to the Spaniards and forbidden to all others. The matter might be looked upon from a twofold standpoint: first, from the spiritual, against which nothing could be said; and second, from the standpoint of temporal jurisdiction, which might be assumed in so far as it related to the propagation of Christianity. Such being the case the Pope as head of the Church could designate the missionaries (as well as their nationality) to preach the Gospel in the newly discovered world, and in his temporal capacity he could forbid missionary activities to any except those of the nationality named, if that seemed to him to be in the interest of the spiritual domain. It will be recalled that, in denying to the Pope jurisdiction in matters material and temporal in the New World, Victoria was careful to reserve from the denial the spiritual domain. Here he applies the distinction on behalf, and to the benefit, of Christianity.[3] No one was better aware than he that he was treading on delicate ground, for he labours the question more than was his practice. He shows himself indeed to be a Spaniard rather than an internationalist, and he allows himself to go so far as to admit that the supreme Pontiff, 'for the good of religion . . . could appoint princes, especially where there were aforetime no Christian princes'.[4]

Let us dwell for a moment on each one of these phases. The Spaniards could be exclusively charged with the mission, 'if the sovereigns of Spain could render more effective help in the spread of the Gospel in those parts'.[5] The Pope could not only 'forbid others to preach, but also to trade there, if this would further the propagation of Christianity, for he can order temporal matters in the manner which is most helpful to spiritual matters'.[6] Then too—and for the first time

[1] *De Indis, infra,* Appendix A, p. xli.

[2] *Ibid.* The scholastics hold that brotherly correction is a work of charity; in this regard see St. Thomas Aquinas, *Secunda Secundae,* question 33, article 1.

[3] *De Indis, infra,* Appendix A, p. xli. [4] *Ibid.,* p. xlii. [5] *Ibid.,* p. xli. [6] *Ibid.*

Victoria uses a material argument for a spiritual purpose, the two dominions having hitherto been kept separate and distinct—were not the Spaniards the first 'to patronize and pay for the navigation of the intermediate ocean'?[1]—an argument which in our day would be called peculiarly 'American'. But as a European is not exempt from human pride, and as the Spaniards 'had the good fortune to discover the New World, it is just that this travel should be forbidden to others and that the Spaniards should enjoy alone the fruits of their discovery'. However, he states the conclusion in this connexion, although it was set forth at length in a previous section, that the failure of the Indians to receive the faith, provided they allowed it to be preached, 'furnishes no lawful ground for making war on them and seizing in any other way their lands'.[2]

But what if the Indians should 'prevent the Spaniards from freely preaching the Gospel'? In that case the Spaniards might resort, after reasoning and persuasion had failed, to war and its consequences, 'until they succeed in obtaining facilities and safety for preaching the Gospel'.[3] The spread of the Gospel was conceived to be to the benefit of the Indians, and if war were necessary to this just end, it should be waged in 'moderation and proportion, . . . and with an intent directed more to the welfare of the aborigines than to their own gain'.[4]

It is evident from the guarded way in which Victoria spoke that he was setting forth a possible title and allowing a resort to force—and indeed to war—with much misgiving, just as, on a previous occasion, allowing war against the Indians he nevertheless tempered justice with mercy, because of the difference between the Spaniards and the Indians. The extreme right was there stated, but it was to be modified in practice. So here, the extreme right to war is admitted, but it is tempered with Christian charity. As Victoria's language was quoted on a previous occasion, it is likewise quoted here, demonstrating that at times the best use of a right may be its non-use: 'Careful attention must, however, be paid to what St. Paul says: "All things are lawful unto me, but not all things are expedient."[5] So everything said above must be taken as spoken absolutely. For it may be that these wars and massacres and spoliations will hinder rather than procure and further the conversion of the Indians.' What, then, was to be the criterion in these matters? 'Accordingly,' Victoria tells us, 'the prime consideration is that no obstacle be placed in the way of the Gospel, and if any such be so placed, this method of evangelization must be abandoned and another one sought for. What we have been showing is what is lawful in itself.' Applying these principles to the matter in hand, he continues:

[1] *De Indis, infra,* Appendix A, p. xlii.
[2] *Ibid. Vide* also *supra,* p. 130; *infra,* Appendix A, pp. xxx, xxxi.
[3] *De Indis, infra,* Appendix A, p. xlii.
[4] *Ibid.*
[5] 1 Corinthians, vi. 12.

'I personally have no doubt that the Spaniards were bound to employ force and arms in order to continue their work there, but I fear measures were adopted in excess of what is allowed by human and divine law. The title under consideration might, then, be a second lawful title whereby the Indians might fall into the power of Spain.' Nevertheless such a title must pass the test imposed by philosopher and churchman. 'But regard must ever be had', Victoria insists, 'to what has just been said lest what in itself is lawful be made in the circumstances wrong, for goodness springs from the one complete cause, but badness from individual defects, according to Aristotle (*Ethics*, bk. 3) and Dionysius (*De divinis nominibus*, ch. 4).'[1]

It might, however, happen that the preaching had not only been heard and had resulted in conversion to Christianity, but that the princes or authority of the converts subjected them to force 'to make them return to idolatry'. Such a use of force could, in the opinion of Victoria, 'justify the Spaniards' in repelling force with force. This was a third title in favour of the Spaniards based, as Victoria says, 'not only on religion, but on human friendship and alliance, inasmuch as the native converts to Christianity have become friends and allies of Christians'.

In his fourth and next title Victoria supposes that 'a large part of the Indians' had been 'converted to Christianity'. What steps could be taken in their behalf? The answer is short and to the point: 'The Pope might for a reasonable cause, either with or without a request from them, give them a Christian sovereign and depose their unbelieving rulers.'[2] Victoria had already remarked in a previous title that the Spaniards might depose rulers who sought to reduce the converts again to idolatry. What was his authority for this? That of the doctors and of St. Thomas, the latter being quoted as expressly saying that 'the Church could free all Christian slaves who are in bondage to unbelievers even if that bondage was in other respects lawful',[3] from which Victoria concludes that the Church, 'in the interests of the faith and to avoid risks, may free all Christians from obedience and subjection to unbelieving lords, provided this be done without scandal'.[4] It is to be observed that Victoria is not so precise here as on other occasions, because 'scandal' is left without definition, and yet it is of the essence.[5]

[1] *De Indis, infra*, Appendix A, p. xliii. [2] *Ibid.*

[3] *Secunda Secundae*, question 10, article 10: 'Potest . . . juste per sententiam, vel ordinationem Ecclesiae auctoritatem Dei habentis tale jus dominii, vel praelationis tolli; quia infideles merito suae infidelitatis merentur potestatem amittere super fideles, qui transferuntur in filios Dei.' [Leonine Ed.]

[4] *De Indis, infra*, Appendix A, p. xliv.

[5] Scandal is defined by St. Thomas Aquinas (II. ii, qu. 43, art. 1) as 'something less rightly done or said, that occasions another's spiritual downfall'. He elaborates his definition—'A thing is said to be less right, not because something else surpasses it in rectitude, but because it has some lack of rectitude, either through being evil in itself, such as sin, or through having an appearance of evil. Thus, for instance, if a man were to *sit at meat in the idol's temple* (1 Corinth. 8. 10), though this is not sinful in itself, provided it be done with no evil intention, yet, since it has a certain appearance of evil, and a semblance of worshipping the idol, it might occasion another man's spiritual downfall. . . . Scandal is therefore fittingly

The fifth title begins a new series of claims. The right of preaching and of conversion and of safeguarding the rights of those converted—even at the expense of war—the dethronement of native princes and the enthroning of Christian princes had been discussed and Victoria's views expressed on each and every one of these points. He now takes up a series of titles, three of which he proves (with doubt as to the fourth), and all of which are in the interest of the aborigines, without reference to their acceptance or rejection of the Christian religion. The fifth title (the first of this group) authorizes the Spaniards to intervene and dethrone the rulers, if need be, to rescue innocent people—for such he considers the barbarians to be in this case—'from an unjust death', Victoria having in mind 'the sacrifice of innocent people or the killing in other ways of uncondemned people for cannibalistic purposes'. Here, as elsewhere, it was necessary for the Spaniards to have lawful jurisdiction, and Victoria finds it granted by the authority of Ecclesiasticus that 'God has laid a charge on every individual concerning his neighbour'[1]—and 'all', in the opinion of Victoria, 'are our neighbours'. Should the barbarians refuse to consider themselves as neighbours and to accept neighbourly assistance in putting an end to these practices, their refusal would be a ground for war: and if the sacrilegious rites in question could not 'otherwise be stopped', that fact would furnish a valid reason 'for changing their rulers and creating a new sovereignty over them'.[2] Victoria was so sure of himself that he would not recognize in the Indians such legal independence as to be able to consign themselves or their children to death.[3]

It may here be noted in passing that there was still another ground, as we shall see later, about which Victoria felt less certain: that of the white men assuming the burden of mandate to fit the natives for admission to the international community upon a basis of equality.

The sixth lawful title is one which needs only to be stated in order to be queried: 'True and voluntary choice' of the Spaniards as rulers by the Indians and by their sovereigns.[4] In this connexion, Victoria accredits the Indians with a knowledge 'of the prudent administration and the humanity of the Spaniards'.[5] If the conduct of the Spaniards had been such as to create the desire on the part of the barbarians to be governed by the foreigners from the Old World, 'this could be done and would be a lawful title, by the law natural too, seeing that a State

described as something done *less rightly*, so as to compromise both whatever is sinful in itself, and all that has an appearance of evil.' [English Dominican Translation, London, 1917.]

[1] 'And he gave to every one of them commandment concerning his neighbour': Ecclesiasticus, xvii. 12.

[2] *De Indis, infra*, Appendix A, p. xliv.

[3] 'Nec obstat quod omnes barbari consentiant in hujusmodi leges & sacrificia, nec volunt se hoc vindicari ab Hispanis; in his enim non ita sunt sui juris, ut possint seipsos, vel filios tradere ad mortem....' Victoria, *De Indis et De Ivre Belli Relectiones*, Carnegie Institution ed., pp. 403–4.

[4] Victoria has previously questioned whether their choice could be 'true and voluntary'. On this point, *vide supra*, pp. 134 *et seq.*

[5] *De Indis, infra*, Appendix A, p. xliv.

can appoint any one it will to be its lord'; and in this connexion, 'the consent of all is not necessary, but the consent of the majority suffices'.[1] It is interesting to note that the barbarians are here spoken of not as individuals or as principalities but as a State (*res publica*), Victoria thus according them, in form as well as in substance, the same rights under this heading as those possessed by the State of Spain and the State of France.

The title which Victoria advanced is as good now as it was then, but the manner of presenting and justifying it has for us an interest transcending its statement. He had spoken of the law of nations as the law natural and as added to by the consent of the majority of mankind. Here we have the law of nations applying to all persons: those who had consented to it, as well as the minority who had not consented, but who were equally bound. The same principle which he had 'argued elsewhere' (referring to his Reading *On the Civil Power*), insisting on its universal application to all humanity, he applies this time in constitutional law. 'The decisions of the majority', he proclaims, 'bind even when the rest are of a contrary mind', and he reinforces his declaration with the statement that nothing 'could be done for the welfare of the State', if this were not so, as it is 'difficult'—he might well have said 'impossible'—'to get all of the same way of thinking'.[2]

To be sure, Victoria had Christians in mind; but the doctrine was of universal as well as lesser application, and in its support he does not invoke the Old Testament for his examples but turns to proven history, choosing this time France instead of Spain for the illustration. 'Accordingly,' he says, 'if the majority of any city or province were Christians and they, in the interests of the faith and for the common weal, would have a prince who was a Christian, I think that they could elect him even against the wishes of the others and even if it meant the repudiation of other unbelieving rulers.' Thus far we have the majority acting only on its own behalf; but that was not sufficient for Victoria. 'I assert', he continues without mincing words, 'that they could choose a prince not only for themselves, but for the whole State, just as the Franks for the good of their State changed their sovereigns and, deposing Childeric, put Pepin, the father of Charlemagne, in his place, a change which was approved by Pope Zacharias.'[3]

In the next and seventh title, the 'allies and friends' again make their appearance. There can be no doubt that a State, Christian or otherwise, might take unto itself an ally, could one be found, in order to enable its cause, whatever it might be, to prevail. Such has been the practice of Christendom—and, indeed, without the help of allies, wars would have been fewer and empires, kingdoms, and States less extensive. The whole thing is put in a nutshell by the great Cardinal Cajetan,

[1] *De Indis, infra,* Appendix A, p. xliv. [2] *Ibid.* [3] *Ibid.*, pp. xliv–xlv.

whom Victoria had criticized in the opening section and whose support he now invokes to the effect 'that the cause of allies and friends is a just cause of war, a State being quite properly able, as against foreign wrongdoers, to summon foreigners to punish its enemies'.[1] Here we might let the matter rest, but for the fact that Victoria at this point adduces some interesting examples which are not merely those of the Old Testament and of the Romans who conquered the world by first protecting and then annexing their allies—although the especial cause of their wars was the defence and protection of their friends—but of the Indians 'recently discovered'. What 'Father' Abraham did, when he 'championed the cause of the King of Salem', and what the Romans had done the Indians could do (and did), namely, 'summon the Spaniards to help and share the rewards of victory with them'; for as Victoria informs us, 'this is what the Tlaxcaltecs are said to have done against the Mexicans, the former arranging with the Spaniards to help them to overcome the latter and to receive whatever could fall to them under the law of war'.[2]

The best comment that can be made on these seven titles which have been set forth is to be found in two paragraphs of Grotius's Commentary *On the Law of Prize*, which is justly considered as the first draft of his larger work *On the Law of War and Peace*. The two paragraphs in question are contained in the separate publication of the twelfth chapter of the Commentary, the *Mare Liberum*, which was published as a separate tractate by Grotius in 1609.

In the first paragraph of the separate publication[3] Grotius says: 'My intention is to demonstrate briefly and clearly that the Dutch—that is to say, the subjects of the United Netherlands—have the right to sail to the East Indies [Victoria was dealing with the West Indies], as they are now doing, and to engage in trade with the people there. I shall base my argument on the following most specific and unimpeachable axiom of the Law of Nations, called a primary rule or first principle, the spirit of which is self-evident and immutable, to wit: Every nation is free to travel to every other nation, and to trade with it.'

This doctrine set forth in this paragraph, of the utmost importance to Grotius—and indeed more important to Victoria—is one with which we are familiar, because it is a summary of the opening paragraph of the third section of Victoria's Reading *On the Indians Recently Discovered*. It was a summary—and it was meant to be a summary—of Victoria's doctrine, because, in a later paragraph of the chapter in question,[4] Grotius mentions Victoria as the author of the 'specific and unimpeachable axiom of the Law of Nations', saying that 'Victoria

[1] *Ibid.*, p. xlv. [2] *Ibid.*

[3] *The Freedom of the Seas*, translation by Ralph van Deman Magoffin, issued with the Latin text by the Carnegie Endowment for International Peace (New York, 1916), p. 7. [4] *Ibid.*, p. 9.

holds that the Spaniards could have shown just reasons for making war upon the Aztecs and the Indians in America, more plausible reasons certainly than were alleged, if they really were prevented from travelling or sojourning among those peoples, and were denied the right to share in those things which by the Law of Nations or by Custom are common to all, and finally if they were debarred from trade'. The reference in his footnote is to the first seven titles of the third section of Victoria's epoch-making Reading *De Indis Noviter Inventis.*[1]

Some there be—especially those who have dipped into the Spanish literature of international law (such as W. S. M. Knight),[2] particularly the writings of Victoria, Ayala, Suárez, and their contemporaries—who look upon Grotius's tractate on the *Freedom of the Seas* as his masterpiece and as his chief claim to the fatherhood of international law.[3] It may well be that the *Freedom of the Seas* is Grotius's masterpiece, but if it is to be regarded as having founded international law, there is something to be said in behalf of Francisco de Vitoria, *prima* professor of theology in the University of Salamanca.

There was an eighth title (already mentioned in passing), about which Victoria was doubtful but about which the twentieth-century world has no doubt. It is but one—although one of the most striking—of the many contributions which Victoria made and which silently, and without reference to him, have found their way into the international law of our day. 'It is this,' he begins succinctly, for it was not his habit to waste words: 'Although the aborigines in question are . . . not wholly unintelligent, yet they are little short of that condition, and so are unfit to found or administer a lawful State up to the standard required by human and civil claims.'[4] Am I my brother's keeper?—a question which Victoria had answered in the affirmative, but of which he was doubtful in the form in which the title set up had been stated. However, it might still 'be maintained that in their [the natives'] own interests the sovereigns of Spain might undertake the administration of their country, providing them with prefects and governors for their towns, and might even give them new lords, so long'—he is careful to add—'as this was clearly for their benefit'. As a moralist and humanitarian

[1] Grotius's citation is actually of Section II, which deals with different matters, but there can be no doubt that his reference is to the *third* section. The great Hollander frequently quoted from a memory which rarely betrayed him—although it would seem to have done so in the present instance. Curiously enough the Simon (1696) edition of Victoria, reproduced photographically in the Carnegie Institute edition, *op. cit.*, has, as the result of a typographical slip in the running head above the passage in question, the very error into which Grotius had fallen—that is, the running head reads Section II when it should be Section III. But we could not and would not trace this printer's slip of a later day to Grotius, however true it may be that the errors of great men are often perpetuated with their greatness.

[2] *The Life and Works of Hugo Grotius*, by W. S. M. Knight, Grotius Society Publications, No. 4 (London, 1925). *Vide* also numerous excellent short papers, chiefly in the *Transactions* of the Grotius Society.

[3] 'Thus in his *Mare Liberum*, probably more than in his *De Jure Belli*, Grotius is so especially associated with the birth of international law as to become entitled to the general tribute he has received in modern times as "Father of International Law".' Knight, *op. cit.*, p. 112.

[4] *De Indis, infra*, Appendix A, p. xlv.

Victoria would have been the last to deny the essential rightness of this argument. 'I say,' he continues, 'there would be some force in this contention; for if they were all wanting in intelligence, there is no doubt that this would not only be a permissible, but also a highly proper course to take; nay, our sovereigns would be bound to take it, just as if the natives were infants.' Here we have the suggestion of guardianship for infants, on condition that the trust should be exercised in behalf of the minors; and the same argument would apply to their 'barbarian parents' because Victoria conceived them to be, notwithstanding their age and experience, less intelligent than 'the boys and youths of other nations'. But whether it be a question of guardianship of minor or adult individuals, or of a people, 'surely this might be founded'—it is Victoria who is speaking—'on the precept of charity, they being our neighbours and we being bound to look after their welfare'.[1]

So far so good. But the claim was not without grave danger of abuse, and Victoria added immediately: 'Let this, however, as I have already said, be put forward without dogmatism and subject also to the limitation that any such interposition be for the welfare and in the interests of the Indians and not merely for the profit of the Spaniards.' This would be the language of the internationalists of our day, four hundred and forty years after the discovery of America. It is the language, however, of the moralist, for Victoria had no law on the question of mandates which he could invoke in its behalf. 'For this', he warns, 'is the respect in which all the danger to soul and salvation lies.'[2]

Victoria, as is the habit with public speakers, began his carefully prepared Reading with an introduction more elaborate in this case than on other occasions, doubtless because of the greater importance which he attached to the subject and its consequences. He also followed the practice of trained speakers of ending his discourses or disquisitions with some observations of a general nature. On this occasion, the conclusion was brief in comparison with the introduction, because he had set forth with great, and indeed elaborate, care the reasons which he felt the subject required him to advance and the conclusions to which he had come. The final conclusion is in the nature of a reply to an objection, which, if it were admitted, would have debarred the Spaniards from trading with the New World. In a few measured phrases he meets and refutes the objection.

The objection, the refutation, and the conclusion of this Reading on what we may call the 'law of peace' are in his own words.

'Now, it seems to follow from all this discussion that, if there be no force in any of the titles which have been put forward, so that the native Indians neither gave cause for just war nor wished for Spanish

[1] *Ibid.*, p. xlvi. *Vide* p. 154 *supra*, note 2.
[2] *De Indis, infra*, Appendix A, p. xlvi.

rulers, &c., all the travel to, and trade with, those parts should be stopped, to the great loss of the Spaniards and also to the grave hurt of the royal treasury (a thing intolerable). My first answer to this is: There would be no obligation to stop trade, for, as already said, there are many commodities of which the natives have a superfluity and which the Spaniards could acquire by barter. Also there are many commodities which the natives treat as ownerless or as common to all who like to take them, and the Portuguese, to their own great profit, have a big trade with similar people without reducing them to subjection. Secondly, there would probably be no diminution in the amount of the royalties, for a tax might quite fairly be placed on the gold and silver which would be brought away from the Indians, as much as a fifth or even more, according to quality, and it would be well-earned, inasmuch as the maritime discovery was made by our sovereign and it is under his authority that trade is carried on in safety. Thirdly, it is evident, now that there are already so many native converts, that it would be neither expedient nor lawful for our sovereign to wash his hands entirely of the administration of the lands in question.'[1]

[1] *De Indis, infra,* Appendix A, p. xlvi.

CHAPTER VII

VICTORIA AND NATURAL LAW

THERE are two occasions when Victoria makes a passing reference to the law of nations, in his readings *On the Indians* and *On the Law of War*. At other times he makes more than a passing reference, expressing his opinion on the origin and sources of the law of nations, the elements entering into its content, the way in which it is modified or developed, and the nature and the extent of the obligation which it imposes. These matters are fundamental in the sense that without them there can be no law of nations; with them there may be a law of nations; and his treatment of these fundamental questions constitutes his system of international law. If the views which he has expressed here and there in the course of the readings can be brought together so as to form a system; if that system, as formulated, was adequate to the international relations of his day, and if it was the structure of international law of a later day and is of our day, he would indeed be the founder of the modern law of nations in the sense that his was a system that had ceased to be a European but had become a universal law. If the system is accepted as adequate to the relations of nations in our day, it is then not merely modern, but present, international law; and if some of its principles are in the course of acceptance, then Victoria is prophet as well as founder of a law adequate to meet the changing order of a progressive world.

In the opening paragraph of the third section of the Reading *On the Indians*,[1] Victoria justifies the right of the Spaniards to visit the Americas, to sojourn in the Americas, and to engage in commerce with them. These things they had a right to do under the law of nations as he viewed it. By natural law the Spaniards might exercise these rights. Therefore natural law was the source of this phase of the law of nations; in so far as this matter is concerned, the law of nature was the acceptable and therefore accepted standard of conduct of nations in their relations one with another.

Victoria employs the expression *jus gentium* in one sentence in order to state the law, and in the next sentence he applies it to nations, using expressly that word, and thereby indicating that he had in mind a true *jus inter nationes*, not merely the law of individuals but of nations composed of those individuals.[2] This conception is definite or indefinite according to the meaning of natural law—of which later.

[1] *De Indis, infra*, Appendix A, p. xxxvi.

[2] 'Probatur primo ex jure gentium, quod vel est jus naturale, vel derivatur ex jure naturali. Instit. de jure naturali, genti *quod naturalis ratio inter omnes gentes constituit vocatur jus gentium*. Sic enim apud omnes nationes habetur in humanum [*inhumanum*, ed.], sine aliqua speciali caussa hospites et peregrinos male accipere.' Victoria, *De Indis*..., Carnegie Institution ed., p. 386. For comment on Victoria's quotation from the *Institutes*, *vide supra*, p. 139, note 3.

In a later passage of the same Reading, Victoria entered into details, as he was dealing with the ways in which title to property could be acquired, the property in question being gold and silver in the mines, and pearls in the rivers and streams. The title here, as before, came under the law of nations, which apparently he felt he should define. He did define it, with the result that his conception of the law of nations of his day is set forth in express terms, and the international law of the future by implication. As in the previous matter, international law is natural law, that is to say, the law of nature was a part of international law, and indeed was the general source from which its special rules would be derived. It might, however, be that these rules of a general nature would not meet the concrete situation; therefore they should be added to. This might be done by usage and by custom: custom being, not isolated instances, but usage which had become habitual and therefore customary. Here we have the element of consent. The appeal to usage or the appeal to custom was a consent to its application, and it was something additional to the rules of natural law; otherwise the appeal would have been to natural law and not to usage or custom. The practice of nations involved the consent of nations and made a law for the nations.

We are here in the presence of an unconscious development of international law; for there is no conscious intention to add specific rules derived from existing principles or to create principles permitting specific rules with which to meet either a present or a future need. Victoria, in the fullness of knowledge of existing principles and rules, stated that a law binding upon nations could be made by the consent or agreement of the nations, using a more general, yet synonymous, expression, 'a consensus of the greater part of the whole world, especially in behalf of the common good of all', which would be 'the majority of mankind' and this 'would certainly have the force of law, even though the rest of mankind objected thereto'.[1] In the opinion of Victoria this would certainly be equivalent to the *consent of mankind*.

However, it was obvious that mankind could not be brought together at a particular time and in a particular place; and just as the members of a national State could adopt a law which would bind the minority as well, and therefore the State as a whole, so also in the opinion of Victoria, the consent of all the inhabitants of the world was not necessary but the consent of a majority of mankind would suffice. The important point here is that a law of a majority of the States would bind the minority and be the law of the international community beyond the legal right of any individual State to make or break. Of

[1] '. . . satis videtur esse consensus, majoris partis totius orbis, maximè pro bono communi omnium. Si . . . major pars hominum constituerit, ut legati ubique essent inviolabiles, ut mare esset commune, ut bello capti essent servi, & hoc ita expediret ut hospites non exigerentur: certè hoc haberet vim, etiam aliis repugnantibus.' Victoria, *De Indis . . .*, Carnegie Institution ed., p. 391.

course individual States could make a treaty which would bind them, but such a treaty would demand only the consent of those States and therefore would not be a law of the international community. We here have the international community as the ultimate source and authority of law and of that system of law which we call the law of nations, just as if Victoria had used the expression: 'We the people of the international community', with the necessary implication that an internal law of a State is invalid if it conflicts with that of the international society.

So far we have been proceeding without a definition of natural law, which Victoria considers as the source of that law of nations which he professed and in professing made. We are, it might be said, stating the unknown in terms of the unknown. What, then, is the law of nature; what did the law of nature mean to the schoolmen, to whom Victoria belonged and of whom he was the most illustrious of his day?

Man has always considered himself as a human being separate and distinct from and superior to the animal. He has therefore insisted that he should be considered as different; and that the difference consists in the assignment to himself of that reason which is denied to the animal world. Claiming the right to be treated as a reasonable animal, he has maintained that law, as a rule of conduct to be applied to him, should bear some relation to the distinction between him and the animal world, that is to say, that the rule of law should be based upon reason; and that it was reasonable that the rule of conduct should change with changing conditions. This is what we call 'natural law'—the law which would seem, because of man's nature, to apply to him; and as conditions change and as he himself develops, the law should change. Therefore the law of nature, or the natural law, or the law applicable to human beings, should have as its source reason, but with a changing and variable content, which may be said to be artificial, in that it takes note of man's civilization.

We would 'naturally' expect that Aristotle would be drawn upon, but that the form of natural law accepted by the schoolmen of Victoria's day would be that of St. Thomas Aquinas. The Greek conception of things[1]—to speak in the most general terms—was that of

[1] The Greek or Aristotelian conception of natura .law is concisely stated by Professor Coleman Phillipson in his comprehensive analysis, *The International Law and Custom of Ancient Greece and Rome* (London, 1911), vol. i, p. 79: 'Aristotle's conception of nature implies the notion of rational design, or "reason", in the universe; and of this "reason" manifestations are perceptible in the physical or material world, though its perfect realization is there never attainable.'

'The Greeks', says Edith Hamilton, 'were the first intellectualists. In a world where the irrational had played the chief role, they came forward as the protagonists of the mind.... The Greeks were the first scientists and all science goes back to them.' And summing the matter up in a sentence or two she adds that 'in their century or two of life [they] remade the universe. They leaped to the truth by an intuition, they saw a whole made up of related parts, and with the sweep of their vision the old world of hodge-podge and magic fell away and a world of order took its place'. *The Greek Way* (New York, 1930), pp. 9, 32, 236.

reasonable individuals living in a universe which evidenced a rational design to which the name 'nature' was given. The law of nature would therefore be a reasonable law to be discovered by the use of reason.[1]

In the Christian conception, the rational design would exist but its source would be God, not nature. The law would be reasonable, and it might be a law which the unaided eye of reason alone could discover; but where reason fell short, Revelation entered and enlarged the content of the law natural. As in the Christian conception a divine order of things replaced the 'nature' of antiquity, it would follow that the law of nature discoverable by reason would also have its origin in divine law, whereas the revealed portion of natural law, not discoverable by the reasonable being, would be an addition, and this addition would be divine law in the technical sense of the term. We would expect, therefore, that the law of nature admitted by St. Thomas Aquinas would not be immutable, at least in so far as it depended upon reason; it would change to meet changing conditions whenever reason suggested a change. It would be a natural law with a variable content, which would increase or vary not merely because of new conditions but because of the development of the reasoning power of mankind, the development of natural law thus being synonymous in large part with the march of civilization. In addition there would be human law: law made by human beings for human purposes, which law, if reasonable, would modify or amplify the law of nature.[2]

Human law, however, is of two kinds: the law within the State,

[1] The Roman conception of natural law is admirably stated by Professor William Archibald Dunning in his study, *A History of Political Theories, Ancient and Mediaeval* (New York, 1910), p. 128: 'Because the ideas and usages of the many peoples subject to Rome were found to have much in common, the *ius gentium*, or totality of these ideas and usages, came to be regarded as identical with the *ius naturale*, and as an actual embodiment of that natural reason, which was the chief element in natural right. When the man whose opinion was law for the Empire declared, in treating of slavery, that "so far as pertains to natural rights, all men are equal", or that "by natural law all men are born free", or that "slavery is an institution contrary to nature", the practical tendency of Stoic doctrine in social matters was made very clear.'

Professor Dunning cites in behalf of his statement the following texts:

Digest, L. xvii. 32 (*ff.* De diversis Regulis Iuris antiqui, 1. *Quod attinet.*): *Idem* (Ulpian) *libro quadragensimo tertio ad Sabinum* Quod attinet ad ius civile, servi pro nullius habentur: non tamen et iure naturali, quia, quod ad ius naturale attinet, omnes homines aequales sunt.

Institutes, I. ii. 2 (*Inst.*, De Iure Naturali, &c., 1. *Sed ius quidem.*): . . . iure enim naturali ab initio omnes homines liberi nascebantur.

Digest, I. v. 4 (*ff.* De Statu Hominum, 1. *Libertas est*): Servitus est constitutio iuris gentium qua quis dominio alieno contra naturam subicitur.

[2] A clear and concise definition of natural law is given by the late Viscount Bryce, in his *Studies in History and Jurisprudence* (New York, 1901), p. 564: 'Those [laws] which prevail everywhere, or at any rate, generally, appear to issue out of the mental and moral constitution common to all men. They are the result of the principles uniting men as social beings, which Nature, personified as a guiding power, is deemed to have evolved and prescribed. Hence they are called Natural. Being the work of Nature, they are not only wider in their area, but also of earlier origin than any other rules or customs. They are essentially anterior in thought as well as in date to the laws each community makes for itself, for they belong to the human race as a whole. Hence they are also deemed to be higher in moral authority than the laws which are peculiar to particular communities, for these may be enacted to-day and repealed to-morrow, and have force only within certain local limits.'

made by a group for its own needs, and the law made by groups as such for their needs, the result being the civil law of the State—which Victoria considered at length in his Reading *On the Civil Power* (analysed elsewhere and reproduced in the Appendix);[1] and the law of nations one and inseparable—a single standard for individuals and nations.

In this conception of things the acknowledged head of the Christian community would decide conflicts between the law natural and the law made by human beings. When Christendom was enlarged by the addition of the barbarians 'recently discovered', the international community necessarily became the final authority and arbiter, voicing 'a consensus of the greater part of the whole world, especially in behalf of the common good of all'.

With the discovery of the Greek texts, with the arguments of Cicero[2] which had survived with Roman law[3]—transmitted in its classical perfection by Justinian—and with the writings of the churchmen, and of course with the Scriptures before his eyes, St. Thomas Aquinas was in a position to give a rounded and systematic form to the elements which entered into his conception of things, and by his genius to impress this conception upon subsequent generations and indeed centuries. The world at large did not have texts at hand.

Having traced thus briefly the development of the natural law of Christendom from its Greek sources, we are now ready to consider Victoria's views on the law of nature and its relation to his international law—matters of the first importance for an understanding of his doctrine with all its implications.

Victoria considers natural law as a source—indeed the preferred source—of the law of nations, and, this being so, he holds that international law is derived from the law natural, with modifications and additions through custom and through the consent of the majority of mankind. We would to-day enumerate treaties as express evidence of 'the majority of mankind'. Further than this he does not go, if we limit ourselves to the Readings *On the Indians* and *On the Law of War*;

[1] *Vide infra*, p. 253, and Appendix C, *infra*, p. lxxi.

[2] Cicero's conception of the universal reason as the controlling guide to the individual, the State, and the nations is thus set forth by Phillipson: 'It is laid down, he [Cicero] says, not only by the law of nature, that is the law of nations, but also by the statutory law of States, that no one shall be allowed, for his own advantage, to inflict an injury on another. Now he who obeys the behests of universal reason, which is the law of gods and men alike—in other words, he who lives according to nature—will never covet his neighbour's goods, or be induced to appropriate for his own profit what he has wrested from another.' Phillipson, *op. cit.*, p. 80.

[3] An excellent exposition of the Roman conception of the Law of Nature is given by Bryce (*op. cit.*, p. 589): 'Speaking broadly, the Law of Nature represented to the Romans that which is conformable to Reason, to the best side of Human Nature, to an elevated morality, to practical good sense, to general convenience. It is Simple and Rational, as opposed to that which is Artificial or Arbitrary. It is Universal, as opposed to that which is Local or National. It is superior to all other law because it belongs to mankind as mankind, and is the expression of the purpose of the Deity or of the highest reason of man. It is therefore Natural, not so much in the sense of belonging to men in their primitive and uncultured condition, but rather as corresponding to and regulating their fullest and most perfect social development in communities, where they have ripened through the teachings of Reason.'

but, if we look elsewhere, we find that what he said was a conclusion of the views which he had expressed at length in a course upon the *Summa Theologica* of St. Thomas, which it was his duty to profess in public. Fortunately, we possess his comment on the 'quaestio' of St. Thomas: whether the right of nations is the same as the natural right (*Secunda secundae*, question 57, article 3). Victoria states that the question is whether the *jus gentium*—to use his exact expression, which is that of the Roman law, instead of its supposed equivalent in our modern terminology—may be distinguished from the natural law: 'St. Thomas marks a distinction, to wit: That right is a natural right, which from its very nature, as it were, balances the right of another. And this can happen in two ways: In one way, in that natural law of itself declares that there is a certain equality and justice—as it were to return a deposit: or, because no wrong is done to you, you do no wrong to another.'[1] The second way may be made clearer by example than by paraphrase. There is the open sea and there is the land of a community held in common. In the open sea the right of each person, or of the groups of persons which we call States, is equal, and it remains equal to the present day, except where it has been renounced. The land, too, might conceivably have remained in common. But let us suppose that, given human nature as it is, the community desires that it be divided. The result would be that the equal right of the individual to the whole had been renounced for an individual right to a specific part. It being the desire of the community that this be done, there is an abstract reason for doing it; there is also a concrete one: that by the division each person having his property separated from the common lot, the peace of the community might be preserved, whereas formerly discord would have arisen by reason of the individual's claiming from the common holding as his what the community would be unwilling to allow. This modification of what has been supposed as a primitive right may result in unequal holdings, but the modified right is nevertheless a right under the *jus gentium*, and is, to quote Victoria's exact language, 'derived from human statute firmly established in reason. . . . Whence it appears that the *jus gentium* may be distinguished from the *jus naturale*'.[2]

The question may be asked whether the division of property by the *jus gentium* takes place under what is called positive—that is to say, human law—or under natural law. St. Thomas was of the opinion that it was rather under positive than natural law, relying upon the statement in St. Isidore's *Etymologies*. The jurists, however, are stated by Victoria to have been in favour of natural law, their view

[1] *De Jure Gentium et Naturali*, fragment published in Beltrán de Heredia, *Los Manuscritos . . . de Vitoria*, p. 207. For translation of this fragment, *vide infra*, Appendix E, p. cxi.

[2] *De Jure Gentium et Naturali, infra*, Appendix E, p. cxi.

being that the *jus gentium* does not come under positive law but under natural law. Following the example of St. Thomas and using the first person, Victoria says: 'I answer to this, and say first of all that the dispute concerns the name more than the thing, for it matters little whether one says this or that.' Victoria says in the second place that the jurisconsults 'make the *jus gentium* too extensive', in extending it to 'too many things' of the natural law which affect men alone.[1] The trouble with the jurists was that they had in mind that Ulpian's rule extended to the animal creation as well as to human beings—a view unacceptable to the schoolman, who regarded the individual, instead of the animal creation, as the starting-point of either system. Victoria's conclusion being that—following the opinion of St. Thomas—'*jus gentium* ought to be placed more under positive law than under natural law'.

Apparently Victoria was free from doubt on the matter and was impatient with the jurists, regarding the theologian as more competent to settle these matters than they—again saying that the dispute is 'one of words'.[2]

But whatever the legal argument might be, and whatever interpretation the jurist or theologian might make, the moralist, as always in Victorian doctrine, was to have the last word. 'The greatest doubt', he declares, 'is a moral one.' If *jus gentium* is a thing of the positive law, as has been said—and not only the jurists of his day but of ours seem to be obsessed with positivism—and not of the natural law, 'is it a sin', he appropriately asks, 'to violate the *jus gentium*?'[3] The answer to the question could not be doubtful to any one at all familiar with Victoria's system.

After stating that he had many times expressed the opinion that human or written laws were 'binding in the court of conscience', he repeats the question in a slightly different form, in order to give it what would be in his opinion a definitive answer: 'But there is a doubt whether it may be a sin to violate the *jus gentium* (to which some have not yet given their sanction), that is to say, to violate a law of nations which is unwritten, or even written, and which does not bind all men who are in the world.' (*Tu es Petrus, et super hanc petram aedificabo ecclesiam meam.*)[4] For purposes of illustration Victoria 'kills' an ambassador—'which is contrary to the *jus gentium*—under circumstances where all are not obliged to observe the *jus gentium*, since the *jus gentium* may not be natural law as we have supposed'. Upon this question, thus posed, depend the law and the prophets. 'Let us imagine', he says, 'that we have a war with the French, and the French send an ambassador whom the Spaniards kill contrary to the *jus*

[1] *Ibid.*, p. cxi.
[2] *Ibid.*, p. cxii.
[3] *Ibid.*
[4] St. Matthew, xvi. 18.

gentium.' (It was the habit of Victoria to consider that his own country might now and then lapse from grace, instead of branding foreigners with suppositious violations of all kinds of laws.) The question arises how—speaking directly to his students—'are you to judge and know that we have not admitted that *jus gentium*, and that we have sinned in killing an enemy?' Victoria's reply indicates that he had previously touched upon a similar point by supposing—'as we have said above in article 2'—that the *jus gentium* is twofold—as positive law is twofold, there being one kind of positive law derived 'from private agreement and consensus, and another kind from public agreement'. So also 'the common consensus of all peoples and nations' makes one kind of *jus gentium* or international law. By way of illustration, Victoria again cites—but without depriving them of life—the familiar case of ambassadors, who are admittedly covered by the *jus gentium* and are admittedly inviolable by the practice of nations. The reason? 'The law of nations so closely approaches to the natural law that the natural law cannot be observed without this law of nations.'[1] Peace is the normal state of affairs. It is therefore to the public advantage to send ambassadors 'to bring about peace', for without them how could there be an end of wars? To act contrary to the *jus gentium* is 'illicit . . . because it is contrary to the common consensus' and 'because of itself it brings on an injury and a certain inequality'. The example which he gives is even more than ordinarily apposite and it states a principle which goes beyond the example; for in holding that inequality is injustice, the necessary implication arises that equality is justice, and therefore as fundamental in his system as is morality. Whence it follows inevitably that 'if one party sends ambassadors to make a peace and they are not violated, and the other party sends ambassadors too', who are violated, then in Victoria's opinion the inequality is injustice —and indeed iniquity—and therefore a mortal sin. Here the *jus gentium* and the natural law are considered as separate systems of law, in that the first does not follow from the second. Victoria's observation is that 'the *jus gentium* does not necessarily follow from the natural law, nor is it necessary simply for the conservation of the natural law, for if it should follow necessarily from the natural law, now it would be the natural law', and there would be one instead of two systems.[2]

The passage which we are analysing shows us not merely Victoria's conception of the two laws—and therefore of international law—but his opinion as a teacher of youth of many years' experience on the value of repetition. The lesson of yesterday is with him as the foundation of the lesson of the morrow. If the *jus gentium* 'necessarily followed from the natural law, through a good sequence, *as we said yesterday*',

[1] *De Jure Gentium et Naturali, infra*, Appendix E, p. cxiii. [2] *Ibid.*, p. cxiii.

the *jus gentium* would be as necessary as natural law and it would therefore be the natural law. Separate as the two statements are, there is a relationship—indeed there is more than a relationship: that in the conservation of the natural law the *jus gentium* plays a vital part. While, however, the two statements are distinct, the *jus gentium*, if 'not wholly necessary' is nevertheless nearly necessary to preserve the fundamental rights of human beings under the law of nature.[1] To return to our example: before there was a division of property, each person had an equal right to the enjoyment of property held in common. When the division took place the equal right of enjoying property was preserved, although the enjoyment itself was limited in practice. The division of the property held in common under natural law was for the purpose of protecting the fundamental right of enjoyment because, given the nature of man, the common enjoyment might, as Victoria had previously intimated, be the source of discords and of wars. The right to the enjoyment of property is thus preserved; from which it follows that the function of the *jus gentium* in relation to the natural law is protective. If, however, natural law is looked upon as persisting and the *jus gentium* as not absolutely necessary—as it is, one might say, incidental to natural law—the force which it has would be that of appositive law, if indeed it is to be considered as separate law. It may therefore cease to exist by the withdrawal of the consent which has made it law. However, the difficulty here may be illustrated by the fact that if a principle is law by a general consent, it can only be abrogated by an equally general consent; and in the matter in hand this is impossible, Victoria says, 'because it is impossible that the consensus of the whole world could be obtained for the abrogation of the law of nations (*jus gentium*)'.[2]

Victoria is here speaking of the law of nations as a system. Parts of that law, he admits, may from time to time be modified or indeed abrogated. As an example he instances the change which had taken place in the status of prisoners of war by the practice of nations. Originally put to death, they were later enslaved; but with the passage of centuries they came to be considered as general property, to be held as captives, and still later to be the subject of ransom and one day exchanged as prisoners of war. The instance which Victoria gives is, one might say, in the middle of this development, which has continued until our day. 'For,' he says, 'if the Spaniards capture Frenchmen in a war, the Frenchmen are captives, but not slaves'—Paludanus being cited to show that the rule of slavery was not applicable among Christians—'because they are able to appear in a court of justice'—the court of justice being inevitable in Victoria's illustrations—'and do other things of that sort, which nevertheless could not be permitted

[1] *Ibid.*, p. cxiii. [2] *Ibid.*

if they were slaves. The acts of a French captive are valid, and a Christian could not sell him at all.'[1]

Therefore the law of nature—and indeed of custom and of pact—should be, and in the long run will be, consistent with the dignity and the nature of the human being for whom it is made—a standard which seems to be in thorough accord with the conception of St. Thomas that the human being and his well-being and ultimate happiness in society, as well as individually, should be the aim and purpose of law, whether it be natural, human, or divine. And according to Victoria, such should be the purpose of the threefold law whether it apply to the individual, wherever situated, to the State, however composed, or to the international community, made up alike of peoples and States.

From all of which, it is an incontrovertible fact stated by St. Thomas—to be admitted in every part of the world—that governments are made for men and not men for governments.

To his students Victoria stated: 'Let this suffice on this question.' Following his example, let it also suffice for us on the relationship between the law of nature and Victoria's system of the law of nations; for indeed there is no more to be said.

What then is the international law of Victoria, composed as it is of natural law, custom, and the consent of the majority of mankind? The answer is in the words of Victoria himself—words already quoted and to be quoted again, and which cannot be repeated too often: 'that international law has not only the force of a pact and agreement among men but also the force of a law; for the world as a whole being in a way one single State, has the power to create laws that are just and fitting for all persons, as are the rules of international law. Consequently, it is clear that they who violate these international rules, whether in peace or in war, commit a mortal sin; moreover, in the gravest matters, such as the inviolability of ambassadors, it is not permissible for one country to refuse to be bound by international law, the latter having been established by the authority of the whole world.'[2]

[1] *De Jure Gentium et Naturali, infra,* Appendix E, pp. cxiii–cxiv.

[2] *De Potestate Civili, infra,* Appendix C, p. xc. For Latin text, *vide* Victoria, *Relectiones Morales,* ed. Simonis (Coloniae & Francofurti, 1696), p. 180.

CHAPTER VIII

THE LAW OF WAR

Scholastic Doctrine

St. Augustine—St. Thomas Aquinas

It has been frequently observed—it may justly be said, by the superficially minded—that too great stress has been laid upon war in tractates and treatises on matters international which have appeared from time to time throughout the centuries. The reason is so simple that, like all elemental things, we overlook it. Peace existed everywhere in the State under normal conditions. And as the rules of peace were to be found fully developed under the cardinal principle of charity, there was no need for philosopher and jurist to expound these rules. War, on the contrary, was abnormal, in the sense that it was not normal. In other words, it was as a transition from the normal; it was not ordinary, but extraordinary; and therefore, it would of itself have made an appeal to the people of any day, just as it has continued to make its appeal even to the year in which we live. It would have been strange had there been tractates and treatises on peace, a status with which people were familiar, as they normally lived in its atmosphere. Obedience to the laws in any organized community—call it 'principality' or 'state' —did not then have, nor has it now, a news value, for it has always been the irregular and the unusual that captures the interest; and a resort to the courts for redress of a wrong was and is of ordinary occurrence, self-redress being permissible only in defence of one's person or property from violation, and only at the time of the immediate danger.

The individual, therefore, was accustomed to this state of things. The State protected rights; the courts gave compensation for damages incurred or imposed punishment for crimes. When Christendom came into being, it found this state of affairs everywhere prevailing in the civilized portion of the ancient world. The Christian accepted a world in which he was born and in which he lived, with its customs and duties ('Render therefore to Caesar the things that are Caesar's');[1] but he had another world, the world of the spirit, and, while his actions were to conform to the laws of the State or the community in which he lived, they were not to be at variance with the principles of that religion which he professed, for which he should live and in which he should die.

There would rarely be a conflict between the two claims of obedience, inasmuch as they applied to different worlds; but when the duty of the Christian seemed to be opposed to the duty of the citizen,

[1] St. Matthew, xxii. 21.

which should prevail? 'Thou shalt not kill', this was the rule of charity. Should a Christian take life? If the prohibition were to be taken in an absolute sense, the answer would necessarily be: 'No.' If, on the other hand, life could be forfeited as punishment for an unjust act, then the answer might be: 'Yes.' Under what circumstances, then, should such answers be given, and who was to be the judge? Thus stated, the difficulty would seem to be more specious than real, because death was in every community a punishment. Looking at it from the larger aspect, however, not as involving the life of an individual as a mere punishment for a crime but as threatening the lives of hundreds of people—indeed thousands and hundreds of thousands—what would become of the prohibition, 'Thou shalt not kill'? The Christian Church answered that the duty was the same in either case: the taking of life was only permissible in the redress of a wrong or as punishment for a crime. Therefore, war involving a resort to arms and the sacrifice of innumerable lives could be justified only if the cause were just. Within the State, the taking of life through process of law was permissible; and between the States the taking of life for a cause that was just was likewise permissible in the sense that a court between the States would have condemned the guilty State, if such a court had existed.

A just cause, therefore, justified the taking of the life of the individual, and likewise the lives of many individuals in war. Judgement was upon the act itself, separate and distinct from the person, the rank, or the number of those who had committed the act—thus applying a single and impersonal standard for man and for State. 'Faith, Hope and Charity, these three: but the greatest of these is Charity.'[1] If charity is the greatest—and the authority that it is cannot be gainsaid—then the taking of the life of a human being could be defended only when the sacrifice of the life was needed in the cause of justice, because the actions of individuals under the rule of charity were to be just, not unjust: as the Gospel says, 'Peace on earth to men of good will'.[2] The right to take life in a just cause, therefore, was an extension of the rule of charity as applicable within the States. Hence the exercise of such a right could be considered and actually was an act of charity, in that through punishment the commission of offences would be curbed and controlled—which control could be and was looked upon by the Church as a charitable act in the sense that it tended to prevent the faithful from going astray. War between States involving the death of many was in the same way an exception to the rule of charity applied internationally. The individual by his wrongful and unjust act excluded himself from the maxim of charity; and the guilty State, by reason of its guilt, was excluded in the same manner. But because the right to

[1] 1 Corinthians, xiii. 13.

[2] St. Luke, ii. 14.

take life was not the rule but the exception, it was to be construed most strictly, and the party claiming the war to be just must prove its justness, as would have been requisite before a court of justice. The king, prince, or other officer of the State should act in the same manner as a judge would have been obliged to act, if there were a court before which the offence could be brought. As in the case of the individual, a demand for redress of a grievance was to be expected, but if the plaintiff were a State, request for such redress should be made of its king, its prince, or appropriate officer. If redress were not granted, action could be taken by the State claiming to have a cause of action, but not without consulting its counsellors, just as a plaintiff in a lawsuit consulted counsel; not without argument of the case from the twofold standpoint of plaintiff and defendant; and not without a formal decision to resort to arms—in plain terms, war.[1] Such was and is the law to be applied, unless the case were one which could not be adjudicated in a court of justice within the State or (if one existed) between the States. Injustice was the source of the claim, and justice the justification for such action. The decision, therefore, must be that of a judge. The judgement must be executed as would be that of a court of justice. Under those circumstances, the Christian might bear arms and plead the justice of the cause as an exception to charity. Otherwise, the Christian should not bear arms; if he did, he made himself a party to a crime.

We are here face to face with a question of conscience, and as far as the Christian is concerned who is called to the colours, to serve in

[1] Shakespeare has given us an interesting example of a ruler's consultation with his counsellors in Act I, Scene ii, of *King Henry V*. Henry has, he believes, a just claim to the crown of France; he knows that if his claim *is* just, he can enforce it by making war against the Dauphin; however, knowing also the necessity of being absolutely certain in so grave a matter, he sends for the Archbishop of Canterbury, who was likewise the Lord Chancellor of his kingdom and his chief counsellor, to give him his advice. The arguments for the war are presented by the Chancellor, and are discussed before the King. The passage of most interest to us, however, is the exhortation of the King when he asks Canterbury's advice:

> And God forbid, my dear and faithful Lord,
> That you should fashion, wrest or bow your reading,
> Or nicely charge your understanding soul
> With opening titles miscreate, whose right
> Suits not in native colours with the truth;
> For God doth know how many, now in health,
> Shall drop their blood in approbation
> Of what your reverence shall incite us to.
> Therefore, take heed how you impawn our person,
> How you awake the sleeping sword of war:
> We charge you, in the name of God, take heed;
> For never two such kingdoms did contend,
> Without much fall of blood; whose guiltless drops
> Are every one a woe, a sore complaint,
> 'Gainst him whose wrongs give edge unto the swords
> That make such waste in brief mortality.
> Under this conjuration, speak, my Lord;
> And we will hear, note, and believe in heart,
> That what you speak is in your conscience washed,
> As pure as sin with baptism.

war, it is a matter for him to decide. He did this at his peril in the earlier days of Christendom, just as is the case to-day with the conscientious objector.

As war is a relationship between States, the existence of States must precede a resort to war. It is therefore advisable to consider the nature of the State which Victoria had in mind and which he considers as authorized under certain conditions to declare and to conduct a just war.

There are two characteristics so marked as to be fundamental: the first is, the State is a collection of human beings; and the second, that the State is looked upon as a community, and the action taken by the governing power is on behalf of the State rather than in behalf of the human beings considered as individuals. The idea of the community, with all its implications of a common interest and a common purpose, runs through the entire Middle Ages.

A majority of the subjects—we of the Western World prefer to speak of 'citizens'—determines the government and elects the head of the State; because a State cannot exist unless there be order—preferably of a permanent nature—which order, being essential, is either by natural or divine law, or by both, and the head of the State being necessary to carry out this natural or divine order, and thus to execute the policy of the State—which is directly or indirectly the will of the majority—it follows that the means to the end is in accordance with the natural or divine order. The favourite expression in this connexion is: 'All power is of God.' But it is the equal right of the entire people, or the majority—inasmuch as it may be difficult or impossible for all to assemble—to exercise this power, whether it be expressed in the formation of government or in the policy which the government as their agent shall pursue, either in response to a specific direction or in accordance with their general consent, express or implied. The power is divine, its manifestation human: in the familiar Latin phrase—*Vox populi, Vox Dei.*

It is not necessary at this time to inquire why the people organize themselves into groups which we call States. The Aristotelian conception that man is a social and a political animal suffices in general; but in dealing with the State of the Middle Ages a word should be said as to the cause and the purpose of the State, in that Aristotle's conception of social and political organization was material, while that of the Christian State was spiritual. The end of such organization according to Aristotle was the well-being of the peoples grouped in a *civitas* forming a civil State. The end of the Christian State, on the other hand, was the preparation of the individuals forming a larger group and province—or Christendom—for the life hereafter, which, in theological parlance, is that of eternal felicity; and such preparation required not merely right conduct, leading to a good life and temporal happiness, but the conduct prescribed by the Church.

We are dealing with the schoolman's conception of the State, set forth in its most perfect and authoritative form by the very head and front of scholasticism—none other than Thomas of Aquinas, Doctor and Saint, in the thirteenth century, the greatest of medieval centuries—a century which believed, as has sometimes happened in history, that it had solved the world's problems and put them in a definitive form. This belief, however, was to be shaken before the end of the century by the life-and-death contest between Boniface VIII and Philip the Fair of France, for whom it appears that Egidius Romanus[1] (St. Thomas's favourite pupil) prepared a tractate of instruction along the lines marked out by St. Thomas, and which he called by the same name as the master had called his—the unfinished *De Regimini Principum*. Nevertheless the belief of the thirteenth century was not without a certain justification. The works of St. Thomas were not merely the masterpieces of their time, but, within the broad frontiers of Christendom, for all time, however much they might be questioned from one century to another. Was not the thirteenth century in possession of the great sources from which St. Thomas might and did draw? Instead of having to rely upon references to Aristotle, the philosopher—and he is said upon competent authority to have furnished the most perfect philosophy in matters political—or to Latin translations made from the Greek texts in the hands of the Spanish Arabs and the translations made by Jewish scholars, the West had been endowed by the Crusades with the Greek texts themselves; the texts were therefore not only at the disposal of St. Thomas but he had actually read them and translated them from the Greek. Then again there were available in fragmentary form the works of Cicero: the *Somnium Scipionis* (later found to be a part of *De Republica*, which came to light in 1820), and the dialogue *De Legibus*, imitating the *Dialogues* of Plato, in which, however, Cicero speaks in his own person. And finally, St. Thomas Aquinas could appeal to the Roman law in the form of the successful codifications by Justinian.

So much for the classical models.

As a theologian, the ecclesiastical models would appeal to St. Thomas because of their reason; the writings of the churchmen by their authority as well, among which were predominant then and now

[1] Egidius the Roman, born Egidius Colonna [1247–1316], tutor of Philip IV of France, Archbishop of Bourges, noted theologian, was a son of the ancient and powerful Roman family of Colonna. He was a student of St. Thomas Aquinas at Paris, and later was appointed to teach there, the first Augustinian to be invited so to do. His learning earned for him the title of *Doctor fundatissimus*. Politically he favoured Boniface VIII in opposition to his pupil, Philip, as is clear from the fact that he is the author of the *Unam Sanctam*.

those of St. Augustine. Even this was not all: there were the Testaments, Old and New; the one for history, the other for doctrine. As a scholar and theologian, as philosopher and historian, St. Thomas Aquinas (who from his social position was of the blood royal and imperial,[1] endowed with an understanding which comprehended at first reading and never forgot, who was an Italian by birth and a Frenchman by education, and by experience and by outlook a citizen of the world) was indeed competent to interpret the past to his present and to supply the world with a new intellectual point of departure.

Therefore it was that Victoria, a Dominican, would have been impressed by the Dominican writings of St. Thomas. As a student he was familiar with them, because they were the favourite text of every branch of the Dominican Order. He had lectured on them in Paris and he lectured on the *Summa* during his professorate in Salamanca. His conception of the State was Aristotelian in origin, with sundry additions, and was based upon the form in which it was left by St. Thomas.

The State as an institution was to be self-sufficient, in the sense that it was organized to carry out its aim and purpose, as set forth by the Philosopher. It was also to be perfect, in the sense that in addition to its temporal end and its spiritual end, it was endowed by the opinion of Christendom with the ways and the means to realize the higher purpose. The purpose of the Victorian State—as that of St. Thomas—was to realize right doing, right thinking, and right living in conformity with the Divine Revelation.[2]

The Reading, which we are shortly to examine, that *On the Law of War*, deals with the first phase of the subject (right doing), as Victoria's elaborate Reading *On the Indians* deals with right thinking and right believing. If there be right doing, we have that tranquillity of order within the State which is peace, according to St. Augustine, St. Thomas Aquinas, and Francisco de Vitoria. This was conceived as the normal state of affairs which did not need justification, and for many centuries it has therefore been less elaborately treated. The purpose of war was to restore this tranquillity of order, and as war was abnormal and at most was a remedy, a resort to war would have to be justified because it was in itself destructive—at least for the time being—of tranquillity and peace. What was the justification? There should be a just cause, in order to redress the wrong or injury which had been committed and to restore the status of peace which is the very end and purpose of a resort to arms; and a just cause means a cause which would have resulted in a favourable judgement in different

[1] Landulph, his father, was Count of Aquino; Theodora, his mother, was Countess of Teano. His family was related to the Emperors Henry VI and Frederick II, and to the Kings of Aragon, Castile, and France.

[2] *Vide infra*, pp. 253 *et seq.*, for a discussion of the Victorian concept of the State; *vide* also *infra*, Appendix C, p. lxxi, for the text of the *De Potestate Civili*.

form from a court of justice, if the litigation had arisen within the State. But since there was no court between the nations with a superior judge, the justice of the cause would have to be determined by advice from within the State, that is, through the judgement reached by the counsellors of the prince,[1] without which the latter would be in error and perhaps in mortal sin should he go to war against a defendant State.

The resort to arms, however, was allowable rather than imperative. The pagan and the unbelievers of Victoria's day did not have the scruples of the Christians; but the scruples of the Christian were very serious, for the doctrine of the Gospel is the doctrine of peace. Was it lawful in accordance with the express terms of the Gospel—not to speak of its implications—for the Christian to resort to arms destructive of the promise of peace? Tertullian, one of the early churchmen, was not only opposed to Christians going to war but his conception of peace went so far as to prevent princes from indulging in litigation before the courts. The view of Tertullian would better be met by a churchman. It was met by a churchman—the churchman being St. Augustine; and the view of St. Augustine prevailed in the practice of Christians: that a just cause was necessary for a just war; and therefore in the absence of a superior judge over both of the States it was permissible to resort to arms in order to redress the injury which the complaining prince had received at the hands of the defendant State. With St. Thomas the views of St. Augustine, transmitted through various channels (notably the *Decretum* of Gratian), prevailed.[2] The views of St. Thomas, based as they were upon St. Augustine, likewise prevailed with Francisco de Vitoria, and indeed throughout Christendom.[3]

*
* *

St. Augustine standing between the Pagan and the Christian worlds interpreted the Pagan to the Christian, and his interpretation, passing into works of authority, became a part of the foundation upon which the new structure was raised.

The old order was indeed changing, 'giving place to new'. The change was rapid, as is the case when the sword is drawn. Rome had been taken, and the Roman Empire was crumbling, if it was not entirely in ruins. Constantine was no more, and with him went the last

[1] *Vide infra*, pp. 221 *et seq.*

[2] *Vide* Professor Ernest Nys, *Notes pour Servir à L'Histoire Littéraire & Dogmatique du Droit International en Angleterre* (Brussels, 1888), especially pp. 18 *et seq.* For an extended treatment of the Law of War, *vide* also Professor Nys's notable volume, *Le Droit de la Guerre et les Précurseurs de Grotius*, *op. cit.*, especially ch. ii.

[3] On the contributions of the early fathers and theologians of the Catholic Church to this subject *vide* particularly the admirable lectures delivered at the *Institut des Hautes Études Internationales*, Paris, in 1929, by Professor Yves de la Brière, under the title *La Conception du Droit International chez les Théologiens Catholiques*. These lectures have been published, although not in definitive form, by the *Centre Européen de la Dotation Carnegie pour la Paix Internationale* (Paris, 1930).

vestiges of an imperial power whose very name was once a conjuration before which 'the heavens were silent, and the earth stood still'.

The qualms of conscience which the Christians of St. Augustine's day had were of military service, and of their duty to the Prince of Peace amid the clash of arms. The great Father of the Church saw an impending anarchy, if the New Testament were to be interpreted so literally—without reference to the *whole* Teaching—that it would prevent the operations of common justice, indeed, bring about the downfall of the entire civil order. Head of the Church he was not: but he was then, is now, and bids fair to remain, with St. Thomas Aquinas, its accredited representative. Under the conditions of the age in which St. Augustine lived, in the fourth and fifth centuries, we should only expect to find in his writings statements here and there of peace, and then but in the nature of a definition of the normal order which was to succeed the wars, if they would but end; for the justification of war in the past, as it is in the present, was the establishment of peace. Peace, to St. Augustine, however, is the end and aim of all. The Perfect Man is at peace, so is the Perfect State; Heaven is at Peace; and God Himself *is* Peace. Did not our General Sherman, who was thought to have been stronger in war than in peace, base the justification of war exclusively upon its ushering in of peace?

It is natural, therefore, that given the accredited position of St. Augustine as Saint and as Doctor, his views would find favour with posterity and would necessarily crowd out the views of others, especially since the multiplication of books by a mechanical process had not then come into being. Manuscript passed from hand to hand, was copied, and selected passages found their way into works of authority—into Gratian's *Decretum*, for example, which during centuries was the only collection to which churchmen turned, deriving from it their knowledge of the Canons of the Church. Passages which the otherwise unknown Gratian[1] had marked and included in his great compilation became classics on the subjects whereof they treated, and Gratian's reading, instead of the original texts, became the point of departure of future thought and development.

St. Augustine has indeed provided us with the seeds from which was to spring our modern law of nations. True, they are not to be found in a single place, nor arranged as it were in the form of a tractate. St. Augustine's works are, as one writer has described them, almost without exception '*livres de circonstance*'. For him, the important

[1] Practically nothing is known of Gratian. A popular medieval legend made him a brother of Peter Lombard, but researches into the life of the latter show the tradition to be without foundation. His *Decretum* did not exist previous to 1139, for it contains decrees of the Second Lateran Council which was held in that year; it was, however, known to Peter Lombard, for he makes use of it in several places in the *Sententiae*. Tradition says that Gratian was a Bolognese, but to support the theory there is but a single proof—the Church of St. Petronius in Bologna contains a medieval monument erected to him. The *Catholic Encyclopaedia* calls him 'the true founder of the Science of Canon Law'.

matter was the most pressing question of the day; girded with a two-edged sword—his brilliant mind and facile pen—he stood ever prepared to do battle for the infant Church against any and all of the many evils, internal and external, which beset it. Only diligent examination of his voluminous works will serve to bring to light the principles of what we of to-day call international law, and with which he sprinkled his manifold controversies. We have chosen a sentence here and a paragraph there, not to show how much St. Augustine did, or how far he went towards founding the law of nations—for that would be misleading—but to bring together in a logical sequence those passages which were the great sources of Victoria's reflection—indeed, which for many ages were the only ruling law upon the subject of war between Christian States.

Victoria both as jurist and as theologian was familiar with the *Decretum*. From his knowledge of the latter alone—apart from his familiarity with the original texts of St. Augustine, which he evinces by direct references to them—Victoria knew of Augustine's weight and influence, in the threefold capacity of Father, Saint, and Doctor of the Church, in lending a Christian interpretation to the leading principles of Roman jurisprudence. What is more to be expected then, than that he would base his first and fundamental contention in the Reading *On the Law of War*—whether it is right for Christians to engage in war—upon that classic passage of St. Augustine which Gratian had embodied in his code of Canons?

'For what', the Doctor asks, 'is to be condemned in war?'[1] It cannot be death, though war and death walk hand in hand. Mere fear of death should not prevent the Christian from waging war, nor fear of causing death. Is not death a part of the normal order? Must not the Christians always be prepared to die? 'It would be characteristic of the timid, and not of the religious,' St. Augustine says with scorn, 'to rail thus against war.'[2] What, then, are those evils which are so intimately connected with war that they are in themselves a justification for making war?

'The desire of doing wrong, the cruelty of revenge, a restless and unquiet mind, the fierceness of rebellion, the lust of power, and such-like things, these are condemned in the law of war.' These must never animate the Christian mind: indeed, when the Christian finds these faults in others, and considerations of order compel him, he is even bound to go to war to punish them. 'Commonly, in order that these may be punished even by the law, by God, or by any legitimate authority ordering it, either wars themselves are made by good men against the violence of their adversaries, or things come to pass in the order of human events where considerations of order either compel

[1] *Contra Faustum*, xxii. 74; quoted in *Decretum*, II. xxiii. 1, ch. 4.

[2] *Ibid.*

men to command something of the kind'—that is to say, that Christian men should go to war—'or force them to obey similar orders'.[1]

If it were not right that Christians should go to war, St. Augustine goes on to say, St. John, when the soldiers came to him to be baptized and asked him what they should do, 'would have answered them saying: Throw down your arms; desert the army itself; persecute, wound, destroy no man.' But this was not John's answer. 'Because he knew them—that when they did these things in battle they were not murderers, but were ministers of the law; that they were not avengers of their own injuries, but were guardians of the public safety, he made answer to them: *Do violence to no man; neither calumniate any man; and be content with your pay.*'[2] Moreover, as St. Augustine points out, Christ Himself ordered that money to be paid to Caesar which John says ought to satisfy the soldiers, and he quotes as evidence the passage —*Render therefore to Caesar the things that are Caesar's; and to God, the things that are God's.*[3] Taxes (or 'tributes', as the Scriptures have it) were paid for this very purpose, 'since because of wars, pay is necessarily furnished the soldier'. Furthermore, Our Lord praised a soldier for his faith—'For just was the saying of that Centurion, *For I also am a man subject to authority, having under me soldiers; and I say to this, Go, and he goeth, and to another, Come, and he cometh, and to my servant, Do this, and he doeth it.*[4] Christ praised his faith, and did not order him to leave his soldiers.'[5]

In another place[6] St Augustine's opponents have brought forward the text, *Put up again thy sword into its place: for all that take the sword shall perish with the sword.* He is ready with his eternal answer: 'He . . . "takes the sword" who, by no authority or legitimate power either ordering it or permitting it, arms himself against the blood of any man.' This is a legal definition, as well as one quite in keeping with Christian theology and doctrine; moreover, for us who seek an international application, it has a most interesting content. Augustine is here condemning *private warfare.*

In a letter to Boniface,[7] Roman General and Governor of Africa, who had requested that he 'write . . . something which might build [him] up unto the Eternal Salvation of which [he] had hope in Our Lord Jesus Christ', we find St. Augustine writing as spiritual adviser to a soldier;—not condemning him for his manner of life, but admonishing him rather to follow his calling in a Christian manner, and to 'hope for salvation'—clearly indicating that Augustine saw no incompatibility between Christianity and military duty. 'Do not think', he says, 'that it is impossible for any one to please God while actively engaged in

[1] *Contra Faustum*, xxii. 74. [2] St. Luke, iii. 14. [3] St. Matthew, xxii. 21.
[4] *Ibid.*, viii. 9, 10. [5] Augustine, *Contra Faustum*, xxii. 74. [6] *Ibid.*, xxii. 70.
[7] Epistle [*ad Bonifacium*] CLXXXIX [old number CCV]; written A.D. 418.

bearing arms. . . .' Instead, he advises him: 'think . . . of this first of all, when thou armest thyself for the fight: that even thy bodily strength is a gift of God; and then, so much wilt thou think of God's gift, that thou wilt not use it against Him.' Physical power being entrusted to man, then, and since 'when faith is pledged, it is to be kept even with the enemy against whom the war is waged', the conclusion is obvious. 'How much more', he exclaims, 'is it to be kept with the friend for whom the battle is fought!'[1]

To what use does God desire us to put that strength with which we have been entrusted? In other words, *what is the object* of war—since it stands proven that we have not been forbidden to take part in it? 'Peace', says St. Augustine, 'should be the object of your desire; war should be waged only as a necessity, and waged only that God may by it deliver men from the necessity, and maintain them in peace. For peace is not sought after, that wars may be made; but war is made that peace may be acquired.' How, then, may one wage war, and still be a consistent seeker after peace? The answer is ready for us.

'Be therefore a peacemaker even in warring: so that by conquering those whom you war against, you may lead them back to the usefulness of peace; for *Blessed are the peacemakers* (saith the Lord), *for they shall be called the children of God*.[2] If that human peace be so sweet which obtains the temporal safety of mortals,' St. Augustine exclaims, 'how much sweeter is that divine peace which obtains for men the eternal felicity of the angels!' Although he does not refer directly to them, it is clear to us that the verses of Ecclesiastes[3] must have been running through his mind when he writes: 'Therefore let necessity and not thy will slay the enemy who fights against thee. Even as you use violence against him who is rebellious and resists, so you ought to be merciful towards the vanquished or the captive, especially in the case where a future disturbance of the peace is not to be feared.'[4]

St. Augustine now considers the fundamental reasons why we may go to war. Here we shall see him at his best[5] and in his glory as the founder of the scholastic method of exposition; and the passage is in itself so full of interest that it should be quoted in full.

The things which this [earthly city] desires cannot justly be said to be evil, for it is itself, in its own kind, better than all other human good. For it desires earthly peace for the sake of enjoying earthly goods, and it makes war in order to attain to this peace; since if it has conquered, and there remains no one to resist it, it enjoys a peace which it had not while there were opposing parties who contested for the enjoyment of those things which were too small to satisfy both. This peace is purchased by toilsome wars; it is obtained by what they style a glorious victory. Now when victory remains with the party which had the juster cause, who hesitates to congratulate the victor, and style it a desirable peace? These

[1] Augustine, *Ep.* [CLXXXIX] *ad Bonifac.*

[2] St. Matthew, v. 9.

[3] Eccles. iii. 1 and 8: 'All things have their season, and in their times all things pass under heaven . . . A time to love and a time to hate. A time of war and a time of peace.'

[4] Augustine, *Ep.* [CLXXXIX] *ad Bonifac.*

[5] *De Civitate Dei*, xv. 5.

things then are good things, and without doubt the gift of God. But if they neglect the better things of the heavenly city, where there will be victory secure in the midst of eternal peace, and so inordinately covet these present good things that they believe them alone to be desirable, or love them better than those things which are believed to be better,—if this be so, then it is necessary that misery follow and ever increase.

Here we have one of those few rare cases where a writer—without the least trace of cynicism—dares to give the true reason for which men make war—'*to obtain earthly peace for the sake of enjoying earthly goods. . . .*' a contest '*for the enjoyment of those things which were too small to satisfy both* [parties to the war]'. As we should expect, however, St. Augustine does not stop there, but adds a trenchant warning concerning the danger of becoming absorbed in the material things of life at the expense of the spiritual.

Who has the power to make war—even the war which he has just described? 'It is of importance [to consider] . . . by what authorities men undertake to make wars. . . .' St. Augustine's consideration of the point leads him to conclude that 'the natural order accommodated to the peace of mortals demands that the authority and counsel for making war should be with the Prince'. And the rest of humanity: is it entirely free from all responsibility in such weighty matters? 'The soldiers owe the service of following up the military commands', answers the Doctor, 'in behalf of the common peace and safety.'[1]

Again the question of military service arises. St. Augustine's day, even as our own, was not quite lacking in those troubled souls whom we, of another world and another day, are accustomed to call 'conscientious objectors'. We are confronted here with that age-old proposition: 'Granted that I owe a duty to the State to assist it in prosecuting a just war, what is my duty, if I believe its cause is not just?' Augustine answers the query for us. 'There is no power but of God, Who either orders or permits. A righteous man, serving it may be under an ungodly king, may do the duty belonging to his position in the state in fighting at the command of his sovereign:—for in some cases it is plainly the Will of God that he should fight, and in others where it is not so plain, the command on the part of the king may be unrighteous' but the soldier acting under orders is innocent, 'because his position makes obedience a duty.'[2]

How now shall our Augustinian war be conducted? Shall it be what we may call a hollow pretext? Or shall it be with the vigour of an outraged Christianity righteously defending itself? St. Augustine seems to hold with the ancient proverb to the effect that 'all things' are 'fair' in war. He speaks here[3] in terms of the 'ambush'—an excellent example, even to-day, of that type of tactics which, outside of war, would be classed among those treacheries most to be abhorred by men.

[1] *Contra Faustum*, xxii. 75.

[2] *Ibid.*

[3] *Liber Quaestionum in Heptateuchum*, vi. 10.

'As to what God ordered, saying to Josue that he should command his troops to make an ambush—that is, a warlike ambush in order to entrap the enemy—we are told that it was not done unjustly for those who made a just war: for a just man ought not to give special consideration to these matters, but only that he begin a just war.' The conclusion is assuredly the Doctor's last word on the subject. 'However, once he has begun a just war, whether he conquers by open battle or by guerrilla warfare, nothing should interfere with justice.' And the just war, he defines as 'wont to be limited to that which avenges an injury, as where any people or state is to be punished for neglect to exact amends from its citizens for their wrongdoing, or to restore what has wrongfully been taken away'.[1]

'In all the things which appear shocking or terrible to human feebleness'—he speaks generally now—'the real evil is the injustice: the rest is only the result of natural properties or of moral demerit.' This is not all. St. Augustine elucidates his thought: 'This injustice is seen in every case where a man loves for their own sake things which are desirable only as means for an end, and seeks for the sake of something else things which ought to be loved for themselves.'[2] This is one of those eternal truths which has made the name of St. Augustine ring from age to age, respected by all men alike and destined to be honoured in the future as it has been in the past for fifteen hundred years, as next to that of St. Paul, the greatest of the names attached to Christian teaching.

Thus, he goes on to say, a man, as far as he is able 'disturbs in himself the natural order which the eternal law requires us to observe. . . . A man is just when he seeks to use things only for the end for which God appointed them: and to enjoy God as the end of all. . . . To love in a friend the love of God, is to love the friend for God. Both justice and injustice, to be acts at all, must be voluntary, otherwise, there can be no just rewards or punishments.'[3]

Peace, St. Augustine has told us elsewhere, is the end and aim of war. He has told us in what that earthly peace consists: now for his basic, his radical definition of that state of being so good that Christians do not hesitate to join it to the Name of God Himself—calling Him the Prince of Peace. We shall quote to some extent then, from that chapter of his *Civitas Dei*[4] which treats

Of the Universal Peace Which the Law of Nature Preserves through All Disturbances, and by which Every one Reaches His Desert in a Way Regulated by the Just Judge.

The peace of the rational soul is 'the ordered harmony of knowledge and action'. The peace of body and soul is 'the well-ordered and

[1] *Ibid. Vide* also *supra*, p. 129, and *infra*, pp. 200–1.
[2] *Contra Faustum*, xxii. 77.
[3] *Ibid.*, 78.
[4] *De Civitate Dei*, xix. 13.

harmonious life of the living creature'. Peace between man and God is the 'well-ordered obedience of faith to eternal law'. Peace between man and man is 'well-ordered concord'. Domestic peace is the 'well-ordered concord between those of the family who rule and those who obey'. Civil peace is a like 'concord between the citizens' of the state. Finally, 'the peace of all things is the tranquillity of order'.

The last phrase which we have quoted is not mere rhetoric. St. Augustine is not a trifler, or a mere pedant probing the eternal problems of the human race, that he may clothe his discoveries in the loveliness of words. St. Augustine is working for men, and in so doing labours for God. He defines his terms, pursuing his definition through the dark and tortuous by-ways of thought, catching it, examining it, stating it in the unchanging terms of everlasting truth.

What is order? 'Order is the distribution which allots things equal and unequal, each to its own place.' This is that Divine Order of which the Fathers speak, requiring that there should be some good even in the worst of men. In the maintenance of this order, God, 'the most wise Creator and just Ordainer of all natures, who placed the human race upon earth as its greatest adornment, imparted to men some good things adapted to this life'; the best of which things, the Doctor and Saint would seem to imply, is 'temporal peace, such as we can enjoy in this life from health and safety and human fellowship'.[1]

Nor is this all. What means have we of protecting this gift of peace? With the other Fathers St. Augustine agrees that God has given us nothing good without also giving us the means of maintaining it. 'God has imparted to men all things needful for the preservation and recovery of this peace, such as the objects which are accommodated to the outward senses, light, night, the air, and waters suitable for us, and everything the body requires to sustain, shelter, or beautify it. . . .' This is the peace of the individual.

What is the peace of Society, as we would say, and upon what is it based? St. Augustine answers that we should love God, and that we should love our neighbour; and as 'in these precepts a man finds three things he has to love—God, himself, and his neighbour—and as he finds that he who loves God thereby loves himself, it follows that he must get his neighbour to love God, since he is ordered to love his neighbour as himself'. Now for the result of the active application of this precept of Charity. 'Consequently he will be at peace,' St. Augustine says, 'or in well-ordered concord with all men, as far as in him lies.'[2]

What sort of concord is this? We have already been told that the concord of the individual peace consists in friendship with God and health of mind and body. The concord of the social peace, according to St. Augustine, is not unlike that of the individual peace. 'And this

[1] *De Civitate Dei*, xix. 13.

[2] *Ibid.*, xix. 14.

is the order of this concord, that a man, in the first place, injure no one; and in the second, do good to every one he can reach.' In this we see the practical Roman in St. Augustine coming again to the fore. The general principle is not sufficient for him; he is only too well acquainted with the habit of fellow men to give honour to good in the abstract, but to fail to observe it in the particular.

Wherein may every man apply the 'order of this concord'? 'Primarily, . . . [a man's] own household is his care, for the law of nature and of society gives him readier access to them and greater opportunity of serving them.' The result? Again the same—friendship and 'health', or earthly happiness.

The *Civitas Dei*, which we have laid under heavy contribution, is a spiritual forerunner of Sir Thomas More's *Utopia*. It has the special distinction in literature, however, of being the first of the Christian tractates in that tradition which deals with the perfect political community, and which is continuous, unbroken, from Plato's day until our own—attesting to the native optimism of mankind which, in spite of all reverses, still persists in hoping, striving, planning for the beautiful 'No Where' of the spirit.

It is indeed fitting, then, that the idea of Victoria's 'international community' should have been conceived in a moment when Christianity was at the cross roads, to be born, as it were, some eleven centuries later, the child of humanity's travail. The 'heavenly city' while it sojourns on earth, 'calls citizens out of all nations, and gathers together a society of pilgrims of all languages, not scrupling about diversities in the manners, laws, and institutions whereby earthly peace is secured and maintained, but recognizing that, however various these are, they all tend to one and the same end of earthly peace. It is therefore so far from rescinding and abolishing these diversities, that it even preserves and adopts them, so long only as no hindrance to the worship of the One Supreme and True God is thus introduced'. The heavenly city—the true *Civitas Dei*—the Doctor goes on to say, while in its stage of pilgrimage 'avails itself of the peace of earth, and so far as it can, without injuring faith and godliness, desires and maintains a common agreement among men regarding the acquisition of the necessaries of life, and makes this earthly peace bear upon the peace of heaven'.[1]

* * *

It was natural that St. Thomas Aquinas, a Saint and Doctor of the Church—the days of the 'Fathers' were past—should have dwelt upon the passages of St. Augustine dealing with the subjects whereof he himself treated in his *Summa*, especially in those sections concerning

[1] *Ibid.*, ix. 17. For a further analysis of St. Augustine's views on peace and war *vide* Herbert Francis Wright, 'St. Augustine and International Peace' published in *Thought*, vol. vi, no. 3 (December, 1931), pp. 399–416.

the questions of peace and of war, which perplexed our long line of ancestors, which perplex us of to-day and which we may hope, but cannot safely predict, will be unknown to our ultimate posterity.

International relations are made up, apparently, of peace and of war, and the two sections of the *Secunda Secundae* of St. Thomas's *Summa* dealing with peace and with war[1] have had such an influence on the early writers on the law of nations, that it would be no stretch of terms to consider St. Thomas as one of its founders; and, in a lesser degree, the advocates of St. Augustine could make a like claim for this Father, this Doctor and this Saint of the Church.

It would be a reflection upon the intelligence of even the most casual reader to inform him that St. Thomas was a schoolman (indeed, he was the greatest among them); and he himself is held to be responsible for the continued use and perfection of the method which we call scholastic exposition—a method, be it said, in which the views of the opponent are first stated with both fullness and accuracy, in order to be refuted by the schoolman, should his wit and ingenuity be equal to the task. Now St. Thomas was not merely equal, but superior; and his method is in fact, though not in name, of our day as well as of future days—for we may not effectively refute the views of our opponents which we have not stated in full, a fact well known to controversialists, whether they be debaters in parliament, advocates in a court of justice, or theologians of whatever sect or faction.

First of peace, in Article 29, *Secunda Secundae*, of the *Summa Theologica* of Saint Thomas. His exact language, as well as that of the text which he invokes, is of the essence, and in a matter of this importance and difficulty, it is better for a third party to eliminate himself: 'Peace is the same as concord', he declares and quotes from St. Augustine (*De Civ. Dei*, xix): '*Peace among men is well ordered concord*'; furthermore, concord '*is union of wills*', and for this definition St. Thomas invokes the statement of Dionysius (*Div. Nom.* xi): that '*peace unites all, and makes them of one mind*'.[2]

So much for the antecedents. Now for the views of St. Thomas, which invariably follow the authorities whom he seeks to refute, beginning with the words, 'I answer that', and constituting, in the opinion of posterity, a demonstration. 'Peace includes concord and adds something thereto. Hence wherever peace is, there is concord, . . .

'For concord, properly speaking, is between one man and another in so far as the will of various hearts agree together in consenting to the same thing.'[3]

[1] Peace is dealt with in *Secunda Secundae* (*Summa Theologica*), question 29, in four articles; War, in the same, question 40, in four articles. See below and following pages.

[2] The translation used throughout the following pages is that of the Fathers of the English Dominican Province: *The 'Summa Theologica' of St. Thomas Aquinas Part II.* (*Second Part*) *First Number*, QQ. I–XLVI (London, 1917), pp. 381 *et seq.*

[3] *Ibid.*, p. 382

St. Thomas now refers to the source of authority, 'Augustine is speaking there of that peace which is between one man and another, and he says that this peace is concord, but that which is well ordered, through one man agreeing with another in respect of something befitting to both of them.' Here we have St. Augustine's famous definition of peace, which pervaded the Middle Ages and which might well be of interest to us of to-day.[1] 'For if one man concord with another, not of his own accord, but through being forced, as it were, by the fear of some evil that besets him, such concord is not really peace, because the order of each concordant is not observed, but is disturbed by some fear-inspiring cause.'[2] What, then, is the peace which St. Augustine had in mind and upon which St. Thomas is relying? 'For this reason he premises that *peace is tranquillity of order*, which tranquillity consists in all the appetitive movements in one man being set at rest together.'[3]

Having demonstrated that peace is the same as concord, St. Thomas now passes to the question whether 'all things desire peace'.[4] 'Peace', he says, strengthening an opinion which he was shortly to destroy, '*unites consent*', vouching Dionysius for the statement. The desire of peace 'is, seemingly, the sovereign good which is the last end. . . . . *Have peace among you*', he adds (appealing to St. Mark for the precept);[5] and as his conclusion he states that '*all things desire peace*', relying again upon St. Augustine and Dionysius.[6]

At this point, St. Thomas speaks *in propria persona* '*I answer that*', and as an example of his method, his complete comment on this point is given: 'From the very fact that a man desires a certain thing it follows that he desires to obtain what he desires, and, in consequence, to remove whatever may be an obstacle to his obtaining it. Now a man may be hindered from obtaining the good he desires, by a contrary desire either of his own or of some other, and both are removed by peace, as stated above. Hence it follows of necessity that whoever

[1] *Vide supra*, pp. 185 *et seq.* [2] *The Summa Theologica, ibid.* [3] *Ibid.*

[4] *Ibid.*, article 2, p. 383. [5] St. Mark, ix. 49.

[6] St. Augustine, *De Civitate Dei*, xix; Dionysius, *De Divinis Nominibus*, xi. Dionysius, who has been cited before [*vide* p. 188, *supra*], is often mentioned as '*Pseudo-Dionysius*' or, more exactly, as '*Dionysius the Pseudo-Areopagite*'.

It is to be assumed that Dionysius did not live before the latter half of the fifth century and that he was probably a Syrian; and what we know of him is to be gathered from his works, which have been held in peculiarly high regard since the end of the sixth century by Christians, both orthodox and heretical.

The Greek Church was especially proud of him; but even in the West, down to the first half of the fifteenth century, his works were regarded as 'exceedingly valuable, and even sacred. It was believed that St. Paul, who had communicated his revelations to his disciple in Athens, spoke through these writings'. [*Vide Catholic Encyclopaedia*, vol. v, p. 17.]

His principal work, *De Divinis Nominibus*, is a disquisition on theology, arranged as a commentary upon the attributes of God as known from the names given to Him in Scripture.

Lorenzo Valla (1407 [?]–57) was the first to express his doubts concerning the works openly. The learned world has long been at loggerheads as to the authenticity of his writings. At present it would seem, however, that Protestant, as well as Catholic, scholarship is in favour of the validity of the works themselves and the reputation of Dionysius may be looked upon as restored.

desires anything desires peace, in so far as he who desires anything, desires to attain, with tranquillity and without hindrance, to that which he desires: and this is what is meant by peace which Augustine defines (*De Civ. Dei*, XIX) [as] *the tranquillity of order.*'

This is indeed true to one whose mind is attuned to peace. What of those whose specialty is war and its justification? 'Even those desire nothing but peace, which they deem themselves not to have. For as we stated above, there is no peace when a man concords with another man counter to what he would prefer. Consequently men seek by means of war to break this concord, because it is a defective peace, in order that they may obtain peace, where nothing is contrary to their will. Hence all wars are waged that men may find a more perfect peace than that which they had heretofore.'[1]

Speaking of perfect peace, St. Thomas says: 'It consists in the perfect enjoyment of the sovereign good, and unites all one's desires by giving them rest in one object. This,' he believes, 'is the last end of the rational creature, according to Ps. cxlvii. 14: *Who hath placed peace in thy borders.*'[2]

In the next section,[3] St. Thomas discusses whether peace is the proper effect of charity, and states the view that peace 'is the effect of justice, according to Isa. xxxii. 17: *And the work of justice shall be peace*'; and he quotes Ps. cxviii. 165: '*Much peace have they that love Thy Law.*'

Having reached this point, St. Thomas expresses his own views. '*I answer that*, Peace implies a twofold union, as stated above (A. 1). The first is the result of one's own appetites being directed to one object; while the other results from one's own appetites being united with the appetite of another: and each of these unions is effected by charity:—the first, in so far as man loves God with his whole heart, by referring all things to Him, so that all his desires tend to one object: —the second, in so far as we love our neighbour as ourselves, the result being that we wish to fulfil our neighbour's will as though it were ours: for which reason it is reckoned a sign of friendship if people *make choice of the same things* (*Ethics*, IX) [quoting the pagan saint, Aristotle], and Tully [the second of the pagan saints] says (*De Amicitia*) that friends *like and dislike the same things.*'[4]

Again, 'Peace is the *work of justice* indirectly, in so far as justice removes the obstacles to peace: but it is the work of charity directly, since charity, according to its very nature, causes peace. For love is *a unitive force* as Dionysius says (*Div. Nom.* iv): and peace is the union of the appetite's inclinations.'[5]

The last and fourth phase of peace which St. Thomas discusses[6] is in reply to the question whether peace is a virtue. It might seem

[1] *The Summa Theologica* (Reply to Objection 2). [2] *Ibid.* (Reply to Objection 4).
[3] Article 3. [4] *Ibid.*, pp. 385–6. [5] *Ibid.* (Reply to Objection 3). [6] *Ibid.*, article 4.

to the uninitiated that this was the most difficult thing to establish, because it would appear to be one of those truths which our Jefferson, if he were called upon, would declare to be 'self-evident'. Did not St. Mark say (ix. 49): '*Have peace among you*'? upon which St. Thomas, momentarily supporting a view for the purpose of drawing a distinction, concludes: 'Therefore peace is a virtue.' Did not St. Matthew (v. 9) say: '*Blessed are the peacemakers, for they shall be called the children of God*'? And again as before, St. Thomas adds: 'Therefore peace is a virtue.'[1]

Assuredly charity is a virtue, which does not need to be proved, inasmuch as it is admittedly one of the three cardinal virtues. Therefore, to quote St. Thomas who is now ready for his distinction: '*I answer that*, . . . Since then charity causes peace precisely because it is love of God and of our neighbour, as shown above (A. 3), there is no other virtue except charity whose proper act is peace, . . .'

St. Thomas does not, however, content himself with a general statement, but replies further to the question of peace as a virtue that 'We are commanded to keep peace because it is an act of charity; and for this reason too it is a meritorious act'; it is even more than that and 'hence it is placed among the beatitudes, which are acts of perfect virtue, . . . It is also numbered among the fruits, in so far as it is a final good, having spiritual sweetness'.[2]

Passing from that tranquillity of order, which is peace, to discord, which is war, St. Thomas has in Question 40, *Secunda Secundae*, made some observations on war—observations which enter into and form an integral and inseparable part of this modern law of nations, which an unregenerate world has replaced by lucubrations of its own and which the purpose of the present tractate is to replace in turn by the views of St. Thomas Aquinas and Francisco de Vitoria and his school, of which Grotius himself was a member.

The great objection to war, on the part of the early theologians, was its sinfulness, some being of the opinion that it was always sinful; others were of the opinion—among them St. Augustine, St. Thomas, and Francisco de Vitoria and his school—that it was not always so, although undoubtedly they must have been of the opinion that it generally was. Leaving aside the objections to its sinfulness, let us content ourselves with the views of St. Augustine and of St. Thomas, which have prevailed: '*On the contrary*'—it is St. Thomas who is speaking[3]—'Augustine says in a sermon on the son of the centurion (*cf. Ep. ad Marcel.* cxxxviii): "*If the Christian Religion forbade war altogether, those who sought salutary advice in the Gospel would rather have been counselled to cast aside their arms, and to give up soldiering altogether. On the contrary, they were told: 'Do violence to no man; . . .*

[1] *The Summa Theologica*, p. 387. [2] *Ibid.*

[3] *Secunda Secundae* (*Summa Theologica*), question 40, article 1, pp. 500–3.

and be content with your pay.'[1] *If he commanded them to be content with their pay, he did not forbid soldiering.*"' Immediately St. Thomas interposes with an '*I answer that*'—an answer, containing, at least in germ, everything that has or can be said on the lawfulness of war. 'In order for a war to be just, three things are necessary. First, the authority of the sovereign by whose command the war is to be waged. For it is not the business of a private individual to declare war, because he can seek for redress of his rights from the tribunal of his superior. Moreover, it is not the business of a private individual to summon the people, which has to be done in wartime. And as the care of the common weal is committed to those who are in authority, it is their business to watch over the common weal of the city, kingdom, or province subject to them. And just as it is lawful for them to have recourse to the sword in defending that common weal against internal disturbances, when they punish evil-doers, according to the words of the Apostle (Rom. xiii. 4): *He beareth not the sword in vain: for he is God's minister, an avenger to execute wrath upon him that doth evil;* so too, it is their business to have recourse to the sword of war in defending the common weal against external enemies. Hence it is said to those who are in authority (Ps. lxxxi. 4): *Rescue the poor: and deliver the needy out of the hand of the sinner;* and for this reason Augustine says (*Contra Faust.* xxii): *The natural order conducive to peace among mortals demands that the power to declare and counsel war should be in the hands of those who hold the supreme authority.*

'Secondly, a just cause is required, namely that those who are attacked, should be attacked because they deserve it on account of some fault. Wherefore Augustine says (Q. X., super Jos.): *A just war is wont to be described as one that avenges wrongs, when a nation or state has to be punished, for refusing to make amends for the wrongs inflicted by its subjects, or to restore what it has seized unjustly.*

'Thirdly, it is necessary that the belligerents should have a rightful intention, so that they intend the advancement of good, or the avoidance of evil. Hence Augustine says (*De Verb. Dom.*):[2] *True religion looks upon as peaceful those wars that are waged not for motives of aggrandisement, or cruelty, but with the object of securing peace, of punishing evil-doers, and of uplifting the good.* For it may happen that the war is declared by the legitimate authority, and for a just cause, and yet be rendered unlawful through a wicked intention. Hence Augustine says (*Contra Faust.* xxii): *The passion for inflicting harm, the cruel thirst for vengeance, an unpacific and relentless spirit, the fever of revolt, the lust of power, and suchlike things, all these are rightly condemned in war.*' Such

[1] St. Luke, iii. 14.

[2] 'The words quoted are to be found not in S. Augustine's works but Can. *Apud* Caus. xxiii.' [Note to Dominican translation.]

are the three principles which St. Thomas propounds, bottomed upon the authority of St. Augustine. To the objections against the three justifications for war, St. Thomas interposes three replies, standing again upon the authority of St. Augustine.

'*Reply Obj. 1.* As Augustine says (*Contra Faust.* xxii): *To take the sword is to arm oneself in order to take the life of anyone, without the command or permission of superior or lawful authority.* On the other hand, to have recourse to the sword (as a private person) by the authority of the sovereign or judge, or (as a public person) through zeal for justice, and by the authority, so to speak, of God, is not to *take the sword,* but to use it as commissioned by another, wherefore it does not deserve punishment. And yet even those who make sinful use of the sword are not always slain with the sword, yet they always perish with their own sword, because, unless they repent, they are punished eternally for their sinful use of the sword.

'*Reply Obj. 2.* Suchlike precepts, as Augustine observes (*De Serm. Dom. in Monte* i), should always be borne in readiness of mind, so that we be ready to obey them, and, if necessary, to refrain from resistance or self-defence. Nevertheless it is necessary sometimes for a man to act otherwise for the common good, or for the good of those with whom he is fighting. Hence Augustine says (*Ep. ad Marcellin.*): *Those whom we have to punish with a kindly severity,* it is necessary to handle in many ways against their will. For when we are stripping a man of the lawlessness of sin, it is good for him to be vanquished, since nothing is more hopeless than the happiness of sinners, whence arises a guilty impunity, and an evil will, like an internal enemy.

'*Reply Obj. 3.* Those who wage war justly aim at peace, and so they are not opposed to peace, except to the evil peace, which Our Lord *came not to send upon earth* (Matth. x. 34). Hence Augustine says (*Ep. ad Bonif.* clxxxix): *We do not seek peace in order to be at war, but we go to war that we may have peace. Be peaceful, therefore, in warring, so that you may vanquish those whom you war against, and bring them to the prosperity of peace.*'

Undoubtedly the names of the great war lords, Alexander, Hannibal, Caesar, Gustavus Adolphus, Frederick the Great, and Napoleon Bonaparte, have leaped, as it were, to the mind of the reader.

Nobody has ever needed to pore over dusty tomes to discover the precursors of Vitoria's Law of Nations. He does not, as other writers have sometimes done, content himself with listing a few references to the authors whom he consulted—a list which in many cases has proved to be far from complete. Instead of that method of 'damning with faint praise'—for what author ever admitted that he did not add something, if not a great deal, of his own—he cites author, book, chapter and verse, with a generous hand, indicating frankly and clearly all upon whom he chiefly relied. And among those cited, if we may judge by the frequency of the citations, he considered, although he did not say so, St. Augustine and St. Thomas Aquinas as unimpeachable authorities of whom he would have deemed it the honour of his life to be considered a disciple; and he might well have felt himself to be the most fortunate of men could he have foreseen that posterity would consider him as adding to the value of their labours.

Perhaps these preliminary observations will enable the reader the better to understand the background of Victoria and to feel the force and the effect of what he expressly said and also of that which lay implicit in his discussion not only of the State but of war and of the reasons (if indeed there be reasons) for a resort to arms.

CHAPTER IX

ANALYSIS OF THE READING *ON THE LAW OF WAR*

VICTORIA had said in the famous passage which Grotius paraphrased with approval in the opening pages of his tractate on the *Freedom of the Seas*,[1] that the Spaniards under certain conditions could well have justified seizure and occupation of the territories of the American principalities as the result of war. When these two are as one, we are obliged to consider their conclusion as the result of a sincere conviction.

Victoria's statement is to be found in the first of the lawful and adequate titles whereby the Indians might have come under the sway of the Spaniards in the following form: 'When the Indians deny the Spaniards their rights under the law of nations they do them a wrong,' so that, 'if it be necessary, in order to preserve their right, that they should go to war, they may lawfully do so.'[2]

It is to be observed that the law of nations is the test of the Spanish right just as the same law of nations is the test of the duty of the Indian principalities in the matter at hand. We are therefore dealing with the law of nations, and the remedy for the violation of the law of nations was then—as unfortunately it still is—an appeal to force, when reason and persuasion have failed of their purpose. Therefore, the Spaniards might resort to war as the final remedy to redress the wrong and to restore the right. If the right existed and the wrong were proved, the remedy might be lawfully applied. In the Victorian conception, there was a law of nations controlling the actions of all States; there were rights and corresponding duties under the law of nations affecting each and every State; the use of force—resulting in war—as a remedy for a wrong under the law of nations was itself a part of the law of nations; and that remedy must needs be consistent in all its parts with the law of nations, otherwise it would be the commission of a wrong to right a wrong. Therefore it was that Victoria felt himself obliged, notwithstanding his many occupations, to discuss the law of war, so that the examination of the question involved in the readings should be a complete survey of the whole subject under the law of nations in its various aspects. Perhaps he was not aware that, by treating a concrete question affecting in its different relations not merely Christendom but the international community, he was not only furnishing an example of the way in which an international situation should be treated but was showing that the rules of law derived from universal justice—whether it be called natural law, divine law, human law, or all three—were then as now an acceptable and adequate standard for the affairs of nations.

[1] *Op. cit.*, p. 9.

[2] *De Indis, infra*, Appendix A, p. xxxix.

He may be considered as the founder of the modern law of nations, which through Grotius has become the accepted law of nations, for he was as assuredly its unconscious founder as Grotius was its conscious expositor. Without the double Reading *On the Indians* and *On the Law of War*, international law would, in the judgement of no less an internationalist than the late Ernest Nys, have lacked its literary masterpiece.[1] It may perhaps be nearer the mark to say that without the discourse on war, international law would have lacked an authoritative and a reasoned discussion of the ultimate remedy through which the rights and duties existing in time of peace could be restored.

Without, however, questioning the value of the tractate on war, the Belgian publicist's judgement is equally sound on the first of the two Readings, which is to be considered as a conscious, measured, and literary statement of the rights and duties of nations in their peaceful, and therefore normal, conditions and to be regarded as a greater service than even a classic discussion of the abnormal state of affairs which we call war.

Theologian and jurist, philosopher and humanist, Victoria's superiority to all internationalists is that he was above and beyond everything a moralist. In his dealings with himself, he was a moralist; with his students, a moralist; and, in applying the same standard to nations which he applied to the individual—not excluding himself—he was a moralist. The moral standard with him was fundamental. He dealt in fundamentals, and he set them forth as only a theologian and jurist, a philosopher and humanist, who was also a moralist could, in stating the standards of nations which, after all, consist of mere individuals more or less artificially grouped. He saw the parts, but he viewed them as a whole: the State, however large, was a part of the international community, and that international community—representing alike the individuals ungrouped and the individuals grouped in States—was the culmination of his thought, as it is the culmination of centuries of development in matters international. This international community—greater than any of its parts—was to possess the power to issue laws and to punish their violation. But the standard of the international community was to be moral; therefore the conception of the law of the international community and of the States and of the individual was to be a moral conception, and the law

[1] 'Je ne crois point, par exemple, qu'il y ait quelque chose de comparable, dans l'histoire littéraire du droit, aux pages si courtes qui composent la double dissertation *De Indis* de François de Victoria, et cependant celui-ci ne put mettre la dernière main à son œuvre, dont on doit la publication au zèle pieux de ses disciples.' Review by Professor Ernest Nys of Dr. Fr. Séraphin de Freitas's *Justification de la Domination Portugaise en Asie*, printed in the *Bibliographie* of the *Revue de Droit International et de Législation Comparée* (tome xv, 1883), p. 198.

Professor Nys was also a great admirer of Suárez—and indeed of the whole Spanish school; and in the same connexion he adds: 'Je ne pense pas, non plus, que Grotius ait jamais produit mieux que la treizième *Disputatio* de la troisième partie de l'*Opus de triplici virtute theologica* de Suárez.'

imposed was of necessity to be moral, in the sense that it should not be unmoral.

No better example of international morality in action is to be found than in the Reading on war. The rules are often harsh, for war is cruel; but in the Reading on war, as in the first disquisition on peace, Victoria restates the rules as they should be in accordance with his moral conception of things. He no doubt looked upon the Reading in question as an imperfect performance, in that the time at his disposal would not permit him to discuss the subject according to 'the amplitude and dignity of the theme',[1] but only according 'to the shortness of time' at his disposal.[2] Therefore he could deal with only the main propositions, and 'with very brief proofs'; and, as the disquisition was in the form of a series of notes on fundamental points, a conscious limitation caused him to 'abstain from touching on the many doubtful matters which might otherwise be brought into this discussion'.[3] The points which he noted were therefore only four in number: 'First, Whether Christians may make war at all; secondly, Where does the authority to declare or wage war repose; thirdly, What may and ought to furnish causes of just war; fourthly, What and how extensive measures may be taken in a just war against the enemy?'[4] It must be said that his treatment of the fourth point covers the subject as it was in his day and generation; but the 'doubtful matters' which he actually did bring into discussion have found their way into subsequent practice, as well as theory. The fifty pages of the Latin text of Victoria's tractate on war constitute with the prior Reading *On the Indians*, if Professor Nys's statement already referred to is to be considered, an incomparable literary masterpiece in the history of law.[5]

War has been a sore question for many years to the Christian, who, thinking in terms of life and the immortal soul, doubts whether he should be a party to taking life. The early Christians found themselves face to face with the question. Tertullian, a name always to be mentioned with respect, was, as we already know, opposed to war; he was indeed of the opinion that Christians might 'not even go to law' for the settlement of their disputes. In an interesting passage Victoria refers to Luther, to the effect that 'although Catholics are fairly in accord on the matter, yet Luther, who left naught uncontaminated, denies that Christians may take up arms even against the Turks'. He

[1] *De Jure Belli, infra,* Appendix B, p. xlix.

[2] From what we know as the result of recent discoveries, Victoria had persuaded himself that he should make a public profession of his doctrines. Having reached that decision he felt that he should not, by allowing his lectures on legitimate and illegitimate titles to stand alone, expose himself to the risk of being forbidden to deliver a subsequent Reading of a general nature which would, so to speak, complete the whole subject. From the language of the first edition of the *Relectiones,* published in 1557, it appears, therefore, that he delivered all three of the readings in the same term, probably in 1539, according to Getino, *op. cit.*, chapter ix, and especially pp. 162–3, note 1.

[3] *De Jure Belli, infra,* Appendix B, p. xlix. [4] *Ibid.* [5] *Supra,* p. 196, note 1.

had relied on certain texts from the Scripture which Victoria had quoted, 'and also on the fact that if the Turks attack Christendom it is the will of God, which may not be resisted'; but 'herein' Victoria says that Luther 'had not as much success as in his other dogmas in imposing on the Germans, who are born soldiers'.[1] It would appear that Tertullian has not had greater luck with his brother Christians than Luther has had with his fellow countrymen. But the majority of Christians in the time of each—and indeed in our present day—admit a resort to arms, although with a growing hesitation and much misgiving.

But the question was one which could not be avoided, and without considering what the effect upon the early Church would have been of a refusal to permit war under certain conditions—indeed under any condition—the fact is that the Christian philosophy permitted war as a means of restoring that tranquillity of order which St. Augustine called peace[2] and which they looked upon as the normal state of things.

It was natural that Victoria should meet and resolve this question at the threshold of his discussion, because if the view of Tertullian, instead of that of St. Augustine, were to prevail, his discussion on the Indians would have ended without reference to war or a law of war.

Important to the early Christians, important to Victoria, the question is still before the world as to when, and under what conditions, Christians may resort to war.

That Victoria should have discussed the question, and as an introduction to his notes, is an admission that it was an arguable one. He therefore argued it and his argument is that of the schoolmen, first stating the case for the opponents of war, to be followed by the views of those Christians who reluctantly felt themselves obliged to allow war as the handmaid of justice.

The war which the Christians accepted was a just war; and the phrase is to-day on the lips of Christians in many countries. Indeed, in many gatherings of the international community, the phrase is making its way again. The question, therefore, which Victoria discussed still preoccupies the Christian and the Gentile of to-day.

The opponents could invoke more than one passage from the Scriptures. Victoria did this for them. 'War might seem altogether prohibited to Christians,' he said in their behalf, 'for there is the prohibition of self-defence [which is firmly embedded not merely in international but in every national system of law, and which seems to be rooted in our human nature] . . . "Whosoever shall smite thee on the right cheek, turn to him the other also"',[3] and again quoting St.

[1] *De Jure Belli, infra,* Appendix B, p. l. [2] *Vide supra,* p. 186. [3] St. Matthew, v. 39.

Matthew: 'I say unto you not to resist evil';[1] and the further warning: 'All they that take the sword shall perish by the sword.'[2]

In the view of the opponents, these were matters of precept, not of mere counsel to be accepted or rejected. Therefore Victoria invoked for them—for his custom was to strengthen the argument of his opponents—the authority of the passages quoted as precept, not as counsel or words of advice; and by way of further strengthening the opposing argument, he added that the doctors and the received usage of the Church were in favour of precept versus counsel.

When Victoria had made up his mind, he did not mince matters. Fair to his opponents, he was fair to himself, and his answer to this point of view is as he himself said in a single proposition: 'Christians may serve in war and make war.'[3]

But Victoria doubtless felt that a categorical counter-statement was not sufficient. He invoked an array of authorities[4] on behalf of his single proposition, which authorities were accepted as settling the matter in favour of the view which Victoria had expressed. It is, however, fair to say that the authoritative opinions which convinced the early Christians and which Victoria set forth are being questioned to-day as they were at the time of their promulgation by St. Augustine. Many there are—and the number is increasing—who wish that the views of the early Christians, which failed of acceptance in the past, may ultimately prevail in the future.

But to the authorities. The conclusion that Christians may serve in war and make war was, as has been intimated, the conclusion of none other than St. Augustine, whose authority in the Christian world is second only to that of St. Paul, and is set forth, as Victoria says, 'in the many passages where he thoroughly considers the question, such as: (*a*) in his *Contra Faustum*,[5] (*b*) in his *Liber 83 Quaestionum*,[6] (*c*) in his *De Verbis Domini*, in his *Contra Secundum Manichaeum*, (*d*) in his sermon on the Centurion's son, and (*e*) in his *Letter to Boniface*'.[7] This is the authority of a churchman. It is, of course, based upon the Gospel. But one of St. Augustine's illustrations was so apt, and had passed through so many successive generations of commentators, that

1 St. Matthew, v. 39.

2 *Ibid.* xxvi. 52. *De Jure Belli, infra*, Appendix B, p. xlix.

3 *De Jure Belli, infra*, Appendix B, p. l.

4 Among the authorities invoked here is St. Augustine: *Liber 83 Quaestionum.* Victoria has referred to this work previously, in his *Relectio de Indis* [*vide infra*, Appendix A, p. xxix]; and refers to it again twice [*vide infra*, Appendix B, pp. li and liv]. None of these four references appears to be correct. The Editor of the edition of 1696 has made marginal note of two of these errors. On his page 420 he remarks '*Videtur locus hic sumptus ex quaest. super Iosue. q. 10*'. Again, on his page 429 he says '*Potius quaestionib. super Josue. q. 10*'. In both these cases, and also in the case of the first citation, the passage may be found in the Migne edition of the *Patrologia Latina*, volume iii of St. Augustine's works, col. 781. The title of that work is *Quaestionum in Heptateuchum Libri Septem*, and the sixth book, from chapter x of which the quotation is taken, is given the sub-title *Quaestiones in Jesum Nave* (sometimes called *Super Josue*).

5 *Vide supra*, pp. 181–2; 184–5.

6 *Vide* note 4 above.

7 *Vide supra*, p. 182 *et seq.*

Victoria made it the subject of special quotation. It is in the words of St. John the Baptist: 'Do violence to no man, neither accuse any falsely.'[1] 'But,' says St. Augustine, commenting on the elder St. John, 'if Christian doctrine condemned war altogether, those looking for counsels of salvation in the Gospel would be told to throw away their arms and give up soldiering altogether; but what is said to them is, "Do violence to no man and be content with your wages".'[2] This was the first authority.

The second proof which Victoria vouches in behalf of Christians serving in and making war is based on reason and analogy, and his authority is, as might be expected, the second great name in the doctrine of the Christian Church regarding war—St. Thomas Aquinas, in his *Summa Theologica*.[3] If force might be used against 'internal wrongdoers and seditious citizens'—upon the authority of the Gospel[4]—it must also be lawful, Victoria adds, 'to use the sword and arms against external enemies',[5] a statement which seems conclusive as to the reason of the thing.

So far Victoria has in his favour the Gospel and the greatest authorities of his Church. But there was also a law upon which he could rely—the law of nature; and the Gospel law did not forbid that which the natural law allowed; it therefore followed that 'what was lawful under natural law and in the written law' was and is 'no less lawful under the Gospel law'.[6]

The case which Victoria makes is clear as regards the use of force for a defensive purpose. This was, however, only the beginning, but a necessary beginning in that it leads to the admission that force may be used in defence of personal property. After this admission the only question outstanding is whether force could be used only at the moment when the personal property was jeopardized or in advance or thereafter, in its defence. With this phase of the subject Victoria deals in what may be called the second group of his proofs, extending the use of force (already proved to be permissible in defence of self and property) to the avenging of wrongs and the repossessing of property.

The authority for offensive warfare is a passage from St. Augustine, already referred to and to be referred to again;[7] and as Victoria must have considered it not merely as fundamental to the present thesis but

[1] St. Luke, iii. 14

[2] *Vide supra*, p. 182 *et seq. De Jure Belli, infra*, Appendix B, p. l.

[3] *Secunda Secundae*, question 40, article 1. *Vide supra*, p. 191.

[4] Romans, xiii. 4.

[5] *De Jure Belli, ibid.*

[6] *Ibid.* Grotius invokes the Spanish school as if it limited war to the redress of injuries under 'municipal jurisdiction', but maintains that he himself justifies it under the law of nature 'which existed before states were organized'. *Vide* Cornelis Van Vollenhoven, *The Framework of Grotius' Book De iure belli ac pacis* (Amsterdam, 1931), p. 85. Victoria had, however, clearly justified war under the law of nature, as appears from the statement above. He would seem to have covered public war in its entirety, rejecting, however, private war waged by individuals against foreign States, a pet doctrine of Grotius which is the very foundation of his commentary, *On the Law of Prize*, and which he later embodied in the great treatise of 1625.

[7] *Vide supra*, p. 185.

to the entire subject, it should be quoted here. It describes wars as just 'which are waged in order to avenge a wrong done, as where punishment has to be meted out to a city or State because it has itself neglected to exact punishment for an offence committed by its citizens or subjects or to return what has been wrongfully taken away'.[1]

The recurrence of the word 'vengeance' may seem strange in the case of a doctor who was likewise a Saint of the Church. But even a defensive war 'could not', in the opinion of St. Augustine and his followers, 'be waged satisfactorily, were no vengeance taken on enemies who have done or tried to do a wrong', for the reason that they would 'only be emboldened to make a second attack, if the fear of retribution did not keep them from wrongdoing'.[2] Avenging a wrong, as the expression is here used, really means punishment for the commission of a wrong, of such a nature and to such a degree as to prevent its repetition. It is not 'vengeance' in the vulgar sense of the word.[3] The end and aim of war is, however, in the opinion of the doctor, something higher than the recovery of property or avenging a wrong, whether to the person or to the property; it is 'the peace and security of the State'. Indeed the end and aim was, in Victoria's opinion, something still higher—not merely the peace and security of the State, but the 'good of the whole world'.[4] We know from many a bitter experience that what affects one State is bound to affect another, and still another State, so that finally the world itself becomes affected. 'For', in the language of Victoria, 'there would be no condition of happiness for the world, nay, its condition would be one of utter misery, if oppressors and robbers and plunderers could with impunity commit their crimes and oppress the good and innocent.'[5]

Victoria has invoked in behalf of the right of Christians to serve in war and to make war the doctors and the saints of the Church, not without a contribution of his own to the matter in hand. But the moralist within him was not satisfied. There was another proof without which the case would not be stated in all its completeness. 'My eighth and last proof', he says, 'is one which in morals carries the utmost weight, namely, the authority and example of good and holy men'—men who 'have not only defended their country and their own property in defensive wars, but have also in offensive wars sought reparation for wrongs done or attempted by their enemies'.[6]

So the case stands to-day.

[1] *Vide* p. 196, note 4; *Quaestionum in Heptateuchum Libri Septem*, Book 6, chapter 10 (*Quaestiones in Jesum Nave* [Super Josue]), *Patrologia Latina*, Migne ed., volume iii, St. Augustine, col. 781: 'Justa autem bella definiri solent, quae ulciscuntur injurias, si qua gens vel civitas, quae bello petenda est, vel vindicare neglexerit quod a suis improbe factum est, vel reddere quod per injurias ablatum est.'

[2] *De Jure Belli, infra*, Appendix B, p. li.

[3] Cf. the comment of Alfred Vanderpol in *La Doctrine Scolastique de la Guerre, Rapport présenté au Congrès de la paix de Clermont-Ferrand*, 1911 (Paris, 1911), p. 5, note; also the comment in his *Le Droit de Guerre d'après les Théologiens et les Canonistes du Moyen-âge, op. cit.*, p. 111.

[4] *De Jure Belli, infra*, Appendix B, p. li. [5] *Ibid.* [6] *Ibid.*

Francisco de Vitoria deals in single and unequivocal propositions: Christians may serve in war and make war.

'In whose hands lies the authority to declare and to make war?'[1] In the hands of the individual, if he be attacked, his life threatened, and his property menaced; in the State—any and every State—for the redress of a wrong. For what purpose may war be declared? Again a single and unequivocal reason: 'to redress a wrong'. These questions, in this order, are stated and answered by Victoria. Let us consider in the same order his reasons. He answers in justification of a single and unequivocal principle. We do not need to trouble ourselves about the right of the individual to protect himself in person or property, repelling force by force, for which Victoria has cited the *Digest*[2] of Justinian as an unimpeachable authority. Because of this, 'any one', he says, 'can make this kind of war, without authority from any one else'.[3]

Here we come to the first of the doubts with which Victoria sprinkled his discourse on war—doubts of the moralist, doubts of conscience—a statement which should not surprise us with reference to a philosopher, as was Victoria, doubt being said to be the basis of philosophy. There is no doubt, however, as to the right of an individual Spaniard or American to resist force by force in the protection of life or property: the doubt arises as to when this defensive force may be used; and whether the justification extends merely to life or to property or can be extended to what, for lack of a better purpose, we call 'reputation'. Now the right of self-defence arises because of the danger to which the person or his property may be exposed, and from the fact that there is no other remedy available at the moment for the protection of one or the other. And such seems to be the concession everywhere made to human nature in its moments of peril. But suppose that moment has passed. Would the individual be justified on the morrow to use force against him who had imperilled his life or threatened his property? The doubt here is more apparent than real because, when the immediate danger has passed, the court of the prince is available to punish the author of the crime against the person or to exact damage for the property lost or injured.

Suppose, however, that the danger to life or property may be avoided by the withdrawal or by the 'flight' of the person attacked. Victoria is here a moralist, in that he cites authorities who consider the reputation of the individual in the community of which he is a member, as well as his own self-respect, as justifying him in refusing to flee, if by flight he might avoid the physical danger but 'smirch his reputation'.[4]

[1] *De Jure Belli, infra,* Appendix B, p. li.

[2] *ff.*, De Iustitia et Iure, 1. *ut vim* (*Digest*, 1. i. 3): 'FLORENTINUS *libro primo institutionum* ut vim atque iniuriam propulsemus: nam iure hoc evenit, ut quod quisque ob tutelam corporis sui fecerit, iure fecisse existimetur, et cum inter nos cognationem quandam natura constituit, consequens est hominem homini insidiari nefas est.'

[3] *De Jure Belli, ibid.*

[4] *Ibid.*, p. lii.

Again, in this connexion, Victoria shows that he is a moralist of the universal type—not merely as a churchman and in matters of his Church but as a jurist, in behalf of legal ethics, and finally, as a man who knew the world in which he lived. Here, since the question is one of law, he invokes a jurist, indeed the prince of jurists, Bartolus—who, commenting on the *Digest*,[1] holds, in Victoria's statement of the case, 'that self-defence is lawful and that there is no obligation to fly, the putting to flight being itself a wrong'.[2] Victoria's conclusion has therefore the threefold interest to which reference has been made, revealing him as the jurist, the moralist, the churchman, with whom conscience is a supreme test: 'This opinion can be safely held and with possibility of demonstration, especially as the civil law admits as much.'[3]

So much for Bartolus. Now for the threefold view of Victoria that 'no one sins who acts under warrant of the law, inasmuch as the law affords justification in the forum of conscience'. And he concludes his opinion—which is in the form of a syllogism, although he avoids entanglement in the process—by stating that 'even if natural law does not allow killing in defence of property', it is 'lawful by the civil law and is available' to all persons within or without the Church.[4]

The double phase of self-defence which we have thus far discussed is of natural law as embodied in the civil law and inherent in every individual or every State; it is likewise a right of the State under international law. But war, even as self-protection, may be said to be abnormal. The ordinary war—which we hesitate and even refuse to call normal—should be looked upon, if permitted at all, as an exception and not as a rule, as an act of State against State, to be declared solely by the State or the authority which represents the State. Victoria is so set on the moral element and has such an enlarged and fundamental conception of the nature and dignity of the human being that he considers again the right of self-protection of the individual in the discussion of the right of the State to declare war. Still, it is not a repetition; his purpose is to raise a distinction, and when the distinction is made, to pass on to the right of the State or of its prince, as its agent, to declare and to conduct war, whether it be in defence or for punishment.

Victoria finds the difference to lie in the fact that 'a private person is entitled . . . to defend himself and what belongs to him, but has no right to avenge a wrong done to him, nay, not even to recapt property that has been seized from him if time has been allowed to go by since the seizure'.[5] In behalf of his 'private person' he uses an illustration, thus completing a discussion which he had begun, but apparently not finished to his satisfaction: 'But defence can only be resorted to at the very moment of the danger, or, as the jurists say, *in*

[1] Bartolus on *Digest*, XLVIII. xix. 1; XLVIII. viii. 9.
[2] *De Jure Belli, infra,* Appendix B, p. lii. [3] *Ibid.* [4] *Ibid.* [5] *Ibid.*

continenti, and so when the necessity of defence has passed there is an end to the lawfulness of war.' Here the jurist is speaking, but the moralist must be heard at length: 'In my view,' he says, 'one who has been contumeliously assaulted can immediately strike back, even if the assaulter was not proposing to make a further attack.' This he had already said, but the illustration which he gives shows his appreciation of the dignity of man; for he adds that the injured person may use force in the avoidance of shame and disgrace, giving as an example one who 'has had his ears boxed', who may, Victoria holds, 'immediately use his sword, not for the purpose of vengeance, but, as has been said, in order to avoid infamy and disgrace'; and similarly, in his opinion, the State may act in its own behalf and in behalf of its subjects for the redress of wrongs.[1]

The authority to which he appeals has stood the test of some twenty centuries and more and is still the youngest and the most recent as it is the oldest of the books of the State. It is the *Politics* of Aristotle, who has given us, in the form of a maxim, an eternal verity—'a State ought to be sufficient unto itself'.[2]

The pagan having been quoted, the logic of the schoolman appears: 'but it cannot adequately protect the public weal and the position of the State if it cannot avenge a wrong and take measures against its enemies.' The reason is that 'wrongdoers would become readier and bolder for wrongdoing, if they could do wrong with impunity'. Therefore, in Victoria's opinion, it is 'imperative for the due ordering of human affairs that this authority be allowed to States'.[3] The action of the State may always be said to be in self-defence, because an attack by force may jeopardize its existence, as well as such property as it holds; but the activity of the State is likewise punitive, and in addition it is preventive, as that of the individual is not. The State is of course an artificial person; it would perhaps be better to say an artificial conception; but whether an artificial person or conception, it cannot act in its own behalf. There must be a natural person in whom authority is lodged and whose action is in behalf, not of the State as a separate entity, but of the individuals of whom the State is composed. Why, then, resort at all to the fiction of an artificial person, when in the end the resort must, in any case, be made to the natural person, and admittedly the status which we call 'State' consists merely and only of natural persons. The person with authority is by Victoria and his authorities designated as a 'prince',[4] who, in the language of our day,

[1] *De Jure Belli, infra*, Appendix B, p. lii.

[2] Book III: *πόλιν δὲ τὸ τῶν τοιούτων πλῆθος ἱκανὸν πρὸς αὐτάρκειαν ζωῆς, ὡς ἁπλῶς εἰπεῖν.*

[3] *De Jure Belli, infra*, Appendix B, p. lii.

[4] 'Princeps' in classical Latin of course meant *chief*; it became during the medieval evolution of the language a title—the 'Chief' or as we have Anglicized it—'Prince' of a people. The same evolution is traceable in other common titles: 'Dux', a leader, has become 'Duke'; 'Papa', a diminutive of father, has become 'Pope'; 'Caesar', a proper name, has become 'Kaiser' or 'Tzar', &c., &c.

would be called the sovereign or head of the State. We must therefore not be astonished if Victoria's authorities are of the old order which, in the opinion of St. Augustine[1] and also in that of Victoria,[2] was 'the natural order, best adapted to secure the peace of mankind'—which order, in the opinion of the one and of the other, 'requires that the authority to make war and the advisability of it should be in the hands of the sovereign prince'. However, Victoria, as will shortly appear,[3] distinguished between the tyrant, whether monarch or dictator, and the just ruler, inasmuch as, in his opinion, the prince—his prince—was only to hold his position 'by the election of the State' and was merely to exercise the authority which had been vested in him as 'its representative'.[4]

But what, we may ask—at least Victoria does—'is a State, and who can properly be called a sovereign prince'? He would have us believe that the whole difficulty lies in this question, but without being meticulously critical, it might be said that the difficulty lies rather in the answer than in the question itself. The difficulty to which he referred was not his but that of his students, for Victoria says, referring presumably to their questions: 'I will briefly reply to them by saying that a State is properly called a perfect community.'[5] But this is a statement of the difficulty rather than its solution. Aristotle had said that 'a State ought to be sufficient unto itself'.[6] Victoria replaces 'sufficient' by 'perfect', which he defines as 'a completed whole, for that is imperfect in which there is something wanting, and, on the other hand, that is perfect from which nothing is wanting'.[7] The distinction between the definitions of Aristotle and Victoria—if indeed there be one—seems rather to be one of words than of fact. But, adopting Victoria's definition, what then is this completed State or community?—a question which Victoria answers as a jurist, versed alike in constitutional and in international law, by saying that 'it is complete in itself, . . . not a part of another community', and that it possesses 'its own laws and its own council and its own magistrates'. The examples? They are twofold: that of the monarchy and that of the republic, such as 'the Kingdom of Castile and Aragon and the Republic of Venice' and others of a like kind.[8]

The definition which Victoria gives is fundamental, embracing

In regard to the word 'State' mentioned in the text in quotation marks, it is to be said that its prototype was the Latin word *status*; the State in Rome was the *respublica* and its existence created a status which in its complete form would be *status reipublicae*. In the same way *imperium* was not empire. It was the power possessed by an individual, Caesar—the transformation of whose name is shown in the first paragraph of this note. Thus it appears, when we of to-day use the word 'State' we are in reality referring not to an abstraction but to the status of organization, that is to say, of inhabitants organized for a political and social purpose. The description *status* has in modern parlance swallowed up the thing —that is, people in a social and political organization.

[1] *Contra Faustum*, xxii. 75; *vide supra*, p. 184. [2] *De Jure Belli*, *infra*, Appendix B, p. lii. [3] *Vide infra*, p. 208 *et seq.* [4] *De Jure Belli*, *ibid.* [5] *Ibid.*, p. liii. [6] *Vide supra*, p. 204, note 2. [7] *De Jure Belli*, *infra*, Appendix B, p. liii. [8] *Ibid.*

not merely a State but a collection of States, provided only that the State, as a single community or as a part of a larger whole, has its own laws, its own council, and its own magistrates. There is, in the Victorian conception, 'no obstacle to many principalities and perfect States being under one prince'; but it is such a prince—and prince alone, or other agent invested with sovereign authority—'and no one else' who possesses the right 'to declare war'.[1]

To the query which might well arise in the mind of an internationalist of the sixteenth century—whether the princes of States under the Emperor Charles V might declare war, without awaiting, or indeed requiring the Emperor's authorization—Victoria's answer was that 'undoubtedly' they could 'make war', for, as he had himself said: 'a State ought to be self-sufficient, and this it would not be, if it had not the faculty in question',[2] a statement which shows that the 'sufficient' State of Aristotle and the 'perfect' State of Victoria were one and the same.

This question, which Victoria answers categorically and, as it were, off-hand, was of current importance, and, although less important in practice, it has not lost its interest in our day in which a League of Nations exists. Fortunately for us, Victoria does not stop here. According the right of war to the principalities of the empire, he brushed aside the claims of such princes as the Duke of Alba or the Count of Benevento, such principalities being, in his opinion, integral parts of the Kingdom of Castile, and therefore imperfect States.[3]

But the illustration bearing on this latter point is not an answer to the entire question involved. There was such a thing as the law of nations which, as Victoria has informed us, is derived from natural law, from custom, and from the agreement of nations, as evidenced by their practice and, as we of to-day would say, through treaties or conventions. If, therefore, any State had acquired the right to wage war under a precept of the law of nations—whether its origin be natural law or derived from natural law, or ancient custom, or treaty, or convention—'this authority', Victoria informs us, could 'not be gainsaid, even if in other respects the State be not a perfect one'.[4] Here we have the law of nations as the source of ultimate authority, binding 'perfect' States to recognize a state of war, although waged by those which they would consider as imperfect communities. Thus is international law not only the source but the standard binding alike upon perfect and

[1] *De Jure Belli, infra,* Appendix B, p. liii. [2] *Ibid.* [3] *Ibid.*

[4] 'Sed cum haec sint magna ex parte aut jure gentium, aut humano consuetudo potest dare facultatem et autoritatem belli gerendi. Unde si qva civitas, aut alius princeps obtinuit antiqva consuetudine jus gerendi per se bellum, nõ est ei neganda haec autoritas, etiam si aliâs non videtur habere Rempublicam perfectã. Item etiam necessitas hanc licentiam & autoritatem concedere posset.' Victoria, *De Indis et De Ivre Belli Relectiones,* Carnegie Institution ed., p. 426.

imperfect communities in this example of the exercise of this greatest and most terrible of all rights of nations—the lawful right to conduct international war.

It was not merely international law which accorded the right but 'necessity' could 'confer this licence and authority'.[1] There is a distinction, however, because international law is applied to international wars, whereas necessity is invoked to justify a resort to acts of force amounting to war within, instead of without, the State. The Government of the United States of America, composed of imperfect States (in that they do not, under the law of nations, possess the right to declare and to carry on war on their own account), found itself confronted with the forcible withdrawal of the States, which fact, however, the United States were unwilling to recognize, and yet under the law of nations the Government of the Union could not itself declare an international war against the States of the Union. This is an illustration from the American Continent in which Victoria was so interested. His illustrations were in point in his day and are doubtless of greater interest to our European friends.

'This', may we not say with Victoria, 'is enough on the present question.'[2]

Admitting that Christians may serve in war and make war—which of course implies, under the Victorian system, that all other persons may exercise the right, if indeed a right it be—and that the authority to make and declare war is vested in the State or the sovereign prince, we come to the all-important question to which others are but incidents: 'What may be a reason and cause of just war?'—a question which 'it is particularly necessary to ask . . . in connexion with the case of the Indian aborigines, which is now before us'.[3]

The question, however, is of a universal nature. It was not only important to the aborigines of America; it was important also to the nations of Europe, especially the Kingdom of Castile and Aragon; and it is still a question of supreme importance to the successors of the aborigines in America, and indeed to the countries which have since loomed large upon a vast and ever receding horizon. Here, as nowhere else, we see the aim and purpose of Victoria. He was interested—deeply interested—in the aborigines; but the law which he was formulating was also meant for people nearer home, and he availed himself of the opportunity afforded him under the question of 'a reason and cause of just war', to denounce, and as it were to stamp under foot the pretexts for wars of his own day, even though they should be those of the emperor *Semper Augustus*, who was at the same time the Catholic sovereign of Spain. Interested as he was in a just war, he had it on his conscience to brand as unjust the wars of which he was an unwilling

[1] *De Jure Belli, infra,* Appendix B, p. liii. [2] *Ibid.* [3] *Ibid.*

witness. The world does not yet know the place which Victoria holds in the movement for international peace.

There were three causes of war which seemed to him to be so pre-eminently unjust that he set them forth in succession, with an unmistakable implication which was not lost upon the emperor and king:

> I. Difference of religion is not a cause of just war. This was shown at length in the preceding Relectio, when we demolished the fourth alleged title for taking possession of the Indians, namely, their refusal to accept Christianity. And it is the opinion of St. Thomas,[1] and the common opinion of the doctors—indeed, I know of no one of the opposite way of thinking.
>
> II. Extension of empire is not a just cause of war. This is too well known to need proof, for otherwise each of the two belligerents might have an equally just cause and so both would be innocent. This in its turn would involve the consequence that it would not be lawful to kill them and so imply a contradiction because it would be a just war.
>
> III. Neither the personal glory of the prince nor any other advantage to him is a just cause of war. This, too, is notorious. For a prince ought to subordinate both peace and war to the common weal of his State and not spend public revenues in quest of his own glory or gain, much less expose his subjects to danger on that account. Herein, indeed, is the difference between a lawful king and a tyrant, that the latter directs his government towards his individual profit and advantage, but a king to the public welfare, as Aristotle says.[2] Also, the prince derives his authority from the State. Therefore he ought to use it for the good of the State. Also, laws ought 'not to be enacted for the private good of any individual, but in the common interest of all the citizens', as is ruled in can. 2, Dist. 4,[3] a citation from Isidore. Therefore the rules relating to war ought to be for the common good of all and not for the private good of the prince. Again, this is the difference between freemen and slaves, as Aristotle says[4] that masters exploit slaves for their own good and not for the good of the slaves, while freemen do not exist in the interest of others, but in their own interest. And so, were a prince to misuse his subjects by compelling them to go soldiering and to contribute money for his campaigns, not for the public good, but for his own private gain, this would be to make slaves of them.[5]

There are but two comments which are perhaps permissible in this connexion: the State, whether of Aristotle or of Victoria, is a free State, composed of free men, not of slaves; and the wars of Victoria's lifetime which sovereigns in Europe were so busily waging with little thought for 'the public good' would, if regarded as just, have reduced his European countrymen to the condition to which the princes of the so-called civilized world were attempting to reduce the American barbarians.

Is there then any cause of war which would commend itself to Victoria's judgement and to his conscience? There is, to quote his exact words, but 'a single and only just cause for commencing a war,

[1] *Secunda Secundae*, question 66, article 8.

[2] *Politics*, Book IV, chap. x: *ἥτις ἀνυπεύθυνος ἄρχει τῶν ὁμοίων καὶ βελτιόνων πάντων πρὸς τὸ σφέτερον αὐτῆς συμφέρον, ἀλλὰ μὴ πρὸς τὸ τῶν ἀρχομένων.*

[3] *Decretum*, Part I, distinction iv, canon 2: 'Erit autem lex honesta, iusta, possibilis, secundum consuetudinem patriae, loco temporique conveniens, necessaria, utilis, manifesta quoque, ne aliquid per obscuritatem inconveniens contineat, nullo priuato commodo, sed pro communi utilitate ciuium conscripta.' This canon is an excerpt from St. Isidore of Seville, *Etymologiae*, Book V, chap. xxi.

[4] *Politics*, Book I, chaps. iii and iv.

[5] *De Jure Belli*, *infra*, Appendix B, pp. liii–liv.

namely, a wrong received'. His proof is not only 'the authority of St. Augustine'[1] and 'the conclusion of St. Thomas'[2] but 'the opinion of all the doctors'.[3]

Victoria's categorical statement of principle is followed by a constitutional statement, which has, however, an international application. In the Victorian conception, and in that of his authorities, it is necessary for the prince to have jurisdiction over foreigners, because, if he is to act as a judge in an international war to redress the 'wrong received', he can only rightly do so if he has jurisdiction. To obtain jurisdiction over foreigners may well have worried him, as it does us of to-day. He solved it in fact and in law by a logic which, it must be said in his behalf, he only used for the advancement of justice, never to make a wrong principle appear as a better reason.

'A prince', he says, 'has no greater authority over foreigners than over his own subjects.'[4] This is a premise universally admitted, as may also be its minor, that 'he may not draw his sword against his own subjects, unless they have done some wrong'.[5] But this double admission creates the desired jurisdiction and thus enables, as we shall shortly see, the prince to pose as a judge over foreigners and to redress by war, if need be, the injuries which they have caused his State or his subjects. 'Therefore', the conclusion of the syllogism is: 'not against foreigners either'.[6] The authority for a conclusion weighty with so many implications? 'He beareth not the sword in vain: for he is the minister of God, a revenger to execute wrath upon him that doeth evil.'[7] Victoria's comment on the matter is that 'we may not turn our sword against those who do us no harm, the killing of the innocent being forbidden by natural law'.[8] This statement appears to be as innocuous as it is clear, but it goes far to extricate the *prima* professor of theology at Salamanca from the consequences of the twentieth chapter of Deuteronomy,[9] which appears here and there as a thorn in his path. 'I omit here any injunctions', he says, 'inconsistent herewith which God has given in special cases'—that of Deuteronomy was very special —'for He is the Lord of life and death and it is within His competence to vary His dispositions.'[10] Modestly and gently, but nevertheless effectively, Victoria leaves to the Creator the law which he himself was unwilling to allow to the creature.

Admitting, however, as Victoria has asserted, that there is but a single and just cause of war, the question necessarily arises as to the extent to which force may be used in a war declared to be just. As the

[1] *Quaestiones in Jesum Nave* [*Quaest. in Hept.*, lib. 6], question 10. *Vide supra*, p. 199, note 4.
[2] *Secunda Secundae*, question 40, article 1. [3] *De Jure Belli, infra*, Appendix B, p. liv.
[4] *Ibid.* [5] *Ibid.* [6] *Ibid.* [7] Romans, xiii. 4.
[8] *De Jure Belli, infra*, Appendix B, p. liv.
[9] Here [Deuteronomy xx] rules are laid down by God for the conduct of wars which the Jews are to wage against His enemies: for instance, *vide* verse 16: 'But of those cities that shall be given thee, thou shalt suffer none at all to live.' [10] *De Jure Belli, ibid.*

end and aim of war is, according to Victoria and those upon whose authority he relies, to be the defence and preservation of the State, that may, therefore, lawfully be done which the defence and preservation of the State require. Why? Because 'a private person may do this in self-defence', and 'therefore much more may a State and a prince'.[1] This would authorize the recovery, in whole or in part, of anything which had been lost to the State—a right which is too 'notorious' to require proof.

Within the State peace and tranquillity existed because courts were at hand in which justice could be administered, wrongs redressed, and crimes punished. As it was necessary that tranquillity and peace should also exist between nations, it was essential by means of a fiction, so common in law, that a court should be presumed to exist, with the prince as judge—and the maintenance of this fiction required that jurisdiction over foreigners could be had, a jurisdiction already suggested and which in a subsequent paragraph Victoria was to justify.

By a series of analogies Victoria demonstrates that the prince engaged in a just war is to be regarded as a judge, with the rights and the duties of a judge in all matters which could be the objects of a suit, civil or criminal, if they could be brought as private causes before a national court. The implication is clear that such matters would assuredly have been objects of a suit before an international court of the princes, if one had existed in his day with jurisdiction over foreigners according to his conception. As thus stated, the matter seems simple. In case of a civil suit, property whereof the Spanish had been unlawfully deprived could be recovered, or, if it were not to be had, damages could be recovered to the extent of the loss and likewise the costs of suit; in a criminal process, punishment for the wrong committed, as well as fines, could be imposed. Let us, however, state the matter in Victoria's language.

'It is lawful to make good out of enemy property the expenses of the war and all damages wrongfully caused by the enemy. . . . Therefore the prince can claim . . . and exact' the expenses and damages of the war. Is not this inevitably so in the Victorian conception of things? Because, he says, 'if there were any competent judge over the two belligerents, he would have to condemn the unjust aggressors and authors of wrong, not only to make restitution of what they have carried off, but also to make good the expenses of the war to the other side, and also all damages'.[2] But does the competent judge exist? Although there was in that day no formal tribunal, Victoria's reply is in the affirmative: 'A prince who is carrying on a just war is as it were his own judge in matters touching the war.'[3]

The prince is therefore in fact, if not in form, a judge.

[1] *De Jure Belli, infra,* Appendix B, p. lv. [2] *Ibid.* [3] *Ibid.*

The doctrine of Francisco de Vitoria is in its entirety that of a judicial system for the entire world, with the princes or sovereign authorities of the States as judges of the violation of rights under the law of nations until there should be a court between, and therefore above, the nations. Hence it is that Victoria's prince may redress rights and punish wrongs just as may a judge of civil or criminal jurisdiction; but he may, in Victoria's language, 'go even farther in a just war', to the extent of doing 'whatever is necessary in order to obtain peace and security from the enemy'.[1]

'Tranquillity and peace'—a recollection without a reference to St. Augustine—are, Victoria truly says, 'among the desirable things of mankind',[2] and happiness is not to be had, if there be no security in material prosperity.

Victoria had given specific examples of what might be done. For our purpose it is better to employ his expression that 'all appropriate measures' may be taken against the enemy, without attempting to define them. It would, however, be an injustice to him if we did not quote another passage in this connexion in his own words, as showing the nature and the extent of the action he has in mind. The 'magistrate not only compels the wrongdoer to make amends to the injured party', he says, speaking as a man of law, 'but, if the former is a source of fear to the latter, he is compelled to give bond or quit the city, so as to remove the danger of which he is the cause'.[3] On this he adds by way of comment: 'Even when the victory has been won and redress obtained, the enemy may be made to give hostages, ships, arms, and other things, when this is genuinely necessary for keeping the enemy in his duty and preventing him from becoming dangerous again.'[4]

The magistrate in matters international as the judge in a civil court is, with such modifications as the milieu suggests or requires, to enter judgement against the defendant enemy for the return of property which may have been seized, to assess damages, not only when the property may not be returned but for losses incurred by its withdrawal, and to enter costs of suit—that is, for the conduct of the war; and as a magistrate in a court of criminal jurisdiction in matters international, he is to punish the enemy defendant for the wrong or wrongs committed and take the appropriate measures to bind him over to keep the peace, whether by bond or otherwise. In like manner, and on an international scale, the prince is the executor of the judgement which he has rendered. And finally, this judgeship—if we may so term it—was not the exclusive right of one State but of any and all States against which a wrong had been committed.

The conception of Victoria in all its parts looks to a permanent

[1] *Ibid.*, p lv.
[2] *Ibid. Vide* also *supra*, pp. 185–6.
[3] *De Jure Belli, infra*, Appendix B, p. lv.
[4] *Ibid.*, pp. lv–lvi.

international organization, with the institution of a permanent international judiciary. It is not improper to observe that the world of our day seems not yet to have grasped the full significance and meaning of the Spanish Dominican's doctrine. Modern nations, to be sure, have long been accustomed to act as judges in controversies affecting them; but too often they have insisted, and still insist, on this as their peculiar and exclusive right, stubbornly maintaining that in all disputes which concern their interests they themselves, even if their cause be the most dubious, are the sole judges competent to enter judgement. Victoria's view was that each and every ruler had the power of a judge only if his cause were just, and that his support of an unjust cause stripped him at once, so far as international law was concerned, of any power to pass on the right or wrong of the controversy. The simple truth is that the Victorian conception is entirely incompatible with the doctrine of sovereignty, by which, in its baldest form, each so-called sovereign nation claims the absolute right to do as it pleases in so far as its strength permits, without reference to the rights of any other nation or to the international community and its rules.

*
* *

But to return to Victoria's argument. In his opinion the question reduces itself to one of jurisdiction, which he has already solved in part in the form of a syllogism, to the effect that the prince has the same authority over foreigners residing within his country as he has over his own countrymen. This, however, is not enough for Victoria; for the prince must have jurisdiction beyond the confines of his country, if he is to exercise his functions as judge and as executor of the judgement which he has rendered in disputes with a foreign State. This jurisdiction he acquires in two ways, one of which is through the right of the prince to resort to reprisals; and the other, through the right of the prince to exercise jurisdiction over foreigners, as the only way to preserve intact the State of which he is the official representative.

Although it is treated on a later page, it seems desirable to consider in the first instance the matter of reprisals—inasmuch as we have for untold generations been familiar with this rough and ready method of acquiring jurisdiction over alleged wrongdoers. The philosopher's method, with which Victoria begins, will then seem more acceptable—at least more easily comprehended—after we are familiar with the historical jurisdiction in fact. 'For instance,' he says in his subsequent treatment of reprisals, 'if French brigands made a raid into Spanish territory and the French King would not, though able, compel them to restore their booty, the Spanish might, on the authorization of their sovereign, despoil French merchants or farmers, however innocent these might be.'[1] The matter is simple enough. The French king had jurisdiction over his subjects within France, whether brigands or merchants. The Spanish authorities could of course apprehend the brigands or merchants of the French king should they be found in Spain, where the wrong had been committed. But supposing that they withdrew? Then it might be said that the Spanish prince would lose his jurisdiction, whereas the French king would undoubtedly possess jurisdiction over his fellow countrymen, whom we suppose to have returned to their native land. Should he of his own accord fail to exercise the jurisdiction which he possessed over his erring countrymen, he should at least do so upon the request of the Spanish prince; but if he should fail to comply with this request, then jurisdiction over guilty and innocent passed to the Spanish sovereign: over the guilty because of the wrong which they had committed and over the innocent because of the failure of the king to do his duty in the premises—and history does not need to be invoked for the statement that the innocent suffer for the fault of the prince.[2]

To return now to the philosophy of the thing. 'Princes have authority not only over their own subjects, but also', Victoria insists, 'over foreigners, so far as to prevent them from committing wrongs, and this is by the law of nations'[3]—which he has defined as a thing of consent and of practice (and it may be said in passing that practice evidences consent which may not have been expressed)—'and', he continues, 'by the authority of the whole world'. We may conceive of the States of the world forming by their existence an international community, which, being the world, would have jurisdiction over the States and their inhabitants.

But this was not enough for the *prima* professor—not merely of theology but of morality and of the law in all its branches. This authority, he considers, is also derived from natural law, which, he has previously said, is the primal source of the law of nations. But the reason for speaking of natural law as separate and distinct from the law of nations is that, in Victoria's opinion, society, based as it is on nature's law, could not hold together 'unless there was somewhere a power and authority to deter wrongdoers and prevent them from injuring the good and innocent'.[4] The purpose of law—whether it be natural or whether it be artificial—is to preserve humankind in society. But Victoria has a further reason: that the State, which by his definition is a 'sufficient' or 'perfect' community, could not be such a community

[1] *De Jure Belli, infra,* Appendix B, p. lxiv.

[2] Victoria closes his present treatise (*De Jure Belli*) with an apt quotation to the same effect (*vide infra,* p. 241): 'quidquid delirant reges, plectantur Achivi.'

[3] *De Jure Belli, infra,* Appendix B, p. lvi. The Latin is: 'Pro cujus probatione notandum, qvòd principes non solum habent autoritatem in suos, sed etiam in extraneos, ad coërcendum illos, ut abstineant ab injuriis, & hoc jure gentium, & orbis totius autoritate.' Victoria, *De Indis et De Ivre Belli Relectiones,* Carnegie Institution ed., p. 432.

[4] *De Jure Belli, infra,* Appendix B, p. lvi.

except by reason of the fact that 'everything needed for the government and preservation of society exists by natural law'. This statement of the case is so fundamental that Victoria more than intimates, indeed he says expressly, that 'in no other way can we show that a State has by natural law authority to inflict pains and penalties on its citizens who are dangerous to it'. But the danger is the chief thing, and the danger may be from without, as well as from within the State; and the authority 'to inflict pains and penalties' outside of its territory would not, under ordinary circumstances, lie with the State but with society at large which undoubtedly has the power to punish 'all wicked and dangerous folk'.[1]

It will be observed that Victoria searched for his authorities in legal and theological questions, but in moral questions he himself spoke as an authority.

In Victoria's day, the international community was not organized with the means and instrumentalities at its disposal to impose its will—at least not as a matter of course; therefore the punishment could best be administered 'through the instrumentality of princes'.[2]

To us of to-day, it would seem that the case of the *Trent*, threatening 'peace and tranquillity'—Victoria's phrase for the aim and purpose of a just war—and provoking an exchange of views of nations had been staged on a large and international scale as a classic illustration of Victoria's conception of the assertion of the rights and duties of the international community, in the absence of a formal international court.

The *Trent Case* arose during the American Civil War, and takes its name from the British packet involved. The ship was bound from Havana, a neutral port, to St. Thomas, another neutral port; among her passengers she carried Messrs. Mason and Slidell, civil agents of the Confederate States of America—to give the seceding States of the American Union their official name—who hoped to reach Europe eventually, where, so it was charged, they intended to transact business on behalf of their government. During her first day out, November 8th, 1861, the *Trent* was overhauled and stopped by the *San Jacinto*, a war vessel of the United States under the command of Captain Wilkes. The Confederate agents, Mason and Slidell, were transferred to the *San Jacinto* which later took them into Boston where they were turned

[1] *Ibid.* The Latin is: 'Imò videtur qvòd jure naturali, qvia aliter orbis stare non posset, nisi esset penes aliqvos vis & autoritas deterrendi improbos & coercendi, ne bonis & innocentibus noceant. Ea autem qvæ necessaria sunt ad gubernationem & conservationem orbis, sunt de jure naturali, nec alia ratione probari potest, qvod respub. jure naturali habet autoritatem afficiendi supplicio & pœnis cives suos, qvi reipub. sunt perniciosi. Qvòd si respublica hoc potest in suos, haud dubium, qvin orbis possit in qvoscunqve pernitiosos & neqvam in homines: & hoc non nisi per principes. Ergo pro certo principes possunt punire hostes qvi injuriam fecerunt reipubl. & omnino postqvam bellum ritè & justè susceptum est, hostes obnoxii sunt principi tanqvam judici proprio: . . .' Victoria, *De Indis et De Ivre Belli Relectiones*, Carnegie Institution ed., p. 433.

[2] *De Jure Belli, infra*, Appendix B, p. lvi.

over to the authorities and imprisoned, and the *Trent* was permitted to continue on her voyage.

Great Britain at once protested. In the language of Victoria, 'the head of the State'—in this case none other than Her Majesty, Queen Victoria—was acting as a judge in the matter, subjecting to her jurisdiction no less a defendant than the United States of America. This would be correct 'Victorian' doctrine for one or the other of the name. But if the matter had stopped there, it would not be worth citing in this connexion. Why then did the incident assume the importance that warrants its inclusion here, since the government of the United States admitted the illegality of its action and restored Messrs. Mason and Slidell to the British authorities? Because it provoked a protest from countries which were, to use a technical phrase, not parties to the judicial proceedings. Why, then, did they express their views? Because the action of Captain Wilkes, as agent of the United States, was in violation of the rights, not merely of Great Britain as a neutral but of every neutral State. Neutrality was and is a recognized principle of the common law of nations; and therefore the violation of that law, although directed against Great Britain alone, nevertheless affected the right of every State forming the international community. In such matters, the right of one is the right of all; and it was the duty of the United States to observe this right towards all. The violation in the case of Great Britain could therefore only be looked upon as an assertion of the right to violate it in respect to each and every other member of the international community.

It is true that Great Britain acted in its own behalf, but it acted also in behalf of the international community. In the language of the *prima* professor of theology of the University of Salamanca, the Queen of England exemplified the 'instrumentality of princes' appearing in behalf of 'society at large'.

However, as has been stated, other 'princes' likewise protested in the matter of the *Trent*.

Under date of December 3rd, 1861, the French Minister at Washington declared that he looked upon the affair 'as a precedent calculated seriously to disquiet all the Powers remaining outside of the present dispute'; and because of that, the French government was not willing to leave the United States in ignorance of its 'point of view'.[1]

The Minister of the Emperor of Austria-Hungary accredited to Washington presented to the government of the United States a communication of December 18th, 1861, in which the Minister of His Imperial Majesty called attention to 'the serious disturbances which the

[1] Montague Bernard, *The Neutrality of Great Britain during the American Civil War*, pp. 196–200; Supplement to *American Journal of International Law*, vol. x (1916), p. 69.

eventuality of a war could not fail to bring on, both with respect to each of the contending parties and with respect to the affairs of the world at large'.[1]

The Prussian government, in its note of December 25th, 1861, stated, through its minister in Washington, that the 'maritime operations undertaken by President Lincoln against the Southern seceding States could not, from their very commencement, but fill the King's Government with apprehensions lest they should result in possible prejudice to the legitimate interests of neutral Powers'. The government of His Prussian Majesty was unwilling to assume that Captain Wilkes had acted under instructions from his government. Should such turn out to be the case, however, its representative added, 'we should consider ourselves under the necessity of attributing greater importance to the occurrence, and to our great regret we should find ourselves constrained to see in it not an isolated fact but a public menace offered to the existing rights of all neutrals'.[2]

Returning now to Victoria, it may be stated that the passage under discussion is but a paragraph of the Reading on war; but it is a categorical assertion on the part of Victoria of the existence of this international community, endowed by him with the right to punish the violations of international law, of which he uses as an example elsewhere the violation of immunity of ambassadors,[3] but which we have illustrated by a concrete example taken from an actual war of—it might be said—but yesterday.

Victoria did not pause to cite numerous instances for the doctrine which he advanced. Apparently the matter seemed too plain in principle for him to enter into detailed discussion. He therefore merely said that the doctrine he advocated was 'approved and confirmed by the authority and examples of good men', and that 'most Christian princes and most religious Emperors have done the same thing'.[4]

Further comment on this passage would seem to be superfluous, indeed impertinent, were it not for a personal opinion with which Victoria ends the discussion and against which we can interpose an American objection as right in theory as the American practice in the case of the *Trent* was wrong. Victoria says that 'shame and disgrace are not wiped away from a State merely by its rout of its enemies, but also by its visiting severe punishment and castigation on them', and 'among the things which a prince is bound to defend and preserve for his State are its honour and authority'.[5] The interposition above referred to is in the language of a great American statesman, Albert Gallatin by name, who, opposing, and rightly, the policy of the United States in Mexico,

[1] Supplement to *American Journal of International Law*, vol. x (1916), p. 72.
[2] *Ibid.*, p. 70. [3] *Vide infra*, p. 268. [4] *De Jure Belli, infra*, Appendix B, p. lvi.
[5] *Ibid.*

finely and truly said that 'the true honour and dignity of the nation are inseparable from justice'.[1]

On as many as three or four occasions, Victoria has shown himself as thinking not only in terms of the individual, who is responsible for his acts; and in terms of the society of which the individual forms a part, through the majority of which society the government (whether it be kingdom, principality, aristocracy, oligarchy, or democracy) is formed, with each citizen or duly authorized agent of the State owing obedience to the State; but above all in terms of the international community, which was as real to him in fact as its necessity is gradually becoming evident to us.

In the opening lines of the third section of the Reading *On the Indians*, Victoria speaks of international law as natural law in the main. In a later passage of the same Reading, he specifies some of the elements which enter into the present content of that law and which add to this content in order to meet the changing, not to say shifting, conditions of the generations as they follow one another. Of this system, then, natural law is the source, with unconscious accretions through isolated acts of usage culminating in conscious practice and taking the form of customary law. Above and beyond all, the States have a right to add to the law of nations (through the action of all, or at least a majority, of the people who are to be bound thereby), which law binds the State, and, since it is made by all or the majority of the groups of people which we call the States, it becomes the law of the international community, and of each member thereof, State or individual.

What, then, is the outcome of this action, conscious or unconscious, of the peoples and the States? Victoria has stated it in a weighty sentence in the very matter at hand, more than intimating that society at large can, through the instrumentality of princes, take the measures necessary for its protection; because the society of States, although evident to him, had not yet assumed that organic form which it needs must assume to be seen by the eyes of groundlings.

In the second section of the Reading *On the Indians*, dealing with the unjustifiable claims of the Spaniards to dominion in America, he mentioned that of the Pope, only to reject it curtly, inasmuch as he had treated that question at length and could therefore content himself with a mere summary of the views which he had expressed in another Reading and on a previous occasion. It is evident throughout the two Readings (*On the Indians* and *On the Law of War*) that he had the State and its various aspects in mind, although he did not refer to his Reading *On the Civil Power*, contenting himself with a statement here and there, the nature and importance of which would be

[1] Albert Gallatin, 'Peace with Mexico,' chap. vii: The Mission of the United States, in *The Writings of Albert Gallatin*, edited by Henry Adams, vol. iii (Philadelphia, 1879), p. 586.

understood by those who had listened to that Reading. Because of the devotion of his auditors, we can at least read and meditate on the views which Victoria expressed on the occasion of the delivery of his tractate on the State, although we may not have it in the exact form in which the *prima* professor of theology laid it before his students. However, irrespective of form, this tractate is one which belongs, not only to those books which are to be 'tasted' or to be 'swallowed', but, in the happy phrase of Lord Bacon, 'to the few to be chewed and digested'.[1]

In this instance, the passage 'to be chewed and digested' is one in which Victoria gives, it would seem, full expression to his conception of the law of nations and the extent to which it either was or should be enforced. The passage is in response to the question 'whether civil laws are binding upon the legislators, and in particular, upon kings'. The reason of the query was that some persons (not Victoria) were of the opinion that the legislators and kings were not bound, 'inasmuch as they are over all the State, and no one can have an obligation imposed upon him unless it be by a superior'.[2] To which view Victoria replies that it is 'more probable' that the kings and legislators in question are bound. The reason and the moral rule were of supreme moment to Victoria, and in the proof of the opinion which he had under-expressed he proceeded to express himself unequivocally, and with a depth of conviction from which warmth was rarely absent. If he stood for a single standard, he was in the habit of invoking plural proofs. 'A legislator of this sort injures the State and the other citizens', he says in the first instance, 'if, being himself a part of the State, he does not bear a part of the burden—in a manner that accords, to be sure, with the person, his quality, and his rank.'[3] This is the first statement by way of proof. What is the second? 'The laws which are made by kings have the same force . . . as if they were made by the whole State; but the laws made by the State are binding upon all': for with Victoria the majority ruled. 'Therefore,' he concluded, 'even those laws which are made by the king, are binding upon the king himself.' But the action of the king may have been voluntary. What of it? Admitting this, he continues: 'Nevertheless, the fact that he is bound or not bound, does not depend upon his own will, just as in the case of pacts; for he who enters into a pact of his own free will, is nevertheless bound thereby.' Here we have the whole matter put upon the highest of planes, the moral plane, the good faith of the high contracting parties—a fact expressed once and for all in the Latin adage, *Pacta sunt servanda*: the fundamental element not merely of the agreements of daily life but of those agreements between nations which have made—and are still making—international law.

[1] *Essays*, L (50): 'Of Studies.' [2] *De Potestate Civili*, *infra*, Appendix C, p. lxxxix. [3] *Ibid.*

From what has been said, a corollary may be inferred; that there is an international law binding upon individual, upon State, and upon the international community—an international law coterminous with the human race, 'namely: that international law has not only the force of a pact and agreement among men, but also the force of a law; for the world as a whole, being in a way one single state, has the power to create laws that are just and fitting for all persons, as are the rules of international law. Consequently', he continues as jurist and as a supreme moralist, 'it is clear that they who violate these international rules, whether in peace or in war, commit a mortal sin; moreover, in the gravest matters, such as the inviolability of ambassadors, it is not permissible for one country to refuse to be bound by international law, the latter having been established by the authority of the whole world.'[1] This is what Victoria had in mind when he said, in the Reading *On the Law of War*, 'If a State can do this to its own citizens, society at large can do it to all wicked and dangerous folk'.[2]

It has been said—but it cannot be said too often—that ethical values were not lost upon Victoria; and because this was so, he hailed before the court of conscience anybody and everybody who violated a law, whether it related to the right of an individual, or were a law of a State or of the international community. The monarch or other chief of the State was bound by the law which he had made, or to which he was a party in the making, or which had been made by the majority over his protest: as a law it bound his conscience; and in the court of conscience the pauper and the king were equally guilty for the violation of one and the same law. The implications of this view are as inevitable as they are unanswerable. Wrongdoers, whether they wore ermine or rags, were but individuals, and as such they were equally and individually liable for the sins they had committed. 'For the sin ye do by two and two ye shall pay for one by one!'[3]

The matter of mortal sin—with which Victoria was professionally familiar and which is so fundamental to his conception of the law of nations (indeed of all law)—should be defined in the sense in which Victoria understood and used this term. 'Just as in natural and divine law that sin is held to be *mortal* which is opposed to reason and to law, but not to the honouring of God or to charity toward one's neighbour, an example being blasphemy, or homicide; whereas that sin is *venial* which is opposed to the honouring of God or to neighbourly charity—as in the case of idle gossip and other acts of that sort: even so will distinctions be made with regard to human laws. . . .'[4]

'The gravity of the sin is to be measured by the nature of the matter itself . . . and therefore it was a sin—and a sin of the same gravity

[1] *De Potestate Civili, infra,* Appendix C, p. xc. [2] *De Jure Belli, infra,* Appendix B, p. lvi.
[3] Kipling's *Tomlinson.* [4] *De Potestate Civili, infra,* Appendix C, pp. lxxxvii–lxxxviii.

—before, as well as after the establishment of the law.'[1] So said his opponents. To this the reply of Victoria was twofold. 'First: that the law binds one not only by prohibiting, but also by commanding affirmatively, and that it may therefore make obligatory a thing which—before the existence of such a law—was advantageous for the State, but not required; so that, after the law has been created, the transgression of it will be a sin, although formerly the same act was not a sin. In the second place, I maintain that it is possible'—Victoria says in his own person—'. . . for a given act to be an evil deed when committed by one person, and not when committed by another; whereas it is evil for all persons, after the law is established.'[2] This is an abstract principle drawn from a concrete situation, for which Victoria gives us a simple and interesting illustration: that of a law 'prohibiting the wearing of silk, or of cloth of gold—an act which formerly was evil only if committed by a poor nobleman, but which, after the law was made, was an evil deed for all persons'. Why should this be so? 'Since', in Victoria's mind, replete with experience, 'there was sufficient reason to make it prohibitory for all, even though there was no inherent impropriety in the mere fact that certain powerful men wore silk or cloth of gold.'[3]

The temporal State is a perfect community, and therefore a self-sufficient State; and it must possess the right 'to exercise jurisdiction and authority over a foreign province', if there be no other way in which the rights of the State may be preserved 'from injury and harm'. This is a statement requiring a concrete illustration, and Victoria, fully aware of this, chooses his own State by way of example to show the wrong he has in mind. 'For if', he says, 'the Spanish were not able to defend themselves against injury from the French', they could 'seize the cities of the latter, set up new princes and rulers therein, punish the guilty, and perform other similar acts on their own authority, as if they were the true rulers of the French, a right which all the doctors must acknowledge'.[4]

There is a further passage from the Reading *On the Civil Power* which is as a link in the chain of Victoria's demonstration: that the 'State as a whole may rightfully be punished for the sin of the monarch', for, as Victoria says, 'when the king has once been set up by the State, any immoderate act of his is charged against the State; since the latter is bound to entrust this power only to him who will be just in the exercise and use of power'.[5] In a word, the reason for this doctrine is that the king's refusal to do justice to the prince of another State, gives the latter the right to sit as the judge of the citizens forming the other State, who

[1] *De Jure Belli, infra.*, Appendix B, pp. lxxxviii–lxxxix. [2] *Ibid.*, p. lxxxix. [3] *Ibid.*
[4] *De Potestate Ecclesiae prior*, Sec. V, *infra*, Appendix D, p. civ.
[5] *De Potestate Civili, infra*, Appendix C, pp. lxxxi–lxxxii.

are liable, whether guilty or innocent, to the punishment which may be inflicted as a result of their sovereign's failure to do justice.

We are now in a position to apply these views, taken from the Reading *On the Civil Power* and also from that *On the Power of the Church*, to the matter in hand. The prince having the right is impressed with the duty to act in behalf of the State, assuming jurisdiction as a judge of the controversy.

Being a philosopher, Victoria was essentially a man of many doubts, and his doubts were those of a philosopher and moralist, a prophet and a genius. 'Many doubts', he begins—we have now returned to the Reading *On the Law of War*—'are suggested by what has just been said.' His first doubt on the preceding proposition is 'whether it be enough for a just war that the prince believes himself to have a just cause'.[1] To one familiar with the introduction which Victoria prefixes to the first section of his Reading *On the Indians*, the reason will be so clear that it only needs to be mentioned in passing. Error might be due to ignorance, but ignorance was of two kinds—'vincible' and 'invincible'. The first could be overcome by the advice of experts in the matter; and a failure to consult them or to abide by their judgement was no defence to the prince, and a war undertaken by him under these circumstances was an unjust war. To hold otherwise would be to admit the justice of both sides, because if princes could plead their ignorance in excuse of their actions, the wise, it is to be feared, would not be consulted, 'for although it is not a common occurrence for princes to wage war in bad faith, they nearly always think theirs is a just cause'.[2] In the Victorian conception, it would not be lawful to take life under such conditions, because each of the contending parties would have a just cause, and this would preclude the taking of innocent life by either party; and were it otherwise, 'Turks and Saracens might wage just wars against Christians, for they think they are thus rendering God service'.[3]

What, then, must the prince do in order to be sure that his cause is just? The answer is easy, if we understand Victoria's point of view: the prince is a judge before he decides the case, enters judgement, and proceeds to enforce it. There is furthermore a striking analogy between the lawsuit of the individual and the suit conducted by the prince. For if the individual litigant resorts to counsel in a case affecting, it may be, solely himself, how much more necessary is it in an international process involving the innocent as well as the guilty—and perhaps the existence of the State itself—'that an exceedingly careful examination be made of the justice and causes of the war and that the reasons of those who on grounds of equity oppose it be listened to'.[4] For this reason, among others, princes are surrounded by counsel, and if they do not consult

[1] *De Jure Belli, infra,* Appendix B, p. lvi. [2] *Ibid.* [3] *Ibid.*, p. lvii.
[4] *Ibid.*

them in this greatest of matters, they not only wage a war which is unjust but they render themselves, in the Victorian conception, liable to punishment—the greatest punishment being the loss of their position, as the people who make may also unmake the head of the State.

It is not, however, sufficient that the cause should be just in a merely legal sense. It should be just from the moral standpoint as well. 'Truth and justice in moral questions are hard of attainment,' Victoria informs the princes of his day, 'and so any careless treatment of them easily leads to error, an error which will be inexcusable, especially in a concern of great moment, involving danger and calamity to many, and they our neighbours, too, whom we are bound to love as ourselves.'[1]

Victoria invokes the authority of a comic poet (Terence):

Omnia enim sapienti verbis prius experiri oportet, quam armis.[2]

So much for the prince.

Next as to the doubt on the subjects of the prince and the attitude which the individual should take as to whether he should serve in a war. If convinced of its injustice, he should not serve, in the opinion of Victoria, who thus recognized the right of the 'conscientious objector'. There is, however, no duty on the part of the subject, as on that of the prince, to examine the question, and he may serve without mortal sin 'on the command of his prince'. The question for the subject is therefore not of knowledge but of good faith. He is not the judge, as is the prince, because he is possessed neither of the advice of counsel nor of the facts of the case. He is in the position of a lictor who 'had to enforce the praetor's decree without question'.[3] Such seems to be the essence of the matter.

The question, however, is larger than it appears to be. We have a clear case for the court of conscience, and if the conscience be aroused, the subject is as guilty as the prince if he act contrary to his conscience. The question is inevitable: What happens to the subject of the prince, although he be a person in command, if he acts contrary to the law of the land upon the order of the prince?

The Supreme Court of the United States was obliged to pass upon this question, arising out of the controversy with France in 1797–1800 over neutral rights. The case was that of *Little* v. *Barreme*,[4] involving the *Flying Fish*, a Danish vessel. Captain Little, in command of the United States frigate *Boston*, relying upon the instructions of the President of the United States, captured a vessel pursuant to those instructions, which, however, were founded upon a misapprehension of the law. Chief Justice Marshall, who had served as an officer in the American Army during the Revolutionary War, felt keenly the embarrassment of the officer, but he was converted by the other members

[1] *De Jure Belli, infra,* Appendix B, p. lvii.

[2] *Vide supra,* p. 149, note 1.

[3] *De Jure Belli, infra,* Appendix B, p. lvii.

[4] 2 Cranch, 170.

of the court to the view that an order of the President of the United States, contrary to an act of Congress relating to the question, neither was nor could be a defence to an action based upon the error.[1]

It is perhaps proper to recall in this place and in this connexion that the advice of a competent person, upon which Victoria invoked the second book of Aristotle's *Ethics*, was a defence in the court of conscience, although it might not be in law, even though the advice should be wrong—the reason being that the individual seeking such advice had done what he could to inform himself and therefore his 'ignorance' was 'invincible'.

To return to the counsel which the prince should consult in order that he might not be in 'vincible' ignorance. Every means being at his disposal, he was responsible in the court of conscience, as well as in a court of law, should he neglect to consult counsellors; if he refused to take their advice, when given, he was legally and morally guilty, and the war, as far as he was concerned, was unjust, whatever it might be in fact. The case would be different, however, with lesser folk, who had not the benefit of competent counsel.

However, it is not the prince alone who can be at fault. 'Senators and petty rulers,' Victoria tells us, 'and in general all who are admitted on summons or voluntarily to the public council or the prince's council ought, and are bound, to examine into the cause of an unjust war.' Should they not do so, 'they are consenting parties thereto'.[2]

Victoria was fully aware of human frailty, and, it appears from the two Readings in question, equally familiar with the frailties of royal and imperial persons, the proof of which is his own statement that 'a king is not by himself capable of examining into the causes of a war and the possibility of a mistake on his part is not unlikely', and that the consequences of such a mistake would be 'great evil and ruin to multitudes'.[3]

We can imagine that this expression by Victoria of the frailties to which the Catholic sovereign and emperor 'ever august' was liable—for they were one and the same person—must not have been wholly agreeable to the Christian prince and religious emperor, when the

[1] 2 Cranch, 178–9: Marshall, Ch.J., delivered the opinion of the Court (February 27th, 1804): '... I confess, the first bias of my mind was very strong in favour of the opinion, that though the instructions of the executive could not give a right, they might yet excuse from damages. I was much inclined to think, that a distinction ought to be taken between acts of civil and those of military officers; and between proceedings within the body of the country and those on the high seas. That implicit obedience which military men usually pay to the orders of their superiors, which indeed is indispensably necessary to every military system, appeared to me strongly to imply the principle, that those orders, if not to perform a prohibited act, ought to justify the person whose general duty it is to obey them, and who is placed by the laws of his country in a situation which, in general, requires that he should obey them. I was strongly inclined to think, that where, in consequence of orders from the legitimate authority, a vessel is seized, with pure intention, the claim of the injured party for damages would be against that government from which the orders proceeded, and would be a proper subject for negotiation. But I have been convinced that I was mistaken, and I have receded from this first opinion. I acquiesce in that of my brethren, which is, that the instructions cannot change the nature of the transaction, nor legalize an act which, without those instructions, would have been plain trespass.'

[2] *De Jure Belli*, *infra*, Appendix B, p. lvii.

[3] *Ibid.*

passage under comment was brought to his attention. That it did reach his eye, appears, as we already know, from a letter from Charles as King of Spain intimating in no uncertain terms that the professors of Salamanca should not discuss matters which did not concern them.[1]

The 'other lesser folk'—the expression is Victoria's—'who have no place or audience in the prince's council or in the public council are under no obligation to examine the causes of a war, but may serve in it in reliance on their betters'. It is to be taken as Victoria's personal view that underlings were inferior in their judgement, his observation on this point being that in such cases 'it is impossible and inexpedient to give reasons for all acts of state to every member of the commonalty'.[2] Public opinion of the 'commonalty' of our day controls prince and counsellors, and directs the policy of States, and time, which answers most things, has given the lie to the view 'that men of the lower orders' —we might add here women as well—'even if they perceived the injustice of a war, could not stop it, and their voice would not be heeded'. But to Victoria it seemed that under these circumstances 'any examination by them of the causes of a war would be futile', and 'unless the contrary be quite certain', a declaration of war on the part of the prince would be sufficient evidence of the justice of the conflict to satisfy the conscience of the 'commonalty' and of the lower orders, who might therefore 'serve in it in reliance on their betters'.[3]

Victoria was, because of his doubt, a man of caution—witness the phrase, 'unless the contrary be quite certain'; but there may be such things—as there doubtless were even in his day—so evident as to be positively known as right or wrong by the man or woman or even the child in the street. And in these matters the individual is himself responsible before that ultimate tribunal, the conscience. This is the view of the Dominican friar of Salamanca, and his phrase, which we have just quoted, is the very language of the confessional.

Victoria has heretofore discussed the question of doubt as if it arose on one side only, without considering whether it also arose on the other; or whether it should reasonably be in the mind of the prince who was acting as the judge or of him who was the defendant. This phase of the matter Victoria treats in a series of propositions relating to the possession of territory by one or the other of the august litigants. The question is a legal one, and it is examined from the standpoint of the lawyer rather than of the jurist (who has been wittily defined as a person who knows a little of every law except his own). The first question supposes that one of the princes seems to be 'in lawful possession'. In such a case, should the other prince who is doubtful as to the legality of the possession, seek 'by war and armed force' to dispossess him? He should not do so, in Victoria's opinion, 'so long as the doubt remains'.[4]

[1] *Vide supra*, p. 84. [2] *De Jure Belli, infra*, Appendix B, p. lviii. [3] *Ibid.* [4] *Ibid.*

The examples which he cites were of his time, but they have not lost their interest for us. 'Suppose the King of France', he says, is in 'lawful possession of Burgundy', but that the right of possession could be considered doubtful. This example had an interest to Victoria, but a peculiar interest to his lord and master; for was not Charles, King of Spain, the grandson of Mary of Burgundy, to whose duchy he would have succeeded had not Louis XI, the King of France, seized possession of it upon the death of the Duchess, then wife of Maximilian, who was grandfather of Charles V? Victoria did not admit the rightfulness of the French claim to possession, but he nevertheless referred to it as a suppositious case. The supposition is here a concession to the King of France. In the next instance it is a concession to the Emperor Charles V who by one title or another was in possession of Naples and Milan. The proof in each case is 'that in doubtful matters the party in possession has the better position'[1]—a situation so favourable as to be recognized in the maxim that 'possession is nine points of the law'.

This is the public law on the question. But because Victoria believed in the unity of law and that the fundamental principles of all law were the same, he made frequent use of analogies from municipal law to prove his arguments regarding international law. What, then, would be the situation in the present instance if it involved a title to possession in a suit at law? A 'lawful judge', Victoria says, 'would never in case of doubt dispossess the party in possession'. Therefore the prince as a judge under international law should not dispossess himself of the territory which he held, nor should he be dispossessed by the other prince (likewise considering himself as a judge in the matter). If this were not so, 'a war could be just on both sides and'—according to the Victorian doctrine—'would never be settled'.[2] Now Victoria was not a short-sighted person, for he could foresee that 'if in a doubtful matter it were lawful for one side to assert his claim by force, the other might make armed defence, and after the one had obtained what he claimed, the other might afterwards claim it back', and the result would follow that 'there would be war without end, to the ruin and tribulation of peoples'.[3]

But the eye of Victoria could look backward as well as forward, for

[1] *De Jure Belli*, *infra*, Appendix B, p. lviii. [2] *Ibid.*

[3] '... qvia in dubiis melior est conditio possidentis: ergo non licet spoliare possessorem re dubia. It. si res ageretur coram judice legitimo, nvnquã in re dubia spoliaret judex possessorẽ: ergo dato, qvòd illi principes, qvi prætendunt jus, sint judices in illa caussa, non possunt licitè spoliare possessorẽ manente dubio de jure. It. in rebus & caussis privatorum nvnquã in caussa dubia licet spoliare possessorẽ [l]egitimũ: ergo nec in caussis principum, leges enim sunt principũ. Si ergo secundũ leges humanas nõ licet in caussa dubia spoliare legitimum possessorẽ, ergo merito potest objici principib. *Patere legem, quam ipse tuleris. Quod* enim *quisqve juris in alium statuit, ipse eodem jure uti debet.* Item aliâs esset bellum justum ex utraqve parte, & bellum nunqvam componi posset. Si enim in caussa dubia licet uni armis repetere, ergo alteri defendere & postqvam unus recuperasset, posset iterum alius reposcere, & sic nunqvã esset finis bellorũ cum pernicie et calamitate populorũ.' Victoria, *De Indis et De Ivre Belli Relectiones*, Carnegie Institution ed., pp. 438–439.

he supposes that a 'city or province . . . has no lawful possessor, . . . and there is a doubt whether the King of Spain or the King of France be the heir and'—it is supposed further—'no certainty in point of law can be attained'.[1] Here we have a hypothetical case which sounds strangely like that of Burgundy. What should be done? 'It seems', Victoria goes on to say, 'that, if one party wants to settle and make a division or compromise as to part of the claim, the other is bound to accept his proposal, even if that other be the stronger and able to seize the whole by armed force'[2]—which might or might not be the case with Charles, King of Spain and Holy Roman Emperor, if we are correct in supposing that Victoria had Burgundy in mind. But to continue the quotation: 'nor would he have a just cause of war'. Here again private law is invoked, to the effect that 'where the matter is in doubt, one party may not seize the whole thing'.[3]

There is a second reason of an international nature, to which Victoria had just referred in his previous proposition: namely, 'the war would be just on both sides'; and there follows the almost inevitable analogy that 'a just judge would not decree and award the whole thing to either party'.[4]

The next hypothetical example is that of a person in peaceable possession who doubts his title. What should he do? Inform himself as to his rights in the premises, examining and weighing the argument against the possession, in order that 'he may thus attain certitude either in favour of himself or the other'. A mere premise will suffice: that one who is 'in doubt and neglects to ascertain the truth is not in possession in good faith'. The conclusion which is reached, after a further example, ends the syllogism: 'Princes are judges in their own cases, inasmuch as they have no superior'; hence it follows that if there were a superior, they would not be judges in their own cases. But to the syllogism: 'It is certain that, if any one raises any objection to a lawful possessor, the judge is bound to examine the case. Therefore in a doubtful matter princes are bound to examine their own case.'[5]

But suppose that the doubt persists, after a thorough examination of the case; is the possessor bound to renounce possession? Victoria replies that he is not so bound but may retain possession, 'so long as the doubt reasonably persists'. What is the authority for this? Again a private law analogy: 'No judge could divest him of it', with the logical conclusion that he is not required to yield possession, in 'whole or part'.[6]

Such is clearly the law of doubt with regard to the prince in the matter of possession; as a judge he does not need to decide against himself, as long as the doubt continues to exist.

But suppose the subject 'doubts whether the alleged cause of a

[1] *De Jure Belli, infra,* Appendix B, p. lix. [2] *Ibid.* [3] *Ibid.* [4] *Ibid.* [5] *Ibid.* [6] *Ibid.*

war is a sufficient one'; or simply 'whether there exists some sufficient cause for declaring war'? Adrian,[1] later Pope as Adrian VI, who had discussed this question, was of the opinion that the subject should not in such case serve in the war, 'even at the command of his prince', because in so doing, he would expose himself 'to the danger of mortal sin'.

Victoria has handled roughly princes, kings, and ambassadors. He now comes to close quarters with the Pope, saying what might have been considered disrespectful by his victim, if he had then been alive: 'However Adrian may twist and turn, he cannot free himself from the authority of St. Augustine, for our proposition is, beyond cavil, the conclusion at which St. Augustine arrives.'[2] What is this proposition? 'If a righteous person be in the military service of a sacrilegious king, he may consistently go to war at his command, provided that it is certain that the command laid on him is not contrary to the Divine precepts or that it is not certain whether it be so.'[3] Upon this Victoria comments that if there is a doubt as to 'whether it be against God's precepts, the subject may lawfully go to war'. Continuing the reference to Adrian he adds: 'Nor does it avail to say that such a person ought to get rid of his doubt and make his conscience acquiesce in the justice of the war, for it remains that, morally speaking, this is impossible, as in other cases of doubt.'[4]

The underlying principle of the school to which Victoria belonged was that war was only permissible when it was for the redress of a wrong. War was a remedy, and the remedy was to cause the right—not the wrong—to prevail. There was a wrong done and there was a wrong-doer, and the remedy applied to both. The wrong was a fact, to be proved as such, and when established, the remedy was at hand, although it was such a 'terrible remedy', to use Victoria's own phrase, that there should be no doubt on the question. If there were a doubt, the court of conscience stood in the way, unless the doubt were removed. It might often be hard to remove a doubt, because the fact might be clear and yet the conscience remain troubled; for it was not every slight cause that permitted a resort to arms; indeed Victoria insisted that force should not be used, even if the cause were just and there was no doubt, if the advantage to the State would be less than the disadvantage to the international community, which, in the ultimate analysis, should weigh right and wrong in the balance for the general good of humanity.

Suppose, however, that there should be not merely a doubt on one side but on both sides. To this question which he himself puts, Victoria replies: 'Apart from ignorance the case clearly cannot occur, for if the

[1] *Quaestiones Quodlibetical*, II, art. 2.

[2] *De Jure Belli, infra*, Appendix B, p. lx.

[3] *Ibid.* Victoria refers here to Gratian's *Decretum*, II. xxiii. I. 4 (C. 23, qu. I, can. *quid culpatur*), which is an extract from St. Augustine. *Vide supra*, p. 180.

[4] *De Jure Belli, infra*, Appendix B, p. lx.

right and justice of each side be certain, it is unlawful to fight against it, either in offence or in defence.'[1] This cannot well be gainsaid by one who accepts the principle that force can only be used against injustice. Obviously in the case supposed, force was excluded.

But there is doubt and doubt. In one case there is a cure for it, as Victoria has previously pointed out, in that a doubt may be one of ignorance, which may be removed by inquiry and examination; on the other hand, the ignorance may be 'invincible'. In the first case, a resort to war would be unjustifiable, in the court of conscience; whereas 'invincible' ignorance would be a justification, if in addition good faith were present. A distinction, however, is to be drawn between the prince who knows that his cause is unjust, and his subjects who may in good faith follow their prince, for the reasons which Victoria has already advanced, as they have—at least in ordinary cases—the right to assume that the prince himself had taken the advice of counsellors and had thus ascertained, not only for himself but for others, the justice of his cause.

Nevertheless in the course of the war, doubts may arise on one side or the other as to the justice of the cause, especially—the cynic would say—if fortune were not crowning their efforts. Princes generally believe—we have Victoria's word for it—that their cause is just, and if Victoria had not said so, history would supply the omission. It is a fact even more incontrovertible, if that were possible, that soldiers taking part in a war on one side or on the other rarely know for what they are contending.

What if a doubt should occur to the prince or a soldier in the course of the war? 'He is bound', Victoria replies, 'when he learns of its injustice to give back what he has taken away and not yet consumed.'[2] Victoria assumes that the individual in question has been acting in good faith and therefore this liability only arises with the doubt. It is the doctrine of unjust enrichment, which obtained in Roman law—in which Victoria seems to have specialized—and it is the law of other systems, based upon the principle that 'a person who is not in fault ought not to be damnified'.[3] The principle seems to prove itself, yet Victoria had and gave interesting examples from which picturesqueness is not absent, instancing a diner out who had attended a 'sumptuous banquet given by a thief where stolen things were consumed'. Such a person would be under 'no obligation', Victoria says, tempering justice with mercy, 'to give redress therefor, save perhaps up to the amount that his meal would have cost him at home'.[4]

One great fear seems to have dominated Victoria, as is shown by

[1] *De Jure Belli, infra,* Appendix B, p. lx.
[2] *Ibid.*, p. lxi.
[3] '.... qvòd qvi non est in culpa, non debet esse in damno: ...' Victoria, *De Indis* ..., Carnegie Institution ed., p. 444.
[4] *De Jure Belli, infra,* Appendix B, p. lxi.

frequent allusions—and indeed examples—the fear lest the cause of war should be not merely unjust on the part of the nation waging it but to the disadvantage of the international community of which it was a constituent part. In this Victoria showed himself to be an internationalist and a humanitarian in the truest and broadest sense of those terms; he demonstrated that his standard of right and wrong was to be measured not merely by the advantage to any king, prince, or country but by the common good of humanity; and that the test of the standard is, in the ultimate analysis, the international community.

There are three admirable and self-revealing passages from his writings which bear directly upon this phase of his international-mindedness.

The first is but a phrase to the effect that 'it is not lawful for slight wrongs to pursue the authors of the wrongs with war, seeing that the degree of the punishment ought to correspond to the measure of the offence (Deuteronomy, ch. 25)'.[1] This statement leads to a sentence on a later page, which is as a prelude to Victoria's final conclusion on the question, that 'a war may be just and lawful in itself and yet owing to some collateral circumstance may be unlawful'.[2] The conclusion, however, is double, not single, and is to be found in two of his readings: the first (which is subsequent in time) is in this very Reading on war: 'Inasmuch as . . . wars ought to be waged for the common good, if some one city cannot be recaptured without greater evils befalling the State . . . it is indubitable that the prince is bound rather to give up his own rights and abstain from war.'[3]

The matter was one with which Victoria was familiar, for it had attracted his attention in his consideration of the civil power of the State and he had given it classic perfection in one of those eternal truths which depend for acceptance neither upon time nor place nor circumstance. 'No war is just,' he there says,[4] 'the conduct of which is manifestly more harmful to the State than it is good and advantageous: and this is true regardless of any other claims or reasons that may be advanced to make of it a just war. The proof is: that if the State has no power to make war except for the purpose of defending itself, and protecting itself and its property, it follows that any war will be unjust, whether it be begun by the king or by the State, through which the latter is not rendered greater, but rather is enfeebled and impaired. Nay more, since one nation is a part of the whole world, and since the Christian province is a part of the whole Christian State, if any war should be advantageous to one province or nation but injurious to the world or to Christendom, it is my belief that for this very reason, that war is unjust.'

1 *Ibid.*, p. lv. 2 *Ibid.*, p. lxi. 3 *Ibid.*
4 *De Potestate Civili, infra,* Appendix C, p. lxxxii.

We feel, as it were, the solemnity of the moment. He has stated the principle, and in accordance with his custom it should be followed by an example. What was it to be: the wrongdoing of some other country, as is the wont with internationalists, or the wrongdoing of his own beloved Spain? We may doubt here and there Victoria's conclusions, but we may not without mortal sin doubt Victoria. 'If, for example,' he says, 'the Spanish should undertake against the French a war which, in other respects, was just, and which was, besides, advantageous to the Spanish kingdom, but which involved Christendom as a whole in still greater harm and loss (suppose, for instance, that the Turks in the meantime take possession of Christian provinces), then the Spanish should cease from waging that war.'[1]

On this question Victoria had no doubt, but he had many doubts as to the 'degree of stress' lawful in a just war—which that of Spain would not be if it prejudiced the international community. The concrete question gave rise to the proper doubt: 'whether it is lawful in war to kill the innocent.'[2] According to certain passages in the Scriptures[3]—which as a schoolman he cited in behalf of the contention—the answer, even in his day, would be in the affirmative. Among other Biblical passages to which he appeals, his view is confirmed by a skilful interpretation of Deuteronomy, where 'women and little ones' were to be spared on the taking of a certain city by force.[4] The further application which he makes of the exception is infinitely to his credit: that even in war it is not allowable to kill children. A small matter this, to us, some four hundred years afterwards, but in his day the battle of Lepanto was still to be fought. Children are exempt from guilt, and it is presumed that the women are guiltless. If, however, they are 'guilty', they share the common fate. A further extension of the exception is in his own words: 'Aye, and this same pronouncement must be made among Christians with regard to harmless agricultural folk, and also with regard to the rest of the peaceable civilian population, for all these are presumed innocent until the contrary is shown.' Going still further, Victoria approaches the subject of neutrality by stating that 'on this principle it follows that it is not lawful to slay either foreigners or guests who are sojourning among the enemy, for they are presumed innocent, and in truth they are not enemies'. In the same manner were 'clerics and members of a religious order' to be treated unless it were shown that they were engaging in hostilities.[5]

But what of the innocent mingled with the guilty, as, for example,

[1] *De Potestate Civili, infra,* Appendix C, p. lxxxii.

[2] *De Jure Belli, infra,* Appendix B, pp. lxi–lxii.

[3] Joshua, vi. 21; 1 Kings (or, 1 Samuel), xv. 3 and 8.

[4] Deuteronomy, xx. 13–14: 'And when the Lord thy God shall deliver it into thy hands, thou shalt slay all that are therein of the male sex, with the edge of the sword,
Excepting women and children, cattle and other things that are in the city . . .'

[5] *De Jure Belli, infra,* Appendix B, p. lxii.

in an assault on a fortress? If its storming be required for the conduct of a just war, it may indeed be taken and the innocent must suffer with the guilty the consequences of the assault. But Victoria the humanitarian comes to the aid of the innocent, even in active combat, applying the principle which he has established 'to see that greater evils do not arise out of the war than the war would avert'; for, he says, summing up the matter, 'it is never right to slay the guiltless, even as an indirect and unintended result, except when there is no other means of carrying on the operations of a just war, according to the passage (St. Matthew, ch. 13) "Let the tares grow, lest while ye gather up the tares ye root up also the wheat with them".'[1]

But suppose the 'guiltless persons' are potential enemies; for example, the 'adult male civilians of the enemy' who may hereafter 'carry a soldier's arms', although they may be presumed as civilians to be innocent. Admitting that they might be killed—because such a procedure had been defended—yet, says Victoria, 'I believe that it is in no wise right, seeing that evil is not to be done even in order to avoid greater evil still, and it is intolerable that any one should be killed for a future fault'.[2]

These are but steps to a larger and more generous conclusion: 'If the innocence of any soldier is evident and the soldiers can let him go free, they are bound to do so.' Here, we might say, is the distinction between warfare and slaughter on a large scale.

Passing from the taking of life, Victoria considers the rights of the enemy. First the innocent are dealt with. Just as the innocent person is to be exempt from the extreme rigour of war, so should be the property of innocent enemy subjects provided it is not such as 'the enemy would use against us'. The distinction in technical terms is between contraband and innocent enemy property. But there were wars and wars: short wars, wars which could be ended without requiring the confiscation of innocent enemy property; and wars which in fact could not be carried on from preparations made in advance but which would in time require for their continuance not only the general stores of the nation but the spoliation of 'all enemy subjects, guilty and guiltless alike', in order to weaken the enemy and bring the war to an end. In such a case, necessity would know no law, and the property, if needed, would not be considered as innocent enemy property.[3] Harsh doctrine this, justified by an overwhelming and immediate necessity! The title to the property thus 'commandeered'—to use the expression of our day—vests at the moment of seizure and therefore need not be restored at the end of the war, although the view to the contrary 'is a pious one and not indefensible'.[4] But the spoliation of foreigners and travellers, although they be on enemy soil, is, Victoria informs us, 'in no wise

[1] *Ibid.*, p. lxiii. [2] *Ibid.* [3] *Ibid.*, p. lxiv. [4] *Ibid.*

lawful, they not being enemies', provided they are not 'obviously at fault'. Here the question is not of enemies but of neutrals, who remain neutrals, unless they have renounced their neutrality.

Victoria has apparently been dealing with land warfare, although in a previous passage he has referred to ships. He takes up maritime conflicts in the familiar form of reprisals, that is to say, the refusal to restore property wrongfully taken by the enemy. If in ordinary course the property may be retaken, the question is ended. But what may the injured party do, if he cannot so 'recoup himself'? Victoria's answer is according to the practice which still exists: 'he may do so wherever satisfaction is obtainable, whether from guilty or from innocent.'[1]

There are land rights and there are water rights, and Victoria extends the remedy to the high seas, recognizing what was the practice in his day, which practice, because abuses inevitably accompanied it (as he himself points out), was renounced almost in our day by the Declaration of Paris of 1856. 'There is, accordingly,' he says, 'no inherent injustice in the letters of marque and reprisals which princes often issue in such cases, because it is on account of the neglect and breach of duty of the other prince that the prince of the injured party grants him this right to recoup himself even from innocent folk. These letters are, however, hazardous and open the way to plunder.'[2]

The lives of children and 'other innocent parties' were, according to Victoria, to be spared. But was it permissible to treat them as prisoners? On this doubt Victoria himself had no doubt: 'It is in precisely the same way permissible to carry the innocent off into captivity as to despoil them, liberty and slavery being included among the good things of Fortune.'[3] This statement seems to require justification, because we of to-day are not inclined to include slavery among the 'good things of fortune'. In primitive times the enemy was to be put to the sword, when captured—which obviated any discussion of captivity. The extreme right of killing was sometimes renounced, in order that the prisoners taken might serve as slaves. Finally the occasional practice became the general rule. Therefore it was international law. Among Christians, however, slavery was renounced, although it still existed in Victoria's day as regarded the Saracens and the Turks.

But supposing the war is of the long-drawn-out variety to which Victoria has referred, so that the indiscriminate spoliation of enemy subjects and the seizure of their goods is 'justifiable': the guilty and the guiltless alike might be carried into captivity; but the harshness of the rule permitting slavery was limited in practice in the wars between Christian nations to the mere right to hold until ransom should be

[1] *De Jure Belli, infra,* Appendix B, p. lxiv. [2] *Ibid.*

[3] *Ibid.* The Latin text is: 'Eodem modo licet ducere innocentes in captivitatem, sicut licet spoliare illos, qvia libertas & captivitas inter bona fortunæ reponuntur.'

paid. Why, then, was the rule different as regards the Saracens? The answer—and a sufficient one—would be that their practice was to treat captives as slaves, and the practice of the Christians was therefore justified by reciprocity—for the reasons advanced by Victoria with that warmth which he only occasionally displays in defence of what seems to us, some centuries later, a harsh practice. But it is to be remembered that in his day the Saracens still constituted a menace to Europe, and that they had only recently been expelled from Spain, in the eventful year of 1492.

But there is a special class of prisoners, known to the law of nations as 'hostages'—in the nature of a pledge for the good faith of the enemy in carrying out their promises and undertakings. Is it lawful to despoil these hostages of their lives? If they are guilty, that is to say, 'have borne arms', the answer is 'yes'. On the other hand, 'if they be children or women or other innocent folk . . . they cannot be killed'.[1]

Passing from the subject of the innocent and the punishment which may be inflicted upon them if they should be proved guilty, Victoria proceeds to discuss the question whether in a just war the lives of all those whose guilt is certain may be taken. He apparently feels that he is here on dangerous, that is to say, uncharitable, ground. Therefore he summons his courage, as it were, by recalling his premise that war is waged: 'Firstly, in defence of ourselves and what belongs to us; secondly, to recover things taken from us; thirdly, to avenge a wrong suffered by us; fourthly, to secure peace and security.'[2] The question before him is twofold: what is permissible in actual battle; and what may be done when the war is over? Victoria had no hesitancy as to the use of the sword in the 'actual heat of battle . . . and, briefly, . . . so long as affairs are in peril.' But may all who have borne arms be killed? 'Manifestly, yes,' says Victoria, stating in two words the views of those who cling to the old order of things, to the word which 'killeth', and reject the spirit which 'maketh alive'. The proof for the affirmative on this question is to be found in the twentieth chapter of Deuteronomy, which, as we have learned before, was as a thorn in Victoria's path but which he here meets fairly and definitely brushes aside as a rule for the special case as set forth in Deuteronomy (the killing of the enemies of the chosen race)—a rule permitting general slaughter on the refusal of the city to surrender, with the safeguarding clause in behalf of 'the women and the little ones'.[3] We may omit the argument for the affirmative, and note how Victoria prepares the way for his humanitarian view on all phases of the question involved. The 'whys' and 'wherefores' of his further argument should be stated largely in his words, inasmuch as he is seen at his best in extricating himself from the word of Holy Writ, which seems to preclude argument,

[1] *De Jure Belli, infra* Appendix B, p. lxv. [2] *Ibid.* [3] *Ibid.*

if it be taken literally and the spirit be sacrificed to the letter. He has yielded a point to his opponents, but only, as we shall soon see, for the purpose of turning the edge of their argument with his proposition that in avenging a wrong, 'it is not always lawful to kill the guilty'.[1] Victoria next begins to eat away the concession which he had made. His first proof is by way of analogy, concerning the practice within the State. 'Even among citizens,' he declares, 'it would not be lawful, not even when the wrong was done by the whole city or district, to kill all the delinquents.' This is inevitable, for such wholesale killing would not be 'for the public good', which is 'the end and aim of both war and peace'.[2] The conclusion of the syllogism, which is in accordance with the equity and humanity of Cicero,[3] is that 'the punishment which we inflict on the guilty must be such as equity and humanity allow'.[4]

The second step is a second concession: that 'sometimes it is lawful and expedient to kill all the guilty'. Here the rule of Deuteronomy is clearly against the fundamental proposition for which he stands—that revenge and punishment should be 'without any cruelty and inhumanity'. The authority of Deuteronomy must be recognized; but it cannot be applied without violating the Victorian principles; and the best, if not the only, way is to limit it to the circumstances which existed at the time of its proclamation but which had ceased to exist in the year 1532. Deuteronomy therefore was to be limited to the past, and at the present might be invoked only against such unbelievers as those from whom it was 'useless ever to hope for a just peace on any terms'. Otherwise, 'it would involve the ruin of mankind and of Christianity, if the victor always slew all his enemies, and the world would soon be reduced to solitude, and wars would not be waged for the public good, but to the utter ruin of the public'.[5] Therefore Victoria, notwithstanding Deuteronomy, utterly repudiates the taking of the lives of enemies 'when no further danger is present'. He speaks emphatically and in the first person, in terms which cannot by any juggling of words be misunderstood: 'I think that they may not be killed, not only not all of them, but not even one of them, if the presumption is that they entered on the strife in good faith.'[6] And good faith was to be presumed on the part of soldiers serving their princes.

The question may further arise whether it is lawful to slay those who have surrendered or have been taken prisoners. 'Speaking absolutely,' Victoria grants, and in accordance with the outworn practice which Deuteronomy sets forth, 'there is nothing to prevent the killing of those who have surrendered or been captured in a just war so long as abstract equity is observed.'[7] However, international law, a thing of

[1] *De Jure Belli, infra,* Appendix B, p. lxvi. [2] *Ibid.*

[3] *De Officiis* (*On Duties*) II. v, last sentence: '. . . ulciscamurque eos, qui nocere nobis conati sint, tantaque pœna afficiamus, quantam æquitas humanitasque patitur.'

[4] *De Jure Belli, infra,* Appendix B, p. lxvi. [5] *Ibid.* [6] *Ibid.* [7] *Ibid.*, p. lxvii.

custom and of practice, is invoked to prove that after victory has been won and all danger is over, the captives in question are not to be killed, if the law of nations is to 'be respected, as is the wont among good people'.[1]

Nevertheless there is a loophole, inasmuch as the custom in the case of a surrender was to provide in the articles of capitulation that the lives of the garrison should be spared. Supposing, however, that a stipulation to that effect had been omitted, Victoria expressed the opinion that in such a case it did not seem unjust for 'the more notorious offenders' to be put to death 'on the order of the prince or a judge'[2]—as the ruler is to be looked upon as one or the other, according to the circumstances.

It would be expected that Victoria as a humanitarian would consider the effect of war upon human beings and that, when he had discussed that phase of the question, he would turn to property, which he would doubtless regard as made for man and not man for property. We can trust both humanist and humanitarian to understand human beings. But there is portable property, like money, garments, silver, and gold, which human beings can carry away; and there are immovables, such as lands, cities, and fortresses, which we call 'real property' and which is stationary. Because of their difference, each is in a class by itself. Victoria therefore treated them separately, first dealing with personal property. But at the outset he expresses a doubt on the whole subject, namely: 'Whether everything that is captured in a just war becomes the property of the captor and seizor.' Yes, is the reply—at least up to the amount required to compensate the human being in question for the property which may have been wrongfully seized, together with the expenses involved in obtaining it, or compensation for both, if the property is not to be reclaimed. The demonstration is short, for compensation or obtaining satisfaction for the wrong committed is, he reminds us, an 'end and aim of war'.[3]

But what are the details of the law of war respecting movables? For in Victoria's opinion (with which Grotius was later to be in agreement) there was a law of war as well as a law of peace, a fact which is evident from the title of the Reading (*De Jure Belli*) under consideration. In the 'just war' with which he is concerned, 'all movables vest in the seizor', but by what law? True to the caption of the Reading, his first thought is of the law to sustain the view which he has expressed. It is the law of nations; and this is true 'even if in amount they exceed what will compensate for damages sustained'. And the law is to be found in the source of law, the *Digest* of Justinian, and 'more expressly' in the *Institutes* of Justinian, stating that 'by the law of nations whatever is taken from the enemy immediately becomes ours, even so far as

[1] *Ibid.*, p. lxvii. [2] *Ibid.* [3] *Ibid.*

that free persons may be made our slaves'.[1] This is the law of property with a vengeance.

But suppose more property is taken than is needed for the lawsuit of which the prince is at once judge and executor. Is he bound to give back his booty, supposing of course that the cause of war be just? No, is the answer; from which it follows 'that what is taken in war is not used as a set-off against the principal debt'. But in a matter of law Bartolus is the authority, and that great commentator is cited as commending this opinion, in his comment on the *Digest*. Apparently booty is here looked upon as the price of war and not as a payment for the property seized or the expenses to which the prince has been put in order to redress the wrong which he and his people have suffered. There is, however, such a thing as law which is as the letter, and equity, which is as the spirit. Therefore, says Victoria, quoting Sylvester (fellow Dominican and theologian)[2] with approval—as was not always the case—this rule regarding booty should be allowed only until a satisfaction sufficient in equity has been taken 'for the damages and wrongs suffered'. This statement might seem to be its own proof; but war is a fact, not a theory, and Victoria was a master in handling facts. 'It is not to be imagined,' he exemplifies, 'that, if the French have ravaged some one district or insignificant town in Spain, the Spanish might also, if they could, ravage the whole of France; they can only retort in a manner proportionate in kind and degree to the wrong done.' According to what standard? As is to be expected, it is none other than 'the estimate of a good man'.[3]

The passage just quoted may well raise a doubt: 'whether it is right to give a city up to the soldiery to sack'; and the doubt had been justified by an example which had shocked the world of his day—and especially Victoria—involving as it did the sack of Rome in 1527 by the army of none other than His Catholic Majesty, Charles V, Holy Roman Emperor, 'ever august'. The answer to this doubt is one to be quoted in its entirety, without interruption or preliminary comment: 'My answer is . . . This is not unlawful in itself, if necessary for the conduct

[1] *De Jure Belli, infra,* Appendix B, p. lxvii. The passages cited above are as follows: I. *si quid bello, ff.,* De Captivis (*Digest,* XLIX. xv. 28): '*Labeo libro quarto pithanon a Paulo epitomatorum* Si quid bello captum est, in praeda est, non postliminio redit.'

I. *hostes, ff.,* De Captivis (*Digest,* XLIX. xv. 24): '*Ulpianus libro primo institutionum* Hostes sunt, quibus bellum publice populus Romanus decrevit vel ipsi populo Romano: ceteri latrunculi vel praedones appellantur. et ideo qui a latronibus captus est, servus latronum non est, nec postliminium illi necessarium est: ab hostibus autem captus, ut puta a Germanis et Parthis, et servus est hostium et postliminio statum pristinum recuperat.'

Dist. I, can. *jus gentium* (*Decretum,* I. i. 9): 'Ius gentium est. . . . seruitutes. . . .' *Inst.,* De rerum divisione, § *item ea quae ex hostibus* (*Institutes,* II. i. 17): 'Item ea, quae ex hostibus capimus, iure gentium statim nostra fiunt: adeo quidem, ut et liberi homines in servitutem nostram deducantur, qui tamen, si evaserint nostram potestatem et ad suos reversi fuerint, pristinum statum recipiunt.'

[2] Sylvester Mazzolini [or Mozoloni or Prierias], 1460–1523. Sylvester's works achieved a great vogue among the jurists and theologians of the Renascence. He is quoted by Grotius with great frequency.

[3] *De Jure Belli, infra,* Appendix B, p. lxviii.

of the war or as a deterrent to the enemy or as a spur to the courage of the troops. So Sylvester, under the word *bellum*, § 10. It is on the same principle as that which justifies the burning of a city for reasonable cause. Nevertheless, inasmuch as such authorization to sack results in many horrors and cruelties, enacted beyond all humane limits by a barbarous soldiery, such as slaughter and torture of the innocent, rape of virgins, dishonour of matrons, and looting of temples, it is undoubtedly unjust in the extreme to deliver up a city, especially a Christian city, to be sacked, without the greatest necessity and weightiest reason.'[1]

If a comment on this passage were permissible, it would be the query: what reason could reasonable people have to resort to an act of barbarism for which there could be no justification? The fact of its lack of all justification to which reference is here made should be its condemnation; and if such acts of destruction and frightfulness still remain possible, on the ground of extreme necessity, the necessity invoked in their behalf is not the least reason why war should be to reasonable people an unpermitted and a polluted thing.

The restriction which Victoria adds is in itself a further condemnation. 'Soldiers', he says, 'may not, without the authority of their prince or general, go looting or burning, because they are themselves not judges.'[2] Strange occupation, this, for judges! The justification for Victoria—there is none for his 'judge'—is that although he was for all time, he was nevertheless a man of his time. But in this matter we of the twentieth century can ill afford to throw stones when we remember the terrible desolation—not to speak of desecration—that has resulted from the international conflicts of our own time.

After this passage dealing with looting and booty, it is as a relief when we come to property that cannot be carried away, such as immovables, concerning which the difficulty seems, in Victoria's opinion, to be 'greater'. The phase of the question which he here discusses is the intervention of the prince, again as judge, not merely to redress wrongs but to punish their commission, to prevent their repetition, and to bind the defendant over to peace—as we would say in our common law. For any one of these purposes—especially the last—'there is no doubt about the lawfulness of seizing and holding the land and fortresses and towns of the enemy, so far as is necessary' to accomplish the ends specified.[3] This is the doctrine of reciprocity, or rather that uncharitable form of it which permits 'an eye for an eye and a tooth for a tooth'; and the compensation exacted is both by divine and natural law, the rule being no less applicable to movables than to immovables.

The erring prince might, just as the ordinary wrongdoer, be bound over to keep the peace—for is not international law, in the words of the

[1] *Ibid.* [2] *Ibid.* [3] *Ibid.*

late Sir Thomas Erskine Holland, but 'public law writ large'?[1] It is, however, not without interest to reproduce Victoria's way of stating that truism: 'In order to obtain security and avoid danger from our enemy it is also lawful to seize and hold a fortress or city belonging to him which is necessary for our defence or for taking away from him an opportunity of hurting us.'[2]

The balance of the Reading, with the exception of the noble ending—which in itself is sufficient to establish and to perpetuate the name of Victoria—deals with what may be called the future conduct of the parties, or what might be termed the ultimate phases of the subject.

From now on to the conclusion, the matter in hand relates to the right 'to mulct the enemy of a part of his territory' for the purpose of 'punishment, that is, in revenge', which should be 'in proportion to the character of the wrong', and on this ground 'to seize a fortress or town'.[3] The proportion to which Victoria refers is to bear—as we would expect—no relation to the strength and the armed force of the victorious party. The matter was important in itself, and indeed fundamental to Victoria's system.

After premising that operations may necessarily have been on a large scale, resulting in the occupation of the enemy's territory and the capture of numerous cities, he then lays down the law and states his own doctrine. 'They ought to be restored', he asserts, referring to the captured cities, 'when the strife is adjusted and the war is over, only so much being retained as is just, in way of compensation for damages caused and expenses incurred and of vengeance for wrongs done, and with due regard for equity and humanity, seeing that punishment ought to be proportionate to the fault.'[4] Here we have the procedure of the lawsuit of private law extended beyond the territorial into the international milieu, showing Victoria possessed of the qualities of an international judge some four hundred years before the present Permanent Court of International Justice was created and installed at The Hague. More than that, we have a demonstration of the fact that according to the Victorian doctrine, force is only to be used as the handmaid of justice, and it is only because the prince is a judge that force can be used at all between States. His whole system, it cannot be said too often, is that of law, whether natural, divine, or human, ascertained in advance by counsel, applied by a technical judge in a national court, and by the prince as a superior judge in disputes between nations—until there should be created a court of the superior.

[1] Thomas Erskine Holland, *Studies in International Law* (Oxford, 1898), p. 152.

[2] *De Jure Belli, ibid.*, p. lxviii.

[3] *Ibid.*

[4] 'Et si necessitas, & ratio belli postulat, ut major pars agri hostium occupetur, & plures civitates capiantur, oportet ut compositis rebus, & peracto bello restituantur, tantum retinendo, qvantum sit justum pro compensatione damnorum & impensarum, & pro vindicta injuriæ, servata æqvitate, & humanitate, qvia pœna debet esse proportionata culpæ. . . .' Victoria, *De Indis* . . ., Carnegie Institution ed., pp. 462–3.

'It would be intolerable', he adds, reinforcing theory by an example within the range of possibility, 'that, if the French raided the flocks of the Spanish or burnt a single district, the latter should be allowed to seize the whole Kingdom of France.'[1] It must have been a pleasure for Victoria to find something in the twentieth chapter of Deuteronomy—here cropping up once more in his path—which he could invoke with approval, as he does in this connexion, to the effect that the chapter in question would justify 'seizing on this score either a part of enemy territory or an enemy city'.[2] Again Victoria discloses his international system as derived from the internal practice of the State; and rightly, because the international community, is it not as a State of larger, indeed universal, proportions? 'Internal wrongdoers', he says, 'may be punished in this way, that is, they may be deprived of house or land or a fortress, in proportion to the character of the circumstances';[3] and if this be so, 'therefore foreign wrongdoers also'.

What would be the procedure of the prince in this matter? As 'a superior judge' he would be competent 'to mulct the author of a wrong by taking away from him a city (for instance) or a fortress'. And the reason for this is one that by now we have learned to expect from Victoria: it is that 'by the law of war he [the prince] is put in the position of a judge'.[4]

There is, however, a doubt 'whether it is lawful to impose a tribute on conquered enemies'. Categorically, yes, 'not only in order to recoup damages, but also as a punishment and by way of revenge'. *Cela saute aux yeux* as our French friends would say—and as would appear from the twentieth chapter of Deuteronomy, which here crops up for the last time in the present disquisition, to the effect 'that when the Jews have approached a city with good cause in order to attack it, if the city receives them and opens its gates, all the people therein shall be saved and shall serve the Jews with payment of tribute'; upon which Victoria laconically remarks: 'This law and usage of war has prevailed.'[5] More laconically we add: it still prevails.

Victoria has confined himself in this connexion to the seizure of territories, with cities and populations, as security for that peace which is the aim and end of war. He has not touched upon the treatment of the erring prince. What procedure, if any, may be taken against his position and his person? The question is as current to-day as it was in Victoria's century, for the modern world has now and then resorted to effective procedures of one kind or another against crowned heads. May the lawful prince be deposed? May a new one be appointed? Or may the principality be retained by the victorious 'judge'? The matter of deposing rulers seemed doubtful—'not unqualifiedly permissible'—to Victoria, and the right, which was assuredly an extreme

[1] *De Jure Belli, infra,* Appendix B, p. lxix. [2] *Ibid.* [3] *Ibid.* [4] *Ibid.* [5] *Ibid.*

one, was not one to be exercised in 'any and every cause of just war'. Victoria admitted freely and fully the doctrine of punishment, even when it appears to be synonymous with revenge, but he always insisted —as he does in this connexion—that it 'should not exceed the degree and nature of the offence'.[1]

The question was delicate in itself, and still more delicate, it would seem, in its application. Therefore, in terms which cannot be improved upon—at least no one appears to have done so—he defines and, in defining, limits the right: 'Punishments should be awarded restrictively, and rewards extensively'—a rule of the three forms of law applicable in this, as well as in all other international suits: human law, natural law, and divine law. In any event, as an extreme right it was to be the exception, not the rule, and only resorted to when there were 'sufficient and lawful causes for effecting a change of princes or for seizing a sovereignty'.[2] What were the circumstances which would justify this extreme measure? Victoria describes them as depending upon 'the number and aggravated quality of the damages and wrongs which have been wrought or, especially, when security and peace cannot otherwise be had of the enemy and grave danger from them would threaten the State if this were not done'.[3] Assuredly the end and purpose of war, as well as of the judge, would be satisfied by the 'adjudication' to the complainant of the entire territory of the defendant prince or State, if need be.

Victoria but stated the law as he found it, justifying its reason by examples from the various forms of law and from history, ancient and modern. The law which he stated was admittedly a hard law, when it was not cruel, and he had doubts at times which seemed necessary to him, if there were to be a relationship between a just war and the justice which includes equity. These doubts have become the *Temperamenta* of every subsequent writer, and they are not his least title to remembrance; indeed their embodiment in international relations was requisite, if there were to be a law of nations which should take note of duties as well as rights, both to be measured by the standard of the good and humane judge and applicable alike to States and human beings whereof the States are composed. Victoria was so anxious that the doubts should be as leaven to the whole lump that he was not satisfied with stating a doubt in the course of the Reading whenever a special case arose in which justice should be tempered with mercy. Lest anything should be overlooked in the limited time which he could devote to the Reading, he added what we would call a 'blanket' and all-inclusive doubt, in which he singled out the last four of his separately stated doubts for special mention.

'Sometimes, nay, frequently, not only subjects, but princes, too,

[1] *De Jure Belli, infra,* Appendix B, p. lxix. [2] *Ibid.* [3] *Ibid.*, pp. lxix–lxx.

who in reality have no just cause of war, may nevertheless be waging war in good faith, with such good faith, I say, as to free them from fault; as, for instance, if the war is made after a careful examination and in accordance with the opinion of learned and upright men. And since no one who has not committed a fault should be punished, in that case, although the victor may recoup himself for things that have been taken from him and for any expenses of the war, yet, just as it is unlawful to go on killing after victory in the war has been won, so the victor ought not to make seizures or exactions in temporal matters beyond the limits of just satisfaction, seeing that anything beyond these limits could only be justified as a punishment, such as could not be visited on the innocent.'[1]

Although the book of Deuteronomy still exists, its application has finally been circumvented if not repudiated.

On the concluding words of Victoria there is no comment which can be made at all equal to their beauty and importance. They stand alone in Victoria's Reading; they stand alone in his system of law; and they will stand alone as long as war is permitted in the enforcement of justice:

All this can be summarized in a few canons or rules of warfare. First canon: Assuming that a prince has authority to make war, he should first of all not go seeking occasions and causes of war, but should, if possible, live in peace with all men, as St. Paul enjoins on us (*Romans*, ch. 12). Moreover, he should reflect that others are his neighbours, whom we are bound to love as ourselves, and that we all have one common Lord, before whose tribunal we shall have to render our account. For it is the extreme of savagery to seek for and rejoice in grounds for killing and destroying men whom God has created and for whom Christ died. But only under compulsion and reluctantly should he come to the necessity of war.

Second canon: When war for a just cause has broken out, it must not be waged so as to ruin the people against whom it is directed, but only so as to obtain one's rights and the defence of one's country and in order that from that war peace and security may in time result.

Third canon: When victory has been won and the war is over, the victory should be utilized with moderation and Christian humility, and the victor ought to deem that he is sitting as judge between two States, the one which has been wronged and the one which has done the wrong, so that it will be as judge and not as accuser that he will deliver the judgement whereby the injured State can obtain satisfaction, and this, so far as possible, should involve the offending State in the least degree of calamity and misfortune, the offending individuals being chastised within lawful limits; and an especial reason for this is that in general among Christians all the fault is to be laid at the door of their princes, for subjects when fighting for their princes act in good faith and it is thoroughly unjust, in the words of the poet, that—

Quidquid delirant reges, plectantur Achivi.[2]

[1] *Ibid.*, p. lxx. [2] *Ibid.*

CHAPTER X

ANALYSIS OF THE READING *ON MATRIMONY*

Notices of Victoria, which fortunately are increasing in number, abound in statements that the *prima* professor of theology at the University of Salamanca was frequently consulted on questions of the day by the high and mighty and by learned and less exalted persons and friends within the Church. For example, there was a communication from no less a person than the Catholic sovereign of Spain, addressed to Francisco de Vitoria, with the request that he take the opinion of his colleagues on the question of the propriety of baptizing infidels[1]—a subject which had already been the occasion for his Reading *On the Indians Lately Discovered.*

The Reverend Father Getino, to whom internationalists—not to say churchmen—are under a great obligation because of his masterly and indispensable biography of Victoria,[2] informs us that it was the custom of the *prima* professor to make the requests which came to him the subject of a course, and in the most important matters, to deliver a reading after his course upon the general subject. As an example Father Getino instances the request addressed to the authorities of the University of Salamanca for an opinion on the divorce which Henry VIII of England was seeking to obtain from Catherine of Aragon.[3] We do not have the text of the course, but we fortunately do possess the *Relectio de Matrimonio* of 1531.[4]

The Reading *On Matrimony*, which is still the authority of the Catholic Church on such matters, dealt in the first section of the second part with two questions: the first, 'Can the temporal prince, like the Church, acting solely on his own authority, make it illicit for certain persons to contract matrimony?' and the second, 'Can the temporal prince create an impediment to matrimony?'[5] It will not escape the attention of the reader that we here have a conflict of authority, for, even supposing that a temporal prince, like the Prince of the Church, is supreme within his legitimate jurisdiction, the question arises as to where the legitimate jurisdiction ends in each case—a problem which has bothered the best of minds throughout the centuries. Victoria's statement was the statement of his Church at the time and still is. This question, even more than that of the State (which Victoria treated in his Reading *On the Civil Power*), was international and its

[1] *Vide supra*, p. 86.

[2] Getino, *op. cit.* The first edition of this work appeared in 1914.

[3] *Vide* Getino, *op. cit.*, pp. 129 *et seq.*

[4] Concerning the date of this *Relectio*, *vide* Beltrán de Heredia, *Los Manuscritos del Maestro Fray Francisco de Vitoria*, *op. cit.*, pp. 137–8.

[5] Translated from *De Matrimonio* as published in Victoria, *Relectiones Morales*, ed. Simonis (Coloniae & Francofurti, 1696), p. 500.

implications are even more than international in a merely material sense. It is therefore the international phase of the question which concerns us.

The question was indeed worthy of a course and of a Reading. It was not only interesting in itself, involving as it did a discussion of the spiritual and temporal power and the line of demarcation between the two; it was interesting to Victoria as a Spaniard, as it involved the right of a princess of Castile and of Aragon, daughter of Ferdinand and Isabella, to the queenship of England. It was also interesting to Victoria as an internationalist in that the petitioner for the divorce was none other than the redoubtable and uxorious Henry VIII of England, *Fidei Defensor*; and it intimately affected Charles I, King of Spain (grandson of the Catholic Sovereigns, Ferdinand and Isabella, and nephew of Queen Catherine of England), as well as Holy Roman Emperor.

As a professor, Francisco de Vitoria was what would be called a drawing card. It is estimated, as has previously been stated, that his students numbered a thousand.[1] It appears also that not only regularly enrolled students and members of the faculty attended his readings, but distinguished laymen and clergymen who were not connected with the University.

The brief introductory passage to this Reading is a salutation to the various categories of auditors who honoured him by their presence.[2] Victoria apparently, and with good reason, approached the subject with a certain misgiving and reluctance, of which his own words are the best evidence:

> Most reverend Fathers, and you who are distinguished in piety as in renown: it is my intention to speak a few words on the subject of matrimony. For my friends and patrons have allowed me no choice as to whether or not I shall discuss this question, to which I had devoted some reflection, and which is perhaps not unworthy of my profession and of your expectations. Since the case centreing in the marriage of those illustrious rulers, the King and Queen of England, has recently been brought to the attention of the University, and since the matter has for some days been exposed to the examination and discussion of that venerable Senate of doctors and teachers, a number of my friends have separately urged me to treat of it in my first *Relectio*. I yielded to their request, since I could not do otherwise, and consequently I must discharge to-day the obligation which I have contracted; although so many objections present themselves to my mind as I enter upon a subject of such great import, that I am more than a little fearful lest time, and the drops of the water-clock, and the kindly attention with which you are wont to favour me, should all fail me before I pierce to the heart of the matter. Therefore, whatever the outcome of my attempt may be, whether you hear words such as you had hoped for, or whether you are left still desirous of those words, it will be your part to guard my good name, applauding or condoning my efforts and the result of my studies, as you have done in the past.[3]

His readings were theological exercises, that is to say, comments

[1] *Vide supra*, p. 75, note 1.

[2] *Vide* Getino, *op. cit.*, p. 131, note: 'A Vitoria le iban a escuchar, no sólo sus discípulos, sino también lo más granado de los profesores.'

[3] *Relectiones Morales, De Matrimonio, op. cit.*, pp. 469–70.

upon a text taken from the Scriptures, with reliance either upon the *Sentences* or the *Summa*.

The text was so perfect ('What therefore God hath joined together, let no man put asunder'—to be found in the Gospel of St. Matthew)[1] that it seemed made to order for the occasion. It was of the utmost importance to Victoria that the question which he was about to discuss should be stated with the greatest clearness and that his statement should not merely be accurate, but meticulously so.

Catherine, a high-minded woman, daughter of the Catholic Sovereigns, married the eldest son of Henry VII, King of England (a son who died without succeeding to the throne), and later married the second son who had already become His Serene Majesty, Henry VIII, King of England. After many years, the latter, desirous of being freed from this marriage, alleged that the union in question was prohibited by divine and natural law and therefore that not even the Supreme Pontiff could permit that he should unite himself with the wife of his brother, the marriage contracted with her having been and being null and void.

Victoria's treatment of this most important subject is impersonally handled, and the names of Henry and Catherine are rarely mentioned. He pursues an impassive and logical line of argument leading to the conclusion that Henry is not justified in claiming an annulment of his marriage with Catherine. Victoria had to decide, and decided, whether Henry VIII was justified in asserting, after many years of matrimony, that his marriage to Catherine was not valid and could not be valid—even by a dispensation of the Pope—on the grounds that she was his brother's widow and that the book of Leviticus[2] forbids marriage with the wife of one's brother.

1. In the first place, Victoria reasons and concludes that when such a marriage has been consummated, no prohibition contained in any form of law suffices to make it invalid.

2. The particular prohibition referred to is not a precept of the Law Evangelical; and prohibitions contained in Leviticus and the other books of the Old Testament are not binding upon Christians.

3. The New Law of the New Testament contains no negative precepts except with respect to those things which are prohibited by natural law; so that our only guide in determining what persons are prohibited from marrying each other is, under the New Law, right reason: the latter, indeed, being inspired of God, is a guide almost as sure as the Scriptures themselves. From the view-point of natural law and natural reason, not all the degrees of relationship mentioned by Leviticus as prohibitive of marriage are actually prohibitive; and the relationship between Henry and Catherine was not, according to

[1] St. Matthew, xix. 6.

[2] Leviticus, xviii. 16.

natural law, prohibitive of marriage. Victoria admits, however, that natural law may be interpreted as prohibiting different acts in three different ways: certain acts are absolutely prohibited; others are prohibited as a general rule, permitting of occasional exceptions; and still others are not, strictly speaking, prohibited but might better be left undone. The case of Henry and Catherine might fall under the second or the third group but not under the first.

4. But even if the prohibition in Leviticus were binding upon Christians, that prohibition nevertheless referred either to the wife of a brother still living or to his widow and the mother of his children. To marry the widow of a brother when the two had had no children was never prohibited by divine law; in fact, it was expressly commanded in case brothers dwelt together, as Victoria points out, in the twenty-fifth chapter of Deuteronomy.[1]

5. In any event, in the opinion of Victoria, a dispensation from the Pope was not necessary to the validity of a marriage contracted with a brother's widow, whether or not she was the mother of his children.

6. A corollary to the conclusion—for which Victoria had chapter and verse—was that infidels who contract marriage within degrees of relationship made prohibitive by the Church are nevertheless actually married, if the union did not violate natural law; since the only prohibition which they had disregarded was one laid down by human law, not considered as binding upon infidels.

Henry was apparently obsessed with the idea of having a son to succeed him. A son did, after intervening marriages, make his appearance, but he met his death at an early age;[2] to be followed by Mary, the daughter of the repudiated Catherine, who, however, had never lost the respect of the English people; and in turn to be followed by Anne Boleyn's daughter, who, in the matter of kingcraft, was superior to any son that ever sat upon the English throne—if indeed the limitation is of England.

The attempt of Henry to persuade the Holy Father to dissolve the marriage on the ground that his queen was the widow of his brother

[1] Verses v–x read thus:

'If brethren dwell together, and one of them die, and have no child, the wife of the dead shall not marry without unto a stranger: her husband's brother shall go in unto her, and take her to him to wife, and perform the duty of an husband's brother unto her.

'And it shall be, that the firstborn which she beareth shall succeed in the name of his brother which is dead, that his name be not put out of Israel.

'And if the man like not to take his brother's wife, then let his brother's wife go up to the gate unto the elders, and say, My husband's brother refuseth to raise up unto his brother a name in Israel, he will not perform the duty of my husband's brother.

'Then the elders of his city shall call him, and speak unto him: and if he stand to it, and say I like not to take her;

'Then shall his brother's wife come unto him in the presence of the elders, and loose his shoe from off his foot, and spit in his face, and shall answer and say, So shall it be done unto that man that will not build up his brother's house.

'And his name shall be called in Israel, The house of him that hath his shoe loosed.'

[2] Edward VI, whose mother was Jane Seymour, and who died in his sixteenth year.

Arthur (who would have succeeded to the throne had he lived, with Catherine as his legitimate spouse) was unavailing. Henry was intent, however, on marrying one Anne Boleyn, whose brown eyes appeared to have captivated him, and was unwilling to have his royal will thwarted. With the aid of a Parliament subservient to his royal pleasure the marriage was dissolved and the inheritance to the Crown vested in the children of his marriage with Anne Boleyn—with the further provision that a failure to accept such action of Parliament would be treasonable and punishable by death; and he also had himself declared the 'Supreme Head' of the Church of England.[1] The result was that Henry became, in fact if not in name, 'Pope' of the Church in England. The expression is used advisedly, because Henry remained Catholic in belief, if Protestant in practice; and the sovereign, the English standard of value, still proclaims the King or the Queen for the time being—Henry's successors, direct or collateral—*Fidei Defensor.*

Arthur, as the eldest son of Henry VII, was born to the throne. Henry came into the world designated for the Archbishopric of Canterbury. He was therefore educated to the cloth, if not so inclined. He was not merely a learned prince for his day, but handled Latin, the language of the Church, with not a little grace. His tractate[2] in defence of the Church against Protestant innovators was agreeable to the Papacy and won him the title of 'Defender of the Faith'. His views on the Papacy in the tractate were markedly different from those which he expressed after he had met Anne Boleyn; for in the tractate against Luther did he not show himself to be a partisan of the Pope's authority? Notwithstanding Sir Thomas More's advice of caution to Henry against going too far, the latter replied: 'We are so much bound to the see of Rome that we cannot do too much honour unto it. Whatsoever impediment be to the contrary, we will set forth that authority to the utmost; for we have received from that see our crown imperial.' 'Which,' More says, 'till his grace with his own mouth so told me, I never heard before.'[3] A few phrases to the same effect are lifted from a letter of the 'Defender of the Faith', written as late as 1526–7, in which he roundly denounced Luther, who was then both a byword and a household word in Germany and whose advice in a matter not unlike his own he would later have been glad to follow—the second marriage of Philip of Hesse with a German lady, whether blue-eyed or brown, we do not know.

So came it than to passe, that Luther at laste, parceyuyng wyse men to espye hym, lerned men to leaue hym, good men to abhorre hym, and his frantyke fauourers to fall to wracke, the nobles and honest people in Almaygne, beynge taught by the profe of his vngratyous practyse, moche more hurt & myschefe to folowe therof, than euer they loked

[1] *Vide Cambridge Modern History, op. cit.*, vol. ii, p. 436. [2] *Assertio Septem Sacramentorum.*

[3] Mark Pattison's article on Sir Thomas More in *Encyclopaedia Britannica*, 11th ed., vol. xviii, pp. 824–5.

after, deuysed a letter to vs written, to abuse them and all other natyons, in suche wyse, as ye by the contentes therof herafter shal well perceyue. In whiche he fayneth hymselfe to be enformed, that we be tourned to the fauour of his secte. And with many flateryng wordes, he laboreth to haue vs content that he myght be bolde to write to vs in the mater, and cause of the gospell. And thervpon without answere had from vs, nat onely publysshed the same letter and put it in print, of purpose that his adherentes shulde be the bolder, vnder the shadowe of our fauour, but also fell in deuyce with one or two leude persons, borne in this our realme, for the translatyng of the Newe testament in to Englysshe, as well with many corruptions of that holy text, as certayn prefaces, and other pestylent gloses in the margentes, for the aduauncement and settying forthe of his abhomynable heresyes, entendynge to abuse the gode myndes and deuotion, that you oure derely beloued people beare, towarde the holy scrypture, & to enfect you with the deedly corruption and contagious odour of his pestylent errours. . . .[1]

The Hessian marriage was frankly bigamous. It need not be said that Luther took a page from Henry's parliamentary book in urging expediency as well as necessity; for just as Henry had himself made by his Parliament 'Supreme Head' of the Church, so Luther had the German prince divinely instituted and supreme in the spiritual as well as the temporal realm. While Henry VIII could claim that he himself was King 'By the grace of God', and Louis XIV could arrogantly say in his own behalf, 'L'État, c'est moi', the doctrine thus expressed was to come to grief at the hands of the Revolutionary Fathers in their Declaration of Independence, when the seeds of popular sovereignty scattered by the generous and unerring hand of the Jesuits to choke the tares of the Lutheran heresy, had been carried across the sea and had come to their full fruition upon the virgin soil of the New World, to be harvested by the successors of the 'Indians lately discovered'.[2]

According to Victoria, the question which he discussed and which he sought to solve in his examination of matrimony was whether the temporal prince could lawfully create an impediment to matrimony so as to render a union unlawful which would have been lawful but for the imposition of such an impediment created by temporal law. The question was an ecclesiastical one which, however, involved temporal considerations. The Reading would necessarily be controversial, for he adopted the method of exposition which the theologians of that day employed, that is to say, he spoke as a schoolman. In so doing he set

[1] Extract from 'A copy of the letters, wherin the most redouted & mighty prince our souerayne lorde kyng Henry the eyght. . . . made answere vnto a certayne letter of Martyn Luther' (Rycharde Pynson, London [1526–7]), in *The Holy Bible*, A Facsimile in a reduced size of the Authorized Version published in the year 1611, with an Introduction by A. W. Pollard, and Illustrative Documents (Oxford, 1911), p. 56.

[2] 'The great merit of Sidney and Locke, therefore, is that they withdrew, as it were, the veil with which Filmer sought to obscure the features of the Cardinal Saint [Bellarmine].

'And hence the glory of St. Robert Bellarmine to transmit the heritage of the past, which, in the hands of George Mason and Thomas Jefferson of Virginia, has already become the hope of the future.' (From an address delivered on the unveiling of the portrait of St. Robert Bellarmine, May 13th, 1931, in the Law School of Georgetown University, Washington, D.C.)

Vide further, on the matter of Cardinal Bellarmine, a letter addressed to His Holiness, Pope Pius XI, on Easter Sunday, 1931, printed under the auspices of the Sacred Congregation of Rites, Rome, 1931, in *Urbis et Orbis*, Concessiones Tituli Doctoris . . . in honorem . . . Card. Bellarmino.

forth a series of arguments which, in his opinion, could be advanced by his opponents in defence of the jurisdiction of the temporal prince, in what might be called the temporal phase of marriage and divorce.

1. The point of approach which Victoria had adopted in the Reading *On the Civil Power* was naturally that which he used in this Reading, which turned, as far as the prince was concerned, likewise upon the cause or reason and the purpose of the exercise of such power. A line or two will make this evident and show the connexion between the two Readings. 'The reason for a given custom is to be deduced from the end which it serves',[1] and the custom was of course to be used in the interest of the State; and the extent to which the power should be exercised might be said to depend upon the extent to which it benefited the State; and hence it followed that there was a justification for the exercise of civil power in the matter of matrimony, which was clearly beneficial to the State.

2. If it should be admitted that the prohibitions regarding consanguinity are properly for the benefit of the State, and since 'political prudence is the rule by which princes and the governors of States are guided, as Aristotle declares in the *Ethics* [VI. viii. 2]',[2] it would follow, in Victoria's statement of the case of the opponent, that the limitation of the relationship within which marriage is beneficial to the State would be 'a function of human and civil power'.

3. If, as is contended, 'matrimony is either a civil contract, or founded upon a civil contract',[3] the Prince might well exercise jurisdiction, of which Victoria cites a number of apt instances.

Victoria, desiring to be fair to the view which he intends to 'demolish'—to use his expression in his Reading *On the Indians*—may be said to appear as holding a brief for the other side. Marriage being a sacrament, it might seem to be exempt, he proceeds, 'from all power that is not spiritual'.[4] This view he brushes aside, on behalf of his opponents, as useless, because marriage existed before it was a sacrament. In the second place, the Prince could assuredly intervene, as 'private individuals' can, to make laws in aid of the sacrament. 'It is also useless', insists Victoria, still in the role of *advocatus diaboli*, 'to argue that marriage is a contract valid in the court of conscience and in the sight of God; and that the temporal prince has no power in the court of conscience, his power being limited to the court of civil contentions.'[5] The fact is that marriage is a contract, and the admission that it is valid in the court of conscience does not remove it from the category of contracts, because the temporal Prince has jurisdiction over contracts in general which are also binding in the court of conscience, such as 'contracts of sale, of donation, and of similar matters'.[6] The

[1] *De Matrimonio, op. cit.*, pp. 501–2. [2] *Ibid.*, p. 502. [3] *Ibid.*, p. 503. [4] *Ibid.*
[5] *Ibid.*, p. 504. [6] *Ibid.*

conclusion is in favour of the Prince, in so far as he regulates marriage as a form of civil contract.

Still appearing in the person of Henry's advocate, Victoria brands as insufficient the argument depriving the civil power of jurisdiction over marriage because it is 'a pact in accordance with natural law; . . . For other pacts, also—for example, donations, promises, and agreements of every sort—are valid and constitute true pacts, even apart from the obligations imposed by civil laws.'[1]

Finally strengthening the case of the opponent, in order that its repudiation may be the more complete, he denounces as groundless the argument that 'civil laws are powerless to forbid anything that is permissible by the law of nature'.[2] The authority advanced is Aristotle's *Ethics* (Book v, chap. vii), to the effect that certain acts were innocent and proper before a law had been passed making them wrong; and that if the power so to do did not exist in the State, 'the civil power would be deficient, and the State would not be self-sufficing, if the latter could not create laws befitting its own welfare and touching upon matters dealt with in no other laws'.[3] Otherwise the State would not be sufficient unto itself and it would not be a 'perfect' community, which would be contrary to the theories of the State which Victoria had already set forth in the Reading *On the Civil Power* and which he was consistently to reiterate throughout the Readings *On the Indians* and *On the Law of War*.

Turning now to the arguments, on behalf of the authority of the Church, that matrimony is a spiritual matter and that the spiritual jurisdiction ousts that of the State in legislation respecting marriage, Victoria expresses in the first person his own opinion on this question. 'I do not doubt that the secular prince, owing to the very nature of his power, possesses control and jurisdiction over matrimony, even to the point of prohibiting intermarriage among persons related by blood or by marriage; neither do I doubt that he can make laws and establish impediments like those established by the Church.'[4] In support of this statement, which goes to the very root of the matter, Victoria adds that 'certain regulations with respect to the making of marriage contracts existed originally in natural law'. Here he takes as an example the very question upon which the opinion of the University had been asked—the matter of marrying a woman who had been the wife of one's brother—and states that 'many regulations are found in Leviticus which were derived from natural law, without the intervention of any spiritual power'.[5]

Stating his individual opinion in accordance with the custom of the schoolmen, Victoria says expressly: 'It is my contention that in spite of the foregoing statements, the Church may prohibit the

[1] *Ibid.*, pp. 504–5. [2] *Ibid.*, p. 505. [3] *Ibid.* [4] *Ibid.*, p. 506. [5] *Ibid.*, p. 507.

exercise of this jurisdiction by civil power: that is, spiritual power—for example, the Pope—may prohibit and prevent the temporal prince from exercising the sort of jurisdiction in question.'[1]

It is interesting—indeed astounding—to observe the extent to which Victoria as a churchman leaned upon the authority of the pagan philosopher in order to justify the power of the Christian Church to assume and to exercise the jurisdiction which it claimed and asserted. In the present case the illustration from Aristotle[2] is the classification of faculties according to their respective ends, the lesser end yielding to the greater, with the inevitable result that the lesser—in the Victorian sense—the material faculty, yields to the exercise of the greater, that is, the spiritual faculty. 'However, I do not mean to say', he informs us, speaking again in the first person, 'that temporal power is entirely or even ordinarily subject to spiritual power. Indeed, nothing is farther from my mind than to suppose that princes are, so to speak, vicars of the Church, or of the Popes; on the contrary, I believe that they have received judicial power from God, even as the Popes themselves have received such power, and that spiritual power cannot interfere with the exercise of this temporal jurisdiction, except in special cases.'[3]

Here we have the classification of the two powers drawn from Aristotle, followed by a recognition of the existence and jurisdiction of the temporal power, as well as of the spiritual, each in its appropriate domain.

However, the question which he is discussing being one over which the Church has jurisdiction, he passes to its consideration from that standpoint: 'But I do contend', he says, 'that the Church may, when acting with due cause, deprive temporal power of the authority to examine into and exercise jurisdiction over certain matters which it would otherwise be authorized to determine and regulate, inasmuch as their very nature pertains to the realm of civil power. The Church might perform such an act, for example, on the ground that the matters in question could not be administered by civil power alone in a manner sufficiently serviceable and suitable to the attainment of spiritual ends.'[4]

It is apparent that Victoria now feels himself in a position to go directly to the question and to draw the line of demarcation upon which the harmonious operation of the two powers depends, in precisely the same manner—as we shall shortly see—as it is drawn between the Federal laws of the United States and the laws of the respective States, which operate without conflict because of the delimitation of their functions. 'The subject under discussion,' he says, 'that is, the question of marriage contracts, affords an example of such a case. For the marriage contract is a matter dependent upon Divine law, and the latter alone can determine and interpret the requirements for marriage,

[1] *De Matrimonia, op. cit.*, p. 507. [2] *Ethics*, I. i. [3] *De Matrimonio, op. cit.*, p. 508. [4] *Ibid.*, p. 509.

and what persons may or may not marry each other, and many other points involved in a contract of this sort. Therefore suitable laws cannot be made concerning matrimony by any person—for example, the secular prince—who is not thoroughly familiar with Divine law. For', he continues, 'human erudition cannot, unassisted, achieve a satisfactory understanding of many questions which occur in connexion with the marriage contract, one of these questions being: What persons may legitimately marry?'[1] The question, however, is not so simple as it sounds. It is not merely who may legitimately marry; but what authority shall determine the question of legitimacy of marriage. The answer is what we must already know: the 'spiritual power, . . . even if marriage were not a sacrament'.[2]

Stating again that the matter is still not so simple as it seems, we conclude this analysis of the *Relectio de Matrimonio* by a further—and perhaps the crowning—quotation from this Reading by the *prima* professor of theology of the University of Salamanca, speaking not merely in his own behalf but in behalf of the University which he was representing: 'Marriage, in so far as it is a necessary function of nature, is an institution of natural law; and in so far as it is a sacrament, it is an institution of Divine law; viewed as a function of the community, it is an institution of civil law: consequently, any dictate of any one of these different sorts of law may render it impossible for a given person to contract matrimony legally.'[3]

The question is of the limitation of two powers, each being freely acknowledged by the other: there is the temporal power, frankly admitted by Victoria; and there is the spiritual power. The question is the line that separates the lawful exercise of these two powers, Victoria being of the opinion that the sacramental nature of marriage, being spiritual in content, is of more importance than the temporal aspect of matrimony as a civil contract. Thus Aristotle might have spoken, had he been a Christian instead of a pagan. As with Victoria, utility in its highest sense was the aim and purpose of temporal jurisdiction, so in the case of a conflict between the power of the State, on the one hand, and the spiritual power on the other, the greater good of the latter would prevail over the material usefulness of the former. It is no answer to this—to use an expression which Victoria has himself employed in argument—to maintain that the two jurisdictions cannot exist side by side. We of the Western World—Victoria's New World—the successors of the aborigines—we of the United States of America—have had and will continue to have experience in this

[1] *Ibid.* [2] *Ibid.*

[3] *Ibid.*, p. 510. For an analysis of the Reading *On Matrimony* from a somewhat different point of view, *vide* Herbert Francis Wright, 'The Divorce of Henry VIII, a contemporary Discussion at one of the Continental Universities', published in the *American Catholic Quarterly Review*, vol. xliv, no. 176 (October, 1919), pp. 556–65.

matter as long as there is a Federal Constitution and a power reserved by each of the States, to be exercised in accordance with their individual judgements. The Federal authority has its visible location in a tract of land but ten miles square, and yet from this tract, known as the District of Columbia, the entire Federal power of the United States radiates, a Federal law—passing through every frontier of each State of the American Union—overriding the power of each of the forty-eight States in each and every matter not reserved to the States. This central power, because of its greater good, usefulness, and value, is vested in the Federal Government to the annihilation of the powers which otherwise would have existed in each individual State were it not for their renunciation of them for this larger purpose. Of this division between the exercise of Federal and State authority a minor but material example is the withdrawal from the State courts of suits affecting citizens of other States and the location of jurisdiction in such a matter in a Federal court because of the mere value of the amount involved.[1]

How natural it is, indeed inevitable, that the exercise of a spiritual power should be withdrawn from a temporal to be vested in a spiritual authority, for the spiritual power, concerned as it is with the imponderables, is superior to any material power which the mind of man can conceive.

[1] *Vide* Sec. 24 of the Judicial Code enacted by Act of Congress, March 3rd, 1911 (c. 231, 36 Stat. 1087).

CHAPTER XI

ANALYSIS OF THE READING *ON THE CIVIL POWER*

NOTWITHSTANDING Victoria's many-sidedness, he was a theologian by inclination and by profession. It is a matter for criticism if the judge enlarges his usual jurisdiction, but with Victoria it is not a matter of criticism but of merit that he extended theology beyond its usual bounds to embrace all subjects with a moral implication, in all parts of the world. Although he was primarily a theologian and in the course of time made, in the words already referred to[1] of Menéndez y Pelayo, every Spaniard a theologian, reviving and making acceptable scholasticism, it is nevertheless a simple fact that he is making a conquest of the world of our day, not by his theology as such but by his readings, which may properly be called disquisitions, on the fundamentals of international law and international relations.

As a Spaniard he was concerned with the nature and extent of the power of his country; as a churchman, he was obliged to familiarize himself with the extent, as well as the nature, of the ecclesiastical power; and as a Spaniard and a churchman, with the extent and limitations of authority both temporal and spiritual, into which the powers of his day seem to have been divided. These were the questions which confronted him whichever way he turned. These were the questions to which he extended his theology, bringing to their discussion a single standard of morality, although applicable to both jurisdictions. To other questions of a public nature, affecting one or the other, he devoted his attention, but they were, it may be said, incidental to a just conception of secular and of spiritual power in what had been an accepted state of things until the horizons were pushed back to disclose a new world which became in itself an integral part of the international community; and it is in connexion with this phase of theology that he occupies to-day a dominating position.

What, then, was, in Victoria's opinion, this theology which dealt with the bases of things temporal as well as spiritual? It was in his Reading *On the Civil Power*, with which we are already familiar, that he expressed himself on the province of theology. 'The duties and functions of the theologian', Victoria would have us believe, having himself in mind, 'extend over a field so vast, that no argument, no discussion, no text, seems alien to the practice and purpose of theology';[2]

[1] *Supra*, p. 68.

[2] *De Potestate Civili, infra*, Appendix C, p. lxxi. An analysis of this *Relectio*, under the title *The 'De Potestate Civili' of Vitoria*, has recently been published by Herbert Francis Wright in the *Proceedings of the Seventh Annual Meeting of the American Catholic Philosophical Association* (Washington, 1932). *Vide* also his address 'Vitoria and the State', published in a volume entitled *Francisco De Vitoria, Addresses in Commemoration of the Fourth Centenary of his Lectures 'De Indis' and 'De Iure Belli', 1532–1932, Delivered at the Catholic University of America, May 1, 1932* (Washington, 1932).

that is to say: it is the universal science.[1] And the reason for this, he continues, vouching the authority of Cicero, the orator (who had himself in mind, it is believed, in his treatise on an orator), is 'that men who are distinguished and skilled in every science and in all the arts are very rare'.[2] To which Victoria adds, on behalf of his own profession, that 'the lack of able and sound theologians is as great as—not to say greater than—the lack of orators which is mentioned by Cicero'. Indeed, is not theology 'the first of all those sciences and studies which the Greeks call θεολογία'? His conclusion to such a premise was inevitable: that 'very few are found who are competent in a subject so difficult'.[3] The world indeed, he added, lay before the theologian who would choose a subject with such an 'infinite number of possibilities'. Among the many 'possibilities', he assured the 'most illustrious and learned gentlemen' who were honouring him with their presence, was the State—regarding which what he said is still true: 'many points remain to be considered, although earnest and erudite men have already accorded it extensive treatment.'[4]

His treatment in a single discussion, on a memorable day in 1528, limited itself to the 'public and private power by which states are governed', which, under the heading of 'reading', 'lecture', or 'disquisition', was a classic, and is to-day beginning to be considered again as such.

It appears to have been the custom in the public addresses which are called *Relectiones* (re-readings, in fact, in the form of single and public lectures) to choose a text from the Bible, to be considered with special reference to the *Sentences* of Peter Lombard or the *Summa Theologica* of St. Thomas Aquinas. In the present instance, the text is from the thirteenth chapter of St. Paul's Epistle to the Romans. It is of but seven words: 'There is no power but of God';[5] and it is as a summary of the origin, the source, and the extent of the power of the State, upon which Victoria was to discourse.

The first of the principal conclusions is: 'All power—whether public or private—by which the secular state is governed, is not only just and legitimate, but is so surely ordained of God, that not even by the consent of the whole world can it be destroyed or annulled.'[6]

The second principal conclusion is: 'Just as the majority of members of a State may set up a king over the whole State, although other members are unwilling, so the majority of Christians, even though there be some who are opposed, may lawfully create a monarch whom all princes and provinces are under obligation to obey.'[7]

[1] *Vide* Beltrán de Heredia, *op. cit.*, pp. 15–16, who quotes Victoria as stating elsewhere: 'Theologia tamen sacra nullum habet terminum, nullam metam, ita ut si quis totam vitam in ejus assiduo studio duxerit non illi pro ipsius satisfecerit dignitati. Ego autem profecto per 26 annos vel plures ei pro virili incubui, vix tamen januas ejus fuisse ingressus me videor; et si alios centum annos haberem vitae, omnes libentissime in ejus studiis transigerem.' *Vide* also *supra*, p. 76.

[2] *De Potestate Civili*, *infra*, Appendix C, p. lxxii. [3] *Ibid.* [4] *Ibid.* [5] Romans, xiii. 1.

[6] *De Potestate Civili*, *infra*, Appendix C, p. lxxii. [7] *Ibid.*, p. lxxxii.

And the last of the three principal conclusions is: 'The laws and constitutions of princes are binding in such a way as to render transgressors guilty in the court of conscience.'[1]

It will be observed that the people choose their kings, and that for this purpose a majority suffices; and in the course of this discussion it will further appear that they may choose any form of government, such as a monarchy or aristocracy or even a democracy, the fundamental conception of Victoria being that the human race is so made that its members must live in society, not in isolation; that such society is in accordance with their nature; and that it is therefore a law of nature that society be organized, and this law of nature is in accordance with the divine order of things, in which power is of God. But the law, whether it be of nature or of God, is immutable in the sense that society demands government, and although a majority of the people can choose the form of government, the entire people could not dispense with government, because without government there would be anarchy and society would cease to exist.

Victoria's method of demonstration may seem old-fashioned to those accustomed to newer catchwords. But his purpose was none other than that of our President Lincoln, when he said that 'this nation'—Victoria would have said every nation—'under God, shall have a new birth of freedom; and that government of the people, by the people, for the people, shall not perish from the earth'.[2] Whether under natural law, as Aristotle would say, or under God, according to Victoria and Lincoln, organization there must be and therefore in a Christian world it is both natural and divine.

The State is to be organized for a social or public purpose. The government is consequently for a public, as distinct from a private, purpose. Therefore we are dealing with public power, and in the view of Victoria, this public power was 'the faculty, authority, or right to govern the civil state'.[3] Victoria had previously said that the public powers are from God, and that they are therefore 'just and legitimate'. If so, 'no power of this sort could be abrogated by the consent of man'.[4] Now this statement might seem strange if it stood alone, as its meaning might not be clear, but it is only a part of Victoria's completed conception; 'for if man', he continues, 'may not renounce the right and the means of defending himself and of using his bodily members for his own advantage'—and human nature whispers he will not—'then neither may he renounce power, since these functions pertain to power by natural and divine law. In like manner, the state may in nowise be deprived of this power to protect itself and to guard against injury from its own citizens or from aliens, a function which it could not

[1] *Ibid.*, p. lxxxiii.
[2] Gettysburg Address, November 19th, 1863.
[3] *De Potestate Civili, infra*, Appendix C, p. lxxxi.
[4] *Ibid.*

fulfil if there were no public powers; and consequently, if all the citizens should agree to dispense with these powers, in order that they might be bound by no law and that there should be no one to command, the agreement would be null and void, being contrary to natural law.'[1]

Of Victoria's conception, it may be said, paraphrasing the famous dictum of an American Chief Justice, that it looks to an international and indestructible community composed of national and indestructible groups.[2]

We are now in a position—forecasting, as it were, conclusions—to appreciate his manner of approach and the process by which he establishes those conclusions, 'imitating', as he says, 'the scholastic manner' in so far as he was 'able' (and it would be impertinent to remark that he was 'able'). Trained speaker that he was, he felt that he must make a number of 'prefatory remarks', which were needed 'to explain it and make it intelligible'.[3] The remarks are not the least valuable part of the discourse, and even in the students' notes from which they are reproduced, they show what a master he was of public discourse, for, although he prepared himself for the occasion, he appears not to have confined himself to his notes.

An example of his style is in a passage which is very material to his purpose, the beauty and indeed the poetry of which not even the imperfect report of his students can obscure or mar: 'For truly,' he said, 'imbued with crude ideas, men wandered in their investigations over all the heavens (as they say), with the result that they were unable to give a satisfactory account of anything according to their own doctrines, and certainly could in no way and by no artifice explain through their philosophizing the construction of all that is best and most great. For how may they object if I seek to know the sort of matter by which the earth is adorned, placed as it is in the very heart of the Universe, solid and globular, entirely rounded in virtue of its own energies, clad with flowers, grass, and trees; or if I ask whence comes the ice-cold, never-failing quality of the streams, the crystal clear liquid, the green mantle of the banks; and whence the composition of the various parts and members of man, derived from one kind of matter? What is the force in that matter which gave to man alone among all living beings, eyes that looked upward; which granted that he should gaze up at the sky; which bade him turn his face towards the stars? And these philosophers make answer as follows: that it could not be otherwise, that man must needs stand erect, while the beasts are low and stooping: not to serve any aim or useful purpose, but merely because different living creatures are dissimilar in matter and construction.'[4]

[1] *De Potestate Civili, infra,* Appendix C, p. lxxxi.

[2] Chief Justice Chase, in *Texas* v. *White* (7 Wall. 725): 'The Constitution, in all its provisions, looks to an indestructible union, composed of indestructible States.'

[3] *De Potestate Civili, infra,* Appendix C, p. lxxii.

[4] *Ibid.*, p. lxxiii.

This might be the view of the materialists. It was not that of Victoria, who continues after interruption: 'But for our intent and present purpose, it will suffice to uphold one sublime truth, the neglect of which must always lead to error. Let us believe that neither the sky nor the land nor the remaining parts of the world, not Man himself, was the beginning of the world; but rather that all that is contained in the heavens was appointed for some useful purpose, and that all things have been created, and necessarily created just as they are, for a purpose, whence are derived the nature and the necessity of all things.'[1]

What then was this universal purpose which with him was one of design, not accident? 'In the course of this inquiry', he says, 'we should note that, while Man is superior to other animals in reason, wisdom, and speech, on the other hand, the Providence that rules us has denied to that eternal, immortal, and wise animal, many things which it has granted to the rest. For Mother Nature, from the very beginning, in order to provide security and protection for animals, furnished each of the others with his own covering, by which he might the better withstand the rigours of wintry frost and cold. She supplied all of these with their own instruments of defence against alien attacks, that they might either offer resistance by means of their natural weapons—as the fiercer animals do; or escape from danger by the swiftness of their flight—after the manner of the weaker animals; or protect themselves with their beaks as if these were spears; or lurk in some hiding-place: and so it is that some of them are lightly held aloft by feathers, while some are provided with claws and still others with horns; but each and every one has his means of self-defence.'

'To Man alone, however, she granted reason and virtue, leaving him frail, weak, needy; drawing him forth from the wreck enfeebled, destitute, in want of everything, reproachful against himself; and scattering hardships throughout his life so that, in truth, from the very moment of his birth he can only presage tears, weeping over his own frailty; as the saying is: "full of trouble".'[2]

The various steps by which Victoria reached his first conclusion can be separated from the narrative and stated under a series of headings:

1. 'Men should not wander singly and in solitude, after the manner of wild beasts, but should dwell in a fellowship in which they might be of aid to one another.'

2. 'The understanding of man'—according to Aristotle—'which can have no existence in solitude, is not to be perfected without instruction and experience.'[3]

3. 'Speech is the messenger of the understanding, and according to Aristotle, it has been bestowed for that sole purpose.'[4]

[1] *Ibid.*, pp. lxxiii–lxxiv.
[2] *Ibid.*, p. lxxiv
[3] Aristotle, *Nicomachean Ethics*, II. i.
[4] *Politics*, I. ii. 10–11.

4. 'If it were possible for wisdom to exist without speech, wisdom itself would under such circumstances be neither pleasing nor communicable.'

5. 'Wherefore Aristotle points out (*Politics* I) that man is by nature a civil and sociable animal.'

6. 'The will, whose chief ornaments are justice and friendship, would of necessity be entirely deformed and, so to speak, crippled, if it were separated from human society.'

7. 'Justice, indeed, cannot be practised except by the multitude; and the same is true of friendship, . . .'

8. 'Unless there be communication of life, all perishes.'

9. 'And even if it were agreed that human life was sufficient unto itself, nevertheless, it could not fail to be bitter and unpleasant when passed in solitude.'

10. 'Therefore, since human societies have been established for this purpose—namely, that we should bear one another's burdens—and since civil society is of all societies that which best provides for the needs of men, it follows that the community is, so to speak, an exceedingly natural form of intercommunication; that is, a form thoroughly in accord with Nature.'[1]

11. 'It is evident, then, that states and commonwealths had not their fount and origin in the invention of men, nor in any artificial manner, but sprang, as it were, from Nature, who produced this method of protecting and preserving mortals. . . . It clearly follows that the same purpose and necessity underlie the existence of public powers.'

12. 'If councils and assemblies of men are necessary to the security of mortals, it is also true that no society can continue to exist without some force and power to govern and provide for it; the use and the utility of public power, and of the community, and of society are absolutely the same.'

13. 'Just as the human body could not be preserved in its integrity, without some directing force to regulate the various members, making them of mutual use and—what is more important—of service to the whole man; even so the state would necessarily lose its integrity, if every individual were solicitous for his own welfare, and ever citizen were heedless of the public good.'

14. 'From what has been said it is easy, indeed, to discern the efficient cause of this power. For if we prove that public power has been set up by natural law, then—since God is the sole author of natural law—it becomes evident that public power is of God and that it cannot be contained within the limits of man's nature or of any positive law. For God, Who has created all things in His wisdom, Who "reacheth . . . from end to end mightily, and ordereth all things

[1] *Potestate Civili, infra,* Appendix C, pp. lxxiv–lxxv.

sweetly, Whose works are all harmoniously disposed", as the Apostle says, has so fashioned the nature and disposition of man that he cannot prosper unless he dwell in a social state.'[1]

15. 'If states and societies are established in accordance with divine or natural law, the same is true of power, without which states could not exist.'[2]

16. 'The State, then, possesses this power by divine Disposition: but the material cause in which, by natural and divine law, power of this kind resides, is the State itself; which by its very nature is competent to govern and administer itself, and to order all its powers for the common good.'

17. 'Inasmuch as this power resides principally in kings, to whom the State has entrusted its authority, it becomes necessary to discuss kingly dignity and power.'[3]

18. 'Not only is monarchy, or royal power, just and legitimate; but, in addition to this, the power of kings is derived from divine and natural law, not from the State itself, nor directly from men . . . and since this power cannot be exercised by the multitude (which could not conveniently make laws and issue edicts, settle disputes and punish transgressors) it has therefore been necessary that the administration of the State should be entrusted to the care of some person or persons (and it matters not whether this power was entrusted to one or to many)'.[4]

19. '. . . it is altogether absurd to suppose that anything expedient to the administration of human affairs is contrary to natural or divine law.'[5]

20. 'It is apparent, then, that kingly power is not derived from the state, but from God Himself. . . . For even though this power is established by the State (since the latter creates the king), nevertheless the State, in this very act, transfers not merely the power, but also its own authority; so that there are not two sorts of power—one, that of the king; the other, that of the community. Therefore, just as we say that the power of the State is established by God and by natural law, so of a surety we must say the same of all kingly power.'[6]

21. 'However, some persons doubt whether this is true of the powers governing any infidel State: whether, that is, the princes and other magistrates found among pagans are legitimate. . . . It should not be a matter of any doubt that legitimate princes and potentates may exist among the heathen . . . Joseph and Daniel were governors under pagan princes. And finally, Christian princes—whether they be secular, or lords of the Church—may not deprive infidels of this power and sovereignty merely on the ground that they are infidels, when no injury has been done by them.'[7]

[1] *Ibid.*, pp. lxxv–lxxvi. [2] *Ibid.*, p. lxxvi. [3] *Ibid.*, p. lxxvii. [4] *Ibid.*, p. lxxviii. [5] *Ibid.*, p. lxxix. [6] *Ibid.*, p. lxxx. [7] *Ibid.*

These twenty-one passages lifted from the remarks justify the three causes of public secular power quoted in the first part of Victoria's Reading *On the Civil Power*.

Just as Victoria had doubts in the Reading *On the Law of War*, so he employed corollaries in the present Reading *On the Civil Power*. In the long run, the effect was the same, notwithstanding the difference in name, because the corollaries were acceptable at the time and the doubts have been accepted in the course of time. The slightest inspection of one or the other would leave the impression that they are interesting and if not the most, certainly not the least valuable portions of the Readings, for their purpose was essentially to broaden, and therefore to humanize, the principles which he laid down.

What could be more interesting, for example, than the first corollary to the first of the principal conclusions of the power of the State—a corollary which Victoria himself says should 'not be despised, and especially not by those who live under a monarchical government'.[1] Victoria was in favour of the monarchical system, although he admitted, somewhat reluctantly, the existence and even the possible advantages of other forms. However, he set his shoulder to the wheel to push forward the monarchy and, if his premises be admitted, the conclusions are inevitable. Still, many a crown has toppled since his day; and the end is not yet. The passage in question is short; it is closely knit; and it shows Victoria in the fullness of his powers, intent on preserving the monarchical form of government for his beloved Spain. Perhaps he felt himself challenged, for were not the people of States which had no king and lived under 'a popular form of government, wont to boast of their liberty'? Hence the corollary—which was not to be despised—that 'there is no less liberty in a monarchy than in an aristocracy, or a democracy'.[2]

As was to be expected, Aristotle was to make his appearance—for Victoria's Aristotle, it may be said again in passing, was the patron saint of the Middle Ages—the various kinds of government being thus divided in the third book of his *Politics*: 'monarchies, or the rule of one; aristocracies, or the rule of a select number; and democracies, or popular rule, that is, the rule of the multitude'.[3] Upon this passage Victoria had a comment, to the effect that 'there is no less liberty under monarchical rule, than under the other forms of rule'. Had he stopped there, it would have been for his opponents to ask where 'liberty' existed under monarchical rule. However, he did not pause to cite examples—which was a favourite method—but proceeded at once to show why the monarchical rule should offer the maximum of liberty: 'Since power itself is the same,'—he adroitly began—'whether it be invested in one or in many, and since it is better to be subject to one

[1] *De Potestate Civili, infra,* Appendix C, p. lxxxi. [2] *Ibid.* [3] III. vii.

than to many (for there are as many masters as there are superior authorities), therefore, there is not less liberty where all are subject to one, than where all are subject to many; especially in view of the fact that where there are many rulers, there are many who are ambitious for power, so that the State—because of their diverse purposes—will necessarily be afflicted with frequent insurrections and dissentions. For, as the poet says, there is no faith in those who share power'[1]—it is usual for Victoria to embroider his text with a line from a poet, but in one of his most serious passages he refers to a comic poet, one Terence[2] by name. He had, however, authority more in his line, if not more apposite. It is that of the Lord, 'speaking through His Prophet: "Many pastors have destroyed my vineyard" (Jeremiah, xii. 10). The best rule, therefore, is the rule of one, just as the whole world is governed by one all-wise King and Master.'[3] There is but one possible comment upon this corollary: It was a pity in his day, and it is a pity in our day, that mankind has not been able to find a temporal ruler at all comparable to the 'one all-wise King and Master'.

The second consequence of the first conclusion is a second corollary, which should be patently unacceptable to the modern world, were it not for the second of the principal conclusions shortly to be mentioned. Therefore the corollary is stated without present comment in Victoria's words that 'the State as a whole may rightfully be punished for the sin of the monarch'. In this instance, Victoria avails himself of surer ground and resorts to a concrete example. 'If any king make unjust war upon another ruler, the injured party may plunder and make lawful war upon and slay the subjects of the unjust king, even if all these subjects be innocent; for when the king has once been set up by the State, any immoderate act of his is charged against the State: since the latter is bound to entrust this power only to him who will be just in the exercise and use of power, and since, in doing otherwise, the State lays itself open to danger.'[4]

Admitting the appositeness of the instance, the right of reprisal seems more than implicit.

The third consequence to be drawn in this connexion is contained in the third and last corollary to the first conclusion, that 'no war is just the conduct of which is manifestly more harmful to the State than it is good and advantageous; and this is true regardless of any other claims or reasons that may be advanced to make of it a just war'. This was a favourite idea—in a lesser man it would be called an obsession—to which later he referred in more than one passage in the Reading *On the Law of War*, with which the reader is already familiar. It is not merely stated here, however, but is restated, on the authority of the

[1] *De Potestate Civili, infra,* Appendix C, p. lxxxi.
[2] *Vide, supra,* p. 149, note 1.
[3] *De Potestate Civili, infra,* Appendix C, p. lxxxi.
[4] *Ibid.,* pp. lxxxi–lxxxii.

maxim that we cannot have too much of a good thing—especially of a thing of this kind. 'If the State has no power to make war except for the purpose of defending itself, and protecting itself and its property, it follows'—in the Victorian system of international law—'that any war will be unjust—whether it be begun by the king or by the State—through which the latter is not rendered greater, but rather is enfeebled and impaired. Nay more, since one nation is a part of the whole world, and since the Christian province is a part of the whole Christian State, if any war should be advantageous to one province or nation but injurious to the world or to Christendom, it is my belief that for this very reason, that war is unjust.'[1]

We are now ready for the second principal conclusion, that 'just as the majority of members of a State may set up a king over the whole State, although other members are unwilling, so the majority of Christians, even though there be some who are opposed, may lawfully create a monarch whom all princes and provinces are under obligation to obey'.

If we were asked to accept this conclusion without the proofs which Victoria scatters with a generous hand in other readings, we would find ourselves in much the same difficulty as with the second corollary. Both the conclusion and the following corollary, however, are acceptable, if they are considered in the light of the comment with which Victoria enriches the conclusion. The simplest and the fairest way is to state under numbered headings the three proofs by which he justifies the conclusion so satisfactorily that thereafter he proceeds at once to the corollary.

1. 'For if the State may entrust its power to some one individual, acting thus for its own advantage, it is certain that the dissent of one or of a few could not prevent the rest from caring for the welfare of the State; otherwise—that is, if the consent of all were required—insufficient provision would be made for the good of the State since unanimous consent is rarely or never found among a multitude.'

This statement lights the way, as it were, to what we would call popular sovereignty, which is not far away in Victoria's scheme of things, for it appears in the very next sentence: 'It suffices, then, in order to do anything legitimately, that the majority should agree on the course in question.'[2] This is made evident by a syllogism permitting the majority, it would seem, to overthrow as well as to install: 'For if two parties disagree, it must necessarily result that the sentiment of one party should prevail; and inasmuch as their desires conflict, the sentiment of the party which is in the minority ought not to prevail; therefore it is the sentiment of the majority which should dominate.' The consequences of this doctrine are stated in the form of a question. 'If the consent of all is required in order to create the king, why is it not also required in

[1] *De Potestate Civili, infra,* Appendix C, p. lxxxii. [2] *Ibid.*

order that he be not so created? Why is unanimous consent more to be required in an affirmative than in a negative matter?'[1] Why, it may be asked, may not the majority on a later and an appropriate occasion unmake what they have made; or, in terms of the concrete, reverse the throne which they set up?

2. 'A king rules over the whole State'; that is to say, Victoria's 'king', for in his monarchical government 'the king rules not only over the individual citizens, but also over the State as a whole'—over the majority which did and the minority which did not elect him—and thus, says Victoria, 'over all the citizens at one time. . . . For if the State were over the king, the result would be a democracy—that is, popular rule; and consequently not a monarchy, which is the rule of one individual: . . . Therefore, the king is over all . . . appeal is not made from the king to the State; and consequently, the State is not greater than the king or superior to him.' [2]

3. 'The majority of Christians may set up a [spiritual] monarch. . . . The Church as a whole is, so to speak, a State, and one body, this conception being in accord with the words of the Apostle: "So we, being many, are one body";[3] consequently, the Church has the power to preserve and protect itself'—otherwise it would not be the 'sufficient' State of Aristotle or the 'perfect' community of Victoria—'and to provide for the best means of self-defence against enemies. . . . And since—as is evident from the very beginning and before such an event actually took place—the human race did at one time possess this power (namely, the power to elect a monarch), we must conclude that it is still able to do so; for the power of which we speak, being derived from natural law, does not pass away.'[4]

It cannot be doubted—to use one of Victoria's phrases—that this is a logical conclusion from his premises. Whether and when the action in question should be taken is a matter for the majority of the human race—not for the present commentator—to determine, dependent upon its desire, and upon the actual creation of the Christian community by such majority of the human race.

Among the many great qualities evident to any and every one who reads the works of Victoria is his poise, which is only another term for balance. It is strikingly exemplified in this passage in which he has expressed, and from his standpoint justified, his preference for a monarchical form of government. He recognizes, nevertheless, the existence of other forms, both in his day and previously, and their proper right to exist if such were the desire of the majority.

The chief consequence which seems necessarily to follow from the preceding conclusion and the illustrations by which it is sustained is in

[1] *Ibid.* [2] *Ibid.*, p. lxxxiii. [3] Romans, xii. 5.
[4] *De Potestate Civili, infra*, Appendix C, p. lxxxiii.

itself a conclusion with which the reader of to-day, irrespective of preference, would find himself in more than substantial agreement: 'In free States such as Venice and Florence, the majority may elect a king even though the rest of the citizens be opposed,'—an 'assertion', he continues, which 'would seem to hold true, not only in view of the fact that such an act is clearly advantageous to the State, but even assuming that an aristocratic or democratic government would be still more expedient'. The majority of mankind has incorporated this corollary in the principle that the majority rules.

If we pass over the question of family relations, which would appear to be one primarily for theologians to handle, there remains but a third and final principal conclusion, that 'the laws and constitutions of princes are binding in such a way as to render transgressors guilty in the court of conscience'.[1] The matter is vital not merely to Victoria as a Dominican but to the Victoria who stands for a moral sanction in his system of the law of nations. This is so evident to those who have made a study of the readings of Victoria which deal with international law, that they are inclined to look upon them as manuals of confession, and indeed enumerate them in a list of such treatises. It is a matter also of importance to Grotius, whose commentary *On the Law of Prize* is considered by one of his countrymen as a Protestant manual of the confessional;[2] and the appeal of his elaborate treatise *On the Law of War and Peace* is to the individual rather than to the nation.

But to return to Victoria and his conclusions. 'There are some', he says, 'who hold that the laws possess no force which renders transgressors guilty in the court of conscience; but rather that they impose only one condition, namely, that princes and magistrates may justly punish the violators of said laws. These same persons deny that the subjects are bound in any other way in the sight of God';[3] we do not need to consider the first part of this statement, and as the second is theological, we may omit comment on that portion in order to state the opinion of Victoria, speaking as an international lawyer.

In spite of the arguments which he had set forth, he said that it seemed to him 'indubitable that civil laws are binding in the court of conscience'.[4] After appealing to Holy Writ, he restates his position, and in the first person: 'I shall add that civil laws are binding under pain of sin and guilt, in the same manner as ecclesiastical laws.'[5] He admitted that 'in some respects human and divine law differ, while in other respects they agree',[6] treating each in turn in order to reach a conclusion on the entire subject. There are various differences, to two

[1] *De Potestate Civili, infra,* Appendix C, p. lxxxiii.

[2] *Vide* Professor Van der Vlugt's lectures delivered at the Hague Academy of International Law under the title of *L'Œuvre de Grotius,* and published in the *Recueil des Cours* of the Academy, 1925, vol. 7, pp. 417–19.

[3] *De Potestate Civili, infra,* Appendix C, p. lxxxiv.

[4] *Ibid.*

[5] *Ibid.*

[6] *Ibid.,* p. lxxxv.

of which we may refer in Victoria's own words: 'In the case of divine law, the Will of the Legislator—since His Will has the force of reason—suffices to render the law just and binding; whereas the Will of the Legislator does not suffice to render human law just and binding.' Why this difference? 'The precepts of the latter must also be advantageous to the State and in harmony with the other laws.' Another difference is that 'divine law binds one more firmly and forcefully'. Yet another difference is that 'divine law is binding where human law is not binding'. These are the 'only differences' which he was 'able to perceive'. Wherein do these laws agree? In the fact that 'divine law so endows a thing with the quality of a virtue or a vice that anything which is in accordance with the mandates of divine law is rendered good and serviceable, although it would not otherwise be possessed of these characteristics; whereas that which is prohibited by divine law has in it something evil and vicious which it would not otherwise have. . . . In like manner, human law has this same power to endow anything with the quality of a virtue, and its opposite with the quality of a vice'.[1]

Omitting likewise the illustrations of a material nature, we come to Victoria's conclusion that 'there is no difference in this respect between human and divine law', for inasmuch as in both cases 'there is merit in an act of virtue, so guilt attends a vicious act'.[2]

This reasoning was contentious in his own day; it is likewise contentious in ours; but some of the successors of the American aborigines recognized the claims of conscience, claiming 'the separate and equal station to which the Laws of Nature and of Nature's God entitle them', thus showing in their Declaration of Independence 'a decent respect to the opinions of mankind'.[3]

Without following Victoria in his proofs, which are largely of a theological nature, we must pause a moment for a question and an answer which should not be omitted: 'Since God says, "By Me kings reign, and princes decree justice," why should not the decrees of those kings and princes be likewise binding in the court of conscience?'[4] And the answer: 'It matters not whether laws be human or divine, in so far as their binding force is concerned.'

Victoria next discusses a phase of the question which must needs have definition, if the reader is to understand the full import of his readings. 'What sort of guilt is incurred by the transgressors of human law: whether mortal, or merely venial?'[5] To the persons within the fold of the Church Universal, these are familiar terms, but to those without the Church a word of explanation will doubtless be useful. And we cannot do better than to resolve the question as far as

[1] *Ibid.*, p. lxxxv.
[2] *Ibid.*, pp. lxxxv–lxxxvi.
[3] Declaration of Independence, July 4th, 1776.
[4] *De Potestate Civili, infra*, Appendix C, p. lxxxvi.
[5] *Ibid.*, p. lxxxvii.

possible in the language of Victoria. Of the binding force of laws, divine and human, he says: 'We must preserve the same attitude towards human and divine laws; and . . . with regard to the manner and extent in which human laws are binding, we ought to consider them as being divine.' The effect would be that 'just as some divine laws are binding on pain of mortal guilt, and others on pain of venial guilt; even so, some human laws bind on pain of venial guilt'. But when is the guilt 'venial' or 'mortal . . . since the civil law itself contains no explanation of this point and since the legislator did not even take the matter into consideration when he framed the law'? Victoria's answer is that 'not even in divine law, and especially not in natural law, is a statement always included as to whether a given precept concerns mortal or venial sin; or as to the relative forcefulness of different precepts, that is, which of them has the more force . . . so that this entire question must be decided according to the particular case involved; just as in natural and divine law that sin is held to be *mortal* which is opposed to reason and to law. . . .'[1] Therefore in each case, the degree of guilt depends upon the extent to which the violation is opposed to reason and to law, whether divine or human.

We are dealing, however, with the civil law, and the words of Victoria on this phase of the question are important and should be quoted, that 'in the case of any decree which promotes to a considerable extent the peace of the citizens, the public well-being and honourable habits of life, transgression is evidently a mortal sin',[2] from which it would follow that in trifling matters the transgression is a venial sin.

By way of example, Victoria refers to the matter of taxation, which is very material and of abiding interest to the successors of those aborigines who were first known to the world forty years before Victoria prepared his Reading *On the Indians*. 'The matter', he says—and we must needs agree with him—'seems absolutely necessary for the defence of the State and for the conduct of other public functions and works'; but most of us would like to differ from him in his conclusion that 'if any one should fail to pay his taxes, he would be committing a mortal sin'.

For the sake of emphasizing the distinction he now supposes that no ordinance had been laid down by the Creator on the two questions of killing and of bearing false witness—but that the following civil laws had been enacted regarding them: 'Thou shalt not kill', and another, 'Thou shalt not bear false witness'. Under this supposition the first civil law, he maintains, would be binding under pain of mortal guilt; the second under pain of venial guilt. This leads Victoria to an important conclusion: that the amount of obligation binding the conscience of a lawbreaker may depend upon the extent of the violation

[1] *De Potestate Civili, infra,* Appendix C, p. lxxxvii. [2] *Ibid.*, p. lxxxviii.

and the nature of the matter involved, rather than upon his mere act of violation, that is to say, 'we should consider rather what the effect would be if that act were commonly practised, either by all or by many'.[1]

The illustration which he makes to drive the point home is of especial interest to a world suffering from economic depression—which was the case after the World War and indeed is at the present writing—for, slight as the offence he now refers to might seem to be on other occasions, its commission at this particular moment of the world's history might result in the financial disorganization of the world. 'For instance,' Victoria remarks, 'if it is prohibited that any one should carry money out of the country, all those who do so are committing a mortal sin, even though a single act of this sort would cause but little harm to the State; nevertheless, the fact that the resources of the country would be exhausted if such should become the common practice, is sufficient to make this a common law, binding on pain of mortal guilt.'[2] In other words, 'sin gains or loses gravity by time or circumstance', as the Catholic Catechism would have us say.

The answer to the objection that the act was wrong in itself, whether committed before or after the law, is twofold, 'first: that the law binds one not only by prohibiting, but also by commanding affirmatively, and that it may therefore make obligatory a thing which —before the existence of such a law—was advantageous for the State, but not required; so that, after the law has been created, the transgression of it will be a sin, although formerly the same act was not a sin.' Thus far the first answer. 'In the second place,' continues Victoria, 'I maintain that it is possible . . . for a given act to be an evil deed when committed by one person, and not when committed by another; whereas it is evil for all persons, after the law is established'; for instance, 'the wearing of silk or of cloth of gold', Victoria says, 'was formerly evil only if committed by a poor nobleman, but . . . after the law was made, [it] was an evil deed for all persons'.[3]

The question might arise—indeed it occurred to Victoria—whether the king possesses power to 'exempt' from liability to guilt, should he so desire. Victoria's answer is in favour of the exemption, for the reason that 'at times the legislator'—meaning the ecclesiastical or secular ruler—does not 'wish to exact obedience to his laws from his subjects, but merely gives an account of what should be done, commenting and directing, rather than issuing commands'. Of the many examples which he says might be given, he instances that of a creditor, who, seeking to collect his money, does not 'always exact it by force, so to speak'.[4]

But a further question presents itself concerning monarchical rule, a question which has caused no end of trouble and the loss of power and

[1] *Ibid.* [2] *Ibid.* [3] *Ibid.*, p. lxxxix. [4] *Ibid.*

position: 'whether civil laws are binding upon the legislators, and in particular, upon kings.' Looking upon legislators and kings as placed over all in the State, it might be contended that they were not bound, because, since they have no superior, the law is not imposed upon them but by them. Victoria, however, did not support this contention, but held that the kings and legislators were 'bound' by the laws; and the proof which he gives is unanswerable and is not merely applicable within the State and between States but is under the superintending power of that international community which it was Victoria's contribution to divine. The matter falls into three parts: first, 'the laws which are made by kings have the same force . . . as if they were made by the whole State; but the laws made by the State are binding upon all; therefore, even those laws which are made by the king, are binding upon the king himself'.[1] This is a syllogism which would indeed have made not only a medieval king but some modern dictators tremble. The second phase of the subject is in the nature of confirmation: 'Under an aristocratic form of government, the decrees of the Senate are binding upon the very senators who issued them; under a popular government the plebiscite is binding upon the whole people; and therefore laws made by the king are in like manner binding upon the king himself.' The third is very simple, but of transcendant importance, as it brings Victoria to the mountain top, within sight of his international community: 'Although the act of creating the law be voluntary on the part of the king; nevertheless the fact that he is thereby bound or not bound, does not depend upon his own will: just as in the case of pacts; for he who enters into a pact of his own free will, is nevertheless bound thereby.'[2]

Now for the epoch-making consequence which Victoria draws in the form of a corollary: 'International law has not only the force of a pact and agreement among men, but also the force of a law; for the world as a whole, being in a way one single State, has the power to create laws that are just and fitting for all persons, as are the rules of international law. Consequently, it is clear that they who violate these international rules, whether in peace or in war, commit a mortal sin; moreover, in the gravest matters, such as the inviolability of ambassadors, it is not permissible for one country to refuse to be bound by international law, the latter having been established by the authority of the whole world.'[3] With this doctrine, organization is effective; without it, it is impossible.

There is a famous maxim in the common law of England—and in other countries—that a law ceases to be obligatory when its reason ceases to exist (*cessante ratione legis, cessat ipsa lex*). Of this Victoria gives two examples, the first, on carrying weapons. The reason may cease in two ways: first, by the cessation of the purpose or circum-

[1] *De Potestate Civili, infra,* Appendix C, p. lxxxix. [2] *Ibid.*, p. xc. [3] *Ibid.*

stances which caused the law to be enacted. His example is: 'In time of war it is forbidden to supply arms to the French, in time of peace that law is not binding.' Again, it may be said that there is no further reason for a law when it has ceased to serve a useful purpose. 'A law, then,' in Victoria's words, 'which ceases to be useful to the State, is no longer a law.'[1] To take a further example of carrying weapons: it might be in the interest of some people to carry weapons for self protection, but to the disadvantage of the many that this should be allowed. This reason being to the advantage of the community would cause the law to prevail, even as against the few who might safely be entrusted with weapons—in accordance with the so-called Benthamite test for law—which is nothing but a paraphrase of Victoria's test—'The greatest good to the greatest number'.

There is a further question: whether the laws of tyrants are binding. The answer might seem to be in the negative. Not so to Victoria, and not so to those who meditate upon his text; 'for, if the State is oppressed by a tyrant and not *sui juris*; and if the tyrant has not the power to create laws, while at the same time it is impossible to put into execution the laws laid down before his time: then, unless obedience is rendered to the tyrant, the State must perish'. The choice is here between despotism and anarchy, and being a man of law and of order, Victoria can only choose the first.

The second reason which Victoria gives for his views on the laws of tyrants is of surpassing interest, in that it shows he had prepared in 1528, when he delivered the Reading on the State, for that larger and all-embracing Reading which he was shortly to deliver upon the law of nations. It was to him 'certain'—and indeed 'obvious'—'that the State would suffer injury if, owing to the fact that princes possessed of no just title have seized the country, there should be no provision for judicial trials, and no way in which to punish or restrain malefactors; for if the laws laid down by a tyrant are not binding, then he is not a legitimate judge'.[2]

Victoria's system of law requires a legitimate judge to adjudicate disputes within as well as between nations. There may indeed be some persons in our day—there were assuredly many in his—who do not agree with the manner in which Victoria's State was created and with the base upon which it rests; but there must be few who would object to the conclusions which he draws. This is the day of democracy; and under Victoria's conception, the will of the majority should always prevail, whether in the making or the unmaking of a monarchy or any other form of government. A man must indeed have been liberal-minded in the sixteenth century to have his doctrine applicable to-day, and, unless human nature changes, in the future as well.

[1] *Ibid.* [2] *Ibid.*, p. xci.

CHAPTER XII

ANALYSIS OF THE READING *ON THE USE OF REASON*

It is frequently said that free will, or the free use of the individual will, is among the doctrines of the Catholic Church; and, on the other hand, that free will—and its exercise—is the patrimony of Protestantism itself. Therefore Victoria's Reading *Concerning the Obligations of Man when He first Attains the Use of Reason* is not only of interest in itself but of the greatest philosophical import; and it enables us to understand in some measure how he, within the pale of the Church, was able to discuss questions going to the very root of the authority of the Church in matters spiritual as well as temporal, and indeed to take issue with the Church and with his sovereign master of Spain, the Holy Roman Emperor, without coming to grief or passing before the Inquisition because of the liberality of the questions, lay and spiritual, upon which he spoke from his chair of theology in the University of Salamanca.

This, however, would not in itself be a sufficient justification for discussing his views here—for we do not have in mind the criticism or justification of any creed or church: analysis of the thirteenth Reading on the obligations of man when he first attains the use of reason is justified by the desirability—and to a certain extent the necessity—of showing the use which Victoria was able to make of the doctrine of freedom of the will as a basic element of his views on organized society.

The text of the Reading was taken from the fourteenth verse of the fifteenth chapter of Ecclesiasticus. Following the opening remarks as to the authenticity of Ecclesiasticus Victoria asks: 'Does every man, upon attaining the use of reason, find the way of salvation and of eternal life open to him?'[1] The answer to this query involves the consideration of three others.

The first of the three is: 'What is meant by the expressions "to have the use of reason", and "to attain the use of reason"?'[2] Victoria concludes that 'to have the use of reason' is 'to have free will',[3] or—since free will involves the use of both reason and will—to be 'master of one's actions'.[4]

The second of the three questions is: 'Of what is a man capable, when he first attains the use of reason?'[5]

Victoria declares that a man does not necessarily have immediate knowledge of God, on such an occasion; and especially not, if the man in question has been reared in the wilds, and without religious education. He adds, however, that there is probably no nation in the whole

[1] *Relectio XIII, De eo, ad quod tenetur homo cum primum venit ad usum rationis,* printed in *Relectiones Morales* (ed. Simonis, *op. cit.*), p. 367. [2] *Ibid.*, p. 368. [3] *Ibid.*, p. 369. [4] *Ibid.*, p. 377. [5] *Ibid.*, pp. 368, 399.

world where there has not always existed, and will not always exist, some knowledge of God, which all persons in the nation will be under obligation to accept. For history speaks of no nation so barbarous that it has no religious rites and does not believe in the existence of God. Moreover, God is the Administrator and Ruler of the whole world; religion is the most important factor in human administration; religion cannot exist without the knowledge of God; and therefore, Divine Providence, which governs all things wisely and in an orderly manner, must have provided the world with this knowledge so necessary to its administration.

'Nevertheless, every person who for the first time attains the use of reason, even though he may not know God, and may not be able to know Him, is capable of acting in a moral manner. All acts which are in harmony with the universal end, and in accord with the Will of God, are good acts; and those which are not in accord with the universal end, are perverse acts.

'And the words of Saint Thomas (I. ii, qu. 21, arts. 3 & 4) would seem also to be pertinent to this point, when he says that man is by nature a civil and social animal. Moreover, he who lives in a social group or a State, is a part of that State. Therefore one who acts in such a way as to promote the welfare and advantage of a private person, is also promoting the public and common welfare; just as one who injures a private person, injures the welfare of the community of which that person is a part; so that he who performs these acts deserves praise and reward [or blame and punishment] not only from the private individual, but also from the whole State or society; and in like manner he deserves praise or blame from the ruler of that society; this is still true, even when the agent has had no thought of benefiting or injuring the social group or the ruler. All of which is certainly in accord with the dictates of natural reason.'[1]

In this connexion Victoria quotes St. Matthew: 'Inasmuch as ye have done it unto one of the least of these my brethren, ye have done it unto me.'[2]

He who attains the use of reason, in Victoria's opinion, is capable of sinning, even before he knows or is able to know God.

The expression 'divine law', he says, may be interpreted in either one of two ways: first, as it exists in God Himself, and thus is entirely unknown to us, and cannot be binding upon us; secondly, divine law as we know it, through natural understanding or through revelation, from which view-point it is binding upon us. We do not need to know that a given precept of divine law exists, neither do we need knowledge of the Creator of that law; we are capable of sinning, if we have the use of reason, and know that a given act is good or bad.

[1] *Ibid.*, pp. 412–13.

[2] St. Matthew, xxv. 40.

'It is impossible', declares Victoria, 'that one should attain such a use of reason as to be capable of venial sin, before he attains it to an extent that renders him capable of mortal sin.'[1]

The third question is the principal one, and gives the *Relectio* its title: 'What are the obligations of man when he first attains the use of reason?'[2]

'Not every one is under an obligation', answers Victoria, 'at the very moment when he first attains the use of reason, to turn expressly, distinctly, and formally to God.'[3]

Nevertheless, 'every person is placed, at such a moment, under some immediate obligation'.[4] That is to say, 'he is under obligation to turn, at that moment, to that which is good, in so far as he is able—that is, in so far as his knowledge permits'. And 'if one is under an obligation to perform a certain act, that fact cannot be unknown to him. Therefore, the obligation must be in conformity with such knowledge as he has. So that we must suppose (as was suggested above) that the first act of deliberation cannot be concerned with a particular moral matter rather than with a general proposition, since understanding must be attained through those things which are best known (*Physics*, I [1, Argument]). For, while in abstract knowledge, acquaintance with the individual precedes acquaintance with the species or *genus*; in matters of practical knowledge, universal principles and conclusions still more universal are best known, and understanding must have its beginning in them. Take for example the principles that, "One ought to live in conformity with right reason"; "It is desirable that a man should live honourably"; "One should not commit injurious acts"; or any other rule of this kind, which one may come to know through natural enlightment, even if he has been reared without knowledge of God and religion.'[5]

Victoria was such a moralist that his system of morals did not depend upon revelation in the Book of Life but upon morality existing separate and distinct from its revealed or written instances; in other words, natural morality.

'Or,' he continues, 'in the case of a person who has been instructed concerning God and religion, take such examples as these: "I must worship God"; "I must obey the law of God"; "One may not act in defiance of the law established by God"; or any similar principle. For it is not possible that the first inquiry or act of deliberation should be concerned with alms, or temperance; neither could it be concerned with the rejection of theft, homicide, or perjury.'[6]

As to the act of deliberation Victoria says: 'I maintain, then, that

[1] *Relectio XIII, De eo, ad quod tenetur homo cum primum venit ad usum rationis, op. cit.*, p. 432.
[2] *Ibid.*, p. 437. [3] *Ibid.*, p. 439. [4] *Ibid.*, p. 441. [5] *Ibid.*, pp. 443–4.
[6] *Ibid.*, p. 444.

when a man has for the first time conceived with sufficient deliberation an opinion of the sort described above, he is bound to form an intention of good behaviour in conformity with that opinion. If he has knowledge of God, he is under the obligation of turning formally to God, saying, for example: "I wish", or "I intend to obey the law of God; I wish to worship God." But if he has no knowledge of God, it suffices that he should intend to live righteously, in conformity with the declaration, "I intend to live in accordance with the dictates of reason; I wish to act honourably; I do not wish to act wrongfully". St. Thomas expressly supports this view, when he says (*De Veritate*, q. 14, a. 2, ad primum), that in the case of a person who has been reared in the wilds, if that person acts according to the impulse within, God in His Providence will aid him in every way that is necessary. St. Thomas explains the expression, "to act according to the impulse within one", saying that it means, "to follow the dictates of natural law, desiring that which is good, and fleeing from that which is evil". That such a procedure suffices, is clear from statements already made. Neither is this conclusion disproved by the assertion of certain persons, to the effect that if any man acts thus [that is, according to the best that lies within him], God will surely enlighten him and give him faith. However that may be—and we shall return to this question presently—the process of acting according to the best of one's ability, precedes the process of enlightment; and therefore, the latter does not fall within the first moment of the use of reason.'[1]

This being the case, 'every person', according to Victoria, 'is under the obligation to receive the faith and the law of Christ, at the time when they are first sufficiently made known to him; neither would it be permissible for him to postpone that acceptance for a certain time; and it would not suffice if he should accept that faith and that law at some time during his life: for he is under the obligation of immediately forming an intention to live in the Law of Christ, and to worship Christ. In like manner, when natural law is for the first time made known to any person, he is bound to accept it; but he can accept it only by intending to obey it and to live in conformity with it; therefore he is bound to form such an intention. The truth of the consequent seems clear, since natural law is no less binding than Christian law, being equally divine. And natural law makes itself known when one comes to the realization that he ought to live in conformity with right reason—that he should not injure his neighbour, for example, or perform similar acts.'[2]

Victoria continues to argue along this line, and stresses the fact that virtuous acts are obligatory for all persons—those who have received religious instruction, and those who have not—at the very time

[1] *Ibid.*, pp. 444–5. [2] *Ibid.*, p. 445–6.

when the use of reason is attained. Near the close of the *Relectio* he remarks that the person who attains the use of reason may be ignorant of any formal command bidding him turn to God, 'but that he nevertheless realizes that one should obey the law of God, or that one should live in accordance with right reason, or that one forms some similar conclusion; since this realization is the first act of deliberation'.[1]

[1] *Relectio XIII, De eo, ad quod tenetur homo cum primum venit ad usum rationis, op. cit.*, p. 448.

CHAPTER XIII

THE LIBERALISM OF VICTORIA

SPEAKING in the first person—if first-personal language be permissible in an undertaking of this kind—for many years past I have wondered why it is that Francisco de Vitoria was so liberal that even in our day his views seem ahead of the times. It is all the more astonishing because as a churchman his views, we may say, were prescribed for him in advance, in that though the circle in which he was permitted to move might be ever so large, it was still a circle. We could the more easily understand his liberalism had he been merely a reformer—in the sense that he was opposed to old ideas and discontented with the present—outlining an impossible future. Reformer he was, to be sure, in that he would submit every act, individual or political, to one and the same moral standard, the right or the wrong of the matter to depend not upon the person but upon the intrinsic nature of the act and its necessary consequences. But there was much more than that in his liberalism.

The statement that his was a balanced mind does not answer the query, because in his day acceptance of things as they were would have been, as it is now, the usual test of balance. We know that he was a learned man profoundly versed in theology with all of its ramifications, without which he held that no question could be adequately decided; but learned people are ordinarily conservatives, because the learning of the world is usually of the past and the eyes of those who spend a great part of their lives in looking backward can rarely penetrate far into the future. But there are pasts and pasts, and the past of his Order was a past of liberalism which was in a very real sense a divination of the future. The past of antiquity was that of direct government; the future was to be that of representative government; and St. Dominic's Order of Preachers is as a bridge between the two.

The basic unit of the Order was the house or monastery, generally called 'convent'; the second unit was the province; and the culmination was the general chapter.

Mr. Ernest Barker, Professor of Political Science in the University of Cambridge, in an illuminating essay on *The Dominican Order and Convocation*—with a tell-tale sub-title, 'A study in the Growth of Representation in the Church during the Thirteenth Century'[1]—assigns to the Order of St. Dominic its place not merely in the Church but in the State, and in so doing enables us to understand why it was that Victoria as a Dominican should be liberal-minded in his conception of the State, and, because of his training and residence in a foreign

[1] Oxford, 1913.

land—as was customary among the Dominicans—he should be internationally minded.

The tendency of the Church in the thirteenth century was towards representation in principle and practice. In his foreword, Mr. Barker states in three short sentences what the essay is to demonstrate: 'The great Orders of the Friars are penetrated by representation. It appears first in the Dominicans: it is copied from them by the Franciscans. In the same century representation begins to appear in the State.'[1] As would therefore be expected, there are several passages in the essay which bear upon the matter in hand, although a direct connexion might not be obvious on a casual reading.

The first step in the process which we wish briefly to trace was the establishment of the Order in Toulouse in 1215.

And the first passage in Mr. Barker's essay to which reference should be made is productive of thought: 'The Dominican is general and universal. He belongs to a house, to a province, but far more to the whole Order; and he has a cure of souls wherever he may preach. He is delocalized, and he is centralized.'[2]

The second step is the organization of the government of the Order and of its branches. Upon this point Mr. Barker says: 'The Order was to be governed by a master-general'; 'the province by a provincial prior [in 1221 the Order was divided into eight provinces]; the convent, which must contain at least twelve friars, by a conventual prior.'[3] This is an interesting detail, indicating, as it does, the pyramidal structure of the whole, its broad base being numerous convents pointing upwards through the provincial organization, the Order culminating in the supreme central organization to which Mr. Barker has referred.

The head of the convent, the prior, is elected by the friars, and is therefore termed the conventual prior. The head of the province, the provincial prior, is elected by a provincial chapter composed of the conventual priors of the province in which the chapter is situated and of two friars elected from each of the convents;[4] that is to say, this provincial chapter is a representative body of the convents within the territory which elect the provincial prior. The general chapter which elects the master-general or head of the Order is likewise a representative body, composed of the provincial priors and of two friars from each of the provinces—elected by the provincial chapter. From top to bottom, or rather from bottom to top, the Order is of a representative character. The office of conventual prior is elective, as is that of the presiding officer in the two higher bodies; and each of the latter officers—of the province and of the general chapter—is elected by elective

[1] Barker, *op. cit.*, p. 7. [2] *Ibid.*, p. 11. [3] *Ibid.*, p. 14.
[4] *Ibid.*, footnote: 'This is slightly altered in the modern constitutions.'

and representative bodies. It would be difficult indeed to find a more perfect combination of representation and election.

There was, however, a second series of bodies with a considerable representative element, known as assemblies. Of the provincial chapter functioning as an assembly—which we shall designate as the provincial assembly—the priors of the various convents within the jurisdiction of the province appear to have been *ex officio* members. In addition, it numbered among its members all the friars who had studied theology for some three years and who were known as the 'general preachers' of the province. The representative element makes its appearance in members elected by each of the convents.

This, however, was not all. There was an advisory, and indeed supervisory, body of four members, known as *definitores*, annually elected by the assembly from 'the more discreet and proper friars'.[1] Mr. Barker states that the office of this committee was 'to treat and define all things with the provincial prior';[2] to hear and amend excesses, if any, of that prior and in case of need to suspend him from his office.

The chapter general, in this second series, which may be designated as the general assembly, is made up of the conventual priors, with their associates and the general preachers of the province where the meeting is held. There is also an inner committee of *definitores* in which both the elective and *official* elements are combined. The general assemblies are held annually. In what we may consider the first two meetings of the assembly, *definitores* are elected; in the third meeting the provincial priors act as *definitores*.

Then there was a body known as *visitatores*,[3] four of whom were elected from the friars of each province and whose duty it was to visit the province and to hear and correct such excesses as would come to their knowledge.

What is the reason for entering into details regarding the organization and government of the Dominican Order? It is threefold, as stated by Mr. Barker:

1. The Order is democratic, being distinct from other religious organizations of the time of a more or less similar nature. 'Authority springs from the general body, and the officials are rather servants of that body than its lords.'[4]

2. The Order is 'a representative democracy,'[5]—a statement which is clear without further comment.

3. 'The Constitutions of the Order are clear-cut in their outline', showing 'legal nicety and precision'.[6]

The importance of the Order because of these three elements is stated in Mr. Barker's conclusion, in his language, inasmuch as it suggests

[1] Barker, *op. cit.*, p. 15. [2] *Ibid.* [3] *Ibid.*, p. 16. [4] *Ibid.*, p. 17.
[5] *Ibid.*, pp. 17–18. [6] *Ibid.*, p. 18.

the purpose for which reference is made to the Order of Preachers: 'It is the most perfect example', he says, adopting the views of a learned German authority, 'that the Middle Ages have produced of the faculty of monastic corporations for constitution-building.'[1] In his proper person Mr. Barker continues: 'Its institutions are adjusted to probable emergencies; they define, for instance, the conditions of a valid majority; they are institutions meant, and likely, to work.'[2] Therefore the conjecture, justified by the event, is 'that they will also be likely to impress men who come into contact with them'—such, for example, as Simon de Montfort, and, not to confine ourselves solely to the de Montfort family, Stephen Langton, Archbishop of Canterbury (the architect of the day in English liberty)—'and that they will tend to be imitated. And if they are imitated, the use of representation is the thing which will in particular be imitated'.[3] The imitation was in the matter of government—representative government, constitutional government, liberal government.

Without attempting to trace the development and application of the idea of representation and to enter into details of its acceptance by Church and State, it is sufficient for present purposes to speak of the result, and the result may be stated in a few words. Through Langton, Archbishop of Canterbury, who was not of the Dominican Order but was its friend; through Kilwardby, a Dominican friar who became Archbishop of Canterbury; and through Peckham, also Archbishop of Canterbury—a Franciscan friar whose Order had adopted the Dominican theory—representation entered into the convocation of the Church, 'with two proctors from each diocese and one from each chapter'[4]—a formula adopted by Edward the First in summoning the clergy to Parliament in 1294,[5] and which still stands in the writs for the election of Parliament.

The Dominican Order was, in Mr. Barker's measured judgement, 'the highest expression of the development of the representative principle in the thirteenth-century Church',[6] and his entire conclusion on this phase of government, both of the Church and the State, he sets forth in a few weighty sentences. The first is that 'the clergy are the forerunners, and that through their habits of organized action and their legal ideas of procuration they lead the movement to representation'.[7] The second shows what we of to-day have been prone to think the ultimate consequences of organized liberty: 'There are two main ideas underlying the English representative system of the thirteenth

[1] Barker, *op. cit.*, p. 18, translated from Hauck, *Kirchengeschichte Deutschlands*, iv. 390.

[2] Barker, *op. cit.*, p. 18. [3] *Ibid.* [4] *Ibid.*, p. 67.

[5] 'The forms of summons in 1294 and 1295 are practically identical. The important difference is that Edward in 1294 summoned the clergy for a different date than that fixed for the laity; he treated it as separate. In and after 1295 the clergy and laity are summoned for the same time.' Barker, *op. cit.*, note 126, p. 68. [6] *Ibid.*, p. 75. [7] *Ibid.*, pp. 72–3.

century—indeed from the thirteenth to the nineteenth century. In the first place, the representation is representation of communities. It is representation not of geographical constituencies containing some thousands of electoral units, but of organized and organic communities, that have a real and regular life of their own. The House of Commons is a federation of these communities through their representatives: it expresses the medieval conception of the State as a *communitas communitatum*. In the second place the representative is a full representative. He binds his constituents. He is a proxy with full powers of attorney; there is no room for a referendum to his constituents. The knights and burgesses, says Edward in 1295, shall have full and sufficient powers for themselves *and their communities*, and business shall in no wise remain undone for want of such power. Both of these ideas are at home with the clergy. Their chapters are real communities, which can federate in a joint assembly, and are conscious of the reasons and the need of such federation, as early as 1226.'[1]

What then, in the view of England and of the Continent, was the role of the Church, especially the Dominican branch of it, which was the highest expression of the representative system, for in institutional history they are but one? A truth reached by two roads is doubly a truth. For England, let Mr. Barker speak: 'The reinforcement of the baronage by shire and borough representatives, which makes a national parliament, finds its precedent in the reinforcement of the episcopate by the proctors of chapters. Representation in a clerical parliament in 1226 is nearly thirty years prior to representation in the lay assembly of 1254';[2] and for the Continent, M. Viollet, whom Mr. Barker quotes as saying: 'Je suppose que ces réunions ecclésiastiques ont pu contribuer à faciliter le développement et la régularisation des grandes assemblées civiles, des réunions d'états. . . . En effet, le premier des trois états, le clergé, se trouva, du premier jour, habitué et comme rompu à ce que nous appellerions aujourd'hui les usages parlementaires. Circonstance heureuse qui a dû contribuer, dans l'Europe entière, sinon à former, du moins à régulariser la tenue des états.'[3]

We are now prepared to see why it was inevitable that Francisco de Vitoria should be a liberal-minded man in government and therefore in law, whether of the Church or of the State, in that he lived and breathed in his formative years an atmosphere of liberalism.

It is only necessary to add, without a word of proof other than his writings, that St. Thomas Aquinas is the head and front of the Dominican Order, whose founder, St. Dominic—universally regarded as a statesman as well as a churchman—has been called the first minister of public instruction in Europe.[4]

St. Thomas Aquinas, it is to be said, was not a stranger to English

[1] Barker, *op. cit.*, p. 73. [2] *Ibid.* [3] *Ibid.*, pp. 73–4. [4] *Ibid.*, p. 30.

development. In a general chapter meeting in the Dominican house at Holborn in London in the year 1263, he was present as a *definitor* of the Roman province.[1] We are thus prepared to understand why St. Thomas Aquinas—being like the other great Dominicans a teacher (as was Victoria later) in the international city of Paris, the centre of the medieval world—was both liberal-minded and international-minded. In a world leaning towards liberalism, it is only the writings of liberals that survive. The writings of St. Thomas have not only survived as the text of the Dominicans but as the supreme text of the Church of which he was to be both doctor and saint; and in the memory of people still living, the study of his writings was prescribed by no less a Pope and statesman than the late Leo XIII.

Victoria was a liberal. He could not help being a liberal. He was an internationalist by inheritance. And because he was both, his international law is a liberal law of nations.

[1] Barker, *op. cit.*, p. 29.

CHAPTER XIV

FRANCISCO DE VITORIA'S CONTRIBUTION TO INTERNATIONAL LAW

PERHAPS the best way to test the importance of Victoria's contribution to international law is to state some of the fundamental principles of the law of nations and to see if they are to be found, and in what form, in the readings of Victoria which relate to international law, which concern international relations, and which possess international implications.

In the first place, the law of nations deals with nations or States. Victoria devotes a Reading to the conception of the State, not merely in national law but in international law as well. A modern conception is that of the equality of States, a conception flouted by the large nations which, with their extensive interests, claim a larger place in the sun of the international firmament—a claim denied, and properly, by the overwhelming majority of States which are the 'lesser powers', so-called by the larger nations.

The corner-stone of Victoria's system was equality of States, applicable not merely to the States of Christendom and of Europe but also to the barbarian principalities in the Western World of Columbus. The modern State is looked upon from within and from without. From within it is a thing of constitutional law; from without, of international law. From within it must be self-sufficient, in order to be a perfect State; from without it is but a member of the international community. These are precisely the elements to be found in Victoria's conception of the State. But the State is to-day being looked upon as an artificial conception and as merely another name at best for a group of people exercising jurisdiction within the so-called frontiers of the so-called State. This is also Victoria's conception. The people forming the group are not 'dumb, driven cattle'; they are not pawns in the hands of the prince: they are human beings endowed with a spiritual nature; and in the view of the Spaniard the end of all things is not dust but a life beyond the grave. This being so, they are masters in their own house. They need society, however, for without it they cannot defend themselves; they cannot procure the well-being and happiness to which they may feel themselves entitled. This is also the doctrine of Victoria. But for the purposes of society, they must have a government, and the government must be one of law; for it is only by law that society can be preserved. The people cannot assemble as a whole; they cannot act as a whole for purposes of government, because all cannot come together at one place and at one time. Nor can they act alone and individually, for if they did there might be as many lines of direction as there are individuals. Hence it is that the will of the majority as a matter of convenience has come to prevail, establishing that form of government to act in their behalf which they conceive to be best fitted to their country—whether a monarchy, an aristocracy, or a democracy —with the right to change from one form to the other, as seems to them best. This is the modern conception of the State. It is also Victoria's conception.

'Many men, many minds' is a proverbial way of saying that people united in society differ individually. The differences result in disputes between members of the groups and controversies between the groups which we call States. Within the State these disputes are not redressed by the individuals themselves, although they may protect their lives or their property against immediate attack, but are laid before a court in which justice is done, property restored or damages awarded—or both —and punishment administered whenever the act is of a criminal nature. Here again the fundamental Victorian doctrine and the modern practice are at one.

But the groups, made up as they are of people, may differ and their controversies must needs be adjusted. These controversies should be settled in the same way as the disputes between individuals, because they are not disputes of the artificial things called States but of the peoples forming them. Therefore the same principles of justice apply to both. It follows that force between States could only justly be used to redress a wrong, and a resort to force was only to be tolerated because there was no court of the States; for the States being equal, there could be no court of the superior in the same way that there were tribunals within each State. This is the Victorian conception. Unhappily it has not been embodied in the practice of the centuries that followed him.

The creation of an international court of justice by the States and for the States, in which their controversies could be decided in the same manner as within the State, would render war both unnecessary and unlawful. The Permanent Court of International Justice, established but a decade ago, upon the initiative of the successors of Victoria's aborigines, is the culmination of that phase of his system of international law.

But there are the States and a larger State, an international community, existing by the mere coexistence of the States, even though there be no formal organization. Before Columbus discovered the American Indies, the States of Christendom—the European world—were the international community. It was Victoria's judgement, ever a liberal one, that the American principalities—as equals of the Christian States—should not be excluded from this international community. Therefore in his theory of international law, they were members possessing the same rights and the same duties as the Christian States of

Europe. In Victoria's conception, the international community, composed of States without reference to geography, race, or religion, replaced the large but still limited international community coextensive with Christendom; this is the opinion of the world to-day.

But this is but a part of Victoria's law of nations. The international community is not a superimposed State; it is coextensive with humanity—no longer merely with Christianity. It is composed of the States and is their representative; it is likewise the representative of the common humanity rather than of the common religion binding the States. It is a union of the States, and the sum total of the States is necessarily more powerful than any of its parts. Its will is the will of humanity, speaking in terms of peoples; its will is international law, speaking in terms of States. But this law reaches the individual through the State, and it controls the actions of the States in their relations with one another.

The international community, therefore, in the Victorian system, possesses the inherent right to impose its will—in the form of law applicable to the individual State—and to punish its violation, not because of a treaty, of a pact or a covenant, but because of an international need. For just as the State is not a 'perfect' State if it be not self-sufficient, so would the international community be imperfect if it were not self-sufficient in a superior and universal sense and if it could not impose its collective judgement, in the form of the law of nations, upon humanity—considered as such—and upon the States as members of the international community. All this is not merely a consequence of Victoria's doctrine; it is the doctrine itself expressly and unmistakably stated in classical terms four centuries before our modern world endeavoured to create by covenant what Victoria had proclaimed as a fundamental principle and which we would call the culmination of his law of nations.[1]

*
* *

There are certain phases of international law mentioned specifically by Victoria and often treated at length which should be enumerated as samples, with but here and there a word of comment.

1. *Title of Discovery.* The discovery, of course, is that of the New World—the greatest discovery of a material nature recorded in history. But did Columbus the Genoan really 'discover' the New World in the

[1] The full consequences of Victoria's doctrine are too broad and far-reaching for discussion here. They are not merely of the past and of the present but of the future as well. Suffice it to say that not a few of our newest and most cherished international principles might be shown to have their roots in the doctrine set forth by Victoria. *Vide*, for example, Herbert Francis Wright's 'International Law: Old Wine in New Bottles' (published in *The Catholic World*, vol. cxxxii, no. 791, February, 1931), in which the germ of the Pact of Paris is traced to Victoria, and it is maintained that other modern principles are directly related to the Victorian system.

sense of Victoria? It already existed and it was possessed by 'barbarians' divided into principalities under 'barbarian' princes. Victoria would have it that this part of the world was merely unknown to the Old World, as were also the aborigines and their rulers. By 'discovery' Victoria meant discovery of unoccupied land; and therefore this title could not apply to the New World. However, Victoria avails himself of the alleged discovery and of the alleged right of occupation to discourse on colonization.

2. *Ambassadors.* The existence of States forms, as it were, a society of States, and they must needs communicate by agents called, under the law of nations, ministers or ambassadors. Such agents should be inviolable and under the protection of the law of nations, as stated by Victoria here and there throughout his writings.

3. *Compulsory Acceptance of Pacific Settlement.* Of this Victoria speaks in language shorter than any summary which could be made: 'If one party wants to settle and make a division or compromise as to a part of the claim, the other is bound to accept his proposal, even if that other be the stronger and able to seize the whole by armed force; nor would he have a just cause of war.' [1]

4. *Conscientious Objectors.* Again the language of Victoria cannot be shortened, 'that subjects whose conscience is against the justice of war may not engage in it, whether they be right or wrong'.[2]

5. *Intervention.* Intervention is recognized by Victoria 'in favour of those who are oppressed and suffer wrong'; and for such a purpose 'the Spaniards can make war'.[3] Victoria, however, knew and stated that intervention was 'war', and that it should be exercised 'always . . . with an intent directed more to the welfare of the aborigines than to their own gain'.[4]

6. *Letters of Marque and Reprisal.* These were admitted by Victoria with much misgiving, as they were 'hazardous and open the way to plunder'.[5] His misgivings, as we have seen, prevailed in the Declaration of Paris of 1856.

7. *Booty and Prize.* Only two short quotations are needed to show Victoria's views on booty and prize: 'It is a universal rule of the law of nations that whatever is captured in war becomes the property of the conqueror.' [6] 'Everything captured in a just war vests in the seizor up to the amount which provides satisfaction for the things that have been wrongfully seized and which covers expenses also. This needs no proof, for that is the end and aim of war.' [7]

In his treatment of this subject, Victoria deals with both 'movables' and 'immovables'.

[1] *De Jure Belli, infra,* Appendix B, p. lix.
[2] *Ibid.*, p. lvii.
[3] *De Indis, infra,* Appendix A, p. xlii.
[4] *Ibid.*
[5] *De Jure Belli, infra,* Appendix B, p. lxiv.
[6] *De Indis, infra,* Appendix A, p. xl.
[7] *De Jure Belli, infra,* Appendix B, p. lxvii.

8. *Neutrals*. 'It is not lawful', Victoria says, 'to slay either foreigners or guests who are sojourning among the enemy, for they are presumed innocent, and in truth they are not enemies.'[1]

'Spoliation of foreigners and travellers on enemy soil, unless they are obviously at fault, is in no wise lawful, they not being enemies.'[2]

Here we have neutrality in the form most embarrassing to the belligerent. In Victoria's day, neutrality was an exception, not the rule. It was to become the rule through the successors of the American aborigines of whose rights and duties he discourses.

9. *Temperamenta*. 'What degree of stress is lawful in a just war?' Victoria answers: 'The deliberate slaughter of the innocent is never lawful in itself.'[3] 'Harmless agricultural folk, and . . . the rest of the peaceable civilian population' should be spared, 'for all these are presumed innocent until the contrary is shown. . . . The same principle', Victoria says, 'applies to clerics and members of a religious order'.[4]

Victoria sets himself like flint against 'killing of guiltless persons . . . when they may be expected to cause danger in the future'[5]—having in mind the Saracens and their children—saying 'that evil is not to be done even in order to avoid greater evil still, and it is intolerable that any one should be killed for a future fault'.[6]

Returning to the farmer and other innocent folk, Victoria adds to what he had previously said on the subject: 'If a war can be carried on effectively enough without the spoliation of the agricultural population and other innocent folk, they ought not be despoiled.'[7]

But there is a further doubt, whether it is lawful to kill, in a just war, 'all the guilty'. To this he replies: 'It is not right to kill all the guilty among the enemy';[8] 'for the measure of the punishment . . . must be proportionate to the offence, and vengeance ought to go no further'.[9]

Such, in his view, is the law of nations which 'must be respected as is the wont among good people'.[10]

Is it right to give a city up to the soldiers to sack? 'It is undoubtedly unjust in the extreme to deliver up a city, especially a Christian city, to be sacked, without the greatest necessity and weightiest reason.'[11]

Is it 'lawful to depose the princes of the enemy and appoint new ones or keep the princedom for oneself'? To which the reply is that the princes may be deposed, but Victoria adds that the deposition of lawful and natural princes 'is not unqualifiedly permissible', as the overthrowing 'of the enemy's sovereignty and the deposition of lawful and natural princes . . . would be utterly savage and inhumane measures'.[12]

The samples numbered 1 to 8 have been given, not as illustrating

[1] *De Jure Belli, infra*, Appendix B, p. lxii. [2] *Ibid.*, p. lxiv. [3] *Ibid.*, p. lxii. [4] *Ibid.* [5] *Ibid.*, p. lxiii. [6] *Ibid.* [7] *Ibid.*, p. lxiv. [8] *Ibid.*, p. lxvi. [9] *Ibid.* [10] *Ibid.*, p. lxvii. [11] *Ibid.*, p. lxviii. [12] *Ibid.*, p. lxix.

those phases of Victoria's doctrine in all their breadth and completeness, but merely by way of example. If they were to be stated in complete form and were to be justified as Victoria justifies them, we would need to reproduce almost in their entirety the two Readings *On the Indians* and *On the Law of War*. But admitting the importance of these samples, which cannot be denied, they are as nothing compared with the *temperamenta* expressed in the form of doubts regarding what Victoria felt could only be considered as the extreme rights which might be exercised by belligerents only as a last resort. He recognized that the practice of nations was more than the expressed consent of nations; it was as a law to nations.

But there was practice and practice. There was a practice which was immoral, as inconsistent with the nature and dignity of man, and a practice which could only be justified if its purpose were to do justice and not to commit injustice. The various *temperamenta* which Victoria recommended are to be found embodied in the treatise of Grotius, which was to become the practice of nations in theory, if not in fact.

These *temperamenta* were designed to mitigate the harshness of war, which was at best an unwilling concession on the part of Victoria which he wished to replace by due process of law, even though in his day there was none but the prince to act as judge, in the absence of a court between the nations.

The creation of such a court is not the least contribution of the successors of those first Americans to whom Victoria extended the law of nations.

* * *

There are certain fundamental principles which have not yet been mentioned but which are integral parts of Victoria's system: one is nationality; another is expatriation; a third is naturalization; a fourth is the equal right to navigate the high seas, to trade with every country, to settle in every country and to possess the rights of other foreigners in every country; and in addition there is a principle, in the form of right or duty—which Victoria was unwilling to accept or reject, as it was not yet an approved principle in his day, although he approved of it—the right or duty of a State, on its own initiative or under, as it were, a mandate from the international community, to prepare backward peoples for dominion upon a footing of equality with enlightened States of the international community.

Victoria's principle of nationality, reduced to practice, has endowed the twenty-one American Republics with a nationality and a citizenship based upon the *jus soli*, that is to say, nationality and citizenship—where the two are identical—are based upon the simple fact of birth within the territory of any State or nation. The acceptance of this principle, which he lays down as a rule of law, would give to each human being—man, woman, or child—one, and only one, nationality; it would give to every human being some nationality; in a word, it would equally obviate statelessness and double nationality.

The principle is universal, in that the standard of *jus soli* would apply equally to citizens of any State and to foreigners domiciled in or passing through the State. The matter of domicile is important, for a child of foreigners born within the State may claim its citizenship only if the foreign parents were domiciled in the State. As to the relinquishment of an old and the obtaining of a new nationality, it is clear that expatriation of foreigners is a prerequisite to naturalization. The right of expatriation is also an integral part of Victoria's law of nations, for he makes it a prerequisite to naturalization, which in his view is the right of every foreigner upon the same terms as those extended to all foreigners. The 'favoured nation' clause is a part of Victoria's system, both in the matter of naturalization and the matter of industry and commerce.

Nationality by birth within a foreign country, naturalization, and the right of expatriation and commerce—all imply freedom of navigation, which is implicit in the Victoria tenet of freedom of the seas already mentioned. Freedom of navigation upon the high seas and of sojourn within each and every country of the international community is requisite for industry and for commerce and for that highest branch of commerce—the traffic of ideas—embraced within the single word 'missionaries'.

Victoria recognized that there were peoples in an imperfect state of civilization; but they were human beings, and human beings, to his way of thinking, should not be subject to exploitation, but should be fitted—if they were not already fit—to enjoy the rights of all human beings, as well as to be subjected to their duties. Therefore it was proper—and indeed praiseworthy—for a State in the plenitude of civilization to take, as it were, these children of nature in hand in order to educate them in their rights and in their duties, that their principalities might be admitted to the international community. The action, however, of the enlightened nation was not to smack of self-interest, much less exploitation; it was to be on behalf of the laggards in the march of civilization. This was a nameless principle in Victoria's system—a principle thought some four centuries later to have been newly created by the Covenant of the League of Nations, and as such christened with the dignified name of mandate.

These things are interesting in themselves, but we will only see their vast importance when we come to consider the masterpiece of Grotius *On the Law of War and Peace*; for with the Readings of Victoria *On the Indians* and *On the Law of War*, the great jurist of Holland had at hand—and indeed before his eyes—a system of international law express in its fundamentals and implicit in its consequences: the first sketch, as an architect would say, of the Temple of International Justice to which Grotius was to add with his own hand the details of the completed drawing.

From this brief and imperfect summary of the principles express or inherent in Victoria's law of nations, we see that it is in part the present law of nations and is in no small part the future law of nations, and that Francisco de Vitoria, *prima* professor of theology in the University of Salamanca, was not merely the founder of the modern law of nations but the prophet of the newer law of nations.

Victoria the Spaniard was born in 1483. A hundred years later, Hugo de Groot was born at Delft.

Vixere fortes ante Agamemnona Multi.[1]

[1] Horace, *Odes*, IV. ix. 25.

'LANDING OF COLUMBUS'

From the woodcut in *La lettera dellisole che ha trouato nuouamente il Re dispagan,* Florence 1493

APPENDIXES

The translations of the Relectiones *De Indis* and *De Jure Belli* are reprinted from *De Indis et de Ivre Belli Relectiones . . .* edited by Ernest Nys, and published by the Carnegie Institution of Washington, 1917. The translation of the Relectio *De Potestate Civili*, and that of Section V of the Relectio *De Potestate Ecclesiae* were prepared especially for this work from Simon's 1696 edition of Victoria's *Relectiones Morales*. The translation of the fragment which we have called for convenience' sake *De Jure Gentium et Naturali* was prepared especially for this work from the text published in Father Beltrán de Heredia's *Los Manuscritos Inéditos del Maestro Fray Francisco de Vitoria, O.P.*, Madrid and Valencia, 1928. In the case of the *De Bello* the translation was made from the text in Father Beltrán de Heredia's *Francisco de Vitoria, O.P., Comentarios a la Secunda Secundae de Santo Tomás*, tomo II, Salamanca, 1932.

The numbers in the inner margin of the texts refer to pages in Simon's 1696 edition of Victoria.

APPENDIX A

THE FIRST RELECTIO

OF THE REVEREND FATHER, BROTHER FRANCISCUS DE VICTORIA

ON THE INDIANS LATELY DISCOVERED

A
TRANSLATION BY
JOHN PAWLEY BATE

The
passage
to be discussed
is from the last chapter
of St. Matthew's Gospel:
Teach all nations, baptizing them
in the name of the Father
and of the Son and of the
Holy Ghost.

SUMMARY OF THE FIRST SECTION

1. How a person in doubt on any matter, to obtain safety of conscience, should consult those whose business it is to give instruction in such matters.
2. After one in doubt has taken such advice he ought to follow what the wise have laid down, else he will not be safe.
3. Whether one in doubt ought, consistently with safety of conscience, to follow the advice given by the wise in a doubtful matter when they lay down that to be now
303 lawful which in other circumstances is unlawful.
4. Whether the Indian aborigines before the arrival of the Spaniards were true owners in public and in private law; and whether there were among them any true princes and overlords.
5. Examination of the error of those who assert that persons living in mortal sin cannot have ownership of anything at all.
6. Mortal sin does not preclude civil ownership of the true kind.
7. Whether ownership is lost by reason of unbelief.
8. The divine law does not make heresy a cause of forfeiture of the heretic's property.
9. Whether heresy causes loss of ownership by human law.
10. A heretic incurs the penalty of confiscation of his property as from the date of the commission of his offence.
11. But although the heretic's offence is patent, the fisc may not seize his property before condemnation.

304 12. Even though condemnation issues after the heretic's death, confiscation of property dates back to the time of the commission of the offence, no matter who is vested with the property.

13. Sales, gifts, and all other modes of alienation by a heretic are void as from the date of the commission of the offence, &c.
14. Whether a heretic before condemnation is the owner of his property in the forum of conscience.
15. A heretic may lawfully live on his own property.
16. A heretic may make a gratuitous conveyance of his property, as by way of gift.
17. A heretic whose offence has rendered him liable to process may not convey his property for value, as by way of sale or dowry.
18. In what case a heretic may lawfully alienate his property for value.
19. Barbarians are not precluded by the sin of unbelief or by any other mortal sins from being true owners alike in public and in private law.
20. Whether the use of reason is a pre-requisite of capacity for ownership.
21. Whether a boy can be an owner before he has the use of reason.

305 22. Whether a person of unsound mind can be an owner.

23. Inasmuch as the Indian aborigines were not of unsound mind, they are not precluded from being true owners on the pretext of unsoundness of mind.
24. These aborigines were true owners alike in public and in private law before the advent of the Spaniards among them.

'Teach all nations, baptizing them in the name of the Father and Son and Holy Spirit' (*St. Matthew*, last chap.). This passage raises the question whether the children of unbelievers may be baptized against the wishes of their parents. This question is discussed by the doctors on the fourth book of the

Sententiae, dist. 4, and by St. Thomas, *Secunda Secundae*, qu. 10, art. 12, and *Tertia Pars*, qu. 68, art. 10. The whole of this controversy and discussion was started on account of the aborigines of the New World, commonly called Indians, who came forty years ago into the power of the Spaniards, not having been previously known to our world. This present disputation about them will fall into three parts. In the first part we shall inquire by what right these Indian natives came under Spanish sway. In the second part, what rights the Spanish sovereigns obtained over them in temporal and civil matters. In the third part, **306**
what rights these sovereigns of the Church obtained over them in matters spiritual and touching religion, in the course of which an answer will be given to the question before us.

Threefold nature of this discussion.

Whether this inquiry is entirely useless.

As regards the first part, it might seem at the very outset that the whole of this discussion is useless and futile, not only for us who have no concern either to inquire whether the men in question have conducted their administration with propriety in every detail or to raise any doubts about that business or to correct any fault that may have been committed, but also for those whose concern it is to attend to and administer these matters. Firstly, this may so seem because neither the sovereigns of Spain nor those at the head of their councils are bound to make completely fresh and exhaustive examination of rights and titles which have already been elsewhere discussed and settled, especially as regards things of which the sovereigns are in *bona-fide* occupation and peaceful possession; this is so because, as Aristotle says (*Ethics*, bk. 3), 'if any one were to be continually inquiring, settlement would be indefinitely postponed'; and sovereigns and their advisers could not attain security and certitude of conscience, and, if they had to trace the title of their rule back to its origin, they could not keep anything they had discovered. Moreover, inasmuch as our sovereigns, namely Ferdinand and Isabella, who were the first to occupy those regions, were most Christian, **307**
and the Emperor Charles V was a most just and scrupulous sovereign, it is not to be believed that they did not make a thoroughly complete and exact investigation into everything that could affect the security of their estate and conscience, especially in such a great matter. On these accounts, then, it may seem not only useless but also presumptuous to raise any question about the matter; it is like looking for a knot in a bulrush and for wickedness in the abode of the righteous.

Lengthy reply of the author.

In meeting this objection we must bear in mind what Aristotle says (*Ethics*, bk. 3), namely, that just as there can be no questioning or deliberation about matters either impossible or necessary, so also there can be no moral investigation about those which are certainly and notoriously lawful and seemly, or, on the other hand, about those which are certainly and notoriously unlawful and unseemly. For no one can properly raise a question whether we ought to live a temperate and brave and upright life or a wicked and base life, nor whether we ought to commit adultery or perjury, or cherish our parents, and other matters of this kind. Certainly such discussion would not be Christian. When, however, some project is on foot concerning which there is a genuine doubt whether it be good or bad, just or unjust, it is then advantageous to take advice and to deliberate **308**

What matters call for consultation.

and to abstain from premature action before finding out and determining how far it is or is not lawful. Such is the case with matters which, when viewed from different sides, look good or bad, as happens in many kinds of barter and contract and other businesses. And in all these cases the circumstances are such that, even if the thing in question were in itself lawful, it would be sinful for any one to do it before deliberating and assuring himself of its lawfulness; and he would not be excused on the ground of ignorance, for the ignorance would manifestly not be invincible, since he does not do what in him lies to inquire into the lawfulness or unlawfulness of the matter. For in order that an act, the goodness of which is otherwise uncertain, be good, it must be done in accordance with the investigation and determination of the wise, it being (*Ethics*, bk. 2) one of the conditions of a good act that it be done in accordance therewith. Accordingly, when, in a doubtful case, the doer omits to take the advice of the wise, he is without excuse. Nay, even if we grant that the act in question is lawful in itself, yet, if there be any doubt thereon, the doer is bound to take the advice, and to act in accordance with the award, of the wise, even though they be themselves in error.

In doubtful matters, abstain from action until its lawfulness is ascertained: to act otherwise is to sin.

309 Accordingly, if any one, without consulting the doctors, were to make a contract, concerning the lawfulness or unlawfulness of which men were doubtful, he would undoubtedly sin, even though the contract were otherwise lawful and even if the doer thought so, not, however, on the authority of the wise, but of his own inclination and judgement. And on the same principle, were one in a doubtful matter to consult the wise and they were to rule against its lawfulness and yet he were to follow his own judgement and do the thing, he would sin even though the thing were otherwise lawful in itself. For example, suppose a man is in doubt whether so-and-so is his wife and he seeks advice whether he is bound to render the marital debt or whether it is right for him to do so, or whether he may exact it from her, and the doctors reply that it is not at all right, and yet he be led by his wife's affection and his own desire to refuse to accept that reply and thinks that his act is lawful, it is certainly sinful for him to approach his wife, although such approach be lawful in itself (as it really is), because he is acting contrary to the conscience which he ought to have. For in those matters which belong to his salvation a man is bound to yield credence to the teachers appointed by the Church, and in a doubtful matter their ruling is law. For just as in the contentious forum the judge is bound to judge in accordance with what is alleged and proved, so in the forum of conscience a man is bound to base his judgement, not on his own sentiments, but on demonstrable reason or on the authority of the wise; else his judgement is presumptuous and exposes him to the
310 risk of going wrong, and indeed he does err in the very fact. This accords with what was laid down in the Old Testament (*Deuteronomy*, ch. 17):

Consult the wise that you may know what is lawful in such matters; act in accord with their judgement.

Sinful to do anything in such doubtful matters without consulting the wise, even though the act be otherwise lawful.

'If there arise a matter too hard for thee in judgement, between blood and blood, between plea and plea, between leprosy and not leprosy, being matters of controversy within thy gates (saith the Lord), thou shalt arise and get thee up to the place which the Lord thy God shall choose, and thou shalt come unto the priests the Levites and unto the judges that shall be in those days and inquire, and they shall show thee the sentence of judgement, and thou shalt do according to the sentence which they of authority in that place shall show thee, and according to the judgement which they shall tell thee thou shalt do, not declining to the right hand or to the left.'

I accordingly assert that in doubtful matters a man is bound to seek the advice of those whom the Church has appointed for that purpose, such as prelates, preachers, and confessors, who are people skilled in divine and human law. For in the Church some are eyes, some feet, and so on (I *Corinthians*, ch. 12): and in *Ephesians*, ch. 4, 'And he gave some, apostles; . . . some, evangelists; and some, pastors and teachers', and in *St. Matthew*, ch. 23, 'The Scribes and the Pharisees sit in Moses' seat; all therefore whatsoever they bid you observe, that observe and do'. And Aristotle (*Ethics*, bk. 1) lays this down as a precept, following Hesiod, 'The man who is ignorant in himself, yet does not listen to another in **311**
order to know what is good, is a foolish and empty person'.

Let merchants take heed hereto.

It is, therefore, not enough for security of life and conscience that a man should deem himself to be doing right, but in doubtful matters he must needs rely on the authority of others whose business is therewith. For it is not enough that merchants should abstain from doing what they themselves deem wrong, if they nevertheless enter into illegal contracts without the advice of the wise.

Cajetan criticized.

And so I do not agree with Cardinal Cajetan when he says that if a doubt arises about something which really is lawful in itself and some preachers or confessors who otherwise have authority to pronounce thereon declare it unlawful or declare it mortal sin when it is venial, yet the man who, following his own inclination in the matter, disbelieves them and determines in his own conscience that it

Let women heed this.

is not a mortal sin, does not sin. As an example, Cajetan takes the use by women of paint and other superfluous adornments, a thing really not a mortal sin, but which he assumes might be pronounced a mortal sin by preachers and confessors. If, says he, a woman is so given to such adornment that she does not yield assent to them, but thinks it lawful or not a mortal sin, she does not commit a mortal **312**

He who follows the advice of the wise is safe in conscience so long as he has no reason for doubting or believing the contrary.

sin when she resorts to such adornment. Now this I declare dangerous. For in those matters which are necessary to salvation a woman is bound to yield assent to the wise and she exposes herself to danger if contrariwise she does what the wise pronounce to be a mortal sin. And, on the other hand, if in a doubtful matter a man has taken counsel with the wise and has accepted their ruling that the thing is lawful, he is safe in conscience—at any rate until he receives a second opinion and is driven to doubt or to believe the contrary by a person of such authority, or by reasons of such cogency, as ought to affect his judgement. This is notorious, for he does all that in him lies and so his ignorance is invincible.

Three propositions deduced from the premises. Proposition I.

The premises, then, establish the following propositions:

First. In doubtful matters a man is bound to seek the advice of those whose business it is to give it, otherwise he is not safe in conscience, whether the doubt be about a thing in itself lawful or unlawful.

Proposition II.

Second. If after a consultation in a doubtful matter it be settled by the wise that the thing is unlawful, a man is bound to follow their opinion, and if he act contrary thereto he is without excuse, even if the thing be otherwise lawful.

Proposition III.

THIRD. On the other hand, if after such consultation it be settled by the wise
313 that the thing is lawful, he who follows their opinion is safe, even if it be otherwise unlawful.

The author adapts the foregoing to the doubt raised about the Indians, and answers it.

When, then, we return to the question before us, namely, the matter of the barbarians, we see that it is not in itself so evidently unjust that no question about its justice can arise, nor again so evidently just that no doubt is possible about its injustice, but that it has a look of both according to the standpoint. For, at first sight, when we see that the whole of the business has been carried on by men who are alike well-informed and upright, we may believe that everything has been done properly and justly. But then, when we hear of so many massacres, so many plunderings of otherwise innocent men, so many princes evicted from their possessions and stripped of their rule, there is certainly ground for doubting whether this is rightly or wrongly done. And in this way the discussion in question does not seem at all superfluous and so we get a clear answer to the objection. Moreover, even if it be granted that there is no doubt about the whole question, it is no novelty for theological discussions to be instituted on points of certainty. For we discuss about the Incarnation of our Lord and other articles of faith. For not always are theological discussions of the deliberative sort, but frequently they are of the demonstrative sort, that is, entered upon, not for purposes of deliberation, but of instruction.

He meets an objection.

314 But some one may come forward and say: Although there were at one time some elements of doubt in this business, yet they have now been discussed and settled by the wise and so everything is now being administered in accordance with their advice and we have no need of a fresh inquiry. To such a person I answer first, God be blessed if it is so; our discussion raises no obstacle thereto; nor would I raise any new complaints. Secondly, I assert that it is not for jurists to settle this question or at any rate not for jurists only, for since the barbarians in question, as I shall forthwith show, were not in subjection by human law, it is not by human, but by divine law that questions concerning them are to be determined. Now, jurists are not skilled enough in the divine law to be able by themselves to settle questions of this sort. Nor am I sure that in the discussion and determination of this question theologians have ever been called competent to pronounce on so grave a matter. And as the issue concerns the forum of conscience, its settlement belongs to the priests, that is, to the Church. Accordingly in *Deuteronomy*, ch. 17, it is enjoined on the king that he take a copy of the law from the hand of the priest. Thirdly, in order that the whole of the matter be adequately examined and assured, is it not possible that so weighty a business may produce other special doubts deserving of discussion? Accordingly
315 I think I shall be doing something which is not only not futile and useless, but well worth the trouble, if I am enabled to discuss this question in a manner befitting its importance.

Firstly.

Secondly.

The decision of this case is not for jurists, but for theologians.

And therefore for priests, that is, for the Church.

Thirdly.

The first question

FOURTH. Returning now to our main topic, in order that we may proceed

about the Indians.

in order, I ask first whether the aborigines in question were true owners in both private and public law before the arrival of the Spaniards; that is, whether they were true owners of private property and possessions and also whether there were among them any who were the true princes and overlords of others. The answer might seem to be No, the reason being that slaves own no property, 'for a slave can have nothing of his own' (*Inst.*, 2, 9, 3, and *Dig.*, 29, 2, 79), and so all his acquisitions belong to his master (*Inst.*, 1, 8, 1). But the aborgines in question are slaves. Therefore the matter is proved; for as Aristotle (*Politics*, bk. 1) neatly and correctly says, 'Some are by nature slaves, those, to wit, who are better fitted to serve than to rule'. Now these are they who have not sufficient reason to govern even themselves, but only to do what they are bidden, and whose strength lies in their body rather than in their mind. But, of a surety, if there be any such, the aborigines in question are pre-eminently such, for they really seem little different from brute animals and are utterly incapable of governing, and **316**
it is unquestionably better for them to be ruled by others than to rule themselves. Aristotle says it is just and natural for such to be slaves. Therefore they and their like cannot be owners. And it is immaterial that before the arrival of the Spaniards they had no other masters; for there is no inconsistency in a slave having no master, as the glossator on *Dig.*, 40, 12, 23, notes. Nay, the statement is expressly made in that passage of the *Digest* and it is the expressed case set out in *Dig.*, 45, 3, 36, pr., where it is said that a slave who has been abandoned by his master and not taken into possession by any one else can be taken into possession by any one. If, then, these were slaves they could be taken into possession by the Spaniards.

Case for a negative answer.

Case for an affirmative answer.

On the opposite side we have the fact that the people in question were in peaceable possession of their goods, both publicly and privately. Therefore, unless the contrary is shown, they must be treated as owners and not be disturbed in their possession unless cause be shown.

A distinction.

If the barbarians had not dominion, different grounds that can be assigned therefor.

In aid of a solution I am loath to recall to notice the numerous utterances of the doctors on the nature of dominion. I have set them out at length when commenting on Restitution, 4, dist. 15, and on *Prima Secundae*, qu. 62, and I pass them by here for fear they should lead me to omit things of greater moment. **317**
And so let me pass them over in order to observe that, if the aborigines had not dominion, it would seem that no other cause is assignable therefor except that they were sinners or were unbelievers or were witless or irrational.

Error of the Waldenses, Wycliffe, and Armachanus about the first ground, i.e., sin.

Fifth. Now, some have maintained that grace is the title to dominion and consequently that sinners, at any rate those in mortal sin, have no dominion over anything. That was the error of the poor folk of Lyons, or Waldenses, and afterwards of John Wycliffe. One error of his, namely, that 'no one is a civil owner, while he is in mortal sin', was condemned by the Council of Constance. This opinion was also held by Armachanus (bk. 10, *Adversus errores Armenorum*, c. 4) and in the Dialogue, *Defensorium pacis*; and Waldensis wrote to controvert him in his *Doctrinale antiquitatum fidei*, vol. 1, bk. 2, ch. 81 and 82, and vol. 11, ch. 3. Armachanus relies on the fact that such dominion is reprobated

In favour of the doctrine of Armachanus and the others named.

Argument 1.

by God: 'They have set up Kings but not by me; they have made princes and I knew it not' (*Hosea*, ch. 8); and then is added the indictment, 'Of their silver and their gold have they made them idols that they may be cut off'. And so, says he, such persons have no lawful dominion in the eyes of God. It is certain, however, that all dominion is by divine authority, for God himself is the creator
318 of everything, and none but they to whom He has given dominion can have it. Now it is not agreeable to reason that He should give it to the disobedient and transgressors of his commandments, just as human princes do not give their property, such as towns and strongholds, to rebels, and if they have given it to them, they confiscate it. But we ought to judge about divine things through the medium of human things (*Romans*, ch. 1). Therefore God does not give dominion to the disobedient. And in token hereof God at times removes such from their exalted position, as in the cases of Saul (I *Sam.*, ch. 15 and 16), and of Nebuchadnezzar and Balthazar (*Daniel*, ch. 4 and 5). **Argument 2.** Again (*Genesis*, ch. 1), 'Let us make man in our own image and likeness that he may have dominion over the fish of the sea', &c. It appears therefore that dominion is founded on the image of God. But the sinner displays no such image. Therefore he has no dominion. **Argument 3.** Further, such a one commits the crime of treason. Therefore he deserves to lose his dominion. Likewise, St. Augustine says that the sinner is not worthy of the bread he eats. **Argument 4.** Also, the Lord had given our first parents dominion over paradise and then deprived them of it because of their sin (*Genesis*, ch. 1). Therefore, &c.

It is true that both Wycliffe and Armachanus speak without distinguishing and seem to be speaking rather of the dominion of sovereignty which belongs to
319 princes. But because their reasoning applies equally to all dominion, they seem to have in view all kinds of dominion generally. And that is how Conrad (bk. 1, qu. 7) understands their teaching, and Armachanus is sufficiently clear in that sense. Those who would follow their teaching may, therefore, say that the barbarians had no dominion, because they were always in mortal sin.

The author replies by this proposition.

Almain's reasoning set out and rejected.

Sixth. But against this doctrine I advance the proposition that mortal sin does not hinder civil dominion and true dominion. Although this proposition was established in the Council of Constance, yet Almain (4, Dist. 15, qu. 2), following Ailly, bases an argument in favour of it, on the fact that a person already in mortal sin who finds himself in extreme need would be in a dilemma, inasmuch as he must eat bread, and if he cannot own any himself he takes another's. Therefore he cannot escape mortal sin. This reasoning is, however, unsatisfactory, in the first place, because neither Armachanus nor Wycliffe seems to be speaking of natural dominion, but of civil; and, secondly, the consequence is denied, it being retorted that in case of necessity a man could take what is another's; and, thirdly, he is in no dilemma, because he can repent. The argument, therefore, must be differently framed.

The author's reasoning or proof 1.

320 First, if a sinner has not civil dominion (which is what they seem to be speaking of), he, therefore, has not natural dominion; but the consequent is untrue; therefore, &c. I prove the consequence; for natural dominion is a gift of God, just as civil dominion is, nay, more so, for civil dominion seems an institute of

human law. Therefore, if for an offence against God a man loses civil dominion, he would for the same reason lose his natural dominion also. But the falsity of the consequent is demonstrated by the fact that the man in question does not lose dominion over his own acts and over his own limbs, for a sinner has a right to defend his own life.

Proof 2. Secondly, Holy Scripture often names as kings those who were wicked and sinners, as appears in the case of Solomon and Ahab and many others; but one cannot be a king without having dominion; therefore, &c.

Proof 3. Thirdly, I employ against the opposing party their own argument: Dominion is founded on the image of God; but man is God's image by nature, that is, by his reasoning powers; therefore, dominion is not lost by mortal sin. The minor is proved from St. Augustine (*De Trinitate*, bk. 9), and from the doctors.

Proof 4. Fourthly, David called Saul his lord and king even when he was persecuting him (I *Sam.*, ch. 16, and elsewhere). Nay, David himself sinned at times, yet did not lose his kingdom on that account.

Proof 5. Fifthly (*Genesis*, ch. 49), 'The sceptre shall not depart from Judah, nor a **321**
leader from between his feet, until he that is to be sent shall come', &c.; yet there were many bad kings; therefore, &c.

Proof 6. Sixthly, spiritual power is not lost by mortal sin; therefore not civil, for it seems much less assuredly to be founded in grace than spiritual power is. Now, the antecedent is obvious, because a bad priest consecrates the Eucharist and a bad bishop consecrates a priest, beyond all doubt. Although Wycliffe denies this, Armachanus admits it.

Proof 7. Seventhly, it is not at all likely, seeing that we are bidden to obey princes (*Romans*, ch. 13; and I *Peter*, ch. 2: 'Be subject to your masters, not only to the good but also to the forward'), and not to take what belongs to another, that God meant that there should be any uncertainty as to who were true princes and owners.

Proof 8. And, in sum, this is manifest heresy. And in the same way that God makes His sun to rise on the good and on the bad and sends His rain on the just and on the unjust, so also He has given temporal goods alike to good and to bad. Nor is this subject discussed, because it is in doubt, but in order that from one crime, to wit, from this insensate heresy, we may learn the character of all heretics.

The second ground for loss of dominion is now considered; the question is whether it is lost by unbelief. The author gives some propositions in reply. Proposition I proved from Scripture.

Seventh. Now it remains to consider whether at any rate dominion may
be lost by reason of unbelief. It might seem to be so, on the ground that heretics **322**
have no dominion, and therefore other unbelievers have not, inasmuch as their condition is not better than that of heretics. The antecedent is evident from the chapter *cum secundum leges* (5, 2, 19, in vi), where it is ruled that the goods of heretics are confiscated by the very fact. My answer is in the following propositions: The first proposition is that unbelief does not prevent any one from being a true owner. This is the conclusion of St. Thomas Aquinas (*Secunda Secundae*, qu. 10, art. 12). It is proved also, firstly, by the fact that Scripture gives the name of king to many unbelievers, such as Sennacherib and Pharaoh and many other kings. Also by the fact that hatred of God is a graver sin than unbelief;

but through hatred, &c. Also, St. Paul (*Romans*, ch. 13) and St. Peter (I *Peter*, ch. 2) enjoin obedience to princes, all of whom at that time were unbelievers, and slaves are there bidden to obey their masters. Also, Tobias ordered that a kid which had been taken from the Gentiles should be restored as having been stolen (*Tobias*, ch. 2); now, this would not be the case, if the Gentiles had no ownership. Also, Joseph made all the land of Egypt tributary to Pharaoh, who was an unbeliever (*Genesis*, ch. 47). The proposition is also supported by the **And by reason.**
323 reasoning of St. Thomas, namely: Unbelief does not destroy either natural law or human law; but ownership and dominion are based either on natural or on human law; therefore they are not destroyed by want of faith. In fine, this is as obvious an error as the foregoing. **Corollary.** Hence it is manifest that it is not justifiable to take anything that they possess from either Saracens or Jews or other unbelievers as such, that is, because they are unbelievers; but the act would be theft or robbery no less than if it were done to Christians.

Proposition II.

EIGHTH. But because heresy presents peculiar difficulties, let a second proposition be: From the standpoint of the divine law a heretic does not lose the ownership of his property. This is generally accepted and is notorious. For since loss of property is a penalty and no penalty is ordained by the divine law for that condition, it is clear that from the standpoint of the divine law property is not forfeited on the ground of heresy. Further, this proposition is evident from the first proposition. For if ownership be not forfeited on the ground of any other unbelief, it follows that it is not forfeited on the ground of heresy, seeing that no special rules upon this point are enacted about heresy in the divine law.

NINTH. But what about human law in this regard? Conrad, indeed (bk. 1,
324 qu. 7, con. 2 and 3), seems to hold that a heretic by the very fact loses the ownership of his property, and so in the forum of conscience he ceases to be capable of dominion. Hence he infers that a heretic cannot alienate and that any alienation made by him is void. This is proved by the afore-mentioned chapter *cum secundum leges*, wherein the Pope premises that for certain crimes wrong-doers by the very fact lose the ownership of their property by civil law, and the Pope rules that the same is to hold for the crime of heresy. And Joannes Andreae seems to hold the same opinion, in his comment on the afore-mentioned chapter *cum secundum leges*. And it seems to be had from the law *Manichaeos* (*Cod.*, 1, 5, 4), whereby heretics are precluded from sale or gift or any dealing with their property. Also, civil laws bind in the forum of conscience, as St. Thomas teaches (*Prima Secundae*, qu. 96, art. 4).[1]

Proposition III.

TENTH. Let the third proposition in the course of our exposition be: A heretic incurs confiscation of his property from the day of the commission of his offence. This is commonly held by the doctors and is the ruling in the *Directorium inquisitorum* (bk. 3, tit. 9), and also in the *Summa* of Baptista de Salis on the word *absolutio* (§ 17), and it seems settled in the afore-mentioned

[1] St. Thomas's Conclusio here is 'Justae leges humanae obligant homines in foro conscientiae ratione egis aeternae a qua derivantur'. *Tr.*

chapter *cum secundum leges* and in the afore-mentioned law *Manichaeos* (*Cod.*, 1, 5, 4).

Proposition IV. ELEVENTH. A fourth proposition: Nevertheless, although the offence be 325
manifest, the fisc cannot seize the property of a heretic before condemnation. This is also generally received, and is the ruling of the afore-named chapter *cum secundum leges*. Nay, it would be contrary to the divine law and to natural law for a penalty to be enforced before condemnation has issued.

Corollary I. TWELFTH. It follows from the third conclusion that, when condemnation has taken place, even though this be after death, the confiscation dates back to the time of the commission of the offence, no matter into whose control the property has come. This corollary is also generally admitted and especially by Panormitanus in his comment on 3, 5, 1 in VI.

Corollary II. THIRTEENTH. And a second consequence is that every sale or gift of or other dealing with such property is void as from the day of the commission of the offence. And so, when condemnation has taken place, all such dealings are rescinded by the fisc and the property is taken by the same fisc, even without any repayment of the price to the purchasers. This, too, is generally admitted, and expressly so by Panormitanus in the passage just named, and is manifest from the afore-named law *Manichaeos* (*Cod.*, 1, 5, 4).

Proposition V. FOURTEENTH. A fifth proposition: Nevertheless a heretic continues to be 326
owner in the forum of conscience until he is condemned. This proposition seems to be at variance with Conrad and with the *Directorium inquisitorum* and Joannes Andreae; it is, however, the proposition of Sylvester, under the word *haeresis*, I, § 8. Adrian also maintains it, discussing the matter at some length (*Quodlibeta*, 6, qu. 2), and Cajetan seems to hold the same view in his *Summa*, Proof 1. under the word *poena*. The proposition is proved, first, by the fact that this deprivation in the forum of conscience is a penalty; therefore, it ought in no wise to be inflicted before condemnation. Nor am I sure whether human law Proof 2. could affect this at all. It is also proved by what is clear from the above-named chapter *cum secundum leges*, namely, that property is confiscated in the same way by the very fact of an incestuous marriage; as also when a free woman who has been ravished marries her ravisher. Nay, if any one fails to pay the accustomed dues on imported merchandise, the goods are forfeit by the very fact; as also in the case of an exporter of contraband merchandise, such as arms and iron, to the Saracens. All the details will be found in the above-named chapter *cum*
secundum leges and in *Cod.*, 5, 5, 3, and *Cod.*, 9, 13, 1, and in *X*, 5, 6, 6, and in 327
Dig., 39, 4, 16 (?). Aye, and the Pope expressly says in the afore-named chapter *cum secundum leges* that, just as confiscation takes place in the cases named, so he intends it to take place in a case of heresy. But no one denies that an incestuous person and a ravisher and one who supplies the Saracens with arms and one who does not pay customs remain true owners of their property in the forum of conscience. Why, then, does not a heretic also? Conrad himself treats as identical the cases named and the case of a heretic. It would, moreover, be over severe to require a man who has just been converted from heresy to give up his property to the fisc.

Fifteenth. It follows as a corollary that a heretic may lawfully live on his own property.

These four corollaries to be noted.

Sixteenth. Secondly, it follows also that he can make a gratuitous conveyance of his property, as by way of gift.

Seventeenth. It follows, thirdly, that if his offence can be brought before the tribunals, he cannot convey his property for value, as by way of sale or dowry. This is manifest, because he would defraud the buyer, making him incur the risk of loss of both the thing and the price, should he, the seller, be condemned.

Eighteenth. Lastly, it follows that, if there were in fact no risk of confiscation, he might even make a conveyance for value. Thus, if some heretic were in
328 Germany, a Catholic could lawfully buy from him. For it would be oppressive if a Catholic could not buy land from a heretic or sell land to him in a Lutheran state; yet it would be necessary to say this, if a heretic were utterly disabled from ownership in the forum of conscience.

Nineteenth. From all this the conclusion follows that the barbarians in question cannot be barred from being true owners, alike in public and in private law, by reason of the sin of unbelief or any other mortal sin, nor does such sin entitle Christians to seize their goods and lands, as Cajetan proves at some length and neatly (*Secunda Secundae*, qu. 66, art. 8).

The principal conclusion is inferred.

Cajetan.

Twentieth. It remains to ask whether the Indians lacked ownership because of want of reason or unsoundness of mind. This raises the question whether the use of reason is a precondition of capacity for ownership in general. Conrad, indeed (bk. 1, qu. 6), propounds the conclusion that ownership is competent to irrational creatures, alike sensible and insensible. The proof
329 consists in the fact that ownership is nothing more than the right to put a thing to one's own use. But brutes have this right over the herbs and plants (*Genesis*, ch. 1): 'Behold I have given you every herb bearing seed which is upon the face of all the earth and every tree in the which is the fruit of a tree yielding seed; to you it shall be for meat and to every beast of the earth.' The stars, too, have the right to shine for light (*Genesis*, ch. 1), 'And God set them in the firmament of the heaven to give light upon the earth and to rule over the day and over the night'. And the lion has dominion over all animals that walk, whence he is called the king of beasts. And the eagle is lord among the birds whence in Psalm 103 the verse about his house being their leader.[1] Sylvester (under the word *dominium*, at the beginning) is of the same opinion as Conrad, saying that the 'elements exercise dominion one over the other'.

Question about the third ground: i.e. whether the Indians lack ownership because of want of reason. Opinion of Conrad.

And of Sylvester.

I answer by the following propositions:

First: Irrational creatures cannot have dominion. This is clear, because dominion is a right, as even Conrad admits. But irrational creatures cannot have a right. Therefore they cannot have dominion. The proof of the minor
330 is that they cannot suffer a wrong and therefore can have no right. The proof of

The author answers by certain propositions. Proposition I. Proof 1. The opinion of Conrad and Sylvester rejected.

[1] This is founded on a mistranslation of the Hebrew; see A.V., Ps. 104, v. 17. *Tr.* [The Translator appears here to have erred as Victoria was using the Vulgate which was based upon the Greek, not upon the Hebrew text. Ed.]

this assumption is that he who kept off a wolf or a lion from its prey or an ox from its pasture would not do it a wrong, nor would he who shut a window to prevent the sun from shining in do the sun a wrong. And this is confirmed by the fact that, if the brutes have dominion, he who took away the grass from a stag would commit theft, for he would be taking what belongs to another against the owner's will.

Proof 2. Also, wild beasts have not dominion over themselves. Therefore much less over other things. The proof of the assumption is that they may be killed with impunity, even for pleasure; and so Aristotle (*Politics*, 1) says that the chase of wild beasts is just and natural.

Proof 3. Also, wild beasts themselves and all irrational animals are more fully within the ownership of man than slaves are. Therefore, if slaves cannot have anything of their own, much less can irrational animals.

Our proposition is also confirmed by the authority of St. Thomas Aquinas (*Prima Secundae*, qu. 1, art. 1 and 2, and qu. 6, art. 2, and *Contra Gentiles*, bk. 3, c. 110), to the effect that only rational creatures have dominion over their acts, the test of a man's being master of his acts being (as St. Thomas says, *Prima Pars*, qu. 82, art. 1, on obj. 3) that he has the power of choice. Hence (as he says in the same place) we are not masters of our appetite as regards its final end. If, then, the brutes have not dominion over their acts, they have it not over other **331**
things. And although this seems to be a dispute about a name, it is assuredly a highly improper and unusual mode of speech to attribute dominion to things irrational. For we do not ordinarily say that a man has dominion save over that which is placed within his control. For when we have not dominion, we speak thus: 'It is not within my control', 'It is not in my power'. Now, as the brutes are rather moved than move themselves, as St. Thomas says (*Prima Secundae*, as above), they for that reason have no dominion.

Sylvester's reasoning rejected. Nor is there any force in Sylvester's remark that dominion sometimes does not signify right, but only power, in which sense we say that fire has dominion over water. For, if this is enough to confer dominion, a robber has dominion over his victim even up to death, because he has power to kill him, and a thief has power to seize his victim's money. Further, as regards the statement that the stars exercise dominion and that the lion is king of beasts, obviously this is said metaphorically and by way of figure.

Doubt concerning a boy to whom dominion does not seem to belong before the use of reason is attained.

TWENTY-FIRST. There might seem some doubt whether a boy, who has not **332**
yet the use of reason, can have dominion, inasmuch as he seems to differ little from irrational animals. And the Apostle says (*Galatians*, ch. 4): 'The heir, as long as he is a child, differeth nothing from a slave'; but a slave has not dominion; therefore, &c. But let our second proposition be: Boys, even before they have the use of reason, can have dominion.

Proposition II. Proof 1. This is manifest, because they can suffer wrong; therefore they have rights over things; therefore also they have dominion, which is naught else than a right.

Proof 2. Also, the property of wards is not part of the guardian's property; but it has owners and no others are its owners; therefore the wards are the owners.

Proof 3. Also, boys can be heirs; but an heir is one who succeeds to the rights of the deceased and who has dominion over the inheritance (*Dig.*, 44, 3, 11, and *Inst.*, 2, 19, 7). Also, as already said, the basis of dominion is in the possession of the image of God, and children already possess the image. The Apostle, moreover, says in the passage of *Galatians* just cited, 'The heir, as long as he is a child, differeth nothing from a slave, though he be lord of all'. The same does not hold good of an irrational creature, for a boy does not exist for the sake of another, as does a brute, but for his own sake.

Proof 4.

333 TWENTY-SECOND. But what about those suffering from unsoundness of mind? I mean a perpetual unsoundness whereby they neither have nor is there any hope that they will have the use of reason. Let our third proposition be: It seems that they can still have dominion, because they can suffer wrong; therefore they have a right, but whether they can have civil dominion is a question which I leave to the jurists.

Proposition III.

TWENTY-THIRD. However this may be, let our fourth proposition be: The Indian aborigines are not barred on this ground from the exercise of true dominion. This is proved from the fact that the true state of the case is that they are not of unsound mind, but have, according to their kind, the use of reason. This is clear, because there is a certain method in their affairs, for they have polities which are orderly arranged and they have definite marriage and magistrates, overlords, laws, and workshops, and a system of exchange, all of which call for the use of reason; they also have a kind of religion. Further, they make no error in matters which are self-evident to others; this is witness to their use of reason. Also, God and nature are not wanting in the supply of what is necessary in great measure for the race. Now, the most conspicuous feature of man is
334 reason, and power is useless which is not reducible to action. Also, it is through no fault of theirs that these aborigines have for many centuries been outside the pale of salvation, in that they have been born in sin and void of baptism and the use of reason whereby to seek out the things needful for salvation. Accordingly I for the most part attribute their seeming so unintelligent and stupid to a bad and barbarous upbringing, for even among ourselves we find many peasants who differ little from brutes.

Proposition IV. The aborigines of the New World not wholly without reason.

TWENTY-FOURTH. The upshot of all the preceding is, then, that the aborigines undoubtedly had true dominion in both public and private matters, just like Christians, and that neither their princes nor private persons could be despoiled of their property on the ground of their not being true owners. It would be harsh to deny to those, who have never done any wrong, what we grant to Saracens and Jews, who are the persistent enemies of Christianity. We do not deny that these latter peoples are true owners of their property, if they have not seized lands elsewhere belonging to Christians.

Principal conclusion deduced from the foregoing.

335 It remains to reply to the argument of the opposite side to the effect that the aborigines in question seem to be slaves by nature because of their incapability of self-government. My answer to this is that Aristotle certainly did not mean to say that such as are not over-strong mentally are by nature subject to another's power and incapable of dominion alike over themselves and other things; for this

Answer to the argument on the negative side adduced in No. 4, above, wherein a passage

of Aristotle's Politics, bk. I, is expounded.

is civil and legal slavery, wherein none are slaves by nature. Nor does the Philosopher mean that, if any by nature are of weak mind, it is permissible to seize their patrimony and enslave them and put them up for sale; but what he means is that by defect of their nature they need to be ruled and governed by others and that it is good for them to be subject to others, just as sons need to be subject to their parents until of full age, and a wife to her husband. And that this is the Philosopher's intent is clear from his corresponding remark that some are by nature masters, those, namely, who are of strong intelligence. Now, it is clear that he does not mean hereby that such persons can arrogate to themselves a sway over others in virtue of their superior wisdom, but that nature has given
them capacity for rule and government. Accordingly, even if we admit that the **336**
aborigines in question are as inept and stupid as is alleged, still dominion cannot be denied to them, nor are they to be classed with the slaves of civil law. True, some right to reduce them to subjection can be based on this reason and title, as we shall show below. Meanwhile the conclusion stands sure, that the aborigines in question were true owners, before the Spaniards came among them, both from the public and the private point of view.

337 SUMMARY OF THE SECOND SECTION

On the illegitimate titles for the reduction of the aborigines of the New World into the power of the Spaniards

1. The Emperor is not the lord of the whole world.
2. Even if the Emperor were the lord of the world, that would not entitle him to seize the provinces of the Indian aborigines and to erect new lords and put down the former lords or to levy taxes.
3. The Pope is not civil or temporal lord of the whole world, in the proper sense of civil lordship and power.
4. Even if the Supreme Pontiff had secular power over the world, he could not give that power to secular princes.
5. The Pope has temporal power, but only so far as it subserves things spiritual.
6. The Pope has no temporal power over the Indian aborigines or over other unbelievers.

338 7. A refusal by these aborigines to recognize any dominion of the Pope is no reason for making war on them and for seizing their goods.

8. Whether these aborigines were guilty of the sin of unbelief, in that they did not believe in Christ, before they heard anything of Christianity.
9. What is required in order that ignorance may be imputed to a person as, and be, sin, that is, vincible ignorance. And what about invincible ignorance?
10. Whether the aborigines are bound to hearken to the first messengers of Christianity so as to commit mortal sin in not believing Christ's Gospel merely on its simple announcement to them.
11. If the faith were simply announced and proposed to them and they will not straightway receive it, this is no ground for the Spaniards to make war on them or to proceed against them under the law of war.
12. How the aborigines, if they refuse when asked and counselled to hear peaceably the preachers of religion, cannot be excused from mortal sin.
13. When the aborigines would be bound to receive Christianity under penalty of mortal sin.
14. In the author's view it is not sufficiently clear whether Christianity has been so proposed and announced to these aborigines that they are bound to believe it under the penalty of fresh sin.

339 15. Even when Christianity has been proposed to them with never so much sufficiency of proof and they will not accept it, this does not render it lawful to make war on them and despoil them of their possessions.

16. Christian princes cannot, even on the authority of the Pope, restrain these aborigines from sins against the law of nature or punish them therefor.

It being premised, then, that the Indian aborigines are or were true owners, it remains to inquire by what title the Spaniards could have come into possession of them and their country.

And first, I shall advert to the titles which might be alleged, but which are not adequate or legitimate.

Secondly, I shall set out the legitimate titles under which the aborigines could have come under the sway of the Spaniards.

The author proposes to set out the titles, both legitimate and non-legitimate, by which the Spaniards might have

seized the territory of the aborigines.

Now, there are seven titles, which might be alleged, but which are not adequate, and seven or eight others, which are just and legitimate.

The first non-legitimate title.

The first title that might be alleged, then, is that the Emperor is the lord of the world, and in such a way that, even if it be granted that in time past there was a defect in his claim, it would by now be purged as regards our present, most Christian Emperor. For, even if we assume that the Indian aborigines may be true owners, yet they might have superior lords, just as inferior princes have
a king and as some kings have the Emperor over them. There can in this way be **340**
many persons having dominion over the same thing; and this accounts for the well-worn distinction drawn by the jurists between dominion high and low, dominion direct and available, dominion pure and mixed. The question, therefore, is whether the aborigines had any superior lord. And, as this question can only arise with regard to either the Emperor or the Pope, let us speak of these.

Is the Emperor lord of the whole earth? For the affirmative. Argument 1. Argument 2. Argument 3.

The first allegation to consider is that the Emperor is lord of the whole world and therefore of these barbarians also. This is supported, firstly, by the appellation, 'Lord of the world', commonly given to the late Emperor Maximilian or to the present Emperor Charles, ever August. Also (*Luke*, ch. 2), 'There went out a decree from Caesar Augustus that a census should be taken of all the world'; but Christian Emperors ought not to be in any worse condition than he; therefore, &c. Also, our Lord seems to have pronounced Caesar to be the true lord of the Jews. 'Render unto Caesar', said he, 'the things that are Caesar's,' &c. (*St. Luke*, ch. 20). But it does not seem that Caesar could have this right, save as Emperor.

Opinion of Bartolus and the glossators, for affirmative.

Therefore Bartolus, commenting on the Extravagans of Henry VII, *Ad reprimendum*, expressly holds that 'the Emperor is the rightful lord of the whole world'. And this is also the opinion of the glossator on *X*, 4, 17, 13. So, too, the glossator on *X*, 1, 6, 34.

Proof 1.

And they prove the allegation first from can. 41, C. 7, qu. 1, where Gregory[1]
says that there is one king among bees, and in the world one Emperor, and also **341**
from *Dig.*, 14, 2, 9, where the Emperor Antoninus says: 'I indeed am lord of the earth', and *Cod.*, 7, 37, 3, § 1, 'everything is understood to belong to the Emperor'.

Proof 2.

The allegation might also be supported by the fact that Adam first and then Noah seem to have been lords of the world: 'Let us make man in our image, after our likeness, and let them have dominion over the fish of the sea and over the fowl of the air and over all the earth', &c. (*Genesis*, ch. 1), and a little later on 'Be fruitful and multiply and replenish the earth and subdue it', &c.; and there is a similar pronouncement made to Noah (*Genesis*, ch. 8). But these two had successors. Therefore.

Proof 3.

Also, there is a proof in the incredibility of God's having instituted in the world anything but the best system of government: 'In wisdom hast thou made them all' (*Psalm* 104). But monarchy is the best system, as St. Thomas admirably shows (*De regimine principum*, bk. 1, ch. 2), and as Aristotle seems to hold (*Politics*,

[1] Victoria has *Hieronymus* here following the *editio Romana* of the *Corpus Juris Canonici*, which attributes this to St. Jerome.

bk. 3). Therefore, it seems to be in accordance with divine institution that there should be one Emperor in the world.

Proof 4.

Also, the things which are outside nature ought to imitate things natural. But in things natural there is always one governor; as in the body, it is the heart; in the soul, it is reason. Therefore in the world there ought to be one governor, just as there is one God.

Bartolus's opinion rejected. Proposition I laid down.

Proof that dominion over the whole world is not in the Emperor by natural law.

1. Now, this contention is baseless. Let our first conclusion, then, be:
342 The Emperor is not the lord of the whole earth. This is proved from the fact that dominion must be founded either on natural or divine or human law; but there is no lord of the earth in any of these; therefore, &c. The minor is proved, first as regards natural law, by what St. Thomas well says (*Prima Pars*, qu. 92, art 1, on obj. 2, and qu. 96, art. 4), namely, that by natural law mankind is free save from paternal and marital dominion—for the father has dominion over his children and the husband over the wife by natural law; therefore no one by natural law has dominion over the world. And, as St. Thomas also says (*Secunda Secundae*, qu. 10, art. 10), dominion and pre-eminence were introduced by human law; they, therefore, were not by natural law. Nor would there be any greater reason why this dominion should be more proper for Germans than for Gauls. And Aristotle (*Politics*, bk. 1) says, Power is of two kinds, the one originates in the family, like that of the father over his sons and that of the husband over the wife, and this is a natural power; the other is civil, for, although it may take its rise in nature and so may be said to be of natural law, as St. Thomas says (*De regimine principum*, bk. 1, ch. 2), yet, man being a political animal, it is founded not on nature, but on law.

Proof that the Emperor is not lord of the whole world by divine law. Proof 1.

How the passage in Daniel is to be taken.

Now, as regards divine law, we do not read that before the coming of our Saviour Christ the Emperors were lords of the whole world, although in the
343 gloss mentioned on the Extravagans, *Ad reprimendum*, Bartolus adduces the passage in *Daniel*, ch. 2, about Nebuchadnezzar, of whom it is said: 'Thou, O King, art a King of Kings; for the God of Heaven hath given thee a Kingdom and power and strength and glory. And wheresoever the children of men dwell, He hath given thee all.' It is, however, certain that Nebuchadnezzar received his sovereignty from God by no special grant, but in the same way as other princes (*Romans*, ch. 13): 'There is no power but of God'; and (*Proverbs*, ch. 8): 'By me kings reign and princes decree justice.' Further, Nebuchadnezzar had not a legal rule over the whole earth, as Bartolus thinks, for the Jews were not legal subjects of his.

Proof 2.

How God is said to have given empire to the Romans.

Another proof that there was by divine law no ruler over the whole world lies in the fact that the Jewish nation was free from the foreigner; nay, the Jews were forbidden by their law to have any foreigner as their lord (*Deuteronomy*, ch. 17): 'Thou mayest not set a stranger to be king over thee.' And, although St. Thomas (*De regimine principum*, bk. 3, ch. 4 and 5) says that the Romans were entrusted with empire by God because of their justice and their patriotism and the excellence of their laws, yet this is not to be taken to mean that they had their empire by divine grant or institution, as St. Augustine also says (*De*

civitate Dei, ch. 18), but that in the divine providence it befell that they should obtain the sovereignty of the world. This, however, was not in the way in which **344**
Saul or David had his kingdom from God, but in some other way, such as by just war or other title.

Proof 3.

This will be plain to any one who considers the titles and modes of succession whereby sovereignty and lordship in the world have come down to our own day. For, to omit everything that happened before the flood, the world was certainly divided after Noah into different provinces and kingdoms, whether this were by ordinance of Noah himself—for he survived the flood three hundred and fifty years (*Genesis*, ch. 9), and sent colonies into different regions, as appears in Berosus of Babylon—or whether, as is more likely, different family-groups by the common agreement of mankind occupied different provinces, as (*Genesis*, ch. 13) 'Abram said unto Lot: ". . . Is not the whole land before thee? . . . If thou wilt take the left hand, then I will go to the right, or if thou depart to the right hand, then I will go to the left."' We are, accordingly, told (*Genesis*, ch. 10) that through the descendants of Noah came diversities of peoples and countries, whether in some regions they first assumed lordship by usurpation, as Nimrod seems to have done, of whom *Genesis*, ch. 10, v. 8, says that he was the first to be a mighty one in the earth, or whether by accord of several to unite in one State they appointed a prince over themselves by common agreement. For it is sure that either in these or in other like modes sovereignty and lordship began in the world and that afterwards, either by right of inheritance or of war or by some other such title, they were continued into our own day, or at **345**
any rate up to the time of the Saviour's coming. Herein it is manifest that before the coming of Christ no one was vested with world-wide sway by divine law and that the Emperor cannot at the present day derive therefrom a title to arrogate to himself lordship over the whole earth, and consequently not over the barbarians.

Reason for saying that after Christ's coming, the Emperor is lord of the whole earth.

It might, however, be alleged that after our Lord's coming there was one Emperor over the world by express grant of Christ, in that He, as regards His manhood, was Lord of the world, according to *St. Matthew*, ch. 28: 'All power is given unto me', &c., which, according to St. Augustine and St. Jerome, is to be understood as regards His manhood. Also, as the Apostle declares (I *Corinthians*, ch. 15), 'He hath put all things under his feet'. Therefore, just as He left on earth one vicar in matters spiritual, so also in matters temporal, and in the latter case it is the Emperor. St. Thomas, too, says (*De regimine principum*, bk. 3, ch. 13) that Christ was from His nativity the true Lord and monarch of the world and that Augustus though unwitting thereof, was acting as His deputy. Now, it is clear that this deputyship was not in matters spiritual, but in matters temporal. Seeing, then, that Christ's Kingdom, if it were temporal, was over the whole world, Augustus was, on the showing, lord of the world and so on the same principle his successors were.

The author demolishes this reasoning.

This reasoning is, however, quite inadmissible: In the first place, because **346**
of the doubt attaching to the statement that Christ as regards His manhood

was temporal Lord of the world. The probability indeed is that He was not, and our Lord seems to have asserted as much in the passage: 'My Kingdom is not of this world.'[1] Accordingly, St. Thomas remarks in this connexion that Christ's dominion is directly appointed for the soul's salvation and for spiritual profit, although it is not excluded in matters temporal in the same fashion as it is appointed in matters spiritual. This shows that in St. Thomas's view His Kingdom was not of the same sort as a civil and temporal kingdom, but that, while He had all kinds of power, even in matters temporal, which would subserve the aim of redemption, yet apart from that aim he had none. Further, even if we grant that He was temporal Lord, it is guess-work to say that He bequeathed that power to the Emperor, there being no mention of any such thing in the whole Bible. And as regards St. Thomas's statement that the Emperor Augustus was Christ's vicegerent, firstly, he does indeed make it in the passage referred to, but in his *Tertia Pars*, where he is professedly discussing the power of Christ, he makes no mention of this temporal power.

Secondly, St. Thomas's meaning is that the Emperor was Christ's vicegerent to the extent that temporal power is subordinate and subservient to spiritual
347 power. In this sense, of a truth, kings are the servants of bishops, just as the smith's art is subject to the knight's and the soldier's, while all the time neither the soldier nor his superior officer is a smith, but is only concerned to give the smith orders about the making of armour. Again, St. Thomas, writing on that passage in *St. John*, ch. 18, expressly says that Christ's Kingdom is not temporal or such a kingdom as Pilate conceived, but a spiritual kingdom, inasmuch as our Lord declares in that passage: 'Thou sayest that I am a King. To this end was I born and for this cause came I into the world, that I should bear witness unto the truth.' This shows it to be a mere fiction to say that by express grant of Christ there is one Emperor and lord of the world.

The author returns to the confirmation of his proposition. The Pope, who granted the Empire, is said to have been Leo III.

A consideration which palpably confirms this is the following: If there had been any such institution by divine law, how comes it that the Empire was divided into Eastern and Western, first among the sons of Constantine the Great and then, later, by Pope Stephen, who conferred the Empire of the West on the Germans, as is held in *X*, 1, 6, 34? For the assertion that the Greeks thereafter were not Emperors is inept and ignorant, as the glossator hereon points out, seeing that the German Emperors never claimed in virtue of this grant to be Lords of Greece, and John Palaeologus, Emperor of Constantinople, was held
348 to be lawful Emperor at the Council of Florence. Moreover, the patrimony of the Church (as the jurists themselves, and even Bartolus, confess) is not subject to the Emperor. Now, if all things were subject to the Emperor by divine law, no imperial gift or any other title could divest the Emperors of them, any more than the Pope can release any one from the power of the Popes. Also, the Kingdom of Spain is not subject to the Emperor, nor is France, as is also held in *X*, 1, 6, 34 above-mentioned, although the glossator adds out of his own head that this is not so much a matter of law as of fact. Also, the doctors agree that States,

[1] St. John, xviii. 36.

which have in times past been subject to the Empire, might be freed from that subjection by prescription; which would not be the case, if this subjection were in virtue of a divine law.

The author proves that the Emperor is not lord of the world by human law either.

Now, in point of human law, it is manifest that the Emperor is not lord of the world, because either this would be by the sole authority of some law, and there is none such; or, if there were, it would be void of effect, inasmuch as law presupposes jurisdiction. If, then, the Emperor had no jurisdiction over the world before the law, the law could not bind one who was not previously subject to it. Nor, on the other hand, had the Emperor this position by lawful succession or by gift or by exchange or by purchase or by just war or by election or by any other legal title, as is admitted. Therefore the Emperor never was the lord of the whole world.

Second proposition. As the gloss on the preface to the Digest.

2. Second conclusion: Granted that the Emperor were the lord of the **349** world, still that would not entitle him to seize the provinces of the Indian aborigines and erect new lords there and put down the former ones or take taxes. The proof is herein, namely, that even those who attribute lordship over the world to the Emperor do not claim that he is lord in ownership, but only in jurisdiction, and this latter right does not go so far as to warrant him in converting provinces to his own use or in giving towns or even estates away at his pleasure. This, then, shows that the Spaniards cannot justify on this ground their seizure of the provinces in question.

Discussion of the second title whereby the Spaniards could obtain possession of the barbarians.

A second alleged title to the lawful possession of these lands, and one which is vehemently asserted, is traced through the Supreme Pontiff. For it is claimed that the Pope is temporal monarch, too, over all the world and that he could consequently make the Kings of Spain sovereign over the aborigines in question, and that so it has been done.

The opinion of some jurisconsults.

In this matter there are some jurists, who hold that the Pope has full jurisdiction in temporal matters over the whole earth, and they even add that the power of all secular princes comes to them from the Pope. This is the tenet of Hostiensis on *X*, 3, 34, 8; also of the Archbishop (pt. 3, tit. 22, ch. 5, § 8); and also of Augustinus Anconitanus. Sylvester holds the same doctrine, making **350**
a much more ample and liberal concession of this power to the Pope, under the word *infidelitas* (§ 7) and under the word *Papa* (§§ 7, 10, 11, and 14), and under the word *legitimus* (§ 4). He has some singular remarks on this topic in the passages mentioned, as, for example, that 'the power of the Emperor and all other princes is sub-delegated as regards the Pope, being derived from God through the medium of the Pope', and that 'all their power is dependent on the Pope', and that 'Constantine gave lands to the Pope in recognition of his temporal power', and on the other hand that 'the Pope gave the Empire to Constantine to his use and profit', nay, that 'Constantine's act was really not a gift, but merely the return of what had previously been taken away', and that, 'if the Pope does not exercise jurisdiction in temporal matters outside the patrimony of the Church, this is not for want of authority, but in order to avoid the scandal of the Jews and in order to promote peace'; and many other things even more

empty and absurd than these. The sole proof that he gives herefor is in the passages 'The earth is the Lord's and the fulness thereof',[1] and 'All power is given unto me, both in heaven and in earth',[2] and the Pope is the vicar of God and of Christ, and (*Philippians*, ch. 2) Christ 'for our sake became obedient even unto death', &c. Bartolus, too, seems to be of this opinion in his comment on the
351 Extravagans, *Ad reprimendum*, and St. Thomas seems to favour it at the end of the second book of the *Sententiae*, the closing words of which are by way of solution of the fourth argument, which is the last of the whole book, namely, that the Pope holds the summit of both kinds of power, both secular and spiritual, and Herveus is of the same opinion in his *De potestate Ecclesiae*.

Summary of the opinion of the aforementioned.

This, then, being laid as a basis, the authors of this opinion say as follows: In the first place, that the Pope has free power, on the footing of supreme temporal lord, to make the Kings of Spain rulers over the Indian aborigines. Secondly, they say that, even if it be assumed that he could not do this, at any rate if these aborigines refused to recognize the temporal power of the Pope over them, this would warrant him in making war on them and in putting rulers over them. Now, each of these things has been done. For, first, the Supreme Pontiff granted the provinces in question to the Kings of Spain. Secondly, the aborigines were notified that the Pope is the vicar of God and His vicegerent on earth and it was claimed that they should, therefore, recognize him as their superior, and their refusal furnishes a good ground for making war on them and seizing their lands, &c. Hostiensis, *place cited*, expressly makes this point, so does Angelus in his *Summa*.

The author replies in a few propositions.

Now, inasmuch as I have fully discussed the temporal power of the Pope in my *Relectio de Potestate Ecclesiastica*, I will put my answer to the above into
352 a few brief propositions:

Proposition I.

3. First: The Pope is not civil or temporal lord of the whole world in the proper sense of the words 'lordship' and 'civil power'. This is the conclusion arrived at by Torquemada (bk. 2, ch. 113), and by Joannes Andreae and by Hugo, on can. 6, Dist. 96. And the most learned Innocent admits, in the above cited *X*, 1, 6, 34, that he has not temporal power over the Kingdom of France. And it seems the definite opinion of St. Bernard in the second book of his *De consideratione*, addressed to Pope Eugenius III. The opposite opinion seems contrary to the precept of our Lord who (*St. Matthew*, ch. 20, and *St. Luke*, ch. 22), says, 'Ye know that the princes of the Gentiles exercise lordship over them', &c. 'But it shall not be so among you.' And contrary also to the precept of the Apostle Peter, 'neither as being lords over [God's] heritage but being ensamples to the flock'.[3] And if Christ the Lord had not temporal power, as has been shown in the foregoing discussion to be more probable and as is also the opinion of St. Thomas, much less has the Pope it, he being Christ's vicar. The above-mentioned thinkers attribute to the Pope that which he has never claimed for himself; nay, he admits the contrary in many passages, as I have shown in the Relectio referred to. And the proof is sufficient, like that given

[1] Psalm, xxiv. 1. [2] St. Matthew, xxviii. 18. [3] 1 Peter, v. 3.

above concerning the Emperor, for no lordship can come to him save either by natural law or by divine law or by human law. Now, it is certain that none comes to him by natural or by human law, and none is shown to come to him by divine law. Therefore the assertion is ungrounded and arbitrary.

The author refutes the arguments of the opposite side.

Further, our Lord's injunction to Peter, 'Feed my sheep',[1] clearly shows 353
that power in spiritual and not in temporal matters is meant. It is, moreover, demonstrable that the Pope has not the whole world for his sphere. For our Lord said (*St. John*, ch. 10) that there should be 'one flock and one shepherd' at the end of the age. This is sufficient proof that at the present day all are not sheep of this flock. Again, assuming that Christ had this power, it is manifest that it has not been entrusted to the Pope. This appears from the fact that the Pope is no less vicar of Christ in spiritual than in temporal matters. But the Pope has no spiritual jurisdiction over unbelievers, as even our opponents admit, and, as seems (I *Corinthians*, ch. 5) to have been the express teaching of the Apostle: 'For what have I to do to judge them also that are without?' Therefore he has it not also in temporal matters. And of a truth there is nothing in the argument that, as Christ had temporal power over the world, therefore the Pope also has it. For Christ undoubtedly had spiritual power over the whole world, not less over believers than over unbelievers and could make laws which bound the whole world, as he did with regard to baptism and the articles of faith. And yet the Pope has not that power over unbelievers and may not excommunicate them or forbid their marriage within the degrees permitted by the divine law. Therefore. Also, the fact that, according to the doctors, Christ did not entrust supremacy in power even to the Apostles shows that there is no force in the conse- 354
quence: Christ had temporal power over the world; therefore the Pope has it too.

Proposition II.

4. Second proposition: Even assuming that the Supreme Pontiff had this secular power over the whole world, he could not give it to secular princes. This is obvious, because it would be annexed to the Papacy. Nor can any Pope sever it from the office of Supreme Pontiff or deprive his successor of that power, for the succeeding Supreme Pontiff cannot be less than his predecessor; and, if some one Pontiff had made a gift of this power, either the grant would be null or the succeeding Pontiff could cancel it.

Proposition III.

5. Third proposition: The Pope has temporal power only so far as it is in subservience to matters spiritual, that is, as far as is necessary for the administration of spiritual affairs. This is also the view of Torquemada (*as above*, ch. 114), and of all the doctors. And the proof of it lies in the fact that an art to which a higher end pertains is imperative and preceptive as regards the arts to which lower ends pertain (*Ethics*, bk. 1). But the end of spiritual power is ultimate felicity, while the end of civil power is political felicity. Therefore, temporal power is subject to spiritual power. This is the reasoning adopted by Innocent 355
in *X*, 1, 33, 6; and it receives confirmation from the consideration that, whenever anybody is entrusted with the charge of any office, he is impliedly granted everything without which the duties of the office cannot rightly be discharged

[1] St. John, xxi. 17.

(*X*, 1, 29, 1). Inasmuch, then, as the Pope is a spiritual pastor by Christ's commission and the discharge of the duties of this office cannot be hindered by the civil power (there being no lack in the provision of things necessary either by God or by Nature), it is beyond doubt that power over things temporal has also been left to him so far as is necessary for the government of things spiritual. And on this principle the Pope can infringe civil laws which tend to breed sinners, just as he has infringed the laws with regard to prescription by a party acting in bad faith, as is clear from *X*, 2, 26, 20. And on this principle also, when princes are at variance with one another about some right of sovereignty and are rushing into war, he can act as judge and inquire into the claims of the parties and deliver judgement, a judgement which the princes are bound to respect, lest those numerous spiritual evils should befall which are the inevitable results of a war between Christian princes. And although the Pope does not do this or does not do it often, it is not because he cannot, as Master Durandus says, but because, for fear of scandal, he wishes to prevent the princes from thinking his motive is ambition or because he is afraid of a revolt from the Apostolic See on the part of
356 the princes. And on this principle the Pope can sometimes depose kings and even set up new kings, as at times has been done. And certainly no one rightly calling himself Christian should deny this power to the Pope. This is the view held by Paludanus and Durandus (*De jurisdictione ecclesiastica*), and by Henricus Gandavensis (*Quodlibeta*, 6, art. 23). It is in this sense, also, that those numerous rules are to be interpreted which say that the Pope has both swords. The earlier doctors make the same assertion, as also does St. Thomas in the second book of the *Sententiae*, as above quoted.

Aye, and there is no doubt that in this way bishops have temporal authority within their bishoprics on the same principle that the Pope has authority in the world. And so they err in speech and in deed, whether princes or magistrates, who strive to prevent bishops from deterring laymen from sin by fines or exile or other temporal punishments. For this is not in excess of their power, provided they do not do it from greed or for gain, but of necessity and for profit in things spiritual. And herein we find a further argument in support of our first conclusion; for if the Pope were lord of the world, a bishop would also be temporal lord in his bishopric, seeing that within his bishopric he also is a vicar of Christ, but this our opponents deny. **Let magistrates and lay princes note this.**

357 6. Fourth conclusion: The Pope has no temporal power over the Indian aborigines or over other unbelievers. This is clear from propositions I and III. For he has no temporal power save such as subserves spiritual matters. But he has no spiritual power over them (I *Corinth.*, ch. 5, v. 12). Therefore he has no temporal power either. **Proposition IV. Proof 1.**

7. The corollary follows that even if the barbarians refuse to recognize any lordship of the Pope, that furnishes no ground for making war on them and seizing their property. This is clear, because he has no such lordship. And it receives manifest confirmation from the fact (as will be asserted below and as our opponents admit), that, even if the barbarians refuse to accept Christ as their **Corollary.** **Confirmation 1.**

Absurdity of the opposite opinion. lord, this does not justify making war on them or doing them any hurt. Now, it is utterly absurd for our opponents to say that, while the barbarians go scatheless for rejecting Christ, they should be bound to accept His vicar under penalty **Confirmation 2.** of war and confiscation of their property, aye, and penal chastisement. And a second confirmation is furnished by the fact that the ground, according to the persons in question, for disallowing compulsion, even if they refuse to accept Christ or His faith, is that it cannot be evidently proved to them by natural reasoning. But the lordship of the Pope admits of this proof still less. Therefore they cannot be compelled to recognize this lordship.

Proof 2, and with authority. Again, although Sylvester discourses at great length on the power of the
Pope, yet, under the word *infideles* (§ 7), he expressly maintains against Hostiensis **358**
that unbelievers cannot be compelled by arms to recognize this lordship and cannot be deprived of their property on this pretext. And Innocent maintains the same in *X*, 3, 34, 8. There is also no doubt that this was the opinion of St. Thomas too (*Secunda Secundae*, qu. 66, art. 8, on obj. 2); Cajetan is express thereon, in his comment on the passage where St. Thomas says that unbelievers cannot be deprived of their property, save only that the subjects of temporal princes can be deprived for reasons known to the law and rendering their subjects **Proof 3.** in general liable to deprivation. Of a truth, Saracens dwelling among Christians have never been deprived of their property on any such pretext or made to **Proof 4.** suffer any harm. Why, if this pretext be enough to justify making war on them, it is as much as to say that they can be deprived by reason of their unbelief. For it is certain that none of the unbelievers recognize this lordship. But there is no doctor even among our opponents who would allow that they can be deprived on the mere ground of unbelief. Therefore the allegation of the doctors in question is utterly sophistical, namely, that if the unbelievers recognize the lordship of the Roman Pontiff, war cannot be made on them, but that it may if they do not recognize it; for none of them does recognize it.

This shows that the title under discussion cannot be set up against the bar- **359**
barians and that Christians have no just cause of war against them either on the ground that the Pope has made a gift of their lands on the footing of absolute lord or that they do not recognize the lordship of the Pope. This is the opinion maintained by Cajetan at considerable length, on *Secunda Secundae*, qu. 66, art. 8, on obj. 2. And the authority of the canonists to the contrary ought not to weigh much, because, as said above, these matters are to be discussed with reference to the divine law, and the majority in numbers and weight hold the contrary view, and among the latter is Joannes Andreae. Our opponents have no text in their favour. And even the weighty authority of the Archbishop of Florence is not to be admitted here, for he followed Augustinus Anconitanus, just as in other places he usually follows the canonists. What has been said demonstrates, then, that at the time of the Spaniards' first voyages to America they took with them no right to occupy the lands of the indigenous population.

Third Title. Accordingly, there is another title which can be set up, namely, by right of discovery; and no other title was originally set up, and it was in virtue of this

title alone that Columbus the Genoan first set sail. And this seems to be an adequate title because those regions which are deserted become, by the law of
360 nations and the natural law, the property of the first occupant (*Inst.*, 2, 1, 12). Therefore, as the Spaniards were the first to discover and occupy the provinces in question, they are in lawful possession thereof, just as if they had discovered some lonely and thitherto uninhabited region.

Not much, however, need be said about this third title of ours, because, as proved above, the barbarians were true owners, both from the public and from the private standpoint. Now the rule of the law of nations is that what belongs to nobody is granted to the first occupant, as is expressly laid down in the aforementioned passage of the *Institutes*. And so, as the object in question was not without an owner, it does not fall under the title which we are discussing. Although, then, this title, when conjoined with another, can produce some effect here (as will be said below), yet in and by itself it gives no support to a seizure of the aborigines any more than if it had been they who had discovered us.

Fourth title discussed.

Its lawfulness proven. Argument 1.

Accordingly, a fourth title is set up, namely, that they refuse to accept the faith of Christ, although it is set before them and although they have been adjured and advised to accept it. This title might seem to be a lawful one for occupying the lands of the barbarians, firstly, on the ground that the obligation of the aborigines to receive the faith of Christ results from the passage: 'Whoso believeth and is baptized shall be saved, but he who believeth not shall be damned.'[1] But damnation is not visited on any one except for a mortal sin, and 'There is no other name given among men whereby we must be saved' (*Acts*,
361 ch. 4). Therefore, as the Pope is the minister of Christ, at least in things spiritual, it would appear that at any rate by the authority of the Pope they can be compelled to receive the faith of Christ, and if they reject the demand to receive it they may be proceeded against under the law of war. Nay, it would seem that princes may do this on their own authority also, seeing that they are God's ministers (*Romans*, ch. 13), and 'revengers [to execute] wrath upon them that do evil'. But those, indeed, do evil who do not accept the faith of Christ. Therefore they can be coerced by princes.

Argument 2.

A second argument is: If the French refused to obey their King, the King of Spain could compel them to obedience. Therefore, if the Indian aborigines refuse to obey God, who is their true and supreme Lord, Christian princes can compel them to obedience; for the cause of God ought not to be in worse condition than the cause of men. And this is confirmed, as Scotus (bk. 4, dist. 4, qu. 9) argues about the baptism of the children of unbelievers, by the fact that persons ought to be compelled to obey a superior lord rather than an inferior lord. If, then, compulsion may be employed to make these aborigines obey their chiefs, much more may it be employed to make them obey Christ and God.

Argument 3. St. Thomas, Secunda Secundae, qu. 10, art. 8.

A third argument is: If the barbarians publicly blasphemed Christ, they could be compelled by war to cease from such blasphemies, as the doctors admit and as is true. For we could take measures of war against them, if they made a

[1] St. Mark, xvi. 16.

mock of the crucifix or in any other way abused Christian practices by way of
insult, as by jesting imitation of the Sacraments of the Church or the like conduct. 362
This is obvious; for if they outraged a Christian sovereign, even one now dead,
we could avenge the outrage; much more, then, if they outrage Christ, who is
the living King of Christians. This is indubitable; for if Christ were alive in the
flesh and pagans wrought an outrage on Him, there is no doubt that we could
avenge the outrage by war. So, therefore, in this case. But unbelief is a greater
sin than blasphemy, for, as St. Thomas asserts and proves (*Secunda Secundae*,
qu. 10, art. 3), unbelief is the gravest of the sins which lie in moral perversity,
because it is directly opposed to faith, while blasphemy is not directly opposed
to faith, but to the confession of faith. Unbelief cuts at the root of turning to
God, that is, at faith, while blasphemy does not. Therefore, seeing that
Christians can proceed by war against unbelievers for their blasphemy of Christ,

Confirmation.

so they can for their unbelief itself. And the contention that blasphemy is not
so great a sin as unbelief is confirmed by the fact that unbelief is, in a Christian,
a capital crime by the civil laws, while blasphemy is not.

Certain propositions in reply. Proposition I.

8. By way of answer let my first proposition be: Before the barbarians heard
anything about Christianity, they did not commit the sin of unbelief by not 363
believing in Christ. This proposition is precisely that of St. Thomas in *Secunda
Secundae*, qu. 10, art. 1, where he says that in those who have not heard of Christ
unbelief does not wear the guise of sin, but rather of punishment, such ignorance
of things divine being a consequence of the sin of our first parent. 'Such un-
believers as these', says he, 'are indeed open to condemnation for other sins, . . .
but not for the sin of unbelief.' Accordingly our Lord says (*St. John*, ch. 15):
'If I had not come and spoken unto them, they had not had sin.' St. Augustine,
in his exposition of this passage, says it refers to the sin of unbelief in Christ.
St. Thomas says the same (*Secunda Secundae*, qu. 10, art. 6, and qu. 34, art. 2, on
obj. 2).

The contrary opinion of Altissiodorensis, and William of Paris, and Gerson, *sc.*, that unbelief is always a sin, quoted.

This proposition is opposed to the teaching of many doctors and especially
to that of Altissiodorensis, 3 p.,[1] on the question, *Utrum fidei possit subesse
falsum*, where he says that ignorance not only of Christ, but of any article of
faith is not invincible ignorance in any one, for if a man does what in him lies,
God will illuminate him either through the doctor that is within him or through
a doctor outside, and so it is always a mortal sin to believe anything contrary
to articles of faith. He takes an illustration from an old woman to whom a bishop
might preach something contrary to an article of faith. And he lays down the 364
general proposition that ignorance of divine law excuseth none. William of
Paris was of the same opinion and supported it by the same kind of argument.
For either, says he, such an one does what in him lies and therefore will receive
illumination, or if he does not this, he is without excuse. And Gerson (*De
spirituali vita animae*, lect. 4) appears to be of the same view. 'Doctors are
unanimous', says he, 'that in matters of the divine law there is no room for
invincible ignorance, seeing that God will always help him who does what in

[1] *Summa aurea sententiarum:* Paris edition (1500), fol. cxxxv, col. 4 at end.

him lies, and He is ready to enlighten the mind as far as will be necessary for salvation and the avoidance of error.' And Hugo de Sancto Victore (bk. 2, pt. 6, ch. 5)[1] says that none is excused by ignorance for breach of the command to receive baptism, for he could have heard and known, had it not been for his own fault, as was the case with Cornelius (*Acts*, ch. 10).

Hugo de S. Victore, of the same opinion.

Adrian gives precision to this doctrine, in his *Quodlibeta*, qu. 4. 'There is', says he, 'a twofold distinction in matters of the divine law. There are some matters to the knowledge of which God does not oblige every one universally, such as the nice problems of the divine law and difficulties with regard to this law and with regard to Holy Scripture and the Commandments; in these matters there may well be a case of invincible ignorance, even if a man does all that in him lies. There are other matters to the knowledge of which God obliges all men generally, such as the articles of faith and the universal commandments
365 of the law; of these it is true, as the doctors assert, that ignorance thereof is not excused. For if any one does what in him lies, he will be illuminated of God through either the doctor that is within him or a doctor from without.'

So also in part Adrian.

Nevertheless, the conclusion above stated is entirely in accord with St. Thomas's doctrine. The proof of it is as follows: Such as have never heard anything, however much they may be sinners in other respects, are under an invincible ignorance; therefore, their ignorance is not sin. The antecedent is evident from the passage (*Romans*, ch. 10): 'How shall they believe in him of whom they have not heard, and how shall they hear without a preacher?' Therefore, if the faith has not been preached to them, their ignorance is invincible, for it was impossible for them to know. And what Paul condemns in unbelievers is not that they have not done what in them lies in order to receive illumination from God, but that they do not believe after they have heard. 'Have they not heard?' says he, 'Yes, verily, their sound went into all the earth.' That is the ground of his condemnation, inasmuch as the Gospel has been preached over all the earth; he would not otherwise condemn them, whatever other sins they might have.

Rejecting the views of these persons, the author proves his own proposition.

This shows that Adrian was also mistaken in another point, with regard to the subject-matter of their ignorance; for in the same note he says, with regard to the subject-matter of morals, that if a man bestows all industry and diligence in getting to know that which behoves him, this is not enough to procure him an excuse for his ignorance, unless by repentance of his sins he specially prepares
366 himself to be illuminated by God. Suppose, then, a man is in doubt about a certain business arrangement and makes inquiry of learned men and tries in other ways to find out the truth and thinks that the thing is lawful; if it really is not lawful and he does it, he is without excuse, if in another respect he is in sin, because he does not do all that in him lies to conquer his ignorance, and although it be admitted that were he to render himself amenable to grace he would not receive illumination, still he is without excuse so long as he does not remove the hindrance in question, that is, his sin. Accordingly, if Peter and John are in

Adrian's mistake about subject-matter of ignorance.

[1] *De Sacramentis Christianae fidei.*

doubt in the same case and business matter and bestow equal human diligence, and each thinks the thing is lawful, but Peter is in grace, while John is in sin, Peter's ignorance is invincible, but John's is vincible, and if they both embark on the business, Peter is excused and John is not. Adrian, I say, makes a mistake here, as I have shown at length in my discussion on *Prima Secundae* on the topic of ignorance. For it would be strange to say that there is no topic of the divine law on which an unbeliever, aye, any one who is in mortal sin, can be invincibly ignorant. Nay, it would follow in the case of the above-named Peter, who was in grace and whose ignorance on some point about usury or simony was invincible, that his ignorance would become vincible merely by his falling into mortal sin, which is absurd.

The author's reasoning against Adrian.

The author's opinion what ignorance is sin, what is not. The author again confirms his proposition.

9. I say accordingly on this point that negligence with regard to the subject- 367
matter is requisite for ignorance, even though it be vincible, to be imputed as, and to be, a sin, as, for example, that the man refused to hear or did not believe what he did hear; and on the other hand I say that for invincible ignorance it is enough that the man bestowed human diligence in trying to learn, even if in other respects he is in mortal sin. And so on this point our judgement is the same concerning one in sin and one in grace, both now and immediately after Christ's coming or after His passion. Adrian could not deny that after our Lord's passion the Jews in India or in Spain were invincibly ignorant of His passion, however much they were in mortal sin; nay, he himself has expressly conceded this in his first *quaestio*, fourth point, on the topic *de observantia legalium.* And it is certain that the Jews who were away from Judaea, whether they were in sin or not, had invincible ignorance about baptism and about the faith of Christ. Just as there 368
could at that time be a case of invincible ignorance on this matter, so there may also be nowadays among those who have not had baptism declared to them.

The mistake of the afore-named authors explained.

But the mistake which the doctors in question make is in thinking that when we postulate invincible ignorance on the subject of baptizm or of the Christian faith it follows at once that a person can be saved without baptism or the Christian faith, which, however, does not follow. For the aborigines to whom no preaching of the faith or Christian religion has come will be damned for mortal sins or for idolatry, but not for the sin of unbelief, as St. Thomas (*Secunda Secundae*, as above) says, namely, that if they do what in them lies, accompanied by a good life according to the law of nature, it is consistent with God's providence and He will illuminate them regarding the name of Christ, but it does not therefore follow that if their life be bad, ignorance or unbelief in baptism and the Christian faith may be imputed to them as a sin.

Proposition II.

10. Second proposition: The Indians in question are not bound, directly the Christian faith is announced to them, to believe it, in such a way that they commit mortal sin by not believing it, merely because it has been declared and announced to them that Christianity is the true religion and that Christ is the Saviour and Redeemer of the world, without miracle or any other proof or persuasion.

Proof.

This proposition is proved by the first: For if before hearing anything of the Christian religion they were excused, they are put under no fresh obligation

by a simple declaration and announcement of this kind, for such announcement is no proof or incentive to belief. Nay, as Cajetan says (on *Secunda Secundae*,
369 qu. 1, art. 4), it would be rash and imprudent for any one to believe anything, especially in matters which concern salvation, unless he knows that this is asserted by a man worthy of credence, a thing which the aboriginal Indians do not know, seeing that they do not know who or what manner of men they are who are announcing the new religion to them. And this is confirmed by what St. Thomas says (*Secunda Secundae*, qu. 1, art. 4, on obj. 2, and art. 5, on obj. 1), namely, that matters of faith are seen and become evident by reason of their credibility. For a believer would not believe unless he saw the things were worthy of belief either because of the evidence of signs or for some other reason of this kind. Therefore, where there are no such signs nor anything else of persuasive force, the aborigines are not bound to believe. And this is confirmed by the consideration that if the Saracens were at the same time to set their creed before them in the same way and without anything more, like the Christians, they would not be bound to believe them, as is certain. Therefore they are not bound to believe the Christians either, when without any moving or persuasive accompaniments they set the faith before them, for they are unable, and are not bound, to guess which of the two is the truer religion, unless a greater weight of probability be apparent on one side. For this would be to believe hastily, which is a mark of levity of heart, as *Ecclesiasticus*, ch. 19, says. Further confirmation is furnished by the passage in *St. John*, ch. 15: 'If I had not wrought signs', &c., 'they would not have had sin.' Therefore, where there are no signs, and nothing to induce belief, there will be no sin.

Confirmation 1. **Confirmation 2.** **Confirmation 3.**

370 11. From this proposition it follows that, if the faith be presented to the Indians in the way named only and they do not receive it, the Spaniards cannot make this a reason for waging war on them or for proceeding against them under the law of war. This is manifest, because they are innocent in this respect and have done no wrong to the Spaniards. And this corollary receives confirmation from the fact that, as St. Thomas lays it down (*Secunda Secundae*, qu. 40, art. 1), for a just war 'there must be a just cause, namely, they who are attacked for some fault must deserve the attack'. Accordingly, St. Augustine says (*Liber 83 Quaestionum*): 'It is involved in the definition of a just war that some wrong is being avenged, as where a people or State is to be punished for neglect to exact amends from its citizens for their wrongdoing or to restore what has been wrongfully taken away.' Where, then, no wrong has previously been committed by the Indians, there is no cause of just war. This is the received opinion of all the doctors, not only of the theologians, but also of the jurists, such as Hostiensis, Innocent, and others. Cajetan (*Secunda Secundae*, qu. 66, art. 8) lays it down clearly and I know of no doctor whose opinion is to the contrary. Therefore this would not be a legitimate title to seize the lands of the aborigines or to despoil the former owners.

Corollary. **Proposition proved from the common opinion of the doctors.**

371 12. Third proposition: If the Indians, after being asked and admonished to hear the peaceful preachers of religion, refused, they would not be excused of

Proposition III.

Proof 1. mortal sin. The proof lies in the supposition that they have very grave errors for which they have no probable or demonstrable reasons. Therefore, if any one admonishes them to hear and deliberate upon religious matters, they are bound at least to hear and to enter into consultation. Further, it is needful for their salvation that they believe in Christ and be baptized (*St. Mark*, last ch.), 'Whoso
Proof 2. believeth', &c. But they cannot believe unless they hear (*Romans*, ch. 10). Therefore they are bound to hear, otherwise if they are not bound to hear, they would, without their own fault, be outside the pale of salvation.

Proposition IV. 13. Fourth proposition: If the Christian faith be put before the aborigines with demonstration, that is, with demonstrable and reasonable arguments, and this be accompanied by an upright life, well-ordered according to the law of nature (an argument which weighs much in confirmation of the truth), and this be done not once only and perfunctorily, but diligently and zealously, the aborigines are bound to receive the faith of Christ under penalty of mortal sin. This is proved by our third proposition, for, if they are bound to hear, they are in consequence bound also to acquiesce in what they hear, if it be reasonable. This is abundantly clear from the passage (*St. Mark*, last ch.): 'Go ye out into all the world, preach the Gospel to every creature; whoso believeth and is baptized shall be **372**
saved, but whoso believeth not shall be damned'; and by the passage (*Acts*, ch. 4): 'No other name is given unto man whereby we can be saved.'

Proposition V. 14. Fifth proposition: It is not sufficiently clear to me that the Christian faith has yet been so put before the aborigines and announced to them that they are bound to believe it or commit fresh sin. I say this because (as appears from my second proposition) they are not bound to believe unless the faith be put before them with persuasive demonstration. Now, I hear of no miracles or signs or religious patterns of life; nay, on the other hand, I hear of many scandals and cruel crimes and acts of impiety. Hence it does not appear that the Christian religion has been preached to them with such sufficient propriety and piety that they are bound to acquiesce in it, although many religious and other ecclesiastics seem both by their lives and example and their diligent preaching to have bestowed sufficient pains and industry in this business, had they not been hindered therein by others who had other matters in their charge.

Proposition VI. 15. Sixth proposition: Although the Christian faith may have been announced to the Indians with adequate demonstration and they have refused to receive it, yet this is not a reason which justifies making war on them and depriving them of
Proof 1. their property. This conclusion is definitely stated by St. Thomas (*Secunda Secundae*, qu. 10, art. 8), where he says that unbelievers who have never received **373**
Proof 2. the faith, like Gentiles and Jews, are in no wise to be compelled to do so. This is the received conclusion of the doctors alike in the canon law and the civil law. The proof lies in the fact that belief is an operation of the will. Now, fear detracts greatly from the voluntary (*Ethics*, bk. 3), and it is a sacrilege to approach under
Proof 3. the influence of servile fear as far as the mysteries and sacraments of Christ. Our conclusion is also proved by the canon *de Judaeis* (can. 5, Dist. 45), which says: 'The holy synod also enjoins concerning the Jews that thenceforth force be not

applied to any one of them to make him believe; "for God has compassion on whom He wills, and whom He wills He hardens."'[1] There is no doubt about the doctrine of the Council of Toledo, that threats and fears should not be employed against the Jews in order to make them receive the faith. And Gregory expressly says the same in the canon *qui sincera* (can. 3, Dist. 45): 'Who with sincerity of purpose', says he, 'desires to bring into the perfect faith those who are outside the Christian religion should labour in a manner that will attract and not with severity; . . . for whosoever does otherwise and under cover of the latter would turn them from their accustomed worship and ritual is demonstrably furthering his own end thereby and not God's end.

Our proposition receives further proof from the use and custom of the Church. For never have Christian Emperors, who had as advisors the most holy and wise Pontiffs, made war on unbelievers for their refusal to accept the Christian **Proof 4.**
374 religion. Further, war is no argument for the truth of the Christian faith. Therefore the Indians cannot be induced by war to believe, but rather to feign belief and reception of the Christian faith, which is monstrous and a sacrilege. And although Scotus (Bk. 4, dist. 4, last qu.) calls it a religious act for princes to compel unbelievers by threats and fears to receive the faith, yet he seems to mean this to apply only to unbelievers who in other respects are subjects of Christian princes (with whom we will deal later on). Now, the Indians are not such subjects. Hence, I think that Scotus does not make this assertion applicable to their case. It is clear, then, that the title which we are now discussing is not adequate and lawful for the seizure of the lands of the aborigines. **Proof 5.** **The opinion of Scotus hereon set forth.**

Another, and a fifth, title is seriously put forward, namely, the sins of these Indian aborigines. For it is alleged that, though their unbelief or their rejection of the Christian faith is not a good reason for making war on them, yet they may be attacked for other mortal sins which (so it is said) they have in numbers, and those very heinous. A distinction is here drawn with regard to mortal sins, it being asserted that there are some sins, which are not against the law of nature,
375 but only against positive divine law, and for these the aborigines cannot be attacked in war, while there are other sins against nature, such as cannibalism, and promiscuous intercourse with mother or sisters and with males, and for these they can be attacked in war and so compelled to desist therefrom. The principle in each case is that, in the case of sins which are against positive law, it cannot be clearly shown to the Indians that they are doing wrong, whereas in the case of the sins which are against the law of nature, it can be shown to them that they are offending God, and they may consequently be prevented from continuing to offend Him. Further they can be compelled to keep the law which they themselves profess. Now, this law is the law of nature. Therefore. This is the opinion of the Archbishop of Florence (pt. 3, tit. 22, ch. 5, § 8), following Augustinus Anconitanus, and of Sylvester (under the word *Papa*, § 7); and it is the opinion of Innocent in *X*, 3, 34, 8, where he expressly says: 'I hold that if the Gentiles who have no other law than the law of nature break that law, they can be punished by the **The fifth title discussed.** **Statement and explanation of the opinion of the Archbishop, Augustinus of Ancona, Sylvester,**

[1] Romans, ix. 18.

and Innocent that this is a lawful title.

Pope. This is shown by the case of the men of Sodom, who were punished by God (*Genesis*, ch. 19). Now, the judgements of God are examples unto us, and so I do not see why the Pope, who is the vicar of Christ, cannot do this.' This is what Innocent said. And on the same principle the Indians can be punished by Christian princes under the authority of the Pope.

The author's answer.

16. I, however, assert the following proposition: Christian princes cannot, even by the authorization of the Pope, restrain the Indians from sins against the

Proof 1.

law of nature or punish them because of those sins. My first proof is that the 376
writers in question build on a false hypothesis, namely, that the Pope has juris-

Proof 2.

diction over the Indian aborigines, as said above. My second proof is as follows: They mean to justify such coercion either universally for sins against the law of nature, such as theft, fornication, and adultery, or particularly for sins against nature, such as those which St. Thomas deals with (*Secunda Secundae*, qu. 154, arts. 11, 12), the phrase 'sin against nature' being employed not only of what is contrary to the law of nature, but also of what is against the natural order and is called uncleanness in II *Corinthians*, ch. 12, according to the commentators, such as intercourse with boys and with animals or intercourse of woman with woman, whereon see *Romans*, ch. 1. Now, if they limit themselves to the second meaning, they are open to the argument that homicide is just as grave a sin, and even a graver sin, and, therefore, it is clear that, if it is lawful in the case of the sins of the kind named, therefore it is lawful also in the case of homicide. Similarly, blasphemy is a sin as grave and so the same is clear; therefore. If, however, they are to be understood in the first sense, that is, as speaking of all sin against the law of nature, the argument against them is that the coercion in question is not lawful for fornication; therefore not for the other sins which are contrary to the law of nature. The antecedent is clear from I *Corinthians*, ch. 5: 'I wrote to you in an epistle not to company with fornicators', and besides 'If any brother among you is called a fornicator or an idolater', &c.; and lower down: 'For what have I to do to judge them also that are without?' Whereon St. Thomas says: 'The prelates 377
have received power over those only who have submitted themselves to the faith.' Hence it clearly appears that St. Paul declares it not his business to pronounce judgement on unbelievers and fornicators and idolaters. So also it is not every sin against the law of nature that can be clearly shown to be such, at any rate to every one. Further, this is as much as to say that the aborigines may be warred into subjection because of their unbelief, for they are all idolaters. Further, the Pope cannot make war on Christians on the ground of their being fornicators or thieves or, indeed, because they are sodomites; nor can he on that ground confiscate their land and give it to other princes; were that so, there would be daily changes of

Confirmation.

kingdoms, seeing that there are many sinners in every realm. And this is confirmed by the consideration that these sins are more heinous in Christians, who are aware

Proof 3.

that they are sins, than in barbarians, who have not that knowledge. Further, it would be a strange thing that the Pope, who cannot make laws for unbelievers, can yet sit in judgement and visit punishment upon them.

Proof 4.

A further and convincing proof is the following: The aborigines in question

are either bound to submit to the punishment awarded to the sins in question or they are not. If they are not bound, then the Pope cannot award such punishment. If they are bound, then they are bound to recognize the Pope as lord and
378 lawgiver. Therefore, if they refuse such recognition, this in itself furnishes a ground for making war on them, which, however, the writers in question deny, as said above. And it would indeed be strange that the barbarians could with impunity deny the authority and jurisdiction of the Pope, and yet that they should be bound to submit to his award. Further, they who are not Christians cannot be subjected to the judgement of the Pope, for the Pope has no other right to condemn or punish them than as vicar of Christ. But, the writers in question admit—both Innocent and Augustinus of Ancona, and the Archbishop and Sylvester, too—that they cannot be punished because they do not receive Christ. Therefore not because they do not receive the judgement of the Pope, for the latter presupposes the former.

Proof 5.

Refutation common to this and the just preceding title.

1.

The insufficiency alike of this present title and of the preceding one, is shown by the fact that, even in the Old Testament, where much was done by force of arms, the people of Israel never seized the land of unbelievers either because they were unbelievers or idolaters or because they were guilty of other sins against nature (and there were people guilty of many such sins, in that they were idolaters and committed many other sins against nature, as by sacrificing their sons and daughters to devils), but because of either a special gift from God or because their enemies had hindered their passage or had attacked them. Further, what is it that

2.

the writers in question call a profession of the law of nature? If it is mere know-
379 ledge, they do not know it all; if it is a mere willingness to observe the law of nature, then the retort is that they are also willing to observe the whole divine law; for, if they knew that the law of Christ was divine, they would be willing to observe it. Therefore, they make no more a profession of the law of nature than they make of the law of Christ. Further, we certainly possess clearer proofs

3.

whereby to demonstrate that the law of Christ is from God and is true than to demonstrate that fornication is wrong or that other things which are also forbidden by natural law are to be shunned.[1] Therefore, if the Indians can be compelled to observe the law of nature because it admits of proof, they can, therefore, be compelled to observe the Gospel law.

Sixth title set out.

There remains another, a sixth title, which is put forward, namely, by voluntary choice. For on the arrival of the Spaniards we find them declaring to the aborigines how the King of Spain has sent them for their good and admonishing them to receive and accept him as lord and king; and the aborigines replied that they were content to do so. Now, 'there is nothing so natural as that the intent of an owner to transfer his property to another should have effect given to it' (*Inst.*, 2, 1, 40). I, however, assert the proposition that this title, too, is insufficient. This appears, in the first place, because fear and ignorance, which vitiate every choice, ought to be absent. But they were markedly operative in the cases of choice and acceptance under consideration, for the Indians did not know what

The author's answer. Proof 1.

[1] Otherwise to be blamed.

they were doing; nay, they may not have understood what the Spaniards were 380
Proof 2. seeking. Further, we find the Spaniards seeking it in armed array from an un-
Proof 3. warlike and timid crowd. Further, inasmuch as the aborigines, as said above, had
real lords and princes, the populace could not procure new lords without other
reasonable cause, this being to the hurt of their former lords. Further, on the
other hand, these lords themselves could not appoint a new prince without the
assent of the populace. Seeing, then, that in such cases of choice and acceptance
as these there are not present all the requisite elements of a valid choice, the title
under review is utterly inadequate and unlawful for seizing and retaining the
provinces in question.

Seventh title. There is a seventh title which can be set up, namely, by special grant from
God. For some (I know not who) assert that the Lord by His especial judgement
condemned all the barbarians in question to perdition because of their abomina-
tions and delivered them into the hands of the Spaniards, just as of old He delivered
The author's refutation. 1. the Canaanites into the hands of the Jews. I am loath to dispute hereon at any
length, for it would be hazardous to give credence to one who asserts a prophecy
against the common law and against the rules of Scripture, unless his doctrine
were confirmed by miracles. Now, no such are adduced by prophets of this type.
2. Further, even assuming that it is true that the Lord had determined to bring the 381
barbarians to perdition, it would not follow, therefore, that he who wrought their
ruin would be blameless, any more than the Kings of Babylon who led their army
against Jerusalem and carried away the children of Israel into captivity were
blameless, although in actual fact all of this was by the especial providence of God,
as had often been foretold to them. Nor was Jeroboam right in drawing Israel
away from Rehoboam, although this was done by God's design, as the Lord had
3. also threatened by his prophet. And, would that, apart from the sin of unbelief,
there might be no greater sins in morals among certain Christians than there are
4. among those barbarians! It is also written (I *St. John*, ch. 4): 'Believe not every
spirit, but try the spirits whether they be of God'; and as St. Thomas says (*Prima
Secundae*, qu. 68), 'Gifts are given by the Holy Spirit for the perfecting of virtues'.
Accordingly, where faith or authority or providence shows what ought to be done,
recourse should not be had to gifts.

Let this suffice about false and inadequate titles to seize the lands of the
The author excuses himself. Indians. But it is to be noted that I have seen nothing written on this question
and have never been present at any discussion or council on this matter. Hence it
may be that others may found a title and base the justice of this business and over- 382
lordship on some of the passages cited and not lack reason in so doing. I, however,
have up to now been unable to form any other opinion than what I have written.
And so, if there be no other titles than those which I have discussed, it would
certainly be of ill omen for the safety of our princes, or rather of those who are
charged with the discovery of these matters; for princes follow advice given by
others, being unable to examine into these matters for themselves. 'What is a man
advantaged', so saith the Lord, 'if he gain the whole world and lose himself, or be
cast away?' (*St. Matthew*, ch. 16; *St. Mark*, ch. 8; *St. Luke*, ch. 9.)

SUMMARY OF THE THIRD SECTION

On the lawful titles whereby the aborigines of America could have come into the power of Spain

1. How the aborigines might have come into the power of the Spaniards on the ground of natural society and fellowship.
2. The Spaniards have a right to travel to the lands of the Indians and to sojourn there so
383 long as they do no harm, and they cannot be prevented by the Indians.
3. The Spaniards may carry on trade among the Indian aborigines, so long as they do no harm to their own country, by importing the goods which the aborigines lack, &c., and taking away gold and silver and other articles in which the Indians abound; and the princes of the Indians cannot prevent their subjects from trading with the Spaniards, &c.
4. The Indians cannot prevent the Spaniards from a communication and participation in those things which they treat as common alike to natives and to strangers.
5. Any children born to Spanish parents domiciled in those parts who wish to become citizens thereof cannot be excluded from citizenship or from the advantages enjoyed by other citizens.
6. What course ought to be adopted if the aborigines desire to prevent the Spaniards trading with them, &c.
7. If the Spaniards, after resort to all moderate measures, cannot attain security among the aborigines or Indians save by seizing their cities and reducing them to subjection, whether they can lawfully do this.

384 8. When and in what case the Spaniards can resort to severe measures against the Indians, treating them as faithless foes, and employ all the rights of war against them and take away their property and even reduce them to captivity, aye, and depose their former lords also and set up new lords.
9. Whether the Indians could have come under the sway of the Spaniards, in the interest of the spread of Christianity. Christians have a right to preach and publish the Gospel in the lands of barbarians.
10. The Pope could entrust to the Spaniards alone the task of converting the Indian aborigines and could forbid to all others not only preaching, but trade too, if the propagation of Christianity would thus be furthered.
11. The Indians are not to be warred into subjection or despoiled of their property, if they give the Spaniards unhindered freedom to preach the Gospel, and this whether they accept the faith or not.
12. How the aborigines who hinder the spread of the Gospel, whether it be their lords or the populace, may be coerced by the Spaniards, so long as no scandal is caused. And what is to be said of those who, while admitting preaching, prevent conver-
385 sion, either by killing or punishing or terrorizing those who have been converted to Christianity?
13. How the Indians might have come under the sway of the Spaniards by the fact that, when they had been converted and become Christians, their princes desired to bring them back to idolatry by force or by fear, and so they were taken into the protection and guardianship of the Spaniards.
14. The Indians might have come under the sway of the Spaniards by the fact that, after

the conversion of a large part of them to Christianity, the Pope, either with or without a request on their part, might on reasonable grounds have given them a Christian prince, such as the King of Spain, and driven out their infidel lords.

15. Whether the Indians could have come under the sway of the Spaniards because of the tyranny of their lords or because of tyrannical laws which injured innocent folk.
16. The Indian aborigines could have come under the sway of the Spaniards through true and voluntary choice.
17. The Indians might have come under the sway of the Spaniards by a title of alliance and friendship.
18. Whether the Spaniards could have reduced the Indians into their power, if it were certainly clear that they were of defective intelligence.

I will now speak of the lawful and adequate titles whereby the Indians might 386
The first lawful title. Proposition I. have come under the sway of the Spaniards. 1. The first title to be named is that of natural society and fellowship. And hereon let my first conclusion be: 2. The Spaniards have a right to travel into the lands in question and to sojourn there, provided they do no harm to the natives, and the natives may not prevent them.

Proof 1. Proof of this may in the first place be derived from the law of nations (*jus gentium*), which either is natural law or is derived from natural law (*Inst.*, 1, 2, 1): 'What natural reason has established among all nations is called the *jus gentium*.' For, congruently herewith, it is reckoned among all nations inhumane to treat visitors and foreigners badly without some special cause, while, on the other hand, it is humane and correct to treat visitors well; but the case would be different, if the foreigners were to misbehave when visiting other nations.

Proof 2. Secondly, it was permissible from the beginning of the world (when everything was in common) for any one to set forth and travel wheresoever he would. Now this was not taken away by the division of property, for it was never the intention of peoples to destroy by that division the reciprocity and common user[1] which prevailed among men, and indeed in the days of Noah it would have been inhumane to do so.

Proof 3. Thirdly, everything is lawful which is not prohibited or which is not injurious
or hurtful to others in some other way. But (so we suppose) the travel of the 387
Spaniards does no injury or harm to the natives. Therefore it is lawful.

Proof 4. Fourthly, it would not be lawful for the French to prevent the Spanish from travelling or even from living in France, or vice versa, provided this in no way enured to their hurt and the visitors did no injury. Therefore it is not lawful for the Indians.

Proof 5. Further, fifthly, banishment is one of the capital forms of punishment. Therefore it is unlawful to banish strangers who have committed no fault.

Proof 6. Further, sixthly, to keep certain people out of the city or province as being enemies, or to expel them when already there, are acts of war. Inasmuch, then, as the Indians are not making a just war on the Spaniards (it being assumed that the Spaniards are doing no harm), it is not lawful for them to keep the Spaniards away from their territory.

[1] [The Latin text has *invicem communicationem*. *Ed.*]

Further, seventhly, there is the Poet's verse, Proof 7.

> Quod genus hoc hominum ? quaeve hunc tam barbara morem
> Permittit patria ? hospitio prohibemur arenae.

[What race of men is this ? or what country is barbarous enough to allow this usage ? We are driven off from the hospitality of its shore.]

Also, eighthly, 'Every animal loveth its kind' (*Ecclesiasticus*, ch. 17). There- Proof 8.
fore, it appears that friendship among men exists by natural law and it is against nature to shun the society of harmless folk.

Also, ninthly, there is the passage (*St. Matthew*, ch. 25): 'I was a stranger and Proof 9.
ye took me not in.' Hence, as the reception of strangers seems to be by natural
388 law, that judgement of Christ will be pronounced with universal application.

Tenthly, 'by natural law running water and the sea are common to all, so are Proof 10.
rivers and harbours, and by the law of nations ships from all parts may be moored there' (*Inst.*, 2, 1); and on the same principle they are public things. Therefore it is not lawful to keep any one from them. Hence it follows that the aborigines would be doing a wrong to the Spaniards, if they were to keep them from their territories.

Also, eleventhly, these very persons admit all other barbarians from all parts. Proof 11.
Therefore, they would be doing a wrong, if they were not to admit the Spaniards.

Also, twelfthly, if it were not lawful for the Spaniards to travel among them, Proof 12.
this would be either by natural law or by divine law or by human law. Now, it is certainly lawful by natural and by divine law. And if there were any human law which without any cause took away rights conferred by natural and divine law, it would be inhumane and unreasonable and consequently would not have the force of law.

Thirteenthly, either the Spaniards are subjects of the Indians or they are not. Proof 13.
If they are not, then the Indians cannot keep them away. If they are, then the Indians ought to treat them well.

Also, fourteenthly, the Spaniards are the neighbours of the barbarians, as Proof 14.
appears from the Gospel parable of the Samaritan (*St. Luke*, ch. 10). But they are bound to love their neighbours as themselves (*St. Matthew*, ch. 22). Therefore they may not keep them away from their country without cause: 'When it is said
389 "Love thy neighbour", it is clear that every man is our neighbour' (St. Augustine's *De doctrina Christiana*).

3. Second proposition: The Spaniards may lawfully carry on trade among the Proposition II.
native Indians, so long as they do no harm to their country, as, for instance, by importing thither wares which the natives lack and by exporting thence either gold or silver or other wares of which the natives have abundance. Neither may the native princes hinder their subjects from carrying on trade with the Spanish; nor, on the other hand, may the princes of Spain prevent commerce with the natives. This is proved by means of my first proposition.

Firstly, because it is an apparent rule of the *jus gentium* that foreigners may Proof 1.
carry on trade, provided they do no hurt to citizens.

Proof 2. Also, secondly, a similar proof lies in the fact that this is permitted by the divine law. Therefore a law prohibiting it would undoubtedly not be reasonable.

Proof 3. Also, thirdly, the sovereign of the Indians is bound by the law of nature to love the Spaniards. Therefore the Indians may not causelessly prevent the Spaniards from making their profit where this can be done without injury to themselves.

Proof 4. A fourth reason is that such conduct would be against the proverb: 'Thou shalt not do to another what thou wouldest not wish done to thyself.'

Proof 5. And, in sum, it is certain that the aborigines can no more keep off the Spaniards from trade than Christians can keep off other Christians. Now, it is clear that if the Spaniards kept off the French from trade with the Spaniards, and this not for the good of Spain, but in order to prevent the French from sharing in **390**
some advantage, that practice would offend against righteousness and charity. If, then, there can be no just legal ordinance to this effect, it also cannot be accomplished in actual fact (for the injustice of a law consists solely in the execution of the law). And, as is said in *Dig.*, 1, 1, 3, 'Nature has established a bond of relationship between all men', and so it is contrary to natural law for one man to dissociate himself from another without good reason. 'Man,' says Ovid, 'is not a wolf to his fellow man, but a man.'

Proposition III. 4. Third proposition: If there are among the Indians any things which are treated as common both to citizens and to strangers, the Indians may not prevent the Spaniards from a communication and participation in them. If, for example, other foreigners are allowed to dig for gold in the land of the community or in rivers, or to fish for pearls in the sea or in a river, the natives cannot prevent the Spaniards from doing this, but they have the same right to do it as others have,
Proof 1. so long as the citizens and indigenous population are not hurt thereby. This is proved by my first and second propositions. For if the Spaniards may travel and trade among them, they may consequently make use of the laws and advantages enjoyed by all foreigners.

Proof 2. Secondly, inasmuch as things that belong to nobody are acquired by the first occupant according to the law of nations (*Inst.*, 2, 1, 12), it follows that if there be in the earth gold or in the sea pearls or in a river anything else which is not appro- **391**
priated by the law of nations those will vest in the first occupant, just as the fish in the sea do. And, indeed, there are many things in this connexion which issue from the law of nations, which, because it has a sufficient derivation from natural law, is clearly capable of conferring rights and creating obligations. And even if we grant that it is not always derived from natural law, yet there exists clearly enough a consensus of the greater part of the whole world, especially in behalf of the common good of all. For if after the early days of the creation of the world or its recovery from the flood the majority of mankind decided that ambassadors should everywhere be reckoned inviolable and that the sea should be common and that prisoners of war should be made slaves, and if this, namely, that strangers should not be driven out, were deemed a desirable principle, it would certainly have the force of law, even though the rest of mankind objected thereto.

5. Fourth proposition: If children of any Spaniard be born there and they wish to acquire citizenship, it seems they cannot be barred either from citizenship or from the advantages enjoyed by other citizens—I refer to the case where the parents had their domicile there. The proof of this is furnished by the rule of the law of nations, that he is to be called and is a citizen who is born within the State (*Cod.*, 7, 62, 11). And the confirmation lies in the fact that, as man is a civil animal, whoever is born in any one State is not a citizen of another State. Therefore, if he were not a citizen of the State referred to, he would not be a citizen of any State, to the prejudice of his rights under both natural law and the law of
392 nations. Aye, and if there be any persons who wish to acquire a domicile in some State of the Indians, as by marriage or in virtue of any other fact whereby other foreigners are wont to become citizens, they cannot be impeded any more than others, and consequently they enjoy the privileges of citizens just as others do, provided they also submit to the burdens to which others submit. And the passages wherein hospitality is commended are to the same effect (I *St. Peter*, ch. 4): 'Use hospitality one to another'; and (I *Timothy*, ch. 3, about a bishop): 'A bishop must be given to hospitality.' Hence, on the other hand, refusal to receive strangers and foreigners is wrong in itself.

Proposition IV. **Proof.** **Confirmation.** **Corollary.**

6. Fifth proposition: If the Indian natives wish to prevent the Spaniards from enjoying any of their above-named rights under the law of nations, for instance, trade or other above-named matter, the Spaniards ought in the first place to use reason and persuasion in order to remove scandal and ought to show in all possible methods that they do not come to the hurt of the natives, but wish to sojourn as peaceful guests and to travel without doing the natives any harm; and they ought to show this not only by word, but also by reason, according to the saying, 'It behoveth the prudent to make trial of everything by words first'. But if, after this recourse to reason, the barbarians decline to agree and propose to use force, the Spaniards can defend themselves and do all that consists with their own safety, it being lawful to repel force by force. And not only so, but, if safety cannot otherwise be had, they may build fortresses and defensive works, and, if they have
393 sustained a wrong, they may follow it up with war on the authorization of their sovereign and may avail themselves of the other rights of war. The proof hereof lies in the fact that warding-off and avenging a wrong make a good cause of war, as said above, following St. Thomas (*Secunda Secundae*, qu. 40). But when the Indians deny the Spaniards their rights under the law of nations they do them a wrong. Therefore, if it be necessary, in order to preserve their right, that they should go to war, they may lawfully do so.

Proposition V. **Proof.**

It is, however, to be noted that the natives being timid by nature and in other respects dull and stupid, however much the Spaniards may desire to remove their fears and reassure them with regard to peaceful dealings with each other, they may very excusably continue afraid at the sight of men strange in garb and armed and much more powerful than themselves. And therefore, if, under the influence of these fears, they unite their efforts to drive out the Spaniards or even to slay them, the Spaniards might, indeed, defend themselves but within the

Note!

limits of permissible self-protection, and it would not be right for them to enforce against the natives any of the other rights of war (as, for instance, after winning the victory and obtaining safety, to slay them or despoil them of their goods or seize their cities), because on our hypothesis the natives are innocent and are justified in feeling afraid. Accordingly, the Spaniards ought to defend themselves, but so far as possible with the least damage to the natives, the war being a purely defensive one.

Sometimes a war is a just war on both sides. There is no inconsistency, indeed, in holding the war to be a just war on both sides, seeing that on one side there is right and on the other side there is invincible **394**
ignorance. For instance, just as the French hold the province of Burgundy with demonstrable ignorance, in the belief that it belongs to them, while our Emperor's right to it is certain, and he may make war to regain it, just as the French may defend it, so it may also befall in the case of the Indians—a point deserving careful attention. For the rights of war which may be invoked against men who are really guilty and lawless differ from those which may be invoked against the innocent and ignorant, just as the scandal of the Pharisees is to be avoided in a different way from that of the self-distrustful and weak.

Proposition VI. 7. Sixth proposition: If after recourse to all other measures, the Spaniards are unable to obtain safety as regards the native Indians, save by seizing their cities and reducing them to subjection, they may lawfully proceed to these extremities. **Proof.** The proof lies in the fact that 'peace and safety are the end and aim of war', as St. Augustine says, writing to Boniface. And since it is now lawful for the Spaniards, as has been said, to wage defensive war or even if necessary offensive war, therefore, everything necessary to secure the end and aim of war, namely, the obtaining of safety and peace, is lawful.

Proposition VII. 8. Seventh proposition: If, after the Spaniards have used all diligence, both in deed and in word, to show that nothing will come from them to interfere with the peace and well-being of the aborigines, the latter nevertheless persist in their hostility and do their best to destroy the Spaniards, then they can make war on **395**
the Indians, no longer as on innocent folk, but as against forsworn enemies, and may enforce against them all the rights of war, despoiling them of their goods, reducing them to captivity, deposing their former lords and setting up new ones, yet withal with observance of proportion as regards the nature of the circum-
Proof 1. stances and of the wrongs done to them. This conclusion is sufficiently apparent from the fact that, if it be lawful to declare the war, it is consequently lawful to pursue the rights of war. And it is confirmed by the consideration that the aborigines ought not to hold a better position merely because they are unbelievers. But all the things enumerated would be lawful against Christians, when once
Proof 2. a just war has arisen. Therefore they are lawful against the aborigines, too. Also, it is a universal rule of the law of nations that whatever is captured in war becomes the property of the conqueror, as is laid down in *Dig.*, 49, 15, 28 and 24, and in *Decretum*, pt. 1, dist. 1, can. 9, and more expressly in *Inst.*, 2, 1, 17, where it is said that 'by the law of nations whatever we take from the enemy becomes ours at once, to such an extent that even men may be brought into slavery to us'.

Further (as the doctors say on the topic of war), a prince who has on hand a just war is *ipso jure* the judge of his enemies and can inflict a legal punishment on them, condemning them according to the scale of their wrongdoing. Everything said above receives confirmation from the fact that ambassadors are by the law of nations inviolable and the Spaniards are the ambassadors of Christian peoples. Therefore, the native Indians are bound to give them, at least, a friendly hearing and not to repel them. This, then, is the first title which the Spaniards might have for seizing the provinces and sovereignty of the natives, provided the seizure be without guile or fraud and they do not look for imaginary causes of war. For if the natives allow the Spaniards to traffic peaceably among them, the Spaniards could not allege in this connexion any just cause for seizing their goods any more than the goods of Christians.

Proof 3. **Confirmation.** **396**

9. Another possible title is by way of propagation of Christianity. In this connexion let my first proposition be: Christians have a right to preach and declare the Gospel in barbarian lands. This proposition is manifest from the passage: 'Preach the Gospel to every creature', &c.,[1] and also, 'The word of the Lord is not bound' (II *Timothy*, ch. 2). Secondly, our proposition is clear from what has been already said, for if the Spaniards have a right to travel and trade among the Indians, they can teach the truth to those willing to hear them, especially as regards matters pertaining to salvation and happiness, much more than as regards matters pertaining to any human subject of instruction. Thirdly, because the natives would otherwise be outside the pale of salvation, if Christians were not allowed to go to them carrying the Gospel message. Fourthly, because brotherly correction is required by the law of nature, just as brotherly love is. Since, then, the Indians are all not only in sin, but outside the pale of salvation, therefore, it concerns Christians to correct and direct them; nay, it seems that they are bound to do so. Fifthly and lastly, because they are our neighbours, as said above: 'Now the Lord has laid a command on every one concerning his neighbour' (*Ecclesiasticus*, ch. 17). Therefore it concerns Christians to instruct those who are ignorant of these supremely vital matters.

Second lawful title. **Proposition I.** **Proof 1.** **Proof 2.** **Proof 3.** **397** **Proof 4.** **Proof 5.**

10. Second proposition: Although this is a task common and permitted to all, yet the Pope might entrust it to the Spaniards and forbid it to all others. The proof is in the fact that, although (as said above) the Pope is not temporal lord, yet he has power in matters temporal when this would subserve matters spiritual. Therefore, as it is the Pope's concern to bestow especial care on the propagation of the Gospel over the whole world, he can entrust it to the Spaniards to the exclusion of all others, if the sovereigns of Spain could render more effective help in the spread of the Gospel in those parts; and not only could the Pope forbid others to preach, but also to trade there, if this would further the propagation of Christianity, for he can order temporal matters in the manner which is most helpful to spiritual matters. And if in this case that is how spiritual matters would be best helped, it consequently falls within the authority and power of the supreme Pontiff. But it seems that in this case this is the course most conducive to spiritual

Proposition II. **Proof 1.** **398**

[1] St. Mark, xvi. 15.

welfare, because, if there was to be an indiscriminate inrush of Christians from other parts to the part in question, they might easily hinder one another and develop quarrels, to the banishment of tranquillity and the disturbance of the concerns of the faith and of the conversion of the natives. Further, inasmuch as it was the sovereigns of Spain who were the first to patronize and pay for the navigation of the intermediate ocean, and as they then had the good fortune to discover the New World, it is just that this travel should be forbidden to others and that the Spaniards should enjoy alone the fruits of their discovery. For, just as in the interests of the preservation of the peace among princes and of the spread of religion the Pope could make such a distribution of the land of the Saracens among Christian princes as would prevent one from crossing over the lands of another, so also for the good of religion he could appoint princes, especially where there were aforetime no Christian princes.

Proof 2.

Proposition III.

11. Third proposition: If the Indians allow the Spaniards freely and without hindrance to preach the Gospel, then whether they do or do not receive the faith, this furnishes no lawful ground for making war on them and seizing in any other way their lands. This has been proved above,[1] where we confuted the fourth alleged title, and it is self-evident, seeing that there cannot be a just war where no **399**
wrong has previously been done (*Secunda Secundae*, qu. 40, art. 1).

Proposition IV.

12. Fourth proposition: If the Indians—whether it be their lords or the populace—prevent the Spaniards from freely preaching the Gospel, the Spaniards, after first reasoning with them in order to remove scandal, may preach it despite their unwillingness and devote themselves to the conversion of the people in question, and if need be they may then accept or even make war, until they succeed in obtaining facilities and safety for preaching the Gospel. And the same pronouncement must be made in the case where they allow preaching, but hinder conversion either by killing or otherwise punishing those who have been converted to Christ or by deterring others by threats and fears. This is clear, because herein the Indians would be doing an injury to the Spaniards (as appears from what has already been said) and these would have a just cause of war. A second reason is that an obstacle would thereby be put in the way of the welfare of the Indians themselves such as their princes have no right to put there. Therefore, in favour of those who are oppressed and suffer wrong, the Spaniards can make war, especially as such vitally important interests are at stake. This proposition demonstrates that, if there is no other way to carry on the work of religion, this furnishes the Spaniards with another justification for seizing the lands and territory of the natives and for setting up new lords there and putting down the old lords and **400**
doing in right of war everything which it is permitted in other just wars, but always with a regard for moderation and proportion, so as to go no further than necessity demands, preferring to abstain from what they lawfully might do rather than transgress due limits, and with an intent directed more to the welfare of the aborigines than to their own gain.

Proof 1.

Proof 2.

Corollary.

Note!

Careful attention must, however, be paid to what St. Paul says (I *Corinthians*,

[1] In the immediately preceding section.

ch. 6): 'All things are lawful unto me, but not all things are expedient.' So everything said above must be taken as spoken absolutely. For it may be that these wars and massacres and spoliations will hinder rather than procure and further the conversion of the Indians. Accordingly, the prime consideration is that no obstacle be placed in the way of the Gospel, and if any such be so placed, this method of evangelization must be abandoned and another one sought for. What we have been showing is what is lawful in itself. I personally have no doubt that the Spaniards were bound to employ force and arms in order to continue their work there, but I fear measures were adopted in excess of what is allowed by human and divine law. The title under consideration might, then, be a second lawful title whereby the Indians might fall into the power of Spain. But regard must ever be had to what has just been said lest what in itself is lawful be made in the circumstances wrong, for goodness springs from the one complete[1] cause, but
401 badness from individual defects, according to Aristotle (*Ethics*, bk. 3) and Dionysius (*De divinis nominibus*, ch. 4).

13. Another title there may be, which is derived from the foregoing, namely: If any of the native converts to Christianity be subjected to force or fear by their princes in order to make them return to idolatry, this would justify the Spaniards, should other methods fail, in making war and in compelling the barbarians by force to stop such misconduct, and in employing the rights of war against such as continue obstinate, and consequently at times in deposing rulers as in other just wars. This can be reckoned a third just title, a title based not only on religion, but on human friendship and alliance, inasmuch as the native converts to Christianity have become friends and allies of Christians and we are under an obligation to do 'good unto all men, especially unto such as are of the household of faith' (*Galatians*, ch. 6).

Third lawful title.

Proof.

14. Another possible title is the following: Suppose a large part of the Indians were converted to Christianity, and this whether it were done lawfully or unlawfully (as by means of threats or fear or other improper procedure), so long as they really were Christians, the Pope might for a reasonable cause, either with or without a request from them, give them a Christian sovereign and depose their other unbelieving rulers. The proof hereof is in the fact that, if this were ex-
402 pedient in order to preserve Christianity because of a fear that under unbelieving rulers converts would apostatize, that is, would lapse from the faith, or that their rulers would seize the opportunity to harass them, the Pope can change rulers in the interests of the faith. And confirmation is found in the fact that, as the doctors assert and as St. Thomas expressly says (*Secunda Secundae*, qu. 10. art. 10), the Church could free all Christian slaves who are in bondage to unbelievers even if that bondage was in other respects lawful. Innocent expressly declares this, in the above-mentioned *X*, 3, 34, 8. Therefore much more will he be able to free other Christians who have been reduced to bondage but not as stringently as

Fourth lawful title.

Proof.

Confirmation 1.

[1] The reference to Aristotle cannot be traced with certainty; but the text follows Dionysius closely. He wrote, literally translated, 'The good is from the one and complete (μία καὶ ὅλη) cause but the bad from many and partial defects'. *Tr.*

Confirmation 2. slaves. Confirmation hereof is also to be found in the fact that a wife is as much bound to her husband as a bondsman is to his lord, and even more so, seeing that marriage is a tie of the divine law and bondage is not. But in the interests of the faith a believing wife is freed from an unbelieving husband, if he persecutes her for her religion, as appears from I *Corinthians*, ch. 7, and *X*, 4, 19, 7. Aye, the custom now is that by the very fact of one spouse being converted to the faith he or she is freed from the other who is an unbeliever. Therefore also the Church, in the interests of the faith and to avoid risks, may free all Christians from obedience and subjection to unbelieving lords, provided this be done without scandal. So we justify this fourth legal title.

Fifth lawful title. 15. Another possible title is founded either on the tyranny of those who bear **403**
rule among the aborigines of America or on the tyrannical laws which work wrong to innocent folk there, such as that which allows the sacrifice of innocent people or the killing in other ways of uncondemned people for cannibalistic purposes. I assert also that without the Pope's authority the Spaniards can stop all such nefarious usage and ritual among the aborigines, being entitled to rescue innocent
Proof 1. people from an unjust death. This is proved by the fact that 'God has laid a charge on every individual concerning his neighbour',[1] and they all are our neighbours. Therefore, any one may defend them from such tyrannical and oppressive
Proof 2. acts, and it is especially the business of princes to do so. A further proof is given by *Proverbs*, ch. 24: 'Deliver them that are drawn unto death, and forbear not to free those that are being dragged to destruction.' This passage is not to be taken as applying only when victims are actually being dragged to death, but the natives can also be compelled to abstain from such ritual. And if they refuse, it is a good ground for making war on them and proceeding against them under the law of war, and if such sacrilegious rites cannot otherwise be stopped, for changing their rulers and creating a new sovereignty over them. In this connexion we find the opinion of Innocent and the Archbishop to be sound, namely, that punishment can be inflicted for sins against nature. And it is immaterial that all the Indians assent to rules and sacrifices of this kind and do not wish the Spaniards to champion **404**
them, for herein they are not of such legal independence as to be able to consign themselves or their children to death. So we may find a fifth lawful title here.

Sixth lawful title. 16. Another possible title is by true and voluntary choice, as if the Indians, aware alike of the prudent administration and the humanity of the Spaniards, were of their own motion, both rulers and ruled, to accept the King of Spain as
Proof. their sovereign. This could be done and would be a lawful title, by the law natural too, seeing that a State can appoint any one it will to be its lord, and herefor the consent of all is not necessary, but the consent of the majority suffices. For, as I have argued elsewhere, in matters touching the good of the State the decisions of the majority bind even when the rest are of a contrary mind; otherwise naught could be done for the welfare of the State, it being difficult to get all of the same way of thinking. Accordingly, if the majority of any city or province were Christians and they, in the interests of the faith and for the common weal, would have

[1] Ecclesiasticus, xvii. 12.

a prince who was a Christian, I think that they could elect him even against the wishes of the others and even if it meant the repudiation of other unbelieving rulers, and I assert that they could choose a prince not only for themselves, but for
405 the whole State, just as the Franks for the good of their State changed their sovereigns and, deposing Childeric, put Pepin, the father of Charlemagne, in his place, a change which was approved by Pope Zacharias. This, then, can be put forward as a sixth title.

Seventh lawful title.

17. Another title may be found in the cause of allies and friends. For as the Indians themselves sometimes wage lawful wars with one another and the side which has suffered a wrong has the right to make war, they might summon the Spaniards to help and share the rewards of victory with them. This is what the Tlaxcaltecs are said to have done against the Mexicans, the former arranging with the Spaniards to help them to overcome the latter and to receive whatever could fall to them under the law of war. **Proof.** For there is no doubt, as Cajetan also asserts (*Secunda Secundae*, qu. 40, art. 1), that the cause of allies and friends is a just cause of war, a State being quite properly able, as against foreign wrongdoers, to summon foreigners to punish its enemies. **Confirmation.** And this is confirmed by the fact that this was a method very much in vogue among the Romans for the extension of their Empire; that is, they brought aid to their allies and friends and so making a just war came, by right of war, into possession of fresh provinces. Yet the Roman
406 Empire is approved by St. Augustine (*De civitate Dei*, bk. 5) and by St. Thomas (*Opusculum* 21) as a lawful one. And Sylvester reckoned Constantine the Great as Emperor, as St. Ambrose did Theodosius. Now, there does not seem any other juridic title whereby the Romans came into possession of the world, save in right of war, and the most especial cause of their wars was the defence and protection of their friends. In just the same way Abraham championed the cause of the King of Salem and of other kings who had struck a treaty with him, and he fought against four kings of that region, though they had done him personally no wrong (*Genesis*, ch. 14). This is the seventh and the last title whereby the Indians and their lands could have come or might come into the possession and lordship of Spain.

Eighth title is doubtful.

18. There is another title which can indeed not be asserted, but brought up for discussion, and some think it a lawful one. I dare not affirm it at all, nor do I entirely condemn it. It is this: Although the aborigines in question are (as has been said above) not wholly unintelligent, yet they are little short of that condition, and so are unfit to found or administer a lawful State up to the standard required by human and civil claims. Accordingly they have no proper laws nor
407 magistrates, and are not even capable of controlling their family affairs; they are without any literature or arts, not only the liberal arts, but the mechanical arts also; they have no careful agriculture and no artisans; and they lack many other conveniences, yea necessaries, of human life. **Probable principle.** It might, therefore, be maintained that in their own interests the sovereigns of Spain might undertake the administration of their country, providing them with prefects and governors for their towns, and might even give them new lords, so long as this was clearly for their

benefit. I say there would be some force in this contention; for if they were all wanting in intelligence, there is no doubt that this would not only be a permissible, but also a highly proper, course to take; nay, our sovereigns would be bound to take it, just as if the natives were infants. The same principle seems to apply here to them as to people of defective intelligence; and indeed they are no whit or little better than such so far as self-government is concerned, or even than the wild beasts, for their food is not more pleasant and hardly better than that of beasts. Therefore their governance should in the same way be entrusted to people of intelligence. There is clear confirmation hereof, for if by some accident of fortune all their adults were to perish and there were to be left boys and youths in enjoyment, indeed, of a certain amount of reason, but of tender years and under the age of puberty, our sovereigns would certainly be justified in taking charge of them and governing them so long as they were in that condition. **408** Now, this being admitted, it appears undeniable that the same could be done in the case of their barbarian parents, if they be supposed to be of that dullness of mind which is attributed to them by those who have been among them and which is reported to be more marked among them than even among the boys and youths of other nations. And surely this might be founded on the precept of charity, they being our neighbours and we being bound to look after their welfare. Let this, however, as I have already said, be put forward without dogmatism and subject also to the limitation that any such interposition be for the welfare and in the interests of the Indians and not merely for the profit of the Spaniards. For this is the respect in which all the danger to soul and salvation lies. And herein some help might be gotten from the consideration, referred to above, that some are by nature slaves, for all the barbarians in question are of that type and so they may in part be governed as slaves are.

Confirmation.

Objection. Now, it seems to follow from all this discussion that, if there be no force in any of the titles which have been put forward, so that the native Indians neither gave cause for just war nor wished for Spanish rulers, &c., all the travel to, and trade with, those parts should be stopped, to the great loss of the Spaniards and also to the grave hurt of the royal treasury (a thing intolerable). My first answer to this is: There would be no obligation to stop trade, for, as already said, there **409** are many commodities of which the natives have a superfluity and which the Spaniards could acquire by barter. Also there are many commodities which the natives treat as ownerless or as common to all who like to take them, and the Portuguese, to their own great profit, have a big trade with similar people without reducing them to subjection. Secondly, there would probably be no diminution in the amount of the royalties, for a tax might quite fairly be placed on the gold and silver which would be brought away from the Indians, as much as a fifth or even more, according to quality, and it would be well-earned, inasmuch as the maritime discovery was made by our sovereign and it is under his authority that trade is carried on in safety. Thirdly, it is evident, now that there are already so many native converts, that it would be neither expedient nor lawful for our sovereign to wash his hands entirely of the administration of the lands in question.

First answer.

Second answer.

Third answer.

APPENDIX B

THE SECOND RELECTIO

OF THE REVEREND FATHER, BROTHER FRANCISCUS DE VICTORIA

ON THE INDIANS, OR ON THE LAW OF WAR MADE BY THE SPANIARDS ON THE BARBARIANS

A
TRANSLATION BY
JOHN PAWLEY BATE

410

SUMMARY

1. Christians may serve in war and make war.
2. In whose hands lies the authority to make or declare war?
3. Any one, even a private person, can accept and wage a defensive war.
4. Whether one who is attacked by a robber or a foe may strike back the assailant, if able to escape by flight.
5. Every commonwealth has authority to declare and make war.
6. A prince has the same authority to declare and make war as a State has.
7. What a State is and who is properly styled a prince.
8. Whether several States or princes, when they have one common lord or prince, may make war of themselves without the authority of the superior lord.

411 9. Petty rulers or princes, who are not at the head of a complete State, but are parts of another State, cannot undertake or make war. And what about cities?

10. What can be a reason or cause of just war? Proof that diversity of religion is not a cause of just war.
11. Extension of an Empire is not a just cause of war.
12. The personal glory, or other advantage, of a prince is not a just cause of war.
13. Wrong done is the sole and only just cause for making war.
14. Not every kind and degree of wrong suffices for making war.
15. When just war exists, everything is lawful which is necessary for the defence of the public good.
16. In just war it is lawful to retake all things that have been lost, or a part thereof.
17. In just war it is lawful to make good, out of the goods of the enemy, all the cost of the war and all damages wrongfully caused by the enemy.
18. After property has been recaptured from an enemy in just war, what the prince may then do.
19. It is lawful for a prince, after gaining the victory in a just war and after retaking property, and even after the establishment of peace and security, to avenge the
412 wrongs done to him by the enemy and to take measures against the enemy and punish them for these wrongs.
20. In order that a war be called just, it is not always enough that the prince believes he has a just cause.
21. The justice of a war must be most thoroughly and carefully examined.
22. Whether subjects are bound to examine the cause of a war; and how, if a subject is convinced of the injustice of a war, he may not serve in it, even though his sovereign commands.
23. If subjects are conscientiously of opinion that a war is unjust, they may not serve in it, whether their opinion be wrong or right.
24. Senators, petty rulers, and, in general, all who, either on summons or coming of their own accord, are admitted to the public council or the king's council, are bound to examine the cause of an unjust war.
25. Who are not bound to examine the causes of war, but may lawfully serve in it in reliance on the good faith of their betters.
26. When ignorance of the injustice of a war would not excuse subjects who serve in it.
27. What is to be done, when there is doubt about the justice of a war; and how if one

prince be in lawful possession, so long as the doubt remains another may not try to turn him out by war and armed force. **413**

28. If there be a city or province concerning which it is doubtful whether it has a lawful possessor, especially where there is a vacancy owing to the death of the lawful lord, &c.—what is to be done in such a case.
29. How a person who is doubtful about his own title, even if he be in peaceable possession, is bound to make careful examination of his case, if perchance he can arrive at certainty either in his own favour or in favour of another.
30. After the examination of a case, so long as a doubt reasonably persists, a lawful possessor is not bound to quit possession, but may lawfully retain it.
31. In a doubtful case, subjects may follow their prince to battle not only in a defensive, but also in an offensive war.
32. Whether a war can be just on both sides, and how, apart from ignorance, this cannot happen.
33. Whether a prince or a subject, who in ignorance has prosecuted an unjust war, is bound to make restitution, if afterwards he becomes convinced of its injustice.
34. Whether it is lawful in war to kill the innocent.
35. Slaughter of the innocent is never lawful in itself and intentionally.
36. Whether it is lawful to kill women and children in a war against the Turks; and what, among Christians, about farmers, civilians, foreigners, strangers, and clergy. **414**
37. The incidental killing of the innocent, even with knowledge, is sometimes lawful, sometimes not.
38. Whether it is lawful to kill the innocent from whom danger in the future is apprehended.
39. Whether it is lawful to despoil the innocent among the enemy, and what things may be taken.
40. If war can be adequately conducted without despoiling farmers or other innocent folk, it seems unlawful to despoil them; and what about foreigners and strangers on enemy territory?
41. How, if the enemy refuse to restore the things which they have wrongfully taken away, and the injured party cannot recoup himself in any other way, he can seek satisfaction where he will, whether from the guilty or the innocent.
42. Whether the innocent and children, who are admittedly not to be killed, may at least be led into captivity and slavery.
43. Whether hostages, taken from the enemy in time of truce or on the termination of a war, may be put to death, if the enemy break faith and do not abide by what has been agreed on.
44. Whether it is lawful in war to kill all the guilty. **415**
45. It is lawful to kill without distinction all who resist in the actual heat of battle either in the storming or the defence of the city, and as long as affairs are in peril.
46. It is lawful to kill the guilty, even after victory has been won and danger has already been removed.
47. It is not always lawful to kill all the guilty, merely in order to avenge a wrong.
48. At times it is both lawful and expedient to kill all the guilty, especially in a war against unbelievers. And what in a war against Christians?
49. Whether it is lawful to kill captives and those who have surrendered, assuming them to have been guilty also.
50. Whether things captured in a just war belong to the captor and seizor; and how these

things vest in the seizor up to a sufficient satisfaction for what has been wrongfully taken away and for expenses.

51. How all movables, by the law of nations, vest in the seizor, even though their value more than compensates the wrong done.

416 52. Whether it is lawful to leave a city to the soldiery by way of booty; and how this is not unlawful, but at times even necessary.

53. Soldiers may not loot or burn without authority; otherwise they are bound to make restitution.

54. It is lawful to seize and hold the lands and fortresses and towns of the enemy, so far as this is necessary by way of compensation for damages done.

55. It is lawful to seize and hold an enemy fortress or city by way of obtaining security and avoiding danger or as a means of defence and in order to take away from the enemy an opportunity to do harm, &c.

56. It is lawful to deprive the enemy of part of his territory on account of the wrong he has done and by way of punishment, that is, revenge; and how on this ground a fortress or town may be seized, so long as due limits are observed.

57. Whether it is lawful to impose the payment of tribute on the conquered enemy.

58. Whether it is lawful to depose the princes of the enemy and put new ones over them or retain the sovereignty for oneself; and how it is not lawful to do this indiscriminately and for every cause of just war whatsoever.

59. When the princes of the enemy may lawfully be deposed, is shown.

60. The canons or rules of belligerency are described.

417 Inasmuch as the seizure and occupation of those lands of the barbarians whom we style Indians can best, it seems, be defended under the law of war, I propose to supplement the foregoing discussion of the titles, some just and some unjust, which the Spaniards may allege for their hold on the lands in question, by a short discussion of the law of war, so as to give more completeness to that *Relectio*. As, however, the other claims on my time will not allow me to deal with all the points which arise out of this topic, the scope which I can give my pen must be proportionate, not to the amplitude and dignity of the theme, but to the shortness of the time at my disposal. And so I will merely note the main propositions of this topic, together with very brief proofs, and will abstain from touching on the many doubtful matters which might otherwise be brought into this discussion. I will deal with four principal questions. First, Whether Christians may make war at all; secondly, Where does the authority to declare or wage war repose; thirdly, What may and ought to furnish causes of just war; fourthly, What and how extensive measures may be taken in a just war against the enemy?

Four principal questions to be discussed.

The first principal question.

The argument on one side of the question.

As regards the first question, war might seem altogether prohibited to Christians,
418 for there is the prohibition of self-defence in the passage (*Romans*, ch. 12), 'Dearly beloved, avenge not yourselves, but give place unto wrath', and our Lord says in the Gospel (*St. Matthew*, ch. 5), 'Whosoever shall smite thee on the right cheek, turn to him the other also' and 'I say unto you not to resist evil', and (*St. Matthew*, ch. 26), 'All they that take the sword shall perish by the sword'. And it is no sufficient answer to say that all these matters are not of precept, but of counsel, for it would be a grave enough impropriety if every war undertaken by

Christians was contrary to our Lord's advice. The opinion of all the doctors is to the contrary and so is the received usage of the Church.

Luther's opinion.

In development of this question be it noted that, although Catholics are fairly in accord on the matter, yet Luther, who left naught uncontaminated, denies that Christians may take up arms even against the Turks, and he relies not only on the above-cited texts of Scripture, but also on the fact that if the Turks attack Christendom it is the will of God, which may not be resisted. Herein, however, he had not as much success as in his other dogmas in imposing on the Germans, who are born soldiers. Tertullian too, seems not averse from this opinion, for in his *De corona militis* he discusses 'whether military service is at all right for a Christian', and in the issue he inclines to hold that military service is 419
forbidden to a Christian, who, says he, 'may not even go to law'.

Tertullian, too, inclines to same opinion.

The author gives his opinion in a single proposition.
(a) Especially book 22.
(b) Quest. 31.
(c) Serm. 19.
Proof 1.
(d) It is in the Sermones De verbis Domini.
(e) Letter 205 to Count Boniface.
(f) Passage seems to be in bk. 22 Contra Faustum, ch. 74.
Proof 2.

1. Passing over outside opinions, however, let my answer to the question be given in the single proposition: Christians may serve in war and make war. This is the conclusion of St. Augustine in the many passages where he thoroughly considers the question, such as: (*a*) in his *Contra Faustum*, (*b*) in his *Liber 83 Quaestionum*, (*c*) in his *De verbis Domini*, in his *Contra Secundinum Manichaeum*, (*d*) in his sermon on the Centurion's son, and (*e*) in his Letter to Boniface. And, as St. Augustine shows, this is proved by the words of John the Baptist to the soldiers (*St. Luke*, ch. 3), 'Do violence to no man, neither accuse any falsely'. 'But,' says St. Augustine, (*f*) 'if Christian doctrine condemned war altogether, those looking for counsels of salvation in the Gospel would be told to throw away their arms and give up soldiering altogether; but what is said to them is, "Do violence to no man and be content with your wages."'

Secondly, there is proof in the reason of the thing (*Secunda Secundae*, qu. 40, art. 1). To draw the sword and use arms against internal wrongdoers and seditious citizens is lawful according to *Romans*, ch. 13, 'He beareth not the sword in vain, for he is the minister of God, a revenger of wrath upon him that doeth evil.' Therefore it is lawful also to use the sword and arms against external enemies. Princes, accordingly, are told in the *Psalms*,[1] 'Deliver the poor and needy, rid 420
them out of the hand of the wicked'.

Proof 3.

Thirdly, this was also allowable by the law of nature, as appears from the case of Abraham, who fought against four kings (*Genesis*, ch. 14), and also by the written law, as appears from the cases of David and the Maccabees. But the Gospel law forbids nothing which is allowed by natural law, as is well shown by St. Thomas (*Prima Secundae*, qu. 107, last art.), and that is why it is called the law of liberty (*St. James*, ch. 1 and 2). Therefore, what was lawful under natural law and in the written law is no less lawful under the Gospel law.

Proof 4 and onward deals with offensive war.

Fourthly, since there can be no doubt that in a defensive war force may be employed to repel force (*Dig.*, 1, 1, 3), this is also proved with regard to an offensive war, that is, a war where we are not only defending ourselves or seeking to repossess ourselves of property, but also where we are trying to avenge ourselves for some wrong done to us. This, I say, is proved by the authority of St. Augustine

[1] Ps. lxxxi in Vulgate. In A.V. Ps .lxxxii.

(*Liber 83 Quaestionum*) in a passage also found in can. *dominus*, C. 23, qu. 2, 'Those wars are described as just wars which are waged in order to avenge a wrong done, as where punishment has to be meted out to a city or state because it has itself neglected to exact punishment for an offence committed by its citizens or subjects or to return what has been wrongfully taken away.' **This is an extract from Quaestiones super Josue, qu. 10.**

A fifth proof with regard to an offensive war is that even a defensive war could not be waged satisfactorily, were no vengeance taken on enemies who have done or tried to do a wrong. For they would only be emboldened to make a **421** second attack, if the fear of retribution did not keep them from wrongdoing. **Proof 5.**

A sixth proof is that, as St. Augustine says (*De verbo Domini* and *Ad Bonifacium*), the end and aim of war is the peace and security of the State. But there can be no security in the State unless enemies are made to desist from wrong by the fear of war, for the situation with regard to war would be glaringly unfair, if all that a State could do when enemies attack it unjustly was to ward off the attack and if they could not follow this up by further steps. **Proof 6. Passages already cited.**

A seventh proof comes from the end and aim and good of the whole world. For there would be no condition of happiness for the world, nay, its condition would be one of utter misery, if oppressors and robbers and plunderers could with impunity commit their crimes and oppress the good and innocent, and these latter could not in turn retaliate on them. **Proof 7.**

My eighth and last proof is one which in morals carries the utmost weight, namely, the authority and example of good and holy men. Such men have not only defended their country and their own property in defensive wars, but have also in offensive wars sought reparation for wrongs done or attempted by their enemies, as appears from the case of Jonathan and Simon (I *Maccabees*, ch. 9), who avenged the death of their brother John on the sons of Jambri. And in the Christian Church we have the conspicuous examples of Constantine the Great **422** and Theodosius the Elder and other renowned and most Christian Emperors, who made many wars of both kinds, although their councils included bishops of great sanctity and learning. **Proof 8.**

2. Second question: In whose hands lies the authority to declare and to make war? **Second principal question.**

3. Herein let my first proposition be: Any one, even a private person, can accept and wage a defensive war. This is shown by the fact that force may be repelled by force (*Dig.*, as above). Hence any one can make this kind of war, without authority from any one else, for the defence not only of his person, but also of his property and goods. **Proposition I.**

4. A doubt, however, arises in connexion with this proposition, namely, whether one who is attacked by a robber or enemy can strike his assailant back if escape by flight is possible. The Archbishop, indeed, says, No; this being in excess of the limits of blameless self-defence, since every one is bound in the exercise of self-defence to do as little harm as possible to his assailant. If, then, resistance would involve the death of or grievous bodily harm to the assailant, but escape by flight is a possible thing, the latter course ought to be adopted. Panormitanus, **Doubt. The Archbishop's opinion.**

Panormitanus' opinion.

however, writing on *X*, 2, 13, 12, draws a distinction. If, says he, the victim would be seriously disgraced by flight, he is not bound to fly, but may repel the wrong by striking back, whereas if flight would not smirch his reputation or honour, as when **423**
a monk or rustic is attacked by a noble and powerful man, he is bound to fly instead.

Bartolus' opinion.

Bartolus, however, commenting on *Dig.*, 48, 19, 1, and 48, 8, 9, holds without distinguishing that self-defence is lawful and that there is no obligation to fly, the putting to flight being itself a wrong (*Dig.*, 47, 10, 15). If, then, armed resistance is permissible in defence of property, as appears from *X*, 2, 13, 12, and from c. 6, tit. 11, bk. 5 in vi, much more is it permissible in order to protect the body from hurt, such hurt being more serious than wrong to property (*Dig.*, 48, 19, 10).

The author adopts Bartolus' opinion.

This opinion can be safely held and with possibility of demonstration, especially as the civil law admits as much, as in *Dig.*, 48, 8, 9. Now, no one sins who acts under warrant of the law, inasmuch as the law affords justification in the forum of conscience. Accordingly, even if natural law does not allow killing in defence of property, this is rendered lawful by the civil law and is available, so long as no scandal is caused, not only to laymen, but to clerics and professed persons.

Proposition II. Distinction between a private person and a State.

5. Second proposition: Every State has authority to declare and to make war. In course of proof of this be it noted that the difference herein between a private person and a State is that a private person is entitled, as said above, to defend himself and what belongs to him, but has no right to avenge a wrong done to him, **424**
nay, not even to recapt property that has been seized from him if time has been allowed to go by since the seizure. But defence can only be resorted to at the very moment of the danger, or, as the jurists say, *in continenti*, and so when the necessity of defence has passed there is an end to the lawfulness of war.

The author's opinion.

In my view, however, one who has been contumeliously assaulted can immediately strike back, even if the assaulter was not proposing to make a further attack, for in the avoidance of shame and disgrace one who (for example) has had his ears boxed might immediately use his sword, not for the purpose of vengeance, but, as has been said, in order to avoid infamy and disgrace. But a State is within its rights not only in defending itself, but also in avenging itself and its subjects and in redressing wrongs. This is proved by what Aristotle says in the third book of his *Politics*, namely, that a State ought to be sufficient unto itself. But it cannot adequately protect the public weal and the position of the State if it cannot avenge a wrong and take measures against its enemies, for wrongdoers would become readier and bolder for wrongdoing, if they could do wrong with impunity. It is, therefore, imperative for the due ordering of human affairs that this authority be allowed to States.

Proposition III. Herein the prince has the same authority as the State.

6. Third proposition: A prince has the same authority in this respect as the **425**
State has. This is the opinion of St. Augustine (*Contra Faustum*): 'The natural order, best adapted to secure the peace of mankind, requires that the authority to make war and the advisability of it should be in the hands of the sovereign prince.' Reason supports this, for the prince only holds his position by the election of the State. Therefore he is its representative and wields its authority; aye, and where there are already lawful princes in a State, all authority is in their hands and without them nothing of a public nature can be done either in war or in peace.

7. Now, the whole difficulty is in the questions: What is a State, and who can properly be called a sovereign prince? I will briefly reply to them by saying that a State is properly called a perfect community. But the essence of the difficulty is in saying what a perfect community is. By way of solution be it noted that a thing is called perfect when it is a completed whole, for that is imperfect in which there is something wanting, and, on the other hand, that is perfect from which nothing is wanting. A perfect State or community, therefore, is one which is complete in itself, that is, which is not a part of another community, but has its own laws and its own council and its own magistrates, such as is the Kingdom of Castile and Aragon and the Republic of Venice and other the like. For there is
426 no obstacle to many principalities and perfect States being under one prince. Such a State, then, or the prince thereof, has authority to declare war, and no one else.

Doubt.

8. Here, however, a doubt may well arise whether, when a number of States of this kind or a number of princes have one common lord or prince, they can make war of themselves and without the authorization of their superior lord.

The author's answer.

My answer is that they can do so undoubtedly, just as the kings who are subordinate to the Emperor can make war on one another without waiting for the Emperor's authorization, for (as has been said) a State ought to be self-sufficient, and this it would not be, if it had not the faculty in question.

Corollary.

9. Hence it follows and is plain that other petty rulers and princes, who are not at the head of a perfect State, but are parts of another State, cannot begin to carry on a war. Such is the Duke of Alva or the Count of Benevento, for they are parts of the Kingdom of Castile and consequently have not perfect States. As, however, these matters are for a great part governed by the law of nations or by human law, Custom can give power and authority to make war. And so if any State or prince has obtained by ancient custom the right to make war of itself or
427 himself, this authority cannot be gainsaid, even if in other respects the State be not a perfect one. So, also, necessity can confer this license and authority. For if within one and the same realm one city should take up arms against another, or one of the dukes against another duke, and the king should neglect or should lack courage to exact redress for the wrongs that have been done, the aggrieved city or duke may not only resort to self-defence, but may also commence war and take measures against the enemy and even kill the wrongdoers, there being no other adequate means of self-defence. For the enemy would not cease from outrage, if the victims thereof were content merely with self-defence. On this principle a private person also may begin an attack on his foe, if there is no other way of safeguarding himself from wrong. This is enough on the present question.

Third principal question.

10. Third question: What may be a reason and cause of just war? It is particularly necessary to ask this in connexion with the case of the Indian aborigines, which is now before us.

Proposition I.

Here my first proposition is: Difference of religion is not a cause of just war. This was shown at length in the preceding *Relectio*, when we demolished the fourth alleged title for taking possession of the Indians, namely, their refusal to accept Christianity. And it is the opinion of St. Thomas (*Secunda*

Secundae, qu. 66, art. 8), and the common opinion of the doctors—indeed, I know of no one of the opposite way of thinking.

Proposition II. 11. Second proposition: Extension of empire is not a just cause of war. This **428** is too well known to need proof, for otherwise each of the two belligerents might have an equally just cause and so both would be innocent. This in its turn would involve the consequence that it would not be lawful to kill them and so imply a contradiction, because it would be a just war.

Proposition III. 12. Third proposition: Neither the personal glory of the prince nor any other advantage to him is a just cause of war. This, too, is notorious. For a prince ought to subordinate both peace and war to the common weal of his State and not spend public revenues in quest of his own glory or gain, much less expose his subjects to Proof 1. danger on that account. Herein, indeed, is the difference between a lawful king and a tyrant, that the latter directs his government towards his individual profit and advantage, but a king to the public welfare, as Aristotle says (*Politics*, bk. 4, Proof 2. ch. 10). Also, the prince derives his authority from the State. Therefore he ought to use it for the good of the State. Also, laws ought 'not to be enacted for the private good of any individual, but in the common interest of all the citizens', as is ruled in can. 2, Dist. 4, a citation from Isidore. Therefore the rules relating to war ought to be for the common good of all and not for the private good of the Proof 3. prince. Again, this is the difference between freemen and slaves, as Aristotle says (*Politics*, bk. 1, ch. 3 and 4), that masters exploit slaves for their own good and not **429** for the good of the slaves, while freemen do not exist in the interest of others, but in their own interest. And so, were a prince to misuse his subjects by compelling them to go soldiering and to contribute money for his campaigns, not for the public good, but for his own private gain, this would be to make slaves of them.

Proposition IV. 13. Fourth proposition: There is a single and only just cause for commencing a war, namely, a wrong received. The proof of this rests in the first place on the authority of St. Augustine (*Liber 83 Quaestionum*,* 'Those wars are described as just wars', &c., as above), and it is the conclusion arrived at by St. Thomas (*Secunda Secundae*, qu. 40, art. 1) and the opinion of all the doctors. Also, an Proof 1. Proof 2. offensive war is for the purpose of avenging a wrong and of taking measures against an enemy, as said above. But there can be no vengeance where there is no pre- Proof 3. ceding fault and wrong. Therefore. Also, a prince has no greater authority over foreigners than over his own subjects. But he may not draw his sword against his own subjects, unless they have done some wrong. Therefore not against foreigners either. This is confirmed by the text already cited from St. Paul (*Romans*, ch. 13) about a prince: 'He beareth not the sword in vain: for he is the minister of God, a revenger to execute wrath upon him that doeth evil.' Hence it is clear that we may not turn our sword against those who do us no harm, the killing of the innocent being forbidden by natural law. I omit here any injunctions inconsistent **430** herewith which God has given in special cases, for He is the Lord of life and death and it is within His competence to vary His dispositions.

*Rather in Quaestiones super Josue, qu. 10.

Proposition V. 14. Fifth proposition: Not every kind and degree of wrong can suffice for commencing a war. The proof of this is that not even upon one's own fellow-countrymen is it lawful for every offence to exact atrocious punishments, such as death or banishment or confiscation of property. As, then, the evils inflicted in war are all of a severe and atrocious character, such as slaughter and fire and devastation, it is not lawful for slight wrongs to pursue the authors of the wrongs with war, seeing that the degree of the punishment ought to correspond to the measure of the offence (*Deuteronomy*, ch. 25).

15. The fourth question is about the law of war, namely, what kind and degree of stress is lawful in a just war. Here let my first proposition be: In war everything is lawful which the defence of the common weal requires. This is notorious, for the end and aim of war is the defence and preservation of the State. Also, a private person may do this in self-defence, as has been proved. Therefore much more may a State and a prince. **Fourth principal question. Proposition I.**

16. Second proposition: It is permissible to recapt everything that has been lost and any part of the same. This is too notorious to need proof. For war is begun or undertaken with this object. **Proposition II.**

431 17. Third proposition: It is lawful to make good out of enemy property the expenses of the war and all damages wrongfully caused by the enemy. This is clear, for the enemy who has done the wrong is bound to give all this redress. Therefore the prince can claim it all and exact it all by war. Also, as before, there is the argument that, when no other way lies open, a private creditor can seize the amount of his debt from the debtor. Also, if there were any competent judge over the two belligerents, he would have to condemn the unjust aggressors and authors of wrong, not only to make restitution of what they have carried off, but also to make good the expenses of the war to the other side, and also all damages. But a prince who is carrying on a just war is as it were his own judge in matters touching the war, as we shall forthwith show. Therefore he can enforce all these claims upon his enemy. **Proposition III. Proof 1. Proof 2. Proof 3.**

18. Fourth proposition: Not only are the things just named allowable, but a prince may go even further in a just war and do whatever is necessary in order to obtain peace and security from the enemy; for example, destroy an enemy's fortress and even build one on enemy soil, if this be necessary in order to avert a dangerous attack of the enemy. This is proved by the fact that, as said above, the end and aim of war is peace and security. Therefore a belligerent may do every-
432 thing requisite to obtain peace and security. Further, tranquillity and peace are reckoned among the desirable things of mankind and so the utmost material prosperity does not produce a state of happiness if there be no security there. Therefore it is lawful to employ all appropriate measures against enemies who are plundering and disturbing the tranquillity of the State. Also, all measures of this kind may be taken against internal foes, that is, against bad citizens. Therefore they are lawful against external foes. The antecedent is clear, for if one citizen does a wrong to a fellow citizen, the magistrate not only compels the wrongdoer to make amends to the injured party, but, if the former is a source of fear to the latter, he is compelled to give bond or quit the city, so as to remove the danger of which he is the cause. This shows that even when victory has been won and **Proposition IV. Proof 1. Proof 2. Proof 3. Corollary.**

redress obtained, the enemy may be made to give hostages, ships, arms, and other things, when this is genuinely necessary for keeping the enemy in his duty and preventing him from becoming dangerous again.

Proposition V.

Power which, in the author's opinion, princes have not only over their own subjects, but also over foreigners by the law of nations, and by natural law too.

19. Fifth proposition: Not only is all this permissible, but even after victory has been won and redress obtained and peace and safety been secured, it is lawful to avenge the wrong received from the enemy and to take measures against him and exact punishment from him for the wrongs he has done. In proof of this be it observed that princes have authority not only over their own subjects, but also over foreigners, so far as to prevent them from committing wrongs, and this is by **433**
the law of nations and by the authority of the whole world. Nay, it seems to be by natural law also, seeing that otherwise society could not hold together unless there was somewhere a power and authority to deter wrongdoers and prevent them from injuring the good and innocent. Now, everything needed for the government and preservation of society exists by natural law, and in no other way can we show that a State has by natural law authority to inflict pains and penalties on its citizens who are dangerous to it. But if a State can do this to its own citizens, society at large no doubt can do it to all wicked and dangerous folk, and this can only be through the instrumentality of princes. It is, therefore, certain that princes can punish enemies who have done a wrong to their State and that after a war has been duly and justly undertaken the enemy are just as much within the jurisdiction of the prince who undertakes it as if he were their proper judge. Confirmation hereof is furnished by the fact that in reality peace and tranquillity, which are the end and aim of war, cannot be had unless evils and damages be visited on the enemy in order to deter them from the like conduct in the future. All this is also proved and confirmed by the authority and examples of good men. For, as said above, the Maccabees made war not only to recover the things which they had lost, but also to avenge their wrongs. And some most Christian princes **434**
and most religious Emperors have done the same thing. Moreover, shame and disgrace are not wiped away from a State merely by its rout of its enemies, but also by its visiting severe punishment and castigation on them. Now, among the things which a prince is bound to defend and preserve for his State are its honour and authority.

Doubt I suggested by what has been said.

Proposition I.

20. Many doubts are suggested by what has just been said. In the first place, there is a doubtful point in connexion with the justice of a war, whether it be enough for a just war that the prince believes himself to have a just cause. On this point let my first proposition be: This belief is not always enough. And for proof I rely, first, on the fact that in some matters of less moment it is not enough either for a prince or for private persons to believe that they are acting justly. This is notorious, for their error may be vincible and deliberate, and the opinion of the individual is not enough to render an act good, but it must come up to the standard of a wise man's judgement, as appears from *Ethics*, bk. 2. Also the result would otherwise be that very many wars would be just on both sides, for although it is not a common occurrence for princes to wage war in bad faith, they nearly always think theirs is a just cause. In this way all belligerents would be innocent

and it would not be lawful to kill them. Also, were it otherwise, even Turks and
435 Saracens might wage just wars against Christians, for they think they are thus rendering God service.

Proposition II. 21. Second proposition: It is essential for a just war that an exceedingly careful examination be made of the justice and causes of the war and that the reasons of those who on grounds of equity oppose it be listened to. For (as the comic poet **Terence.** says) 'A wise man must make trial of everything by words before resorting to force', and he ought to consult the good and wise and those who speak with freedom and without anger or bitterness or greed, seeing that (as Sallust says) 'where these vices **Sallust.** hold sway, truth is not easily distinguished'. This is self-evident. For truth and justice in moral questions are hard of attainment and so any careless treatment of them easily leads to error, an error which will be inexcusable, especially in a concern of great moment, involving danger and calamity to many, and they our neighbours, too, whom we are bound to love as ourselves.

Doubt II. 22. Second doubt: Whether subjects are bound to examine the cause of a war or whether they may serve in the war without any careful scrutiny thereof, just as the lictors had to enforce the praetor's decree without questioning. On this **Proposition I.** doubt let my first proposition be: If a subject is convinced of the injustice of a war,
436 he ought not to serve in it, even on the command of his prince. This is clear, for no one can authorize the killing of an innocent person. But in the case before us the enemy are innocent. Therefore they may not be killed. Again, a prince sins when he commences a war in such a case. But 'not only are they who commit such things worthy of death, but they, too, who consent to the doing thereof' (*Romans*, ch. 1). Therefore soldiers also are not excused when they fight in bad faith. Again, it is not lawful to kill innocent citizens at the prince's command. Therefore not aliens either.

Corollary. 23. Hence flows the corollary that subjects whose conscience is against the justice of a war may not engage in it whether they be right or wrong. This is clear, for 'whatever is not of faith is sin' (*Romans*, ch. 14).

Proposition II. 24. Second proposition: Senators and petty rulers and in general all who are admitted on summons or voluntarily to the public council or the prince's council ought, and are bound, to examine into the cause of an unjust war. This is clear; for whoever can save his neighbour from danger and harm is bound to do so, especially when the danger is that of death and greater ills, as is the case in war. But the persons referred to can avert the war, supposing it to be unjust, if they lend their wisdom and weight to an examination into its causes. Therefore they are bound so to do. Again, if by their neglect an unjust war be entered on, they are consenting parties thereto, for that which a man could and ought to prevent is
437 imputed to him, if he does not prevent it. Again, a king is not by himself capable of examining into the causes of a war and the possibility of a mistake on his part is not unlikely and such a mistake would bring great evil and ruin to multitudes. Therefore war ought not to be made on the sole judgement of the king, nor, indeed, on the judgement of a few, but on that of many, and they wise and upright men.

Proposition III. 25. Third proposition: Other lesser folk who have no place or audience in the prince's council or in the public council are under no obligation to examine the causes of a war, but may serve in it in reliance on their betters. This is proved, first, by the fact that it is impossible and inexpedient to give reasons for all acts of state to every member of the commonalty. Also by the fact that men of the lower orders, even if they perceived the injustice of a war, could not stop it, and their voice would not be heeded. Therefore, any examination by them of the causes of a war would be futile. Also by the fact that for men of this sort it is enough proof of the justice of war (unless the contrary be quite certain) that it is being waged after public counsel and by public authority. Therefore no further examination on their part is needed.

Proposition IV. 26. Fourth proposition: Nevertheless the proofs and tokens of the injustice of the war may be such that ignorance would be no excuse even to subjects of this sort who serve in it. This is clear, because such ignorance might be deliberate and adopted with evil intent towards the enemy. Also, were this otherwise, un- **438**
believers would be excused when they follow their chieftains to war against Christians and it would be unlawful to kill them, it being certain that they deem themselves to have a just cause of war. Also, the soldiers who crucified Christ, ignorantly following Pilate's order, would be excused. Also, the Jewish mob would be excused which was led by the elders to shout 'Away with Him, crucify Him'.

Doubt III. **Proposition I.** 27. Third doubt: What should be done when the justice of the war is doubtful, that is, when there are apparent and probable reasons on both sides. First proposition: As regards the princes themselves, it seems that if one be in lawful possession, the other may not try to turn him out by war and armed force, so long as the doubt remains. For example: Suppose the King of France to be in lawful possession of Burgundy and that it be doubtful whether he has or has not right thereto. The Emperor may not try to oust him by arms; nor on the other hand may the French King seize Naples or Milan, if there be doubt who is entitled to it. The proof is that in doubtful matters the party in possession has the better position. Therefore it is not lawful to dispossess the possessor in favour of a doubtful cause. Further, if the matter were being heard by a lawful judge, he would never in case of doubt dispossess the party in possession. Therefore, if we postulate that those princes who are asserting a right are judges in their own cause, they may **439**
not lawfully eject a possessor so long as there is any doubt about the title. Further, in the suits and causes of private persons it is never permissible in a doubtful matter to dispossess a lawful possessor. Therefore not in the causes of princes; for the laws are the princes' laws. Therefore, if by human law it is not permissible in a doubtful matter to dispossess a lawful possessor, it can quite validly be objected to princes, 'Obey the law thyself hast made, seeing that a man ought to adopt the same law for himself which he has enjoined on others'. Also, were it otherwise, a war could be just on both sides and would never be settled. For if in a doubtful matter it were lawful for one side to assert his claim by force the other might make armed defence, and after the one had obtained what he claimed, the other might afterwards claim it back, and so there would be war without end, to the ruin and tribulation of peoples.

28. Second proposition: If the city or province in regard of which the doubt arises has no lawful possessor, as, for instance, if it were open by reason of the death of the lawful lord and there is a doubt whether the King of Spain or the King of France be the heir and no certainty in point of law can be attained, it seems that, if one party wants to settle and make a division or compromise as to part of the claim, the other is bound to accept his proposal, even if that other be the stronger and able to seize the whole by armed force; nor would he have a just cause of war. The proof is that when the merits of a quarrel are equal, one side **Proposition II.**
440 does no wrong by claiming an equal part of the thing in dispute. Further, in private disputes also, where the matter is in doubt, one party may not seize the whole thing. Also, in the same way the war would be just on both sides. Also, a judge would not decree and award the whole thing to either party.

29. Third proposition: He who is in doubt about his own title is bound, even though he be in peaceable possession, to examine carefully into the cause and give a quiet hearing to the arguments of the other side, if so be he may thus attain certitude either in favour of himself or the other. This is proved by the fact that a man who is in doubt and neglects to ascertain the truth is not in possession in good faith. So also, in a matrimonial cause, if the man who is in lawful possession entertains a doubt whether in truth the woman is his or the other's, it is certain that he is bound to examine the question. Therefore the same principle applies in other causes. Also, princes are judges in their own cases, inasmuch as they have no superior. But it is certain that, if any one raises any objection to a lawful possessor, the judge is bound to examine the case. Therefore in a doubtful matter princes are bound to examine their own case. **Proposition III.**

30. Fourth proposition: After examination of the case the lawful possessor is not bound to quit possession so long as the doubt reasonably persists, but may lawfully retain it. This is manifestly so, for, firstly, no judge could divest him of **Proposition IV.**
441 it. Therefore he is not bound to give it up, either the whole or part. Also, in a matrimonial cause where the matter is doubtful, the man is under no obligation to give up his possession, as is laid down in *X*, 5, 39, 44, and in *X*, 4, 21, 2. Therefore the like is not required in other causes. And Adrian expressly holds (qu. 2, *Quotlib.* 2) that a party in doubt may retain his possession, and he applies this rule to princes in a doubtful matter. But concerning subjects who are in doubt with regard to the justice of a war, Adrian indeed says (*Quotlib.* 2, on the first principal argument) that a subject in such a case, that is, one who is in doubt whether the alleged cause of a war is a sufficient one or simply whether there exists some sufficient cause for declaring war, may not serve in such a war, even at the command of his prince. The proof is that he exposes himself to the danger of mortal sin. Also, what is not of faith is sin, a doctrine which, according to the doctors and to truth, is to be understood as condemnatory, not only where the conscience is assured or based on opinion, but also where it is in doubt. Sylvester seems to hold the same doctrine, under the word *bellum*, I, § 9. **Adrian's opinion about subjects.**

31. But let this be my fifth proposition: In the first place, there is no doubt that in a defensive war subjects may, even though the matter be doubtful, follow **Proposition V,**

wherein the opinion of Adrian is refuted.

their prince to the war; nay, that they are bound to follow him, and also in an offensive war. The first proof is in the fact that, as has been said, a prince is not **442** able, and ought not, always to render reasons for the war to his subjects, and if subjects cannot serve in war except they are first satisfied of its justice, the State would fall into grave peril and the door would be opened to wrongdoing. Also, in doubtful matters the safer course ought to be adopted. Now, if subjects in a case of doubt do not follow their prince to the war, they expose themselves to the risk of betraying their State to the enemy, and this is a much more serious thing than fighting against the enemy despite a doubt. Therefore they ought rather to fight. Also, this is manifestly proved by the fact that the lictor is bound to carry out the decree of the judge, even though he has his doubts about its justice, for there would be serious danger in the opposite course. Also, St. Augustine writing against the Manichæans, defends this line of argument, where he says: 'If a righteous person be in the military service of a sacrilegious king, he may consistently go to war at his command, provided that it is certain that the command laid on him is not contrary to the Divine precepts or that it is not certain whether it be so' (C. 23, qu. 1, can. *quid culpatur*). Here we have St. Augustine expressly declaring that if it is not certain—that is, if there is a doubt—whether it be against God's precepts, the subject may lawfully go to the war. And however Adrian may twist and turn, he cannot free himself from the authority of St. Augustine, for our proposition is, beyond cavil, the conclusion at which St. Augustine arrives. Nor does it avail to say that such a person ought to get rid of his doubt and make **443** his conscience acquiesce in the justice of the war, for it remains that, morally speaking, this is impossible, as in other cases of doubt. Now, Adrian's mistake seems to be in thinking that, if I am in doubt whether this war is just for my prince or whether there be a just cause for this war, it immediately follows that I am in doubt whether or no I ought to go to this war. I admit that I am no wise justified in doing what my conscience doubts about and that, if I am doubtful about the lawfulness of doing any given thing, I sin if I do it. But any doubt of mine about the justice of this war does not necessarily involve a doubt whether I ought to fight or serve in this war. Nay, it is quite the other way about. For although I may doubt whether the war is just, yet the next point is that I may lawfully serve in the field at my prince's command. It is precisely the same as with a lictor who has his doubts whether the judge's decree is just, it does not follow therefrom that he doubts whether or no he ought to carry it into execution; he knows that he is bound to carry it into execution. So, also, if the doubt be whether this woman be my wife; I am, consequent upon such doubt, bound to render her conjugal rights.

This passage is in bk. 22, Contra Faustum, c. 75, though not in quite the same words.

The cause of Adrian's error.

Doubt IV.

32. The fourth doubt is: Whether a war can be just on both sides. The following is my answer: First proposition: Apart from ignorance the case clearly cannot **444** occur, for if the right and justice of each side be certain, it is unlawful to fight against it, either in offence or in defence. Second proposition: Assuming a demonstrable ignorance either of fact or of law, it may be that on the side where true justice is the war is just of itself, while on the other side the war is just in the sense

Proposition I.

Proposition II.

Although their prince knows the injustice of the war, the subjects on each side may sometimes lawfully fight.

of being excused from sin by reason of good faith, because invincible ignorance is a complete excuse. Also, on the side of the subjects at any rate, this may often occur; for even if we assume that a prince who is carrying on an unjust war knows about its injustice, still (as has been said) subjects may in good faith follow their prince, and in this way the subjects on both sides may be doing what is lawful when they fight.

Doubt V.

33. Hence arises the fifth doubt: Whether one who has in ignorance gone in an unjust war and subsequently is convinced of its injustice is bound to make amends therefor. This may be asked both about a prince and about a subject.

Proposition I.

My first proposition is: If the injustice of the war had been within reach of proof by him, he is bound when he learns of its injustice to give back what he has taken away and not yet consumed—that is, to the extent to which he has been enriched; but he need make no amends as regards what he has consumed, because the rule of law is that a person who is not in fault ought not to be damnified, just as one who in good faith attended a sumptuous banquet given by a thief where stolen things
445 were consumed would be under no obligation to give redress therefor, save perhaps up to the amount that his meal would have cost him at home. Sylvester, however, says, under the word *bellum*, I, § 9, that if our man was in doubt about the injustice of the war yet followed his lord's authority, he is liable to make good everything, because it was with bad faith that he fought.

Sylvester's opinion.

Proposition II; against Sylvester's opinion.

Now, let my second proposition, in conformity with the foregoing, be: Our man is not bound to make good what has been consumed, any more than the other side would be, because (as has been said) his fighting was lawful and in good faith. Sylvester's contention would, however, be sound if the man had really been in doubt whether it was lawful for him to go to the war, for he would then be acting against his conscience. Now, much attention must be paid to the admitted fact that a war may be just and lawful in itself and yet owing to some collateral circumstance may be unlawful. For it is admitted that one may be entitled to recapture a city or a province and yet that, because of some scandal, this may become quite unlawful. For inasmuch as (according to what has been said before) wars ought to be waged for the common good, if some one city cannot be recaptured without greater evils befalling the State, such as the devastation of many cities, great slaughter of human beings, provocation of princes, occasions for new wars to the destruction of the Church (in that an opportunity is given to pagans to invade and seize the lands of Christians), it is indubitable that the prince is bound rather to give up his own rights and abstain from war. For it is
446 clear that if the King of France, for example, had a right to retake Milan, but by the war both the Kingdom of France and the Duchy of Milan would suffer intolerable ills and heavy woes, it would not be right for him to retake it. This is because that war ought to take place either for the good of France or for the good of Milan. Therefore, when, on the contrary, great ills would befall each side by the war, it could not be a just war.

Note!

Doubt I, arising from

34. With regard to another question, namely, what degree of stress is lawful in a just war, there are also many doubts. The first is: Whether it is lawful in war

the last principal question. Argument for the affirmative. to kill the innocent. It seems that it is; because, in the first place, the Sons of Israel slew children at Jericho, as appears from *Joshua*, ch. 6, and afterwards Saul slew children in Amalek (I *Samuel*, ch. 15), and in both these cases it was by the authority and at the bidding of God. 'Now, whatever is written is written for our instruction', as appears from *Romans*, ch. 15. Therefore, if a war of the present day be just, it will be lawful to kill the innocent.

Proposition I. Proof 1. 35. With regard to this doubt, let my first proposition be: The deliberate slaughter of the innocent is never lawful in itself. This is proved, firstly, by *Exodus*, Proof 2. ch. 23: 'The innocent and righteous slay thou not.' Secondly, the basis of a just war is a wrong done, as has been shown above. But wrong is not done by an inno-Proof 3. cent person. Therefore war may not be employed against him. Thirdly, it is not **447** lawful within a State to punish the innocent for the wrongdoing of the guilty. Proof 4. Therefore this is not lawful among enemies. Fourthly, were this not so, a war would be just on both sides, although there was no ignorance, a thing which, as has been shown, is impossible. And the consequence is manifest, because it is certain that innocent folk may defend themselves against any who try to kill them. Confirmation. And all this is confirmed by *Deuteronomy*, ch. 20, where the Sons of Israel were ordered to take a certain city by force and to slay every one except women and little ones.

36. Hence it follows that even in war with the Turks it is not allowable to kill children. This is clear, because they are innocent. Aye, and the same holds with regard to the women of unbelievers. This is clear, because so far as the war is concerned, they are presumed innocent; but it does not hold in the case of any individual woman who is certainly guilty. Aye, and this same pronouncement must be made among Christians with regard to harmless agricultural folk, and also with regard to the rest of the peaceable civilian population, for all these are presumed innocent until the contrary is shown. On this principle it follows that it is not lawful to slay either foreigners or guests who are sojourning among the enemy, for they are presumed innocent, and in truth they are not enemies. The same principle applies to clerics and members of a religious order, **448** for they in war are presumed innocent unless the contrary be shown, as when they engage in actual fighting.

Proposition II. 37. Second proposition: Sometimes it is right, in virtue of collateral circumstances, to slay the innocent even knowingly, as when a fortress or city is stormed in a just war, although it is known that there are a number of innocent people in it and although cannon and other engines of war cannot be discharged or fire applied to buildings without destroying innocent together with guilty. The proof is that war could not otherwise be waged against even the guilty and the justice of belligerents would be balked. In the same way, conversely, if a town be wrongfully besieged and rightfully defended, it is lawful to fire cannon-shot and other missiles on the besiegers and into the hostile camp, even though we assume that there are some children and innocent people there.

Note! Great attention, however, must be paid to the point already taken, namely, the obligation to see that greater evils do not arise out of the war than the war

would avert. For if little effect upon the ultimate issue of the war is to be expected from the storming of a fortress or fortified town wherein are many innocent folk, it would not be right, for the purpose of assailing a few guilty, to
449 slay the many innocent by use of fire or engines of war or other means likely to overwhelm indifferently both innocent and guilty. In sum, it is never right to slay the guiltless, even as an indirect and unintended result, except when there is no other means of carrying on the operations of a just war, according to the passage (*St. Matthew*, ch. 13) 'Let the tares grow, lest while ye gather up the tares ye root up also the wheat with them.'

Short and decided answer of the author.

An incidental doubt.

38. Here a doubt may arise whether the killing of guiltless persons is lawful when they may be expected to cause danger in the future; thus, for example, the children of Saracens are guiltless, but there is good reason to fear that when grown up they will fight against Christians and bring on them all the hazards of war. Moreover, although the adult male civilians of the enemy who are not soldiers are presumed to be innocent, yet they will hereafter carry a soldier's arms and cause the hazard named. Now, is it lawful to slay these youths? It seems so, on the same principle which justifies the incidental killing of other guiltless persons. Also (*Deuteronomy*, ch. 20) the Sons of Israel were ordered when assaulting any city to slay 'every adult male'. Now, it cannot be presumed that all of these would be guilty.

The author's answer.

My answer is that although this killing may possibly be defended, yet I
450 believe that it is in no wise right, seeing that evil is not to be done even in order to avoid greater evil still, and it is intolerable that any one should be killed for a future fault. There are, moreover, other available measures of precaution against their future conduct, namely, captivity, exile, &c., as we shall forthwith show. Hence it follows that, whether victory has already been won or the war is still in progress, if the innocence of any soldier is evident and the soldiers can let him go free, they are bound to do so.

On the argument for the affirmative.

To the argument on the opposite side my rejoinder is that the slaughter in the instances named was at the special command of God, who was wroth against the people in question and wished to destroy them utterly, just as he sent fire on Sodom and Gomorrah which devoured both guiltless and guilty together. He, however, is Lord of all and has not given this licence as a common law. And the same answer might be made to that passage in *Deuteronomy*, ch. 20. But, inasmuch as what is there enjoined is in the form of a common law of war for all future time, it would rather seem that the Lord enjoined it because all adult males in an enemy State are deemed guilty, and guiltless cannot be distinguished from guilty. Therefore all may be killed.

On the passage last cited from Deuteronomy.

Doubt II.

Proposition I.

39. The second doubtful point is whether in a just war it is lawful to despoil innocent enemy-subjects. Let my first proposition be: It is certainly lawful to
451 despoil the innocent of goods and things which the enemy would use against us, such as arms, ships, and engines of war. This is clear, because otherwise we could not gain the victory, which is the aim of war. Nay, it is also lawful to take the money of the innocent and to burn and destroy their grain and kill their horses,

Corollary. if this is requisite in order to sap the enemy's strength. Hence follows the corollary that if the war goes on for an indefinitely long time it is lawful utterly to despoil all enemy-subjects, guilty and guiltless alike, for it is from their resources that the enemy is feeding an unjust war, and, on the other hand, his strength is sapped by this spoliation of his citizens.

Proposition II. 40. Second proposition: If a war can be carried on effectively enough without the spoliation of the agricultural population and other innocent folk, they ought

Sylvester. not to be despoiled. Sylvester maintains this (under the word *bellum*, I, § 10) on the ground that war is founded on a wrong done, and therefore the rights of war may not be enforced against the innocent if the wrong can be redressed in another quarter. Aye, and Sylvester adds that, even if there were good reason to despoil the innocent, yet when the war is over the victor is bound to restore to

Sylvester's dictum a pious one, but does not seem to the author necessary. them whatever is left. This, however, I do not think necessary, because, as said above, whatever is done in right of war receives the construction most favourable to the claims of those engaged in a just war. Hence, whatever has been lawfully 452
seized is not in my opinion subject to restitution. All the same, Sylvester's remark is a pious one and not indefensible. But the spoliation of foreigners and travellers on enemy soil, unless they are obviously at fault, is in no wise lawful, they not being enemies.

Proposition III. 41. Third proposition: If the enemy refuse to restore things wrongfully seized by them and the injured party cannot otherwise properly recoup himself, he may do so wherever satisfaction is obtainable, whether from guilty or from innocent. For instance, if French brigands made a raid into Spanish territory and the French King would not, though able, compel them to restore their booty, the Spanish might, on the authorization of their sovereign, despoil French merchants or farmers, however innocent these might be. This is because, although the French State or Sovereign might initially be blameless, yet it is a breach of duty, as St. Augustine says, for them to neglect to vindicate the right against the wrongdoing of their subjects, and the injured sovereign can take satisfaction

Letters of reprisal not unjust in themselves, however hazardous. from every member and portion of their State. There is, accordingly, no inherent injustice in the letters of marque and reprisals which princes often issue in such cases, because it is on account of the neglect and breach of duty of the other prince that the prince of the injured party grants him this right to recoup 453
himself even from innocent folk. These letters are, however, hazardous and open the way to plunder.

Doubt III. 42. The third doubtful point is: Assuming the unlawfulness of the slaughter of children and other innocent parties, is it permissible, at any rate, to carry them off into captivity and slavery? This can be cleared up in a single pro-

Answer contained in a single proposition. position, namely: It is in precisely the same way permissible to carry the innocent off into captivity as to despoil them, liberty and slavery being included among the good things of Fortune. And so when a war is at that pass that the indiscriminate spoliation of all enemy-subjects alike and the seizure of all their goods are justifiable, then it is also justifiable to carry all enemy-subjects off into captivity, whether they be guilty or guiltless. And inasmuch as war with pagans

is of this type, seeing that it is perpetual and that they can never make amends for the wrongs and damages they have wrought, it is indubitably lawful to carry off both the children and the women of the Saracens into captivity and slavery. But inasmuch as, by the law of nations, it is a received rule of Christendom that Christians do not become slaves in right of war, this enslaving is not lawful in a war between Christians; but if it is necessary having regard to the end and aim of war, it would be lawful to carry away even innocent captives, such as children and women, not indeed into slavery, but so that we may receive a money-
454 ransom for them. This, however, must not be pushed beyond what the necessity of the war may demand and what the custom of lawful belligerents has allowed.

Christians may not enslave Christians under the law of war.

Doubt IV.

43. The fourth doubtful point is: Whether it is lawful at any rate to kill hostages who have been taken from the enemy, either in time of truce or on the conclusion of a war, if the enemy break faith and do not abide by their undertakings. My answer is in a single proposition: If the hostages are in other respects among the guilty, as, for instance, because they have borne arms, they may rightfully be killed in that case; if, however, they are innocent, as, for instance, if they be children or women or other innocent folk, it is obvious from what has been said above that they cannot be killed.

Answered in a single proposition.

Doubt V. Four points to be noted.

44. The fifth doubt is: Whether in a just war it is lawful to kill, at any rate, all the guilty. Prefatory to an answer be it noted that, as is shown by what has been said above, war is waged: Firstly, in defence of ourselves and what belongs to us; secondly, to recover things taken from us; thirdly, to avenge a wrong suffered by us; fourthly, to secure peace and security.

Proposition I.

45. This premised, let my first proposition be: In the actual heat of battle, either in the storming or in the defence of a city, all who resist may be killed indiscriminately; and, briefly, this is so as long as affairs are in peril. This is
455 manifest, because combatants could not properly effect their purpose save by removing all who hinder and resist them. All the doubt and difficulty, however, is to know whether, when we have won our victory and the enemy is no longer any danger to us, we may kill all who have borne arms against us. Manifestly, yes. For, as shown above, one of the military precepts given by the Lord (*Deuteronomy*, ch. 20) was that when a city of the enemy had been taken all dwellers in it were to be killed. The words of the passage are: 'When thou comest nigh unto a place to fight against it, then proclaim peace unto it. And it shall be if it make thee answer of peace, and open unto thee, that all the people that is found therein shall be saved and shall be tributaries unto thee and shall serve thee. But if it will make no peace with thee, but will make war against thee, then thou shalt besiege it. And when the Lord thy God hath delivered it into thine hands, thou shalt smite every male thereof with the edge of the sword, but not the women and the little ones.'

Wherein consists the difficulty of this doubt.

Argument for the affirmative.

Proposition II.

46. Second proposition: Even when victory has been won and no danger remains, it is lawful to kill the guilty. The proof is that, as said above, war is ordained not only for the recovery of property, but also for the avenging of wrongs. Therefore the authors of a past wrong may be killed therefor. Again,

this is permissible against our own wrongdoing citizens. Therefore also against foreigners; for, as said above, a prince when at war has by right of war the same **456** authority over the enemy as if he were their lawful judge and prince. And a further reason is that, although there be no present danger from the enemy, yet security for the future cannot be had, unless the enemy be restrained by the fear of punishment.

Proposition III.

47. Third proposition: Merely by way of avenging a wrong it is not always lawful to kill all the guilty. The proof is that even among citizens it would not be lawful, not even where the wrong was done by the whole city or district, to kill all the delinquents; nor in a common rebellion would it be permissible to slay and destroy the whole population. Accordingly, for such a deed, St. Ambrose interdicted Theodosius from the Church. For such conduct would not be for the public good, which is nevertheless the end and aim of both war and peace. Therefore, it is not right to kill all the guilty among the enemy. We ought, then, to take into account the nature of the wrong done by the enemy and of the damage they have caused and of their other offences, and from that standpoint to move to our revenge and punishment, without any cruelty and inhumanity. In this connexion Cicero says (*Offices*, bk. 2) that the punishment which we inflict on the guilty must be such as equity and humanity allow. And Sallust says: 'Our ancestors, the most religious of men, took naught from those they conquered save what was authorized by the nature of their offences.'

Proposition IV. Here an incicental answer is given to the principle advanced, in favour of Proposition I.

48. Fourth proposition: Sometimes it is lawful and expedient to kill all the **457** guilty. The proof is that war is waged in order to get peace and security. But there are times when security cannot be got save by destroying all one's enemies: and this is especially the case against unbelievers, from whom it is useless ever to hope for a just peace on any terms. And as the only remedy is to destroy all of them who can bear arms against us, provided they have already been in fault. That is how the injunction in *Deuteronomy*, ch. 20, is to be interpreted. Otherwise, however, in a war with Christians, where I do not think this would be allowable. For, as it needs must be that scandals come (*St. Matthew*, ch. 18) and also wars between princes, it would involve the ruin of mankind and of Christianity if the victor always slew all his enemies, and the world would soon be reduced to solitude, and wars would not be waged for the public good, but to the utter ruin of the public. The measure of the punishment, then, must be proportionate to the offence, and vengeance ought to go no further, and herein account must be taken of the consideration that, as said above, subjects are not bound, and ought not, to scrutinize the causes of a war, but can follow their prince to it in reliance on his authority and on public counsels. Hence in the **458** majority of cases, although the war be unjust on the other side, yet the troops engaged in it and who defend or attack cities are innocent on both sides. And therefore after their defeat, when no further danger is present, I think that they may not be killed, not only not all of them, but not even one of them, if the presumption is that they entered on the strife in good faith.

Doubt VI.

49. Sixth doubt: Whether it is lawful to slay those who have surrendered

or been captured, supposing them also to have been guilty. My answer is that, speaking absolutely, there is nothing to prevent the killing of those who have surrendered or been captured in a just war so long as abstract equity is observed. Many of the rules of war have, however, been fashioned by the law of nations, and it seems to be received in the use and custom of war that captives, after victory has been won (unless perchance they have been routed) and all danger is over, are not to be killed, and the law of nations must be respected, as is the wont among good people. But I do not read or hear of any such custom with regard to those who have surrendered; nay, on the capitulation of a fortress or city it is usual for those who surrender to try and provide for themselves in the conditions of the capitulation, as that their heads shall be safe and that they shall be let go in safety; that is, they fear that an unconditional surrender would mean their
459 deaths. We read of this being several times done. Accordingly, it does not seem unjust that, if a city capitulates without taking any such precautions, the more notorious offenders should be put to death on the order of the prince or a judge.

The author's answer.

50. Seventh doubt: Whether everything that is captured in a just war becomes the property of the captor and seizor. My first proposition hereon is: There is no doubt that everything captured in a just war vests in the seizor up to the amount which provides satisfaction for the things that have been wrongfully seized and which covers expenses also. This needs no proof, for that is the end and aim of war. But, apart from all consideration both of restitution and satisfaction, and looking at the matter from the standpoint of the law of war, we must distinguish according as the things captured in war are movables (like money, garments, silver, and gold), or are immovables (like lands, cities, and fortresses).

Doubt VII. Proposition I.

51. This being assumed, let my second proposition be: All movables vest in the seizor by the law of nations, even if in amount they exceed what will compensate for damages sustained. This is clear from *Dig.*, 49, 15, 28, and 24, and from can. 9, Dist. 1, and it is more expressly laid down in *Inst.*, 2, 1, 17, where it is said that 'by the law of nations whatever is taken from the enemy immediately becomes ours, even so far as that free persons may be made our
460 slaves'. And St. Ambrose says (*Liber de Patriarchis*) that when Abraham slew the four kings their spoil belonged to him as the conqueror, although he refused to take it (*Genesis*, ch. 14, and can. 25, C. 23, qu. 5). And this is confirmed by the authority of the Lord (*Deuteronomy*, ch. 20), where He says concerning the storming of a town: 'All the spoil thereof thou shalt divide with the army and thou shalt eat of the spoil of thine enemies.' Adrian holds this opinion in his *quaestio* on restitution, in the special *quaestio* on war. So, also, Sylvester, under the word *bellum*, § 1 and § 9, where he says that he who fights a just cause is not bound to give back his booty (can. 2, C. 23, qu. 7). Hence it follows that what is taken in war is not used as a set-off against the principal debt, as the Archdeacon also holds (can. 2, C. 23, qu. 2). And Bartolus is of the same opinion, in his comment on *Dig.*, 49, 15, 28. And this is understood to be so even if the enemy be ready to make amends in other ways for the damages and wrongs suffered. Sylvester, however, limits this, and rightly, allowing it only until a

Proposition II.

Corollary.

satisfaction sufficient in equity has been taken for the damages and wrongs suffered. For it is not to be imagined that, if the French have ravaged some one district or insignificant town in Spain, the Spanish might also, if they could, ravage the whole of France; they can only retort in a manner proportionate in kind and degree to the wrong done, according to the estimate of a good man.

Incidental doubt. Answer thereto. Proposition III. Sylvester.

52. But on this conclusion a doubt arises, namely, whether it is right to give a city up to the soldiery to sack. My answer is, and let this be my third proposition: This is not unlawful in itself, if necessary for the conduct of the war **461** or as a deterrent to the enemy or as a spur to the courage of the troops. So Sylvester, under the word *bellum*, § 10. It is on the same principle as that which justifies the burning of a city for reasonable cause. Nevertheless, inasmuch as such authorization to sack results in many horrors and cruelties, enacted beyond all humane limits by a barbarous soldiery, such as slaughter and torture of the innocent, rape of virgins, dishonour of matrons, and looting of temples, it is undoubtedly unjust in the extreme to deliver up a city, especially a Christian city, to be sacked, without the greatest necessity and weightiest reason. If, however, the necessities of war require it, it is not unlawful, even if it be likely that the troops will perpetrate foul misdeeds of this kind, which their generals are none the less bound to forbid and, as far as they can, to prevent.

Proposition IV.

53. Fourth proposition: Despite all this, soldiers may not, without the authority of their prince or general, go looting or burning, because they are themselves not judges, but executive officers; and those who do otherwise are bound to make restitution.

Proposition V.

54. Now, with regard to immovable property and things, the difficulty is greater, and let my fifth proposition be: There is no doubt about the lawfulness of seizing and holding the land and fortresses and towns of the enemy, so far as **462** is necessary to obtain compensation for the damages he has caused. For instance, if the enemy has destroyed a fortress of ours, or has burnt a city or vineyards or olive gardens, we may in turn seize his land or fortress or city and hold it. For if it is lawful to exact compensation from the enemy for the things of ours which he has taken, it is certain that by the divine law it is not more lawful to take recompense therefor in movables than in immovables.

Proposition VI.

55. Sixth proposition: In order to obtain security and avoid danger from our enemy it is also lawful to seize and hold a fortress or city belonging to him which is necessary for our defence or for taking away from him an opportunity of hurting us.

Proposition VII.

56. Seventh proposition: It is also lawful, in return for a wrong received and by way of punishment, that is, in revenge, to mulct the enemy of a part of his territory in proportion to the character of the wrong, or even on this ground to seize a fortress or town. This, however, must be done within due limits, as already said, and not as utterly far as our strength and armed force enable us to go in seizing and storming. And if necessity and the principle of war require the seizure of the larger part of the enemy's land, and the capture of numerous cities, they ought to be restored when the strife is adjusted and the war is over, **463**

only so much being retained as is just, in way of compensation for damages caused and expenses incurred and of vengeance for wrongs done, and with due regard for equity and humanity, seeing that punishment ought to be proportionate to the fault. Thus it would be intolerable that, if the French raided the flocks of the Spanish or burnt a single district, the latter should be allowed to seize the whole Kingdom of France. Now, the lawfulness of seizing on this score either a part of enemy territory or an enemy city appears from *Deuteronomy*, ch. 20, where permission is granted in war to seize a city that has refused to accept terms of peace. Again, internal wrongdoers may be punished in this way, that is, they may be deprived of house or land or a fortress, in proportion to the character of the circumstances. Therefore foreigner wrongdoers also. Again, a superior judge has competence to mulct the author of a wrong by taking away from him a city (for instance) or a fortress. Therefore a prince who has suffered wrong can do this too, because by the law of war he is put in the position of a judge. Again, it was in this way and by this title that the Roman Empire grew and developed, that is, by occupation, in right of war, of cities and provinces belonging to enemies who had injured them, and yet the Roman Empire is defended as just and lawful by St. Augustine, St. Jerome, St. Ambrose, St. Thomas, and other reverend doctors. Nay, it might be held approved by God in the passage,
464 'Render unto Caesar the things that are Caesar's,' and by St. Paul, who appealed unto Caesar and who in *Romans*, ch. 13, gave an admonition to be subject to the higher powers and to princes and to pay tribute to those who at that time, all of them, derived their authority from the Roman Empire.

57. Eighth doubt: Whether it is lawful to impose a tribute on conquered enemies. **Doubt VIII.** My answer is that it is undoubtedly lawful, not only in order to recoup damages, but also as a punishment and by way of revenge. **Answer.** This is clear enough from what has been said above and from the passage in *Deuteronomy*, ch. 20, which says that when the Jews have approached a city with good cause in order to attack it, if the city receives them and opens its gates, all the people therein shall be saved and shall serve the Jews with payment of tribute. And this law and usage of war has prevailed.

58. Ninth doubt: Whether it is lawful to depose the princes of the enemy and appoint new ones or keep the princedom for oneself. **Doubt IX.** First proposition: **Proposition I.** This is not unqualifiedly permissible, nor for any and every cause of just war, as appears from what has been said. For punishment should not exceed the degree and nature of the offence. Nay, punishments should be awarded restrictively, and rewards extensively. This is not a rule of human law only, but also of natural and
465 divine law. Therefore, even assuming that the enemy's offence is a sufficient cause of war, it will not always suffice to justify the overthrow of the enemy's sovereignty and the deposition of lawful and natural princes; for these would be utterly savage and inhumane measures.

59. Second proposition: **Proposition II.** It is undeniable that there may sometimes arise sufficient and lawful causes for effecting a change of princes or for seizing a sovereignty; and this may be either because of the number and aggravated

quality of the damages and wrongs which have been wrought or, especially, when security and peace cannot otherwise be had of the enemy and grave danger from them would threaten the State if this were not done. This is obvious, for if the seizure of a city is lawful for good cause, as has been said, it follows that the removal of its prince is also lawful. And the same holds good of a province and the prince of a province, if proportionately graver cause arise.

Note! Note, however, with regard to Doubts VI to IX, that sometimes, nay, frequently, not only subjects, but princes, too, who in reality have no just cause of war, may nevertheless be waging war in good faith, with such good faith, I say, as to free them from fault; as, for instance, if the war is made after a careful examination and in accordance with the opinion of learned and upright men. And since no one who has not committed a fault should be punished, in that case, **466**
although the victor may recoup himself for things that have been taken from him and for any expenses of the war, yet, just as it is unlawful to go on killing after victory in the war has been won, so the victor ought not to make seizures or exactions in temporal matters beyond the limits of just satisfaction, seeing that anything beyond these limits could only be justified as a punishment, such as could not be visited on the innocent.

Three rules of warfare. I. 60. All this can be summarized in a few canons or rules of warfare. First canon: Assuming that a prince has authority to make war, he should first of all not go seeking occasions and causes of war, but should, if possible, live in peace with all men, as St. Paul enjoins on us (*Romans*, ch. 12). Moreover, he should reflect that others are his neighbours, whom we are bound to love as ourselves, and that we all have one common Lord, before whose tribunal we shall have to render our account. For it is the extreme of savagery to seek for and rejoice in grounds for killing and destroying men whom God has created and for whom Christ died. But only under compulsion and reluctantly should he come to the necessity of war.

II. Second canon: When war for a just cause has broken out, it must not be waged so as to ruin the people against whom it is directed, but only so as to obtain one's rights and the defence of one's country and in order that from that **467**
war peace and security may in time result.

III. Third canon: When victory has been won and the war is over, the victory should be utilized with moderation and Christian humility, and the victor ought to deem that he is sitting as judge between two States, the one which has been wronged and the one which has done the wrong, so that it will be as judge and not as accuser that he will deliver the judgement whereby the injured State can obtain satisfaction, and this, so far as possible, should involve the offending State in the least degree of calamity and misfortune, the offending individuals being chastised within lawful limits; and an especial reason for this is that in general among Christians all the fault is to be laid at the door of their princes, for subjects when fighting for their princes act in good faith and it is thoroughly unjust, in the words of the poet, that—

Quidquid delirant reges, plectantur Achivi.
(For every folly their Kings commit the punishment should fall upon the Greeks.)

APPENDIX C

RELECTIO

OF THE REVEREND FATHER, BROTHER FRANCISCUS DE VICTORIA

CONCERNING CIVIL POWER

A

TRANSLATION BY

GWLADYS L. WILLIAMS

The text
is from the first verse
of the thirteenth chapter
of Romans :
There is no power but
of God.

SUMMARY

1. All power—whether public or private—by which the secular State is governed, is not only just and legitimate, but is so ordained of God, that not even by the consent of the whole world can it be destroyed or annulled.
2. The twofold nature of power: public, and private.
3. The purpose of civil power.
4. The wretchedness of man is recounted. And a discussion follows concerning what should be done in provision for his needs.
5. States and commonwealths had not their fount and origin in the invention of man, but sprang, as it were, from nature.
6. The efficient cause of civil power.
7. The source whence the State derives civil power. And an account of the material cause
181 of that same power. In whom it resides, by natural and divine law.
8. Not only is monarchy, or royal power, just and legitimate; but, in addition to this, the power of kings is derived from divine and natural law, not from the State itself, nor directly from men.
9. Whether those powers are legitimate which govern the States of infidels. That is to say, whether the princes and magistrates found among pagans are legitimate.
10. Three causes of public secular power are expounded.
11. There is no less liberty in a monarchy than in an aristocracy, or a democracy.
12. The State as a whole may rightfully be punished for the sin of the monarch.
13. Circumstances under which no war is just.
14. Just as the majority of members of a State may set up a king over the whole State, although other members are unwilling, so the majority of Christians, even though there be some who are opposed, may lawfully create a monarch whom all princes and provinces are under obligation to obey.
15. In what manner the laws and constitutions of princes are binding in the court of conscience. And remarks with regard to the precepts laid down by parents for their children, and by husbands for their wives.
16. How human and divine law differ; and how they agree.
17. Both divine and human law have a binding force that renders transgressors guilty.
182 18. The kind of guilt incurred by transgressors of human laws: whether it is mortal, or merely venial.
19. How one may distinguish between human laws which involve the transgressor in mortal guilt, and those which involve him in venial guilt.
20. Whether the king has the power to exempt one from liability to guilt, if he should so wish.
21. Whether civil laws are binding upon the legislators, and in particular, upon kings.
22. Whether the obligation to obey a law ceases to exist, when the reason for the law ceases to exist.
23. Whether the laws of tyrants have a binding force.
24. The commands of parents are binding, even as civil laws are binding. And the same is true with regard to commands given by husbands to their wives.

The duties and functions of the theologian extend over a field so vast, that no argument, no discussion, no text, seem alien to the practice and purpose of theology. And this may account for the fact that the lack of able and sound theologians is as great as—not to say greater than—the lack of orators which is mentioned by Cicero, and which he explains by saying that men who are distinguished and skilled in every science and in all the arts are very rare. Theology, indeed, is the first of all those sciences and studies which the Greeks call θεολογία.

Consequently, there is no occasion for surprise, if very few are found who are competent in a subject so difficult. In this immense domain, then, and in the extensive field composed of the writings of all scholars, an infinite number of **183**
possibilities present themselves; but I have selected one passage for special notice: surely if it merits my consideration and treatment of it, it is worthy—most illustrious and learned gentlemen—of your attention. The passage, then, concerns the State: a matter with regard to which many points remain to be considered, although earnest and erudite men have already accorded it extensive treatment. Since the topic is too broad to be disposed of in a single discussion, I have chosen as the subject for to-day the public and private power by which States are governed.

The intention of the author in this *Relectio*.

The text to be read and commented upon is from the 'Master of the Sentences',[1] (2d 44), and is based upon the words of Paul (*Romans*, 13: 1): 'There is no power but of God.' Although a multitude of topics might be brought up in connexion with this passage, nevertheless, our entire discussion shall be limited for the present to laic or secular power, in order that we may not be more discursive and rambling than is needful. The whole *Relectio*, then, will be restricted to three conclusions.

The first principal conclusion.

First. The first conclusion is this: All power—whether public or private—by which the secular State is governed, is not only just and legitimate, but is so surely ordained of God, that not even by the consent of the whole world can it be destroyed or annulled. Before passing to the proof of this conclusion, I must make **184**
a number of prefatory remarks which are needed to explain it and make it intelligible. To be sure, I have not undertaken to treat of all the points which could be introduced into a discussion so extensive; on the contrary, I shall confine myself to a very few words, only such as are necessary to our purpose, expressing myself briefly and concisely, and imitating the scholastic manner in so far as I am able.

Aristotle, near the beginning of the *Physics*, I.

The causes of secular power are to be investigated: first, the causes of public secular power; then, those of private secular power.

Second. Since the nature of power is twofold—public, and private—we shall treat first of public, and presently, of private power. And since (as Aristotle declares) we believe that when we have informed ourselves of the causes of anything, we are acquainted with the thing itself, it seems to me worth while to investigate the causes of civil laic power, as that power will be the subject of the whole lecture. Once these causes have been ascertained, the force and effect of the power in question will doubtless be easily evident. First of all, we should take note of the admonition of that same Aristotle in the *Physics*:[2] not only in matters relating to Nature, but also in all man-made constructions, 'necessity' should be considered from the view-point of purpose, which is first of all causes, and the principal one. This doctrine, whether invented by Aristotle (near the end of Book 2 of the *Physics*) or taken by him from Plato, was a most important philosophical

[1] Peter Lombard. [2] II. ix.

argument, and shed a great deal of light on all subjects. His predecessors, who were not devoid of learning, but were, on the contrary, philosophers of the first rank,

Confutation of those who attributed the necessity of things to matter.

185 attributed the necessity of things to matter, as if conceiving (to use the example employed by Aristotle himself) that the house was built in a given manner of necessity: the stones and foundations are below the level of the ground, while the wood—being lighter—rises above, not because such an arrangement best serves human purposes, but because heavy objects are borne downward by their very nature. In like manner, man's feet are at the lowest part of his body, not in order that he may walk, but because that part of him is especially heavy. Again, the bones of living creatures are within, not for the reason that the body needs them to give stability to the flesh and the limbs, but because that material is harder and more solid.

For truly, imbued with crude ideas, men wandered in their investigations over all the heavens (as they say), with the result that they were unable to give a satisfactory account of anything according to their own doctrines, and certainly could in no way and by no artifice explain through their philosophizing the construction of all that is best and most great. For how may they object if I seek to know the sort of matter by which the earth is adorned, placed as it is in the very heart of the Universe, solid and globular, entirely rounded by virtue of its own energies, clad with flowers, grass, and trees; or if I ask whence comes the ice-cold, never-failing quality of the streams, the crystal clear liquid, the green mantle of the banks; and whence the composition of the various parts and members of man,

Ovid: Book I of the *Metamorphoses*.[1]

186 derived from one kind of matter? What is the force in that matter which gave to man, alone among all living beings, eyes that looked upward; which granted that he should gaze up at the sky; which bade him turn his face towards the stars? And these philosophers make answer as follows: that it could not be otherwise, that man must needs stand erect, while the beasts are low and stooping: not to serve any aim or useful purpose, but merely because different living creatures are dissimilar in matter and construction.

From this source was derived the foolish opinion expressed by Epicurus, and by his disciple Lucretius.[2] The latter[3] declared that eyes were not made for seeing, nor ears for hearing, but that all things come to pass through chance and from that multiform dance of the atoms, whirling through infinite space: a theory whose stupidity and absurdity could not be surpassed by any statement or conception. Neither could anything be easier than to refute such folly. Cicero did so at length in the *De natura Deorum*;[4] and Lactantius, also, in the *De opificio Dei*. But for our intent and present purpose it will suffice to uphold one sublime truth, the neglect of which must always lead to error. Let us believe that neither the sky nor the land nor the remaining parts of the world, not man himself, was the beginning of the world; but rather that all that is contained in the heavens was appointed for some useful purpose, and that all things have been created, and

[1] lines 85–6.

[2] Lucretius, *De rerum natura*, v. 145 *et seq.*

[3] The text has the singular form of the verb, *dicebat*, with no specific subject expressed. It might be permissible, in view of the fact that the Latin edition contains many obvious errors, to read *dicebant*, 'They declared.' *Tr.*

[4] I. ii. 3.

necessarily created just as they are, for a purpose, whence are derived the nature 187
and the necessity of all things.

Inquiry is made regarding the purpose of civil or secular power.

THIRD. Consequently, we must undertake an inquiry and investigation regarding the purpose that underlies the establishment of the power which we are about to consider. In the course of this inquiry we should note that, while man is superior to other animals in reason, wisdom, and speech, on the other hand, the Providence that rules us has denied to that eternal, immortal, and wise animal, many things which it has granted to the rest. For Mother Nature, from the very beginning, in order to provide security[1] and protection for animals, furnished each of the others with his own covering, by which he might the better withstand the rigours of wintry frost and cold. She supplied all of these with their own instruments of defence against alien attacks, that they might either offer resistance by means of their natural weapons—as the fiercer animals do: or escape from danger by the swiftness of their flight—after the manner of the weaker animals; or protect themselves with their beaks as if these were spears; or lurk in some hiding-place: and so it is that some of them are lightly held aloft by feathers, while some are provided with claws, and still others with horns; but each and every one has his means of self-defence.

The want and the wretchedness of man.

FOURTH. To man alone, however, she granted reason and virtue, leaving him
frail, weak, needy; drawing him forth from the wreck enfeebled, destitute, in 188
want of everything, reproachful[2] against himself; and scattering hardships throughout his life so that, in truth, from the very moment of his birth he can only presage tears, weeping over his own frailty; as the saying is: 'Man is full of trouble.' Therefore, in order that proper provision might be made for these needs, it was necessary that men should not wander singly and in solitude, after the manner of wild beasts, but should dwell in a fellowship in which they might be of aid to one another. 'Woe to him that is alone,' saith the Wise Man, 'for if he fall, there shall not be another to lift him up; but where there are many, they will succour one another.'[3] Therefore, on this same point, Aristotle (2 *Ethics*) admonishes us that the understanding of man, which can have no existence in solitude, is not to be perfected without instruction and experience. Even in this respect, indeed, we seem inferior to brutes, inasmuch as they are able to learn by themselves those things which it is needful for them to know; while men are utterly incapable of learning thus. Again, speech is the messenger of the understanding, and according to Aristotle,[4] it has been bestowed for that sole purpose —speech, which in itself renders man superior to the other animals, and which would be of no value outside the sphere of human society: furthermore, if it were possible for wisdom to exist without speech, wisdom itself would, under such

Job. xiv. 1.

[1] The text reads *communitate* ('fellowship'). Is this perhaps a misprint for *immunitate*, or even *commoditate* ('comfort')? *Tr.*

[2] *incrinem*. A misprint for *criminans*? *Tr.*

[3] Evidently a paraphrase of Ecclesiastes, iv. 9–10: 'Two are better than one; because they have a good reward for their labour.

'For if they fall, the one will lift up his fellow: but woe to him that is alone when he falleth; for he hath not another to help him up.' *Tr.*

[4] *Politics*, I. ii. 10–11.

189 circumstances, be neither pleasing nor communicable.[1] For we find this saying in *Ecclesiasticus* (41. 17):[2] 'wisdom that is hid, and a treasure that is not seen, what profit is there in them both?' Wherefore Aristotle points out (*Politics*, I)[3] that man is by nature a civil and sociable animal. And truly the will, whose chief ornaments are justice and friendship, would of necessity be entirely deformed and, so to speak, crippled, if it were separated from human society[4]: justice, indeed, cannot be practised except by the multitude;[5] and the same is true of friendship, without which (as Cicero[6] declares in various passages) we should have no use for water or fire or sun, and without which (according to the opinion of Aristotle[7]) there is no virtue. Unless there be communication of life, all perishes. And even if it were agreed that human life was sufficient unto itself, nevertheless, it could not fail to be bitter and unpleasant when passed in solitude. For nothing solitary is acceptable to Nature, and she impels us all to mingle with one another. Cicero[8] says: 'If any man should climb to the heavens and behold the nature of the Universe and the beauty of the stars, that harmonious plan would not be sweet to him, without his friend.' Wherefore Timon of Athens, who deliberately withdrew from the society of men, is judged by Aristotle, *Politics*, I,[9] to have been of an inhuman and brutish disposition, persons of this sort being classified as wild beasts. Saint Augustine remarks, in his book *On Friendship* (chapter 8):[10] 'For
190 I should say that they are not men, but beasts, who assert that one should so live that he will neither afford consolation to any man, nor be a burden or a sorrow to any one; who neither receive pleasure from the good fortune of other persons, nor inflict sadness upon others by their own perversity, taking care to love no one, and to be loved by none.' Therefore, since human societies have been established for this purpose—namely, that we should bear one another's burdens—and since civil society is of all societies that which best provides for the needs of men, it follows that the community is, so to speak, an exceedingly natural form of intercommunication: that is, a form thoroughly in accord with Nature. For even though the various members be of mutual assistance, nevertheless a single family is not self-sufficing, least of all for the resistance of violence and injury; and this, it seems, was the reason that motivated Ham and Nimrod when they were the very first to compel men to form a city, as we read in *Genesis* (10).[11]

Neither in intellect nor in will can man be perfected, without friendship and communication with others.

This book *On Friendship* has been relegated to the end of Volume IV of the works of Augustine, not being considered as truly his.

FIFTH. It is evident, then, that States and commonwealths had not their fount and origin in the invention of man, nor in any artificial manner, but sprang, as it were, from Nature, who produced this method of protecting and preserving

Commonwealths had not their origin in art, but in nature.

[1] The 1696 edition mentions two readings here: *inscibilis* ('unknowable') and *insociabilis* ('unsociable'). *Tr.* [2] Cf. Ecclesiasticus, xx. 32. [3] ii. 9. [4] II. i.

[5] Apparently Victoria uses such terms as *multitudo* and *multi* in the sense of 'more than one'; cf. the reference to Ecclesiastes, iv. 9–10, on p. lxxiv. *Tr.*

[6] *On Duties*, II. xvi. 51–2. [7] *Nicomachean Ethics*, VIII. i. 1. [8] *On Friendship*, xxiii. 88.

[9] An erroneous reference, perhaps due to a printer's error, since Aristotle's *Politics* is referred to a few lines above. What Victoria's reference actually was can only be conjectured—possibly he cited Aristophanes. *Vide The Lysistrata*, lines 805–20. [10] Vol. vi, col. 836, Migne ed.

[11] There are several verses in this chapter of Genesis which refer to the power of Nimrod (v. 8 'And Cush begat Nimrod: he began to be a mighty one in the earth'), and to the cities which first formed his kingdom. In the same chapter, the lineage of Nimrod is traced back to Ham. However, there is no statement precisely like that made by Victoria. Cf. also 1 Chronicles i. 10, which is substantially the same as Genesis x. 8 quoted above. *Vide* also reference to Genesis on p. lxxvii. *Tr.*

mortals. And under this head of the discussion it clearly follows that the same purpose and necessity underlie the existence of public powers. For if councils and 191
assemblies of men are necessary to the security of mortals, it is also true that no society can continue to exist without some force and power to govern and provide for it; the use and the utility of public power, and of the community, and of society are absolutely the same. For if all were equal, and subject to no power, each individual would draw away from the others in accordance with his own opinions and will; the commonwealth would of necessity be torn apart; and the State would be dissolved—unless there were some providential force to provide for the common welfare and consider the common good. For, 'Every kingdom divided against itself shall be brought to desolation';[1] and 'Where there is no ruler', so saith the Wise Man, 'the people shall perish'. Just as the human body could not be preserved in its integrity, without some directing force to regulate the various members, making them of mutual use and—what is more important—of service to the whole man; even so the State would necessarily lose its integrity, if every individual were solicitous for his own welfare, and every citizen were heedless of the public good. We have pointed out, then, the ultimate and principal cause of civil power, and the utility—even more, the overwhelming necessity—of secular power, which none but the gods resist.

A neat comparison of States with the human body.

The principal cause and purpose of civil power is the greatest utility; nay, more . . . [Incomplete note.]

Sixth. From what has been said it is easy, indeed, to discern the efficient cause of this power. For if we prove that public power has been set up by natural 192
law, then—since God is the sole author of natural law—it becomes evident that public power is of God and that it cannot be contained within the limits of man's nature or of any positive law.

The efficient cause of this same power is God; and an exposition of the nature of this cause.

For God, who hath created all things in His wisdom, who 'reacheth . . . from end to end mightily, and ordereth all things sweetly',[2] whose works are all harmoniously disposed, as the Apostle says, has so fashioned the nature and disposition of man that he cannot prosper unless he dwell in a social state. Moreover, Cicero[3] quotes Scipio as saying that 'nothing is more acceptable in the sight of God our King, who ruleth all the world and who hath created all that is in the earth, than are those groups called "States", in whatsoever society framed by the laws of man they may be found'. And if States and societies are established in accordance with divine or natural law, the same is true of power, without which States could not exist. In order that all doubt on the subject may be removed, we shall confirm by reasoning and by testimony the assertion that power also is derived from divine law. In the first place, Aristotle declares that all things, whether heavy or light, are moved by their Creator, from no other cause than the natural inclination and necessity for motion which they have received from Him. If, then, God created for men such a necessity and inclination that they cannot 193
subsist except in a social state and under some ruling power, it must be true that these very conditions are also derived from God. For those things which are

[1] St. Luke, xi. 17. Cf. St. Matthew, xii. 25; St. Mark, iii. 24.

[2] Evidently a reminiscence from the Book of Wisdom, viii. 1, in which, however, the subject of the verb is 'She', referring to Wisdom. *Tr.*

[3] *The Republic*, VI. xiii. 13.

natural to us all, without doubt flow naturally from God; since the author of the form or shape—as that same Aristotle says—is the author also of the consequences necessarily attendant upon the form or shape. Wherefore Paul likewise admonishes us: 'Whosoever therefore resisteth the power, resisteth the ordinance of God.'[1] **Romans xiii.**

The material cause of this same power is the State itself, by natural and divine law: a proposition which is subtly confirmed.

SEVENTH. The State, then, possesses this power by divine DISPOSITION; but the material cause in which, by natural and divine law, power of this kind resides, is the State itself, which by its very nature is competent to govern and administer itself, and to order all its powers for the common good. The proof of this fact is as follows: since by natural and divine law there must be a power for the government of the State, and since—if common, positive, and human laws are laid aside—there is no reason for depositing that power in one person rather than in another; it necessarily follows that the community is self-sufficing and that it has the power to govern itself. For if—before men gathered together into a State—no one person was the superior of the others, it is in no way reasonable that in the assembly, or civil council, one individual should assume power over the others; especially not, in view of the fact that every man has by natural law the power and the right to defend himself, there being nothing more natural than to repel force by
194 force. And certainly there is no reason to prevent the State from exercising this power over its citizens (as if they were the various members of one body), in order to preserve the integrity of the whole, and in a spirit of devotion to the public good. Furthermore, the slaying of a man is prohibited by divine law, as we learn from the Patriarch, in the Ten Commandments; therefore, the authority to slay must be derived from divine law; but the State—as is evident from usage[2] and custom—has the authority to kill a man; consequently, it has that authority by divine law. Neither will it suffice to say that divine law does not absolutely prohibit the slaying of any man, but only that of an innocent man; because the conclusion to be drawn is that no private individual is permitted to kill any man, howsoever wicked. Therefore, the State has a certain authority to slay, which a private individual does not possess; and since that authority cannot be derived from positive law, it must be derived from divine law.

As to whether kingly power is of God. Those who deny that it is of God, rely upon the following arguments.

Inasmuch as this power resides principally in kings, to whom the State has entrusted its authority, it becomes necessary to discuss kingly dignity and power. There are certain persons, even some Christians, who not only deny that royal power is of God, but who even assert that all kings, rulers, and princes are tyrants and plunderers of our liberty; so incensed are these persons against every form
195 of domination and power, with the sole exception of democratic power. And they attempt to prove these statements by citing authorities and by reasoning. In the first place, they argue that man was created free. For in the happy age of innocence there was neither master nor servant. Their second argument is that in the beginning, it was said of men: 'let them have dominion over the fish of the sea, and over the fowl of the air',[3] &c.; and again: 'God created man' that he might

First argument.

Second argument.

[1] Romans, xiii. 2.

[2] 1696 text has *visu*, probably for *usu*, although the former might be translated as 'from what we see'. *Tr.*

[3] Genesis, i. 26.

'have dominion over the fish of the sea', &c.;[1] but it was not said 'let him have dominion over other men'.

Third argument.

The third argument is that in the book of natural law, we do not read that there was any prince among the worshippers of the true God.

Fourth argument.

In the fourth place, the same persons argue that the office of princes had its origin in tyranny. For Nimrod, the son of Ham and one of the line rejected by Noah, was the first to assume the tyrant's power (*Genesis*, 10).[2] Neither do the

Gregory.

They rely also upon the authority of the Fathers.

holy doctors pass over this point in silence. For Gregory declares that it is against Nature and a momentous matter that one man should wish to be ruler; since by natural law all men are equal. And Isidore[3] says: the common possession of all, and the liberty granted by natural law, is the use of one's own liberty. And even if kingly power was not prohibited before the establishment of the Evangelical Law, at least liberty was granted to Christians by Christ. This is apparent in the passage where the Master says: 'of whom do the kings of the earth take . . .tribute ? of their own children, or of strangers ?' And Peter answered: 'Of strangers.'[4] Whence those persons whose arguments we are reviewing deduce the certainty that Christians are under no obligation to pay tribute, unless this be needful for the 196

And upon the authority of the Scriptures.

avoidance of scandal. And this is confirmed by the admonition of the Apostle: 'Owe no man anything, but to love one another.'[5] And again: 'Ye are bought with a price; be not ye the servants of men.'[6] Furthermore, in the Epistle to the *Ephesians*,[7] Paul says: 'One Lord, one faith, one baptism.' Therefore it is not permissible that we as Christians should set up princes over ourselves. In view of all these arguments, it is by no means strange that factious, corrupt persons, full of pride and ambition, stir up sedition against princes.

The author replies that monarchical power is not only just, but is also derived from divine and natural law.

Eighth. Therefore, in reply to all these assertions, we, in company with all wise men, will rather say: not only is monarchy, or royal power, just and legitimate; but, in addition to this, the power of kings is derived from divine and natural law, not from the State itself, nor directly from men. The proof is as follows: since the State possesses power over its own parts, and since this power cannot be exercised by the multitude (which could not conveniently make laws and issue edicts, settle disputes and punish transgressors), it has therefore been necessary that the administration of the State should be entrusted to the care of some person or persons (and it matters not whether this power is entrusted to one or to many); it has not been impossible, then, to transfer a power identical with the power of the State.

The same conclusion may be proved by citing authorities. For it is agreed that royal dominion is not contrary to natural law, as our opponents believe: since natural law is immutable—a proposition demonstrated by Aristotle 197
(5 *Ethics*)[8] and set forth also in the Decrees; and since, consequently, if royal dominion were opposed to natural law, it would not have been just in any century or any age; and since the fact that such dominion actually was just as evident from the Old Testament, wherein praise is bestowed upon Melchisedec,

[1] Genesis, i. 25–6.
[2] See page lxxv, note 11. *Tr.*
[3] *Etymologies*, v. iv.
[4] St. Matthew, xvii. 25, 26.
[5] Romans, xiii. 8.
[6] 1 Corinthians, vii. 23.
[7] Ephesians, iv. 5.
[8] v. vii.

King of Salem; upon Joseph, the steward and tax collector of Pharaoh's kingdom; upon Jacob, a just man, who accepted land for cultivation from Pharaoh; and upon Daniel and his companions, the former being made governor of the province by Nebuchadnezzar: favours which these holy men would certainly not have accepted, if they had conceived of royal dominion as being tyrannical. Again, in *Deuteronomy* (10),[1] conditions are laid down for kings, in accordance with which they are to reign over the children of Israel; neither are the latter forbidden to set up kings over themselves, provided only that he whom they set in this post be not a stranger. In the same chapter the Israelites are bidden to obey the precept and decree of the priest, under pain of capital punishment;[2] and it matters not whether the person in authority be priest or king, if he have the same power. Furthermore, the Levites are constituted judges, endowed with the power of life and death. In the books of *Kings*, too, we read that certain kings were set up by God Himself, and that others were designated by Him; whereas, assuredly, the Lord would not have done these things, had they been contrary to natural law. Again, the Maccabees, who are considered by all to have been men of the utmost valour and sanctity, either accepted the princely power of their forefathers when it was conferred upon them, or appropriated it for them-
198 selves for just reasons. In truth, it is altogether absurd to suppose that anything expedient to the administration of human affairs is contrary to natural or divine law. Therefore, as Job wisely says, 'God doth not cast away the mighty whereas he himself also is mighty'.[3] Neither is evangelical liberty opposed to kingly power, as seditious individuals insinuate to the ignorant masses. For nothing, as is shown in another passage, is prohibited by the Gospels if it be permitted by natural law; indeed, evangelical liberty consists principally in this very fact. Consequently, if it was permissible for States to set up kings before the Gospels were proclaimed, it is not to be supposed that since they have been proclaimed, that same practice is prohibited. Moreover, if kings were not legitimate sovereigns, it is certain that the Apostle of Christ would never have admonished us to obey them; yet it is evident that the words of Paul (*Romans* 13. 1) can have no other meaning, 'Let every soul be subject unto the higher powers'. And again: 'There is no power but of God'; and, 'Whosoever therefore resisteth the power, resisteth the ordinance of God'.[4] Many other things in this same vein did he write in the Epistle to *Titus*, saying (*Titus*, 3. 1): 'Put them in mind to be subject to principalities and powers.' And in the First Epistle to *Timothy* (2. 1–2), we read: 'I exhort therefore, that, first of all, supplications . . . be made for . . . kings, and for all that are in authority; that we may lead a quiet and peaceable life . . .' Peter, also (First Epistle, 2. 13) delivers this admonition: 'Submit

[1] Apparently an incorrect citation. Deuteronomy xvii is evidently the chapter which Victoria has in mind both here and below. See Note 2. *Tr.*

[2] See Deuteronomy, xvii. 8–13.

[3] Job, xxxvi. 5. The words quoted above are taken from the Douay version, since they seem better fitted to this context than the corresponding verse of the King James version: 'Behold, God is mighty, and despiseth not any: he is mighty in strength and wisdom.' The word *timidus* in the quotation made by Victoria, 'Deus tanquam timidus adjicit potestatem, cum ipse sit potens', does not seem to be brought out in either version, but might be translated, 'after the manner of the timorous'. *Tr.*

[4] Romans, xiii. 2.

yourselves to every ordinance of man for the Lord's sake: whether it be to the king', &c. It is apparent, then, that kingly power is not derived from the State, 199
but from God Himself, according to the opinion of the Doctors of the Holy Catholic Church. For even though this power is established by the State (since the latter creates the king), nevertheless the State, in this very act, transfers not merely the power, but also its own authority; so that there are not two sorts of power—one, that of the king; the other, that of the community. Therefore, just as we say that the power of the State is established by God and by natural law, so of a surety we must say the same of all kingly power; and this conclusion, as we see, is quite in accord with the Scriptures and with that custom by which kings are designated as the ministers, not of the State, but of God. Solomon records the words of God: 'By me kings reign.'[1] And our Lord made answer to Pilate thus: 'Thou couldest have no power at all against me, except it were given thee from above',[2] that is, from Heaven. We see, then, that those writers are mistaken who concede that the power of the State is derived from divine law, but who do not admit that the same is true of kingly power. For if men, or the State, had power not from God, but if instead—by agreement and for the sake of the public good—all men should will to set up over themselves some power, the latter, to be sure, would be derived from men, like that which the members of a religious order confer upon their abbot. But such is not the case, for the power of self-government exists in the State and would continue to exist therein even if all the citizens were unwilling; and the kings who rule over States are appointed to exercise this power.

The doubt concerning civil power among infidels.[3] The argument for the negative. The opinion of Richardus.

Ninth. However, some persons may doubt whether this is true of the powers 200
governing any infidel State; whether, that is, the princes and other magistrates found among pagans are legitimate. It might seem that they are not; for if any Christian were unfaithful, he would certainly be deprived of all public power on this account, as the laws command; therefore, as long as the factor of infidelity exists in him, it is an impediment to the assumption of sovereignty or power. And Richardus—a man of remarkable ability, in other respects—expresses the opinion, in his book on the *Poverty of Christ*, that not only lack of faith but any mortal sin whatsoever is a bar to the possession of any power or dominion or jurisdiction, whether public or private; moreover, he holds that the claim to any power whatsoever, and the foundation of it, are in Divine Grace; but I shall omit

The reply of the author.

his arguments, because they are too weak to call for discussion. Indeed, it should not be a matter of any doubt that legitimate princes and potentates may exist among the heathen, since the bidding of the Apostle, in the passages above mentioned, is that one should obey potentates and princes and be subject to them at all times, and since it is certain that in those days all such powerful persons were infidels. Moreover, Joseph and Daniel were governors under pagan princes. And finally, Christian princes—whether they be secular, or lords of the Church—may not deprive infidels of this power and sovereignty merely 201
on the ground that they are infidels, when no injury has been done by them.

[1] Proverbs ,viii. 15. [2] St. John ,xix. 11. [3] *Fideles* in 1696 Edition. *Tr.*

Tenth. The three causes of public secular power, indeed, are correctly set forth in the following definition given by certain authors: Public power is the faculty, authority, or right to govern the civil State. The proof of this statement is clearly evident in what has already been said. In so far as relates to public power: we have shown that public powers are from God, and that they are therefore just and legitimate; and from all this is derived the proof of the last part of the conclusion stated above, wherein we declared that no power of this sort could be abrogated by the consent of men. For if man may not renounce the right and the means of defending himself and of using his bodily members for his own advantage, then neither may he renounce power, since these functions pertain to power by natural and divine law. In like manner, the State may in nowise be deprived of this power to protect itself and to guard against injury from its own citizens or from aliens, a function which it could not fulfil if there were no public powers; and consequently, if all the citizens should agree to dispense with these powers, in order that they might be bound by no law and that there should be no one to command, the agreement would be null and void, being contrary to natural law.

A definition of public secular power, which names three causes of that power.

202 Eleventh. The foregoing conclusions involve a corollary not to be despised, and especially not by those who live under a monarchical government. For States which have no king and which function under a popular form of government, are wont to boast of their liberty. The corollary, then, is as follows: That there is no less liberty in a monarchy than in an aristocracy, or a democracy. For Aristotle (*Politics*, 3)[1] classifies the various sorts of rule thus: monarchies, or the rule of one; aristocracies, or the rule of a select number; and democracies, or popular rule—that is, the rule of the multitude. I hold, then, that there is no less liberty under monarchical rule, than under the other forms of rule. The proof is as follows: since power itself is the same, as has already been demonstrated, whether it be invested in one or in many, and since it is better to be subject to one than to many (for there are as many masters as there are superior authorities), therefore, there is not less liberty where all are subject to one, than where all are subject to many; especially in view of the fact that where there are many rulers there are many who are ambitious for power, so that the State—because of their diverse purposes—will necessarily be afflicted with frequent insurrections and dissensions. For, as the Poet says, there is no faith in those who share power. And the Lord says, speaking through His Prophet: 'Many pastors have destroyed my vineyard.'[2] The best rule, therefore, is the rule of one, just as the whole
203 world is governed by one all-wise King and Master.

Corollary I.

Twelfth. The second corollary to be inferred from the conclusions above set forth is: That the State as a whole may rightfully be punished for the sin of the monarch. Wherefore, if any king make unjust war upon another ruler, the injured party may plunder and make lawful war upon and slay the subjects of the unjust king, even if all these subjects be innocent; for when the king has once been set up by the State, any immoderate act of his is charged against the

Corollary II.

[1] III. vii.

[2] Jeremiah, xii. 10.

State; since the latter is bound to entrust this power only to him who will be just in the exercise and use of power, and since, in doing otherwise, the State lays itself open to danger.

THIRTEENTH. The third corollary is as follows: No war is just the conduct of which is manifestly more harmful to the State than it is good and advantageous; and this is true regardless of any other claims or reasons that may be advanced to make of it a just war. The proof is: That if the State has no power to make war except for the purpose of defending itself, and protecting itself and its property, it follows that any war will be unjust, whether it be begun by the king or by the State, through which the latter is not rendered greater, but rather is enfeebled and impaired. Nay more, since one nation is a part of the whole world, and since the Christian province is a part of the whole Christian State, if any war
should be advantageous to one province or nation but injurious to the world or to **204**
Christendom, it is my belief that, for this very reason, that war is unjust. If, for example, the Spanish should undertake against the French a war which, in other respects, was just, and which was, besides, advantageous to the Spanish kingdom, but which involved Christendom as a whole in still greater harm and loss (suppose, for instance, that the Turks in the meantime take possession of Christian provinces), then the Spanish should cease from waging that war. And these are the points which pertain to the exposition of the first conclusion.

The second principal conclusion.

FOURTEENTH. Second conclusion: Just as the majority of members of a State may set up a king over the whole State, although other members are unwilling, so the majority of Christians, even though there be some who are opposed, may lawfully create a monarch whom all princes and provinces are under obligation to obey.

Proof of the first part of this conclusion.

The first part of this conclusion has been rendered sufficiently evident by the foregoing discussion. For if the State may entrust its power to some one individual, acting thus for its own advantage, it is certain that the dissent of one or of a few could not prevent the rest from caring for the welfare of the State; otherwise—that is, if the consent of all were required—insufficient provision would be made for the good of the State, since unanimous consent is rarely or never found among a multitude. It suffices, then, in order to do anything legitimately, that the majority should agree on the course in question.
This point can be satisfactorily demonstrated. For if two parties disagree, it must **205**
necessarily result that the sentiment of one party should prevail; and inasmuch as their desires conflict, the sentiment of the party which is in the minority ought not to prevail; therefore it is the sentiment of the majority which should dominate. Moreover, if the consent of all is required in order to create the king, why is it not also required in order that he be not so created? Why is unanimous consent more to be required in an affirmative than in a negative matter?

Proof of the second part.

The second part of the conclusion under consideration is that such a king rules over the whole State: that is, in a monarchical government, the king rules not only over the individual citizens, but also over the State as a whole, which is to say, over all the citizens at one time. Even though the philosophers express varying opinions and many points may be in dispute with regard to such a

State, nevertheless I am able to prove that part of our conclusion. For if the State were over the king, the result would be a democracy—that is, popular rule—and consequently not a monarchy, which is the rule of one individual: this statement is clearly corroborated by the opinion of Aristotle (*Politics*, 3).[1] Again, the State may bestow upon any person power not only over the individual citizens, but over all the citizens simultaneously; and that person will then be
206 possessed of royal power identical with the sovereignty (neither democratic nor aristocratic) that is possessed by one sole ruler. Therefore, the king is over all. Finally, appeal is not made from the king to the State; and consequently, the State is not greater than the king, or superior to him.

Proof of the third part.

The third part of this conclusion is the statement that the majority of Christians may set up a [spiritual] monarch. The proof is as follows: The Church as a whole is, so to speak, a State, and one body, this conception being in accord with the words of the Apostle: 'So we, being many, are one body';[2] consequently, the Church has the power to preserve and protect itself, and to provide for the best means of self-defence against enemies. Furthermore, since temporal ends are subordinate to spiritual ends and must serve them—a point which will be more fully discussed in another passage—if the existence of one sole monarch should be expedient to the defence and propagation of the Christian faith, I see no reason why they who have the spiritual authority to do so, should not oblige Christians to create one monarch; just as the princes of the Church, acting in behalf of their faith, deprive heretical princes of a sovereignty that is in other respects legitimate. And since—as is evident from the very beginning and before such an event actually took place—the human race did at one time possess this power (namely, the power to elect a monarch), we must conclude that it is still able to do so; for the power of which we speak, being derived from natural law, does not pass away.

Corollary.

The following corollary is attached to this conclusion: In free States such
207 as Venice and Florence, the majority may elect a king even though the rest of the citizens be opposed. This assertion would seem to hold true, not only in view of the fact that such an act is clearly advantageous to the State, but even assuming that an aristocratic or democratic government would be still more expedient. For the State has the power of self-government, and the act of the greater part is the act of the whole; therefore, the State may accept the form of government that it desires, even if this be not the best form. Rome, for example, possessed an aristocratic government, which is not the best type.

The third principal conclusion.

Fifteenth. Third conclusion: The laws and constitutions of princes are binding in such a way as to render transgressors guilty in the court of conscience; and the precepts laid down by parents for their children, and by husbands for their wives, have this same force. If time permitted, many points neither futile nor unworthy of mention might be brought up in this connexion and in support of this conclusion. But inasmuch as a lengthy discussion would be inopportune, I shall dispose of the whole matter in as few words as possible. First of all, there

[1] III. vii–viii.

[2] Romans, xii. 5.

The contrary opinion of certain persons is cited.

are some who hold that the laws possess no force which renders transgressors guilty in the court of conscience; but rather that they impose only one condition, namely, that princes and magistrates may justly punish the violators of said laws. These same persons deny that the subjects are bound in any other way in the sight of God; just as many members of religious orders say, with regard to their constitutions, that the latter render them liable to punishment, but not to guilt. **208**
Those who argue after this fashion do not make their assertions in an irrational and foolish manner; on the contrary, they support their stand by reasons and arguments not without validity. The first argument is: that any conclusion at variance with this stand would imply that secular power is spiritual, since secular power would then be binding in the court of conscience. Secondly: the aim of the State and of secular power is merely temporal—let us say, peaceful conditions, and the community life of the citizens—and therefore does not pertain to the conscience. In the third place: secular power would as a result be most defective in one respect, for it would make one liable to guilt, and it would not be able to grant absolution. In the fourth place: one would, under such circumstances, be punished twice for his sin; for the princes would punish him in this world, and God would punish him further in the next world. Fifthly: secular power cannot impose a spiritual penalty; and therefore it cannot render one liable to guilt, since there is no reason, apparently, to suppose that it can perform the one act, and not the other. Sixthly: one of two things would follow—either the prince would have the power to render one not liable to guilt, or he would have the power to render one liable; in opposition to the former assumption is the fact that *spiritual* prelates have the power to render one not liable, as is made evident in the various religions; and if the second assumption held good, in what way could it be made known when the princes wished to exercise this power of rendering one liable to guilt, since they themselves make no declarations concerning the matter?

(Margin notes: Argument I. II. III. IV. V. VI.)

The author defends the conclusion set forth.

Nevertheless, in spite of these arguments adduced by certain authoritative doctors, it seems to me indubitable that civil laws are binding in the court of conscience. For Paul apparently testifies openly to this fact in *Romans*, 13. 5, saying: 'Wherefore ye must needs be subject, not only for wrath, but also for **209**
conscience sake.' And Peter says:[1] 'Submit yourselves to every ordinance of man for the Lord's sake: whether it be to the king, as supreme . . . ', an admonition which would seem entirely unintelligible if laws were binding only in the courts of civil contentions, and not in the court of conscience. But some may retort, that to be bound in the court of conscience, and to be rendered liable to guilt, are not one and the same thing; especially since the members of religious orders admit that they are bound in the court of conscience by their laws, but maintain that the latter do not render them liable to guilt. In view of this argument, I shall add that civil laws are binding under pain of sin and guilt, in the same manner as ecclesiastical laws. This is clearly proven by the words of Paul (*Romans*, 13. 2); 'and they that resist shall receive to themselves damnation.' But none

The author expounds his opinion more clearly.

[1] 1 Peter, ii. 13.

shall receive damnation unless it be that he is guilty; and thus it follows that those who transgress laws are in truth guilty in the sight of God.

Sixteenth. However, in order that the foregoing statements may be more satisfactorily clarified and confirmed, we must note that in some respects human and divine law differ, while in other respects they agree.

In what respects divine and human law differ.

They differ, indeed, inasmuch as divine law is derived from God alone, and consequently may not be abolished nor abrogated by any one; whereas human law is, so to speak, established by man, and may therefore be abolished or annulled by man. The two kinds of law differ also in the fact that, in the case of divine law,
210 the Will of the Legislator—since His Will has the force of reason—suffices to render the law just and binding; whereas the will of the legislator does not suffice to render human law just and binding, for the precepts of the latter must also be advantageous to the State and in harmony with the other laws. Yet another difference is the fact that divine law binds one more firmly and forcefully. For in many cases divine law is binding where human law is not binding. These are the only differences which I am able to perceive.

In what they agree.

The two kinds of law agree, however, in the fact that divine law so endows a thing with the quality of a virtue or a vice that anything which is in accordance with the mandates of divine law is rendered good and serviceable, although it would not otherwise be possessed of these characteristics; whereas that which is prohibited by divine law has in it something evil and vicious which it would not otherwise have. Manifest examples of this fact are Baptism, Confession, and the other Sacraments, in which there is good only because Christ commanded that they be observed. Again, the consumption of meats, and certain other acts prohibited by the Old Law, involved no vice other than the fact that they were forbidden by the Law. Wherefore it becomes evident that nothing is a vice, except for the reason that it is prohibited in the Law; and nothing a virtue, except for the reason that the Law orders or commends it. For all goodness on the part of the human will—as the Doctors prove beyond any doubt—consists in conforming to the Divine Will and to divine law; while all wickedness springs
211 from non-conformance with divine law, that is, non-conformance with the rule by which all human acts should be guided. In like manner, human law has this same power to endow anything with the quality of a virtue, and its opposite with the quality of a vice. For just as drunkenness becomes intemperance for the reason that it is prohibited in divine law; even so does fasting become an act of virtue because it is commended by the same law; while abstinence from certain sorts of food is likewise a virtue for the reason that it is prescribed by human law. Again, not to confine ourselves to examples drawn from ecclesiastical laws, we may note an example of another sort, namely: that the buying of public office is a sin of ambition because it is prohibited by human law. And the wearing of silk is a sin of luxury only because it is forbidden. When the expenditure for a banquet is so lavish as to exceed the bounds set by law, that is intemperance; but the same expenditure, prior to the existence of the law, may have been temperance and magnificence. There is no difference in this respect between

human and divine law. For in both cases, just as there is merit in an act of virtue, so guilt attends a vicious act.

The author shows that there is inherent in human law a force which renders transgressors guilty, even as in the case of divine law.

Seventeenth. Therefore, even as divine law has a binding force that renders transgressors guilty, so human law has the same force. Lest it seem that this statement is made arbitrarily, we shall prove it as follows: Human law is derived from God; therefore it is binding even as divine law is binding. The proof of this proposition is: that among the works of God are numbered not only those things which He Himself fashions, but also everything that He creates, when acting through secondary causes; consequently, not only that law is divine which God Himself ordained, but also that law which was made
by men as agents of the Divine Power; just as the term 'pontifical laws' **212**
includes not only those established by the Pope himself, but also those which his subordinates have created by his authority. Thus the constitutions of certain universities and colleges are said to be 'pontifical', although it is clear that they were not drawn up by the Pope himself but were composed by others acting on his authority. Or, to demonstrate our point more clearly, we may argue thus: Let us suppose that the Pope has the authority to create laws that are binding in the court of conscience; if he should entrust to some agent the transmission of these laws to a certain community, and the task of enjoining obedience on the part of that community, would not the precepts of his deputy have a binding force in the court of conscience? Therefore, since God says, 'By me kings reign, and princes decree justice',[1] why should not the decrees of those kings and princes be likewise binding in the court of conscience? To make the force of our argument still more evident: it seems altogether absurd for every one to admit that, if the Pope enjoins obedience to the papal legate on the part of a given community, the precepts of that legate will have a binding force which renders guilty those who disregard them; and nevertheless to deny that when Christ enjoins obedience to princes, the laws of these princes also have a binding force which renders transgressors guilty. In short, they who concede that pontifical laws have such force as to render transgressors guilty, can in nowise deny that civil laws also have that binding force. For the Lord created secular princes for the government of the secular state in exactly the same manner in which He
created pontifical princes for the spiritual state. And the words of the Lord, 'He **213**
that despiseth you despiseth me',[2] refer not only to ecclesiastical authorities, but to civil magistrates also. Neither is obedience to secular princes less earnestly enjoined in the Scriptures than is obedience to the princes of the Church. Therefore it matters not whether laws be human or divine, in so far as their binding force is concerned; just as a Sacrament established by the Apostles or by the Church, if they possessed the power to establish it, has the same validity as if it had been instituted by Christ; and just as the Old Law, although it was given through the Angels and not directly by God Himself, was no less binding than is the Law of the Gospel, which was received directly from Christ, a fact that is not to be disputed.

[1] Proverbs, viii. 15. [2] St. Luke, x. 16.

EIGHTEENTH. However, a question may arise as to what sort of guilt is incurred by the transgressors of human laws: whether mortal, or merely venial. The fact that such guilt may at times be mortal is readily apparent in the words of Paul, already quoted: 'and they that resist shall receive to themselves damnation.'[1] Moreover, the earth swallowed up Dathan and Abiram, because they opposed Moses and Aaron:[2] whereas they would not have been punished by death, if their sin had been venial.

The doubt as to whether human law at times binds one on pain of mortal guilt; or whether it never does so.

On the other hand, it might seem that human laws could never be binding on pain of mortal guilt, for the reason that in the case of conflict between a divine
214 precept concerning a merely venial sin, and any human law whatsoever, one ought to transgress the human law rather than be disobedient to the divine ordinance; and nevertheless if the human law concerned a mortal sin, that law should be obeyed rather than the precept regarding a venial sin, since one should flee from mortal guilt more than from venial guilt. This grave doubt has been answered by what we said a little while ago. We have asserted that we must preserve the same attitude towards human and divine laws, in so far as their binding force is concerned; and that, with regard to the manner and extent in which human laws are binding, we ought to consider them as being divine. For a human law which, if it were divine, would involve transgressors in venial guilt, actually has that force; and one which, if it were divine, would involve transgressors in mortal guilt, already so involves them. As we have said, with regard to this point there is no difference between divine law and human law; since the latter is binding in the same way, but with not so much force, as if it were ordained by GOD. Consequently, just as some divine laws are binding on pain of mortal guilt, and others on pain of venial guilt, even so, some human laws bind on pain of venial guilt, and some bind on pain of mortal guilt.

Arguments on both sides of the question.

The reply of the author.

NINETEENTH. But how may one distinguish between human laws which involve the transgressor in venial guilt, and those which involve him in mortal guilt; since the civil law itself contains no explanation of this point, and since the legislator did not even take the matter into consideration when he framed the law? The answer to this query is: that not even in divine law, and especially not
215 in natural law, is a statement always included as to whether a given precept concerns mortal or venial sin; or as to the relative forcefulness of different precepts, that is, which of them has the more force. For even as the command is given: 'Thou shalt not kill', so too are given these commands: 'Neither shalt thou steal', and 'Neither shalt thou bear false witness', and, 'every idle word that men shall speak, they shall give account thereof'.[3] In both human and divine law, then, there are the same rule and the same means of measuring the relative gravity of sins; so that this entire question must be decided according to the particular case involved; just as in natural and divine law that sin is held to be *mortal* which is opposed to reason and to law, but not to the honouring of GOD or to charity towards one's neighbour, an example being blasphemy, or homicide; whereas that

Whence one may draw a distinction between human laws binding on pain of mortal guilt, and those binding on pain of venial guilt.

The author replies. The distinction pertains to the nature of the act, as in the case of natural and divine law.

[1] Romans, xiii. 2. [2] Numbers, xvi; Numbers, xxvi. 9–10; Deuteronomy, xi. 6; Psalms, cvi. 17.
[3] St. Matthew, xii. 36.

sin is *venial* which is opposed to the honouring of God or to neighbourly charity—as in the case of idle gossip and other acts of that sort; even so will distinctions be made with regard to human laws. For in the case of any decree which promotes to a considerable extent the peace of the citizens, the public well-being, and honourable habits of life, transgression is evidently a mortal sin. But if the decree be concerned with a matter less essential and, as it were, trifling, transgression is a venial sin. Examples of this sort in connexion with human laws are less easily evident than in the case of divine laws. But we may consider the matter of taxation, which seems absolutely necessary for the defence of the State and for the conduct of other public functions and works: consequently, if any one should fail to pay his taxes, he would be committing a mortal sin. If, then, no laws at all had **216**
been laid down by God; if He had entrusted to men the whole task of law-making; and if there were a civil law, 'Thou shalt not kill', and another, 'Thou shalt not bear false witness', the first law would be binding on pain of mortal guilt; the second, on pain of venial guilt. Just as such a distinction exists now in the case of these divine laws, even so, if any person should trespass against the civil law in hunting, or by wearing cotton, his act would not be considered a mortal sin. Other and more opportune examples might be mentioned: for this distinction is one which depends, not upon the will of the legislator, but upon the nature and quality of the act[1] in question.

Rebuke of the younger theologians who measure the gravity of sins by the amount of obligation.

From the foregoing statements, it becomes evident that certain of the younger theologians are greatly in error when they say that the gravity of sins is to be deduced and measured in accordance with the amount of obligation; for the correct procedure is quite the contrary. The amount of obligation should be deduced from the extent of the matter in question [i.e. of the act and its consequences]. We have no inherent knowledge that the obligation not to kill is greater than the obligation not to steal, unless that knowledge arises from the nature of the matter involved, and not by the contrary procedure. Neither is it pertinent to the question to consider whether the particular act which is commanded or prohibited would, if committed only once, be a great benefit or a great evil to the State; we should consider rather what the effect would be if that act were commonly practised, either by all or by many. For instance, if it is prohibited that any one should carry money out of the country, all those who do so are committing a mortal sin, even though a single act of this sort would cause but little harm to the State; nevertheless, the fact that the resources of the country would be exhausted if such should become the common practice, is sufficient to make this **217**
a common law, binding on pain of mortal guilt; just as one act of fornication causes but little harm, while the same deed would be extremely injurious if it were a widespread practice. Wherefore either of these acts would be a mortal sin.

The argument against the author's opinion.

On the other hand, there are those who argue with great vehemence that if the gravity of the sin is to be measured by the nature of the matter itself, then it is not the law that makes the transgressor guilty; for if the transgression is

[1] The Latin *materia* ('matter') seems to be most fittingly translated throughout this passage by the more restricted English term, 'act'. *Tr.*

injurious to the State after the law is established, it must have been injurious before the existence of that law; and therefore it was a sin—and a sin of the same gravity—before, as well as after the establishment of the law. The answer to this argument is, first: that the law binds one not only by prohibiting, but also by commanding affirmatively, and that it may therefore make obligatory a thing which—before the existence of such a law—was advantageous for the State, but not required; so that, after the law has been created, the transgression of it will be a sin, although formerly the same act was not a sin. In the second place, I maintain that it is possible—as is evident from the examples already propounded—for a given act to be an evil deed when committed by one person, and not when committed by another; whereas it is evil for all persons, after the law is established. Take for example the prohibition against the wearing of silk, or of cloth of gold—an act which formerly was evil only if committed by a poor nobleman, but which, after the law was made, was an evil deed for all persons; since there was sufficient reason to make it prohibitory for all, even though there was no inherent impropriety in the mere fact that certain powerful men wore silk or cloth of gold.

A doubt that is easily answered. The reply of the author.

218 TWENTIETH. However, there still remains the question as to whether the king has the power to exempt one from liability to guilt, if he should so desire. The answer is, that without doubt he is empowered to do so; precisely after the manner of the maker of ecclesiastical laws, who at times sets up statutes that are in no way binding, an example of this being found in certain of the statutes set up by the Superior of a religious order among his brethren. It would be most unreasonable to say that the constitutions established by ecclesiastical prelates are not always binding in such a way as to render the transgressor guilty, but that the constitutions of secular princes cannot fail to be binding in this manner. For at times the legislator, whether he be ecclesiastical or secular, does not wish to exact obedience to his laws from his subjects, but merely gives an account of what should be done, commenting and directing, rather than issuing commands. Many instances of this sort are evident in both civil and ecclesiastical laws and ordinances: just as a creditor seeking to collect his money does not always exact it by force, so to speak.

The question as to whether legislators and kings are bound by their own laws.

The author replies that in all probability they are so bound.

Proof I.

Proof II.

Confirmation.

TWENTY-FIRST. Finally, this question arises: Whether civil laws are binding upon legislators, and in particular, upon kings. For some persons are of the opinion that these legislators and kings are not so bound, inasmuch as they are over all the State and no one can have an obligation imposed upon him unless it be by a superior; but it is more probable that kings and legislators are bound by the laws. The proof of this is, first: that a legislator of this sort injures the State, and the
219 other citizens if, being himself a part of the State, he does not bear a part of the burden—in a manner that accords, to be sure, with the person, his quality, and his rank. But since this obligation is indirect, we shall offer another proof. The laws which are made by kings have the same force—a fact we have already expounded—as if they were made by the whole State; but the laws made by the State are binding upon all; therefore, even those laws which are made by the king, are binding upon the king himself. This argument is confirmed as follows: Under an

aristocratic form of government, the decrees of the Senate are binding upon the very senators who issued them; under a popular government the plebiscite is binding upon the whole people; and therefore laws made by the king are in like manner binding upon the king himself. Moreover, although the act of creating the law be voluntary on the part of the king; nevertheless, the fact that he is thereby bound or not bound, does not depend upon his own will: just as in the case of pacts; for he who enters into a pact of his own free will, is nevertheless bound thereby. From all that has been said, a corollary may be inferred, namely: that international law has not only the force of a pact and agreement among men, but also the force of a law; for the world as a whole, being in a way one single State, has the power to create laws that are just and fitting for all persons, as are the rules of international law. Consequently, it is clear that they who violate these international rules, whether in peace or in war, commit a mortal sin; moreover, in the gravest matters, such as the inviolability of ambassadors, it is not permissible for one country to refuse to be bound by international law, the latter having been established by the authority of the whole world.

Corollary concerning the binding force of international law.

The doubt as to whether the obligation to obey a law passes away, when the reason for the law passes away.

TWENTY-SECOND. Concerning the third conclusion, the following doubt 220
arises: Whether the obligation to obey a law ceases to exist, when the reason for the law ceases to exist. For example, it is forbidden to carry weapons by night, by reason of the dangers that arise thereby; but I know that no danger will result from the fact that I am armed: do I, then, sin in carrying weapons? The answer is as follows: The reason for a law may cease to exist in either one of two ways. In one way, when the reason which caused the law to be established entirely ceases to exist: if for example, in time of war it is forbidden to supply arms to the French, in time of peace that law is not binding; for if the very reason which requires that the law be binding, that it endure, and that it serve the purpose for which it was created, should pass away; then all reason for creating or even for preserving the law in question likewise passes away. This statement is confirmed by the fact that a thing is brought to corruption by the very causes that generated it. A law, then, which ceases to be useful to the State, is no longer a law. In the second place, the reason behind a law may cease to exist with special reference to one individual, but not absolutely with respect to all or to many persons, so that—as in the case which we have been considering—the individual to whom the reason for the law does not apply is nevertheless bound by the law. For the fact that dangers often arise from the practice of carrying weapons by night, is sufficient reason for prohibiting that practice to all; otherwise the law would be entirely inefficacious, since every individual would suppose that it had not been laid down for him, but for others; and in like manner, with regard to other precepts, the reason should be viewed not from a particular but from a universal standpoint.

The reply of the author.

The reason for a law may cease to exist in either one of two ways: if in the first way, the law ceases to be binding; if in the second way, the law does not cease to be binding.

A doubt arises as to whether or not the laws of tyrants are binding.

TWENTY-THIRD. Another question arises, namely: Whether the laws of 221
tyrants are binding. It might seem that they are not binding, since tyrants have no power at all. Nevertheless, the contrary is true: For if the State is oppressed by a tyrant and is not *sui juris*; and if the tyrant has not the power to create laws, while at the same time it is impossible to put into execution the laws laid down

before his time: then, unless obedience is rendered to the tyrant, the State must perish. It seems indeed that those laws which are acceptable to the State are binding, even when they have been created by a tyrant—not, to be sure, because he established them, but by the agreement of the State; for it is better to obey the laws created by a tyrant, than to obey no law at all. It is certain and obvious that the State would suffer injury if, owing to the fact that princes possessed of no just title have seized the country, there should be no provision for judicial trials, and no way in which to punish or restrain malefactors; for if the laws laid down by a tyrant are not binding, then he is not a legitimate judge.

The reply. The laws of a tyrant are binding when they are acceptable to the State.

TWENTY-FOURTH. The last part of the third conclusion is this: the commands of parents are binding, even as civil laws are binding; and the same is true with regard to the commands given by husbands to their wives. The proof of this, in so far as children are concerned, is as follows: just as we are commanded to obey those who are set in authority over us, so are we exhorted to obey our parents, as is evident from the admonition in *Ephesians* (6. 1) and *Colossians* (3. 20): 'Children, obey your parents'; if it be sinful, then, not to obey those who are set over us, so is it a sin if we be not obedient to our parents. Again, among the crimes and sins
222 enumerated in *Romans* (1. 30) into which GOD allowed men to fall is the sin of those who are 'disobedient to parents'. Furthermore, since the laws prescribe such obedience, and since the laws are binding on pain of guilt, he is guilty who does not obey his parents. This precept, indeed, seems also to be included in the command to honour one's parents. And, just as it was stated above, that laws are sometimes binding on pain of mortal guilt, sometimes, however, on pain of venial guilt; so it would appear that the same could be said regarding the precepts laid down by parents. Wherefore, surely, if a father should issue a command that was of great import in the management of the household, transgression of the command would evidently be a mortal sin; nay, more, this would also seem to be true with regard to commands referring only to the management of the son. However, as we have said, not every law is binding on pain of guilt: for example, any law by which the king guides, rather than commands, does not bind in this way; and the same assertion has far more force when applied to the precepts of parents; for the latter, when they issue commands, do not always wish to exact the obedience owed them, but sometimes merely desire to make their wishes clear.

Demonstration of the truth of the last part of Conclusion III (the last conclusion).

The commands of parents are binding upon their children: at times on pain of mortal guilt.

It should be noted, however, that the family is a part of the State, and that consequently the laws may determine in what respects children are bound to obey their parents, and in what respects they should not. For example, the State has determined the age-limit up to which such an obligation exists; and similarly, in other instances made exceptional by the laws of the State, failure to obey one's
223 parents is not a sin. In like manner, it is for the laws to determine the particular punishment with which a father may chastise a disobedient child, and to restrain the father from going beyond the limits set.

The State, by means of the laws, may determine in what respects children are bound to obey their parents, and what punishments may be inflicted by the latter.

The same points can also be proved with regard to the commands laid down by husbands for their wives. For it is necessary to the existence of the family that there be one Head, whom the other members of the family are bound to obey;

Proof of the same state-

ment with regard to the commands laid down by husbands for their wives.

and this is the husband, who is the head of the household and of the wife, as we read in *Ephesians* (5. 23). Again, in the same chapter[1] it is said: 'Wives, submit yourselves unto your own husbands, as unto the Lord.' In a later passage are the words: 'But let . . . the wife see that she reverence her husband.'[2] Moreover, wives are bound to render obedience because the laws so command; and it is for the laws also to determine in what way and to what extent a wife shall be bound to obey her husband, and also whether or not the husband may inflict corporal punishment upon his wife: even as we have said that the same questions are to be decided with respect to children and parents.

DEO GRATIAS

[1] Ephesians, v. 22.

[2] Ephesians, v. 33.

APPENDIX D

RELECTIO

OF THE REVEREND FATHER, BROTHER FRANCISCUS DE VICTORIA

CONCERNING THE POWER OF THE CHURCH

Part I, Section V

A
TRANSLATION BY
GWLADYS L. WILLIAMS

The
passage
to be discussed
is the nineteenth verse
of the sixteenth chapter of St. Matthew:
And I will give unto thee
the keys of the
kingdom
of
heaven.

SUMMARY

1. It is shown that spiritual power is greater and more excellent than civil power.
2. As to whether the Pope is lord of the world.
3. Temporal power is not derived from the Pope, as inferior spiritual powers are derived from him.
4. Civil power is not subject to the temporal power of the Pope, as if he were a temporal sovereign.
5. It is not for the Pope to judge, ordinarily, concerning the disputes of princes, or claims to dominion; and he may not ordinarily be appealed to in civil suits.
6. The Pope has not the power to depose a secular prince, even with due cause, by virtue of any temporal authority.

63 7. Civil laws do not [ordinarily] require the confirmation of the Pope; neither can he invalidate them.

8. The Pope possesses no strictly temporal power: that is, no power which is directed to a strictly temporal end.
9. Temporal power is not wholly dependent upon spiritual power in the way in which an inferior art or skill is dependent upon one that is superior.
10. Civil power is, in a sense, subject to the power of the Pope—not to his temporal, but to his spiritual power.
11. In a sense, the Church possesses temporal power and authority over the whole world.
12. The Pope, for the purpose of achieving spiritual ends, has the most ample temporal power over all princes, over all kings, and over the Emperor.
13. The sort of temporal power that the Pope may be understood to possess.
14. When the Pope should be heeded, in opposition to the King, and when he should not be heeded, in matters pertaining to some civil law, or to some point of temporal administration.
15. As to whether Christ was Lord of the whole world.
16. Christ was not King by hereditary succession.
17. Christ did not receive temporal dominion as a gift of God, after the manner of secular princes.
18. By what title the kingdom of Christ was established throughout the whole world.

66 [64] We have discussed the nature, purpose, and origin or author of spiritual power: not, indeed, in a manner worthy of the subject-matter, but rather in accordance with the narrow limits imposed by time and by our own ability. It seems to me that I shall not stray too far from the matter in hand if I undertake to compare civil with spiritual power, before passing to the discussion of the latter.

I have decided, then, to treat principally of two questions: first, whether civil power is subject to spiritual power; and secondly, whether ecclesiastical officers are subject to civil power. For the affirmative and negative sides of both questions are defended respectively by a goodly number of persons not lacking in renown.

Two questions: the first is discussed here; the second, in the immediately following section.

We have, then, this question: is spiritual power to be set over temporal or civil power? And since—as we suppose for the time being, and as we shall later prove—the Pope is sovereign with respect to all ecclesiastical power, the question also arises: is the Pope in like manner superior to all temporal princes and powers?

It is indubitable that spiritual power is more excellent than civil power.

First. I shall not revive the dispute as to which of the two sorts of power is the more perfect; for it is indubitable that the spiritual is the more excellent, the more eminent, and possessed of the supreme dignity: since different faculties, like different arts and forces, and like all things which serve a purpose, are to be valued according to the purpose which they serve; and since the purpose of spiritual 65
power excels that of temporal power to the same extent that perfect blessedness and ultimate felicity excel human or earthly felicity. As Innocent says (*Decretals*, I. xxxiii. 6): 'Spiritual things are more worthy than temporal things, in the same degree that spirits are superior to bodies.' And (in the *Epistle to the Hebrews*, chapter 7) the Apostle proves the dignity of the Evangelical priesthood, by referring to the fact that Melchisedec, who was the Priest of God, blessed Abraham (*Genesis* 14. 18–20); for there can be no doubt that he who gives the blessing is greater than he who is blessed; and Abraham was a temporal prince, that is, he performed the functions pertaining to temporal power. Spiritual power, then, is in every way greater and more august than temporal power, and should be accorded a veneration and obedience in like manner greater than the veneration and obedience accorded to temporal power. Therefore, passing over this comparison of the two sorts of power, let us turn to the other question, namely: is the Pope superior to civil powers, in jurisdiction and in authority? There are some persons, indeed, who favour the Popes so zealously as to believe that kings and other temporal princes are merely his vicars or deputies—ministers, as it were, of the papal power—and that all temporal power is derived from the Pope. Other persons, on the contrary, exempt princes from ecclesiastical power to such a degree, 66
that they leave scarcely any part of that power in its integrity, desiring that all disputes—even those of a spiritual nature—should be brought before a civil court, and settled therein. But we, tempering the force of the two conflicting opinions, shall answer the question stated above, by setting forth several propositions.

The question which is to be discussed here. Two mutually contradictory opinions are mentioned.

The author replies with three propositions. I.

Second. The first proposition is this: the Pope is not lord of the world. The proof of this proposition is to be found in *Matthew*, 20. 25–26 and *Luke*, 22. 25–26:[1] 'Ye know that the princes of the Gentiles exercise dominion over them; and they that are great exercise authority upon them. But it shall not be so among you.' And there is the closely following phrase:[2] 'Even as the Son of man came not to be ministered unto, but to minister, and to give his life a ransom for many.' It seems that in this passage the Lord forbade [to His Disciples] even the desire for individual dominion over one another; so far was He from bestowing [world-wide] sovereignty upon them.

Saint Bernard refers to the passage in question, saying (*'De confid.' ad Eugenium*, bk. 2): 'For what did the Holy Apostle transmit to you, other than this? "That which I have," he said, "I give unto you." And what is this gift? One thing I know: it is not gold or silver. You may claim the latter for any other reason that you will, but not by Apostolic right; for he was not able to give you that

[1] The passage in the Gospel of St. Luke reads as follows: 'The kings of the Gentiles exercise lordship over them; and they that exercise authority upon them are called benefactors. But ye shall not be so.' *Tr.*

[2] St. Matthew, xx. 28.

which he himself did not possess; but that which he had, he gave, namely, the care of the Churches. And what does he say concerning worldly dominion? Hearken to his own words: "Neither as being lords over *God's* heritage, but being examples to the flock."[1] And lest you should chance to think that this admonition was given merely by reason of humility, and not in the spirit of truth, remember
67 the words of the Lord, in the Gospel: "The princes of the Gentiles exercise dominion over them", &c. Clearly, worldly dominion is forbidden to the Apostles. How is it then, that you dare either to usurp the office of apostle by means of dominion, or to seize dominion in the name of the Apostles? One or the other of these two things [that is, either the office of apostle, or dominion], is expressly forbidden to you. If you wish to possess both at the same time, you shall lose both. Do not suppose that you are excepted from among the number of those of whom God said: "They have reigned, but not by me; princes have arisen and I knew them not." The Apostolic rule prohibits dominion, and proclaims the obligation of service.' And below [Saint Bernard adds]: 'Go ye out into the field: the field is the world; and go ye not as lords, but as stewards of God.'

Moreover, the Pope admits that dominion over certain lands has been granted him by the Emperor (*Decretum*, II. xii. I. 15). The same principle is evident in the following statement (*Decretum*, I. xcvi. 6): 'In truth, the Emperor should not arrogate to himself pontifical rights; neither should the Pope usurp the title of the Emperor'. Furthermore, the Pope does not have dominion over the lands of infidels, since he possesses power only within the Church; dominion over those who are outside the Church does not pertain to him, according to the Apostle (I *Corinthians*, 5).[2] Again, infidels may in truth be rulers, since the Apostle (*Romans*, 13)[3] commands that tribute be paid them, even by the faithful, and declares that their power is derived from God and that their laws must be obeyed; nevertheless, they do not receive this dominion from the Pope; for surely he is unwilling that they should possess it, and labours to overthrow the sovereignty of pagans; therefore, he is not lord of the world. Whence it becomes clear that
68 many jurisconsults are in error—for example, the Archbishop Panormitanus, Angelus, Ancharanus, Sylvester, and a host of others—for they hold that the Pope is lord of the world in the strictly temporal sense; and that he possesses a temporal authority and power of jurisdiction throughout the world and over all princes. In my opinion, this statement is indubitably and manifestly false, although the authorities cited declare it to be manifestly true. I believe that it is merely a fabrication intended as flattery and adulation for the Popes. More sagacious jurisconsults, such as Joannes Andrea[4] and Hugo, hold the opposite view on this

[1] I Peter, v. 3.

[2] Verses 12–13 read as follows: 'For what have I to do to judge them also that are without? do not ye judge them that are within? But them that are without God judgeth. . . .' *Tr.*

[3] Verses 1–7 bear on this point. *Tr.*

[4] The text of the 1696 edition reads 'Ang.'; but Victoria apparently does not refer in any other passage to a Joannes Angelus; whereas, in the *De Indis* (p. 240 of the Classics of International Law edition) Iohanis Andrea and Hugo are cited together as denying the Pope's temporal sovereignty over the whole world. Other misprints occurring in the citations make it still more probable that 'Ang.' appears here for 'And.' *Tr.*

point. Neither did Saint Thomas ever attribute such dominion to the Pope, although he was a most zealous supporter of the papal authority. In the second place, another assertion made by the same persons is not only clearly false, but even ridiculous: that is, the assertion that the donation granted to Sylvester, and that other grant made by Philippus Augustus, were not in point of fact, donations, but acts of restitution; while, on the other hand, Pope Sylvester actually donated the empire of the East to Constantine, in the interests of peace. In like manner, these persons maintain that the fact that the Pope does not exercise a temporal administration throughout the Christian world is not due to any defect in his authority, but results from his desire to strengthen the bond of unity and peace among his children. It is certain that such a belief has no foundation in the Scriptures; neither do we read anywhere that this power was given to the Apostles by Christ, that they exercised it, or that they spoke of possessing any such power; **69**
and furthermore, the Pope himself has never recognized the existence of the power in question, but has testified to the contrary in many statements, from which we have already drawn several quotations. The learned Innocent says quite clearly (in *Decretals*, IV. xvii. 13), that he has no power over the Kingdom of France in temporal matters.

II. THIRD. The second proposition is as follows: temporal power is not derived from the Pope, as inferior spiritual powers are—for example, bishoprics, or curateships, or other spiritual powers. The proof of this second proposition lies in that which precedes it. For the Pope does, in a certain sense, confer power and authority upon bishops and inferior ecclesiastical officers, a point which we shall discuss later; but he confers no power upon kings and princes, because no person gives that which he does not have; and since—as we have already proved—the Pope himself is not a secular sovereign, he cannot bestow secular sovereignty upon others, and consequently cannot make temporal kings or princes; that is, he cannot do so through any temporal power. The proof of this assertion is to be found also in the preceding part of our discussion, where we quoted the admissions made by **70**
the Popes themselves. The same point may be proved by means of the following argument: temporal power existed before the keys of power were given to the Church, for there were true princes and temporal lords before the advent of Christ; neither did Christ come to take away that which belonged to others; therefore, [He did not transfer this temporal power to the Church], neither did the Church have need of such temporal dominion; therefore, [there is no reason to suppose that it possesses that dominion]. This second proposition is not altogether identical with the first, because it might pertain to the office of the Pope to set up kings, even if he himself were not a sovereign: just as he gives dominion over and claim to certain prebendships and temporal goods of which he himself is not the owner; and just as the Emperor creates and ordains Dukes, although he himself is not endowed with the authority pertaining to that position, a position which he cannot reserve to himself. But I maintain that the Pope is not set over temporal kings and princes, even in the sense of creating or being able to create them; and I am as free from doubt with regard to this proposition as I was with

Let heretics note that this Catholic does not heap adulation upon the Pope, and yet he attributes supreme spiritual power to him: and he believes indeed that all temporal or civil powers are subject to the Pope, in so far as is necessary for the attainment of spiritual ends; as we shall see, later, in the eighth proposition.

regard to the first; although my opponents commonly assert that the Pope created all temporal power, delegating it and making it subject to his own authority. They claim, too, that the Pope made Constantine Emperor. But all these assertions are fictitious and highly improbable; neither are they supported by any reasonable argument, or by the testimony of any of the fathers of the Church or even by the theologians. The fact is that certain legal commentators bestowed this power
71 upon the Pope, because of their own poverty both of material possessions and of doctrine. Finally, dominion over private property is not derived from the Pope; and therefore public dominion is not derived from him.

III. To the heretic who strives to misinterpret the words he reads: Note at this point the sense which the author himself assigns to his own statement of opinion.

FOURTH. The third proposition is this: civil power is not subject to the temporal power of the Pope; although I do not say that it is in no way subject to him. For it is certain that all powers are subject to the Pope, by virtue of his spiritual power, which makes us all his sheep, while he himself is the shepherd. Nevertheless, I assert that civil power is not subject to him because of any temporal sovereignty on his part.

This proposition differs somewhat from both the first and the second. For granting that the Pope is not lord of the world, and that he does not possess the power to create worldly sovereigns; he might nevertheless be superior to such sovereigns, just as the Emperor is superior to certain kings without being the ruler of their kingdoms, and without possessing the power to create kings within their provinces; or just as the King of France in recent times was superior to the Count of Flanders, although he was not strictly speaking a sovereign over the latter and did not appoint the Counts of that territory. Indeed, any king is superior to all the private individuals within the kingdom, and yet it is not he who makes them masters of their own property. I maintain, then, that princes, or kings, are not subject to the Pope even in this last sense.

This proposition requires no proof, since it is obviously true, in the light of the preceding propositions. However, we may confirm it, as follows: the temporal State is perfect, and complete in itself; therefore, it is not subject to any outside
72 force, since if it were thus subject, it would not be complete; therefore, it can create for itself a prince who is in no way subject [to any temporal authority]. Moreover, we do not read of any temporal dominion possessed by the priests among the people of Israel, at the time when the latter had kings and priests. From what source, then, can such a power have sprung, this power which the Scriptures do not mention? But the most valid proof of all is this: the possession of such temporal power by the Pope is not proved in any way whatsoever; therefore, he does not possess it. Furthermore, if the Pope did possess the power in question, why should a bishop not have the same temporal power over his bishopric?

FIFTH. There is a corollary which obviously follows upon these propositions, namely: it is not for the Pope to judge, ordinarily, concerning the disputes of princes, or laws relating to sovereignty, or claims to dominion over various kingdoms; neither may he be appealed to, ordinarily, in civil suits. All this is evident from the propositions already set forth: for if the Pope is not a [temporal] Lord, and not superior to princes [in a temporal sense], there is no reason for appealing to him in ordinary civil disputes. And I say that the Pope is not possessed of such secular power, either with regard to its use and execution, or even with regard to the authority inherent therein. For those who defend the temporal power of the Pope admit, indeed, that he does not ordinarily put it to use; but they add that this is due, not to any defect in the papal authority, but merely to the fact that he himself has given and transferred the power and its exercise to temporal princes.

The opinion of the author is as follows: the Pope does not possess inherently the supreme temporal power or dominion received by Christ, to whom every other temporal power was commonly and inherently subject.

Whereas I maintain that the Pope possesses neither the ability to use the power in **73**
question, nor the power itself; and that consequently it does not befit him to pass judgement in temporal disputes, whether in the first instance, or after an appeal has been made to him: that is to say, in ordinary cases, such an act does not befit him; for I do not deny that there are cases in which recourse may be had to the Pope; neither do I deny that he may on particular occasions rescind a civil judgement. However, he would do so, not by virtue of any temporal power, but acting entirely through his spiritual power, as I shall presently explain. Pope Alexander III admitted this fact, when he said (in *Decretals*, IV. xvii. 7): 'Being mindful of the fact that it pertains to the King, and not to the Church, to pass judgement concerning material possessions; and in order that we may not seem to disparage the right of the English, who assert that it is for them to judge concerning the possessions in question: we leave that judgement to be rendered by the king, while we command your fraternity', &c. And Bernard wrote to Eugene: 'You have power over sins [that is, you have power with regard to moral questions]; but not over material possessions: it was in the former sense, indeed, that you received the keys to the kingdom of heaven.' He adds: 'These insignificant worldly matters are subject to their own judges and their earthly princes.' In like manner, Innocent III (in *Decretals*, II. i. 13) says: 'For we shall not attempt to pass judgement with respect to fiefs, since that is a question concerning which the king should judge.'

Sixth. A second corollary of the three propositions stated is this: the Pope has not the power to depose a secular prince, even with due cause, as he has the power to depose a Bishop. In all these statements, the phrase 'by virtue of any temporal authority', is to be understood; for they do not apply to cases involving **74**
spiritual power, or to certain specific occasions, as I shall explain later. The truth of this corollary is evident from what we have already said.

Seventh. A third corollary of the first, second, and third propositions is as follows: in ordinary cases, civil laws do not require the confirmation of the Pope; nor can he invalidate them. This statement is obviously true, in the light of the foregoing discussion: for, if civil power is not dependent upon the Pope, the acts of civil power cannot be dependent upon him.

Proposition IV. In this proposition one must understand the restricting

Eighth. The fourth proposition is this: the Pope possesses no strictly temporal power. Allow me to add in explanation of this statement, that civil or temporal power is that power which is directed towards a temporal end; while spiritual power is that which is directed towards a spiritual end. I mean to say, then, that the Pope possesses no power directed towards a temporal end; in other

words, no strictly temporal power. This is the opinion held by Cajetan (*Apol.* c. 6, ad octavum argumentum Almain). The proposition may be proved thus: we have stated above that spiritual and temporal power differ with respect to the end towards which each is directed, for the end of spiritual power is in itself spiritual; but the Pope is merely a personage, or Priest, in whom the supreme power of the Church [that is, supreme spiritual power] resides; and therefore, the Pope has no power which tends to a temporal end. This argument may be confirmed as follows: without possessing any purely temporal power, he would still be the Pope, since he would be endowed with the supreme ecclesiastical power; therefore, there
75 is no need to deposit any temporal power in him. A second confirmation is this: the necessity and reason for things is to be deduced from the end which these things serve; but no end at all would be served in depositing this temporal power in the Pope; therefore, [such an act would be neither necessary nor reasonable]. And although several followers of Thomas Aquinas are to be found among those who support the opposite opinion, nevertheless, it is my belief that Saint Thomas agrees with the statements set forth above, a belief which I support by these arguments: first, as we have already said, he never attributed power of this sort to the Pope, although he himself was a zealous supporter of the Popes; secondly, and chiefly, according to Saint Thomas, ecclesiastical officers are exempt from the payment of tribute because that privilege has been conferred upon them by secular princes—a point to which I shall later return; whereas there would be no need of a privilege granted by secular princes for the exemption of ecclesiastical officers, if the Pope were the supreme temporal ruler—as our opponents assert—and if kings derived their power from him.

phrase: 'by virtue of the fact that he is Pope, that is, the Pastor of the Church of Christ'; for, in any other sense, the Pope—as we know—may be temporal lord of Rome or of certain States; and we know, too, that not a few of the German bishops are dukes or counts.

Concerning this point, more will be said later.

Proposition V.

Ninth. The fifth proposition is as follows: Temporal power is not wholly dependent upon spiritual power, in the way in which an inferior art or skill is dependent upon one that is superior: as skill in handling the reins, for example, is the servant of equestrian skill; as skill with nautical instruments serves the skill of the seaman; as that involved in the use of weapons is subservient to military skill. My reason for setting forth this proposition is the fact that the Doctors do indeed draw such a comparison between the two sorts of power in question. The proof of the proposition is this: the existence of civil power is not absolutely due to the existence of spiritual power; whereas an inferior art does exist precisely because of the existence of the superior art; therefore, the comparison is not quite exact. Both parts of the antecedent are obviously true. For there would be no
76 art of weapons, if there were no military art; and no skill with the reins, if there were no equestrian skill; since all art of this kind [that is to say, all such art as is involved in handling weapons and in the management of reins] is organic, that is to say, instrumental; and if the purpose ceased to exist, there would be no use for the instrument, and—what is more—there would be no instrument. But such is not the case in a comparison of civil with spiritual power: for even if the latter did not exist, and if there were no state of supernatural blessedness, there would still be a certain order in the temporal state, and a certain power; just as order and power exist among natural creations, even those which are irrational, so that some

Even if there were no spiritual power, and no state of supernatural bliss, there would

still be some kind of temporal or civil power.

of these creations are active, and others passive, solely in order to serve the universal good. There is a great difference, then, between the two comparisons. Therefore, we should not conceive of the one power as being derived from the other, as existing solely because the latter exists, and as forming, so to speak, an instrument or part of that superior power in the way in which that of the praetor, for example, forms a part of the kingly power. On the contrary, civil power is complete and perfect in itself, and directed to its own immediate end.

Nevertheless, as we have already remarked, it is in a certain sense subordinated to spiritual power. The confirmation of this statement is as follows: according to the opinion of the wisest philosophers, it would be the duty of a brave man to lay down his life for the State, even if there were no felicity to be attained after this earthly existence; that is, the State would continue to exist, even if the end to which spiritual power tends, were removed; and consequently some orderly relationship of princes and subjects would also continue to exist, since, without 77
this relationship, there would be no State.

Proposition VI.

TENTH. The sixth proposition is this: notwithstanding the truth of the foregoing statements, civil power is, in a sense, subject to the power of the Pope—not to his temporal, but to his spiritual, power. The proposition may be proved thus: if the end of a given faculty is subordinate to the end of another faculty, then the first faculty is itself subordinate to the second. ([Aristotle,] *Ethics*, I [i].) Saint Thomas (II. ii, qu. 40. art. 3 [art. 2, reply to obj. 3]) makes this same comparison. But the end of temporal power is, in a sense, subordinate to the end of spiritual power; and therefore the former power is subordinate to the latter. The proof of this assumption is as follows: human felicity[1] is imperfect, and is subordinate to the perfection of supernatural blessedness; just as the art of manufacturing weapons is subordinate to that of soldiers and generals, while the art of ship-building is subordinate to that of the seaman, and the art of making ploughshares to that of agriculture, and so on. We should not suppose, then, that civil and spiritual power are like two distinct and separate States, such as the French and English nations. Our contention may be confirmed and

Civil administration, when detrimental to spiritual administration, must be altered.

expounded in the following manner: if a given form of civil administration should prove detrimental to spiritual administration, then—even if the form of administration in question were well-fitted to the attainment of the ends of civil power itself—the king or prince would nevertheless be obliged to alter that form: a point 78
which I shall presently prove. Therefore, civil power is, in a sense, subject to spiritual power. On the other hand there are those who argue that, in like manner, if spiritual power were injurious to the State, the Pope would be obliged to alter his method of administration. The reply to this argument is as follows: it is not true [that one power is thus subjected to the other], except in cases where such subjection is necessary or extremely useful; and in such cases, it is the temporal interests which must be subordinated to the spiritual interests, even though the former be entirely sacrificed. It will not suffice to answer that, even if the

[1] The text reads *specialitas*, 'peculiarity'; evidently a slip for *felicitas*. The marginal note in the 1696 edition makes the suggestion: 'Forte potestas' ('Perhaps the word should be *power*'). *Tr.*

foregoing statements are true, their truth is not due to any subjection or dependence on the part of civil power, but rather to the fact that the end of spiritual power is more perfect than the end of civil power; so that, for charity's sake, spiritual good should be allowed to prevail over temporal good. Such an argument I say, is not valid. For if temporal power were in no sense subject or subordinate to spiritual power, then—even granting that spiritual good is greater than temporal good—there would arise no obligation to preserve the former to the detriment of the latter. We may prove our assertion thus: the ruler of one State is not bound to further the welfare of another State—although the latter may be much the greater of the two—by any means which will be detrimental to his own State, and indeed, it is his duty not to do so. Furthermore, a private individual is not bound to endure injury to his own interests in order to preserve a foreign State.

Within the Church, the civil State is subordinate to the spiritual State.

79 Therefore, if the civil and spiritual States were entirely independent of each other, like two temporal States, or like two unrelated arts, the temporal prince would not be bound to serve spiritual interests, to the detriment of the temporal State. And it is useless to argue that the king is obliged to serve spiritual interests, out of regard for his subjects; that in case the subjects should suffer spiritual injury, it would be necessary for him to succour them even to the great detriment of temporal interests and the temporal government; that if the king did not act thus, he would be doing the subjects an injury; but that all this is due to the fact that they are his subjects. I maintain that this argument, also, is invalid. For such an obligation on the part of the king does not exist merely with respect to his own subjects; on the contrary, if great spiritual injury to Africa should result from the civil administration of the Spanish State, the Spanish prince would be bound to correct that form of administration. The obligation, then, is derived from dependence and subordination. This statement is confirmed as follows: the whole Church is one body; not two bodies, resulting from the two States, civil and spiritual, but one only. This fact is made evident in the statement of Saint Paul to which we have already referred. For Christ is the Head of the whole Church, and it would be monstrous if there should exist a body with no head, or if one head were joined to two bodies; on the contrary, that which exists is a single body

The civil and spiritual States comprise not two bodies, but one.

80 in which all the members are mutually connected and properly subordinated, the ignoble parts serving those parts which are more noble; so also in the Christian State, all offices, ends, and powers are properly subordinated and connected. And since it can in no wise be said that the spiritual members serve those which are temporal, one must say that, on the contrary, the temporal members serve those which are spiritual, and are dependent upon them. Another proof is this: it would seem that a priest of the New Law possesses no less dignity than a priest of the Old Law; and the latter had the power, in certain cases, to pass judgement in temporal disputes, a fact which we have already proven (*Deuteronomy* 17);[1] [therefore, the priests of the New Law also have that power].

In the Church the temporal State serves the spiritual State, and not vice versa.

Section 5; number 6.

ELEVENTH. The seventh proposition is this: in a sense, the Church possesses temporal power and authority over the whole world. The truth of this proposition

Proposition VII.

[1] *Vide* verses 8–13. *Tr.*

is made evident, first (in *Decretum*, I. xxii. I), in which Pope Nicholas says: 'Christ entrusted to the blessed Peter, who bears the keys of eternal life, the laws of both earthly and celestial empire.' And with regard to this statement, the *Gloss* (*Argumentum*) says: 'That is, the Pope possesses both swords, namely, the spiritual, and the temporal sword.' The same assertion appears in *Decretum*, I. lxvi. 33 [I. lxiii. 33]; *Ibid.*, II. xv. 6. 4; and *Ibid.*, 5, respectively. The blessed Bernard also makes an express statement to this effect in a letter to Eugene; and nevertheless he by no means attempts to flatter the Pope, or win his favour, in this letter; on the contrary, he restrains the papal ambition in so far as he is able. Moreover, the proposition under discussion may be proved by the following argument: it was necessary for convenience in ecclesiastical administration, and for the spiritual ends of the Church, that some temporal power should exist **81**
therein; therefore, such power must be deposited in the Church. The antecedent will be proved and expounded in our discussion of the eighth proposition, which is as follows:

In what sense the Pope possesses both swords.

Proposition VIII.

TWELFTH. The eighth proposition: the Pope, for the purpose of attaining spiritual ends, has the most ample temporal power over all princes, over all kings, and over the Emperor. First, we may prove that the Church possesses temporal power for the attainment of spiritual ends, by the following argument: temporal things, as we have already said, are in a sense necessary for and subordinated to spiritual ends; consequently, Christ would not have made sufficient provision or taken sufficient care for spiritual matters, if He had not left some power which would be fitted, when need should arise, to regulate and employ temporal things in such a way as to promote spiritual ends; but this function does not pertain to the office of secular princes, who are ignorant of the comparative relationship between temporal and spiritual matters, and are not entrusted with the care of the latter; therefore, the task of employing temporal things for spiritual ends is a function of ecclesiastical power; and consequently, if it should at any time be necessary to use the material sword and temporal authority for the purpose of preserving and administering spiritual interests, the Pope would have the power to do so. I hold, indeed, that he has this power in the highest degree: for to whatever extent, and at whatever time such acts may be necessary for spiritual **82**
ends, the Pope is able not only to perform all the acts that may be performed by secular princes, but also to create new princes, depose others, divide empires, and do many things. However, in expounding this matter more fully, we must take into consideration several difficulties.

A doubt which arises.

THIRTEENTH. For example, it is doubtful whether one should conceive of this temporal power on the part of the Pope as being exercised only indirectly, by means of spiritual power and the spiritual sword; or whether the Pope may exercise temporal power directly. If, for instance, it should become necessary for purposes of defence to have the Spanish go forth to war against the Saracens, would the Pope merely have power to urge the king, by means of reproof and injunctions, to undertake this war; or would he himself, acting on his own authority, be able to declare war and call the Spaniards together for this purpose,

in such a way that they would be bound to follow him even as they would follow the king? Or, to take a more familiar example, suppose that the Emperor should create a law to the effect that the possessor may make a claim by prescription even when acting in bad faith; suppose that this law is not so unjust in itself as to lose all force without being revoked, and that nevertheless, since it affords occasion for injury and rapine, doing more harm than good, it is expedient that the law should be rejected and abolished. The question then arises as to whether the Pope, acting directly on his own authority, can revoke this law and create another that is contrary to it, or whether he can only admonish the Emperor, urging the latter
83 to revoke and abolish the law. I answer, first: that the Pope has not, in ordinary cases, the power to revoke that law while acting directly on his own authority; for such an act is one which pertains to civil power, and the Pope should not and cannot usurp civil power, except in cases of necessity; if he should do so, he would inflict an injury upon civil princes, since he would be usurping their office. This statement may be proved as follows: if the Pope were able to exercise civil power solely on the ground that a given act involving such power would assist in the attainment of spiritual ends, then the Pope would on every occasion be able to exercise all civil power, since temporal administration in its entirety is a necessary factor in attaining spiritual ends; and as a result, the office of prince would cease to exist. Therefore, in order that a given act may fittingly be performed by the Pope, it does not suffice that the act in question should be necessary, in a general sense, to the attainment of spiritual ends; on the contrary, the particular case involved should also be one of necessity; that is, a case in which civil power ceases to function, not one in which it still has the ability to perform its offices. In my opinion, then, the Pope should first avail himself of his spiritual power, that is, he should command that the law in question be revoked; and if the secular prince refuses to obey this command, then the Pope himself can and should revoke the law, acting on his own authority; and the revocation will be effective. And I hold, in like manner, that if a Christian people should elect an infidel prince, and the
84 Pope should justly fear that the nation might be turned from its faith by this prince, then, even though the latter would be their true ruler, from the viewpoint of divine law, the Pope ought nevertheless to admonish the people—and even command them—to rid themselves of such a ruler; and if the people were unwilling or unable to obey the Pope, in that case he could, on his own authority, remove the prince; and thus he who had formerly been a true prince would be deprived of his princely office by the authority of the Pope. I hold also that in regard to other temporal affairs, the Pope cannot anticipate the acts of temporal power; neither has he any authority to act in cases which threaten no injury to spiritual interests, however negligent temporal power may be, on these occasions, in the administration of the State: but in cases which do threaten grave harm to spiritual interests, the Pope has power to apply a remedy in the manner already set forth. Similarly, if two princes are waging war against each other over some province, to the manifest detriment and injury of religion, the Pope not only has the power to forbid the continuation of this war; but—if the contending rulers

The author replies to the doubt which has been expressed.

When the civil State is in need of correction or admonition, it is fitting that the Pope should first avail himself of his spiritual power—commanding, and compelling by means of censure; and then, if he accomplishes nothing by this means, he may make use of his temporal power, having been compelled by necessity to do so. This must be understood as referring to Christian States which are directly subject, not to the Pope himself, but to other princes.

The case of necessity in which the Pope may avail himself

of his temporal power in the manner indicated above, is—according to the author—a case in which the temporal State is administered in such a way as to threaten injury to the spiritual State.

cannot come to an agreement in any other way—he can also act on his own authority as their judge, deciding in favour of the one, and against the other. The reason for all this is that the spiritual State—like the temporal State—must be perfect and, consequently, self-sufficient; and a temporal State has this right, 85
namely, that when it cannot in any other way preserve itself from injury and harm, it may exercise jurisdiction and authority over a foreign province: for if the Spanish were not able to defend themselves against injury from the French in any other manner, it would be permissible for them to seize the cities of the latter, set up new princes and rulers therein, punish the guilty, and perform other similar acts on their own authority, as if they were the true rulers of the French, a right which all the Doctors must acknowledge; and therefore, if spiritual power were not in any other way able to preserve the spiritual State from harm, it could, on its own authority, perform all the acts [including those which pertain to the civil State], that might be necessary to its safety; otherwise, spiritual power would be a cripple, and insufficiently prepared to attain its natural end.

A second doubt.

FOURTEENTH. A second doubt which arises is this: granting that the Pope does not possess temporal power in the ordinary sense, but only in case of necessity, if he should declare that some civil law or some other point of temporal administration is not fitting or expedient to the government of the State, and should therefore command that the law in question be abolished, and if the king should make a conflicting declaration, which declaration is to be heeded? The answer is as follows: if[1] the Pope should say that the administrative point under discussion is not expedient to the temporal government of the State, no heed ought to be paid to him; since the prince, and not the Pope, is the one to pass judgement on this matter; so that, even granting that the statement of the Pope 86
might be true, the case would in no way fall under the papal authority. In other words, if the point in question is not opposed to spiritual welfare or to the interests of religion, that fact suffices to bar the exercise of papal power. But if the Pope declares that a given administrative factor is detrimental to spiritual welfare—saying, for example, that a certain law cannot be obeyed without mortal sin, or that it is contrary to divine law, or that it encourages sinful practices —then one must abide by the papal decision; since it is not for the king to pass judgement in spiritual matters, a fact which we have already noted. All this is true provided that the Pope is not manifestly in error, or acting fraudulently; for he should be mindful of the requirements of temporal administration, and should not make a hasty decree, without any respect to temporal interests, merely because that decree seems, on first thought, to promote the interests of religion. For neither princes nor the people are bound to conform to the best possible plan of Christian life, nor can they be forced to do so; on the contrary, they can be obliged only to observe the law of Christianity within certain limits and boundaries. The confirmation of this statement is as follows: Christ left in one Church two distinct powers for the conservation and increase of temporal as well as

The reply of the author.

With regard to the welfare or injury of temporal things, the king should be heeded.

With regard to the welfare or injury of spiritual things, the Pope should be heeded.

[1] The text has simply *Responsi Papa*; part of the phrase—which may have been *Respondeo si Papa*, or some similar combination of words—has apparently been omitted. *Tr.*

spiritual interests, and it is possible that doubts and controversies may not infrequently arise between these two powers; therefore, it would seem that the
87 Church had been imperfectly provided for, if there were no tribunal where doubts of this kind might be resolved; otherwise, the Church would become an illustration of the rule that, 'Every kingdom divided against itself is brought to desolation' (*Matthew*, 12. 25 and *Luke*, 11. 17). Neither is it reasonable to say that this tribunal should be constituted of secular princes, for the latter cannot judge aright concerning spiritual matters; and consequently, it is evident that the office in question pertains to the princes of the Church. Furthermore, no matter how great the accompanying detriment to the administration of temporal affairs, if any act is necessary to the spiritual life of the subjects, temporal considerations must be laid aside; and therefore—since the examination of spiritual questions pertains to the office of ecclesiastical prelates—it is for the prelates to pass judgement in cases involving a comparison of temporal and spiritual interests. It is apparently in this sense—the sense which we have discussed above—that Pierre de la Palu concedes authority in temporal matters to the Pope, although he extends that power more generously than is necessary. (See his treatise *On the Power of the Church*.) And Boniface VIII says (in *Extravagantes Communes*, I. viii. 1): 'With regard to this question, indeed' (that is, the question of the papal power) 'we learn from the Gospel that there are two swords, the spiritual and the temporal: for the Apostles said: "Lord, behold, here are two swords,"[1] &c.' And later, Boniface [*Extrav. Comm.*, I. viii. 1] adds: 'There is no power but of God; but all those things which are of God are well-ordered; yet they would not be well-ordered if one sword were not subordinated to the other, so that the one which is, so to speak, inferior, is forced by some other agency into the
88 service of higher things.' Innocent III makes a similar statement (in *Decretals*, IV. xvii. 13.)

The Pope has two swords: the spiritual, and the temporal.

However, there are a number of arguments which may be adduced in opposition to some of the statements that we have made; and certain authors have been moved by these arguments to take the contrary view with regard to several of the propositions stated.

There is a question as to whether Christ was Lord of the whole world.

Arguments against the first three propositions, adduced by those who entertain an opinion contrary to that of the author.

FIFTEENTH. The first argument, then, and one which is opposed in particular to the first three propositions, is as follows: Christ our Redeemer was Lord of the world, an office befitting his humanity; but the Pope is the Vicar of Christ; therefore, the Pope is truly lord of the world, and so possesses power of every sort over all princes, and over every temporal power. The truth of the antecedent is evident, for Christ Himself is King of kings and Lord of lords (*Revelation* 18)[2], and of Himself, He says: 'All power is given unto me in heaven and in earth' (*Matthew*, 28. 18). And the Prophets also declare: 'And he is the governor among the nations' (*Psalm* 21)[3], 'And his kingdom ruleth over all' (*Psalm* 102; and

[1] St. Luke, xxii. 38.

[2] This is the chapter number given in the Latin text. The reference is probably to Revelation xix. 6; see also Revelation, xvii. 14. *Tr.*

[3] xxii. 28 of the King James version, which has been used throughout these translations whenever possible. The Douay version, xxi. 29, reads thus: 'And he shall have dominion over the nations.' *Tr.*

Psalm 46).[1] The truth of the consequent is proved by the simple command given to Peter: 'Feed my sheep' (*John*: the last chapter). Therefore it would seem that Peter, even as Christ, has unlimited authority, in order that he may feed the sheep of Christ—authority, that is, in both spiritual and temporal matters. Moreover, Christ said to the Apostles: 'As my Father hath sent me, even so send I you'
(*John*, 20. 21). But He Himself was sent, possessing both sorts of power; therefore, 89
both sorts still exist in the Church. Furthermore, it seems that He set Himself up as King; for He was accused of doing so, and apparently did not deny the accusation (*Luke*, 23; *John*, 19; *Matthew*, 27).

The author replies to this argument, before he mentions the others.

To this first argument, I reply: that the fact that Christ possessed temporal power, or that he was Lord of the world, does not in itself suffice to prove that He endowed the Church with such power: just as the doctors admit that Christ possessed the power of excellence, which He nevertheless did not transmit to the Church; since the Church cannot institute new sacraments, or abandon those which have already been established, or remit sins without administering the Sacrament, while Christ possessed the power to do all these things. Even if we grant, then, that Christ had dominion over the whole world, it was expedient that He should have such dominion, both because of the authority of His person, and because He was destined to renew the world; neither was it possible for Him to abuse power; it was not expedient, however, that He should transmit that power to the Church, since the ecclesiastical dignitaries might have used it wrongfully, to the injury of the Church—in other words, the transference of the power was not advisable, for the very reason which causes the doctors who oppose our opinion to admit that the *exercise* of such power by the Pope is not expedient [although they maintain that he does *possess* it]. And what need was there for the existence of that theoretical[2] power, which the Church
was never to use? 90

The author's second reply to the same argument.

Sixteenth. In the second place—having dealt more fully in another passage with this matter of the temporal power of Christ—I shall merely say for the present, that Christ was not king by hereditary succession: this fact is evident, since we read of no such kingdom in the Gospel, and vainly seek to invent it; moreover, it would seem that no woman can succeed to the throne, and therefore Christ [as the Son of Mary] could not do so.

The third reply to the same argument: wherein copious proof is given of the fact that the kingdom of Christ was not temporal.

Seventeenth. In the third place, I answer that, in my opinion, Christ did not receive temporal dominion as a gift of God, after the manner of secular princes; for His kingdom is of another sort. These two statements may be proved as follows: throughout the Scriptures, wherever mention is made of the kingdom of the Messiah, it is always apparent that this kingdom is of a different kind from those which are temporal, and that it is directed to a different end: a fact that is clearly brought out in the *Second Psalm*: 'But I am appointed king by him over

[1] ciii. 19 of the King James version; and xlvii. 9, 'God reigneth over the heathen'. The Douay version reads as follows: (cii. 19) 'And his kingdom shall rule over all'; (xlvi. 9) 'God shall reign over the nations.' *Tr.*

[2] The Latin reads: *potestate Mathematica*, literally: 'Mathematical power.' *Tr.*

Sion his holy mountain, preaching his commandment.'[1] Christ himself deemed this same passage worthy to be expounded in the Gospel (*John*, 18. 36–37): 'My kingdom is not of this world. . . . To this end was I born, and for this cause came I into the world, that I should bear witness unto the truth.' Which is the same as to say, 'preaching his commandment'. Surely, if one takes this passage literally, it seems that Christ excluded from it entirely any suggestion of temporal rule. For when Pilate asked: 'Art thou the king of the Jews?' the Lord answered: 'Sayest thou this thing of thyself, or did others tell it thee of me?'[2] These words
91 clearly prove our point. For Pilate, being ignorant of the Law and of religion, could have had in mind no other than a temporal kingdom, such as those of secular princes; and consequently, if he put this question on his own initiative, asking whether Christ was king, he must have meant the term to refer to such a temporal kingdom, in which event the question would have called for a different answer from that which Christ gave; but if the words of Pilate were inspired by the accusation of the Jews, who said that Jesus was setting himself up as king, then the answer ought not to have been the same [as if Pilate had asked the question of his own accord]. And so, when Pilate had said: 'Thine own nation, and the chief priests have delivered thee unto me',[3] the Lord admonished him that he should not be deceived by the calumnies of the Jews, but should understand that the kingdom which the Jews were unwilling for Christ to rule was not of such sort as Pilate might have supposed, being, on the contrary, the kingdom of the Messiah, and not of this world: that is, did not exist for the same reason as other kingdoms, neither was it directed towards the same end, but rather to the proclamation of truth; as if Christ had said, 'Do not be deceived; my kingdom, which the Jews accuse me of desiring, is not such a kingdom as yours'. Therefore, if one considers the matter well, the conclusion is that He did not deny the charge; neither did the Jews at any time accuse Him of claiming any kingdom other than that of the Messiah; for these are their words (*Luke*, 23. 2): 'We found this fellow perverting the nation, and forbidding to give tribute to Caesar, and saying that he him-
92 self is Christ a King.' It is true, however, that the Jews conceived of the kingdom of the Messiah as a temporal kingdom; and their opinion would seem to be shared by those who hold that it is by hereditary law that the Messiah has sovereignty over the Jews, although Christ clearly rejected such a title.

The kingdom of Christ had not a human origin; and its title and purpose are those of redemption. Christ, in so far as pertained to his spiritual purpose—namely, that

EIGHTEENTH. Therefore, the rule of Christ over the whole world originated from no human source—not from hereditary right, nor from election, nor from any similar claim; neither did it serve any temporal end, for its end was redemption, as the blessed Apostle Paul said: 'He humbled himself, and became obedient unto death, even the death of the cross. Wherefore GOD also hath highly exalted him, and given him a name which is above every name: That at the name of Jesus every knee should bow, of things in heaven, and things in earth, and things under the earth' (*Philippians*, 2. 8–10). And for that purpose of redemption,

[1] Verse 6. The wording given above is taken from the Douay version, as that of the King James version differs widely from the Latin phrase used by Victoria. *Tr.*

[2] St. John, xviii. 33–4.

[3] St. John, xviii. 35.

of redemption —had full temporal power, which, moreover, He transmitted to the Church, that the latter might make use of it when necessity should demand.

which is a spiritual end, He possessed full power, even in temporal matters; and
was able to bring about changes in all the kingdoms of the world, to set up new
princes, to humble others, to make subjects,[1] and to do all things which may have
been necessary to the purpose of redemption for which He had come into the
world. Neither do we deny that the Church has this same power on certain occa-
sions. For surely, if all Christians should wish to choose pagan princes, the Pope
would have the power to prevent them from so doing, and to appoint Christian
princes for them. However, our principal contention is also proved by the state- 93
ment: 'For GOD sent not his Son into the world to condemn the world; but that
the world through him might be saved' (*John*, 3. 17). And in another passage, are
the words: 'Who made me a judge, or a divider, over you?' (*Luke*, 12. 14).
The same contention may be proved by reasoning: for Christ did not avail himself
of such power; and that power is vain which is not put to use. But our opponents
assert that Christ must have possessed this power to complete his dignity and
perfection. As if a dignity so great as to be desired by our Lord could pertain to
those things all of which Paul 'counted but dung' (*Philippians*, 3. 8)! And in
truth, the words of Christ have taught us to scorn not only the use of temporal
things, but even the right of possession in them: so far was He from laying claim
to temporal things by His deeds.

The second argument of those who oppose the opinion of the author.

[A third argument.]

NINETEENTH. Our adversaries draw another argument from the words,
'Lord, behold, here are two swords' (*Luke*, 22. 38). On this point, see Cajetan
(*in jentaculo*). Boniface, in the *Extravagantes* already mentioned, interprets the
statement as a reference to a spiritual and a temporal sword. The blessed Bernard
(bk. 4. 'de consideratione.' *ad Eugenium*) does likewise. A third argument adduced
by our opponents is this: Pope Zacharias deposed the king of the French, although
that king was a Christian, and set up in his place Pepin, the father of Charlemagne:
a fact which is attested by Gelasius (*Decretum*, II. xv. 6. 3). Pope Stephen trans-
ferred the kingdom of the Greeks to the Germans, in the time of the Emperor
Constantine; and it was he who appointed the first Emperor—Charles, surnamed
the Great: all of which is attested by Innocent III (in *Decretals*, I. vi. 34; see also 94
Decretals, II. ii. 10). Clement (*Constitutions*, II. xi. 2) touches upon this same
point. Moreover, Innocent IV forbade to the king of Portugal the administration
of his own kingdom, as we read in the chapter beginning *grandi* (*Sext*, I. viii. 2).

The reply of the author to these two arguments.

To all these arguments, we answer that they prove nothing beyond the fact which
we have already stated, namely, that in particular cases the Pope has the power
to perform all the acts in question: in cases, that is, where such acts are necessary
in order to rid the kingdom of scandal, in order to defend religion against pagans,

The fourth argument.

or for other and similar purposes. In the fourth place, the same persons argue that
it is a function of ecclesiastical power to examine into every case of mortal sin;
or at least, that ecclesiastical power includes the power to pass judgement by way
of fraternal correction (*Matthew*, 18).[2] Therefore, since there is in every suit,
however secular the matter may be, one party that acts injuriously, the Church
will have power to judge every suit, and to examine into every secular controversy

[1] *facere privatas*, a misprint for *facere privatos*?—*Tr.*

[2] *Vide* verses 15–20.

and dispute: an authority which, however, implies the possession of civil power.
We answer that on many occasions and in many suits, the question as to whether **One reply of the author.**
or not a given party is committing the injury, is a matter of civil law; and that con-
sequently the adjudication of that suit does not pertain to the power of the
Church; since the case ought, on the contrary, to be decided in the proper court,
namely, the civil court. However, after the case has been decided, if one or
another party refuses to obey; then, by reason of the sin involved, recourse may
be had to the Church: a measure which must not be resorted to before the suit
95 is settled in a civil court. In the second place, we reply that the process by which **A second reply.**
so many suits are brought to the Church for adjudication, has for its end merely
the act of fraternal correction, and not the satisfaction of the injured party; the
opposite is true, in the civil courts. Consequently, the judgement that is
rendered through the power of the Church is not temporal but spiritual; and the
Pope should not and cannot use such judicial power for the purpose of defrauding
or obstructing civil jurisdiction. As for the statement concerning the two swords,
it is clear that it should by no means be taken literally. On the contrary, when
Christ was pointing out to the Apostles the fact that they would meet with opposi-
tion, and that they must needs have some means of defence, they—mistaking His
meaning—said: 'Lord, here are two swords',[1] &c. (See Torquemada, bk. 2, c.
113, 114, 115.) Finally, the following argument may be adduced by our oppo- **The last argument.**
nents: the Popes distribute the provinces of infidels among other nations, as is
evident if we recall the islands discovered by the Spaniards. But the answer
to this argument is easily deduced from what we have already said. Nevertheless
we must not fall into the error made by Occam (*Dialog.* bk. 6, c. 8; *in fine Dialog.*) **The error of Occam and Gerson.**
and Gerson (lect. 4. *de vita spirituali*), that is, the belief that the Pope cannot
punish all sins by sentence of excommunication: not those sins, for example, which
are opposed solely to the law of Nature; but only those which are directly in
opposition to the Gospel, such as sins against the Sacraments and against faith.
This is contrary to the teachings of Paul (2 *Corinthians*, 5),[2] for he passes sentence
of excommunication upon incest, notwithstanding the fact that it is a sin against
Nature [and not against the Law of the Gospel].

[1] St. Luke, xxii. 38.

[2] *Sic.* The reference is evidently to 1 Corinthians, v, and particularly verses 1–5. *Tr.*

APPENDIX E

DE JURE GENTIUM ET NATURALI

ON ST. THOMAS AQUINAS, SUMMA THEOLOGICA,
SECUNDA SECUNDAE, QUESTION 57, ARTICLE 3.

A

TRANSLATION BY

FRANCIS CRANE MACKEN

2. 2, q. 57, a. 3: Whether the law of nations may be distinguished from the natural law. St. Thomas marks a distinction, to wit: That right is a natural right, which, from its very nature, as it were, balances the right of another. And this can happen in two ways: In one way, in that natural law of itself declares that there is a certain equality and justice—as it were to return a deposit—or, because no wrong is done to you, you do no wrong to another. In the other way [i.e. according to the *jus gentium*], some thing is made equal to another in relation to a third thing, just as property may be private—one may not say in equity or justice—but such a division of property is ordered for the peace and concord of men which cannot be preserved unless every one should have his property clearly defined. And therefore it is the *jus gentium* that property should be private. Therefore, having posited this, the first proposition is: That which is, in the first way, equal and absolutely just, is called natural law; that is, it is of natural right. The second proposition: That which is equal and just in the second way, as it were a certain disposition of things with relation to a third just thing, is *jus gentium*. And so that which is not in itself just, but is derived from human statute firmly established in reason, is called *jus gentium*, so that, on its own account it does not imply equity, but on account of something else, as, in the matter of war, and other things. Whence it appears that the *jus gentium* may be distinguished from the *jus naturale*.

Here there is a doubt under which law the *jus gentium* is contained: whether under positive law or under natural law. On this point St. Thomas says [1. 2, q. 85 or 95, a. 4] in solution of the first doubt, that the *jus gentium* is contained more under positive than under natural law. And it is proven by Isidore in the book of the *Etymologies*. But the opinion of the Jurisconsults seems to be opposed to this, who, after they posit the definition of the *jus gentium*, give many examples, and among these examples they mention duty to God, and that we should obey our parents and our country, and that we should ward off violence and injury. But it is clear that all these things are of the natural law—to worship God, to honour our parents, to love our country—all these things are of the natural law from their very nature, because they are right of themselves, and not as a means for something else. This is not the case with the declaration of war, and the appropriation of property. Therefore the law of nations is not contained under positive law, but more under natural law.

I answer to this, and say first of all that the dispute concerns the name more than the thing, for it matters little whether one says this or that. I say secondly, that the Jurisconsults make the law of nations too extensive, and include too many things under it, because as appears in that title, *De Justitia et Jure*, they make the *jus gentium* extend to all those things in which brute animals do not participate—so that they make it extend to all those things which are common to man alone. But they call natural law only those things which are extended to all created things. And so, according to them, natural law is common to all animals, rational and irrational. And therefore, to their way of thinking, fornication is not prohibited in accordance with the natural law, because it is not something common to all created things. And in the same way, worshipping God, honouring parents—which things do not affect brute beasts—are called the *jus gentium* and not natural law. From this they infer that the *jus gentium* falls under natural law. But this, I say, is to extend the *jus gentium* too far, because many things are of the natural law which do not affect all created things. That is clear, because it is the natural law that fire rises and burns, but this is not common to all created things, because it is not common to stones. Also, to return a deposit is of the natural law, and to worship God is of the natural law, but these things are not common to all created things, but only to men, because they are of themselves good things. Therefore we say with St. Thomas that the natural law is an absolute good, and not a relative good: but the *jus gentium* is only relatively good, therefore it is said that the *jus gentium* has not equity of itself, from its own nature, but was established as inviolable, from agreement among men. And so I answer the principal doubt with this conclusion: That *jus gentium* ought to be placed more under positive law than under natural law. Whence the theologians do not posit those examples which the Jurisconsults posit, concerning the worship of God and the honouring of parents, but others: either concerning personal property, or other things which have not of themselves equity, that is to say of their own nature; such as the manumission of slaves, the propriety of possessions, the conservation of the kingdom, &c. The dispute is one of words, and therefore one may speak as a jurist or as a theologian, interpreting the terms loosely or closely—however one may consider they ought to be taken.

But the greatest doubt is a moral one. If the *jus gentium* is of the positive law as has been said, and not of the natural law, is it a sin to violate the *jus gentium*? It is answered that, speaking of those things which are done in a legitimate manner according to the *jus gentium*, that is: concerning human written law there is no doubt but that to act contrary to it is a sin, because those laws, as we have said many times, are binding in the court of conscience. But there is a doubt whether it may be a sin to violate the *jus gentium* (to which some have not yet given their sanction), that is to say, to violate a law of nations which is unwritten, or even written, and which does not bind all men who are in the world. Let us make this clear by the case of the killing of an ambassador—which is contrary to the *jus gentium*—under circumstances where all are not obliged to observe the *jus gentium*, since the *jus gentium* may not be natural law as we have supposed. So let us imagine that we have a war with the French, and the French send an ambassador whom the Spaniards kill contrary to the *jus gentium*. How then are you to judge and know that we have not admitted that *jus gentium*, and that we have sinned in killing an enemy? To this, it is answered by the supposition that the *jus gentium* is twofold, just as positive law is twofold, as we have said above in article 2. There is one kind of positive law taken from private agreement and consensus, and another kind taken from public agreement. In like manner we say of the *jus gentium* that a certain kind of *jus gentium* is from the common consensus of all peoples and nations, and in that way ambassadors have come to be admitted under the *jus gentium*, and are inviolable among all nations. For the *jus gentium* so closely approaches to the natural law that the natural law cannot be preserved without this *jus gentium*. And so of peace—by the law of nature, if wars should arise, it is the public business to bring about a peace by the sending of ambassadors. And otherwise, if ambassadors should not be admitted by the *jus gentium*, they could not put an end to wars. It is the same thing with persons taken captive in a just war, because they are made slaves in accordance with the *jus gentium*, among all peoples and nations. Whence, from this, it is always illicit to violate the *jus gentium*, because it is contrary to the common consensus. Secondly I say, that to act contrary to the *jus gentium* and to violate it is illicit, because of itself it brings on an injury and a certain inequality which is inferred, because, if the French hold our ambassadors to be inviolable, we ought certainly to hold theirs to be inviolable also. Whence, if one party sends ambassadors to make a peace and they are not violated, and the other party sends ambassadors too, and they are violated, it follows that there is inequality and injustice.

But it is doubted whether the *jus gentium* follows necessarily from the natural law, or whether it may be so necessary for the conservation of the natural law that the natural law cannot be observed without it. I answer that the *jus gentium* does not necessarily follow from the natural law, nor is it necessary simply for the conservation of the natural law, for if it should follow necessarily from the natural law, now it would be the natural law. It is clear, because if it necessarily followed from the natural law, through a good sequence, as we said yesterday, it follows, because just as the natural law is necessary, so is the law of nations: and consequently it might be the natural law. Just as simple fornication is contrary to the natural law, because it follows in good sequence from the natural law. Nevertheless, however necessary the *jus gentium* is to the conservation of the natural law, it is not wholly necessary, but nearly necessary, because the natural law can be but badly preserved without the *jus gentium*. For the natural law would be preserved with great difficulty, if there were no *jus gentium*. Indeed the world could go on, if possessions should be in common as is the case among the religious: however, it would be with great difficulty, for men would be likely to rush into discords and wars.

But it may be argued: After that, the *jus gentium* is not necessary law and natural law, but positive law; therefore as such it can be abrogated. I answer denying the consequence, because, when once anything is established from a virtual consensus of the whole world, and admitted, it is necessary that the whole world should likewise agree as to its abrogation; but that, however, is impossible, because it is impossible that the consensus of the whole world could be obtained for the abrogation of the law of nations [*jus gentium*]. Secondly, I say that the law of nations can well be abrogated in part, although not entirely, just as the law of nations is that those taken in a just war may be made slaves; but Paludanus says that this does not hold among Christians. For if the Spaniards capture

Frenchmen in a war, the Frenchmen are captives, but not slaves, because they are able to appear in a court of justice and do other things of that sort, which nevertheless could not be permitted if they were slaves. The acts of a French captive are valid, and a Christian could not sell him at all. Behold here the *jus gentium* is in part violated, for by the *jus gentium*, those taken in a just war are to be made slaves. Let this suffice on this question.

APPENDIX F

DE BELLO

ON ST. THOMAS AQUINAS, SUMMA THEOLOGICA, SECUNDA SECUNDAE, QUESTION 40.

A

TRANSLATION BY

GWLADYS L. WILLIAMS

ERRATA

Page	
cxv.	Notes 4 and 5 should be transposed.
cxvi.	Note 2. *For* editor. *read* editor. *Tr.*
cxvii.	line 2 from foot of text. *For* if its *read* if it is
	note 1. *For* §§ 8–10. *read* §§ 8–10. *Tr.*
cxxii.	Note 2. For *in noxa:* read *in noxa.*
cxxiii.	line 2 from foot. *For* in which *read* in which]
	last line. *For* only]. *read* [only].
cxxvi.	Note 1, line 5. *For* has *read* hast
cxxviii.	Notes 2 and 3 should be transposed.

INDEX

Armachanus. For *Curatorium* read *Curatorum*
Ayala. *For* law, x *read* law, 10*a*
Beltrán. For *Tomas*, 12*a* read *Tomás*, 13*a*
Brierè. *read* Brière
Bustamente y Sirnén. *read* Bustamante y Sirvén
Cajetan. *For* Italian theologian, 129 *read* Italian theologian, 103, 129
Castillian language. *read* Castilian language
Christian Faith: Indians: *For* forced by war 128 *read* forced by war, 128
Declaration of Paris. *For* 1865 *read* 1856
Fitzralph. For *Curatorium* read *Curatorum*
Germany. *For* 12–13 *read* 124 *n*
Morality. *read*
Morality:
international, in Victoria's reading on the Indians, 197
Thomas Aquinas: *Summa.* For *Secundae,* read *Secundae)*
Vitoria: Cajetan. *For* Tomaso *read* Thomas
Zacharias. *For* Childeric *read* Childéric

ON ST. THOMAS AQUINAS, *SUMMA THEOLOGICA*
QUESTION 40: ON WAR
ARTICLE I
On whether or not it is always a sin to wage war.

1. The assertion is made that it is not always a sin to wage war. The truth of this assertion is evident from the words of Augustine. For he, in his *Sermon on the Centurion*[1] who held a military post, proves that truth, by referring to the words of John the Baptist (*Luke*, 3. 14). John did not bid soldiers abandon their military occupation; yet he instructed them as to those matters which were necessary for their salvation. Accordingly, Saint Thomas asserts that the making of war is proper for the king, for a public personage; but not for a private individual. Moreover, war ought to be made for some reasonable cause, and not from the desire to do harm. See the text [of St. Thomas's discussion].

2. This is a grave matter, in which it is of the deepest import to know what is permissible and what impermissible.

As to the principal question—namely, whether it is permissible for Christians to fight,—Tertullian, a very early author, says in his work *De corona militis*[2] that this is not permissible. Moreover, he proves this assertion on the ground that Peter was justly using his sword in the defence of Christ, and that nevertheless, Christ said: 'Put up again thy sword' (*Matthew*, 26. 52). The same fact is further evident from the words of Christ: 'for all that take the sword shall perish with the sword.'[3] Neither does this passage refer to robbers; for such an interpretation is not to the point, since Peter was performing a licit act. Tertullian[4] makes many other statements to this effect. He adduces the fact that, according to Paul, Christians ought not to suffer suits at law, but should, on the contrary, submit to being defrauded, in preference to litigation.[5] Again, how is it permissible for a Christian to wage war, since, if he is struck, it is his duty to turn the other cheek? Hence, the waging of war is not permissible for Christians. Moreover, as to the argument built upon the words of John the Baptist, Tertullian declares that a different principle applies to those persons who are already of the soldiery when faith comes to them; for they may retain their military office, since they cannot break the oath which they swore to their king, lest they suffer capital punishment. As to others among the number of the faithful, however, it is not permissible for such persons to wage war, nor did John the Baptist actually counsel anyone to perform military service. Tertullian also says that many sins result from the fact that military watch is kept on the Lord's day, when it is not permissible to labour

[1] August. *Epistola*, cxxxviii, chap. ii, n. 15 (in Migne, *Patrologia Latina*, vol. 33, col. 532). *Tr.*

[2] Tertullian, *De corona*, chap. i and xi (*Patrologia Latina*, vol. 2; col. 76 and 93). *Tr.*

[3] From the same verse in *Matthew*. *Tr.*

[4] Evidently a reference to *I Corinthians*, chap 6. *Tr.*

[5] Tertullian, *op. cit.*, chap xi. *Tr.*

even for Christ, and when one should abstain from all work. Thus you may see in what honour those feast days were held, at which heretics now scoff.

However, as you know, Tertullian had certain opinions which were strange even to the point of heresy; and the opinion set forth above may perhaps have been one of these. One may well maintain that Tertullian was ill advised[1] when he made the assertion in question. I, indeed, rejoice that there are wars in defence of the state. But I should not wish that a particular person for whom I benevolently desired eternal life should engage in military service.

Thus, in the light of the arguments set forth by St. Thomas, the conclusion that warfare is permissible for Christians is now established as a certainty. For, as Paul says, the prince bears the sword for the defence of the state. If the French attack the Spanish, the [Spanish] prince is bound to defend the latter people, and to slay the French, if need be; even in defiance of the fact that certain newly arisen heretics, indeed, artfully maintain that it is not permissible for Christians to engage in war, basing their assertion on the words: 'Dearly beloved, avenge not yourselves, but *rather* give place unto wrath' (*Romans*, 12. 19). This stand, however, is heretical.

3. Doubt arises with respect to the regulations or conditions of war. The first condition is that the war must be [declared by][2] a public personage; the waging of war pertains to princes (*principes*). What is to be understood by the term 'princes'? For it would seem that this title refers solely to those who have no superiors, inasmuch as St. Thomas says that, if one does have a superior, one may not [on his own authority] declare war, but may ask his superior for the right to do so. However, we have the following argument to the contrary: St. Thomas declares that those persons to whom it pertains to punish inferiors and protect the state from private individuals by such punishment, may declare war; yet kings, even though they may be subject to emperors, have the function of punishing private individuals and of protecting the state; therefore, it is permissible for such [subordinate rulers] to declare war.

I reply [first,] that, in the case of defensive warfare, (as Cajetan, who treats of the matter admirably, says,) any king whatsoever and any commonwealth whatsoever—for example, this city—may defend themselves. If the inhabitants of Toledo attack the inhabitants of Salamanca, the latter may defend themselves on their own authority. There can be no doubt on this point. Secondly, I hold that the power of the prince is derived from the state. Therefore, in cases in which it is permissible for a state to wage war, it is in like manner permissible for a king to wage war. Thirdly, I hold that there is a distinction between private persons and states; for, granting that a private person may defend himself and his property, it is nevertheless impermissible for him to avenge himself or to reclaim his own property save through the judge. For if it were permissible for him to do so in a different manner, that is, if any person whatsoever were the

[1] *dans consilium.* Apparently an error; perhaps a misprint for *sans consilium,* where one would have expected *sine consilio? Tr.*

[2] The bracketed phrase '[*indictum a*]' was supplied at this point by the editor.

judge of his own cause, it would not be possible to govern the world. For such [a state of affairs] would be contrary not only to divine law, but also to natural law. The state, on the other hand, has complete power to avenge itself, to recover its own property, and to punish its enemies. This truth is evident, because, if the state had not this power, there would be disorder in the world, and injury would be suffered at the hands of the wicked. Wherefore it follows, that, with respect to these three points,—namely, avenging itself upon its enemies, recovering its property, and punishing its enemies,—the state possesses the same power over its enemies as that which it possesses over its subjects. And if the state has this power, so also has the prince; for he draws his power from the state.

4. A question arises, however, as to what that is which we call a state. I reply that, according to Aristotle,[1] a state should be self-sufficing. Therefore, that which has the power to do these three things (the power to avenge itself, &c.)—that is a state.

But what groups do have these three powers? Cajetan answers that one applies the term state [to a given group], not because it has one head, but because it is a perfect state, not part of another state; and because it does not conduct its affairs in conjunction with any other state whatsoever. This holds true, moreover, regardless whether or not [that group] has a superior. Thus the Duke of Milan may declare war if need be; because, even though he is subject to the emperor, the state of Milan is nevertheless perfect and does not share its being with any other state. The foregoing also makes evident the way in which a king who is subject to the emperor may declare war; and, furthermore, what persons may declare it.

5. As to the causes for waging war, a king may do so for these purposes: the recovery of his own property; vengeance; [and the punishment of his enemies], —as we have already declared. A question is raised, however, as to whether he may engage in war because of a treaty and for the purpose of aiding some other prince who is suffering injury.

I reply, [first,] that he may, for the reason that a man's friends are in a certain sense one with himself. Secondly, it is evident that he may, since, if we should suffer injury, it would be permissible to call upon the Portuguese for aid; and therefore, it is in like manner permissible for us to aid them.

6. But is it permissible to defend subjects against their king, when they suffer unjustly because of him? Is it permissible to wage war against one's king?

I reply that, [in the first place,] if the case is doubtful, such an action is not permissible; for it would result in disorder to the state if it were permissible for other princes to wage war in defence of any persons at all who might make complaint[2] concerning their king; there is, besides, the additional argument that the judge of the case is the prince himself. In the second place, I hold that, if its clearly evident that the subjects are suffering unjustly because of their king, it

[1] *Politics*, Bk. I, chap. ii, §§ 8–10.

[2] The Latin phrase apparently has a singular antecedent for the subject of the plural verb, as follows: *si liceret principibus aliis pro quocumque bellare qui de rege conquererentur*. *Tr.*

is permissible for [foreign] princes to wage war against that king. And, in general, when subjects have a right to war against their king, it is licit for [foreign] princes to war in defence of that people. The reason supporting this assertion is that the people in question are an innocent people, and that, by natural law, princes may and can defend the [whole] world, lest injury be inflicted upon it. Such, indeed, was the conduct [of one prince], in the time of Pedro, King of Spain. He was a tyrant; and the King of the French warred against this King Pedro in behalf of another son.

7. There arises in this connexion, and in the case of a foreign possession,—take for example the Duchy of Milan,—a doubt as to whether it is permissible for the King of Spain to defend the Duke of Milan against the King of France.

I answer that, if the possession were our own, such defence would be altogether permissible. In a doubtful case, the position of the possessor is the better. The judgement in this case is the same as it would be in the case of a private person. I am in doubt as to whether or not this cloak is mine; I should exercise diligence in seeking to know the truth; as long as a doubt remains, I may licitly retain the cloak. On the other hand, If I doubt whether a cloak is mine, and if another person is in possession of it, then, as long as I remain in doubt, it is not permissible for me to seize the cloak. The reason for this is that the other person has the right to hold the possession; therefore, it is not possible that I should have the right to take it; for a war cannot be just on both sides. Accordingly, in answer to this query, I hold that in a doubtful case [the war in question] is not permissible. When, however, the Duke has entered upon the war on just grounds, it is licit to defend him by warfare. Moreover, conversely, I hold that it would not be licit in such a case to aid the invader; for by giving [such] aid, one would expose himself to [moral] peril, since the matter is doubtful; one would be doing the possessor an injury.

8. There follows a discussion concerning subjects, concerning the question of whether they are under an obligation to know that a war is just, before they may enter into it; or whether it suffices that they be summoned by their prince.

It would seem that they are under an obligation to possess that knowledge; for otherwise, if they are not obliged to know that the war is just, it will be necessary to excuse all those who follow the King of France against the Spanish, and conversely. And if they are not under that obligation, but are proceeding justly, it will not be permissible to slay them, inasmuch as they will be innocent. In favour of the contrary view, there is the argument that the soldiers themselves are not judges; and therefore, they are not under an obligation to possess the knowledge in question.

I reply, [first,] that, if it is evident that the war is unjust, or if this is known to be the case, or if the subjects are conscious that the war is unjust, they may not fight, even when the prince exercises compulsion upon them. The reason for this is that such a prince is committing a mortal sin, and one must obey God rather than obey him. In the second place, I hold that the common people, who are not admitted to the council of the prince, are not under obligation to ascertain the just cause of the war, but may [simply] follow their king. This fact is evident, because they cannot all be informed of the cause of the war. Thirdly, I hold that the magnates who are admitted to the council of the prince, are obliged to inquire into the cause of the war, for this is the proper course of action for them. And besides, it is their duty to admonish the king as to whether or not the war ought to be waged; for they should aid him with their counsel. In the fourth place, I hold that when the cause of war is not clearly unjust, but doubt does exist, it is permissible for soldiers to engage in the war. The proof of this assertion is as follows: under such circumstances, the soldier is confronted by two conflicting doubts; if he does go to battle, he is in danger of prosecuting an unjust war; if he does not go, he exposes himself to the danger of deserting his king and country in their time of need; when one is placed between two perils, he ought to choose that which is less evil; and it is less evil to injure enemies than to injure one's own state; therefore, . . . A second proof is the fact, which we have already pointed out that these soldiers are not under an obligation to inquire into the cause of the war, since it is not for all persons to know this cause. Therefore, when they are in doubt, soldiers may go forth to war. It is true, as we have remarked in our discussion of ignorance, that if the ignorance is crass and, so to speak, wilful, it does not serve as an excuse. Accordingly, I hold that if there are indications that the war is not just,—[if, for example,] I am in doubt, but close my eyes, saying: 'What do I know of the matter?' because I feel affection for my king,—then I may not be acquitted of sin. Therefore, when we say that in a doubtful case the subjects may engage in war, it is to be inferred that we mean, 'when the doubt favours [the justice of the war].' It should also be noted that when it later becomes clear that the war was unjust; when we were previously in doubt; when we have followed our king in good faith; when, [as I have already assumed,] it becomes evident to us afterwards that the war was unjust; under these circumstances—so I maintain—the soldiers are obliged to make restitution for that which they have borne away, if they have become the richer thereby. I do not say that they are so bound with respect to damage inflicted,—because they have burned a city, or have committed some other sort of destruction; but they are indeed bound to restore those things which they have in their possession and by which they have grown more rich. The king will perhaps be under an obligation to make restitution for the entire loss.

I also maintain that those who are prepared to go forth to every war, who have no care as to whether or not a war is just, but follow him who provides the more pay, and who are, moreover, not subjects [of that person], commit a mortal sin, not only when they actually go to battle, but whenever they are thus willing. I further contend that, when the case is doubtful, allies—for example, the Swiss—may not, when they themselves are not subjects, furnish aid to the other side. However, it should be observed in this connexion that there may exist a doubt as to the right of the matter; as to whether, [for instance,] a particular city belongs to France. But let us suppose that the city is in the possession of our king; it is then indubitable that the war in which the city is defended by the Spanish king, is a just war; and accordingly, any persons whatsoever may offer aid to the Spanish king.

9. A doubt is raised as to whether it is permissible to slay in warfare. I reply that if this act is necessary to victory, it is permissible, just as it is permissible to slay individuals who disturb the state.

10. However, a question arises in this connexion. Let us suppose that the Spanish have been victorious; they are no longer fearful of danger; but their enemies are fleeing: is it permissible to pursue the latter and slay them, assuming, as I have suggested, that their death is no longer necessary to the victory [of the Spanish]?

I answer, [first,] that it is entirely permissible to slay them. The reason for this is that the king possesses power not only to recover his property, but also to punish his enemies, even after they have entered into [their own] city; just as the king might slay certain citizens who had set fire to the city, and not merely confiscate their goods. This fact is evident because, if it were not permissible to slay those persons, it would not be possible to avoid wars; [for the enemy][1] would come back forthwith. Secondly, I hold that it would not be permissible to slay all of the enemy; on the contrary, moderation should be observed. Even as the king might not punish all the citizens of a particular city, in case they had rebelled against him, whereas he might punish certain ones; just so, he may not slay the whole number of his enemies. Rather, should we inquire into the matter of whether or not the war in question is the first which those persons have unjustly waged against us; and furthermore, into the matter of whether they were impelled to the war without any cause whatsoever, or with cause. Thirdly, I hold that it is not permissible to slay any of the enemy, after victory has been won, in cases in which they were fighting licitly, provided that there is no longer any danger threatened from them. Let us suppose that the King of Spain justly besieges the city of Bayonne; the inhabitants licitly defend themselves, for if they did not defend themselves, they would be traitors. I hold that, if the King of Spain takes the city, and if danger no longer threatens from those inhabitants, he may not slay them. The reason for this is that they are innocent. I maintain [that such is the case], provided that peril in war is not threatened, for if these persons are in the actual process of waging war, it is permissible to repel force with force; and even assuming that the enemy are innocent, it is permissible to slay them in cases such as that posited.

11. Doubt arises as to whether innocent children may be slain in this war. I have engaged in discussion with a certain member of the Royal Council, who declared it to be advisable that all persons should be slain in order that wars be satisfactorily waged.

I hold, first, that all persons who are able to bear arms should be considered as injurious, since it is presumed that they are defending the king who is our

[1] ... *si non liceret eos occidere, non possent vitari bella; redirent statim iterum.* Some readers might prefer to derive the subject of *redirent* from *bella,* rather than from *eos*; in either case, the meaning would not be materially affected. *Tr.*

enemy. It is permissible to slay them, unless the contrary is manifestly true, that is, unless it is manifest that they are not injurious. Secondly, I hold that when it is necessary for the attainment of victory to slay the innocent, it is permissible to do so. For example, a city is besieged; it is necessary to bombard it; the death of the innocent is a consequence of this bombardment; let them die, since that consequence is incidental. On this point there can be no doubt; it is as if a fortress were being besieged. In the third place, I maintain that if the city had been captured, and if these innocent persons had approached the scene of victory, because they were [supposedly] no longer in peril, it would not be permissible for the king to slay such persons—for example, children, persons dedicated to a religious life, and clerics who were not giving assistance [to the enemy]. The reason for this restriction is clear; for these persons are innocent, neither is it needful to the attainment of victory that they should be slain. It would be heretical to say that it is licit to kill them under such circumstances. Accordingly, the innocent may not be slain by [primary] intent, when it is possible to distinguish them from the guilty.

12. A doubt is raised, however, as to whether or not it is permissible in a just war to give a city over to plunder, pillage, and the sword. It would seem that this is permissible, since otherwise, possession of the city could not be obtained The soldiers are thus made more eager, and the enemy more fearful. Accordingly, such a course of action is proper, for the sake of attaining victory.

On the other hand, there is the argument that the death of the innocent follows in consequence; therefore, such conduct is not permissible.

I reply, [first,] that if this course of action is not necessary to the war as a whole, they who permit it sin in the gravest manner. Secondly, I hold that if such a course is necessary, the leaders may permit it, but the soldiers may not adopt it on their own authority. For example, [in wars] against the Moors, the leaders may give over the [enemy] cities to plunder. This conduct, indeed, is permissible not for the reason that [the enemy] are Moors, but because they are holding our possessions and because the war is just. Therefore, this same conduct will be permissible even among Christians. In the third place, I maintain that, in such a case, the leaders ought to admonish the soldiers not to slay innocent persons. However, even though these leaders know that in consequence of this permission the soldiers may commit many evil deeds, they are nevertheless quite able to give the permission.

13. In connexion with this doubt, and with the preceding doubt, however, one should note this passage in *Matthew* (13. 29) '. . . lest while ye gather up the tares, ye root up also the wheat with them.' From these words, it is inferred that, at times, the guilty should not be punished, lest the death of the innocent should follow, in consequence. Accordingly, Saint Thomas (II. ii, qu. 11, a. 3, *ad tertium*), maintains that on certain occasions, heretics are not to be punished; not, that is, when it is impossible for them to be punished without resultant scandal and peril to the innocent. In this connexion, then, I make the following assertion: the presumption is always that in a given city there are certain innocent persons;

and therefore, it is not pious or Christian to slay the whole number of the inhabitants since, in that case, the innocent are slain. Therefore, after the attainment of victory, and for the purpose of wreaking vengeance, the leaders ought rather to slay the guilty.

On the other hand, there is the argument that in Amalek, Saul slew all the inhabitants, even the children, and there remained not even one watering against a wall; nay, more, because he spared some things, Samuel threatened that the Lord would take his kingdom from him.

I reply that [Saul] did this at the command of the Lord, Who is the Lord of life; just as He slew innocent persons in Sodom, and nevertheless did so to their advantage, since, as Jerome says, those innocent persons have found salvation. In this connexion, we should call to mind the well-known story of the Emperor Theodosius, which relates that he gave over the city of Thessalonica to the sword and to plunder, because it rebelled against him; and that it was Ambrose who excommunicated Theodosius until the latter should repent. [Ambrose] acted thus, not because [Theodosius] slew the principal personages of the city, for that was licit; but because he slew the innocent. Wherefore, it follows that in war it is not permissible to slay the lowly, nor pilgrims[1] who are not a cause of the war, and do not lend aid in it.

14. A doubt arises in this connexion. Let us suppose that at the present time there are certain innocent persons in a [conquered] city; they are doing no harm; but if we permit them to live, they will do harm, later; is it permissible to slay them? It would seem to be impermissible, inasmuch as they are not in fact injurious.

On the other hand, what does it avail to leave them in peace for the present, if they are to war against us at a later date?

I reply that to slay them is not permissible, whatever military persons may say. The children of infidels may not be slain, for they have not committed any injurious act.

15. A question is raised as to whether, in a just war, these persons may be—not slain—but despoiled; and this point is more doubtful.

I reply, [first,] that, when it is necessary to the completion of victory to take their engines, and sheep, oxen, and other herds, then, even granting that the persons in question are innocent, it is permissible to seize all these goods. The reason for the foregoing is manifest; since it is permissible for any person to wage war justly, and it is likewise permissible to apply all the means necessary to the attainment of victory. I hold, secondly, that when a state or a kingdom is guilty of an injury[2] [the seizure in question is licit]. For example, the French have despoiled the Spaniards, and therefore, if the King of the French and his kingdom are unwilling to give satisfaction, the Spaniards may enter [that kingdom] and

[1] The Latin reads: . . . *non licet occidere pauperes, oratores qui non sunt causa,*' &c. If the comma were deleted, after *pauperes,* the translation might be: '. . . it is not permissible to slay humble suppliants who are not a cause,' &c. Both *pauperes* and *oratores* have various meanings, although both terms are a little difficult to translate in this context. Is there perhaps an error in the Latin text at this point? *Tr.*

[2] The text has *innoxa,* evidently for *in noxa*; Cf. note 2, p. cxxv of this translation. *Tr.*

seize all their own property, taking it even from the hands of innocent persons. The reason for this is that, otherwise, they could not recover their own possessions. In this case, moreover, it is a question not of individual persons, but of a state. Afterwards, the guilty individuals among the French are bound to repair the losses of the innocent French.

16. There is doubt as to whether that which one captures in a just war is the property of the person who captures it.

We shall discuss this point at length, below [(On II. ii, qu. 66, a. 8)], in treating of rapine. For the present, I shall assert, in the first place, that if the Spaniards have been despoiled of a hundred thousand ducats, they may seize that amount. This fact is very well known; it is permissible to recover one's own property. I assert, secondly, that it is permissible not only to do this, but also to seize all that by which compensation may be made for the expenses of a war. This point is clearly true, since the war is waged for that very purpose, namely, that one may keep himself free from loss; therefore, it is permissible to seize property equivalent to the entire expense of the war. In the third place, I assert that, in addition to seizing his own property and compensation for expenses, the Spanish king may furthermore punish the French, to the extent, say, of twenty thousand ducats. The reason supporting this assertion is the fact, pointed out above, that he may punish those persons temporally, just as he might inflict corporal punishment upon private individuals. There is the further argument that, as we have said, he may proceed even as far as to take vengeance for the sin committed by the French. Fourthly, I make the assertion that it is not permissible, even in a just war, to seize all the goods of the enemy, without distinction. Not all things captured in war are the property of the conqueror. It is licit to seize, not everything possible, but [only] those things by means of which compensation may be made for loss and for the expenses [of the war], and the sin of the enemy punished. The reason for this is that the king has not greater power over the enemy than he has over the persons who are subject to him; and if the Duke of Alba should slay a man, he could not be punished by being deprived of his dukedom; that would be a grave penalty. Similarly, then, even if we assume that the French plunder the Spaniards, that sin may not be punished by a penalty of unrestricted gravity. Fifthly, I assert that, as long as a just war continues, those movable goods which are seized, would seem to be, by the *jus gentium*, the property of the one who seizes them. This may be the case; since one is not condemned, in confession, to restore those goods which he seizes while the war is being waged. I mean to say, 'while a just war is being waged'; for if we are already the conquerors, if the sum of the expenses has been recovered, if—moreover—sins have been punished and vengeance upon the enemy has been achieved; then, whatever we may have borne away in actual warfare is ours, but it is not now permissible to indulge in further plunder. However, throughout the duration of a just war,—one in which we are, accordingly, fighting not unjustly,—all those things which we have seized are ours; [a statement in which I refer to movables only]. My sixth assertion is that the case is otherwise with respect to immovables.

The Spaniards, fighting against the French, capture ten cities as certain prize in the course of a just war; those cities do not belong to the Spanish king, neither may he retain them. Conceive of the King of France as a subject; such a penalty would then be excessive and grave. Indeed, when the loss has been repaired, the expenses [of the war] met, and the sin punished, it is by no means permissible for the King [of Spain] to keep the cities in question. Seventhly, I assert that, if the King of Spain captures one city of France, and if the retention of that city serves as vengeance and as a punishment for the sin committed by the French, the Spanish King may retain it, and need never give it to the King of France; for he may punish the latter. This should be done, moreover, according to the judgement of the victor, not according to that of the vanquished. Assume that under these circumstances the King of France offers some other form of satisfaction; the other King may refrain from accepting it, and may in preference retain the city. This is so, for the reason that he is the judge in the case.

17. A doubt arises as to whether or not it is permissible to seize men in warfare, taking them captive.

I maintain, [in the first place,] that this is permissible. This fact is evident by the *jus gentium*. No [authority] censures this practice, nor does any condemn the captor to make restitution; on the contrary, such captors may retain these men until the latter are ransomed. Secondly, I maintain that it is no longer permissible to slay them, for they are captives; nor is such slaughter needful to the attainment of victory.

18. A question is raised, however, as to whether or not captives taken in war are slaves.

I reply, [first,] that sometimes this would seem to have been the case, in accordance with the *jus gentium*; for in the time of the Romans this was apparently the practice, that captives in war should be slaves. Secondly, I hold, in agreement with de la Palu (in 4. d. 15. qu. [3]a. [5] conclus. [1]), that in our times Christians may not be made slaves, even in a just war in which it is assumed that they have licitly been captured. The reason for this is that they may give testimony, and, furthermore, they may have their own possessions; and this is not permissible for slaves. Thirdly, I hold that, in the case of other persons,—for example, in that of pagans and Moors,—captives made in war are slaves. That is to say, they are slaves if a just war is waged against them; for if a war is not just, the captives may not be made slaves. This is the proper conclusion.

19. A doubt arises as to whether or not it is permissible in war to perform [injurious] acts which are not to our own advantage. For example, a question is raised as to whether the Spaniards may licitly set fire to the cities of the French, and to their fields; for this does not promote the welfare of the Spaniards.

I reply that to do so wantonly is diabolical; this fire is the fire of hell; for such an act is not needful in the attainment of victory. Conduct of this sort is not pious among Christians: [persons who perform such acts] destroy cities which for many years to come they shall not rebuild; even as Socrates said to Alexander, who destroyed a certain city:—Truly, in many years you will not build up its like.

20. There is doubt with regard to hostages, to persons given as a pledge. A pact has been made between [two] kings, and several men are delivered into the power of one of these, so that, if the other king does not observe the pact, they may be slain; just as befell some Frenchmen, a few years ago, in Spain. The question is whether such [hostages] may be slain, if another person does not keep[1] the promise he has made. It would seem that they may; for they have been given as pledges for this very purpose, namely, that they may be slain if the agreements are not observed.

On the other hand, it may be argued that they are innocent. Why should they be slain for another's sin? They neither foster it, nor do they play a part in the injury.[2]

I reply that they may by no means be slain, but that they should be held as captives; and I also maintain that the law and the pact in question would be iniquitous. The reason for this view is that these persons are innocent.

21. There remains for discussion only the doubt as to the fourth argument cited in the text, tending to prove that war is not licit. The proof is this: warlike exercises are forbidden by the Church; this fact is evident, since tournaments are prohibited, and since those who fight in tournaments are accordingly denied ecclesiastical burial if they die; hence, neither is war licit. This view is further confirmed by the fact that, in Spain, we see certain persons dying in these jousts and tournaments,—the heir of Oñate and many other persons; the same is true of the *cañas*;[3] therefore, such exercises are not licit.

The reply to the foregoing is that warlike exercises of this sort are in themselves licit. [You will exclaim:] 'Oh, slaughter is their result!' I answer that many builders die, that they fall to their death while building, and that nevertheless, no one says that this occupation is forbidden. Those deaths, then, are not an inherent part [of the warlike exercises in question]; on the contrary, [the participants] do not commonly die in these exercises. But if the deaths of men did commonly follow upon any such exercise, that particular exercise would be forbidden; otherwise, it would not be forbidden.

ARTICLE II

Whether it is permissible for clerics and bishops to engage in battle.

1. It is said that this is not permissible. This fact is clearly true, from the following passage in *Matthew* (26. 52): 'Put up again thy sword into its place,' which applies to bishops. The point, moreover, is clear, because, in the first place, all the offices in a state do not pertain to the same persons; on the contrary, certain offices pertain to specific persons. Clerics and bishops have been allotted divine offices. Therefore, they ought not to seek others. In the second place, clerics have been constituted in order that they may offer sacrifices on the altar.

[1] *servant*, evidently for *servat*. *Tr.*
[2] *innoxa*, evidently for *in noxa*. Cf. note 2, p. cxxii of this translation. *Tr.*
[3] Jousts with red spears. *Tr.*

Therefore, they that offer up for all men, Christ, Who shed His blood for all men, should not seek to shed blood. Hence, it is not permissible for clerics to engage in battle.

2. A doubt arises—since Saint Thomas proves this opinion on the basis of the Gospel—as to whether the prohibition is laid upon the persons in question, by divine law.

I reply, [first,] that this prohibition is not directly imposed either by natural or by divine law; to no one is fighting prohibited by divine law because of the fact that he is a cleric. But this [to refrain from fighting] is befitting [a cleric], as is evident from the passage above cited, according to which Christ would lay down [for clerics] the prohibition that he did lay down for Peter, even though a layman might yield [to the impulse to do battle]. Secondly, I hold that it is most fitting from the viewpoint of both natural law and divine law, that clerics should not do battle.

3. But [another question arises]: may the Pope grant dispensations on this point?

I reply that it would not be proper to grant such dispensations in the case of the entire body of clergy, but that the Pope may well grant the dispensation, when there is cause, in the case of a particular cleric—for example, in the case of one who is a good leader. On this point, see the *Decretum*, II. xxiii. 8. 21 and 1. Moreover, this same view is proved by the example of David, for the Lord did not will that David should build Him a house, because David was a man of blood (*II Kings*, 7)[1]. This passage, however, proves, not that [fighting] is prohibited [to clerics], but that it is most fitting that clerics should not be men who have shed blood.

4. Does this prohibition, however, apply to all clerics? It would seem that those who have had only their first tonsure do not sin [in fighting], since as a matter of fact these clerics do engage in battle. It may be that such conduct is indeed prohibited to all, but that this [prohibition] is a matter of positive law; and, [in point of fact,] clerics of the first tonsure do, at the present time, commonly engage in battle. Other clerics, who have fully received holy orders, would sin [in fighting]. From this it follows that, since it is not licit for clerics to engage in battle, they are to be considered as innocent persons; it is not permissible to slay or to despoil them. I would say, that is, that it is not permissible unless they aid the enemy; for if they do so, they may licitly be slain, especially in the actual conflict of battle. Furthermore, if we know that there are, in a given place,

[1] This thought is not clearly set forth in the Biblical passage cited. Verse 13 of chapter 7 of *II Kings* states: 'He [the son of David] shall build a house to my name, and I will establish the throne of his kingdom for ever.' The passage in question is found in *I Paralipomenon*, 22. 7–10 which reads: 'And David said to Solomon: My son, it was my desire to have built a house to the name of the Lord my God. But the word of the Lord came to me, saying: Thou has shed much blood, and fought many battles, so thou canst not build a house to my name, after shedding so much blood before me: The son, that shall be born to thee, shall be a most quiet man: for I will make him rest from all his enemies round about: and therefore he shall be called Peaceable: and I will give peace and quietness to Israel all his days. He shall build a house to my name, and he shall be a son to me, and I will be a father to him: and I will establish the throne of his kingdom over Israel for ever.'

See also *II Kings*, 16. 8, *III Kings*, 5. 5; *ibid.*, 8. 19. *Tr.*

a hundred armed clerics, desirous of doing battle, it is permissible to slay them. The reason for this is, that one may licitly perform all necessary acts, and that the act in question is necessary. Secondly, I assert that after victory is won, and even though the clerics have engaged in battle, they may not licitly be slain; first, because capital punishment has not been established with respect to them, by law; secondly, because they are exempt. The king, even assuming that he seizes them, is not judge with the power to slay [such persons].

5. A doubt arises as to whether it is permissible to despoil churches, and to carry off the property therein. I hold, [first,] that if the enemy store up their goods in churches, it is entirely licit to seize those goods; and that such stored possessions do not enjoy ecclesiastical immunity. Secondly, I hold that it is not licit to seize ecclesiastical goods, for they are the property of innocent clerics; and furthermore, they have been consecrated to God. It should be noted, however, that if the enemy make improper use of those ecclesiastical goods in attempts against us, it is permissible to seize such goods in anticipation. Similarly, I hold that it is not licit to demolish churches; that is, not unless the enemy are using the churches as citadels; or again, if we fear that the enemy may fortify the churches, to be used as citadels, it is licit to seize these churches in anticipation, and to demolish them. I would point out that this should be understood as referring to cases of great necessity; if the necessity is not great, the churches should be preserved.

6. The following question arises, however: it is necessary to the attainment of victory to set fire to a church; but the church will be consumed; the crosses, the cups, the Eucharist will be destroyed in flame; is this act permissible?

I reply, [first,] that if the act is not necessary, even though it may be in some fashion advantageous,—for not all advantageous acts should be performed in war,—if, then, the act is not necessary, it is a monstrous sacrilege that Christians, who adore their unique sacrament of the Eucharist, should destroy it by fire.[1] Secondly, I hold that if the act in question is necessary to the consummation of the war, [it should be borne in mind that] Christ cannot be destroyed by fire; for He no longer dies; He may not be consumed save in the Eucharist.[2] Moreover, the fault is not ours, but the enemy's, for they are sacrilegious in their misuse of the church and of the Eucharist, retaining the latter in that place, when they know that we are setting fire to the church. Accordingly, I maintain that, just as it is permissible to slay innocent persons incidentally when such conduct is necessary, so is it permissible to set fire to a church, [under similar circumstances], even though the Eucharist may be consumed. It would be as if the enemy should maliciously place the Eucharist upon the wall [of a fortification].

7. A doubt arises as to whether clerics may do battle in defence of their own goods.

1 The translation at this point is unsatisfactory, as the Latin text is apparently incorrect or incomplete, probably the latter. The text reads as follows: *est sacrilegium immane quod christiani, qui adorantes eucharistiae unicum eorum sacramentum, comburant illud. Tr.*

2 *Non potest cremari magis quam in stomacho. Tr.*

I reply, [in the first place,] that it is permissible for them to do battle and to slay, for the purpose of defending the goods of the Church and their own goods; neither are they irregular if they do so. I hold, secondly, that it is permissible for them to engage in warfare in defence of the goods of the community and in defence of the state, when such a course of action is necessary. For [let us suppose that] a certain city is besieged; its clerics are experienced [in warfare]; it is permissible for them to fight. Cajetan,[1] however, declares that such clerics are irregular, even though they may act rightly in committing slaughter. Sylvester holds that when this conduct on their part is necessary, they are not irregular. And in my opinion, the matter is as set forth in the *Constitutions of Clement*, V. iv; that is, a cleric committing slaughter in defence of his own goods is not irregular, and consequently, he will be absolved from irregularity if he does so in defence of the goods of the community.

With respect to the same point, Cajetan[2] declares that clerics may not [*sic*] do battle for the purpose of attaining victory when the king would be able to conquer with the clerics, and would not be able to do so without them. I, [for my part,] hold that they may not engage in warfare. The reason in support of this view is as follows: the conclusion in question is to be understood as referring to a just war; for if it is unjust, then it is not licit even for laymen; in a just war, then, it is not licit for clerics to fight when this is not necessary to the defence of the community. Sylvester,[3] however, notes that, before the commencement of the war, it is permissible for clerics to exhort the soldiers to brave conduct; and I believe that it is [then] permissible that the former should bid the latter commit slaughter. But, in my opinion, those clerics would be irregular, who in the actual conflict of battle, should say: 'Commit slaughter.' So Sylvester[4] declares; even though some persons of religious calling have followed the contrary course, encouraging the soldiers [with exhortations] during the actual conflict of battle.

A question presents itself with regard to bishops who have temporal domains; is it permissible for them to do battle?

I answer that they themselves ought not to fight; but that, through their generals, they may promote (*movere*) wars, not merely undertake (*suscipere*) them. This fact is clearly true, since they are temporal lords; therefore, for the purpose of ruling the state, it is permissible for them to undertake and to promote wars.

8. There is a question in connexion with soldiers, as to whether or not they are irregular.

I declare that if they have committed slaughter, it is true that they are

[1] *Commentarium in S. Thomae Summam Theologicam*, II. ii, qu. 40, art. 2, contained in Thomas Aquinas, *Opera Omnia*, vol. v. (Rome, 1773) p. 425. *Tr.*

[2] *Summa Sylvestrina, quae Summa Summarum Merito Nuncupatur* (Venice, 1601), on word *bellum*, III. 3. *Tr.*

[3] Victoria apparently refers to Cajetan's *Commentarium in S. Thomae Summam Theologicam*, II. ii, qu. 40, art. 2. Cajetan, however, in his Commentary affirmatively states that clerics may do battle in cases of necessity; for instance, when a besieged city would be overthrown without the help of the clerics. He goes on to say 'a cleric is even bound to fight in such a crisis'. *Tr.*

[4] Sylvester, *op. cit.*, word *bellum*, III. 3. *Tr.*

irregular. However, if they have not committed slaughter, and if the war was just, they have contracted no irregularity; this is a matter of positive law. If, on the other hand, the war is unjust, and its injustice is evident, I maintain that the soldiers are irregular, even though they do not commit slaughter, if they are nevertheless present and prepared to slay if able, and if they do give aid.

9. There is a doubt as to the clerics who take part in the war for the purpose of receiving confessions: is it permissible for them to despoil the enemy after victory is won?

I hold that this is permissible for the soldiers only, and not for the clerics. Wherefore, the latter are bound to make restitution,—I would not say, to the enemy, but to the soldiers—or else they are bound to give up their spoil to the general; just as it would not be licit for me, who am not fighting, to enter the camp of the enemy and seize booty.

10. A doubt arises in connexion with enemies who flee for refuge to a church, after victory is attained. We have conquered; we have taken the city; the enemy hasten to the church: is it permissible to slay them? It would seem that this is not permissible, since they are no longer doing harm.

I answer that, if peril no longer threatens from them, they enjoy complete ecclesiastical immunity. This assertion is proved by the fact that, as we have already pointed out, our king has no greater dominion and power over them than if they were his subjects; and he may not drag his subjects from a church; therefore, he may not treat his enemies thus. If, however, peril threatens, it is permissible to burn them and the church, should this be necessary. There ought to be no doubt on that point. In this connexion, see the arguments set forth by Saint Thomas.

ARTICLE III

Whether it is permissible to lay snares in warfare.

1. Is it permissible to make use of fraud, or deceit, in war? The answer is that it is never permissible to lie. Furthermore, it is not permissible to make use of fraud which is contrary to an agreement entered into with the enemy. However, it is permissible to refrain from revealing certain truths to the latter. All these points are made clear in the text [of Saint Thomas].

2. A doubt arises as to whether faith must always be kept with the enemy. I shall suppose, as a specific case, that ten agreements are entered into, by the French and the Spanish. If the French break all of these agreements, we are free from every obligation to observe any of them, in view of the fact that the former do not observe them. But what if they fail to observe one of the agreements, and do observe the other nine? With respect to that one, we are no longer bound to keep faith. But there arises a question as to whether or not we are bound to keep faith with respect to the other nine agreements.

I reply that we are by no means bound to keep faith with respect to these. So long as fraud is not involved, [the contracting parties] are bound to observe the agreements. If one party breaks one agreement, there is no longer an obligation to keep any of the agreements. The reason for this is that the pact is interpreted as including the provision that no one shall transgress any one of the agreements in question.

3. A question arises as to whether or not faith should be kept with the enemy when it cannot be kept without detriment to the state. The answer would seem to be in the negative.

I reply that faith is always to be kept with the enemy. The reason for this is as follows: just as it would be ruinous to human converse if we should once admit that lying is licit; and again, just as many evils would follow if fornication were once permitted; even so, if we once admit that faith ought to be broken with the enemy for some particular cause, many evils would result, and there would be no end to wars; just as, if the King of France were captured a second time, he could not be freed, since it would be said that he would not keep faith. Accordingly, I hold, [first,] that faith should be kept with the enemy, even if this be [somewhat] detrimental to the state. In the second place, [however,] I hold that faith should not be kept with them if to do so would be in the highest degree detrimental to the state, with the result that it would perish; for in that case it would not be just for us to seek to have faith kept; just as, if the King of France demanded a hundred thousand ducats, and we could not observe good faith with him save by the destruction of all Spain, we should by no means be bound [to meet the request], and the demand upon our good faith would be unjustly made.

4. A doubt presents itself with respect to the person who has made a promise in war as the result of fear falling upon a man [by nature] steadfast.

For example, the King of France was captured, and made many promises; he would not have made the promises, save through fear of death, or being held here permanently: is he bound to keep those promises? I hold that he is bound, and that if the contrary were true, there would be no end to wars. On the other hand, there is the argument that he made the promise because of fear falling upon a steadfast man; and a man is not bound to keep the promises which he makes because of such fear; therefore, . . .

To this, I reply that he is absolutely bound to observe the conditions of his promises; otherwise, the state would be thrown into disturbance, and wars would never cease. I furthermore reply, to the argument set forth [above], and [my statement] is confirmed by what we have [already] said,—that there are two ways in which one may make a promise owing to fear that falls upon a steadfast man. In one sense, injury may be done a person, in the process of instilling fear into him; as when certain persons force another, under pain of death, to promise that he will take a wife, because otherwise he will be slain; though a grave injury is indeed involved in arousing this fear in him. I hold that this man is not bound to observe the promise he has made. In the second case, fear may be justly instilled into one; as when a given person is condemned to capital punishment for the crime of heresy, and is told that he will be slain unless he takes a particular woman to wife; he makes the contract in order to escape death, but would not make it otherwise; the marriage is valid. Thus, in the case of the King of France, no injury was involved in the fact that he was captured in war; for that was just. Neither is injury involved in demanding his agreement to certain conditions of peace, conditions which he would not agree to observe were it not for the purpose of escaping from death or from the necessity of remaining permanently among the Spanish. Therefore, he is bound to observe his promises; a point which should be noted.

ARTICLE IV

Whether it is permissible to engage in warfare on holy days.

1. Finally, this question arises with respect to war; is it permissible to engage in warfare on holy days, or is the holy day violated, by warfare?

The first conclusion is that we may licitly engage in war on holy days, for the defence of the state, when such conduct is necessary.

The second conclusion is this: unless such need exists, it is not licit to engage in war on holy days. No one entertains any doubt as to this conclusion.

2. With respect to the first conclusion, Tertullian, as we have said above,[1] holds that it is in nowise licit for Christians to engage in warfare or to fight on holy days. But when the observance of a holy day depends upon positive law,—in accordance with the stipulations and regulations of which law the festival is observed—it is not improper, that, if the welfare of the state is sufficiently at stake, the holy day should not be observed with respect to this abstinence from warfare on the part of Christians. Cajetan[2] also says that, even if one should engage in war on a holy day when it was not necessary to do so, he would not be committing a mortal sin if he did not, as a result, omit to perform the divine offices. The reason for this is that warfare is not inherently evil; moreover, it is not servile labour; it is, then, illicit on a holy day when there is no need for it, [simply] because it is not in keeping with the purpose of the holy day. This argument is confirmed by the fact that dances and weddings disturb the mind as much as does war, and nevertheless one engages in them on holy days without anxiety as to mortal sin; therefore, . . .

[1] Page cxv of this translation. *Tr.*

[2] Cajetan, *op. cit.*, qu. 40, art. 4. *Tr.*

INDEX

www.ingramcontent.com/pod-product-compliance
Ingram Content Group UK Ltd.
Pitfield, Milton Keynes, MK11 3LW, UK
UKHW050955290926
15470UKWH00006B/1825

9 781584 771104